Classical Economics

Classical Economics

Samuel Hollander

Basil Blackwell

Copyright © Samuel Hollander 1987

First published 1987

Basil Blackwell Ltd
108 Cowley Road, Oxford OX4 1JF, UK

Basil Blackwell Inc.
432 Park Avenue South, Suite 1503
New York, NY 10016, USA

British Library Cataloguing in Publication Data

Hollander, Samuel
   Classical economics
   1. Classical school of economics
   I. Title
   330.15′3   HB94

   ISBN 0-631-13412-3
   ISBN 0-631-15968-1 (Pbk)

Library of Congress Cataloging-in-Publication Data

Hollander, Samuel
   Classical economics

   Bibliography: p.
   Includes index
   1. Classical school of economics.   I. Title
   HB94.H65   1987   330.15′3   87-8004

   ISBN 0-631-13412-3
   ISBN 0-631-15968-1 (pbk.)

Typeset in 10 on 12pt Times
by Unicus Graphics Ltd, Horsham, Sussex
Printed in Great Britain by TJ Press Ltd, Padstow, Cornwall

Contents

With love, to my grandson Ro'i Melech
and his parents Frances and Ami Bogot

Preface

This text will, I hope, make available to advanced undergraduate and graduate students the substance of my rather hefty studies of Smith, Ricardo and Mill. To that end I have combined the arguments of those studies into appropriate sub-sections. (Thus chapters 4, 5 and 6 can be read as a single unit; similarly 7, 8 and 9; 10 and 11; 12, 13 and 14.) I have also dispensed with footnotes; noteworthy material has been placed where it belongs, namely in the text.

It seemed to me in preparing this work that the assertive, all-knowing tone of the typical textbook had to be avoided; the student must be given the evidence on which the various interpretations are based. This procedure has added inevitably to the length of the work. Greater brevity might have been achieved by concentrating on what is currently in the limelight – the 'Italo-Cambridge' vs the 'neo-classical' perspectives on classicism. I have attended to this controversy, but have chosen to extend the horizon further. It would leave a false impression to neglect the law of markets, the monetary controversies, methodology, ideology and influence, all of which played a part in the making of 'classicism'. Needless to say, readers can always be selective.

It is a pleasure to express my warm thanks for the advice and encouragement of friends in preparing this volume. I am much indebted to Alan Abouchar, William Baumol, Helen Boss, Avi Cohen, Tony Endres, Kieren Furlong, Cigdem Kurdas, Ian McDonald, Dusan Pokorni and Hamish Stewart. I owe a particular debt to Tom Kompas and Eric Stubbs who have kept a friendly eye on the manuscript since its inception. I am also obliged to my students Colette Bergeron, Michael Gasiorek, Kevin Reilly, Paul Rochon, Margaret Sanderson and, especially, Mahmud Jamal, for their assistance.

I wish to acknowledge the permission of the University of Toronto Press to draw freely on my *Economics of Adam Smith* and *Economics of David Ricardo*; of *Oxford Economic Papers* for use of two articles

(1977, 1980) in preparation of chapter 16; and of *History of Political Economy* and *The American Economic Review* for use of articles (1981, 1984 respectively) in preparation of chapter 15.

A Connaught Senior Fellowship, held in 1984–85, proved indispensable for my investigations. The Humanities and Social Sciences Committee of the Research Board, University of Toronto, very kindly supported completion of this study with a research grant.

This book is dedicated to my daughter and son-in-law and to my first grandchild. His early arrival cost me several weeks, but in compensation he has since raised my productivity enormously.

S.H.

Somebody who reads only newspapers and at best books of contemporary authors looks to me like an extremely near-sighted person who scorns to wear eye glasses. He is completely dependent on the prejudices and fashions of his time since he never gets to see or hear anything else. And what a person thinks on his own without being stimulated by the thoughts and experiences of other people is even in the best case rather paltry and monotonous.

Albert Einstein

1 Introduction

1.1 Why Study the History of Economics?

Economic theories have to be selective; were they all-inclusive they would be ineffectual. No geographer would construct a three-dimensional map on a scale of 1 inch to 1 inch. But what, in economics, to select for special attention partly depends on circumstances – on the world environment, factual knowledge and our particular interests at any time (Hicks, 1976). From this it follows that an economic theory may be 'rejected' because it is inappropriate for the particular problems with which we are currently concerned, rather than because it is 'wrong'. It may often appear when there is a change in economic thought that one theory has displaced another because the first has somehow been proved, in some definitive sense, faulty, when nothing more than a change in 'concentration of attention' is involved. It is important, therefore, if this is so, to try to discover whether, how and why changes in concentration have occurred over time. Not to do so is to remain under the possibly false impression that what one has learned in basic theory courses is all there is to know; that earlier perspectives have been definitively disposed of as erroneous, when there is much that remains 'valid' albeit forgotten or neglected by the profession.

There is good reason to support this view. A number of instances illustrate that theoretical constructs, lost from sight, have indeed proved to be of permanent usefulness as old problems re-emerge.

In a study entitled *Britain's Economic Problem: Too Few Producers* (Bacon and Eltis, 1978), two economists have attempted to account for Britain's slow growth rate in terms of the distinction between 'productive' and 'unproductive' labour, a theme characterizing Adam Smith's *Wealth of Nations* (1776), whereby growth depends in part upon the distribution of the labour force between the (capital) goods and the service sectors. After the 1870s this distinction lost favour amongst Western ('neo-classical') economists increasingly interested with the allocation of scarce resources between competing uses as a problem in its own right. For of what concern is it whether labour is engaged in 'productive' or 'unproductive' work, since services as well as goods are desirable? The distinction was set aside to be belatedly resuscitated when the problem under investigation reverted to that of particular concern to the eighteenth- and nineteenth-century 'classical' writers.

There are economists who today maintain that inflationary and deflationary business fluctuations arise from monetary disturbances in a world of uncertainty. This perspective was extensively studied by nineteenth-century economists in response to the inflation of the Napoleonic War period, the post-war decision to return to the gold standard and later debate regarding the running of a monetary system. Yet monetary disequilibrium theory was abandoned during the 1930s under the influence of Keynes's *General Theory* (1936) without any attempt to scrutinize the early literature.

Various eighteenth-century economists attempted to trace the precise course whereby an injection of money flows through the economic system in an effort to avoid a mechanical 'quantity theory' approach. It is an approach that insists upon recognition of a linkage between the structure of the economy – the pattern of activity as reflected in relative prices – and the aggregative dimension with its corresponding level of prices. Neglect of this perspective in our own day, so it has been argued, has had disastrous consequences, including simultaneous inflation and unemployment.

In this general context an historical episode of profound socio-political significance comes to the fore. The General Strike of 1926 followed wage reductions designed to increase the competitiveness of British exports and counter the effects of the return to gold in the previous year at the pre-war par of exchange. The decision of 1925 to appreciate the pound was partly a matter of keeping faith with British creditors – to permit holders of sterling to redeem their pounds at the old rate and not suffer a depreciation in terms of gold – for the Bank of England regarded the return to full convertibility as the end all of existence and ruled out exchange depreciation, taking for granted that this position had behind it a long-standing tradition characterizing the major classical writers. Yet the fact is that in correspondence with the prime minister in 1811 and before Parliament in 1819, David Ricardo, the central figure of classical economics and a fervent champion of the gold standard, protested that he would never recommend a return to gold at the original par if the pound had been very much depreciated, a policy that would inevitably set in motion a real deflation of output and employment. Had the policy-makers of the 1920s realized that this was the true classical position, they would not have been able to appeal to a false tradition in support of deflation; while J. M. Keynes, who opposed their policy, failed to reinforce his argument by appeal to the literature. How different the economic history of Britain might have been had he known of Ricardo's caution.

Unfortunately Keynes had a totally distorted view of classical macro-economics, neglecting the allowances made for excess commodity supply in the aggregate, which will be elaborated in this text. Yet even he asserted the permanent validity of classical allocation theory, and warned in 1946 against hasty recourse to import and exchange rate controls which his own writings had encouraged. Government intervention was required 'not to defeat but to implement the wisdom of Adam Smith'; 'I find myself moved, not for the first time, to remind contemporary economists that the classical teaching embodied some permanent truths of great significance... There are in these matters deep undercurrents at work, natural forces, one can call them, or even the invisible hand, which are operating towards equilibrium...' (1946 [1980], 444–5). Similarly, in the *General Theory* itself: 'if our central controls succeed in establishing an aggregate volume of output corresponding to full employment as nearly as is practicable, the classical theory [of resource allocation] comes into its own again from this point onwards' (1936 [1973], 378).

Some episodes in the history of classical economics enhance one's technical mastery of a subject. This is even true of price theory, the most polished of all branches of modern economics. And this is not surprising, for we are tracing out the mental processes of supremely intelligent economists who struggled with inherently difficult issues – the easily forgotten fact, in this instance, that price is a *relative* notion – and thereby sharpening our appreciation in a manner that few modern theory textbooks (where so much that requires investigation is taken for granted) can achieve. The *Wealth of Nations* contains some truly fascinating applications of price theory – for example, the implications of economic development for the price structure – not to be found in modern texts. More generally, the relation between allocation and growth is a major classical theme which is in danger of being lost from sight. We shall also find, in contrasting Ricardo with Smith on the distinction between relative and absolute prices, much of relevance to the modern debate regarding the responsibility of wage pressure for general inflation. Similarly, the nature of economic 'cost' as alternative product foregone is revealed strikingly in the classical literature.

The great works of economics will inevitably be used, even misused; and unless they are studied seriously their misuse will go undetected. Too often one sees the intellectually unedifying picture of politicians (and others with an axe to grind) using the works of the masters for their own ends, possibly without having read them. Thus, for example, 'conservatives' (sporting Adam Smith neckties) frequently cite Smith as champion of some extreme form of *laissez-faire*, with little justification, since in Smith's writings may be discerned the elements of a moderate kind of interventionism and harsh statements regarding capitalist institutions. Those with a taste for irony will be pleased to learn that early British socialism has its roots in the *Wealth of Nations*.

Our subject also helps to assure that alternative general methodologies or world views of economic process differing from those in which the student is trained are not neglected. Here we must introduce Thomas Kuhn's famous work on the *Structure of Scientific Revolutions* (1970), especially his notions of 'normal science' and 'paradigm change'. Scientists engaged in normal science work within the bounds of a particular general model or world view of their subject in which they have been trained (a 'paradigm') but do not raise questions about its validity. They are engaged in puzzle solving, or the application of the standard rules of the game to new problems as they appear. (There is no limit to the publishable articles that can be added to an academic curriculum vitae by grinding out such applications.) Paradigm testing – questioning the rules of the game – is a very rare activity. When it occurs, it is in response to a failure of the currently accepted model to deal with severe anomalies. This is not to say that the appearance of anomalies will automatically throw into question the relevance of the paradigm. Anomalies can be ignored for quite a long time, certainly if no alternative approach is proposed. Moreover, the decision to abandon a paradigm in favour of an alternative need not be made on 'objective' grounds of logical argument and demonstration. This point has been made much earlier by Max Planck, the celebrated German physicist: 'A new scientific truth does not triumph by convincing its opponents and making them see the light, but rather because its opponents eventually die, and a new generation grows up that is familiar with it' (1949, 33–4). A subjective element is involved in the choice, reflecting in some cases the absence of an unambiguity of advantage of one approach over the other and even a degree of incommensurability.

This perspective is a helpful one for our subject, having in mind an on-going debate between 'neo-classical' economists who follow the general equilibrium or demand–supply approach which governs the training of most Western economists, and an alternative school, referred to henceforth as the 'Italo-Cambridge' or simply the 'Cambridge' school, which takes off from the position of the Italian writer Piero Sraffa who spent over half a century at Trinity College, Cambridge.

Modern general-equilibrium economics envisages 'distribution' as a problem in the pricing of productive factors, assuming production functions which allow for factor substitution and the isolation of the physical contributions of factors at the margin in each activity. The demand prices of factors are also in part dependent on the prices of final goods, which are imputed back to the productive factors thus arriving at the value of the marginal factor product in each activity. Conversely, the technological conditions described by the production function together with the supply conditions governing the flows of productive factors to each activity, determine costs of production. These cost conditions govern the supply of final goods which combined with the demand conditions determine their prices. The system is one of mutual interdependence of factor and commodity markets such that changes in the demand or supply conditions in either will have ramifications throughout.

In sharp contrast, the Italo-Cambridge school rejects general-equilibrium analysis in favour of a kind of sequence analysis. More precisely, given technology and the structure of production (output levels), knowledge of the wage rate – determined by sociological considerations exogenous to the economic system – suffices for the determination of the profit rate and a set of relative prices satisfying the condition that the profit rate is uniform across all sectors. (Alternatively, the profit rate may be known initially, in which case we can solve for wages and relative prices.) On this view there is no relationship of mutuality between final prices and distribution; rather a key aspect of distribution – either the wage or profit rate – is given to the economic system prior to pricing. Most strikingly, the machinery of demand–supply analysis, including the 'law of demand' (the negatively sloped demand curve), plays no role, and equilibrium prices need not satisfy the equation of supply and demand (see p. 563 and appendix 1 for elaboration).

As one might expect from a Kuhnian perspective, adherence to one or other of the foregoing world views is not solely a matter of objective choice. Cambridge adherents are by and large critical of capitalist institutions, while general-equilibrium economists are somewhat more favourably disposed. It is not perhaps surprising that the pedigree of the alternative approaches has become a hotly debated theme amongst historians of economics. But there is more to the matter than this. Those modern economists who utilize an aggregate production function involving 'capital' and labour find themselves on the defensive. Various paradoxes (brought to light in Cambridge) relating to choice of techniques (labour–capital ratios) upon variation in factor prices threaten the central notion of a diminishing marginal rate of substitution; and the realization that a 'quantity of capital' is not measurable apart from the rate of profit (that is, independently of distribution) implies that to explain the rate of profit in terms of the marginal product of capital involves circular reasoning (see appendix 1). Uncertainties of this kind have encouraged research in the history of the discipline, designed to appreciate better the origins of the present impasse and to suggest alternative approaches. It is most pertinent that Piero Sraffa (1898–1983), who in *Production of Commodities by Means of Commodities* (1960) did more than anyone to define the Cambridge notions of sequence analysis, found in Ricardo's early work propositions relating to profit rate determination which he believed might be interpreted along these lines.

Little wonder then that Ricardian economics should be the centre of attention. Indeed, for Cambridge historians such as Maurice Dobb (1973), Ricardo stands at the head of the line of thought, also said to include Karl Marx, wherein distribution is prior to pricing, rather than on the general-equilibrium line. On this view, general-equilibrium economists include Adam Smith (1776), various 'dissenters' from Ricardo writing during the 1820s and 1830s, and John Stuart Mill (1848); in the post-classical period, the 'marginalists' of the 1870s – W. S. Jevons (1871 [1924]) in Britain, Léon Walras (1874) and Carl Menger (1871) on the Continent; Alfred Marshall (1890 [1920]); and twentieth-century neo-classicists.

A similar place in the history of economics, though from a totally different perspective, have been accorded Ricardo by J. A. Schumpeter, author of a celebrated text, the *History of Economic Analysis* (1954). Schumpeter had the greatest admiration for the algebraic statement of general-equilibrium as formulated by Walras. Since, on Schumpeter's reading, Ricardo (unlike Adam Smith and J. S. Mill) 'was completely blind to the nature, and the logical place in economic theory, of the supply-and-demand apparatus' (1954, 601), his *Principles of Political Economy* constituted a 'detour' on the path towards neo-classical general equilibrium. On Schumpeter's view 'progress' in economics was actually inhibited by Ricardo. Paul Samuelson (1978), the dean of modern neo-classicism, ranks Ricardo behind Adam Smith in competence, thereby adding his vote to the Schumpeterian view.

The Dobb and Schumpeter perspectives have much in common, since both envisage the development of economics from the eighteenth century in terms of a dual process reflecting two paradigms. The only difference lies in the distribution of praise and blame. What to Schumpeter is sound economics is scarcely economics at all to Dobb.

The present text envisages matters very differently. It will be my major theme that the notion of alternative 'paradigms' does not adequately describe the development of nineteenth-century economics. First, in Ricardian economics (and this also applies to Marx) there is a fundamentally important core of general-equilibrium economics accounting for resource allocation in terms of the rationing function of relative prices; nineteenth-century cost price analysis turns on the demand–supply mechanism. Ricardo as price theorist was in the tradition of Adam Smith, and in major respects corrected Smith using the latter's own tools to do so. There was no Kuhnian 'revolution' or paradigmatic change in 1817 from this perspective. Secondly, and a related point, there is no justification for attributing to Ricardo (or Marx) the assumption of a wage rate given exogenously from outside the economic system. Like Smith (and J. S. Mill), Ricardo and Marx were not 'fix-wage' theorists. With wages variable it is legitimate to introduce into the model one of the key relationships of general-equilibrium economics – that between commodity and factor markets; that is a mutual relationship between pricing and distribution. This is not to say that Smith's interests or those of Ricardo or Marx were identical with each other or those, say, of Walras or the present-day theorist. They shared a common 'core' – the theory of allocation. But each focused on a different aspect of the economic system and each had a different objective in writing; for the late nineteenth-century general-equilibrium economists were preoccupied with allocation for its own sake, whereas a major concern of Smith and Mill was economic development, and Smith, Ricardo and Mill were much interested in the secular behaviour of the profit and wage rates. This is certainly not to say that the post-classicists eschewed the growth problem; only that there was a change in major focus. The changing concentration of attention – the application of allocative theory in unfamiliar contexts – adds considerably to the interest of the history of classical economics. The evidence of strong continuity of doctrine over the past two centuries does not render irrelevant the contributions of the great classical masters.

1.2 The Role of the Historian

One school of thought would have the historian of economics provide an account of the gradual march towards 'truth' and the successive shedding of errors which prevented a more rapid accumulation of truth. Schumpeter's *History* is characterized by such a perspective, which denies any long-term role in the development of economic analysis for bias or ideology; for what is involved is an 'objective' progression of ideas into which the scientist's personal biases, philosophies, religious beliefs and so forth do not enter. More specifically, it is *economic analysis* (historical, statistical and theoretical techniques and the results which they help generate), as distinct from *economic thought* (opinions concerning public policy bearing on economic subjects that float in the public mind) or *systems of political economy* (comprehensive sets of economic policies based upon some normative, unifying principle, such as socialism or liberalism), which, in Schumpeter's view, constitutes 'scientific' economics. And economic analysis is amenable to judgement by professionals who can say unambiguously of a piece of work whether it is 'good' analysis or not, and of a particular individual whether he is a 'good' analyst or not. It is implied too that there is only one 'truth' towards which the subject progresses – in Schumpeter's case the truth embodied in the general-equilibrium model. Thus Schumpeter's view of progress is strictly constrained within a Kuhnian paradigm.

At the other end of a broad spectrum of approaches to the history of economic thought is that view which insists that no theory can objectively be said to stand higher than another in the time sequence, for theory is of necessity biased. This is the Marxist view. We have legal, philosophical and sociological theories which rationalize and support class bias (the class in power) and, similarly, we have economic theories to explain and justify the *status quo*. Much of nineteenth-century economics, on this view, reflects the ideology of the industrial and commercial bourgeoisie.

The development of marginal utility theory, as formalized in the early 1870s by Walras, Jevons and Menger, has been interpreted by Marxist historians in precisely these terms. So too have the discussions of embryonic neo-classicism by the so-called 'dissenting' critics of Ricardo, during the 1820s and 1830s. T. R. Malthus's population doctrine (1798, 1803), has similarly been charged with bias by Marxist historians. Malthus is represented as wishing to see working class earnings driven down to the minimum of subsistence or, at best, as denying that long-run improvement of living standards could ever be achieved under any institutional arrangement. The same is said of the contribution by G. P. Scrope (1831, 1833) and Nassau Senior (1836), whereby interest is a necessary payment to reward the painful act of 'abstaining' from present consumption, just as labour imposes a pain cost that requires a compensation. This approach to interest is regarded by Marxists as pure apologetics.

The obvious problem arises how it comes about that the Marxists themselves do credit some economics as 'sound' and do rank contributions according to 'scientific' criteria. Their 'relativism' apparently is a partial one; all theory, except Marxian theory, is riddled with illusion. Here a qualification is required regarding the significance of the year 1830, a revolutionary year in France, and regarded by Marx as a watershed (see p. 377). Until that date economics was developing 'scientifically', for Marx had particular respect for Ricardo in England

and Simonde de Sismondi in France; it is only after 1830 that economics 'lost its way' – a development interpreted as a reactionary response to the revolutionary events – and required rescue, Marx himself providing the life-line in *Capital* (1867).

The Marxist criterion of 'science' requires recognition of the distinction between the relationship of men in production (class relations) rather than the relationship of men to things, for example the individual's connection with the goods he purchases. Once again the notion of 'progress' only seems to have validity within the confines of a specific paradigm. This book will show, however, that Marx's economics shares much common ground with the 'bourgeois' writers. It is also doubtful whether the charge of bias in the various historical episodes listed above – the 'dissention' from Ricardo in the 1820s and 1830s, Malthus's population doctrine, and the abstinence approach – can be substantiated. The same applies to the development of the marginal utility theory in the 1870s which Marxists account for in terms of apologetics.

There remains to note at this point one further historiographical issue – the relation between the history of economics and economic history. Some historians maintain that the development of economic analysis is closely related to contemporary economic events, including economic policy. It seems obvious that economic problems sometimes do become matters of interest to economists: but to say that is to say little. A true 'environmental' approach would have to demonstrate that every major economic event leads to a change in economic theory, and conversely that every major change in economic theory is related to a particular event (cf. Stigler, 1965b). It is doubtful whether this strong hypothesis can be supported. There are some kinds of 'events', however, that are singularly significant, although they are not strictly individual events, but rather pervasive aspects of the economic system. From earliest times economists have been concerned with *value*, and, as we shall see, their interest extended with time from market exchange rates (the going rate of exchange between commodities) to the nature of the 'costs of production' that underlie supply curves, an extension that can perhaps convincingly be related to changes in the general economic environment. Similarly, a concern with economic growth during the eighteenth and nineteenth centuries can doubtless be related to broad empirical developments; and the monetary preoccupations of the period obviously reflect contemporary problems.

It is when one focuses on specific pieces of theory that it is more difficult to justify environmental relationships. This is particularly the case since economics became a professional or university discipline; thereafter, economics often takes off on its own under internal pressures, proceeding in isolation from the real world. But it is also true of several episodes we shall encounter, including Ricardo's demonstration in 1821 of the possibility of technological displacement of labour. Diminishing agricultural returns in agriculture, a key aspect of nineteenth-century economics, is frequently related by historians to British experience during the Napoleonic War, when increasing reliance was placed on domestic resources for the supply of grain. It is not clear, however, whether the argument is justified or not. For both Ricardo and later J. S. Mill were much impressed by the impact of new industrial and agricultural technology. Moreover, impressive formulations of the theory had been made 40 years before Ricardo and his contemporaries wrote on the matter.

More generally, great economists – at least those with any concern for application – have been able to discern the trend pattern of economic data; thus an aspect of Adam Smith's greatness was his capacity to observe potentially profound but still incipient structural changes that normally might pass unnoticed. It is, therefore, insufficient for us to know what was the nature of the economy at any period; we must also know something about the lives of individual innovators in economic theory to be able to say anything worthwhile about the origins of their contributions. That is why biography – knowledge of what a particular economist had learned and the techniques he was familiar with, his personal style, his empirical experience and so forth – is important if one is going to appreciate fully the history of economics (cf. Jaffé, 1965).

1.3 On Method

One of our concerns in this book will be classical methodology. As background, it is helpful to have at hand some modern perspectives regarding the nature of assumptions in economic models and the testing of theory by prediction.

Much neo-classical writing, including Lionel Robbins's famous book *On the Nature and Significance of Economic Science* (1932), takes the position that the axioms of economic theory are, so to speak, intuitively self-evident, being derived from a form of introspection. By contrast, a view championed by Milton Friedman (1953) has it that there need be little concern for the empirical 'accuracy' of the axioms (however derived), science demanding only accurate prediction. For model building necessarily entails abstraction from reality, and the efficacy of such abstraction is amenable to evaluation only in terms of the accuracy of prediction. In answer to critics of the competitive model who observe that the real world is one characterized by monopoly, it is urged that the ultimate test lies in the purported fact that various predictions based on the competitive model are borne out. We may proceed, therefore, 'as if' the economic world behaves according to the assumptions regardless of whether or not we believe that actually to be the case.

From this latter perspective it is predictive ability that gives economists the right to represent their subject as scientific. Some authorities, pre-eminently Sir Karl Popper (1934, ch. 5), have preferred to state the issue in terms of 'falsification'; only those statements that now (or conceivably sometime in the future) are subject to falsification have the right to be called scientific, while all other statements constitute dogma. For on this view there is no such thing as confirmation, a corroboration never proving the truth of a theory but only providing temporary support, since subsequent observation may always overthrow it.

But what precisely is being put to the test? Since it is often possible to obtain the same prediction on the basis of different models, it is meaningless to subject an isolated theorem to test. What must be tested is the entire body of interconnected relationships which underlie that theorem, allowing for the so-called *ceteris paribus* conditions presumed to hold when the theorem is derived – a complex matter indeed, for it is never easy to discern which particular assumption or assumptions may have been responsible for deviations from the expected outcome.

Now the classical economists, including Adam Smith and Ricardo and certainly J. S. Mill, who formally addressed economic method, were aware of much of this. It will be one of my tasks to demonstrate how sophisticated they were and how much of what is believed to be 'new' methodology is old hat. The economists were conscious of the fact that a full test, to constitute a genuine refutation, would require information regarding an entire constellation of causal relations and that any partial test must necessarily be inadequate.

Because of a sharp awareness of the inevitable intervention of disturbing causes – even assuming that all relevant causes have been formally allowed for, which is a strong assumption indeed – the sights of the classical economists were, very sensibly, set at modest levels. They refused to make historical predictions regarding specific variables. Moreover, they were not so naive as to believe that the elasticities of various functional relations could be easily specified, whereas the balance of causal and often conflicting influences playing upon a variable depends strategically upon the precise quantitative strengths of those influences. To avoid misunderstanding regarding the intended scope of their models they wrote of 'tendencies' to describe individual cause–effect relations, rather than specific outcomes. The inadequacy of data to allow specification of precise elasticity values at any time and the instability of functional relations over time set economics apart from the physical sciences in practice even though the general procedures had much in common. As a partial insurance, J. S. Mill insisted that we must at least have confidence in the capacity of our models to explain what has occurred; there must be no unexplained residuals if we are to rely on theory for future policy proposal.

The classicists, moreover, championed direct investigation of the structural characteristics of economic models – the social, anthropological and demographic factors at play – a very different perspective from that encouraged by Friedman's methodology or that which represents the axioms as intuitively self-evident. For they believed (perhaps because of their recognition of the difficulties impeding accurate testing by prediction) that the usefulness of the theoretical propositions in economics hinged critically upon the empirical validity of the axiomatic foundation; their postulates were always intended to reflect a specific time- and space-bound reality.

1.4 Scope and Plan of the Present Work

The objective of this book is to trace out the major theoretical contributions of the British classical school relating predominantly to value and micro-economic distribution, growth and its implications for macro-economic distribution, and money. As already mentioned, the issue of methodology will also be kept in mind.

Textual interpretation is no easy matter. In the first place, we are obliged to take the texts seriously – an unnecessary observation were it not for a strange prejudice to the contrary amongst some commentators. For this reason I shall avoid mere assertion by use of direct quotation as far as it practicable. Yet a subjective element necessarily enters into the interpretative exercise. This is not to open the door to anarchy; it is rather to recognize the need for common sense and balanced judgement. For interpretation is an art; even if we had clear-cut exegetical rules at hand – and we do not – we would have to exercise judgement in their application. But while we cannot always be absolutely certain of our exegesis, some interpretations are more likely than others. That at least is the presumption with which I shall proceed. Were it not so, the entire exercise would be futile.

Some historians appear to believe that the investigator must pretend to lack knowledge of the future beyond the period under study, and this because of concern with the danger of anachronistic readings. Now it is self-evident that we must strenuously avoid superimposing on an early writer reference frameworks that were developed only after his death or even after a particular moment in his career. But this does not require that we avoid modern vocabulary and categories in tracing the filiation of ideas. One is writing after all for modern readers. More important, there is also a danger of denying the presence in an early writer's work of modern concepts merely because they are expressed differently. Again, to trace the filiation of ideas requires common sense and good judgement, not a refusal to use modern categories and a pretence at innocent ignorance.

The main body of this book is organized by general topic: value and micro-economic distribution or allocation theory; capital, employment and growth; money; and method. To some extent this is an artificial device, for our modern classifications do not formally correspond to those of earlier economists. None the less, if we proceed cautiously little harm will be done. The classicists did, after all, deal conspicuously with the theory of allocation, assuming stationarity of population and capital or at least constant average wage and profit rates; and with the growth process involving expanding population and capital and variable wage and profit rates, assuming an equilibrium distribution of the factors between sectors. Similarly they separated out monetary analysis for consideration. Where there exist interconnections between allocation, growth and money, the appropriate allowances will be made.

At the same time we shall also be concerned with the contribution by individual authors to the topic in question – pre-eminently Adam Smith (1723–90), David Ricardo (1772–1823) and John Stuart Mill (1806–73) and, on specific topics, Thomas Robert Malthus (1766–1834) and Karl Marx (1818–83) – in order to define what each successive economist adopted from his predecessors and contemporaries and what he discarded. (For brief biographies, see appendix 2.) We must then be sensitive to the possible danger of importing a bogus impession of conscious progressive development. What, for example, may now be represented as the filling in by a writer of a *lacuna* or the correction of a deficiency in the work of some predecessor, may not then have appeared in that light; and what matters for the historian is how at the time the state of knowledge was perceived – though that is not all that matters. Again, caution is advised.

Suggested Reading

The Suggested Reading appended to each chapter is intended to be 'representative' rather than exhaustive. One objective of the selection is to point readers to a variety of alternative perspectives. A number of works dealing wholly or in large part with 'classical economics', its origins and aftermath might be consulted for this purpose: Myint (1948), part 1; Mitchell (1967), vol. I; Dobb (1973); Eagly (1974); Sowell (1974); O'Brien (1975); Deane (1978), ch. 1–7; Blaug (1985), ch. 1–8; Schumpeter (1954), 181–94 on Smith and 463–90, 527–74, 575–687 on the period 1790–1870.

Blaug (1985) and Spiegel (1983), and Hollander (1973, 1979, 1985) on Smith, Ricardo and Mill respectively, all contain excellent bibliographies. J. C. Wood has included various articles on Smith, Ricardo and Malthus in the Croom Helm series *Assessments of Leading Economists* (Wood, 1984, 1985, 1986).

Much of the discussion that follows regarding Adam Smith, David Ricardo and J. S. Mill derives from my full-length studies of these classicists. Also highly recommended are Skinner (1979) on Smith, J. H. Hollander (1910) on Ricardo, and Schwartz (1972) on Mill. See also appendix 2 for suggested biographies of the main authors.

Viner (1960), Robbins (1961), Grampp (1965), Samuels (1966), Coats (1971), provide broad coverage of the classical economists on economic policy. Robbins (1968) treats the theory of economic development in the history of economics, giving much attention to the classicists.

On those in the so-called 'second rank' of the classical school, see Bowley (1937) on Senior; Robbins (1958) on Torrens; Rauner (1961) on Bailey; O'Brien (1970) on McCulloch; and Moss (1976) on Longfield.

Schumpeter (1954), 1–47, explains his approach to the history of economics. For the opposing 'Marxian' view, emphasizing the ideological dimension, see Meek (1967), 196–224, and Dobb (1973), ch. 1. The introductory chapter to Blaug (1985) deals with a variety of alternative approaches to the history of economics.

Caldwell (1984) provides extracts from some major twentieth-century contributions to economic methodology. This book and also Caldwell (1982) contain excellent discussions of the work of Robbins, Friedman, Popper and also of Kuhn and various other contributors to the 'growth of knowledge' tradition. Blaug (1985), ch. 17, provides 'a methodological postscript' which touches on the falsifiability criterion in classical and later economics (see also Blaug, 1980).

The forementioned 'postscript' also treats the broad utility of the study of the history of economics. On this issue, Winch (1962), Gordon (1965) and Boulding (1971) are interesting.

Hicks's essay on '"Revolutions" in Economics' and Leijonhufvud's on 'Schools, "Revolutions", and research programmes in economic theory', both of which appear in Latsis (1976), are important for our themes. See also the succinct 'Introduction' to Deane (1978). Hutchison (1978a) deals at length with various episodes illustrating 'revolutions and progress in economic knowledge'.

2 The Precursors of Adam Smith: an Overview

2.1 Introduction

This chapter presents a bird's-eye view of some pre-Smithian literature by way of introduction to our subject. We shall proceed at a rapid pace, some of the main features of the pre-classical period being indicated only in general terms. We first treat (section 2.2) the 'Scholastic' tradition of the medieval Christian theologians with specific reference to their approach towards *value*, an issue arising within an ethical framework involving justice in exchange. This discussion is followed by reference to the natural-law philosophers and ethical jurists of the seventeenth and early eighteenth centuries. In all this we discern significant 'gaps' in the appreciation of the operation of the pricing mechanism, although this is not stated by way of criticism since neither the theologians nor the philosophers wrote as economists. Section 2.3 takes up the 'mercantilist' perspective on economic thought. This turns on the desirability of a long-term favourable foreign trade balance as a means of attracting the precious metals, regarded as an index of the national stock of 'wealth'. This is followed in section 2.4 by some indication of analytical progress relating to 'automatic adjustment mechanisms' discernible within mercantilist writings, particularly in the international sphere. Sections 2.5 and 2.6 extend the discussion to eighteenth-century thought relating to allocation theory and economic growth – the main themes of this book. All this, together with the work of the French Physiocrats (chapter 3), sets the stage for Adam Smith's *Wealth of Nations*.

2.2 The Scholastic Tradition

Scholastic economic thought turns to a considerable degree on the interpretation and evaluation of obscure passages by Aristotle

(384–322 BC) in his *Nicomachean Ethics* on the 'just' rate of exchange between commodities. There is much debate to this day regarding the Schoolmen's position on justice in exchange – whether the emphasis was placed on production costs or on demand (utility), and the nature of the relation envisaged between these perspectives. We shall here indicate some very broad lines of Scholastic thought.

Competitive market price was analysed by St Thomas Aquinas (1225?–1274), the most celebrated of the Schoolmen, in terms of demand–supply (utility–scarcity), with a recognition that even expected changes in supply can play upon the current price. He took the competitively determined market price of a commodity as an index of commutative justice. Sale at a market price which permitted a 'gain', an excess over the price initially paid by the seller for the product (or its raw materials), was regarded as morally satisfactory provided costs were reflected thereby – the 'gain' in fact constituting a return to labour, risk-taking or transportation. An excess simply 'because the price of a thing has changed with the change of place or time' would be justified only where the individual had not originally purchased the commodity in question with the intention of reselling it, that is where he is not strictly a trader at all. Conversely, a market price which *failed* to cover 'legitimate' expenses was not obligatory, so that a trader might with justice charge a price higher than that ruling in the market should an opportunity to do so present itself.

This result, which reflects both an absence of pure profit and of loss, will be attained in the long run by the classical or neo-classical competitive process, and it is doubtless this fact that has encouraged the view that the early Scholastics 'discovered' the condition of long-run competitive equilibrium (e.g., Schumpeter, 1954, 93). But Aquinas did not reach these conclusions by means of analytical reasoning. He did not explain how the market price would come to reflect normal costs by tracing through the consequence of a failure to cover supply price, or indicate the manner in which resources will move between occupations in response to relative profitability. This problem in fact did not concern him. He was prescribing certain 'just' courses of action according to which the market price was a satisfactory criterion provided that it did not permit pure profit on the one hand, and did not lead to losses on the other. While preoccupation with the ethics of pricing might lead to the analysis of economic phenomena, it does not seem to be the case that Aquinas took the step from ethics to analysis. A similar conclusion may be applied to Duns Scotus (d. 1308); to identify the just price with the competitive common price and also with the 'normal' cost of the good may at most be said to 'imply' the law of cost but cannot be regarded as an analytical statement thereof.

Recent research suggests that Aquinas' teacher Albertus Magnus (d. 1280) may actually have gone further than his pupil in his recognition that a selling price below cost would damage society, specifically by driving the producers out of business (Langholm, 1979, 63–4); 'on the whole, his pupils must be said to have responded less than brightly to this really remarkable suggestion. Thomas Aquinas was quite deaf to it' (p. 80). And more generally, Scholastic economics was entirely unequipped to appreciate 'the notion of adjustment of productive resources towards an equilibrium of industries' (p. 82).

Later Scholastic writers (particularly the Jesuits) formally took issue with the willingness of their predecessors to legitimize charges exceeding the 'common estimation' by individual sellers who had undergone – through no 'fault' of their own – abnormally high costs. Reliance upon the common estimation was to be the rule whether or not losses, or pure profits, resulted. This becomes clear from criticisms of Duns Scotus by Molina (1536–1600) and by Lugo (1593–1660). For all that, the later Schoolmen did not divorce the 'common estimation' from production costs. An individual in a random case may indeed be permitted to enjoy profits or be obliged to suffer losses by reliance upon the going competitive price, but in their view this price will 'tend' to reflect normal costs: 'a merchant cannot compensate himself for expenses he has incurred when other merchants who have incurred smaller expenses commonly sell the same goods at a lower price. He must reckon it his bad luck that he has brought goods at a great outlay to a place where their common price was less' (Lugo, in Dempsey, 1943, 153). A particularly comprehensive statement to the same effect was made by Lessius (1554–1623).

Thus, despite formal criticism in later Scholastic writings of the cost orientation of their predecessors, costs none the less appeared as the predominant factor in the 'common estimation'. A formal emphasis upon 'utility' as the cause or source of value is also to be noted. For example: 'the value of things is not considered as resident in their entity but in their utilities and advantages' (Molina, cited in Dempsey, 1943, 149). But such formal statements occur repeatedly in the work of Aquinas (and indeed of Aristotle) and should not be exaggerated. Utility was a necessary condition of exchange value, not a sufficient condition or the determinant of exchange value. Yet the analytical implications of the emphasis on costs must be carefully adjudicated. The distinction between normal and abnormal costs, and the argument that it is the former which contribute to the determination of the 'common estimation', suggests perhaps a step towards appreciation of the notion of supply price, but there is still inadequate investigation of the process of long-run cost-determination of price, and little to suggest an appreciation of the function of prices in the general allocation of resources. For it is not at all made clear how the price reflecting the 'common appraisal' – which takes into account expenses that are ordinarily and usually incurred – is in fact arrived at. (Indeed certain formulations allow for evaluation by 'experts'.)

The Scholastics did not apply the supply–demand apparatus to the problem of income formation and developed no integrated theory of distribution. There is one particular price, treatment of which in terms of demand and supply was entirely ruled out: the price of money. That interest must not be charged was originally a biblical injunction, but unsuccessful attempts were made to rationalize the injunction by 'proving' the sterility of money.

Finally, it must be emphasized that the fundamental concern of the Scholastic authorities was to assure the avoidance of monopsonistic and monopolistic exploitation. If this end could be achieved by means of the market, well and good. But the price determined by the civil authority might be preferable in some circumstances. There is no evidence that the Scholastics were market enthusiasts because of a belief in 'economic freedom' or because they recognized the function of the competitive price mechanism in the organization of general economic activity.

Much the same analytical *lacunae* regarding value are discernible in the writings of the seventeenth-century natural-law philosopher Samuel Pufendorf (1632–94) which were well known to Adam Smith. In the first place, the formal references to utility are made. The 'foundation' of ordinary price 'is the aptitude of a thing or action, by which it can either mediately or immediately contribute something to the necessity of human life, or to making it more advantageous and pleasant' (1672 [1934], 676). But the emphasis is on cost price. The cost (or natural) price is defined 'as a just price which is commonly set by those who are sufficiently acquainted with both the merchandise and the market', taking account of the labour and expense 'commmonly' incurred and also a moderate 'profit' (pp. 685–8). This 'common' cost price, be it noted, may be determined not by the market process at all, but by experts. A temporary price determined in the market is also recognized; but as in the case of the later Scholastics, no account is given of the relationship envisaged between the cost and the (temporary) market prices.

Francis Hutcheson (1694–1746) used Pufendorf as a text in his Glasgow lectures on moral philosophy which were attended by Adam Smith as a student. The published version of Hutcheson's lectures contains a chapter dealing with price, but the subject is carried no further than it had been by Pufendorf. The hiatus in the analysis of price determination by the Scholastic writers and the ethical jurists remained to be filled.

2.3 The Mercantilists

In the first chapter of Book IV of the *Wealth of Nations* (1776), Adam Smith describes British mercantilism as a body of policy recommendation originating with merchants and manufacturers – pamphleteers rather than a genuine 'school' of writers – who mistakenly identified the stock of national wealth with the precious metals. From their perspective, national policies were required which assured the attraction of the metals. If there were no domestic mines, the only way that gold could be attracted was by a favourable balance of trade. The principle of a *long-term* favourable balance of trade governed their recommendations.

Our primary concern here will be with the post-1620 period. During the sixteenth century the emphasis was on a favourable trade balance on each individual trade transaction rather than nationally, as in the later period. The earlier objective was to assure against a depletion in the national gold stock rather than to generate an increase. There was also a peculiar concern to avoid exchange depreciation to which end close regulation of individual transactions in the foreign exchanges and in metals was recommended. (The term 'bullionism' has been coined to cover the earlier period.)

John Stuart Mill viewed mercantilist doctrine in the same light as Adam Smith, and in the 'Preliminary Remarks' to his *Principles of Political Economy* (1848 [1965], II, 4–7) explained the basic error in terms of false analogies, particularly the fallacy of composition – the identification of the individual and the nation: the individual is wealthy who has accumulated gold, and the nation also, being an aggregate of the individuals, is similarly wealthy. One might add also the erroneous notion that one man's gain in trade is another man's loss, similarly transferred to the level of the nation – a stark contrast with the subsequent classical attitude towards trade envisaged as a matter of cooperation which benefits all parties.

While Smith and Mill probably exaggerated when they charged the pamphleteers with literally *identifying* the precious metals and wealth, there is no doubt that they drew too close a relationship. Many conceived the precious metals as a store of wealth. For they favoured savings (sometimes on moral or religious grounds and from class prejudice), but in the naive sense of storing up, or not consuming, goods, which process they perceived to be best achieved in the form of durable commodities with high unit value. It is this perspective that generated much of the basic case for a metallic inflow. Two citations from a 1690 work by Sir William Petty (1623–87) will illustrate the emphasis on saving and on the suitability of the metals as stores of wealth which gave to them their superior importance:

But above all the particulars hitherto considered, that of superlucration [saving] ought chiefly to be taken in; for if a Prince have never so many Subjects, and his Country be never so good, yet if either through sloth, or extravagent expences, or Oppression and Injustice, whatever is gained shall be spent as fast as gotten, that State must be accounted poor... (1899, I, 254).

The great and ultimate effect of Trade is not Wealth at large, but particular abundance of Silver, Gold, and Jewels, which are not perishable, nor so mutable as other Commodities, but are Wealth at all times, and all places: Whereas abundance of Wine, Corn, Fowls, Flesh, etc., are Riches but *hic &nunc*, so as the raising of such Commodities, and the following of such Trade, which does store the Country with Gold, Silver, Jewels, etc. is profitable before others (pp. 259–60).

A confusion of loanable capital with money also contributed to the significance attached to the national stock of metal. We shall illustrate this theme by reference to interest rate determination. It had long been observed by the pamphleteers that the interest rate declined along with the inflow of precious metals into Europe from the Americas. (The law which prescribed a maximum interest rate was periodically modified, the legal maximum tending downwards.) The analysis of this phenomenon sometimes entailed the unsatisfactory argument that as the money supply increases so each pound becomes worth less in purchasing power, and a lower interest is paid for loanable funds. (This is not a sensible argument: if £100 borrowed has lower purchasing power, so too does the £10 paid in interest for the loan.) Some of the pamphleteers maintained that an increase in the money supply depresses the interest rate, because it affects the supply side of the loanable funds market more than the demand side and conversely upon a reduction. Characteristically, the mercantilists failed to distinguish between money and capital, whether lent out or employed by its owner. John Locke (1632–1704) provides an illustration:

Now, I think, the natural interest of money is raised two ways: first, when the money of a country is but little, in proportion to the debts of the inhabitants, one amongst another.... Secondly, that, which constantly raises the natural interest of money, is, when money is little, in proportion to the trade of a country. For in trade everybody calls for money, according as he wants it, and this disproportion is always felt (Locke, 1691; in Viner, 1937, 31).

The mercantilists also made out a case for high employment turning mainly on the beneficial effects for the trade balance flowing from a fully employed work force (though also because of the danger to social stability of idleness). It was specifically employment designed to improve the balance of trade that concerned them, not high employment as such or as a means to high consumption by labourers as the classicists were later to champion. The wage rate was said to reflect sub-sistence levels, not only descriptively but prescriptively: it was recom-mended that the wage should be at a minimum to ensure that resources are not absorbed in producing goods that otherwise might be exported. (There was also a considerable opinion that the labour supply curve for any given body of workers was backward bending, such that as wages rise the supply of labour effort falls off.) Indeed, the mercantilists went so far as to recommend a large population even if it implied large numbers living in workhouses. The recommendation of a high popula-tion strongly suggests the objective of low wages as a stimulus to the bal-ance of trade surplus, to the end always of attracting a large stock of specie (precious metals). The following extract from Charles Davenant (1656–1714) illustrates this theme:

> In order to have hands to carry on labour and manufactures, which must make us gainers in the Balance of Trade, we ought not to deter, but rather invite men to marry, which is to be done by privileges and exemption for such a number of children, and by denying certain offices and dignities to all unmarried persons…A country that makes provision to increase in inhabitants, whose situation is good, and whose people have a genius adapted to Trade, will never fail to be gainers in the Balance, provided the labour and industry of their people be well managed and carefully directed (1699 [1771], II, 191–2).

This statement captures mercantilism in a nutshell. There was to be a large population and direction of resources to assure a positive trade balance. As a second illustration consider: 'plenty of people must also cause *cheapnesse of wages*: which will cause the cheapnesse of the Manufacture…' thereby improving sales prospects abroad (Petyt, 1680; in McCulloch, 1856a, 349). A third example: 'I conceive the true original and ground of Trade, to be great multitude of people crowded into small compass of Land, whereby all things necessary to life become deer, and all men who have possessions, are induced to Parsimony; but those who have none, are forced to industry and labour, or else to want' (Temple, 1673, 211). That the prices of wage goods should be high in consequence of population pressure on scarce land thereby depressing real wages and satisfying 'the true and original grounds of trade', is a class attitude if ever there was one.

The mercantilist attitude towards technical progress is relevant here too, for they envisaged innovation as assuring an effective increase in population. To quote Sir William Petty: 'introducing…Facilitations of Art…is equivalent to what men vainly hoped from *Polygamy*. For as much as he that can do the Work of five men by one, effects the same as begetting four adult Workmen' (1899, I, 118). In fact some of these writers denied that technical progress was at all useful in a closed economy.

In these respects we have both a 'failure of ideas' and class bias. There are, however, other interpretations. Historically orientated German economists of the late nineteenth century, under the leadership of Wilhelm Roscher and Gustave Schmoller, argued that similar problems to those of contemporary Germany had been involved, the internal and external controls characterizing mercantilism reflecting the expression by new nation states of their power and unity. These policies were pre-eminently political matters having little to do with the intellectual matters that Smith and Mill had described. Other economic historians play down intellectual error, class bias and the political dimension, and argue in terms of the economic conditions of the time. From this perspective there is little merit to the catch-all designation 'mercantilism'. In the British case, for example, devaluations by foreign countries in the early seventeenth century had, it is argued, caused domestic employment crises; in addition, many countries, especially the Baltic producers of naval supplies, were unwilling to accept British goods for one reason or another. These economic conditions generated protectionist recommendations designed to assure surpluses in some trade areas and the accumulation of hard currency to finance purchases of national importance in others.

J. M. Keynes in his *General Theory* (1936) interpreted the concern with a monetary inflow by way of the trade balance as a means to stimulate employment, reading 'Keynesianism' into the literature. There is some justification for this position. The notion that 'the more readie money...that our merchants should make their returne by, the more employment would they make upon our home commodities, advancing the price thereof, which price would augment the quantitie by setting more people on worke' (Malynes, 1601, 109) is suggestive. However, the direct effect of high exports on employment was more significant. Encouragement was to be afforded the most labour-intensive export sectors and the importation of raw materials for making up by domestic labour; 'valuable' industries were ranked from this perspective. These kinds of arguments may reflect aspects of 'under-development'; they imply that without metallic inflows from abroad, or direct stimulation of particular industries coupled with the encouragement of raw material imports, it would be impossible to maintain full employment. This orientation is still conspicuous in the mid-eighteenth century, as in the work of Sir James Steuart (1712–80), against which Adam Smith was to protest vehemently.

An element of white-washing is unfortunately implicit in some of the foregoing rationalizations of mercantilism. Thus Keynes's interpretation as a reflection of the mainstream of thought is unconvincing given the widespread championship of population expansion even in periods of chronic unemployment and under-employment. This same preoccupation is also scarcely suggestive of an economics of underdevelopment. The faulty intellectual components of much pre-Smithian literature, and its pervasive class bias, must not be minimized.

2.4 Instances of Analytical Progress: Automatic Adjustment Mechanisms

Much of the earliest mercantilist writing was pre-analytical; it might be described as the argumentation typical of a popular newspaper. The case for exchange control by the state and for export monopolies, the nature of the balance of trade and of money, were formulated at this level. But there is discernible the introduction of elementary analysis and this of a type that indicates a groping towards the idea of a self-regulating market system. This trend is to be found even amongst ' writers who, from a policy point of view, were protectionists. It is essential to separate a writer's ability as a theorist from the particular policy prescriptions that he recommends, for there were those who understood the price mechanism but did not wish to see it given its head.

An example of analytical advance relates to the balance of trade. It was conceived that the balance of trade may be represented in terms of domestic demand for foreign goods and foreign demand for domestic goods, which can be translated into the demand for foreign exchange and the supply of foreign exchange respectively, the combination of which yields an exchange rate or the price of foreign exchange in terms of the home currency. A statement of what is involved will be found in the pamphlet by the seventeenth-century British writer Thomas Mun (1571–1641) entitled *England's Treasure by Forraign Trade* (1664; written c.1630). This most sophisticated of mercantilists also analysed the effect of gold flows on internal and foreign price levels and the implications for activity of hoarding. He further distinguished between the aggregate and the micro-economic dimensions (even if the main concern is a net aggregate money inflow it is unnecessary to control every single transaction); between the short and the long run (a particular trade which involves the immediate export of gold might yet generate a long-run net inflow); and between visible and invisible trade items. Now it so happens that Mun was a spokesman for the East India Company, which at that time was exporting bullion and importing luxury items – the exact reverse of the standard mercantilist recommendations. It could certainly be said that he was not a dispassionate economist analysing trade. Yet his bias does not gainsay the quality of his argument, the validity of which must stand or fall independently of such considerations. Mun's contribution, amongst others of the early 1600s, reflects the transition from the more stringent type of mercantilism sometimes labelled 'bullionism', which was concerned to assure a favourable balance on every individual transaction (see above, p. 19).

Mun's work, and also that of John Locke (1691) and various others, pointed the way towards later developments in international trade theory by Adam Smith's close friend David Hume (1711–76), one of the discoverers (in 'Of the Balance of Trade', *Political Discourses*, 1752d) of the so-called 'specie-flow mechanism' whereby the free-flowing movement of precious metals between trading nations assures an equilibrium such that exports balance imports. (Gervaise, 1720, had earlier provided a brilliant statement.) The analysis typically involved the following propositions (see Viner, 1937, 75): (*a*) that the net international balance of payments is paid in specie; (*b*) that price levels are a function of the money supply; and (*c*) that imports and exports are a function of the relative price levels of home and foreign commodities. These three propositions were then integrated into a self-regulating mechanism: an increase in the money supply internally (derived let us say from newly discovered mines) will generate an increase in domestic prices and, consequently, shifts of the demand and supply curves in the foreign exchange market reflecting increased domestic demand for foreign goods and reduced foreign demand for domestic goods. If the disturbance is large enough there will follow an outflow of gold to meet the net foreign debt. This outflow in turn lowers somewhat the internal price level and raises prices abroad, domestic commodities becoming increasingly competitive compared with foreign commodities, assuring ultimately a new equilibrium where exports and imports are again in balance. Here we have an embryonic notion of the gold standard mechanism, the implication of which is that there is no particular advantage to a large stock of precious metals so that there need be no concern for the adequacy of the national money supply. Some of the elements constituting the mechanism, including the quantity theory, had already been established earlier, as in Mun's work, but Mun, of course, did not reach the final conclusion and continued to recommend a permanent foreign trade surplus.

The Hume mechanism is governed by the profit motive of individuals responding to price differentials – 'a moral attraction, arising from the interests and passions of men' (1752d, 65). Hume, from this perspective, may be regarded as one of the first of the classicists. But even earlier there are instances of an appreciation of the irrelevance of the money stock as a policy concern because of the operation of an automatic adjustment mechanism of sorts. Thus we find the proposition in *Discourses Upon Trade* (1691) by Dudley North (1653–1734) that a country never retains more money than it 'needs', for which reason there was no problem about the international balance. An initial excess will generate a fall in its value to the metallic content so that coins are melted down: 'There is required for carrying on the Trade of the Nation a determinate Sum of Specifick Money, which varies, and is sometimes more, sometimes less, as the Circumstances we are in require.... This ebbing and flowing of Money supplies and accommodates itself, without any aid of Politicians' (in McCulloch 1856a, 538–9). Even Sir William Petty had written in 1662 that 'there is a certain measure, and due proportion requisite to drive the trade of a Nation, more or less than which would prejudice the same' (1899, I, 35), and in 1665 that 'Money is but the fat of the Body-politick, whereof too much doth as often hinder its Agility, as too little makes it sick' (1899, I, 113); but he neglected to trace the impact of money on the level of prices, and thus lacked the automatic mechanism now under discussion.

*   *   *

As we have seen, simple demand–supply (utility–scarcity) analysis was well established by 1700. It comes as no surprise that this analysis provided the solution to the so-called 'paradox of value' discussed below (p. 61), as by John Law (1705, 4). The range of application of the analysis had been extended by seventeenth-century writers not only to the foreign exchange market, but also to the rate of interest – the identification of interest as a price amenable to analysis on a par with the rent of land indicating a significant break from Scholastic attitudes. (Wages, however, were as before treated as exogenously given.) But in addition to these extensions some individual writers delved deeper into the motives behind resource allocation, paralleling at a more general level the growing appreciation, even within mercantilism, of automatic mechanisms of international adjustment.

The notion of 'economic man' was familiar to the earliest writers. As the Scholastics phrased it, 'everyone will do that which makes for his own interest'. And in the mercantilist literature the significance of self-interest was also realized. None the less, government interference of all kinds was supported either because it was feared that the profit motive would generate ruinous results unless controlled – the usual view – or because positive social advantages would flow from this particular motive only if directed along suitable channels.

A most interesting *sixteenth-century* example is provided by John Hales (1549), who seems to have appreciated, to an unusual degree for his day, the role of relative prices and profits in domestic resource allocation. The imposition of maximum wheat prices, he argued, would generate scarcity by reducing relative profitability; whereas the removal of price maxima would stimulate wheat production at the expense of wool, by 'provok[ing] every man ... to turn the lands which he enclosed from pasture to arable land; for every man will gladder follow that wherein they see more profit and gains' (cited Grampp, 1965, I, 78). Yet even he questioned whether self-interest always produced social harmony (p. 85).

During the late seventeenth and early eighteenth centuries a growing number of economic writers came to oppose government direction of resources, on the grounds that, since governments are incompetent, and subject to pressure groups of various orders, it might lead to a worse result than unregulated trade. This too is only a negative kind of appreciation of the strength of the profit motive. There is discernible, however, a more positive view according to which unregulated trade actually serves the public interest. On this view the profit motive does not lead to a chaotic result, but organizes economic activity satisfactorily. To talk about 'unregulated' trade is, however, somewhat misleading because no responsible writer ever denied the need for a legal and institutional framework within which trade is to be carried on. Unregulated trade means rather that within the framework defining which activities are *precluded*, the profit motive must be given its head.

An example of our theme is provided by the Reverend Joseph Lee (*A Vindication of a Regulated Enclosure*, 1656). Lee wrote as follows: 'The advancement of private persons will be the advantage of the publick ... whatsoever benefit we make to ourselves, tends to the publick good' (22–3). The context is the contemporary enclosure of land for sheep; the problem was the displacement of labour. Significantly, his support of enclosure was qualified, Lee allowing regulation designed to avoid potential conflict between private and public interests, and to assure that benefits are not limited to a particular class. Thus only if the economy as a whole enjoys full employment could the case for enclosure be made; appropriate timing was essential. Secondly, where monopoly was prevalent the law must intervene; his case assumed competitive conditions. Thirdly, he recommended that labourers' cottages be protected by contract; the advantages flowing from the change must not be at the expense of the propertyless. We are touching here on a profoundly important question of applied economics or, as John Stuart Mill later phrased it, the 'art' of political economy.

A notable, if less 'responsible', statement of the social advantage of free (internal) trade is by North: 'there can be no Trade unprofitable to the Publick; for if any prove so, men leave it off; and whenever the

Traders thrive, the Publick, of which they are a part, thrive also...All favour to one Trade or Interest against another, is an Abuse, and cuts so much Profit from the Publick' (1691; in McCulloch, 1856a, 513–14). There are in North's pamphlet some other relevant observations, one regarding the automatic control of interest rate fluctuations. North argues from the perspective of opportunity cost that the supply of loanable funds is pretty elastic, for as the interest rate falls so the (lending) opportunities foregone when specie is melted down into plate tend to decline, inducing a switch of metal holdings from the monetary form; conversely, as the interest rate increases, plate tends to be melted into money to be lent out (p. 519). This assures an elastic response of supply to variations of the interest rate so that the interest rate will not change significantly despite significant movements in the demand for loanable funds. The market process itself regulates the magnitude of fluctuations.

2.5 The Eighteenth Century: Allocation Theory

When we come to the eighteenth century we encounter some brilliant analyses of the organizing function of the profit motive, which accord a conspicuous role in allocation to relative prices and alternative costs. *The Fable of the Bees; or Private Vices, Publick Benefits* (1714) by Bernard Mandeville (1670–1733) may be mentioned here, for some commentators read the work as a pioneer of *laissez-faire* individualism and have even charged Adam Smith with plagiarism. In fact, Mandeville insisted that private activity ruled by self-interest had desirable social consequences only if under the 'dextrous management' of government; there is a strong mercantilist flavour to his position:

> The great Art...to make a Nation happy and what we call flourishing, consists in giving every Body an Opportunity of being employ'd; which to compass, let a Government's first care be to promote as great a variety of Manufactures, Arts, and Handicrafts, as Human Wit can invent; and the second to encourage Agriculture and Fishery in all their branches...; for as the one is an infallible Maxim to draw vast Multitudes of People into a Nation, so the other is the only Method to maintain them (1714 [1924], 197).

> Every Government ought to be thoroughly acquainted with, and stedfastly to pursue the Interest of the Country. Good Politicians by dextrous Management, laying heavy Impositions on some Goods, or totally prohibiting them, and lowering the Duties on others, may always turn and divert the Course of Trade which way they please....But above all, they'll keep a watchful Eye over the Balance of Trade in general, and never suffer that all the Foreign Commodities together, that are imported

in one Year, shall exceed in Value what of their own Growth or Manufacture is in the same exported to others. Note, that I speak now of the
Interest of those Nations that have no Gold or Silver of their own Growth
(pp. 115–16).

Richard Cantillon's *Essay on the Nature of Commerce in General*
(1755) provides a much better illustration of our general theme.
Cantillon (1680–1734), sometimes described as 'first of the moderns',
applied economic theory to the problem of resource allocation and
traced through the consequences of a change in tastes on the part of
landowners – empirically the sector governing taste patterns and
expenditure flows – from servants to horses. The switch in demand
between products creates excess demand in the one case and excess
supply in the other at the initial (cost) prices; appropriate changes in
market prices follow, with consequent movements of land and labour
services between uses until a new pattern of equilibrium outputs is
established. This constitutes a nice early formulation along 'Marshallian' lines of the way in which resources are transferred between sectors
as demand patterns alter: 'farmers will not fail to change from year to
year the use of the land till they arrive at proportioning their production
pretty well to the consumption of the Inhabitants' (1755 [1931], 63).
More specifically:

> When a Landowner has dismissed a great number of Domestic Servants,
> and increased the number of his Horses, there will be too much Corn for
> the needs of the Inhabitants, and so the Corn will be cheap and the Hay
> dear. In consequence the Farmers will increase their grass land and
> diminish their Corn to proportion it to the demand. In this way the
> Fancies or Fashions of Landowners determine the use of the Land and
> bring about the variations of demand which cause the variations of Mar-
> ket prices. If all the Landowners of a State cultivated their own estates
> they would use them to produce what they want; and as the variations of
> demand are chiefly caused by their mode of living the prices which they
> offer in the Market decide the Farmers to all the changes which they
> make in the employment and use of the land (p. 65).

Now Cantillon does not explicitly define a demand schedule, but his
adjustment process makes little sense unless one attributes to him an
implicit appreciation of the law of demand. It is important to establish
that the conception of a price–quantity relation was part and parcel of
the eighteenth-century approach to resource allocation. And this is not
surprising, for market demand–supply analysis involving price–quantity
relations had been understood much earlier on. Moreover, even before
1700 an empirical schedule had been constructed relating price
increases to output reductions, evidently implying a price–quantity
demand relationship:

We take it, that a defect in the harvest may raise the price of corn in the following proportions:

Defect		*above the Common Rate*
1 Tenth		3 Tenths
2 Tenths	Raises	8 Tenths
3 Tenths	the	1.6 Tenths [1 and 6 tenths]
4 Tenths	Price	2.8 Tenths [2 and 8 tenths]
5 Tenths		4.5 Tenths [4 and 5 tenths]

So that when corn rises to treble the common rate, it may be presumed, that we want [i.e., lack] above 1/3d of the common produce; and if we should want 5/10ths, or half the common produce, the price would rise to near five times the common rate (Davenant, 1699 [1771], II, 224–5).

The eighteenth-century writers were incorporating the law of demand into a broader picture of the allocation of resources, with attention now paid to the consequences of a divergence of market price from cost price and the process whereby the former tends to the latter.

A word now about cost price itself. Cost price in Cantillon's work, or 'intrinsic value', includes the land and labour requirements per unit of output (1755 [1931], 29). He sought to render commensurable the different inputs, and sum the coefficients in real (rather than money) terms as Sir William Petty had attempted to do in 1691 (1899, I, 176ff.). Cantillon's own solution was to translate the labour requirements per unit of output into land requirements per unit which are then added to the direct land requirement (1755 [1931], 41). The translation was achieved by assuming that workers in any industry are paid a fixed wage, so many corn units per hour, and that a specific quantity of land is required per unit of corn. The assumptions relating to the fixed corn wage and the constant land and labour coefficients of production implying constant-cost conditions – or horizontal long-run supply curves – also prove to be historically important.

Cantillon's treatment of profits is also exceptional. A distinction is made between 'hired people' and 'undertakers' ('entrepreneurs'), the former receiving contractually fixed incomes and the latter uncertain incomes as the difference between sales proceeds and contractual payments (pp. 39–41, 51–5). Cantillon's profit applies, strictly speaking, to any uncertain income, and not solely to the income of capitalist employers; thus it includes also the 'return' to beggars and thieves. But as far as the employer is concerned it is a residual or surplus which in corn terms, Cantillon tells us, constitutes for the majority of farmers and master manufacturers about three times the produce of land needed to maintain standard labour (p. 41). So while profits are received as an uncertain residual income, there none the less exists, on average, a normal profit which is included in long-run (cost) price and which does not represent merely 'wages of management'. On this view, in agriculture there is apart from the 'true Rent' paid to the landlord, and the farmer's costs and own subsistence needs, a net income 'which ought to remain with him to make his undertaking profitable' (p. 121). This conception implies a break with the earlier (Scholastic) version of profits that was more suitable to trading relations − the simple notion of buying cheap and selling dear, or 'profit upon alienation' in Sir James Steuart's terminology, which as Karl Marx later insisted cannot explain the emergence of net profit in the economy as a whole (Marx, 1862−3 [1954], I, 42).

At the same time, a serious complexity deserves special notice. Cantillon also writes as if profits (as well as wages) are transfer payments out of rent: 'except the Prince and the Proprietors of Land, all the Inhabitants of a State are dependent...[and] derive their living...from the property of the Land-owners' (1755 [1931], 55). In fact an entire chapter (Part I, xii) is devoted to the proposition that 'All Classes and Individuals in a State subsist or are enriched at the Expense of the Proprietors of Land' (p. 43). This latter perspective, and also an analysis 'Of the Circulation of Money' (Part II, iii), were to have some influence on the French Physiocrats. Here too Sir William Petty's name must again be mentioned. He had already hit in 1662 upon the concept of an agricultural surplus remaining after seed and subsistence have been allowed for, neglecting the problem of comparing non-homogeneous outputs and inputs:

> Suppose a man could with his own hands plant a certain scope of Land with Corn, that is, could Digg, or Plough, Harrow, Weed, Reap, Carry home, Thresh, and Winnow so much as the Husbandry of this Land requires; and had withal Seed wherewith to sow the same. I say, that when this man hath subtracted his seed out of the proceed of his Harvest, and also, what himself hath both eaten and given to others in exchange for Clothes, and other Natural necessities; that the remainder of Corn is the natural and true Rent of the Land for that year; and the *medium* of...so many years as makes up the Cycle, within which Dearths and Plenties make their revolution, doth give the ordinary Rent of the Land in Corn (1899, I, 43).

Other contemporaries were defining cost price along lines to become standard in the *Wealth of Nations*. Thus, for example: 'I can most clearly perceive that the value of all commodities, or the price, is a compound of the value of the land necessary to raise them, the value of the labour exerted in producing and manufacturing them, and of the value of the brokerage which provides and circulates them' (Temple, 1758; cited

Meek, 1967, 29). As Meek shows, William Temple meant by 'broker-age' profits on industrial and agricultural investment.

Sir James Steuart in his *Inquiry into the Principles of Political Economy* (1767) undertook analyses of the market–natural price relationship similar to those of Cantillon. But he did not recommend that the allocative consequences of changes in taste patterns be allowed to occur. We have here further illustration of the need to separate contributions to economic theory from particular policy objectives. The major theoretical contributions were not all made by writers who favoured free enterprise. Steuart was a 'mercantilist' as far as social control is concerned. As noted above, Steuart also retained the unsatisfactory notion of 'profit upon alienation'.

2.6   The Eighteenth Century: Economic Growth

The late seventeenth- and eighteenth-century literature thus indicates a growing concern with the relation between market price based on simple demand–supply (utility–scarcity) analysis and costs, and with the nature of costs. The new emphasis upon resources used up in production and the allocative consequences of divergencies of market from cost price, is in fact part of a general advance from the limited perspective on economic problems by the early writers to the sophisticated classical approach. This preoccupation with the 'real' dimensions of the system manifests itself not only in value or price theory (our primary concern thus far) but also in the new promising attention given to economic growth. We shall touch briefly on capital and its functions, technological progress, interest rate determination and its trend path, population and the limits to growth.

With an appreciation of the nature of capital as productive capacity, the concern with money waned. Capital as a productive factor not only included machines and structures, but also wage goods and materials the function of which was to permit the adoption of lengthy or round-about productive processes (frequently entailing specialized tasks) by tiding over the interval between the time that production commences and the time that it ends. Thus Josiah Tucker (1712–99): 'The inhabitants of a poor country, who ... generally live from hand to mouth, dare not make such costly experiments or embark on such expensive or long-winded undertakings as the inhabitants of a rich country can attempt and execute with ease' (1774, 24). The 'poor' country does not possess the stored-up capital goods which allow individuals to undertake lengthy processes including (be it noted) research.

The notion of capital in its function of permitting indirect processes may seem particularly appropriate for the simplest agricultural system, where society must survive from harvest to harvest. But this is too restricted a view. For output to be forthcoming in a continuous stream, as modern economics has it, it is necessary for the 'pipelines' (including structures and machinery at all stages of production) to be in place and to be appropriately filled; capital goods exist, therefore, which evidently have been built in the past. Moreover, nearly all the labour devoted to any particular batch of goods emerging at retail at any particular moment has been applied in the past. There is an important element of truth in the concept of the need for capital to tide over lengthy processes even if one does not insist on the strict notion of an agricultural 'year' and if allowance is made for continuous production.

Our writers portray concern with the sources of increased productivity, as the discussion of capital already indicates. Thus Tucker focused upon the advantages of specialization (the division of labour) having in mind productivity gains deriving from the allocation of tasks between men, women and children according to their respective strengths (1757 [1931], 242–3). But this interest extended to technological progress more generally, and in this context he raised the possibility of labour displacement, although the problem was minimized on the grounds that the use of cost-reducing machinery in any industry would in time allow an expansion of demand for the product and the reabsorption of initially displaced workers and even an expansion of the work force: 'The System of Machines, which so greatly reduces the Price of Labour [labour costs], as to enable the Generality of a People to become Purchasers of Goods, will in the End, though not immediately, employ more Hands in the Manufacture, than could possibly have found Employment, had no such Machines been invented' (pp. 241–2). Here we again see that the responsiveness of quantity demanded to price was appreciated and effectively used in application even prior to the *Wealth of Nations*.

Sir James Steuart in his *Inquiry* made a most significant contribution to the understanding of technological change. He distinguished between fixed capital (structures and machinery) and circulating or working capital (the latter including wage goods), the demand for labour deriving from circulating capital alone. Technical change, provided it did not reduce aggregate circulating capital, would not entail labour displacement (1767 [1966], I, 121–5). This is a potent insight. The next step along the road was by Ricardo in 1821, when he demonstrated that it was possible for there to occur a 'conversion' of circulating into fixed capital – technical progress taking the form of a reduction of circulating in favour of fixed capital – the end result being a reduction in the aggregate demand for labour.

*   *   *

We turn next to interest rate determination, having in mind, by way of contrast, the standard mercantilist perspective (see above, p. 20). Whatever the precise rationale, the pamphleteers traced a close relationship between the money supply and the interest rate. In the late seventeenth century and increasingly thereafter, by contrast, much more stress came to be placed on the nature of the demand and supply of loanable funds in their *non-monetary* aspects. The emphasis is upon the determinants of savings – some initial surplus, the consumption patterns of different classes and the concentration of ownership in different groups – and, on the side of investment, the nature and intensity of competition in production and trade and the alternative uses of funds. Money remained important in the determination of the interest rate but largely in the short run. This trend constitutes both a break from scholastic usury analysis, by identifying the yield from 'stock' (material goods utilized for deriving an income) and the yield from land; and from standard mercantilism, by avoiding the assumption that the savings process consists in the accumulation of a stock of money.

An outstanding illustration of the new position appears in Dudley North's discussion of the 'Abatement of Interest' designed to refute the recommendation that the legal maximum rate be reduced as a stimulus to trade. Lending and borrowing are related to a skewed wealth distribution and to differential skills and preferences:

> Now as there are more Men to Till the Ground than have Land to Till, so also there will be many who want Stock to manage; and also (when a Nation is grown rich) there will be Stock for Trade in many hands, who either have not the skill, or care not for the trouble of managing it in Trade... Thus to be a Landlord, or a Stock-Lord is the same thing; the Landlord hath the advantage in this: That his Tenant cannot carry away the Land, as the Tenant of the other may the Stock; and therefore Land ought to yield less profit than Stock, which is let out at greater hazard (1691; in McCulloch, 1856a, 517–18).

North's general position is that the equilibrium interest rate will fall with an increase in the supply of loanable funds relative to the demand, 'wherefore it is not low Interest makes Trade, but Trade increasing, the Stock of the Nation makes Interest low'.

Subsequently these ideas were further elaborated. In Cantillon's *Essay* (1755 [1931], 199ff.) interest in a primitive society is represented as a function of the 'needs of borrowers' (time preference of consumers) governing the demand for funds and the 'fear and avarice' of lenders governing the supply price. In an advanced society capital productivity is introduced (in addition to the time preference of consumers); interest is paid because of the profits that can be derived from investment of borrowed funds. The emphasis is upon *pure* profits – a surplus – as the source of interest and as the motive for borrowing, that is, upon an excess over the cost of the upkeep of entrepreneurs quite distinct from the wages of superintendence. Changes in expectations regarding profits might alter the interest rate even if the money supply is constant; conversely an increase in the money supply has no unambiguous effect upon the interest rate. Cantillon's examination of the precise processes by which an increase in the money supply might affect the interest rate represents a pioneering achievement of the first order. Unlike North, who denied any relation between the money supply and the (long-run) interest rate, or Locke, who defined an unambiguous inverse relation, Cantillon emphasized alternative patterns depending upon the particular point of injection of the increased money supply. Similarly, David Hume's analysis 'Of Interest' (1752c) recognized that differential effects on interest will follow an increase in the money supply depending on the hands through which it passed.

In Hume's scheme interest is a function of the 'demand for borrowing', the supply of funds and the 'profits from commerce'. Cantillon emphasized borrowing for business purposes; for Hume the demand for loanable funds derived largely from the consumption requirements of 'prodigal' landlords in particular. Hume none the less envisaged an inverse relationship between the extent of capital accumulation (specifically by merchants) and the rate of profit on (commercial) capital. Great stocks, he contended, imply heavy competition so that profits are likely to decline with accumulation; but a low yield will entail a greater willingness to *lend* so that the interest rate is likely to be reduced too. Thus, with the extension of commerce, 'there must arise rivalships among the merchants, which diminish the profits of trade, at the same time that they encrease the trade itself. The low profits of merchandize induced merchants to accept more willingly of a low interest, when they leave off business, and begin to indulge themselves in ease and indolence' (1752c, 55). It may be noted, in addition, that in Hume's view not only does a low interest rate result from expansion, but a converse relationship is defined according to which a low interest is likely to stimulate industry insofar as cost prices of goods decline and the quantity demanded of products rises ('Of Public Credit', 1752e [1955], 93–4).

The notion in North, Cantillon and Hume of a secular decline in the profit rate with capital accumulation – and an expected consequential decline in the interest rate – is of supreme importance. Smith, Ricardo and Marx were all to formulate the theorem, one of the most celebrated in economic literature, each providing a different rationale.

In conclusion let me emphasize a fundamental characteristic of the literature discussed above, namely, the absence of any clearly defined relationship between the interest rate and saving. It was taken for granted that the total available supply of investible funds – as distinct from the supply of loanable funds – was determined by sociological and institutional factors and thus did not vary with the interest rate.

* * *

Eighteenth-century economists examined the determinants of population growth with increasing precision. They thought in terms of the notion of a food 'surplus' over and above the requirements of the food producers themselves as a stimulus to population growth, the demand for labour tied to the surplus. Steuart provides an example: 'A people...who have an industrious turn, will multiply in proportion to the superfluity produced by their farmers; because the labour of the necessitous will prove an equivalent for it' (1767 [1966], I, 40). In this context we find a 'Malthusian' conception expressed in terms of a mechanical analogy: Given the production of food at a particular level (for a sufficient length of time) population will be constant at a particular level, with the wage rate at 'subsistence'. With an increase in food the wage rate rises above subsistence, generating population growth until a new equilibrium is established. Conversely, should there be a fall in food output, the wage rate declines below the subsistence level generating a reduction in the supply of labour which proceeds until equilibrium is re-established:

> Thus the generative faculty resembles a spring loaded with a weight, which always exerts itself in proportion to the diminution of resistance: when food has remained some time without augmentation or diminution, generation will carry numbers as high as possible; if then food come to be diminished, the spring is overpowered; the force of it becomes less than nothing. Inhabitants will diminish, at least in proportion as the overcharge. If, upon the other hand, food be increased, the spring which stood at 0, will begin to exert itself in proportion as the resistance diminishes; people will begin to be better fed; they will multiply, and, in proportion as they increase in numbers, the food will become scarce again (pp. 32–3).

In Steuart we also encounter the phenomenon of the limits of growth in land scarcity, taking the form of diminishing agricultural returns at the extensive margin of cultivation (p. 116). There are in the background clouds threatening long-run expansion. Richard Cantillon similarly identified land as the limiting factor: 'the multiplication of Animals', he wrote 'has no other bounds than the greater or less means allotted for their subsistence' and could increase to infinity 'if we could find lands to infinity to nourish them' (1755 [1931], 67). Petty in 1662 had clearly enunciated the intensive and extensive margins and recognized some of the implications for differential rent (1899, I, 48–9, 52). As we shall see, these features were, in some form or other, absorbed into classical doctrine.

It remains to note a growing concern on the part of some writers with *measurement* of economic data. Numerical investigation of industrial structure by occupational and social grouping, population size and distribution by sex and geographic area, total and per capita income, and net savings was undertaken by Gregory King (and used by Davenant, 1699 [1771], II, 182–5). Sir William Petty's exercises in 'political arithmetick' are also conspicuous. We have seen (p. 20 above) that Petty was not responsible for literally identifying wealth and the precious metals. In the 1660s he estimated gold and silver to comprise only £6 million out of a total national capital stock – including land, houses, shipping, cattle and inventories – of £250 million (1899, I, 105–8). A yet broader measure of wealth, including 'the value of the people', he estimated at nearly double the more conventional index (pp. 108–10).

In the context of taxation policy, Petty treated the relative advantages of encouraging alternative sectors according as they produced more or less durable commodities (including both producer and consumer goods). Thus in 1690 he condemns those who 'do nothing at all, but *eat* and *drink*, *sing*, *play*, and *dance*; nay to such as study *Metaphysicks*, or other needless *Speculation*; or also employ themselves in any other way, which produce no material thing, or things of real use and Value in the Commonwealth' (1899, I, 270). By their activity 'the Wealth of the Publick will be diminished'. For all that, he allows for those active 'in governing, directing and preserving those, who are appointed to Labour and Arts', and concedes some service activities to be indirectly productive should they 'qualifie and dispose Men to what is itself more considerable'.

The Physiocratic doctrine of *agricultural* productivity – to which we turn in the next chapter – entails a severe narrowing of scope compared to Petty's perspective. The emphasis on 'materiality' in the classification of 'productive' sectors was to become a conspicuous feature of classicism.

2.7 Summary and Conclusions

The new 'Principles of Political Economy' of the eighteenth century were a different breed from the seventeenth-century pamphlets. Of the growing sophistication of economic analysis there can be no question.

As for value theory, we have emphasized the weight already placed in pre-Smithian literature on the relationship of market price to cost price, costs including 'normal' profits. This preoccupation implies a concern with the allocation of resources in terms of alternative opportunities; for when we describe the process by which some industries contract and others expand in consequence of deviations of market from cost price, it is precisely the process of resource allocation involving alternative opportunities that is at stake – the movement between uses of resources seeking the highest rewards. Earlier demand–supply analysis was thus incorporated into an embryonic general-equilibrium context. As for economic growth, we have encountered discussion of a population mechanism turning on deviations between the actual and the sub-sistence wage, the demand for labour deriving from the community's surplus; recognition of a threat to growth emanating from land scarcity; analysis of the interest rate in terms of savings propensities and capital productivity; and the notion of a declining return on capital with accumulation.

For a full appreciation of the 'origins' of the new trends it would be necessary to consider the divergence from scholastic attitudes which characterized the Enlightenment, including the scientific developments of the times reflected in a great admiration for Newtonian physics. The mechanical analogies of the eighteenth-century economists may be fruitfully approached in these terms. Changes in social attitude related to the Enlightenment are also significant, David Hume providing an important illustration. Even if it were true, as many pamphleteers had argued, that an increase in wages is undesirable because it reduces competitiveness abroad and damages the balance of trade, this outcome was 'not to be put in competition with the happiness of so many millions' ('Of Commerce', 1752a [1955], 16).

The transition from the monetary perspective of the mercantilist pamphleteers – their near-identification of wealth and money – may partly be explained by changes in the nature of the economy. With the growing significance of bank notes and other exchange media it would be increasingly difficult to think of money in terms of the precious metals, thereby undermining the mercantilist perspective on wealth. The transition from mercantilism constitutes a rich mine for those concerned with the relationship between economic and social history and the history of economic thought.

There remains to note that self-consciousness regarding method provides one sure index that a subject has achieved a certain maturity. Petty pointed out that his *Political Arithmetick* of 1690 adopted a 'not yet very usual' method, 'for instead of using only comparative and superlative Words, and intellectual Arguments, I have taken the course...to express my self in Terms of *Number, Weight,* or *Measure*; to use only Arguments of Sense, and to consider only such Causes, as have visible Foundations in Nature (1899, I, 244). Cantillon was careful to separate pure theory from normative policy declarations and value judgements; he formulated his assumptions explicitly; he listed the *ceteris paribus* conditions; and he complicated his arguments step by step, starting with a simplified model and then relaxing the simplifications one by one (1755 [1931], 333–60). As for Steuart, he warned of the danger of misusing theory, complaining of 'the habit of running into what the French call *Systèmes*' or excessively complex sequences of cause–effect relationships, based upon assumptions adopted without adequate empirical justification and generating results which are applied irresponsibly: 'chains of contingent consequences, drawn from a few fundamental maxims, adopted, perhaps rashly', and applied by the author 'far beyond the limits of the ideas present to his understanding, when he made his definition' (1767 [1966], 8). The careless selection of axioms and careless transfer from theory to application are defects of modern model building which Schumpeter was to label the 'Ricardian vice'. Far from originating with Ricardo – a charge which is itself of doubtful validity – irresponsible theorizing and application were recognized as potential problems even before the *Wealth of Nations*.

Suggested Reading

Aquinas' *Summa Theologica*, Questions 77 and 78 and his *Commentary on Aristotle's Nicomachean Ethics*, vol I, are recommended as a small sampling of original Scholastic thought. Viner (1978), ch. 2, deals with the religious and social preconceptions of the Scholastics. On aspects of Scholastic economic analysis see Schumpeter (1954), 90–107; de Roover (1957); Hollander (1965); B. Gordon (1975), chs 6, 8, 9; Worland (1977); and Langholm (1979).

Adam Smith's account of the 'mercantile system' in the *Wealth of Nations*, Book IV, ch i and viii, is essential reading.

J. R. McCulloch's *Early Tracts on Commerce* (1856a) contains examples of primary mercantilist writings including Mun (1664) and North (1691). Viner (1937), chs 1 and 2, is still the *locus classicus* for commentary on mercantilist theory. See also Schumpeter (1954), Part II, ch. 7. A summary statement by Eli

Heckscher of his famous *Mercantilism* (1937, 2nd edn 1955) and a variety of other important interpretive essays will be found in Coleman (1969). On the process of 'decay' of mercantilism, Viner (1963) and Heckscher (1955), I, 221–325, are suggested. For background on economics and ideology in the mercantilist period, see Appleby (1978); and on the self-interest axiom, see Grampp (1965), ch. 1, and Myers (1983).

Seventeenth-century theories of interest are analysed in Tucker (1960), ch 1, and Bowley (1973), chs 1 and 2. On Petty, Hull's 'Introduction' to the *Economic Writings* (1899) is still worthwhile. Endres (1985) treats Petty and Davenant as political arithmeticians. See also Letwin (1963), chs 5 and 7 on Petty and North.

For a general discussion of economic theories in the eighteenth century see Letwin (1963), ch. 8. Low (1952) deals with early eighteenth-century opinion on economic progress; Low (1954) and Tucker (1960), ch. 2, with the interest rate in a growth context; and Bowley (1973), chs 3 and 6, with opinion on the price mechanism and wages.

On Mandeville's place in the history of economics, see Landreth (1975) and Hayek (1978), 249–66. Mandeville and *laissez-faire* is discussed by Viner (1958), 332–42, and Rosenberg (1963). Spengler (1954), with considerable justice, considers Cantillon to be 'the first of the moderns'. Cantillon figures centrally in Bowley and Tucker. On Hume, Rotwein's 'Introduction' to Hume's *Economic Writings* (1752 [1955]) and Taylor's study of Hume as predecessor of Adam Smith (1965) are useful studies. On Steuart, with particular reference to economic methodology, see Skinner (1965, 1981). Skinner's 'Introduction' to Steuart's *Inquiry* (1767 [1966]) and Vickers' review of the reissue of the *Works* (1970) are also important. Meek (1967), 3–17 offers a 'Marxian' perspective on Steuart. Extracts from Cantillon, Hume, Steuart and Josiah Tucker are printed in Meek (1973a).

The dichotomy between 'productive' and 'unproductive' labour emerges in the mercantilist literature and plays a part in subsequent developments. For the first full treatment of the subject, dealing with Petty, the classicists, Marx and modern Soviet economics, see Boss (1988).

3 The Physiocrats

3.1 Introduction

French Physiocracy (*physiocrate* means 'the rule of nature'), unlike mercantilism, constitutes a genuine 'school', perhaps the first school of economic thought. The movement, a reaction against French mercantilism, considered land to be the sole source of income. It flourished during the 1750s and 1760s under the guidance of François Quesnay (1694–1774), but physiocratic attitudes are not limited to France during this particular period. There are even indications of agricultural bias in the *Wealth of Nations*. In the first decade of the nineteenth century, William Spence (*Britain Independent of Commerce*, 1807), a British writer, argued that the source of Britain's wealth lay in agriculture and that international commerce was not essential. Conversely, as already noted in chapter 2, the Physiocrats drew upon some of Cantillon's formulations.

In section 3.2 we take up the notion of 'surplus' which is central to physiocratic thought, and also Quesnay's device of *tableaux économiques* which he used to represent national product flows and income distribution within a framework allowing a 'surplus' in agriculture alone. With this background we consider in sections 3.3 and 3.4 the physiocratic perspectives on pricing and economic growth. Section 3.5 is devoted to Quesnay's outstanding contemporary A. R. J. Turgot, who was to attract the attention of Ricardo, and who markedly improved the quality of economic analysis.

3.2 Surplus and the *'Tableau Economique'*

In their model-building the Physiocrats assumed the economic system to be comprised of three sectors – 'productive', 'proprietory' and 'sterile'. The productive sector, or the class of farmers, is so designated because it is assumed that only farm labour yields a 'surplus' over costs. The proprietory sector includes those who expropriate the surplus – the Church, army, state and private landlords. Labourers engaged in manufacturing constitute the third sector; their labour fails to generate a surplus, for which reason it is labelled 'sterile'.

A preliminary word first on the nature of surplus, an ambiguous concept rather too loosely used in economic discourse. We may distinguish between four possible usages – there are doubtless others – each helpful in its own way. The most obvious usage is a physical surplus of output over input, which to be definable unambiguously requires that output and input be comprised of the same substance. Surplus can also be regarded as an income available for net accumulation (disposable surplus); a payment exceeding the marginal supply price of a factor (economic rent); and a formal residual (as distinct from a contractual) income.

The notion of disposable surplus has a counterpart in a conception of 'costs' considered as the returns to productive factors required to maintain the dimensions of an economy unchanged with neither growth nor decline. The 'surplus' is then any income over and above the amount which just suffices to cover 'necessary' consumption requirements and capital replacement. Such an excess is potentially available for net accumulation. This seems indeed to be the notion of surplus in most of the representations by the Physiocrats. There is supposedly an income yielded in agriculture – and in agriculture alone – which is disposable in the sense of being available for net accumulation. It does not follow that the surplus will necessarily be used for accumulation – it might be consumed – but it is available for that purpose.

There is an alternative way of envisaging 'costs' which is more appropriate in a growing system. Consider, for example, capital supply growing at a particular rate with the return to capital above some minimum requirement, the amount required to keep this factor unchanged in supply. The excess over the minimum cannot be regarded as a surplus, using the term now in the sense of an 'economic rent', because it is a *necessary* return (at least at the margin), required to induce the particular growth rate in question. But while the income exceeding subsistence is not an economic rent, precisely because there would ensue a fall in the factor growth rate if it is reduced, it might yet be available for net accumulation. In other words, in order for a specific growth rate of a factor to be forthcoming, the suppliers of that factor (at least marginal suppliers) insist on a particular return, but that return might none the less be high enough to allow them to save if they so wish. There is then a surplus in the first sense (a disposable source) but not in the second (an economic rent). It is only in a growing system that the two can diverge; in a 'stationary state' there is no surplus in either sense – since profits are at a minimum nothing is available for accumulation, and should that income be reduced the result would be net decumulation. Now profit was formerly regarded by the Physiocrats as a 'cost' element including a return to cover the replacement of capital used up and the wages of management. But part was interest, and a variety of questions arise regarding interest: is it, or does it include, a 'surplus' and in what sense? These matters will be briefly postponed.

There can also be a surplus in the sense of a formal residual, or an income received as the leavings from sales proceeds after contractual obligations have been met. That was Cantillon's way of thinking about profit (see above, pp. 29–30), and it was to be Ricardo's too. Conceivably, an income may be a residual without being a surplus in either of the other more substantive senses. For example, if profits, paid as a residual, are reduced by taxation, there may be negative consequences for the rate of accumulation of capital and for the demand for labour with depressing effects on the wage rate. A change in the profit rate thus plays on wages, and wages are as much affected by profit as profits are affected by wages, a mutuality of interdependence indicating that profits are no more a genuine surplus than are wages notwithstanding the different forms of payment.

*   *   *

With this behind us we can turn to Quesnay's *tableaux économiques*. These are representations of the circular flow of national income – expenditure and annual reproduction – and its distribution between broad sectors. The models exclude both foreign trade and intra-sectoral flows. The earliest versions portray, in 'zig-zag' fashion, successive rounds of expenditure during any annual production period, as in figure 3.1, an English rendition (Kuczynski and Meek, 1972) of a table produced by Quesnay in 1759, now known as the 'third edition'. The essential axiom is that each pound of working capital invested (or 'advanced') by the 'productive' (agricultural) sector generates sufficient income to cover costs and yield a surplus of one pound, whereas each pound of working capital invested by the 'sterile' (manufacturing) sector generates income sufficient only to cover costs.

It is here assumed that the sum of 'annual advances' (working capital) in agriculture during the *past* year amounts to £600, yielding a net revenue of £600 which has been paid to landlords, as indicated on the first line of data. Landlords spend their revenue (at the beginning of the current year), one-half on agricultural produce and one-half on manufactures; as shown by the diagonal lines emanating from £600 in the

Objects to be considered: (1) three kinds of expenditure; (2) their source; (3) their advances; (4) their distribution; (5) their effects; (6) their reproduction; (7) their relations with one another; (8) their relations with the population; (9) with agriculture; (10) with industry; (11) with trade; (12) with the total wealth of a nation.

PRODUCTIVE EXPENDITURE relative to agriculture, etc.	EXPENDITURE OF THE REVENUE after deduction of taxes, is divided between productive expenditure and sterile expenditure	STERILE EXPENDITURE relative to industry, etc.
Annual advances required to produce a revenue of 600*l*. are 600*l*.	Annual revenue	Annual advances for the works of sterile expenditure are

600*l*. produce net·········	600*l*. ··one-half goes here	300*l*.
Products ····one-half goes here		Works, etc.
300*l*. reproduce net····· one-half	300l. ······ one-half goes here	300*l*.
goes here		
150 reproduce net one-half, etc.	150 etc. one-half	150
75 reproduce net·········	75	75
37··10s. reproduce net······	37··10	37··10
18··15 reproduce net·······	18··15	18··15
9···7··6*d*. reproduce net····	9···7··6*d*	9···7··6*d*.
4··13···9 reproduce net·····	4··13···9	4··13···9
2···6··10 reproduce net·····	2···6··10	2···6··10
1···3··5 reproduce net······	1···3···5	1···3···5
0··11··8 reproduce net······	0··11···8	0··11···8
0···5··10 reproduce net·····	0···5··10	0···5··10
0···2··11 reproduce net·····	0···2··11	0···2··11
0···1··5 reproduce net······	0···1··· 5	0···1··· 5

etc.

TOTAL REPRODUCED ...... 600*l*. of revenue; in addition, the annual costs of 600*l*. and the interest on the original advances of the husbandman amounting to 300*l*., which the land restores. Thus the reproduction is 1500*l*., including the revenue of 600*l*. which forms the base of the calculation, abstraction being made of the taxes deducted and of the advances which their annual reproduction entails. etc.

Figure 3.1 Quesnay's *tableau économique*.
(Source: Kuczynski and Meek, 1972.)

centre column to the left- and right-hand columns (the upside-down writing is *not* a printer's error). The landlords' purchase of food amounting to £300 finances farmers' advances, allowing them to set *this* year's production in motion; this activity generates output covering expenditure and also a surplus of £300, as shown in the centre column. Account must also be made of the expenditures by landlords on manufactures; this allows renewed production by the 'sterile' class, but here no surplus results. However, one-half of the manufacturers' cost outlays entail by assumption the purchase of agricultural produce as indicated by the appropriate diagonal line; this outlay (of £150) permits further agricultural activity which yields an equivalent surplus. Similarly, one-half of farmers' expenditures is supposedly devoted to manufactures though in this case no surplus results.

The cumulative sum of agricultural output produced this year amounts to £1500 (see explanatory note to the table): £600 net revenue *plus* £600 replacement of the annual advances *plus* £300 (not formally allowed for in the table) 'interest on the original advances' or interest on fixed capital, which we take up shortly. Manufacturing output amounts to £600 all of which is replacement of costs. The table actually indicates annual manufacturing advances of only £300 (see first line of the data) but there is presumably an abstraction from a part of the purchases that the sterile class makes or else 'sterile' activity would yield a surplus. Some commentators suggest that Quesnay abstracted from purchases of inputs abroad (Meek, 1962, 283); but this solution clashes with Quesnay's presumption that the model describes a closed economy.

The diagram in figure 3.1 formally relates to a single landowner's expenditure (although we have interpreted it for simplicity as applying to the landlord class as a whole). Quesnay subsequently devised a simplified version (*Analyse du tableau économique*, 1766; in Daire, 1846, 57–78) altering the figures to apply explicitly to three classes (we now have *milliard* francs) and giving only the total annual receipts and expenditures, in effect summarizing the results achieved by the successive rounds of spending. A rendition by Shigeto Tsuru (1956) captures most of the main features (figure 3.2).

We assume that at the close of a particular year (say, December 1770) farmers have produced five milliard francs' worth of agricultural produce (three of food and two of raw materials), and that the sterile sector has produced two milliards' worth of manufactures; the landlords have produced nothing. The argument can proceed in barter terms, but money helps to carry out the exposition more easily. There is by supposition two milliards' worth of money in the hands of the farmers at the end of the year indicated by the solid thick line. (For simplicity, we abstracted from money flows in our summary of the 'third edition',

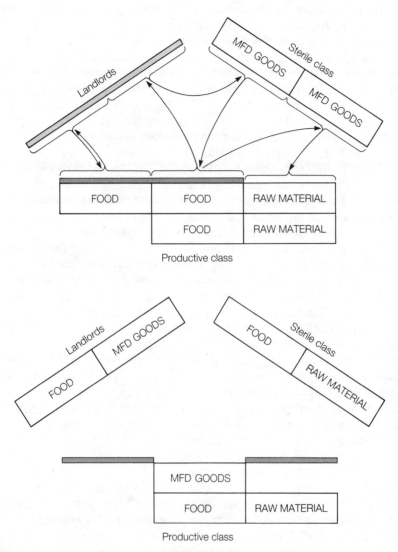

Figure 3.2   Physiocratic intra-class flows.
(Source: Tsuru in Sweezy, 1942, 366.)

proceeding entirely in terms of product flows.) Landlords, by dint of property ownership, have a claim on two milliards' worth of the national product, and farmers pay over to them in cash two milliards as rent, as indicated by the arrows emanating from the solid line. The landlords now disburse this sum in the following way: they buy one milliard of food (the exchange takes place at the end of the year) and one milliard of manufactures, choosing to enjoy their command over the national income half in food and half in manufactured goods. For simplicity the first cash flow can be envisaged as ceasing upon return to its source. But the sterile class has one milliard in cash which it uses to buy raw materials; the agricultural class in turn acquires manufactured goods with the one milliard of money – in effect an exchange of manufactures for raw materials; the sterile class then uses the one milliard it again receives to buy food, at which stage the second money flow ceases. The arrows indicate the money flows during the process.

After the exchanges have taken place (still in December of 1770) we find that the landlords are in possession of one milliard of food and one milliard of manufactured goods, that the sterile class has exchanged its two milliards of manufactured goods for one of food and one of raw materials, and that the agricultural class has acquired by exchange one milliard of manufactures, and retained one of food and one of raw materials. The latter items might have entered into an exchange between the different farmers but intra-class exchanges are neglected.

The production process commences anew in January 1771. In agriculture, the food and raw material – used as working capital in the maintenance of labour and as seed – supported by one milliard's worth of manufactures will by December again have yielded five milliards of agricultural output. Apparently it is possible for two units of working capital (supported by one of manufactures) engaged in agriculture to generate an output of five milliards, a surplus of two milliards. The food and materials used as working capital in manufacturing will have merely been 'transformed' into two milliards of manufactured goods.

There are certain assumptions underlying the diagrams, which are not clear from the diagrams themselves. The Physiocrats represented capital by the term *avances* – advances. (They were familiar with Cantillon and might have derived the idea from him.) One category (*avances foncières*) entails drainage, fencing and permanent land improvements; a second (*avances primitives*), livestock, tools and buildings; and a third (*avances annuelles*), working or circulating capital, taking the form of food and raw materials. The two categories of fixed capital (which are not formally represented) are said to constitute five times the working capital in agriculture, so that there is in the background a stock of fixed capital of ten milliard. (Fixed capital in the 'third edition' is thus $5 \times £600$ or £3000, the interest of £300 amounting to 10 per cent.)

The one milliard of manufactures which enters into agricultural costs seems to be understood as the counterpart of interest on fixed capital (though in some versions it appears as replacement of fixed capital used up). But if it constitutes interest, what about the maintenance of fixed capital? Moreover, assuming it to be interest, questions arise regarding its nature. Is it an income which farmers could, if they wished, devote to net accumulation – is it *disposable*? And secondly, is it a surplus in our second sense, such that if it were taxed, it would not lead capitalists to alter the rate at which they are accumulating? We will presently consider some of the literature in a bid to answer these questions; at this stage it suffices to be aware of an ambiguity surrounding the one billion of manufactures utilized in agriculture.

Manufacturing too requires food and raw materials to maintain the processes of production during the year. But in this case an output is yielded which only replaces these costs. There is no surplus. There is also no fixed capital. These sharp contrasts with the agricultural sector raise the relationship between events and theory: was the model intended to represent contemporary French conditions, with agriculture including the advanced capital-intensive sector and manufacturing the more primitive domestic sector? We shall return to this matter later (section 2.6).

Let us now examine the key issue, the notion of a net product in agriculture alone, such that two milliard of working capital produces a surplus of two milliard. This notion is not a deduction based upon a set of axioms and some rationalizing process. It is rather an assumption with which we start the exercise. It is a characteristic which reflects a fundamental weakness of Physiocracy, for there is little economic rationale for that assumption. Indeed, we have here a serious confusion between *physical* surplus, which by itself has no economic import, and *value* surplus, which alone is significant economically. The Physiocrats apparently had in mind some kind of physical surplus (albeit represented in money terms), writing frequently of the 'gift of nature' (or providence) permitting one to sow a grain of corn seed and to reap two at the end of the year. A glance at the author's garden (or a consideration of Soviet agriculture) would have sufficed to convince them that this is by no means a ubiquitous phenomenon! Some land is very poor; some farmers are very poor; and capital goods may be poor. There might, therefore, be no physical surplus. Secondly, what meaning does a physical surplus have when the output is not composed of the same physical substance as the input? How is the comparison to be made except by recourse to a theory of value whereby the prices of the relevant products are determined? To talk about physical surplus is in fact to talk about biological creativity and biological creativity is of no relevance to economics. The Physiocrats, however, insisted that manufacturing (say of tables from wood) was a sterile activity in that it merely altered the 'form' of agricultural produce, but was not creative – manufacturing was transformation not production: 'façonner et produire sont deux: on ne façonne les matières brutes, qu' après qu' elles ont été produites: rien n'est plus évident' (Baudeau, 1767, in Daire, 1846, 868). Raw materials are here said to be made up by manufacturing after they have been 'produced' in the agricultural sector, a proposition which is supposedly 'self-evident'.

The underlying notion that nature is active in agriculture alone is untenable. Natural forces are at play in the manufacturing sector as well. The Physiocrats failed to understand that, on their assumption that land is required in agriculture alone, land rent will only be generated if that land is *scarce* – scarcity imposing limits upon the level of agricultural output achievable and (given the demand for agricultural products) assuring a price sufficiently high to generate rent. Were agricultural land expanded in supply, the rent of land would fall – in the extreme case to zero – a real transfer taking place from landlords to the other factor owners. What appears to be a necessary 'surplus' is in fact nothing but an extraction from other factors due to land scarcity. Evidently, land must be productive for it to yield a return, but it must also be scarce – productivity is a necessary but insufficient condition. Conversely, were the natural forces utilized in manufacturing to become scarce, the level of manufacturing output would be constrained, assuring a price which allows a return to the owners of those natural forces (provided of course that they could be appropriated as private property). This rent would necessarily be at the expense of the other factors.

The physiocratic notion that agricultural activity alone yields a surplus is thus based upon a serious analytical error, since it neglects the economic principle of scarcity, or pricing in terms of demand and supply. One of the best clarifications in the literature of this principle is by Ricardo (see below, pp. 97–8). Were the Physiocrats at all aware of this kind of criticism? Their references to the 'gifts of nature' imply not. But when one actually digs down into the texts it becomes apparent that they recognized the possibility that, under certain circumstances, the price of agricultural output (corn) might fall very low, even reducing rent to zero, an allowance that has profound significance for their policy recommendations. To appreciate this point requires some familiarity with the physiocratic theory of commodity pricing.

3.3 The Price Mechanism

Quesnay and his followers recognized the phenomenon of general economic interdependence which characterizes an exchange economy, an interdependence subject to regular laws. They devised their formal models precisely to represent an interdependent economic system (albeit in rather general terms). This was an impressive intellectual achievement. But how far did Quesnay go towards an appreciation of the functioning of the price mechanism in free competition, the organizing function of prices? That he accorded 'self-interest' – in the sense of maximizing behaviour – the role of fundamental motive force governing the operation of the market-exchange system is not in doubt. Our question is whether his logic turned on a clearly formulated theory of competitive price with an eye to an 'optimal' allocation of resources.

A citation from Quesnay's paper 'Impôts' regarding the manufacturing sector (and capturing nicely the distinction between sectors) is relevant here:

> ... the wealth which constitutes the costs of agriculture differs greatly, as regards its employment, from industrial wealth. It is the former which causes revenue to be generated, whereas the product of industrial wealth is confined to goods which are worth only the expenses which they entailed. The worker who makes a piece of cloth purchases the raw material and incurs expenses for his needs while he is making it. The payment he receives when he sells it returns to him the purchase price and his expenses; the gain which his labour procures for him is confined to the restitution of the expenses he has incurred.... The competition of workers who are trying to procure for themselves a similar gain in order to get a living restricts the price of manufactured goods to the level of this gain itself. Thus this gain, or restitution of expenses, is not, like the revenue of landed property, an original form of wealth representing a pure profit (Quesnay, 1757, in Meek, 1962, 105).

The reason manufacturing prices reflect material and wage costs and no more is here given in terms of the competitive process; in particular, there are other workers at hand whose entry, or perhaps potential entry, assures that prices merely cover costs with no 'surplus'. (The reference to the worker's 'needs' suggests that wages are at 'subsistence'; that the long-run aggregate labour supply curve is infinitely elastic at the subsistence level, an implication also suggested by the physiocratic theory of tax incidence. From this perspective labour is, so to speak, a reproducible factor at constant cost.)

Matters are very different in agriculture. Assuming a closed economy, market prices are erratic because of the extreme volatility of the harvest in the face of an inelastic demand for food, ruling out any regular tendency towards production costs. For while 'the revenue of a kingdom is regulated by the price of its produce' – a significant statement because we are clearly not really dealing with *physical* net revenue notwithstanding repeated references to the 'gifts of nature' – 'in a state in which there is no external trade at all, either of export or of import, the price of [agricultural] produce cannot be subject to any rule or any order' (Quesnay, 'Hommes', 1757, in Meek, 1962, 93). There is, in short, no assurance that market prices tend towards cost prices in the agricultural sector. The allocative function of prices breaks down.

There is a further distinction which relates to the nature of long-run cost price in the two sectors. Quesnay defines the 'fundamental price' of agricultural output as 'the expenses or costs which have to be incurred in their production or preparation', to which, however, must be added 'a gain sufficient to encourage people to *maintain* or increase their production' (Meek, ibid., 93; emphasis added). Full cost thus includes a profit, and only if the market price suffices to yield this sum does the commodity sell at a *bon prix* (its proper level) – an unlikely occurrence in a closed system. Agricultural profits are thus included as a necessary payment even for the maintenance of activity, leading Quesnay to warn against taxing those profits (as well as wages): 'The profits of the farmers and the gains of the men whom the farmers employ in cultivation ought to be distinguished from the revenue which this same cultivation brings in every year for the proprietors; for it is the costs and profits of the husbandmen which assure cultivation and the revenue' (Quesnay, 'Impôts', 1757, in Meek, 1962, 106). By contrast, costs in manufacturing seem to include wage and material costs alone.

The deductions to be made from these contrasts are profoundly significant. First, the notion of a tendency of capital to move between industries (whether agricultural or manufacturing) in consequence of capitalists' maximizing behaviour such that profits on capital tend to an equality throughout the system – a key characteristic of Smithian and nineteenth-century economics – was not apparently a feature of physiocratic theory. A 'relativist' approach focusing on the backwardness of contemporary French manufacturing might prove a fruitful source of hypotheses for this distinction.

Secondly, there is no guarantee in a closed economy that the corn price suffices to yield a profit over wage, material and capital costs. And that must be true *a fortiori* of rent, the immediate source of which is the surplus in price over and above paid-out costs and the profits of the farmer. We may conclude that Physiocracy is based on quicksand. While the Physiocrats wrote of 'the gift of nature', they obviously appreciated that it is *value* that matters in economics not physical product, allowing that the value of agricultural produce might (in a closed economy) fall disastrously, eradicating the entire net value product. Indeed there existed a danger that excess supply might force corn prices to near zero levels – 'que l'abondance ne fasse tomber les productions en non valeur' (Quesnay, 1958, II, 571) – destroying the revenues of landowners and the sovereign.

The Physiocrats recommended free trade in corn as a means of guaranteeing stable corn prices, since world market conditions are more stable than local conditions: 'On the assumption of freedom of external trade the price will always be regulated by the competition of neighbouring nations in the produce trade' (Quesnay, 'Grains', 1757, in Meek, 1962, 87). But it was obviously much more than that. From their perspective free trade in corn was a necessary condition of the entire rental income, without which there was no guarantee at all of a net revenue. The policy was thus recommended on the specific presumption that France was a net exporter of corn, the world price exceeding the price attainable (on average) in a closed system. This episode provides a splendid illustration of the dangers of selective quotation, for nothing seems clearer than Quesnay's apparently general maxim 'that complete freedom of trade should be maintained; for THE POLICY FOR INTERNAL AND EXTERNAL TRADE WHICH IS THE MOST SECURE, THE MOST CORRECT, AND THE MOST PROFITABLE FOR THE NATION AND THE STATE, CONSISTS IN FULL FREEDOM OF COMPETITION' ('Maximes Générales', 1767, in Meek, 1962, 237). Yet in the same context we also read '*that the prices of produce and commodities in the kingdom should never be made to fall*; for then mutual foreign trade would become disadvantageous to the nation' (1962, 235). The Physiocrats, who have the reputation of being free trade reformers, were as much interventionist as the mercantilists. Had France been a net importer of corn they would not have recommended a free trade policy.

More generally, the Physiocrats opposed mercantilist regulations which had diverted resources from the agricultural sector by encouraging the importation of raw materials for domestic manufacture and the export of luxury goods, on the grounds that the manufacture of goods utilizing imported raw materials only yields a revenue covering wage costs but no 'surplus'. But Quesnay lacked a rigorous analytical explanation of how resources would be allocated in the absence of government intervention, and hinted that intervention (involving more than foreign trade policy) in favour of agriculture might be desirable. For economic policy 'should be concerned only with encouraging productive expenditures and trade in raw produce' (1962, 233). Without such encouragement (it is implied) no mechanism exists to allocate resources optimally.

3.4 Economic Growth

The major preoccupation of the Physiocrats was economic development rather than allocation as such. (In neither exercise was the device of *tableaux* very useful.) For Quesnay, the key to growth lay in the accumulation of capital. The conception of capital as *advances* figures conspicuously, the term suggesting the essential role of capital in permitting time-consuming activities to proceed. Land, for example, has to be prepared for successful cultivation: 'And is it not also clear that the land never makes any advances, that on the contrary it makes us wait a long time for the harvest?' ('Grains', 1757, in Meek, 1962, 82). Working capital (*avances annuelles*) includes subsistence made available to support workers over the annual agricultural year, although the notion of capital extends to more complex forms, including structures and equipment.

The source of new capital was identified in the community's disposable surplus. Quesnay denied the need for society to concern itself with an increased supply of money by way of the external balance as a means of achieving faster growth. But the problem of surplus considered as the source for accumulation must be examined a little more closely. In the manufacturing sector, it will be recalled, competition reduces prices to the level of costs where costs are understood as some indispensable minimum relating to necessary consumption and material replacement. This presumption rules out the possibility that even though costs are covered there might none the less be included a disposable element. What about agriculture? Assuming that the price adjustment mechanism is not thwarted by violent fluctuations in the harvest – a strong assumption – agricultural prices also cover costs, with the major difference that profits are included in costs as a necessary expense. What we have to consider now is whether those profits contain a disposable surplus, or whether the only disposable surplus in the system is land rent.

According to the late Professor Meek, as physiocratic doctrine matured, so the notion of an element in the farmer's income available for net accumulation came to be recognized. For example, 'the interest of the cultivator is the mainspring of all economic operations and all agricultural progress', Quesnay wrote in 1766 (Meek, 1962, 164n.). In fact, Quesnay attributed to the landowners the role of consumer rather than investor, in an extraordinary defence of their social function: 'The proprietors are useful to the state only through their consumption; their revenue exempts them from labour; they produce nothing; and if their revenue was not circulated among those in the remunerative occupations, the state would be depopulated through the greed of these unjust and treacherous proprietors' ('Impôts', 1757, in Meek, 1962, 104).

Concern with the net value product – the need to assure a high demand for agricultural products – explains in part the physiocratic preoccupation with the dangers of hoarding by proprietors, particularly where large fortunes are accumulated. (Here again we find the Physiocrats abandoning their conception of physical surplus.) But, in addition, a further distinction was made between 'productive' and 'unproductive' consumption, or consumption by those who do and consumption by those who do not make a contribution to the national product:

> Every man who shares in the wealth of the kingdom, but who does not contribute to it in any way, is useless to the state. But, it will be asked, is not every man profitable to the state by virtue of his consumption? Yes, when he makes restitution for this consumption through his work, or through his utility in contributing directly or indirectly to the production of what he consumes or appropriates for himself; for if he does not return to the stock of wealth the value of what he takes out of it, the stock must necessarily diminish ('Hommes', 1757, in Meek, 1962, 98).

On this view, labour in manufacturing falls within the 'productive' sector; the original classification was proving a liability. Quesnay, moreover, allowed that contributions to the national product could be indirect, permitting also the inclusion of some activities by members of the government, Church and army, apart from those 'improving' landlords who undertook investments. It was the class of 'idle *rentiers*' who made no 'productive' contribution, for they did not reproduce the wealth that they consumed. At the same time the level of activity would be threatened were the 'idle' to hoard their incomes. Quesnay partly overcame the dilemma by conceding that while landlords' consumption was necessary in this latter sense, it would be preferable were their purchasing power transferred by loan for investment purposes.

* * *

In their approach to capital and the source of additions to the real capital stock, the Physiocrats advanced beyond their mercantilist predecessors and contemporaries. The contrast extends further. Much emphasis is placed in physiocratic writing on the need for efficiency, and accordingly on technical progress, the objective being (in the first instance) a maximization of the net value product. The mercantilists, as we know, were only interested in efficiency in so far as foreign sales were affected; technical progress in a closed economy would have been of no great importance.

There is some discussion of population in physiocratic doctrine. If the surplus agricultural output were maximized there would be an appropriate growth in population. But this was not something the state need particularly concern itself with, as the mercantilists had maintained. As for the attitude to labour, another contrast arises. Quesnay attacked those who opposed the education of peasants; investment in education was significant in the light of his great interest in efficiency. And far from adopting the mercantilist notion of a backward-bending labour supply curve, he believed that there would be a positive response in the supply of effort to any increase in real wages.

3.5   The Contribution of A. R. J. Turgot

One of our main criticisms of Physiocracy has been its failure to provide an adequate explanation of the competitive mechanisms of adjustment. A. R. J. Turgot (1727–81), a French contemporary of Quesnay, went a considerable way towards correcting this deficiency. His demonstration of the organizing function of the competitive price mechanism is on a par with that of Adam Smith; both Ricardo and John Stuart Mill expressed deep admiration for him.

Turgot, in *Réflexions sur la Formation et la Distribution des Richesses* (1770), gives an account of the rates of return to various employments of capital – including rental earnings on investments in the purchase of land, the return to loanable funds, the earnings on capital invested in agriculture, manufacturing, and commerce – observing that these returns are maintained in 'a sort of equilibrium' by competitive pressures, any monetary differentials that may persist in equilibrium reflecting non-monetary advantages or disadvantages of the various investments. The analysis is phrased in terms of a mechanical analogy – as we know, already a characteristic eighteenth-century practice:

> The different employments of capital produce, therefore, very unequal products; but this inequality does not prevent the exercise of a reciprocal influence one upon the other, or the establishment between them of a sort of equilibrium, as between two liquids of unequal gravity which communicate with one another at the bottom of a reversed syphon of which they occupy the two branches; they will not be on a level, but the height of one cannot increase without the other also rising in the opposite branch (1770 [1963], 83–4).

This is a statement of great historical significance, for the notion of profit rate uniformity (subject to non-monetary differentials) pervades Smithian and nineteenth-century classical economics.

Turgot subscribed to the general physiocratic view that wages would tend to subsistence – including an allowance 'to provide for accidents' and 'to bring up families' – and that if wages were taxed money wages would rise to compensate. The precise rationalization given runs expressly in terms of 'equilibrium' – general equilibrium – again adopting a mechanical analogy:

In a nation where trade and industry are free and vigorous, competition fixes this profit [the wage rate] at the lowest possible rate. A kind of equilibrium establishes itself between the values of all the productions of the land, the consumption of the different kinds of commodities, the different sorts of works, the number of men employed at them, and the price of their wages.

Wages can be fixed and remain constantly at a definite point only in virtue of this equilibrium, and of the influence which all the parts of the society, all the branches of production and commerce, exercise upon one another. This granted, if you change one of the weights, a movement cannot but result from it in the whole of the machine which tends to restore the old equilibrium. The proportion which the current value of wages bears to their fundamental value was established by the laws of this equilibrium and by the combination of all the circumstances under which all the parts of the society are placed.

You augment the fundamental value [by a tax on wages or wage goods]; the circumstances which have before fixed the proportion which the current value bears to this fundamental value cannot but cause the current value to rise until the proportion is re-established. I am aware that this result will not be sudden; and that in every complicated machine there are frictions which delay the results most infallibly demonstrated by theory (Letter to Hume, 1963, 108–9).

For Turgot then (and this also holds for Ricardo and J. S. Mill) pure theory does not allow for 'frictions' which must, however, be recognized in application.

Turgot, moreover, provided what is apparently the first explicit recognition of incremental (marginal) analysis – this is in the context of diminishing returns at the intensive margin of agricultural cultivation (1767 [1844], I, 420–2). He distinguished between the total, the average and the marginal product and defined the relationship between them. Although he did not incorporate the analysis into his statement of general equilibrium, the formulation indicates the high potential of economics in the 1770s.

As already noted, the notion of a net income in farmers' profits came ultimately to be recognized in standard physiocratic writings. But Turgot went yet further, totally blurring the distinction between agriculture and manufacturing, as in the following statement relating to the manufacturing sector: 'As fast as this capital comes back to him by the sale of his products, he uses it for new purchases in order to supply and maintain his Manufactury by this continual circulation: on his profits he lives, and he places on one side what he can spare to increase his capital and put into his business, adding to the amount of his advances in order to add still more to his profit' (1770 [1963], 54). Clearly manufacturing profits contain a disposable surplus. The passage from Turgot describing the notion of profit rate equalization also reflects the abandoning of any sharp distinction between the two sectors.

Wealth itself is defined by Turgot to include land, movable riches (that is the sum of capitals employed in industry, agriculture and commerce) and durable personal goods. He includes specie in the totality of movable riches, but insists that it amounts to only a very small fraction thereof, and is certainly not identifiable with the wealth of society. Turgot approached the interest rate in terms of the demand for loanable funds by borrowers and the offers of lenders, the latter dependent on the supply of capital (movable riches) 'accumulated, saved bit by bit out of the revenues and profits ... It is these accumulated savings that are offered to borrowers, and the more there are of them the lower is the rate of interest, at least if the number of borrowers is not augmented in proportion' (1770 [1963], 78–9). Turgot has much in common with Cantillon or Hume in that they focused on the productivity of capital goods and savings propensities in the analysis of the interest rate diverting attention away from the purely monetary determinants.

The flexible working of the loanable funds market provided Turgot with the rationale for one of the most important propositions in classical literature, namely that in the process of accumulation, savings are converted into investment *without lag*. This is sometimes referred to as the Turgot–Smith theorem:

> We have seen that money plays scarcely any part in the sum total of existing capitals; but it plays a great part in the formation of capitals. In fact, almost all savings are made in nothing but money; it is in money that the revenues come to the proprietors, that advances and the profits return to undertakers of every kind; it is, therefore, from money that they save, and the annual increase in capitals takes place in money: but none of the undertakers make any other use of it than to convert it *immediately* into the different kinds of effects upon which their undertaking depends; and thus this money returns to circulation, and the greater part of capitals exist only in effects of different kinds (pp. 98–9).

Thus either people consume or they save, and the savings process, although a monetary process, entails no leakages, the inducement of a lower interest rate assuring increased borrowing for investment purposes to match any increase in savings.

3.6   General Overview and Analytical Significance

We return by the way of summary to the main lines of physiocratic thought. David Hume described the Physiocrats as a set of men 'the most chimerical and arrogant that now exists since the annihilation of the Sorbonne' (*Letters*, 1932, II, 205). Adam Smith (below, p. 321) also complained of Quesnay's fanaticism, commenting critically on an excessively close analogy between society and the human body. (Quesnay was a doctor and there is reason to believe that the circular-flow process of the *tableaux* might have been suggested to him by consideration of the blood flow.) That there is something of the fanatic in physiocracy is suggested by the emphasis upon the doctrine of 'evidence', encountered in the assertion that 'nothing is more evident' than the distinction between *façonner et produire*'.

The economic error involving biological creativity is perhaps more easily understood, though not justified, if we consider the cultural environment, for the Physiocrats were riddled with standard eighteenth-century biases in favour of agriculture – the notion of the Noble Savage and the pristine rural life. Furthermore, the notion of a disposable surplus generated uniquely in agriculture fits in well with the reality of the day, including the subsistence level at which labourers generally survived and the use of capitalistic organization and methods in agriculture rather than in manufacturing – agriculture in certain areas was (relatively speaking) the advanced capitalistic sector, while manufacturing operated on primitive, domestic lines. None the less, though these 'relativist' perspectives help throw some light on Physiocracy, they do not excuse analytical error, as was said in the earlier discussion of mercantilism. That Turgot avoided many of the weaknesses in question points clearly to this conclusion.

We turn next to a most interesting interpretation of the so-called Single Tax doctrine. This physiocratic doctrine has traditionally been interpreted as a theory of incidence supposing that the only surplus in the system is land rent. Thus, a tax imposed for example on wages (wages assumed to be at subsistence) must ultimately fall on rental income – the burden falling initially on labourers who are only compensated by higher money wages after population has contracted. (Quesnay emphasized contraction in consequence of emigration; Meek, 1962, 194.) But according to Ronald Meek this interpretation fails to capture the essence of the matter. The Physiocrats, Meek insists (pp. 392ff), were attempting to free farmers from having to pay any tax; for their earnings, it was recognized, contained a disposable surplus, and it was farmers not landlords who actually constituted the investing group in society. The formal claim that there is no source for taxation except in land rent was designed to avoid the imminent danger that irresponsible revenue-seeking governments would be attracted by any taxable income even if otherwise destined for investment. It is relevant too that the contemporary tax system imposed no obligation at all on land rents. The physiocratic position would thus be a reformist one. Where they exaggerated was in proposing that only land rents should be taxed.

From the perspective of intellectual history, the significance of Physiocracy lies in the balance it provides in the development of economics. This is clear from the various comparisons we have made with the mercantilists and their preoccupations with the balance of trade, the adequacy of the money supply and the size of population. The Physiocrats set these matters aside so that the weight of preoccupation altered. We have emphasized the treatment of capital accumulation – the key to growth being investment in capital goods to tide over time-consuming processes, and the funds for which derived from society's disposable surplus. Here is a major transformation of perspective in line with contemporary British contributions.

It is significant too that Karl Marx gave the Physiocrats a very good press, describing them in his *Theories of Surplus Value* as 'the true fathers of modern political economy' (1862–3 [1954], I, 44). Marx himself was interested in the generation of a surplus by capitalist employers in all sectors, not just in agriculture. None the less, he regarded Physiocracy as a step in the right direction.

Analytical parallels are sometimes drawn between aspects of Physiocracy and modern theory, particularly late nineteenth-century or 'Walrasian' general-equilibrium economics (Schumpeter, 1954, 242). However, doubts arise, for unlike the Physiocrats, who proceeded in terms of broad sectoral groupings and sought to pin-point leading sectors in the system, Walras set down precise equations to describe the various markets. Parallels have been drawn with Keynesian economics – a common predilection for social aggregates and discussion of the dangers flowing from faulty government policy and from hoarding (p. 243). On the other hand, there is not the same concern with employment in Quesnay as there is in Keynes. The most interesting of all of the parallels is with input–output tables (Phillips, 1955). (The 1923–4 Soviet National Economic Balance actually invokes the *tableau économique* for inspiration and analogy.) Whether, from a historical point of view, one should read it as such is another matter: we must avoid jobbing backwards. It seems that more is hidden than revealed by the input–output approach, for it disguises the notion of surplus accruing uniquely to land, by envisaging the landlords as 'producing' two units of rental service in the course of which activity they consume one unit of food and one unit of manufactures – most uncharacteristic from a physiocratic perspective.

Suggested Reading

Important samples of Quesnay's work will be found in Quesnay (1958), vol. II, and selections in English in Meek (1962, Part 1). Various versions of the *tableau* are reproduced and discussed in Kuczynski and Meek (1972). The writings of several of Quesnay's followers are printed in Daire (1846). For English translations from the works of Quesnay and de Mirabeau, see Meek (1973a).

Adam Smith's position on Physiocracy is summarized in the *Wealth of Nations*, Book IV, ch. IX, 'Of the Agricultural System', and is, of course, essential reading. Higgs (1897) is still to be recommended for a general overview of the physiocratic school. Fox-Genovese (1976) investigates the social background to physiocratic thought. Important commentary on key aspects of physiocratic economics is provided by Meek (1962), including the relation between Physiocracy and English classicism (Part II, ch. 4). Meek's ch. 3 and Spengler (1945) consider Physiocracy and the question of aggregate demand. Eltis (1984), ch. 2 and Spengler (1960) analyse physiocratic growth theory.

Turgot's place in the history of economics is the subject-matter of Groenewegen (1983). For Schumpeter's position on Quesnay and Turgot, see (1954), Part II, ch. 4. Turgot's life and work is discussed in Meek (1973b), which contains an English translation of Turgot's *Reflections*.

4 Smith on Value and Distribution

4.1 Introduction

In contrast to his French contemporaries who frequently neglected demand by focusing upon the physical dimension of output, Adam Smith elaborated in his *Wealth of Nations* the consumer's concept of wealth and the mechanism connecting production with demand, or the allocation of scarce productive factors within a competitive framework. The first concern of this chapter is the process whereby the demand–supply mechanism generates a pattern of market prices which reflects relative scarcity in the case of given commodity supplies (section 4.2). This mechanism is then shown in section 4.3 to be at work in the generation of long-run or cost prices, where allowance is made for changing commodity supplies by transfer of productive factors between industries. The celebrated 'labour theory of value' turns out to be a special case of long-run cost price determination and thus to depend on the possibility of supply adjustments (section 4.4). Various applications of demand theory are taken up in section 4.5.

A second major topic is micro-economic distribution in the sense of the determination of the returns to factors of production in particular industries rather than their average returns in the economy as a whole. This topic is approached in sections 4.6, 4.7 and 4.8 from the perspective of the demand for a factor (land, labour and capital) based upon its productivity, and its relative scarcity. One and the same general theory is shown to apply in both factor and commodity markets.

The chapter closes with a Smithian 'model' of value and distribution. David Ricardo, accepting much of Smith's basic analysis of resource allocation, found this model to be unsound. His criticisms mark the transfer from eighteenth- to nineteenth-century classicism.

Here I must repeat a word of warning (pp. 12–13 above). Adam Smith did not model his book after Hicks's *Value and Capital* (1939)! He wrote within an eighteenth-century intellectual milieu unfamiliar to the modern economist. Thus, for example, he sometimes formulated his analysis in terms of the operation of an invisible hand (divine providence?) guiding the (competitive) economy – 'organized' by self-interested participants seeking to maximize their utilities and revenues – towards an 'optimum' allocation of resources. (All this with an eye to what Smith took to be the opposing 'mercantilist' tradition.) Still a price-theoretic orientation to the *Wealth of Nations* which in substance, if not expression, has a 'modern' flavour cannot be gainsaid; no one has yet been able to show that the unfamiliar formulation affects the substance of the analysis.

It must also be allowed that Smith began his work not with the theory of price but rather with a discussion of the 'Division of Labour' – its origin and its relation to the size of the market – a topic which falls within the domain of economic development. This and related matters, including government policy, will be taken up in the last four sections of chapter 7.

4.2   Utility and Scarcity

Some commentators believe that Smith rejected utility as a determinant of value, basing themselves on a passage in the *Wealth of Nations* that came to be called the 'water–diamond paradox' or the 'paradox of value':

> The word VALUE, it is to be observed, has two different meanings, and sometimes expresses the utility of some particular object, and sometimes the power of purchasing other goods which the possession of that object conveys. The one may be called 'value in use'; the other, 'value in exchange'. The things which have the greatest value in use have frequently little or no value in exchange; and on the contrary, those which have the greatest value in exchange have frequently little or no value in use. Nothing is more useful than water: but it will purchase scarce any thing; scarce any thing can be had in exchange for it. A diamond, on the contrary, has scarce any value in use; but a very great quantity of other goods may frequently be had in exchange for it (1776 [1937], 28).*

* All extracts from the *Wealth of Nations* (1776) are from the 1937 New York edition, edited by E. Cannan. Henceforth throughout this chapter references to the *Wealth of Nations* are given by page number only.

These commentators have, in fact, discerned a totally novel orientation in the *Wealth of Nations*. For historically, so runs their argument, the emphasis had been on utility and scarcity as the determinants of exchange value; Smith's teacher, Francis Hutcheson (and those who had influenced him, including the Scholastics), indeed Smith himself in early lectures, had emphasized utility and scarcity, whereas in the *Wealth of Nations* Smith made only brief explicit reference to these phenomena, concentrating rather on production costs.

As we know already, however, even the Scholastics were pre-occupied by cost price, and certainly by the mid-eighteenth century cost pricing and the relationship of pricing to allocation had become standard themes. Several of Smith's contemporaries (Cantillon, Steuart, Hume and Turgot for example) had put a great deal of weight on cost price and other long-term 'real' magnitudes. There indeed remained unresolved problems regarding the relationship of market to cost price, and the implications for resource allocation of that relationship, but Smith did not change the orientation of thought. On the contrary, his concern with these matters fell within the mainstream of development of contemporary economic thought.

More important is the fact that there is no evidence of a downplaying in the *Wealth of Nations* of demand or of its underpinnings in utility. Let us consider more closely the 'water–diamond paradox'. Smith did not state the 'paradox' as a technical problem the solution to which eluded him, because, as seems to be believed, he lacked the notion of marginal utility. The term 'value-in-use' in this context does not in fact refer to desirability, the economist's notion of utility. Rather, Smith is making the point that the physiological need for water has no significance for the problem of pricing. This valid position tells us nothing of the role in pricing of 'utility' in the economist's sense.

What then can we say of Smith's position regarding the role of utility? Smith could scarcely have made it clearer that a condition for exchange value, and thus for inclusion in the national income, is that the product has utility in the economist's sense of desirability:

> Unless a capital was employed in manufacturing that part of the rude produce which requires a good deal of preparation before it can be fit for use and consumption, it either would never be produced, because there would be no demand for it; or if it was produced spontaneously, it would be of no value in exchange, and could add nothing to the Wealth of the society (p. 341).

This statement flies in the face of standard Physiocracy by pointing away from a physical conception of 'wealth' (national income).

Consider next a discussion of the causes of price variation over time with reference to the materials required by clothing and lodging. These commodities evidently constitute a class of goods which possess high value-in-use in a physiological sense. But their 'usefulness' (desirability) per unit varies with quantity. Smith is absolutely clear that relative scarcity is the essential point:

> In the one state [the early stage of economic development]...there is always a super-abundance of those materials, which are frequently, upon that account, of little or no value. In the other there is often a scarcity which necessarily augments their value. In the one state a great part of them is thrown away as useless...In the other they are all made use of, and there is frequently a demand for more than can be had...(pp. 161–2).

Here Smith provides, so to speak, the 'answer' to the so-called paradox of value.

Smith further elaborated on the motives behind consumer demand, and included 'value-in-use' (functional usefulness) as one only of the various sources of desirability. Thus 'the demand for [precious] metals arises partly from their utility [value-in-use], and partly from their beauty' (p. 172). Conspicuous consumption also comes into play: 'The merit of their beauty is greatly enhanced by their scarcity. With the greater part of rich people, the chief enjoyment of riches consists in the parade of riches, which in their eye is never so complete as when they appear to possess those decisive marks of opulence which nobody can possess but themselves.' And to these sources of desirability is added the utilitarian demand for the precious metals arising from their monetary function: 'That employment...by occasioning a new demand, and by diminishing the quantity which could be employed in any other way, may have...contributed to keep up or increase its value.' There is a whole range of sources of utility – beauty, conspicuous consumption, and various utilitarian functions of the product, but not those latter alone, and certainly not its physiological properties alone.

An explicit marginal concept – a notion of incremental value – can be extremely helpful in the appreciation of price determination traced back to individual choice. But to formulate the role of relative scarcity in price determination in Smith's fashion carries us a very long way; formal marginal analysis merely makes sharper what was already very well understood. In any event, the history of demand theory is not to be identified with the history of utility theory; and Smith did make formal use of the notion of marginal demand price as we shall see (below, p. 68).

A notion of 'real value' expressed in terms of 'labour commanded' helps explain the attribution to Smith of a neglect of utility considerations:

> The value of any commodity...to the person who possesses it, and means not to use or consume it himself, but to exchange it for other com-

modities, is equal to the quantity of labour which it enables him to purchase or command. Labour, therefore, is the real measure of the exchangeable value of all commodities.

The real price of every thing, what every thing really costs to the man who wants to acquire it, is the toil and trouble of acquiring it. What every thing is really worth to the man who has acquired it, and who wants to dispose of it or exchange it for something else, is the toil and trouble which it can save to himself, and which it can impose upon other people (p. 30).

But by no means does 'labour', in this context, imply some physical magnitude divorced from utility considerations; on the contrary, the object of the proposed index is to obtain a measure of economic welfare. In a negative sense, it constitutes a rough measure of the effort counterpart of national or private income – the number of labour units commanded by the national income or any individual's income providing a rough and ready indication of the cost in terms of labour effort of that income. Conversely, it provides a more direct measure of the real purchasing power over commodities represented by an individual's or society's income – also a utility notion – bearing in mind that 'every man is rich or poor according to the degree in which he can afford to enjoy the necessaries, conveniences and amusements of human life' (p. 30). This welfare perspective of labour commanded has no relevance for the analytics of price determination and should not be confused with the notion of labour embodied in commodities – labour input – which, under strictly defined circumstances, governs long-run prices (see p. 71 below). The discussion of a *measure* of value in terms of labour command is not part of a theory of the *determination* of value.

4.3 Price Determination

The conditions assuring a competitive market structure include, for Smith, large numbers and the absence of collusion. An example of a competitive structure is provided by the internal corn trade which was 'the least liable to be engrossed or monopolized by the force of a few large capitals', the impediment to engrossment deriving both from the disproportion between the annual output and the ability of 'a few private men' to purchase it, and from the existence of many independent producers who could each take on the function of dealer (p. 492). The satisfaction of the condition of large numbers of independently operating buyers and sellers guarantees the eradication of excess demands or excess supplies by way of price competition. But the process (to be discussed presently) whereby market prices tend in the long run towards cost prices – the extension of the price mechanism from the problem of exchange to that of production – also requires knowledge of profit opportunities available to resource owners, and freedom of movement between industries.

A word next, by way of contrast, regarding monopoly pricing. An observation that monopoly price 'is upon every occasion the highest which can be ... squeezed from the buyers, or which, it is supposed, they will consent to give' (p. 61) is injudicious. It should, however, be read in conjunction with a more specific discussion relating to the determination of the price of coal, wherein Smith defines a range of possible prices between a minimum determined by long-run costs and a maximum determined by the price of wood (corrected for the costs of transporting coal to the market), from which the seller or group of colluding sellers might choose: 'Coals, in the coal country, are every where much below this highest price. If they were not, they could not bear the expence of a distant carriage, either by land or by water. A small quantity only could be sold, and the coal masters and coal proprietors find it more for their interest to sell a great quantity at a price somewhat above the lowest, than a small quantity at the highest' (pp. 166–7). Cases of artificial reduction of output to force up price are also noted: 'were it possible, indeed, for one great company of merchants to possess themselves of the whole crop of an extensive country, it might, perhaps, be in their interests ... to destroy or throw away a considerable part of it, in order to keep up the price of the rest' (p. 491). Evidently, Smith was unable to specify the actual 'monopoly price', but it is quite clear that the 'maximum which can be squeezed from the buyers' is subject to the interest of sellers who face a negatively sloped demand curve.

*   *   *

Let us turn to the details of competitive price determination. Assuming several scarce factors (labour, capital and land), the cost of any commodity is said to be the sum of the unit wage, unit profit and unit rent costs. The chapter treating this issue (*Wealth of Nations*, Book I, vii: 'The Natural and Market Prices of Commodities') contains an embryonic account of general-equilibrium theory, for which even the most critical commentators such as Schumpeter have great respect.

Smith begins by defining the 'natural rates' of wages, profit and rent. These rates are simply the average returns to the three factors, which, for purposes of the analysis of commodity pricing, are taken as data. (There will be more to say on the nature of these 'natural' rates when we turn to macro-economic distribution in the growth context.) The term 'natural' was sometimes used by classical economists to refer to the wage paid in full 'stationary state' equilibrium when the system as a whole is at a final standstill. Similarly, the 'natural' return to capital. But that was not always the case and Smith understood the term to reflect the average factor returns ruling even in a growing system. With this in mind he thus defined the 'natural price' of a commodity:

> When the price of any commodity is neither more nor less than is suffi-
> cient to pay the rent of the land, the wages of the labour, and the profits of
> the stock employed in raising, preparing, and bringing it to market,
> according to their natural rates, the commodity is then sold for what may
> be called its natural price ... (p. 55).

'Natural price' is, therefore, cost price where the factors are paid the going rates. The 'market price', by contrast, is the actual price, which can diverge from the natural price depending upon market conditions. Only in long-run equilibrium does the market price equal the natural price: 'When the quantity brought to market is just sufficient to supply the effectual demand [quantity demanded at cost price] and no more, the market price naturally comes to be either exactly, or as nearly as can be judged of, the same with the natural price' (p. 57). For purposes of the argument in this chapter the natural or cost price of a commodity is assumed constant. Smith, in effect, defined the long-run supply curve in the 'Marshallian' sense of a locus of outputs and corresponding supply prices in the case of constant costs.

How then is the market price determined? The process by which the market price rises above or falls below the natural price entails 'compe-tition' in a race to obtain limited supplies or get rid of excess supplies. Smith's agents, and this is true throughout the classical period, are accorded some price-making ability. Competition, thus envisaged as a process of reaching equilibrium, has no counterpart in most modern elementary price-theory textbooks, which assume competitive con-sumers and sellers to be 'price-takers' reacting to given prices.

We must now look at the details of the analysis (p. 56). The market price (OP_m in figure 4.1) is 'regulated by the proportion between the quantity which is actually brought to market [OQ_s], and the demand of those who are willing to pay the natural price [OP_n]', labelled by Smith the 'effectual demand' [OQ_d]. Thus in a market period during which the supply is given at OQ_s, the market price is 'regulated' by the 'proportion' OQ_s/OQ_d. Since in this case there is an excess demand at OP_n, the actual price rises above cost price, let us say to OP_m.

The two equilibrium points E_n and E_m fall along a demand curve, the market price determined by the given market supply and the conditions of demand which define the slope of the curve passing through E_n. This statement requires substantiation. For not only is supply in the market

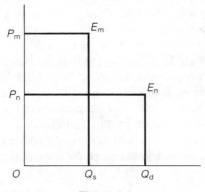

Figure 4.1

period apparently a specific quantity, but Smith's 'effectual demand' is a single point on the demand curve; it is a specific quantity demanded at a given price, not the entire demand curve. The market price is, moreover, formally said to be determined by the *ratio* between two quantities, rather than by equality of quantity demanded and quantity supplied. Yet we have given illustrations of Smith's appreciation of the demand schedule; and the argument used to substantiate his proposition regarding market price in the present context also indicates that he had in mind genuine curves or schedules relating to demand and to supply:

> When the quantity of any commodity which is brought to market falls short of the effectual demand, all those who are willing to pay the whole value of the rent, wages, and profit, which must be paid in order to bring it thither, cannot be supplied with the quantity which they want. Rather than want it altogether, some of them will be willing to give more. A competition will immediately begin among them, and the market price will rise more or less above the natural price, according as either the greatness of the deficiency, or the wealth and wanton luxury of the competitors, happen to animate more or less the eagerness of the competition. Among competitors of equal wealth and luxury the same deficiency will generally occasion a more or less eager competition, according as the acquisition of the commodity happens to be of more or less importance to them. Hence the exorbitant price of the necessaries of life during the blockade of a town or in a famine (p. 56).

Apparently no consumer actually makes purchases at cost price: 'rather than want it altogether' he must enter into competition for the scarce commodity; there are, in brief, no exchanges at non-equilibrium prices, all transactions occurring at the market price OP_m. The extent to which the market price will exceed the cost price depends upon the magnitude of the excess demand at that cost price (Q_d-Q_s) and, given that difference, upon consumers' 'wealth and wanton luxury'. Smith is here examining the conditions that determine the *slope* of the demand curve passing through E_n. He is saying that the higher the consumers' income, the steeper or less elastic the demand curve. (He may have had in mind a greater carelessness in budget allocation the smaller the proportion of an income spent on a particular commodity.) Moreover within any particular income group, commodities which have poor substitutes will be more inelastic in demand than luxury goods.

In the case of excess supply at cost price, competition forces the price below cost:

> When the quantity brought to market exceeds the effectual demand, it cannot all be sold to those who are willing to pay the whole value of the rent, wages and profit, which must be paid in order to bring it thither. Some part must be sold to those who are willing to pay less, and the low price which they give for it must reduce the price of the whole (p. 57).

It is inviting to interpret Smith here as referring to the notion of marginal demand price, the market price for the entire stock determined by the price which marginal buyers are prepared to pay. This is a nice statement of what is involved along a demand curve, where price discrimination is precluded. It may be said that Smith's reference to 'some part' of the produce exchanging at below cost prices implies that there are exchanges that do occur at cost price. But this interpretation is unlikely considering the explicit reference to a reduction in 'the price of the whole' and also the preclusion of non-equilibrium exchanges in the reverse case of excess demand.

Further remarks suggest that the supply curve cannot be represented accurately by a vertical line, which would imply given stocks to be sold during the period come what may. The possibility was recognized of withdrawing supplies to add to inventory as prices fall, and conversely drawing from inventory as prices rise, thus generating a supply curve with a positive slope. Thus, given an excess supply at cost price, the market price will fall

> according as the greatness of the excess increases more or less the competition of the sellers, or according as it happens to be more or less important to them to get immediately rid of the commodity. The same excess in the importation of perishables, will occasion a much greater competition than that of durable commodities; in the importation of oranges, for example, than in that of old iron.

Supply elasticity will thus depend on the possibility of withdrawing products from the market and holding them in stock. We may therefore attribute to Smith a positively sloped (market) supply curve as well as a negatively sloped demand curve.

The judicious use of prices is also the key to the process of rationing given stocks over time. The negatively sloped demand curve is central to this analysis, on the basis of which Smith concluded that government intervention in the corn trade was ruinous precisely because of neglect of the effects of low price on the rate of consumption (pp. 490–1).

*　　*　　*

So much for market price determination. We have next to consider the adjustment of market to natural (cost) price. The equilibration process by which market price comes to equal natural price in any industry turns on the presumption that factor owners are alert to available opportunities throughout the system, so that there is a tendency towards equalization of the returns to factors. To say that market price falls short of natural price is simply to say that *factors can earn more in other industries.* In that case they will transfer elsewhere, with the consequence that the short-run supply curve will shift towards the left until the market price comes to equal the natural price:

> If at any time [quantity supplied] exceeds the effectual demand, some of the component parts of its price must be paid below their natural rate. If it is rent, then the interests of the landlords will immediately prompt them to withdraw a part of their land; and if it is wages or profit, the interest of the labourers in the one case, and of their employers in the other, will prompt them to withdraw a part of their labour or stock from this employment. The quantity brought to market would soon be no more than sufficient to supply the effectual demand. All the different parts of the price will rise to their natural rate, and the whole price to its natural price (p. 57).

In the converse case, where market price exceeds cost price, there occurs expansion of supply: 'The quantity brought [to market] will soon be sufficient to supply the effectual demand. All the different parts of its price will soon sink to their natural rate, and the whole price to its natural price' (p. 58). Smith's demand–supply analysis falls within a context of 'general-equilibrium' wherein factor returns tend to equality across the board.

It has been maintained by one authority that 'in a market economy either there may be a tendency towards uniformity of wages and the rate of profit in different lines of production, or prices may be governed by supply and demand, but not both. Where supply and demand rule, there is no room for uniform levels of wages and the rate of profit' (Robinson, 1961, 57). Now this position would hold true in the event of immobility of factors between alternative uses, where we assume that the supply of each and every type of capital good, of labour, and of land is given, so that the return to each of these inputs is in the nature of a 'rent' determined by demand conditions. But this was not Smith's assumption. He was trying to explain the motives which assure that there will be movement of factors between industries until long-run equilibrium is achieved, with the returns to each of the three major classes of factors at a common level. Far from demand–supply analysis being inoperative, it is required to assure a tendency towards uniformity of returns.

Smith's repeated references to 'soon' and 'immediately' in his account of equilibration may be significant. Ricardo has been often described as an irresponsible applied economist who neglected time lags, and carried out his analysis in comparative-static terms – comparing long-run equilibria with little concern for the transition between them. Smith has always had a good press in this regard. Yet in this context at least he seems to be suggesting a very rapid transfer between equilibrium positions.

For all that, Smith recognized that disturbances are likely to be of frequent recurrence, so that while there are pressures at work 'tending' to bring the system rapidly towards repose assuming a once-and-for-all change in data, there can be long periods during which market prices diverge from long-run prices:

> The natural price ... is, as it were, the central price, to which the prices of all commodities are continually gravitating. Different accidents may sometimes keep them suspended a good deal above it, and may sometimes force them down even somewhat below it. But whatever may be the obstacles which hinder them from settling in this centre of repose and continuance, they are constantly tending towards it (p. 58).

Impressive though it is, the general-equilibrium analysis of *Wealth of Nations*, Book I, vii is constrained in various ways. There is, first, no formal discussion of the variability of proportions between factors in each establishment – substitution along an isoquant in modern parlance. And secondly, the average factor returns are given data, while in a true general-equilibrium system the average returns would be determined as part of the analysis. This presumed constancy implies (although Smith does not make the point) a uniformity of factor proportions from one sector to the other. If factor proportions differed, then shifts in the demand between products of differing factor intensity would play upon the labour market causing the wage to change. We shall revert to this matter in our discussion of Smith's nineteenth-century successors.

Smith claimed subsequently that a general wage rate increase 'necessarily increases the price of many commodities [manufactures], by increasing that part of it which resolves itself into wages, and so far tends to diminish their consumption both at home and abroad' (p. 86); and conversely, that a reduction in wages 'would necessarily be attended with a proportionable one in that of all home-manufactures...' (pp. 836–7). It follows logically that the *structure* of prices alters with changes in the wage rate should the labour intensity vary between products. But in all cases – even if labour intensities are uniform, which Smith may here have assumed – the *level* of prices will be affected. Now it is true that an increase in the wage of a particular kind of labour, required by one (or a very few) industries will generate an increase in the cost price of the commodity in question. But it is not true that a wage increase applicable to all types of labour will cause the price level to rise. It was Ricardo's great achievement to recognize that Smith had extended illegitimately a proposition valid only for partial-equilibrium analysis (see p. 88 below).

4.4 The Labour Theory of Value

By the 'labour theory of value' is intended the proposition that commodities exchange in long-run equilibrium in proportion to their labour input: 'It is natural that what is usually the produce of two days' or two hours' labour, should be worth double of what is usually the produce of one day's or one hour's labour' (p. 47). Thus if it takes two hours to catch one deer and one hour to catch a beaver, one deer will exchange for two beaver. The labour theory would apply where the only factor required is labour or if there are others whose services are free. But the impression given by Smith is of a single-factor case, and one where constant returns to scale prevail.

It is easy to justify the assertion in terms of Smith's own competitive model of long-run price determination. At an exchange rate of (say) one deer to one beaver some actors in the play will be dissatisfied. For example, some deer-producing beaver consumers will decide to hunt fewer deer, releasing two hours of labour per unit, and with those two hours catch two beavers thus acquiring more beaver by production than is possible by exchange; equally, some beaver-producing deer consumers would be stimulated to further expand beaver output, for therewith they can obtain by exchange one deer for each hour of labour. In consequence the output of deer falls and the output of beaver increases, and correspondingly the exchange rate turns against beaver until equilibrium is achieved. (To tell this story is to presume mobility of labour between sectors and the absence of monopoly constraints on output in any of the sectors.)

When wage rates differ between types of labour, prices in long-run equilibrium will no longer reflect relative labour quantities but relative labour costs, each hour weighted by the appropriate wage rate (p. 47). Again, be it noted, it is the demand–supply mechanism that yields this result, by assuring that wage rates reflect relative labour scarcity.

The labour theory of value, in either its pristine 'quantity' version or its more complex 'cost' version, Smith took to be a very special case. When allowance is made for interest on capital and rent on land, prices of commodities must cover not merely labour cost but also rent and interest, and for this general case Smith devised the analysis of Book I, vii, 'Of the Natural and Market Price of Commodities' discussed above. But in fact he was too hasty. A labour theory refers to rates of exchange *proportionate* to labour inputs; absolute prices might even in the three-factor case yet be proportionate to the labour input. This elaboration, which is due to Ricardo, will be dealt with later.

4.5 Variable-cost Conditions and the Dynamics of Consumption

The tradition that Smith 'played down' demand analysis derives partly from almost exclusive concentration upon chapter vii of Book I, which assumes constant-cost conditions in all industries. An increase in demand for a product then leaves the long-run (cost) price unchanged. But Smith designed the chapter to elucidate the various propositions regarding resource allocation, for which purpose the 'strong' assumption was adequate. It is quite clear, however, that it did not represent his typical position regarding cost conditions. The issue can best be appreciated as an aspect of the dynamics of consumption.

Smith categorized agricultural produce (other than corn) into broad classes according to the secular pattern of price movement. The first category includes all those items which are more or less fixed in supply – for example, rare birds – and which face a demand that is continually increasing as (real) incomes rise: 'The quantity of such commodities, therefore, remaining the same, or nearly the same, while the competition to purchase them is continually increasing, their price may rise to any degree of extravagance, and seems not to be limited by any certain boundary' (p. 218). By contrast, in the second category are instances of products amenable to increase in response to secularly rising demand. The analysis of these latter cases is further testimony to Smith's recognition of the economic significance of scarcity, and at the same time illustrates the fact that the explanation of price in terms of supply and demand (relative scarcity) was not regarded as an alternative to that in terms of costs; the scarcity approach was not, in other words, restricted to the analysis of market price. I refer to Smith's observation (pp. 219–20) that in the course of economic development the extension of tillage and consequent reduction in the supply of cattle hitherto available on the wilds as free goods, combined with increasing population and real purchasing power per head and consequent expansion in demand for butcher's meat, tend to force up cattle prices, ultimately rendering the production of butcher's meat profitable. At this time some land areas, initially prepared for cereals, will be utilized for commercial cattle raising. A (long-run) price ceiling is thus ultimately imposed as demand for butcher's meat continues to rise: 'When it has got so high it cannot well go higher. If it did, more land and more industry would soon be employed to increase their quantity' (p. 220).

A third category includes cases where output variation in response to expanding demand is 'either limited or uncertain' (pp. 228ff). This covers wool and hides which are treated as joint products with the carcass. Even in an underdeveloped economy there is often sufficient demand, emanating from the world market if not domestically, for wool and hides to assure commercial preparation. The secular increase in domestic real incomes, therefore, has a much smaller (relative) effect upon the demand for such products than upon that for butcher's meat. But the suppy of wool and hides will be affected – an 'uncertain' response – along with that of butcher's meat as the latter is increased in response to expanding demand.

An account of the fisheries – which also fall into the third category – contains a very nice formulation of diminishing (average) returns:

> But it will generally be impossible to supply the great and extended market without employing a quantity of labour greater than in proportion to what had been requisite for supplying the narrow and confined one. A market which, from requiring only one thousand, comes to require annually ten thousand ton of fish, can seldom be supplied without employing more than ten times the quantity of labour which had before been sufficient to supply it. The fish must generally be sought for at a greater distance, larger vessels must be employed, and more expensive machinery of every kind made use of. The real price of this commodity, therefore, naturally rises in the progress of improvement (p. 235).

In the specific case of corn production, constant rather than increasing costs are said to prevail. Here, however, cost conditions are defined with allowance made for technical progress: 'In every different stage of improvement ... the raising of equal quantities of corn in the same soil and climate, will at an average, require nearly equal quantities of labour ...; the continual increase in the productive powers of labour in an improving state of cultivation being more or less counterbalanced by the continually increasing price of cattle, the principal instrument of agriculture' (p. 186). The implications for costs of land scarcity as such are not recognized. This is a striking feature that marks off Smithian economics from nineteenth-century classicism.

In the case of manufactured goods Smith emphasized a downward secular trend in (real) costs. Considering the role accorded scale economies in the first chapter of the *Wealth of Nations* ('Of the Division of Labour'), these instances take on particular importance. An increase in demand from an initial state of full industry equilibrium raises price in the short run only, while the new long-run equilibrium price will be below the initial level. Demand therefore plays a fundamental role in determining long-run as well as short-run prices: 'The increase of demand, besides, though in the beginning it may sometimes raise the price of goods, never fails to lower it in the long run. It encourages production, and thereby increases the competition of producers, who, in order to undersell one another, have recourse to new divisions of labour and new improvements of art, which might never otherwise have been thought of' (p. 706). In this analysis, there is no true theory of the firm, Smith simply taking it for granted that the size of the average production unit will rise along with the expansion of the industry.

4.6   The Theory of Distribution: Factor Productivity

Distribution from a micro-economic perspective is governed for Smith by the demand–supply mechanism applied to the factor's labour, capital and land, the demand for which in each case turns upon productivity considerations. This assertion requires justification, for it is often said that Smith believed labour to be the sole productive factor, alone responsible for wealth but suffering deductions at the hands of capitalists and landowners. And, indeed, we do read that in the 'early and rude state of society which precedes both the accumulation of stock and the appropriation of land ... the whole produce of labour belongs to the labourer' (p. 47); and that this idyllic state came to be transformed:

> As soon as stock has accumulated in the hands of particular persons, some of them will naturally employ it in setting to work industrious people, whom they will supply with materials and subsistence, in order to make a profit by the sale of their work, or by what their labour adds to the value of the materials. In exchanging the complete manufacture ... something must be given for the profits of the undertaker of the work who hazards his stock in this adventure. The value which the workmen add to the materials, therefore, resolves itself in this case into two parts, of which the one pays their wages, the other the profits of their

employer upon the whole stock of materials and wages which he advanced (p. 48).

Similarly with regard to rent: 'As soon as the land of any country has all become private property, the landlords, like all other men, like to reap where they never sowed, and demand a rent even for its natural produce' (p. 49).

These statements attributing output to labour made in the context of the transfer to the modern state cannot, however, be taken as a denial of a positive contribution of 'capital' to production in modern society. What Smith has to say regarding capital productivity makes it certain that his statements defining profits as 'deductions from the produce of labour' were intended as a criticism of contemporary capitalism – the ownership of capital by a separate class of capitalists.

In the relevant analyses of Book I (ch. vi: 'Of the Component Parts of Price'; ch. viii: 'Of the Wages of Labour'; ch. ix: 'Of the Profits of Stock'), capital or 'stock' is understood as materials, tools and subsistence which is 'stored up somewhere beforehand', and which permit time-consuming processes to be undertaken by specialist labour. But the clearest statement is to be found in the 'Introduction' to Book II:

> In that rude state of society in which there is no division of labour, in which exchanges are seldom made, and in which every man provides everything for himself, it is not necessary that any stock should be accumulated or stored up beforehand, in order to carry on the business of the society. Every man endeavours to supply by his own industry his own occasional wants as they occur...
>
> But when the division of labour has once been thoroughly introduced, the produce of a man's own labour can supply but a very small part of his occasional wants. The far greater part of them are supplied by the produce of other men's labour, which he purchases with the produce, or what is the same thing, with the price of the produce of his own. But this purchase cannot be made till such time as the produce of his own labour has not only been completed, but sold. A stock of goods of different kinds, therefore, must be stored up somewhere sufficient to maintain him, and to supply him with the materials and tools of his work, till such time, at least, as both these events can be brought about (p. 259).

In a broad sense Smith can thus be said to have recognized the essence of 'capitalistic' production, namely the use of methods involving indirect processes which evidently yield a higher product than more direct methods, but which require a period of waiting and accordingly 'capital' in the form of wage goods as well as hand tools and materials.

In a more precise sense Smith recognized that certain refinements in the degree of specialization entail extensions in the period of production; for the invention of machines is portrayed as the outcome of the division of labour, and the use of machinery increases the 'roundaboutness' of the process with resultant increases in labour productivity:

> The quantity of materials which the same number of people can work up, increases in a great proportion as labour comes to be more and more subdivided; and as the operations of each workman are gradually reduced to a greater degree of simplicity, a variety of new machines come to be invented for facilitating and abridging those operations. As the division of labour advances, therefore, in order to give constant employment to an equal number of workmen an equal stock of provisions, and a greater stock of materials and tools than would have been necessary in a ruder state of things, must be accumulated beforehand (p. 260).

Much attention is paid to items in the capital structure apart from wage goods. In the extract above, for example, the emphasis is deliberately diverted from wage advances; in the case of a given work force, extensions of the period of production as a means to increased output require additional materials (the materials–output ratio being apparently a technological constant), not additional subsistence. Similarly, considerable attention is devoted to machinery, the function of which is to 'facilitate and abridge labour' or to 'increase the productive powers of labour', and industrial structures which (unlike private dwellings) are the means of 'procuring a revenue, not only to their proprietor who lets them for a rent, but to the person who possesses them and pays that rent for them' (p. 265). Clearly then fixed capital is productive and, so it seems, the sourse from which profit is paid. The category also includes land improvements and human capital or 'acquired and useful abilities'. Smith's capital, it is sometimes said, is primarily subsistence goods and raw materials whereas machinery, tools and skill are simply more complex forms. This may be so, but it would be illegitimate to conclude that Smith's theory of production can be appreciated without taking into account fixed capital, since it is through the use of machinery that many of the effects of the extensions of the time period of production are enjoyed, technology requiring embodiment in real capital goods.

Fixed capital is only introduced if it is expected that revenue will cover depreciation and yield at least the normal rate of return: 'When any expensive machine is erected, the extraordinary work to be performed by it before it is worn out, it must be expected, will replace the capital laid out upon it, with at least the ordinary profits' (p. 101). Similarly, 'the expence which is properly laid out upon a fixed capital of any kind, is always repaid with great profit, and increases the annual produce by a much greater value than that of the support which such improvements require' (p. 271). 'Wear and tear' as an annual expense is also explicitly allowed for (pp. 266–7).

From these passages, and having in mind also the diversion of attention from capital envisaged merely as advanced wages, it appears that Smith was groping towards a relationship between the productivity of capital goods and the rate of return on capital. Such a relationship has a counterpart in that between the productivity of land and the rental income. For when Smith was not considering the imaginary original society and the imaginary transfer to the modern state, he was emphatic that land is productive: 'rent may be considered as the produce of [the] powers of nature, the use of which the landlord lends to the farmer. It is greater or smaller according to the supposed extent of those powers, or in other words, according to the supposed natural or improved fertility of the land' (pp. 344–5). Similarly: 'The rent of land is paid for the use of a productive subject. The land which pays it produces it' (p. 794). It is accordingly likely that the various references to the 'deduction' made by rent from the contribution of the labourer allude to a change in property relationships which Smith frowned upon – land was originally held 'in common' so that there was no distinction between a labouring and land-owning class – rather than constituting a denial of the productivity of land.

As for labour itself, Smith writes in terms of what, after 1870, came to be known as the 'imputation' principle – the imputing of the value of the factor from that of the product it yields. Thus wages are regulated by the 'quantity and supposed value of the work' (p. 74); and the demand for labour is related to the demand for final output, such that a reduction in taxes upon subsistence or raw materials allows workers 'to work cheaper, and to send their goods cheaper to market. The cheapness of their goods would increase the demand for them, and consequently for the labour of those who produced them' (pp. 890–1). These references to the value-product of labour apply at the micro-economic level of analysis in contrast to the 'wages fund' approach of aggregative analysis.

The rationale behind factor demand thus lies in factor productivity, a principle applying to land and capital as well as labour. Productivity could not, however, have been regarded by Smith as a sufficient condition for factor pricing as the Physiocrats so often implied, having in mind his appreciation of the scarcity requirement in the case of commodity pricing. But we may be more explicit about this matter by reference to his discussion of land rent, where it is made clear that productivity is a necessary but insufficient condition for a revenue product (see, however, below pp. 98, 156, 175 for physiocratic residues).

4.7 Factor Supply: Land

Rent (to be distinguished from interest paid to the landlord for land improvements) Smith asserted, 'depends upon the demand' for the product and conceivably could be reduced to zero with no withdrawal of land services:

> Rent...enters into the composition of the price of commodities in a different way from wages and profit. High or low wages and profits, are the causes of high or low price; high or low rent is the effect of it. It is because high or low wages and profit must be paid, in order to bring a particular commodity to market, that price is high or low. But it is because its price is high or low; a great deal more, very little more, or no more than what is sufficient to pay those wages and profit, that it affords a high rent, or a low rent, or no rent at all (pp. 145–6).

On this account, wages and profits 'enter into' costs while rent amounts to a demand-determined surplus. This is extraordinary considering the analysis of Book I, vii, where Smith treated rent on an exact par with wages and profits in his determination of cost price (see p. 65 above). Is it possible to avoid attributing to Smith a grotesque inconsistency?

If the passage quoted above related to aggregate rather than industry conditions, the dilemma might be resolved. In the aggregate, wages and profits are 'necessary' payments, but rent is not, because a given stock of land is available notwithstanding even a zero return. By contrast, the rent per acre in any use enters into costs since the land must meet the return potentially available in alternative uses. But this is an unlikely solution because of the explicit reference in the passage to 'a particular commodity'; and because, as we will see, profit (or rather interest) in the aggregate is in fact identified by Smith with rent – neither are 'necessary' payments.

There is another possible way out. We shall find presently (see p. 82 below) that the pricing of corn is distinguished from that of other agricultural products. Agricultural products, other than corn, have their cost prices determined in the manner of Book I, vii as the sum of wages, profits and rent per unit, whereas the rent of corn land is treated as a surplus. But this too is conjecture, for the passage does not suggest a specific concern with corn.

Only were Smith for some reason presuming that land in some particular use has no alternative opportunities will his proposition that rents are yielded as a demand-determined surplus hold up. It is likely that a solution to our problem will be found just here. Smith distinguished between food-producing and materials-producing land, implying the preclusion of land transfer between these broad uses at least. The former is said 'always' to yield a rent (p. 146). Food-producing land apparently 'always' yields rent because when food increases in supply, there follows a corresponding increase in population and thus in the demand for food. Materials-producing land, by contrast, 'sometimes does, and sometimes does not, afford Rent', as illustrated by the empirical observation that at early stages of development (despite the expropriation of land into private hands) the owners of forest land, or of quarries and mines, cannot obtain a rent for the services of their properties. Competitive bidding for the abundant supplies is too weak to generate a positive return – an observation of obvious relevance to the so-called 'paradox' of value.

An example is given from woodland: 'When the materials of lodging are so super-abundant, the part made use of is worth only the labour and expence of fitting it for that use. It affords no rent to the landlord, who generally grants the use of it to whoever takes the trouble of asking it' (p. 163). An increase in the level of purchasing power, however, entails a rising demand for wood and minerals and accordingly for the use of forests and mines, so that a rent comes to be generated. But even in a developed economy 'the demand for [such products] is not always such as to afford a greater price than what is sufficient to pay the labour, and replace, together with its ordinary profits, the stock which must be employed in bringing them to market' (pp. 164–5). Thus, for example, marginal mines – in terms of low productivity or poor location – may yield no rent. Our passage would apply precisely to such a case, assuming, of course, that land suitable for mines has no alternative use – or at least no effective alternative under going market conditions. For if land for mining had to meet competition from other uses a rent would have to be paid even for the least productive mines or else such units would not be used for mining; rent would 'enter into' costs, as in the world of Book I, vii.

The attempt to define the circumstances under which rent will be generated in terms of the scarcity of land (relative to demand for its output) as well as its productivity is most significant when considered in historical perspective. The physiocratic analysis was fragile, failing to provide a sound explanation for the existence of a surplus revenue over the 'costs' of agricultural produce. The reference to rent-free marginal mines is also significant in terms of a comparison with later Ricardian theory, especially when considered in conjunction with various other casual allusions in the *Wealth of Nations* to the phenomenon of 'differential rent': 'The rent of land not only varies with its fertility, whatever be its produce, but with its situation, whatever be its fertility'; thus on good land, a given area 'not only maintains a greater number of cattle, but as they are brought within a smaller compass, less labour becomes requisite to tend them, and to collect their produce' (p. 147), so that a cost differential is generated which, Smith explains, is eradicated in the form of rent. But this phenomenon does not play the conspicuous role it was later to play in Ricardian theory. In fact, most of Smith's contemporaries and successors were scarcely aware of its presence in the *Wealth of Nations*. (We shall return to this matter in the discussion of the theory of growth, p. 164).

4.8   Factor Supply: the Wage and Profit Structures

Smith's discussion of the wage rate structure, to which we turn next, deals with constraints upon the supplies of labour to particular industries; it is the competitive market process that governs the relative supplies of different types of labour and generates appropriate differentials. Much work had already been done on this topic by Cantillon, Steuart and others, but Smith took the issue further. An equilibrium pattern of wages for Smith is one in which differential money wages reflect the differential disutilities attached to the various occupations. Money wages per hour may differ, for it is the money wage per disutility unit that tends to equality. A preliminary statement in *Wealth of Nations* Book I, v, is developed at length in Book I, x, and to this we turn.

Here five characteristics are listed which compensate for money wage differentials:

> The five following are the principal circumstances which, so far as I have been able to observe, make up for a small pecuniary gain in some employments, and counterbalance a great one in others: first, the agreeableness or disagreeableness of the employments themselves; secondly, the easiness and cheapness, or the difficulty and expence of learning them; thirdly, the constancy or inconstancy of employment in them; fourthly, the small or great trust which must be reposed in those who exercise them; and fifthly, the probability or improbability of success in them (p. 100).

The argument is based on several assumptions: that labour movement between occupations is unimpeded by institutional constraints (pp. 99, 118ff); that the different occupations are well known so that there is knowledge of available opportunities (p. 114); that they are long established because novelty involves disutility for workers who must, in the short run, be compensated; and that they involve full-time employment because part-time workers are likely to accept a particularly low monetary reward per hour.

Training costs (alluded to in item two of the list) are treated as a form of investment in human capital formation, which requires a return as does any other: 'The work which [a person] learns to perform, it must be expected, over and above the usual wages of common labour, will replace to him the whole expence of his education, with at least the ordinary profits of an equally valued capital' (p. 101). Learning costs include foregone earning opportunities, maintenance undertaken by the individual or by his parents, and payments for training to the employer; but in addition, over the working lifetime of the individual, there must be a net differential representing a return on investment. The wage differential therefore includes an interest rate.

If we are to take seriously Smith's effort to define an equilibrium wage structure such that money wages are equal per unit of disutility, it would have to be the case that interest represents compensation for some kind of disutility. Some nineteenth-century economists were later to conceive formally of interest as the reward for abstinence from present consumption. (Strictly speaking it is the *marginal* pain cost that is relevant.) And if that is the case, the analysis is complete in the sense that the wage paid to skilled workers covers the actual disutility involved in training and the disutility for which the interest is a payment. But it will emerge that for Smith, as for other eighteenth-century writers, interest was *not* a 'necessary' payment in the foregoing sense (see below, p. 161), thereby weakening the general argument.

Regarding regularity of employment, even if the whole year is considered (so that allowance is made for seasonal variations) there will yet have to be a net return paid to workers in seasonal industries, to compensate for 'those anxious and desponding moments which the thought of so precarious a situation must sometimes occasion' (p. 103). The very fact that an industry is subject to cyclical or seasonal fluctuations is itself upsetting and requires compensation.

The item 'trust' will be a valid consideration in Smith's scheme only if the adoption of responsibility entails a psychic burden. If people enjoy taking on responsibility then the differential would not work in the direction proposed. The monetary return allows also for the differing degrees of chance of success, implying that taking risk is painful. Yet some of Smith's observations suggest otherwise, for he refers to a tendency of people to overestimate their chance of outstanding success and crowd into professions which promise a small likelihood of a very great reward.

There is a parallel analysis of the profit rate structure. Profit rate equalization is said to presume knowledge of new profit opportunities deriving from changes in the pattern of demand and also from new technologies, the discovery of new types of inputs, and so forth. As a possible source of compensating profit rate differentials Smith considers the constancy or inconstancy of employment, but only to dismiss it: 'whether the stock of capital is or is not constantly employed depends, not upon the trade, but the trader' (p. 105). This is difficult to appreciate, since in the context of the wage structure instability of the trade was regarded as a relevant phenomenon.

4.9   A Model of Value and Distribution

There is to be found in the *Wealth of Nations* a model relating to value
and distribution which was much discussed in the subsequent literature.
To understand this model and the modifications made to it by Ricardo,
is to grasp much of post-Smithian economics. Some features, especially
the determination of the general wage and profit rates, are of a macro-
economic nature and must be taken on faith for the present. But the
model yields results of the first importance for our present topic of
allocation economics and therefore has to be considered at this
juncture.

In the model, the money price of corn is accorded special treatment.
Smith does not apply a simple cost of production theory to corn in the
manner of Book I, vii but focuses on the international flow of the
precious metals (silver), observing that in equilibrium, across the trading
world, there is a common silver price of corn – or to be more precise
that the number of ounces of silver paid for a bushel of corn *tends* to an
equilibrium assuming the free international flow of the precious metals
and of goods – a version of the Hume specie-flow mechanism. Two
categories of disturbances to the silver price of corn are examined. (The
discussion is found in a lengthy 'Digression on Silver' attached to *Wealth
of Nations*, Book I, xi: 'Of the Rent of Land'.) First, there are improvements in productivity of the mines in a particular country stimulating
an increase in the supply of silver, and thus in the silver demand for, and
silver price of corn. There would follow a reallocation of the higher
money stock throughout the trading world, until a new equilibrium is
reached. Secondly, there are disturbances impinging on the side of the
(corn) demand for silver in some country. These occur if aggregate
activity increases internally stimulating an increase in the corn price of
silver or, in other terms, a fall in the silver price of corn. A lower silver
price of corn is, in fact, a necessary condition for an inflow of precious
metals into a country to finance a larger GNP: 'Gold and silver naturally
resort to a rich country, for the same reason that all sorts of luxuries and
curiosities resort to it; not because they are cheaper there than in poorer
countries, but because they are dearer, or because a better price is given
for them. It is the superiority of price which attracts them...' (p. 217).
Once a new equilibrium state is established, there is no longer any
motivation for any movement of precious metals: 'as soon as that superiority ceases they necessarily cease to go thither'.

We have thus far the determination of the silver price of corn. We
come next to the average money wage rate, which is determined by the
money price of corn, and by aggregate labour market conditions,
specifically by the rate of growth of labour demand:

The money price of labour is necessarily regulated by two circumstances; the demand for labour, and the price of the necessaries and conveniencies of life. The demand for labour, according as it happens to be increasing, stationary, or declining, or to require an increasing, stationary, or declining population, determines the quantity of the necessaries and conveniencies of life which must be given to the labourer; and the money price of labour is determined by what is requisite for purchasing that quantity (p. 85).

We postpone treatment of the profit rate and assume provisionally that we appreciate its determination in order to focus on the general cost and price conditions throughout the system. In manufacturing industry for which (in standard physiocratic and classical fashion) land is supposed not to be required, production costs include wages, profits and raw materials. The cost prices of the raw materials themselves (agricultural products in general other than corn) are determined in the manner of *Wealth of Nations* Book I, vii. These products have to meet the competition of alternative land use, which is corn production. The rent of corn land itself emerges as a residual, the difference between the silver price of corn and wage plus profit costs. The price of corn thus governs an entire structure of other prices. If the price of corn rises then the prices of all the other agricultural products will also have to rise; conversely if it falls, the prices of all other products fall. For if the price of corn rises so rents will rise and these other products have to meet the competition of higher rents in corn production. (In this context, possibly for empirical reasons, Smith traces a one-way relation from the corn sector rather than a relation of mutual interdependence.)

The price of corn therefore plays upon manufacturing prices by way of materials costs as well as by way of the money wage rate. This sequence is outlined in Book IV, v, 'Of Bounties'. The analysis establishes Smith as a genuine 'model builder', for here he brings together a complex string of arguments leading to the striking theorem that the 'money price of corn regulates that of all other home-made commodities':

> It regulates the money price of labour, which must always be such as to enable the labourer to purchase a quantity of corn sufficient to maintain him and his family either in the liberal, moderate, or scanty manner in which the advancing, stationary or declining circumstances of the society oblige his employers to maintain him.
>
> It regulates the money price of all the other parts of the rude produce of the land, which, in every period of improvement, must bear a certain proportion to that of corn.... It regulates, for example, the money price of grass and hay, of butcher's meat, of horses, and the maintenance of horses, of land carriage consequently, or the greater part of the inland commerce of the country.

By regulating the money price of all the other parts of the rude produce of land, it regulates that of the materials of almost all manufactures. By regulating the money price of labour, it regulates that of manufacturing art and industry. And by regulating both, it regulates that of the complete manufacture. The money price of labour, and of every thing that is the produce either of land or labour, must necessarily either rise or fall in proportion to the money price of corn (pp. 476–7).

The passage neglects to mention profits. However, since the capital outlay rises (wages and raw material costs having increased) the costs relating to capital increase accordingly (p. 816). Depreciation is also left out of account.

The fundamental implication of the model, which it must be noted applies generally and not only in the stationary state, is that an increase in the general money wage rate will be reflected in an increase in the prices of *manufactured* goods proportional to the labour input. As for agriculture, the impact will be on rent, prices remaining unchanged. For rent is a residual yielded on corn land and will be squeezed as wages rise; the fall in rent will, of course, apply also to other land-using commodities, no net change occurring in their prices.

4.10 Conclusion

One of the policy applications of Smith's analysis was to the contemporary corn-export subsidy or 'bounty'. Any such subsidy will cause the domestic price of corn to rise as the export of corn is encouraged, which in turn plays on both the money wage rate and materials prices and thus on the price of manufactured goods. This sequence led Smith to declare that the bounty cannot encourage agricultural relative to manufacturing activity as was its intention, since there is no relative increase in the money price of corn, and merely a nominal fall in the purchasing power of silver:

> The real effect of the bounty is not so much to raise the real value of corn, as to degrade the real value of silver; or to make an equal quantity of it exchange for a smaller quantity, not only of corn, but all other home-made commodities; for the money price of corn regulates that of all other home-made commodities (p. 476).

Equally strongly: 'our country gentlemen', the farm interests governing Parliament, 'did not perhaps attend to the great and essential difference which nature has established between corn and almost every other sorts of goods.... The nature of things has stamped upon corn a real value which cannot be altered by merely altering its money price. No bounty upon exportation, no monopoly of the home market can raise that value' (p. 482).

Adam Smith's artistry with the price mechanism is remarkable (see section 4.5 and the later discussion on pp. 170ff). Yet we are faced with a paradox: his notion of the ineffectiveness of intervention designed to stimulate agriculture by export subsidies in the case of a corn-exporting country (or by duties in that of a corn-importing country) was, with good reason, to be severely criticized on price-theoretic or allocative grounds. David Ricardo could not fathom the theorem, which negates Smith's own principles of competitive allocation economics. Ricardo's corrections mark the transition to nineteenth-century classical theory, although considering his application of Smithian tools it would be too strong to describe the transition as a 'revolution'.

Suggested Reading

From here on suggested primary sources will be marked by an asterisk and these are followed by recommended commentaries. Where appropriate reference will be made to J. C. Wood's *Critical Assessments* on Smith (1984), Ricardo (1985) and Malthus (1986). It should be repeated that the selections do not necessarily take a position coinciding with that of the present author.

*   *   *

*Smith (1776 [1937]) *An Inquiry into the Nature and Causes of the Wealth of Nations*, Book I, chs iv–vii on value; chs viii–xi on distribution.

On value theory, see Robertson and Taylor (1957) in Wood (1984), item 81; and Dobb (1973), ch. 2. Hollander (1973), ch. 4 (and ch. 9 which focuses on trade), and also Kaushil (1973) in Wood (1984), item 98, take the position developed in the present chapter. Williams (1978), ch. 2 deals with Smith and the theory of the firm. On distribution, see an important article by Rosenbluth (1969) in Wood (1984), item 94; Dobb (1973); and Hollander (1973), ch. 5. For a summary of the Smithian theory of value and distribution and its status 1776–1816 see Hollander (1979), ch. 1.

The classicists' position on demand, with partial reference to Smith, is discussed by V. E. Smith (1951). Stigler's *Essays in the History of Economics* (1965), chs 5 and 8, cover the development of utility theory and of perfect competition, and contains important references to Smith. Gordon (1959) deals with the question: 'What was the Labour Theory?' and Buchanan (1929) writes on 'the historical approach to rent and price theory' with pertinent allusions to Smith. Bowley (1973), ch. 4 covers utility and the paradox of value, and ch. 5 the problem of market structure in classical economics with pertinent sections on Smith.

5 Ricardo on Value and Distribution

5.1 Introduction

While preparing the *Principles of Political Economy* for publication (1817), David Ricardo explained what was preoccupying him: 'In reading Adam Smith, again, I find many opinions to question, all I believe founded on his original error respecting value. He is particularly faulty in the chapter on bounties' (Ricardo, 1951, VII, 100).* In a letter to J. R. McCulloch – at this time a 'Smithian' economist – he was equally explicit: 'Your system proceeds upon the supposition that the price of corn regulates the price of all other things, and that where corn rises or falls, commodities also rise or fall, – but this I hold to be an erroneous system although you have great authorities in your favour, no less than Adam Smith, Mr. Malthus and Mr. Say' (p. 105). Here we have the key to Ricardo's *Principles* in Ricardo's own words: and this was the reason for closing the previous chapter with Smith's model which relates general prices to the price of corn via the money wage and materials costs, and with his corn–export bounty application.

To appreciate Ricardo's criticism we have to understand his theory of value. He did not object to Smith for holding a cost of production theory of long-run competitive price. He objected rather to the manner in which Smith treated the switch from a simple economy with one scarce factor to a complex economy with a variety of factors, particularly his conclusion that labour quantity had no further relevance in value determination with the appearance of rent and profit. In Smith's model rent is included in the production costs of agricultural products.

---

* All extracts from the works of Ricardo are from the *Works and Correspondence* (1951), vols I–XI, edited by P. Sraffa. Throughout this chapter references to the *Works* will be given by volume and/or page number only.

This Ricardo denied, holding *marginal* cost to be relevant to exchange rate determination: 'until a country is cultivated in every part [an allusion to the extensive margin] and up to the highest degree [an allusion to the intensive margin], there is always a portion of capital employed on the land which yields no rent ... it is this portion of capital, the result of which, as in manufactures, is divided between profits and wages, that regulates the price of corn' (I, 252). In short, assuming rent-free land at the margin of cultivation, 'the appropriation of land, and the consequent creation of rent' would not 'occasion any variation in the relative value of commodities' (p. 67). As for the implications of the payment of profits, all depended on the technological structure of the various industries; under some circumstances a labour theory of relative-price determination might still apply.

Ricardo's exposition of value theory in the first chapter of the *Principles* begins with the proposition that long-run equilibrium exchange values will reflect relative labour embodiment if labour is the sole factor. That relative production costs reflect relative labour input alone is true, even in this simple case, only if there occurs no change in the structure of rewards paid to the different types of labour used in producing the various commodities. This complication Ricardo avoids by assuming a given structure which assures that when wages change, they change proportionately for all types of labour. (Adam Smith, incidentally, had also adopted this assumption in the growth context; 1776 [1937], 143.) Since all commodities are affected uniformly, their relative cost prices and exchange rates remain unchanged.

To adopt a labour theory of value is not necessarily to deny the presence of costs other than labour costs. It is to say that cost prices are *proportional* to relative labour input. Now some production processes require working capital only, others a combination of fixed and working capital, while the durability of fixed capital or machinery and the circulating period of working capital will differ from product to product. (In a letter Ricardo reduced all of these characteristics to differences in the *time* that labour is invested in a process; Ricardo, VIII, 193.) Yet, provided the capital structures of the various products are everywhere the same, a change in the wage rate will impinge on all commodities equally, leaving relative production costs, and therefore prices, unaffected. Only when allowance is made for non-uniformity of the technological characteristics will a wage increase alter the structure of prices, for the exchange rates of relatively labour-intensive commodities rise in terms of commodities involving a lesser labour intensity. (It will be clarified presently that by a 'wage change' is intended a change in money wages provided money itself has constant purchasing power – excluded are purely nominal changes in money wages.)

But surely the price of machinery rises when wages rise, so that there should be no differential impact once the machines are replaced at their new cost? Ricardo's answer (I, 62) is that it cannot be presumed that the price of machinery rises at all, for machines are products like any other and the same principles apply: all will depend upon the factor proportions utilized in the capital goods sector, and there is no presumption that machine-makers can 'pass on' to users the increased wage burden (on this, see also appendix 1, p. 447).

To summarize thus far: according to Smith, a wage increase raises the costs and thus the prices of manufactured products. According to Ricardo, it is solely the structure, not the level of prices, that is altered. Smith had failed to follow through consistently the relativity dimension of pricing; for what is true of a disturbance affecting one industry alone – an increase in the wage raises costs and the price of that commodity – is not true of a disturbance affecting all industries. It was Ricardo's valid contention that Smith had fallen into error in approaching a general-equilibrium problem in terms appropriate for partial-equilibrium analysis.

Since a wage increase cannot be passed on in higher prices, as Smith maintained, its effect – apart from possibly disturbing the price structure – must be to reduce profits. This theorem on distribution we shall henceforth refer to as the 'inverse wage–profit relation'. It will be remembered, however, that Smith's proposition whereby a wage increase raises general prices applies solely to manufacturing; in agriculture the incidence of higher wages is on land rent. This too Ricardo rejected, on the principle that rent is excluded from marginal cost which alone is relevant in pricing. No part of the burden of increased wages can fall on land. The general pricing principles were common to all sectors.

It is easy to appreciate, intuitively, why a wage increase leaves relative prices unaffected when its impact on the various industries is uniform, but alters the structure of prices should it impinge differentially. It is a matter of the relative impact on unit costs in the different sectors. But we can be much more precise. Ricardo's analysis turns on the Smithian principles of resource allocation including demand–supply analysis and profit rate equalization. More generally, the present chapter demonstrates that Ricardian economics must be envisaged in terms of a general-equilibrium model wherein distribution and final commodity prices are mutually interdependent. Those interpretations that ascribe to Ricardo the determination of distribution 'prior' to that of values or prices have little merit.

The following two sections (5.2, 5.3) treat demand–supply analysis and its relation to cost pricing. The discussion, which proceeds within the context of resource allocation, is extended in section 5.4 to cover Ricardo's major theorem on distribution (the inverse wage–profit relation). Cost and its relation to rent is treated in section 5.5. Section 5.6 takes the analysis of resource allocation yet further, in dealing with the impact of various disturbances to the system; here the general-equilibrium dimension to Ricardian theory is developed.

One section (5.7) is devoted to the famous comparative cost theory of trade. Location of this discussion in the present chapter reflects its message for the issue of resource allocation.

In the remainder of the chapter we return to a closed economy and look more closely at the distribution issue. Section 5.8 examines the role of the 'measure of value' in Ricardo's central exposition of value and distribution in the first six chapters of the *Principles*. Sections 5.9, 5.10 and 5.11 deal with various specific aspects of the distribution analysis that have attracted the attention of commentators.

5.2 Demand–Supply Analysis

A tradition exists that demand theory played a small part, if any at all, in Ricardian analysis. Nothing could be further from the truth. Ricardo went to some lengths to make the point 'that the production of no commodity, except from miscalculation, precedes the demand or anticipated demand for it' (VIII, 273–4). This apparently obvious point had to be made, since in T. R. Malthus's opinion increased food production preceded increased population: 'The point in dispute is this, Does the supply of corn precede the demand for it, or does it follow such demand?…I [am] of the latter opinion' (p. 255). But much more is involved than recognition of demand as a necessary condition for exchange value.

The responsiveness of quantity demanded to price variation was clearly recognized by Ricardo in the *Principles*, although there would perhaps be ranges of inelasticity: 'Whatever habit has rendered delightful, will be relinquished with reluctance, and will continue to be consumed notwithstanding a very heavy tax; but this reluctance has its limits, and experience every day demonstrates that an increase in the nominal amount of taxation, often diminishes the produce' (I, 241). Ricardo recognized elsewhere that price elasticity – defined in terms of the proportionate response of quantity demanded to price and consequential changes in total expenditure – varies over the range of prices, exceeding unity at high levels and declining to values less than unity at lower levels. The extract that follows, from a Parliamentary intervention of 1822, considers the entire range of prices, commencing in effect at an infinitely high level:

> He would put a case to the House, to show how a superabundant supply of an article would produce a sinking of its aggregate value much greater than in proportion to the surplus supply. He would suppose, that in a particular country a very rare commodity was introduced for the first time – superfine cloth for instance. If 10,000 yards of this cloth were imported under such circumstances, many persons would be desirous of purchasing it, and the price consequently would be enormously high. Supposing this quantity of cloth to be doubled, he was of opinion that the aggregate value of the 20,000 yards would be much more considerable than the aggregate value of the 10,000 yards, for the article would still be scarce, and therefore in great demand. If the quantity of cloth were to be again doubled, the effect would still be the same; for although each particular yard of the 40,000 would fall in price, the value of the whole would be greater than that of the 20,000. But, if he went on in this way increasing the quantity of the cloth, until it came within the reach of the purchase of every class in the country, from that time any addition to its quantity would diminish the aggregate value (V, 171).

The closing sentence implies that at low prices the opportunities to attract *additional* purchasers by *further* price reductions are limited – a clear notion of marginal demand price. This rationalization of the inelastic range appeared also in early correspondence of 1813 involving the differential characteristics of regular commodities and of the monetary metals:

> Coffee, Sugar, and Indigo, are commodities for which, although there would be an increased use, if they were to sink much in value, still as they are not applicable to a great variety of new purposes, the demand would necessarily be limited; not so with gold and silver. These metals exist in a degree of scarcity, and are applicable to a great variety of *new* uses – the fall of their price, in consequence of augmented quantity, would always be checked, not only by an increased demand for those purposes to which they had before been applied, but to the want of them for entirely new employments (VI, 91–2).

It does not seem that Ricardo appreciated the modern 'substitution effect', the response of quantity demanded to relative price changes assuming unchanged purchasing power. Variation of quantity demanded upon price change he attributed to our 'income effect'. Now the income elasticity of demand for corn he presumed to be very low and sometimes zero for simplicity; and he maintained with pellucid clarity in the *Principles* that it is the zero income elasticity of demand which accounts for zero price elasticity:

An increase in the cost of production of a commodity, if it be an article of the first necessity, will not necessarily diminish its consumption; for although the general power of the purchasers to consume, is diminished by the rise of any one commodity, yet they may relinquish the consumption of some other commodity whose cost of production has not risen (I, 343–4).

That Ricardo lacked the formal conception of marginal utility is clear from an illustration of the observation that 'value-in-use' and 'value-in-exchange' must be kept separate: 'If by an improved machine I can with the same quantity of labour, make two pair of stockings instead of one, I in no way impair the utility of one pair of stockings, though I diminish their value' (p. 280n.). In this passage the emphasis is on the physiological properties of commodities (rather than the psychological dimension), which suggests a hierarchical ranking of utility, and rules out the incremental dimension. None the less, Ricardo fully appreciated the solution to the paradox of value formulated on the first page of the *Principles*: 'Let water become scarce, says Lord Lauderdale [1804], and be exclusively possessed by an individual, and you will increase his riches, because water will then have value' (p. 276). Indeed, he came close to stating explicitly the substance of the distinction between total and marginal utility:

> A man is rich or poor, according to the abundance of necessaries and luxuries which he can command; and whether the exchangeable value of these for money, for corn, or for labour, be high or low, they will equally contribute to the enjoyment of their possessor. It is through confounding the ideas of value and wealth, or riches [,] that it has been asserted, that by diminishing the quantity of commodities, that is to say of the necessaries, conveniences, and enjoyments of human life, riches may be increased. If value were the measure of riches, this could not be denied, because by scarcity the value of commodities is raised; but if Adam Smith be correct, if riches consist in necessaries and enjoyments, then they cannot be increased by a diminution of quantity (pp. 275–6).

A reduction in output, Ricardo here states, reduces 'wealth' or 'riches' – it reduces *total utility* – but it raises 'value' which clearly is determined at the *margin*.

The principle of scarcity value was applied by Ricardo in a passage which again comes close to distinguishing between total and marginal utility – the latter equalling zero in the case at hand:

> M. Say accuses Dr. Smith of having overlooked the value which is given to commodities by natural agents, and by machinery, because he considered that the value of all things was derived from the labour of man; but it does not appear to me, that this charge is made out; for Adam

Smith no where undervalues the services which these natural agents and machinery perform for us, but he very justly distinguishes the nature of the value which they add to commodities – they are serviceable to us, by increasing the abundance of productions, by making men richer, by adding to value in use; but as they perform their work gratuitously, as nothing is paid for the use of air, of heat, and of water, the assistance which they afforded us, adds nothing to value in exchange (pp. 286–7).

Also striking is Ricardo's reply to a charge that the British economists neglected the scarcity property of valuable goods, as in this letter to Malthus:

[J. B. Say's] brother Louis Say has published a thick volume of remarks upon Adam Smith's, his brother's, Your and my opinions. He is not satis-fied with any of us. His principle object is to shew that wealth consists in the abundance of enjoyable commodities, – he accuses us all of wishing to heap up what we call valuable commodities, without any regard to quantity, about which only the Polit. Economist should be anxious. I do not believe that any of us will plead guilty to this charge. I feel fully assured that I do not merit it should be made against me (IX, 248–9).

Quite evidently, Ricardo placed himself with Smith, Malthus and J. B. Say amongst those who adopted the consumer's concept of wealth with all that it implies from the scarcity perspective.

Ricardo is frequently said to have rejected demand–supply analysis. From the above evidence, this is obviously a misconception. What he actually complained of was 'the opinion that the price of commodities depends *solely* on the proportion of supply to demand, or demand to supply' (I, 382), a complaint alluding to those formulations which appeared to exclude a role for cost conditions in the mechanism. Thus his observation to Say: 'You say demand and supply regulates the price of bread; that is true, but what regulates supply? the cost of produc-tion...' (IX, 172). The essence of the matter is also captured in a letter to Malthus: 'You say demand and supply regulates value – this I think is saying nothing... – it is supply which regulates value – and supply is itself controlled by comparative cost of production' (VIII, 279).

It is worth noting that Robert Torrens (1790–1864) regarded all of this as received doctrine:

Political Economists seem on all hands agreed, that the quantity in which commodities exchange for one another depends, in any given instance, upon the proportion of demand and supply. It is also on all hands agreed, that with respect to all commodities which industry can indefinitely increase, the cost of production is the circumstance which, by limiting the quantity of them brought to market, regulates the proportion of supply to demand, and ultimately determines the exchangeable value (1822 [1935], 9).

5.3   Cost Price and Allocative Economics

If one's concern is capital accumulation or the growth of population, it is often sensible to assume as a first approximation that profit rate and wage rate uniformity have both been achieved; namely, that the various sectors of the economy are throughout in equilibrium. If allocation is the issue we must look at the motivation for the use of factors in one sector rather than another. That hinges on differential wages and differential profits – the fact that capitalists (labourers) have an eye to what their capital (labour) can yield elsewhere. To talk of 'costs' is to take account of precisely this aspect of the economic problem. The classical notions of wages and interest as compensation for effort and abstinence respectively, are pertinent at the macro-economic level where the determinants of aggregate factor supplies are under investigation; in the micro-economic context costs refer to foregone opportunities, as they do for the later neo-classicists (with the qualification that the earlier writers limited this conception to products alone, excluding foregone leisure). Indeed, the cost price analysis of Ricardo, as of Smith, is preeminently an analysis of the allocation of scarce resources (capital and labour), proceeding in terms of general equilibrium.

To demonstrate this position regarding Ricardian micro theory let us begin with a statement by J. B. Say, in his *Traité d'économie politique* (4th edn., 1819) of mutual interdependence between product and factor markets, incorporating the principle of opportunity cost and also that of imputing the values of factors from the values of their products (or derived demand) – in broad terms only because of the absence of a formal marginal conception whereby the physical contributions of individual factors can be isolated:

> It is utility which determines the demand for a commodity, but it is the cost of its production which limits the extent of its demand. When its utility does not elevate its value to the level of the cost of production, the thing is not worth what it cost; it is a proof that the productive services might be employed to create a commodity of a superior value. The possessors of productive funds, that is to say, those who have the disposal of labour, of capital or land, are perpetually occupied in comparing the cost of production with the value of the things produced, or which comes to the same thing, in comparing the value of different commodities with each other; because the cost of production is nothing else but the value of productive services, consumed in forming a production; and the value of a productive service is nothing else than the value of the commodity, which is the result. The value of a commodity, the value of a productive

service, the value of the cost of production are all, then, similar values when every thing is left to its natural course (cited by Ricardo, I, 282–3).

Now Léon Walras (1874), who developed the algebraic formulation of general-equilibrium relations, believed Say to have been on the right road by this formulation of general interdependency (1954, 425). But so did Ricardo, who commented on the passage: 'M. Say maintains with scarcely any variation, the doctrine which I hold concerning value' (I, 283). His sole complaint related to Say's treatment of the services of land on a par with those of capital and labour, given Ricardo's own presumption that rent must be excluded from marginal cost. Similarly: 'In your doctrine of productive services I almost fully agree, but I submit to you, whether, as rent is the effect of high price, and not the cause of it, it should not be rejected when we estimate the comparative value of commodities' (VIII, 279). The notion of opportunity cost in fact pervades Ricardo's work, and his cost prices make no sense except in these terms. To this matter we now turn.

'Cost of production' or 'natural price' includes profits as well as wages each at its average or ordinary rate (I, 291). Under the technological conditions defined in the first chapter of the *Principles*, namely uniform factor proportions, a state of general equilibrium such that prices reflect costs throughout the system, will be one satisfying both profit rate uniformity and proportionality of prices to labour inputs. More accurately, under the stated circumstances, uniformity of profit rates requires that proportionality. The following passage (drawn from a discussion of subsidized labour for some firms in a manufacturing industry) summarizes the point beautifully, and does so in a context expressing that what is relevant is *marginal* labour input:

> The manufacturer enjoying none of these facilities might indeed be driven altogether from the market, if the supply afforded by these favoured workmen were equal to all the wants of the community; but if he continued in the trade, it would be only on condition that he should derive from it the usual and general rate of profits on stock, and that could only happen when his commodity sold for a price proportional to the quantity of labour bestowed on its production (p. 73n.).

Now it is the possibility of capital (and labour) movement between uses, or commodity–supply adjustment, which assures the tendency to cost price and proportionality to labour input. This can be illustrated from the discussion of an exogenous change in tastes, starting out from an equilibrium in which 'all commodities are at their natural price, and consequently... the profits of capital in all employments are exactly at the same rate' (p. 90):

Suppose now that a change of fashion should increase the demand for silks, and lessen that for woollens; their natural price, the quantity of labour necessary to their production, would continue unaltered, but the market price of silks would rise, and that of woollens would fall; and consequently the profits of the silk manufacturer would be above, whilst those of the woollen manufacturer would be below, the general and adjusted rate of profits. Not only the profits, but the wages of the workmen, would be affected in these employments. This increased demand for silks would, however, soon be supplied, by the transference of capital and labour from the woollen to the silk manufacture; when the market prices of silks and woollens would again approach their natural prices, and then the usual profits would be obtained by the respective manufacturers of those commodities.

It is then the desire, which every capitalist has, of diverting his funds from a less to a more profitable employment, that prevents the market price of commodities from continuing for any length of time either much above, or much below their natural price. It is this competition, which so adjusts the exchangeable value of commodities, that after paying the wages necessary to their production, and all other expenses required to put the capital employed in its original state of efficiency, the remaining value or overplus will in each trade be in proportion to the value of the capital employed (pp. 90–1).

In circumstances of differential factor ratios the same assumption of factor mobility dictates a divergence of cost prices from labour inputs, as Ricardo explained in his first chapter. But the entire notion of cost price presumes factors that have alternative uses; and whether or not costs are proportional to labour inputs, only those returns that reflect alternative opportunities are allowed for in costs. Embodiment of labour, or the pain cost attached to labour and abstinence, are not the relevant considerations.

The principle of profit rate equalization which provides the key to Ricardo's analysis of resource allocation turns on standard demand–supply analysis. Since 'it is through the inequality of profits, that capital is moved from one employment to another' (p. 119), an economy-wide change in labour productivity or any other disturbance impinging equally on all commodities, has no differential effects on profitability at the initial long-run cost prices and therefore will generate no changes in supply, leaving those prices unchanged. By contrast, a disturbance limited to a single industry, such as a change in input coefficients or a tax or subsidy, will generate an alteration in output and consequent alteration in price, to re-establish the original return on capital in that industry. Applications of the distinction in question extend far and wide, one of the most important bearing upon the fundamental nature of trade:

If any cause should raise the price of a few manufactured commodities, it would prevent or check their exportation; but if the same cause operated generally on all, the effect would be merely nominal, and would neither interfere with their relative [cost] value, not in any degree diminish the stimulus to a trade of barter, which all commerce, both foreign and domestic really is (p. 228).

5.4   Alternative Opportunities and the Inverse Wage–Profit Relation

The principle that cost prices reflect alternative opportunities also provides us with the rationale for Ricardo's fundamental theorem of distribution – the inverse wage–profit relation. In the event of uniform factor proportions there will occur no price changes when the general wage is altered: 'The cause that operates on one, operates on all; how then can it be said that the relative values of commodities will be affected?' (II, 179). Since prices do not vary at all, profits must be affected inversely. In the case of differential factor proportions between industries the impact of a general wage change is more substantial. At the initial prices the profit rate must decline across the board; but the decline will evidently be sharper in 'labour-intensive' than in 'capital-intensive' industries and accordingly, consistent with Ricardo's analysis of economic process as outlined above, reallocation of resources between sectors is set in motion to assure equalization of the return on capital. In the new equilibrium the prices of commodities produced by labour-intensive processes will have risen relative to those produced by capital-intensive processes – outputs contracting in the first category and expanding in the second – and the profit rate will again be equalized everywhere at a lower level than in the initial equilibrium.

From the perspective of price-theory all this is of the first importance. Standard partial-equilibrium analysis – the demand–supply diagram applied to a single industry – would be inappropriate for the analysis of the foregoing case. Ricardo's great insight lies in the realization that in the new equilibrium, while some prices will indeed be higher than originally, others will be lower, supply conditions deteriorating, as it were, in the former case but actually improving in the latter. This realization reflects a deep understanding of the notion of the relativity of exchange value and the operation of the demand–supply mechanism within a general-equilibrium framework.

One further detail requires elaboration. Again consider our standard disturbance – an experimental wage increase where differential factor ratios apply. It is conceivable, even probable, that the reallocation of activity set in motion by the disturbance will play back upon aggregate labour demand (and thus upon the wage) requiring further allocative adjustment before full equilibrium is achieved. This playback occurs because, in the classical view, aggregate labour demand hinges not on total capital but on the circulating capital component, which obviously varies not only with technology (see below, p. 188), but also with the pattern of activity. The pattern of activity – again with a playback on the wage – might also be affected directly should expenditure patterns differ between classes as Ricardo allowed: 'if in the division of the gross produce, the labourers commanded a great proportion, the demand would be for one set of commodities – if the masters had more than a usual share, the demand would be for another set' (VIII, 272–3). Not only then does the new (lower) profit rate emerge along with the new set of outputs and prices, but it is impossible to 'forecast', as it were, the new profit rate immediately following the initial disturbance without knowledge of the entire system of demand curves for final products. Ricardo failed to spell out the playback on distribution; but there is nothing in the logic of his system to preclude it. There is, in brief, no solution to distribution prior to pricing. (For restatements of this issue, see also pp. 104, 439 below).

5.5 Cost and Rent

We can sharpen our understanding of Ricardo's position on cost price by considering the contrast between cost and rent. I shall first establish Ricardo's awareness that the phenomenon of differential rent, which plays so large a role in his system, is but a special case of a more general phenomenon, namely land scarcity.

Rent is provisionally defined as payment to the landlord 'for the use of the original and indestructible powers of the soil' (I, 67), a productivity phenomenon. But in the following passage – which incidentally alludes to the solution of the 'paradox of value' in terms of demand–supply – the ultimate rationale is more specifically expressed in terms both of productivity and scarcity:

> On the first settling of a country, in which there is an abundance of rich and fertile land ... there will be no rent; ...
>
> On the common principles of supply and demand, no rent could be paid for such land, for the reason stated why nothing is given for the use of air and water, or for any other of the gifts of nature which exist in boundless quantity ... no charge is made for the use of these natural aids [in production], because they are inexhaustible, and at every man's disposal. In the same manner the brewer, the distiller, the dyer, make incessant use of the air and water for the production of their commodities; but as the supply is boundless, they bear no price (p. 69).

Using these principles Ricardo rejected a physiocratic residue in the *Wealth of Nations*, namely Smith's assertion that in manufactures '*nature does nothing, man does all*; and the reproduction must always be in proportion to the strength of the agents that occasion it' (cited p. 76n.). Factor productivity, Ricardo insisted, is a necessary but insufficient condition for a positive return: 'Does nature nothing for man in manufactures?...There is not a manufacture which can be mentioned, in which nature does not give her assistance to man, and give it too, generously and gratuitously'.

Now differential rent (reflecting productivity differentials) is simply a special case of scarcity rent, falling within the general demand–supply framework: 'If all land had the same properties, if it were all unlimited in quantity, and uniform in quality, no charge could be made for its use, unless it possesses peculiar advantages of situation' (p. 69); conversely, '[if] air, water, the elasticity of steam, and the pressure of the atmosphere, were of various qualities; if they could be appropriated, and each quality existed only in moderate abundance, they, as well as the land, would afford a rent as the successive qualities were brought into use' (p. 75).

Ricardo also understood that rent would be generated even on marginal units of output where scarcity manifests itself in an extreme form – the functional relation between output and costs terminating or the supply curve becoming vertical; and he traced through some of the analytical consequences – 'Marshallian' consequences – for taxation:

> The corn and raw produce of a country may, indeed, for a time sell at a monopoly price; but they can do so permanently only when no more capital can be profitably employed on the lands, and when, therefore, their produce cannot be increased. At such time, every portion of land in cultivation, and every portion of capital employed on the land will yield a rent, differing, indeed, in proportion to the difference in the return. At such time too, any tax which may be imposed on the farmer, will fall on rent, not on the consumer. He cannot raise the price of his corn because by the supposition, it is already at the highest price at which the purchasers will or can buy it. He will not be satisfied with a lower rate of profits, than that obtained by other capitalists, and, therefore, his only alternative will be to obtain a reduction of rent or to quit his employment (pp. 250–1).

(It will be noted that in this passage Ricardo refers to the *intensive* as well as the *extensive* margin of cultivation.)

It is not surprising, in the light of all this, to find Ricardo maintaining that 'rent is the effect of high price....It is...from the price which the produce is sold, that rent is derived; and this price is got not because nature assists in the production, but because it is the price which suits the consumption to the supply' (p. 77n.). Rent appears even in the price

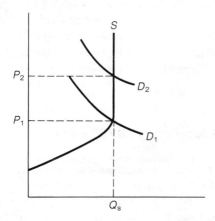

For ranges of demand until D_1, rent appears solely as a producer's surplus and is zero at the margin. Beyond D_1, rent is paid even on marginal units.

Figure 5.1

covering the last unit, if the demand curve is high enough (above D_1 in figure 5.1), as a pure demand-determined surplus. Over the range of output below Q_s (or equilibrium prices below P_1), rent emerges as a producer's surplus (the producer's 'triangle'), dependent upon the location of the demand curve and is not paid on marginal units.

Ricardo nowhere explicitly stated that rent is excluded from marginal cost in the standard case because of a presumption of one-use land – the absence of alternative opportunities. But that is the economic logic involved, and not the fact that the supply conditions of land in the aggregate differ from those of capital and labour. That he appreciated the logic is clear. Consider, for example, a generalization of the rent concept from land to capital – the recognition that once the assumption of capital mobility between uses is abandoned it is the rent analysis that becomes appropriate:

> As a part of this capital, when once expended in the improvement of a farm, is inseparably amalgamated with the land, and tends to increase its productive powers, the remuneration paid to the landlord for its use is strictly of the nature of rent, and is subject to all the laws of rent. Whether the improvement be made at the expense of the landlord or the tenant, it will not be undertaken in the first instance, unless there is a strong probability that the return will at least be equal to the profit that can be made by the disposition of any other equal capital; but when once made, the return obtained will ever after be wholly of the nature of rent, and will be subject to all the variations of rent (p. 262).

Also relevant is the recognition in the context of foreign trade that once resource mobility is precluded the general rules of cost price break down so that, even assuming uniform capital–labour ratios, commodities will no longer exchange in proportion to relative labour inputs (below, p. 106).

5.6   Resource Allocation and Distribution

The discussion of allocation mechanisms can be extended by examining the process of reabsorption into the system of factors released by a variety of disturbances. The implicit assumption is that factors are released in proportion; the 'law of markets' (see p. 241) then assures their reabsorption with no pressure at all on the factor returns.

In the case of taxation, displaced factors are reabsorbed in consequence of the expanded government expenditure financed from tax proceeds: 'If, however, less salt was consumed, less capital was employed in producing it; and, therefore, though the producer would obtain less profit on the production of salt, he would obtain more on the production of other things. [A tax]…does not diminish demand, it only alters the nature of it. It enables Government to consume as much of the produce of the land and labour of the country, as was before consumed by the individuals who contribute to the tax…' (p. 237). In the special case of corn taxation, where because of zero demand elasticity resources are not released, government spending is satisfied indirectly as consumer demand for a variety of products other than corn falls in consequence of the tax on corn – the income effect once again: 'it is not necessary that my demand for corn should diminish, as I may prefer to pay 100 *l.* per annum more for my corn, and to the same amount abate in my demand for wine, furniture, or any other luxury. Less capital will consequently be employed in the wine or upholstery trade, but more will be employed in manufacturing those commodities, on which the taxes levied by Government will be expended'.

A second example relates to the important case of freer corn importation: 'If corn, in consequence of permanent abundance, fell to 3 *l.* 10 *s.*, the capital employed on No. 6 [land] would cease to be employed; for it was only when corn was at 4 *l.* that it could obtain the general profits, even without paying rent: it would, therefore, be withdrawn to manufacture those commodities with which all the corn grown on No. 6 would be purchased and imported' (p. 268). Released resources are thus transferred to the export sector with no effect on 'general profits'. In addition, there also occurs a net expansion of manufacturing for domestic consumption, 'as on any other supposition no advantage would be gained by importation, and low prices' (p. 418).

Also revealing is the analysis of innovation, which in his third edition Ricardo modified. In the original analysis it is presumed that labour released by innovation would be accompanied by a complement of capital. Accordingly, Say's Law assured reabsorption with no downward pressure on the wage rate. Given the capacity for output expansion there can be no demand deficiency:

> If, by improved machinery, with the employment of the same quantity of labour, the quantity of stockings could be quadrupled, and the demand for stockings were only doubled, some labourers would necessarily be discharged from the stocking trade; but as the capital which employed them was still in being, and as it was the interest of those who had it to employ it productively, it appeared to me that it would be employed on the production of some other commodity, useful to society, for which there could not fail to be a demand ... (p. 387).

In the case of technical change in agriculture the same principle applies: 'capital will be withdrawn from the land, for though there would not be an increased demand for corn, there would be an increased demand for other things' (II, 135–6). Again there is no pressure on factor returns.

We turn now to disturbances in particular sectors which involve the attraction of resources rather than their release. Once again reliance is upon the law of markets – in this case to assure against a rise in factor returns. The analysis of the corn export bounty provides an illustration.

It was Smith's contention (see above, p. 84) that the agricultural rate of profit would not rise relative to the manufacturing rate in consequence of a corn export bounty, for the initial (domestic) corn price increase will generate a corresponding rise in manufacturing prices by way of the money wage rate and the cost of materials. Ricardo, by contrast, insisted convincingly that, whether or not money wages rise during the process of adjustment to the disturbance, a profit differential would be created in favour of agriculture by the rise in the market price of corn, and accordingly resources would be attracted from manufacturing: 'It is ... the inequality of profit, which is always the inducement to remove capital from one employment to another; and, therefore, more corn would be produced, and fewer commodities manufactured' (I, 307). Assuming, as Ricardo did assume in this context, constant-cost industries including agriculture, the adjustment process continues until 'the price of corn will again fall in the home market to its natural and necessary price, and profits will be again at their ordinary and accustomed level' (p. 302). The procedure is a striking example of the Ricardian method of simplifying by removing inessentials the more clearly to make a point; subsequently he complicated the analysis by allowing for increasing costs in agriculture, but the substance of the argument is unaffected (p. 312).

The analysis is of prime importance. The Smithian procedure flew in the face of basic allocation principles. Ricardo himself objected strongly to Smith's conclusions in the chapter on bounties (above, p. 86), but his correction posed a problem. A reduction in manufacturing output might be expected to generate an increase in the prices of manufactured goods and a rise of manufacturing profit rates until an equality with the (increased) return in agriculture is reached. The adjustment process would then come to an end with the general rate of return higher than its original level. (In that event the basic Ricardian theorem that 'profits depend upon wages' would be demonstrably in error since with no alteration in wages the general profit rate would have increased.) The solution is that the prices of manufactured goods are not in fact raised during the process, for allowance must be made for an increased inflow of imports – the counterpart of the expanded export of corn: 'Manufactures would not rise, because fewer would be manufactured, for a supply of them would be obtained in exchange for the exported corn' (p. 307).

*   *   *

One outcome of the analysis thus far is that the profit rate in agriculture does not play the strategic role envisaged in various modern formulations of 'classical' economics. Our case studies reveal this key fact. Thus technological improvement in the agricultural sector releases labour and capital for employment in other sectors, and they are reabsorbed elsewhere with no alteration in their respective returns; the price of corn falls to the lower cost level (without supply adjustment in this case) and the return in agriculture (temporarily raised) comes back into line with the given general rate. Despite a change in the 'margin of cultivation', the profit rate remains constant. Similarly, freer corn importation leaves the general profit rate unchanged despite a contraction of the domestic margin; the process involves a fall in the price of corn and the transfer of resources to the manufacturing sector with no effect on the general profit rate. Precisely the same kind of argument holds for the case of a corn export subsidy.

Now Ricardo certainly insisted that if the price of luxury goods (silks, velvets, etc.) rose there would be no effect on profits, 'for nothing can affect profits but a rise in wages; silks and velvets are not consumed by the labourer, and therefore cannot raise wages' (p. 118). But this is a quite separate analytical issue. Ricardo himself tried to keep the issues apart, proceeding in his treatment of the corn export bounty on the (provisional) assumption that agriculture is a constant-cost industry, so that there is no long-run change in the corn price at all, and thus no change in the wage. The subsequent allowance for rising money wages, in consequence of increasing corn costs, is a separate complication. It is essential not to confuse the effects on the profit rate induced by a change in the margin of agriculture itself – there are none – and the effects of a change in the price of corn working upon the general profit rate by way of money wages. It is clearly the attribution to Ricardo of a fixed commodity wage assumption which precludes this essential distinction, since an increase in the corn price *must* be followed by a rise in the money wage if the commodity wage is given.

*   *   *

In the foregoing discussion of resource allocation (given aggregate labour and capital) we have seen that a technological change in any industry may have the effect of releasing labour, which is reabsorbed elsewhere in the system without pressure on the wage rate. Reabsorption of labour at a constant wage is assured by the operation of the law of markets. In chapter 31 of the *Principles* ('On Machinery'), added in 1821, Ricardo introduced a new issue by raising the possibility of labour-displacing technological change. Because the aggregate demand for labour turns on the wages-fund component of total capital, the new technology entails an actual fall in labour demand assuming given total capital (below, p. 188). Reliance on the law of markets to assure reabsorption at constant wages is no longer possible, for now there is a technological problem to be overcome.

Ricardo said little about the further consequences of excess labour at the original wage; he was satisfied with a demonstration of the theoretical possibility of the disturbance in question. But how must we approach the problem consistently with his general theory? That the commodity wage falls would be the first step. The profit rate consequently rises across the board at going prices. The precise sequence of events which then follows turns upon the pattern of factor proportions, the fall in wages raising the return on capital relatively more in labour-intensive than in capital-intensive industries at going prices. On the principle that capital movements are governed by profit rate differentials, capital will be transferred between industries such that the net aggregate demand for labour rises.

Even should factor proportions be initially identical throughout the system, the innovation itself creates a difference between the ratios in the affected industry and those in the remaining industries. In this case, too, profit rate differentials are created by the fall in wages generating capital movements and thus assuring a net increase in the aggregate demand for labour. Reabsorption will, however, be ruled out in the case of identical factor proportions throughout, if it is assumed that the innovation is introduced into all industries. Here there is no solution to excess labour supply apart from net capital accumulation or a reduction in labour supply.

A further extension of the Ricardian analysis involves the consequences of a change in the pattern of tastes, one which Ricardo himself did not formally make. We have seen earlier (pp. 94–5 above) that changes in the pattern of demand affect the factor returns in particular industries generating appropriate adjustments of industry size, while the general levels of profits and wages remain unaffected. It is the assumption of uniform factor proportions which permits the neglect of any 'playback' on the wage rate itself emanating from changes in the pattern of demand, and allows the treatment of the factor returns as parameters in the analysis of price. (In the *Wealth of Nations* too, changes in demand affect the factor returns in the particular industries involved but not the general return.) Let us, however, ourselves apply Ricardian principles to an exogenous change in the pattern of demand, assuming differential machinery–labour ratios, given aggregate capital (machinery and working capital combined) and aggregate labour. An increase in the demand for a 'machinery-intensive' good at the expense of that for a labour-intensive good will disturb the profit rate and the price structures. There will follow in consequence an expansion of the first category of commodities and a contraction of the second. But as a result the fixed capital or machinery component of total capital will rise at the expense of wage capital as resources are transferred between industries. The wage rate, given the total labour force, must rise and the general profit rate correspondingly fall. Of course, if the wage rate is a *datum* these conclusions are precluded. But Ricardo always insisted that the commodity wage is a *variable* governed by 'the relative amount of population to capital' (II, 265). On this view, the adjustment process following a variation in the pattern of final demand must affect the average factor returns by acting on the breakdown of aggregate capital between its component parts.

But not only is distribution dependent upon the pattern of final demand, that is upon output levels: we know too that a change in the price of labour will play back on the pattern of activity and therefore on relative cost prices (above, p. 96). So there is a powerful general-equilibrium or 'neo-classical' dimension to the Ricardian system.

5.7 The Comparative-Cost Theory of Trade

Adam Smith had included among the advantages of free international trade the more efficient utilization of resources:

If a foreign country can supply us with a commodity cheaper than we ourselves can make it, better buy it of them with some part of the produce of our own industry, employed in a way in which we have some advantage. The general industry of the country... is certainly not employed to the greatest advantage, when it is... directed towards an object which it can buy cheaper than it can make. The value of its annual produce is certainly more or less diminished, when it is thus turned away from producing commodities evidently of more value than the commodity which it is directed to produce. According to the supposition, that commodity could be purchased from foreign countries cheaper than it can be made at home. It could, therefore, have been purchased with a part only of the commodities, or, what is the same thing, with a part only of the price of the commodities, which the industry employed by an equal capital would have produced at home, had it been left to follow its natural course (1776 [1937], 424).

Opportunities for mutually beneficial trade, on this account, merely presume the existence of 'absolute' cost differentials.

David Ricardo's chapter 'On Foreign Trade' (*Principles*, ch. 7) expounds the celebrated 'comparative-cost' doctrine, a significant advance over Smith in the understanding of competitive resource allocation, and therefore requiring attention. The general principle – already stated by Robert Torrens (1815) – is that international specialization 'distributes labour most effectively and most economically' (I, 134). These are efficiency gains which pertain even if commodities cost absolutely more to produce abroad than domestically, provided that the cost differentials are not uniform. In Ricardo's illustration labour input per unit of cloth and wine respectively (labour for one year) are 100 and 120 in England, and 90 and 80 in Portugal (p. 135). The opening of trade opportunities between the two initially autarchic economies implies the exchange of (Portuguese) wine for (English) cloth despite the higher productivity of Portuguese labour in the production of both commodities, since the productivity advantage is greater in the case of wine than cloth. The essence of the matter is the determining role played by comparative rather than absolute advantage:

This exchange might even take place, notwithstanding that the commodity imported by Portugal could be produced there with less labour than in England. Though she could make the cloth with the labour of 90 men, she would import it from a country where it required the labour of 100 men to produce it, because it would be advantageous to her rather to employ her capital in the production of wine, for which she would obtain more cloth from England, than she could produce by diverting a portion of her capital from the cultivation of vines to the manufacture of cloth.

Ricardo was expressing the notion, in terms of modern geometric terminology, that the respective 'production possibility' limits are for each country widened by specialization and trade.

Ricardo took for granted that the terms of trade would settle at a ratio of 1:1, approximately half-way between the internal cloth/wine cost ratios in England and Portugal of 1.2:1 and 1:0.88. At a 1:1 exchange rate England obtains by importation, for each 100 labour hours devoted to cloth, 1 unit of wine which would have required 120 labour hours to produce domestically; Portugal for 80 labour hours devoted to wine obtains by importation 1 unit of cloth which would have cost her 90 labour hours to produce domestically. But this is not a necessary outcome. The international terms of trade will settle somewhere between the limiting (autarchic) ratios, depending on the pattern of international demand. This extension was one of J. S. Mill's great achievements (see below p. 140).

While Ricardo failed to justify his specific presumption regarding the terms of trade, the underlying principle is crucial – namely, that within each country capital mobility assures profit rate equalization and thus (assuming, of course, identical capital–labour ratios) proportionality of exchange ratios to relative labour–input ratios; whereas capital immobility across frontiers permits divergencies of the international terms of trade from relative labour inputs:

> In one and the same country, profits are, generally speaking, always on the same level; or differ only as the employment of capital may be more or less secure and agreeable. It is not so between different countries.... Such an exchange [as that between English cloth and Portuguese wine] could not take place between the individuals of the same country. The labour of 100 Englishmen cannot be given for that of 80 Englishmen.... The difference in this respect, between a single country and many, is easily accounted for, by considering the difficulty with which capital moves from one country to another, to seek a more profitable employment, and the activity with which it invariably passes from one province to another in the same country (pp. 134–6).

5.8   The Measure of Value

We now return to the main lines of Ricardian theory. We have seen how the competitive mechanism of resource allocation operates to assure the inverse wage–profit relation. But Ricardo dug deeper. Not all wage changes impinge on the return to capital; a purely nominal change in the money wage rate reflecting a variation in the general purchasing power of money would not do so. Ricardo sought to demonstrate that only 'real' changes counted – and by 'real' he intended changes in the labour absorbed in the production of wages (I, 47–9). An increase in the real wage rate in this sense might reflect a larger wage basket produced by unchanged labour per unit of output. But an unchanged wage basket also will require a greater labour input if productivity has fallen; indeed, even a reduced wage basket requires a greater labour embodiment if productivity falls more steeply than the commodity wage. All these cases of 'real' wage increases will impinge on the profit rate. Ricardo sought also to demonstrate by use of a (hypothetical) measuring device that a 'real' wage change necessarily entails a change in the *proportionate* share of wages in the income divided between labour and capital. While the allocative mechanism assures the inverse wage–profit relation, as we have seen, these two features of the distribution relation are far more clearly exposed by application of his measure of value. It is to this matter we turn next.

In section VI of the chapter 'On Value' Ricardo designed a measure in terms of which to express all prices. He sought to isolate a commodity (we will call it X) such that merely by observing changes in the exchange rate between X and other commodities (A, B, C ...) – variations in their prices in terms of X – one would automatically know, without intimate knowledge of their respective productive processes, how the labour embodied (the *'real value'*) in the other commodities has altered: 'When commodities varied in relative value, it would be desirable to have the means of ascertaining which of them fell and which rose in real value, and this could be effected only by comparing them one after another with some invariable standard measure of value, which should itself be subject to none of the fluctuations to which other commodities are exposed' (I, 43).

The conditions that must be satisfied for commodity X to serve as an accurate measure of labour embodiment, and changes thereof, include the following: first, the labour embodied in X itself must be unchanged. (Use of a ruler for the measurement of length requires that the unit on the ruler itself be fixed.) Secondly, the labour–capital ratio required by X must be given once and for all; otherwise, though the labour input in X may be constant, there could be disturbances to the X-prices of commodities emanating from changes in X's capital input. But even on these strong assumptions, X (our sought-after ideal 'money') 'would not be a perfect standard or invariable measure of value, because ... it would be subject to relative variations from a rise or fall of wages, on account of the different proportions of fixed capital which might be necessary to produce it, and to produce those other commodities whose alterations in value we wished to ascertain' (p. 44). Thus a third assumption must be that the capital–labour ratios of *all* commodities are the same as that of X. Then only will it be the case that a change in the exchange rate between (say) X and A, will be due solely to a change in the labour input in A. For it cannot be due to anything else. In particular, it cannot be due to a change in the wage rate, for that would affect X and A equally, the X–A exchange rate remaining unaffected.

Now Ricardo appreciated that commodities do *not* have the same capital–labour ratios. His was an extreme assumption which he sometimes modified in various ways. One was to reduce the disturbance to a minimum by assuming a commodity X which has the average capital–labour ratio in the system as a whole (I, 45–6; also VIII, 193). In that case, upon a general wage increase, the price of A will rise in terms of X, if A's process is more labour-intensive than X's, and the price of B will fall if B's process is less labour-intensive than X's, because the costs of X are then affected less than the costs of A and more than those of B. There will be products that have the same capital–labour ratio as X and their prices will remain unchanged. Notice that if the average is appropriately selected, it should, in principle, be the case – since increases in terms of X are cancelled by price decreases – that 'deviations from value' (Marx's term) balance out, the value of the total output to be distributed remaining constant in the face of wage rate changes, thus facilitating the demonstration of the inverse wage–profit relation. This feature was to be much emphasized by J. R. McCulloch as well as by Karl Marx (below, p. 374).

Ricardo was frustrated by the difficulties of defining an ideal measure. When it came to the main chapters on distribution and his demonstration of the wage–profit theorem, he cut the knot by assuming that all products in the system in fact require the same capital–labour ratio. He cheated a little, justifying the procedure partly as a practical course of action – he had to get on with the job – but also because changes in the wage rate are (empirically) constrained in magnitude while there is scarcely any limit to potential changes in the quantity of labour input required to produce particular commodities. But the problem did not disappear; Ricardo died with an unfinished manuscript on his desk dealing with the measure (1823).

We turn to the chapter 'On Profits' – the culmination of the theoretical core of the *Principles* presented in the first six chapters. It emerges from the analysis here that the profit rate is a direct function of the proportionate share of profits in the value of the marginal product, the latter divided between labour and capital, and an inverse function of the share of wages. Notice that Ricardo's interest in income shares is not in the threefold division of aggregate national income between rent, wages and profits.

The argument runs thus. Ricardo presumes that the price of corn is determined by marginal labour costs excluding rent: 'the price of corn is regulated by the quantity of labour necessary to produce it, with that portion of capital which pays no rent' (I, 110). But what is meant by the price of corn? It is the price of corn in terms of the measure of value: 'for the purpose of making the subject more clear, I consider money to be invariable in value, and therefore every variation of price to be referable to an alteration in the value of the commodity'. When the money price of corn is observed to rise in terms of the ideal measure, or 'gold', it can be due only to a change in its labour input, for the labour embodied in gold is unchanged by assumption. We must add, however, the implicit assumption in line with the first chapter, 'On Value', that the capital–labour ratio is the same in gold and in corn.

In a growing system, with expanding population, resort is made to increasingly unproductive land, or land at increasing distances from the market (the extensive margin), and the more intensive cultivation of given land of uniform quality. In consequence, labour productivity in corn falls, and this is reflected in an increase in the gold price of corn. In manufactures, a constant labour input is assumed; the prices of manufactures do not, therefore, change during the growth process.

What happens to wages in the course of the process? Ricardo presumes the commodity wage to be constant, so that when the money price of corn rises, the money wage must rise to assure a constant basket. And here we arrive at the key issue – the consequences of an increase in the money wage. If commodity prices remain unchanged, then obviously profits are squeezed; and given the assumptions outlined thus far, it is clear that prices are indeed unaffected.

It helps to have in mind the hypothetical data used by Ricardo to expound the foregoing argument. He assumes that ten men operating on land 1 produce 180 quarters of corn, the price of corn initially at £4 per quarter yielding a total revenue of £720. (To say that a quarter of corn is worth £4 is to say that there is as much labour in a quarter of corn as there is in the gold embodied in £4.) At a larger population a second group of ten men is applied on land 2, the yield of which is only 170 quarters. Productivity has fallen, and the money price of corn, which reflects changes in the labour input only, rises correspondingly, the total value of 170 quarters remaining at £720. The money value of the marginal product is unchanged because the price of corn rises in inverse proportion to the fall in the physical output; alternatively expressed, the gold value of the declining marginal product is constant because 'value' refers to (marginal) labour input and the same input – an input of ten men – is responsible for the last additions of output.

This formulation raises the matter of differential rent. The farmer utilizing type-1 land finds that the price of corn having risen per quarter, the total value of his output (180 quarters) exceeds the value of the current marginal output. But this differential is transferred by the competitive mechanism to the landowner. Both the value of the output due to the marginal application of labour and the value of intra-marginal output net of rent is £720.

In his fifth chapter, 'On Wages', Ricardo defined the 'natural rate of wages' – the so-called subsistence wage – as the rate required to keep population constant. At a real wage below the natural rate, the death rate rises, the birth rate falls, and population size contracts; and conversely, population expands at a wage above subsistence. In the illustration given in 'On Profits' he assumes for pedagogic simplicity that wages are throughout at subsistence. Thus each worker receives £24 per annum, permitting expenditure of £12 on manufactures and £12 on food – the equivalent of three quarters of corn at £4 per quarter. This constitutes a fixed-proportions subsistence basket. The total wages of ten men originally amount to £240 and total profits, therefore, to £720 (the value of the marginal product) less £240 or £480. When the price of corn has risen, the worker must receive sufficient income to permit the purchase as before of £12 worth of manufactures and three quarters of corn, so that aggregate wages of the group of ten rises to £247 and the residual – either the residual on marginal land, or the residual on intra-marginal land net of rent – falls to £473.

Profits decline from £480 to £473. The profit rate, which is calculated relative to a capital stock of £3000, thus falls from 16 to 15.7 per cent. (Since the capital stock probably includes various agricultural products, it is likely to rise, as the corn price rises, above £3000 if valued at replacement cost so that the profit rate falls somewhat more rapidly.) Manufacturing capitalists also have to put up with the same increase in the money wage rate. Assuming that manufactures are produced with the same capital–labour ratio as 'gold' there is no effect on manufacturing prices when the money wage rises, and profits are squeezed everywhere.

In this exercise Ricardo was attempting to get behind the veil of money to the labour resources used up in production. More specifically, at larger population sizes the proportion of the labour resources – ten men – embodied in the total marginal product which is devoted to the production of commodity wages rises; for the absolute increase in the 'money' wages of our ten marginal men from £240 to £247 reflects an increase in the labour embodied in their wage basket and necessarily entails a proportionate increase of the given marginal labour input, whose output is shared with capitalists. Conversely, the proportion embodied in profits declines, the profit rate – to adopt Marxian terminology – varying inversely with 'the value of labour power' (labour embodied in wages) relative to the value of commodities in general (labour embodied in the aggregate which is shared with capitalists).

In this structure an increase in 'gold' wages – gold produced with constant labour input and thus acting as a proxy for labour – reflects an increase in the proportionate share of wages. Some commentators have argued that this identification of gold wages with proportionate wages lacks generality because everything depends on a presumed constancy of aggregate value, in other words, upon constancy of the aggregate work force which constitutes the total amount of value in the system. For one can only be sure that an increase in the value of wages (the labour embodied in wages) implies an increase in proportionate wages, if the total amount of value (the labour force) is constant. This is a misconception. Nothing depends upon the total work force. Our interest is in a specific quantum of labour (value), whether it be that of the ten men (as in Ricardo's formal exposition) or of one man for a given time period such as one day's labour. An increase in money ('gold') wages, that is, in the labour embodied in wages, refers to an increase in the money wages paid to ten men or to one man, and this necessarily corresponds to an increase in the proportionate share since the quantum of value is given by construction.

We can summarize the entire argument in *per capita* terms – let us say a day's labour of one man. The Ricardian scheme relates the return on capital to the 'value' of *per capita* daily wages – that is, to the labour embodied in those wages – that value being measured in terms of Ricardian 'gold' or money. This in turn is to relate the rate of profit *to the fraction of the work day devoted to the production of wages goods*, a very 'Marxian' conception as we shall see later in chapter 15.

So far we have neglected the potential impact of higher materials' costs. Ricardo, however, did allow that

> there are few commodities which are not more or less affected in their price by the rise of raw produce, because some raw material from the land enters into the composition of most commodities. Cotton goods, linen, and cloth will all rise in price with the rise of wheat; but they rise on account of the greater quantity of labour expended on the raw material from which they are made, and not because more was paid by the manufacturer to the labourers whom he employed on those commodities (pp. 117–18).

So far so good. However, should all manufacturing industries, and agriculture too, utilize materials, then (on Ricardo's own principles) it would *not* be possible to pass on higher materials' costs by raising prices. The burden would necessarily fall on capitalists, creating doubts about the validity of the inverse relation which links profits uniquely to the wage. Ricardo failed to note this problem, perhaps because he assumed implicitly that farming, unlike manufacturing, does not require materials.

5.9   Profits an 'Exploitation' Income?

The foregoing theorem is sometimes interpreted as an approach whereby labour alone 'creates value' while profits are an imposition on the workers – a category of 'surplus value' in the sense of an exploitation income. This is questionable. The theorem relating the profit rate to the proportion of the work day devoted to the production of *per capita* wages tells us by itself virtually nothing about the 'nature' of profits, since it is essential to know upon what this proportion depends. This is clear from Ricardo's insistence that the value of output (both domestic and imported) must be measured by a 'quantity of our domestic labour' (II, 436), and full allowance made, in stating the principle of distribution, for the differences of skill that exist between labourers in different countries: 'I apply my doctrine to the same country only, and fix on a standard which is common in that country. I should not estimate profits in England by the labour of a Hindoo.... unless I had the means of reducing them to one common standard' (pp. 272–3). In stating the formula for profit rate determination we thus take for granted a certain social and productive organization within which labour operates. Accordingly, all forces affecting labour efficiency which are relevant for the proportionate distribution of the value of (marginal) output must be taken into account. These facts scarcely suggest that by his formula Ricardo intended to maintain that profits are 'due to' labour and a 'deduction' from the product of labour. It might more accurately be said that land and the general determinants of labour productivity are 'responsible' for profits.

There is also nothing to suggest that some normative distinctiveness of labour led Ricardo to the view that the entire net product should morally be paid as wages on the ground that the capitalist recipients of profits undertake no 'effort' or task requiring compensation. On the contrary: 'One class gives its labour only to assist towards the production of the commodity and must be paid out of its value the compensation to which it is entitled, the other class makes the advances required in the shape of capital and must receive remuneration from the same source' (IV, 365).

That profits are not a genuine 'residual' is also clear from the fact that a reduction in the rate of return on capital plays a part in wage rate determination by way of its effect upon accumulation and therefore labour demand (on this matter see below, p. 182). Since there exists a mutual relationship between wages and profits, it may equally be said that 'wages depend upon profits' as the reverse. Indeed, Ricardo himself refers to a 'natural equilibrium between profits and wages' (I, 226). The formula that formally defines a one-way dependency of profits on wages simply reflects the fact that within the structure of Ricardo's theoretical system wages are the only contractual income – the old Cantillon approach reflecting the practical businessman's perspective according to which profit is what remains from sales proceeds after meeting contractual obligations (see above, p. 29).

T. R. Malthus also insisted that profits depend upon labour's proportionate share and praised Ricardo for his formulation of the inverse profit–wage relation (below, p. 403). But the theorem is 'neutral' regarding the actual determination of the profit rate. Whether, for example, the profit rate is affected by the kind of phenomenon which Malthus had in mind – 'the deficiency of aggregate demand' – can only be answered from external considerations.

5.10 The Inverse Relation a 'Truism'?

The inverse relation between profits and wages – 'profits depend upon wages' – may seem to be a mere truism, since by a change in wages is meant a change in *proportionate* wages. But this is not so. It is obviously true that an increase in a proportionate share must imply a decrease in the residual proportionate share. But Ricardo's efforts were not devoted to proving this proposition; his concern was with the preceding stages of the argument. In the first place, he struggled (unsuccessfully as he himself realized) to devise a means of assuring constancy in the value of the total to be shared between wages and profits. Secondly, setting this problem aside and presuming an approximately unchanged value of the produce to be distributed, Ricardo sought to demonstrate that only *certain* categories of wage rate variation may be identified with variations in the wage share. A money wage increase which reflects increased labour embodiment, whatever may be happening to the commodity wage, is identifiable with an increased wage share of output net of rent; while a money wage increase which is purely nominal, reflecting an alteration in the cost (supply) conditions of the monetary medium, leaves the share of wages unchanged. This is a constructive distinction of the first importance. Thirdly, the identification of an increase in the 'real' wage with an increase in the wage share in output net of rent cannot be a truism since it does not hold good universally. An increase in the labour embodied in wages may not involve an increase in the wage share should the value of output-as-a-whole (net of rent) be increasing; an increased wage share is unambiguously implied only if the value of *per capita* wages rises. Finally, the statement of the inverse relation between wages and profits envisaged as proportions is only a step towards the ultimate objective, which was to define the determinants of the rate of return on capital. And the rate of profit, while dependent upon, is not identified with, the share of profits in the value of *per capita* output (net of rent), since the capital stock is not reduced entirely to wage advances.

But when all is said and done, the full significance of what constitutes the outstanding relationship in Ricardo's work can only be evaluated if we keep in mind the instigating force behind his investigations – the objection to received Smithian doctrine. Smithian analysis did not distinguish between those 'nominal' wage rate increases which do not and those 'real' wage rate increases which do involve a change in the distributive shares, and in fact proposed that even wage increases falling within the latter category may be passed on by employers in the form of higher prices in the manufacturing sector and lower rents in agriculture.

5.11   The Inverse Relation and the Monetary Mechanism

Assuming an unchanged labour input in the production of the monetary metal, wage rate increases are non-inflationary – when wages rise, either there results no disturbance to prices at all (the case of uniform factor proportions) or there results a change in the structure of prices (the case of differential factor proportions). In neither case can capitalists pass on the increased wage cost in the form of generally higher prices as Smith believed. To what extent does all this hinge upon the Ricardian measure of value? Ricardo himself was conscious of the inability to specify a real-world candidate corresponding to his 'gold' or even to specify the full set of theoretical conditions to be satisfied in principle. His purpose was to show that the profit rate varies with a variation in the proportionate share of wages in the marginal product and he devised his measure to that end. Yet he also made his point along alternative lines more in tune with the real-world monetary system. Thus, on occasion he accepted, for the sake of argument, Smith's proposition whereby an increase in wages does lead to an increase in prices generally, but pointed out that this could only be temporary, because in terms of the international flow of precious metals there can be no permanently maintained exogenous increase in prices in one country; gold (in the everyday sense of the term) will flow out to correct the imbalance which must appear in trading relationships and the price level then falls again (I, 104–5).

There was a further line of defence. Even if all prices rise with wages, this does not mean that real profits are maintained, since the purchasing power of profits will be eroded (pp. 126–7). The origins of Ricardo's preoccupation with the effect of wage increases on prices and profits can in fact be discerned in the course of the great monetary debate of 1810–11.

5.12 Summary and Conclusion

Having in mind the allocative dimension demonstrated in the earlier sections of this chapter, it will be clear that it is unjustified to say of Ricardo that he had little comprehension of the way markets work and relative prices operate in allocating resources; neither can it be said that there is a crucial sense in which distribution is 'prior to' exchange. The Ricardian general-equilibrium system satisfies the following conditions. Full equilibrium implies equality of the profit rate on capital (and equal wages) throughout the system and is satisfied when prices everywhere equal costs. Secondly, equilibrium in commodity markets is characterized by zero excess demand at cost-covering prices, namely the condition that quantity supplied equals quantity demanded. Thirdly, while the machinery–labour ratio in each industry is governed by technological determinants, the economy-wide ratio is a variable, partly dependent upon the pattern of demand for final goods. (Ricardo actually recognized machinery–labour substitution, see below, p. 187, but in dealing with allocation theory, he assumed it away, relying on factor substitution by way of changes in the structure of outputs.) Thus, changes in the pattern of final demand can bring about variations in the wage rate by affecting the average division between fixed and circulating capital and thus the demand for labour; conversely, a change in the wage rate plays on the structure of prices via its impact on activity or output levels. Finally, Say's law of markets closes the system.

The Ricardian system is one of mutual dependence between distribution and pricing, but this interdependence is sometimes veiled. The problem is created in part by the ambiguous methodological status of the 'fundamental theorem of distribution', for it is on occasion Ricardo's practice to derive a new general profit rate in consequence of a change in wages by use of the standard measuring procedure and then to apply the new rate in the calculation of the price structure. But this does not constitute an account of the causal linkages at play; it is merely a formal device designed to yield appropriate predictions regarding the new equilibrium values of key variables following a disturbance to the wage rate. The technical difficulties involved are severe. Depending on the particular measuring procedure adopted, a different 'forecast' emerges; moreover, what may be an 'ideal' measure given the initial pattern of equilibrium outputs, and thus the weighting of various industries, will not necessarily remain so should that pattern alter following a wage change (see below, p. 452).

Suggested Reading

* Ricardo, *Principles of Political Economy*, in *Works and Correspondence* (1951), ed. P. Sraffa, I, chs 1–7, 19, 20, 22, 24, 30.
*   'Absolute Value and Exchangeable Value', *Works*, IV, 357–412.

Ricardian value theory is analysed in Marshall's famous Appendix I to his *Principles of Economics* (1920); Stigler (1965), ch. 12, in Wood (1985), item 27; Hollander (1979), ch. 6 also in Caravale ed. (1985) ch. 2; and Rankin (1980) in Wood (1985), item 85. For the value and distribution analysis as a whole, see Sraffa's 'Introduction' to Ricardo's *Works* (1951), particularly his proposed 'rational reconstruction' (xxx–xxxiii) of Ricardo's 1814 correspondence and 1815 *Essay on Profits*; Knight (1956) in Wood (1985), item 50; Stigler (1965c), in Wood (1985), item 50; Dobb (1973), ch. 3; and Hollander (1979), 'Introduction' and chs 3, 4, 5 and 6.

Buchanan (1929); Smith (1951); Gordon (1959); Stigler (1965), chs 5 and 8; and Bowley (1973), chs 4, 5 and 6 are again relevant.

The Ricardian approach to trade is examined in Viner (1937), ch. 8; Allen (1965), 3–33; and Chipman (1965). For a discussion of the comparative-cost theory from the perspective of international monetary economics, see Hollander (1979), 459–73.

6 Mill on Value and Distribution

6.1 Introduction

Ricardo's fundamental theorem on distribution (the inverse profit–wage relation), we have seen, was not divorced from the corpus of allocation analysis. Ricardianism and neo-classicism have in common a similar 'central core' amounting to allocation theory based on the demand–supply mechanism. We now carry the story further. A primary theme of this chapter is John Stuart Mill's Ricardianism – the inverse profit–wage relationship based upon the standard measure, and the linkages between distribution and the competitive allocation mechanism isolated in the investigation of Ricardo. Various theoretical contributions by Mill fit into the existing structure as 'improvements' and do not constitute elements of a different general model. To demonstrate this is important considering assertions in the secondary literature that Mill effected, or wished to effect, or ought to have effected, a breakaway from Ricardian analysis – complaints that imply the need for psychological explanations to account for his unwillingness to recognize the innovatory character of his own work (below, p. 419).

First the chapter will address short-run and long-run price formation under various cost and market conditions. Particular attention is paid to consumer behaviour (section 6.3), and to a novel approach towards price adjustment following the introduction of new technology into a competitive (constant-cost) industry (section 6.5). Then we will turn (section 6.8) to the analysis of the wage rate structure, a key issue in classical allocation theory. Mill's recognition of the principle of derived demand (section 6.9) confirms the role accorded final demand in employment decisions by firms. Section 6.10 digresses to consider the treatment of international values, for there is much here relevant for Mill's general perspective on demand theory and equilibration.

The concluding section considers aspects of the theory of distribution, particularly the linkages with the theory of value and allocation. Following Mill and Ricardo, the emphasis will be almost entirely on wages per man, profits per cent and rent per acre, as distinct from wages, profits and rent as shares in the total national product. While the logic of this economic reasoning turned upon the principles of competitive allocation theory, Mill – always in the Ricardian manner – also maintained the fundamental theorem in terms of the quantity theory of money.

6.2 Short-run Price Formation

Mill's central analysis of price determination in the *Principles of Political Economy* (1848) runs in terms of the equation of quantity demanded and supplied, and is applied in the first instance to commodities the supply of which is 'not susceptible of being multiplied at pleasure' ([1965], III, 468).* The exposition concentrates largely upon the role played by the negative slope of the demand curve in the process of correction of excess demand and supply:

> Meaning by the word demand, the quantity demanded, and remembering that this is not a fixed quantity, but in general varies according to the value, let us suppose that the demand at some particular time exceeds the supply [by one-third], that is, there are persons ready to buy, at the market value, a greater quantity than is offered for sale. Competition takes place on the side of the buyers, and the value rises.... At what point ... will the rise be arrested? At the point whatever it be, which equalizes the demand and the supply: at the price which cuts off the extra third from the demand, or brings forward additional sellers sufficient to supply it.....
>
> The converse case is equally simple. Instead of a demand beyond the supply, let us suppose a supply exceeding the demand. The competition will now be on the side of the sellers: the extra quantity can only find a market by calling forth an additional demand equal to itself. This is accomplished by way of cheapness; the value falls, and brings the article within the reach of more numerous customers, or induces those who were already consumers to make increased purchases (pp. 466–7).

Allowance is also made for the withdrawal of supply into stocks upon price reductions as part of the adjustment mechanism: 'but whether the

---

* All extracts from the works of Mill are from the *Collected Works of John Stuart Mill*, edited by J. M. Robson (see Bibliography). Throughout this chapter references to the *Collected Works* are given by volume and/or page number only.

demand and supply are equalized by an increased demand, the result of cheapness, or by withdrawing a part of the supply, equalized they are in either case.'

Mill's analysis provided a resolution of the apparent 'paradox, of two things each depending upon the other' – that while 'demand ... partly depends on the value', at the same time 'value depends on the demand' (p. 466). The solution, Mill conceded, 'must have been frequently given', but he added, 'I cannot call to mind any one who had given it before myself, except the eminently clear thinker and skilful expositor, J. B. Say'. The solution, of course, turns upon the distinction between demand in the sense of quantity demanded and demand in the sense of the entire schedule, the equilibrium price being the solution to the *equation* of quantity demanded and quantity supplied (pp. 467–8).

The negatively sloped demand curve and the equilibrating function of price in the short run, were part and parcel of Ricardian analysis and well established already in the *Wealth of Nations*. The formal equation of demand and supply and the distinction between displacement of and movements along the demand curve, certainly constitute an improvement in rigour. But their merit lies less in substantive content than in conspicuous location amongst the basic theoretical principles; for Ricardo made many of his statements regarding the theory of allocation in informal contexts relating to applied problems. Mill quite rightly regarded his own analysis as a clarification of sometimes obscure, or ambiguous, or incomplete formulations in the original statements of 1817.

Considering the price mechanism just outlined, it is scarcely surprising that (despite the absence of any notion of incremental utility) the so-called 'paradox of value' posed no problem (II, 30). Another interesting application of demand–supply analysis is to the joint production case discussed in the chapter 'Of Some Peculiar Cases of Value' (Book III, xvi): 'Since cost of production here fails us, we must revert to a law of value anterior to cost of production, and more fundamental, the law of demand and supply. The law is, that the demand for a commodity varies with its value, and that the value adjusts itself so that the demand shall equal the supply' (III, 583):

> Equilibrium will be attained when the demand for each article fits so well with the demand for the other, that the quantity required of each is exactly as much as is generated in producing the quantity required of the other. If there is any surplus or deficiency on either side; if there is a demand for coke, and not a demand for all the gas produced along with it, or *vice versâ*; the values and prices of the two things will so adjust themselves that both shall find a market.
>
> When, therefore, two or more commodities have a joint cost of production, their natural values relatively to each other are those which

create a demand for each, in the ratios of the quantities in which they are
sent forth by the productive process (p. 584).

This specific theorem is said not to be itself important, 'but the illustration it affords of the law of demand, and of the mode in which, when
cost of production fails to be applicable, the other principle steps in to
supply the vacancy, is worthy of particular attention'. We shall see in
section 6.4 below that, on his own terms, Mill should have avoided
formulations which, taken literally, imply that demand–supply analysis
is an alternative to cost price analysis.

6.3 Consumer Behaviour

In what follows we look briefly at Mill's account of consumer behaviour
with special reference to the rationalization of the law of demand – the
price–quantity relationship.

The closest Mill comes to the notion of diminishing marginal utility is
in the context of a proposal to limit the right of bequest, where the
distribution of generalized purchasing power is at stake: '[The] difference to the happiness of the possessor between a moderate independence and five times as much, is insignificant when weighed against
the enjoyment that might be given... by some other disposal of the four-
fifths' (II, 225). This seems to imply the principle of diminishing utility
applied to income although the incremental dimension is not necessarily intended. In fact, a number of impediments were at play which may
have detracted from a marginal utility conception of pricing. First, there
is Mill's materiality dimension of wealth which focuses on the acquisition
of a stream of future utilities rather than on immediate utility. Secondly,
there is a notion that retail purchases are not made on maximizing
principles. This latter point should be put in context.

One of the most famous declarations in the *Principles* maintains that
'only through the principle of competition has political economy any
pretension to the character of a science' (p. 239). This is repeated in a
'warning' at the outset of Book III ('On Exchange') that the analysis of
price formation which follows presumes competition, for 'only so far as
[prices] are thus determined, can they be reduced to any assignable law'
(III, 460). On these grounds the analysis – which turns on the axiom
'that there cannot be for the same article, of the same quality, two prices
in the same market' – is limited to the wholesale sector, for Mill
represents individual consumers as typically failing to act in maximizing
fashion:

> The values and prices... to which our conclusions apply, are mercantile
> values and prices; such prices as are quoted in price-currents; prices in

the wholesale markets, in which buying as well as selling is a matter of business; in which the buyers take pains to know, and generally do know, the lowest price at which an article of a given quality can be obtained.... Our propositions will be true in a much more qualified sense, of retail prices; the prices paid in shops for articles of personal consumption. For such things there often are not merely two, but many prices, in different shops, or even in the same shop; habit and accident having as much to do in the matter as general causes. Purchases for private use, even by people in business, are not always made on business principles: the feelings which come into play in the operation of getting, and in that of spending their income, are often extremely different. Either from indolence, or carelessness, or because people think it fine to pay and ask no questions, three-fourths of those who can afford it give much higher prices than necessary for the things they consume; while the poor often do the same from ignorance and defect of judgement, want of time for searching and making inquiry, and not unfrequently, from coercion, open or disguised.

In this passage we have a perfect instance of the counteracting forces to 'wealth maximization', of which so much is made in the early essay on definition and method (see below, p. 340).

The same perspective had been taken in a discussion of 'Competition and Custom' (Book II, iv), where it was also emphasized that the single price axiom turning upon wealth maximization, in the sense of pecuniary interest, does not appy at the retail level because of the failure of consumers to act as maximizers:

Not only are there in every large town, and in almost every trade, cheap shops and dear shops, but the same shop often sells the same article at different prices to different customers: and, as a general rule, each retailer adapts his scale of prices to the class of customers whom he expects. The wholesale trade, in the great articles of commerce, is really under the domination of competition. There, the buyers as well as the sellers are traders or manufacturers, and their purchases are not influenced by indolence or vulgar finery, nor depend on the smaller motives of personal convenience, but are business transactions (II, 242–3).

Strictly speaking, the retailer may be said to act in maximizing fashion by resorting to price discrimination, but our concern here is the consumer whose failure to act 'on business principles' makes such discrimination possible.

Not only is (pecuniary) maximization ruled out for the typical consumer, but some kinds of behaviour lead to what from a simple marginal utility perspective seems perverse. The reference to 'vulgar finery' in the foregoing passage suggests conspicuous consumption, an issue emerging in a variety of other contexts. Thus, we have the pronouncement that 'I know not why it should be a matter of congratulation that persons who are already richer than any one needs to be, should have doubled their means of consuming things which give little or no pleasure except as representative of wealth' (III, 755). And there is a striking application to the taxation of luxuries entailing, in effect, an upward-sloping demand curve:

> a great portion of the expenses of the higher and middle classes ... is not incurred for the pleasure afforded by the things on which the money is spent, but from regard to opinion, and an idea that certain expenses are expected from them, as an appendage of station; and I cannot but think that expenditure of this sort is a most desirable subject of taxation.... When a thing is bought not for use but for its costliness, cheapness is no recommendation. As Sismondi remarks, the consequence of cheapening articles of vanity, is not that less is expended on such things, but that buyers substitute for the cheapened article some other which is more costly, or a more elaborate quality of the same thing; and as the inferior quality answered the purpose of vanity equally well when it was really expensive, a tax on the article is really paid by nobody: it is a creation of public revenue by which nobody loses (p. 869).

The view that utility turns on relative not absolute income was quite common among classical writers. It led Nassau Senior to the law of diminishing marginal utility, only to dismiss it (1836, 6–13).

Mill asserted in his essay on method (1836) that 'we know not of any *laws* of the *consumption* of wealth as the subject of a distinct science: they can be no other than the laws of human enjoyment' (IV, 318n.). The 'laws of human enjoyment', he maintained, are not the concern of economists. But we know that Mill does refer to 'general principles of demand', pre-eminently the negatively sloped demand curve. One might be justified in supposing that the negative slope is attributed solely to wholesale purchasers. Yet we also find in Mill's *Principles* a rationalization of this property that seems to apply to final consumers. Mill apparently applies the methodological distinction between 'scientific' economics – based on the standard maximization axiom – and 'applied' economics which allows for qualifications; it is with the former that he is here concerned. Equally, however, we must bear in mind that though the majority of consumers 'give much higher prices than necessary for the things they consume' a price increase normally has some restrictive impact on consumption that requires analysis, the imperfections merely precluding a single price for all consumers.

The rationale for a negative slope runs in terms of the 'income effect' generated by price variation. Depending upon the kind of commodity involved, more or less of any increase in purchasing power generated by a fall in price will be devoted to the commodity in question rather than to others. From this perspective 'absolute necessaries' are demand-inelastic: 'In the case of food, as those who had already enough do not require more on account of its cheapness, but rather expend in other things what they save in food, the increased consumption, occasioned by cheapness, carries off, as experience shows, only a small part of the extra supply caused by an abundant harvest' (III, 467). Conversely, in the event of price increases, 'it is other things rather than food that are diminished in quantity by them, since, those who pay more for food not having so much to expend otherwise, the production of other things contracts itself to the limits of a smaller demand' (p. 475).

All this is important, although already well dealt with by Ricardo (see above, pp. 90–1). But Mill's correspondence shows how easy it would have been for him to have incorporated a wider range of considerations had he wished to devote more attention to the rationalization of the price–quantity relationship at the level of the individual. Specifically, he formulated a truly beautiful statement of the substitution effect in consumption resulting from changes in relative price (purchasing power held constant), which verbally describes a twist in the budget constraint about the initial equilibrium point:

> You say [he wrote to J. E. Cairnes in 1865], if a tax is taken off beer and laid on tobacco in such a manner that the consumer can still, at the same total cost as before, purchase his usual quantity of both, his tastes being supposed unaltered, he will do so. Does not this assume that his taste for each is a fixed quantity? or at all events that his comparative desire for the two is not affected by their comparative prices. But I apprehend the case to be otherwise. Very often the consumer cannot afford to have as much as he would like of either: and if so, the ratio in which he will share his demand between the two may depend very much on their price. If beer grows cheaper and tobacco dearer, he will be able to increase his beer more, by a smaller sacrifice of his tobacco, than he could have done at the previous prices: and in such circumstances it is surely probable that some will do so. His apportionment of self-denial between his two tastes is likely to be modified, when the obstacle that confined them is in the one case brought nearer, in the other thrown farther off (III, 1089).

Nothing in this very modern-sounding approach to the logic of choice clashes with what is in the *Principles*; the new materials merely provide a further rationalization for the negative slope of the demand curve.

6.4 Demand–Supply Analysis, Cost Price and Profit Rate Equalization

We turn now to the precise relationship between demand–supply and cost price analysis. It is helpful to have in mind here the opinion, expressed by Malthus in 1824 ([1963], 188), and repeated ever since, that Ricardo had limited demand–supply analysis solely to the market period and cases of monopoly, treating long-run cost price quite independently – i.e. that the two theories were mutually exclusive. J. S. Mill rejected Malthus's attribution as soon as it appeared, insisting in an 1825 *Westminster Review* article that in the opinion of the Ricardo school long-run cost prices were arrived at by way of supply variation (IV, 33–4).

In Mill's key chapter 'Of Demand and Supply, in their Relation to Value' (Book III, ii), there will be found a reference to 'another law' than that of demand and supply – namely cost price – 'for that much larger class of things, which admit of indefinite multiplication' (III, 468). But this statement is immediately followed by the caution that in dealing with production costs it was essential 'to conceive distinctly and grasp firmly' the 'exceptional' case of 'commodities not susceptible of being multiplied at pleasure' – the case of given supplies. Indeed, 'the principle of the exception stretches wider, and embraces more cases than might at first be supposed'. As is well clarified in correspondence of 1869, Mill simply wished to deter analysts from 'stopping short at demand & supply as the final regulators of price, without going on to that which in the last resort, adjusts the demand and supply to one another, viz. Costs of production' (XVII, 1596).

Mill's appreciation of the relativity of exchange value is nowhere expressed more clearly than in his discussion of costs. 'Value is a relative term', he wrote in his chapter on the 'Ultimate Analysis of Cost of Production' (Book III, iv), it is 'not a name for an inherent and substantive quality of the thing itself' (III, 479). Accordingly, Ricardo's emphasis upon labour was justifiable, notwithstanding that the primary costs to be met by the capitalist–employer are wage costs, since 'in considering…the causes of *variations* in value, quantity of labour is the thing of chief importance; for when that varies, it is generally in one or a few commodities at a time, but the variations of wages (except passing fluctuations) are usually general, and have no considerable effect on value' (p. 481). None the less, wage differentials (as well as relative labour inputs) will be reflected in the cost price structure, and changes thereof will generate changes in the price structure: 'Although, however, *general* wages, whether high or low, do not affect values, yet if wages are higher in one employment than another, or if they rise and fall permanently in one employment without doing so in others, these inequalities do really operate on values' (p. 480).

Once allowance is made for differential time periods of production from industry to industry – the fact that 'one commodity may be called upon to yield profit during a longer period of time than the other' (p.

482) – it follows that 'commodities do not exchange in the ratio simply of the quantities of labour required to produce them' (p. 484). This is in line with a rejection of the labour theory in his 1825 article; there Mill insisted, against a misreading by Malthus, that Ricardo had always understood 'that commodities which have the same quantity of labour bestowed on their production, will differ in exchangeable value, if they cannot be brought to market in the same time', and had allowed for the potential impact upon exchangeable values of general wage rate variations (IV, 31–2). As Mill phrases the matter in the *Principles*: 'even a general rise of wages ... does in some degree influence values. It does not affect them in the manner vulgarly supposed, by raising them universally. But an increase in the cost of labour, lowers profits; and therefore lowers in natural value the things into which profits enter in a greater proportion than the average, and raises those into which they enter in a less proportion than the average' (III, 485).

In his *Leading Principles* J. E. Cairnes (1823–75) criticized Mill's inclusion of wages and profits within costs; wages and profits were not 'costs' in the legitimate sense of that term – namely, 'sacrifices incurred by man in productive industry' – but constituted rather 'the return made by nature to man upon that sacrifice'. 'Labour' and 'abstinence' were the true costs of production (1874, 48–9). For his part, Mill observed in correspondence that the difference was a matter of 'the most convenient or most scientific mode of expressing the same doctrine' according to whether the context involved the economic system as a whole or the motives of the individual participants in activity: 'the cost to society, as a whole, of any production, consists in the labour and abstinence required for it. But, as concerns individuals and their mutual transactions, wages and profits are the measure of that labour and abstinence, and constitute the motives by which the exchange of commodities against one another is immediately determined' (XVII, 1894–5). Here we have a conscious distinction between aggregative and micro-economic theorizing. The formulation confirms that the theory of costs was treated by Mill from a micro-economic perspective involving relative value and the motives underlying allocation.

As we know, long-run equilibrium prices satisfy the condition that the return to capital in each sector meets the alternative available elsewhere: 'under the régime of competition, things are, on the average, exchanged for each other at such values, and sold at such prices, as afford equal expectation of advantage to all classes of producers; which can only be when things exchange for one another in the ratio of their cost of production' (III, 582). This condition of course hinges upon the capital mobility axiom: 'The value at any particular time is the result of supply and demand ... [but] unless that value is sufficient to repay the

Cost of Production, and to afford, besides, the ordinary expectation of profit, the commodity will not continue to be produced'; for 'the *necessary* price' includes a return on capital 'as great . . . as can be hoped for in any other occupation at that time and place', and in the event of a return in excess of the going rate 'capital rushes to share in this extra gain, and by increasing the supply of the article, reduces its value' (pp. 471–2). But Mill was quite aware that the adjustment is not instantaneous, and allowed for sluggish correction following changes in the pattern of demand (II, 408). Before capital can be extricated from a declining trade (or increased in the case of expansion) the returns thereon are not in the nature of profit, but rather that of Marshallian 'quasi-rent', a notion already firmly established by Ricardo. Profit equalization occurs, so to speak, at the margin of investment. A striking instance of this will be found in the account given of taxes on house rents. Such taxes, 'for some time after the tax was first imposed' fall on the owners, reducing net profits on their investment below the going rate so that 'houses would not be built'; 'by degrees, however, as the existing houses wore out, or as increase of population demanded a greater supply, rents would again rise; until it became profitable to recommence building, which would not be until the tax was wholly transferred to the occupier' (III, 834).

We may consider land rent from the cost perspective. The conditions of land supply in the aggregate distinguished rent from the other factor returns: 'In the case of an implement (a thing produced by labour) a price of some sort is the necessary condition of its existence: but the land exists by nature. The payment for it, therefore, is not one of the expenses of production' (II, 58). It is purely a matter of scarcity in the case of an agent subject to 'engrossment and appropriation', as Mill's important statement of the basic technical failing of Physiocracy shows:

> The rent of land being a price paid for a natural agency, and no such price being paid in manufactures, these writers imagined that since a price was paid, it was because there was a greater amount of service to be paid for: whereas a better consideration of the subject would have shown that the reason why the use of land bears a price is simply the limitation of its quantity, and that if air, heat, electricity, chemical agencies, and the other powers of nature employed by manufacturers, were sparingly supplied, and could, like land, be engrossed and appropriated, a rent could be extracted for them also (p. 29).

This perspective is precisely that of Ricardo (see above, pp. 97–8).

Thus far we have concentrated on the aggregative dimension. When Mill focused upon individual sectors – and in this he reverted to Smith – the picture was very different:

No one can deny that rent sometimes enters into cost of production. If I buy or rent a piece of ground, and build a cloth manufactory on it, the ground-rent forms legitimately a part of my expenses of production, which must be repaid by the product. And since all factories are built on ground, the rent for it must, on the average, be compensated in the values of all things made in factories (III, 487).

Allowance is also made for the use of particular inputs 'which cannot be increased *ad libitum* in quantity, and which therefore, if the demand goes beyond a certain amount, command a scarcity value'. In these cases, scarcity value indirectly 'enters into the cost of production, and consequently into the value, of the finished article' (p. 486). (The term 'scarcity' is here used in the technical sense of limited supplies.) But in fact scarcity manifests itself much more generally, for it is at the root of the profit equalization principle itself – the allocation of scarce capital between competing uses.

6.5 The Adjustment Mechanism: an Elaboration

We consider next a valiant and original attempt by Mill to get a grip on the complex issue of long-run price and output adjustments. Let us take as the standard case the adjustment to a new equilibrium following a technological change that reduces natural (long-run cost) price. Mill allows a price-setting role to individual (competitive) entrepreneurs who, aware of the likelihood of entry into the industry by firms in response to super-normal profit, act to forestall them. It is not, therefore, that increase in supply works to reduce price to the lower cost level, but that price is lowered directly, at a rate depending upon the threat of entry by new firms as estimated by existing entrepreneurs; these include in their calculations the risk of entry from the viewpoint of prospective entrants, which in turn hinges partly upon demand elasticity:

> The latent influence by which the values of things are made to conform in the long run to the cost of production, is the variation that would otherwise take place in the supply of the commodity. The supply would be increased if the thing continued to sell above the ratio of its cost of production.... The value of the thing would in a little time, if not immediately, fall ... because if it did not, the supply would ... be increased, until the price fell .... If, indeed, the supply *could* not be increased, no diminution in the cost of production would lower the value: but there is by no means any necessity that it *should*. The mere possibility often suffices; the dealers are aware of what would happen, and their mutual competition makes them anticipate the result by lowering the

price....Nobody doubts...that the price and value of all these things [even things in inelastic demand] would be eventually lowered by any diminution of their cost of production; and lowered through the apprehension entertained of new competitors, and an increased supply; though the great hazard to which a new competitor would expose himself, in an article not susceptible of any considerable extension of its market, would enable the established dealers to maintain their original prices much longer than they could do in an article offering more encouragement to competition (III, 473–4).

It is expectation of increased supply that brings about the price reduction to cost, for which reason precisely 'if...the supply *could* not be increased, no diminution in the cost of production would lower the value'. (Mill does not consider the possibility that potential entrants will contemplate displacing existing firms even if there should be some technical inability to expand global industry supply, and that those in the industry will protect themselves by cutting prices.) In the usual case of non-zero elasticity of demand there does occur actual output expansion by existing firms which, at the lower cost prices, are faced by larger markets. In the limiting case of zero demand elasticity, there will be no such increased market opportunities – a possibility Mill emphasized in order to counter the view that there necessarily occurs an output expansion to assure that price falls to cost: 'Whether there will be a greater permanent supply of the commodity after its production has been cheapened, depends on...whether a greater quantity is wanted at a reduced value. Most commonly a greater quantity is wanted, but not necessarily'. This led Mill to add that

the value of things which can be increased in quantity at pleasure, does not depend (except accidentally, and during the time necessary for production to adjust itself,) upon demand and supply; on the contrary, demand and supply depend upon it. There is a demand for a certain quantity of the commodity at its natural or cost value, and to that the supply in the long run endeavours to conform (p. 475).

As explained, it is not a matter of the supply curve shifting outwards with price sliding down the demand curve, but rather, output of each firm expanding to meet the quantity demanded at cost price. It is scarcely surprising that many readers have been misled into believing that Mill's cost price is divorced entirely from demand and supply.

There arise a number of complications. Unless the firms can react immediately by expanding output, there will be excess demand at the new cost price and one must suppose upward pressure on the price. This kind of complexity is actually raised by Mill in his treatment of a tax:

Again, reverse the case, and suppose the cost of production increased....The value would rise; and that, probably, immediately. Would the supply be diminished? Only if the increase of value diminished the demand. Whether this effect followed, would soon appear, and if it did, the value would recede somewhat, from excess of supply, until the production was reduced, and would then rise again (p. 474).

In this case, as before, price changes 'immediately' (although the counterpart to the logic of fear of entry is not clarified). At the higher price, in the first instance, supply exceeds demand (supposing quantity demanded falls with price increases), generating some downward pressure on the price. Only after output is actually reduced can the higher price level be permanently maintained. The implication is that in our case of technological change prices will rise somewhat from the initial (lower cost) level under pressure of excess demand, although firms would be reluctant to accept improved offers for fear of attracting new entrants and would be engaged in attempting to expand capacity to meet the demand probable at the cost price even if current price should be held temporarily somewhat above it.

Mill's firms are supposed to engage in a passive form of collusion to satisfy what amounts to an implicit market-sharing arrangement. A characteristic of the analysis is its failure to indicate the long-run optimum size of the firms, each of which is apparently presumed to have the technical ability to expand at constant cost without limit. What constraint does exist is self-imposed.

In adopting the price-adjustment mechanism Mill diverged from tradition, but key features of the standard approach are unaffected. In the first place, it remains true that in comparing long-run equilibria following the adoption of new technology a lower price will usually be accompanied by a higher output. Secondly, profit rate differentials are still the originating factor in the adjustment – though it is now existing firms who take the initiative to eradicate them by changing price. It would, moreover, be going too far to attribute to Mill sole reliance on internal adjustment. That mechanism applies where the disturbance is amenable to treatment in partial-equilibrium terms, the economy-wide profit rate taken by firms in a particular industry as given. It would not apply to a disturbance such as a general wage change. It is difficult to see how it would operate effectively alone in variable-cost industries where there is no unambiguous level of costs to which firms can attempt to adjust price; and the mechanism will be totally irrelevant in the case of newly established industries.

Mill apparently chose to emphasize price adjustment in order to weigh a neglected component and indicate that actual supply variation as the *initiator* of price change was not always essential. A detailed account of the role of credit in the profit rate equalization process is compatible with both kinds of adjustment – expansion and contraction by entry and exit of firms in response to profit rate differentials, and expansion and contraction by existing firms to satisfy excess demand at cost price (II, 407).

6.6　Variable-cost Conditions

Thus far we have followed Mill in assuming constant-cost industries. In the event of increasing costs, variations in conditions of demand lead to changes in long-run cost price as well as output. Agriculture, of course, provides the main example. The 'law of value', in this case, is that natural price is 'determined by the cost of that portion of the supply' – 'even the smallest' – 'which is produced and brought to market at the greatest expense' (III, 490). Elsewhere, the increasing cost case is put thus: 'the permanent value is determined by the greatest cost which it is necessary to incur in order to obtain the required supply' (p. 582). In some formulations equal weight is placed on the intensive and extensive margins: 'the real expenses of production are those incurred on the worst land, or by the capital employed in the least favourable circumstances' (II, 429); while in an early defence of Ricardian rent doctrine (1828) Mill had insisted that 'what the theory requires is, that of the whole *capital* employed in agriculture, there should always be one portion which yields no rent; one portion which barely replaces itself, with the ordinary profits of stock. *This* principle is the real foundation of the theory of rent' (IV, 171). It was not necessary that 'no-rent land' should exist as some critics believed. Moreover, the common objection that 'best' land is characteristically not taken up first was misplaced. For fertility must be interpreted not in terms of absolute produce but produce relative to costs and potentially productive land may need much preparatory investment (p. 173).

Decreasing costs (increasing returns) is a more complex matter. At the enterprise level, opportunities for specialization hinge on size; but even when specialization has reached a technical maximum, output expansion may lead to higher productivity as the labour force is used increasingly to capacity (II, 131). Various other overhead costs are taken into account, including that of direction; and the adoption of machine-intensive processes usually turns on size (p. 133). It is recognized that an increase in industry output is compatible with a larger number of small firms, but a high industry output is said to encourage the establishment of large firms – concentration increases with industry size.

An important test of scale economies is provided by the market:

> Whether or not the advantages obtained by operating on a large scale preponderate in any particular case over the more watchful attention, and greater regard to minor gains and losses, usually found in small establishments, can be ascertained, in a state of free competition, by an unfailing test. Wherever there are large and small establishments in the same business, that one of the two which in existing circumstances carries on the production at greatest advantage will be able to undersell the other (p. 133).

And Mill observed – in 'Marshallian' fashion – that taxation, by restricting demand, may prevent increasing returns from coming into effect: 'The higher price necessitated by the tax, almost always checks the demand for the commodity; and since there are many improvements in production which, to make them practicable, require a certain extent of demand, such improvements are obstructed, and many of them prevented altogether' (III, 840).

It is sometimes said that by his organization and weight of emphasis Mill unjustifiably played down the role of demand in price formation, with the result that the theory of value is made to look too simple. In proceeding so, runs the argument, he followed Ricardo rather than Bailey (1825) and Senior (1836), who sought to explain the varied relationships between demand, costs of production and value.

This, however, is not a fair criticism. The analysis of a tax imposed on a decreasing-cost industry indicates vividly the emphasis on the role of demand in long-run price formation. But the criticism also neglects classical terminology. Mill, it is true, did not formally give equal weight to the operation of demand and of supply in the case of products produced under conditions of increasing cost, writing that 'their value is not, correctly speaking, a scarcity value, for it is determined by the circumstances of the production of the commodity, and not by the degree of dearness necessary for keeping down the demand to the level of a limited supply' (III, 490). This, however, is not to play down demand and deny the scarcity dimension; the formulation reflects classical verbal usage whereby 'scarcity' value – also sometimes called 'monopoly' value – applies to cases of totally inelastic supply. Thus, should there be an absolute limit to further output expansion from land with increasing demand, 'both the land and its produce would really rise to a monopoly or scarcity price', rent appearing even on the marginal units of output (491; cf. II, 428). In all this, of course, Mill followed Ricardo (see above, p. pp. 98–9).

Mill, indeed, had himself protested at the sort of reading we are now considering. As early as 1828 he had defended the differential-rent theory against the strictures of Senior (1821), who supposed that Sir Edward West, Malthus and Ricardo 'considered the cultivation of inferior land as the *cause* of a high price of corn'; the reverse was true, for the cultivation of inferior land was the *effect* of high price 'itself the effect of demand' as 'explicitly laid down by the distinguished authors previously referred to, and particularly by Mr Ricardo' (IV, 174). Similarly, in the *Principles* he insists that differential rent is essentially a scarcity phenomenon, again correctly attributing this view to Ricardo: 'Mr Ricardo does not say that it is the cultivation of inferior land' that 'causes' rent on the superior, 'but the *necessity of cultivating* it, from the insufficiency of the superior land to feed a growing population' (II, 428).

6.7 Imperfect Competition

Mill recognized that increasing returns may be incompatible with competition. In the context of increasing returns he observed that 'where competitors are so few, they always end up agreeing not to compete. They may run a race of cheapness to ruin a new candidate, but as soon as he has established his footing they come to terms with him' (II, 142). Public utilities provide good examples of imperfect competition; it is to gas and water companies that Mill alludes in referring to a trade which 'from the nature of the case, [is] confined to so few hands, that profits may admit of being kept up by a combination among the dealers' (p. 405). Mill justified government regulation of public utilities. But governments were also charged with unjustifiable encouragement of barriers-to-entry:

> The usual instrument for producing artificial dearness is monopoly. To confer a monopoly upon a producer or dealer, or upon a set of producers or dealers not too numerous to combine, is to give them the power of levying any amount of taxation on the public, for their individual benefit, which will not make the public forego the use of the commodity. When the sharers in the monopoly are so numerous and so widely scattered that they are prevented from combining, the evil is considerably less: but even then the competition is not so active among a limited as among an unlimited number. Those who feel assured of a fair average proportion in the general business, are seldom eager to get a larger share by foregoing a portion of their profits (III, 927–8).

The implication is clear that price will be higher the smaller the number of firms in the industry. A 'strict or absolute' monopoly – a single seller – was easily dealt with as the limiting case, Mill providing a nice statement of the total revenue function, which (unless marginal cost should be zero) implies revenue rather than profit maximization as the objective:

> The monopolist can fix the value as high as he pleases, short of what the consumer either could not or would not pay; but he can only do so by limiting the supply. The Dutch East India Company obtained a monopoly price for the produce of the Spice Islands, but to do so they were obliged, in good seasons, to destroy a portion of the crop. Had they persisted in selling all that they produced, they must have forced a market by reducing the price, so low, perhaps, that they would have received for the larger quantity less total return than for the smaller: at least they showed that such was their opinion by destroying the surplus (p. 468).

Cost of production determines the minimum. In all of this Mill was following closely along Adam Smith's path (see above, p. 65).

Analytical tools are also applied to 'monopolistic competition' in the modern sense of that term, as in the case of markets subject to unrestrained freedom of entry, where the result is not determined by price competition, but by 'custom or usage' (II, 243). Thus, 'retail price, the price paid by the actual consumer, seems to feel very slowly and imperfectly the effect of competition; and when competition does exist, it often, instead of lowering prices, merely divides the gains of the high price among a greater number of dealers'. More specifically, 'custom' indicated a particular mark-up over the wholesale price, and what competition existed avoided price cutting (pp. 409–10). Mill touched also on the efficiency losses in retailing flowing from the limitation on price competition, the inefficiencies reflecting excessive numbers: 'the share of the whole produce of land and labour which is absorbed in the remuneration of mere distributors, continues exhorbitant ... there is no function in the economy of society which supports a number of persons so disproportioned to the amount of work to be performed'. A source of the problem, in addition to the price rigidity imposed by 'custom', was seen to be the ability to differentiate, by location if not by product – an ability likely to be undermined by the transport revolution which breaks down the dependency of consumers on local dealers (p. 243).

Mill may have lacked a formal 'barriers-to-entry' classification of market structures such as that of Bailey and Senior, yet his analysis of price and non-price competition turns strategically on the absence of barriers, whereas that of 'strict' monopoly and of imperfect competition requires them. In fact, Mill took a major step forward by recognizing the implications for market structure of the 'natural' barriers generated by scale economies. There is too the adjustment of prices to cost in the standard (constant-cost) case where potential entry plays a key role (see above, p. 127). Barriers are also of the essence in the analysis of the wage rate structure, to which we turn next.

6.8 The Wage Structure

Recognition of heterogeneous labour led Smith, Ricardo and J. S. Mill to abandon the pure labour theory even prior to allowance for capital and land, and to adopt a labour–cost theory which incorporates the impact of changes in the wage structure on long-run cost prices. Karl Marx writhed in circular reasoning to avoid the conclusion that reducing 'skilled' to 'unskilled' labour by use of an index of wage rates implies the rejection of a pure labour theory; in effect he too abandoned the theory even before introducing the problems flowing from differential 'organic composition of capital' (cf. *Capital*, I [1965], 43–4).

Heterogeneity of labour can refer either to productivity differentials, reflecting natural or learned qualities, or to attitudes to work. In Smith's account of the manner in which free competition assures that earnings in different occupations tend to keep in line (see above, p. 80), the emphasis is upon the characteristics of the job and the attitude towards them by labour – the 'five circumstances' discussed relate to 'the employments themselves', so that different monetary returns in long-run equilibrium merely reflect the varying degrees of attractiveness attached to each occupation. Nothing is said of natural differences of 'talent or genius'; and skill and productivity are merely implied in the discussion of learning. These characteristics are true also for Mill, who in the chapter on 'Differences of Wages in Different Employments' (Book II, xiv) lays out the general principle thus:

> There is no difficulty in understanding the operative principle in all these cases. If, with complete freedom of competition, labour of different degrees of desirableness were paid alike, competitors would crowd into the more attractive employments, and desert the less eligible, thus lowering wages in the first, and raising them in the second, until there would be such a difference of reward as to balance in common estimation the differences of eligibility. Under the unobstructed influence of competition, wages tend to adjust themselves in such a manner, that the situation and prospects of the labourers in all employments shall be, in the general estimation, as nearly as possible on a par (II, 381–2n.).

This summary of 'the operative principle' was withdrawn in the third edition (1852), Mill having grown dissatisfied with the Smithian analysis. Smith had recognized immobility due to 'policy' or institutional impediments to mobility, but there were two major deficiencies to his treatment. First, the pure logic of the competitive structure presumed the labour market *as a whole* to be in equilibrium; in the event of general unemployment the differentials become totally distorted:

> But when the supply of labour so far exceeds the demand that to find employment at all is an uncertainty, and to be offered it on any terms a favour, the case is totally the reverse. Desirable labourers, those whom every one is anxious to have, can still exercise a choice. The undesirable must take what they can get. The more revolting the occupation, the more certain it is to receive the minimum of remuneration, because it devolves on the most helpless and degraded, on those who from squalid poverty, or from want of skill and education, are rejected from all other employments. Partly from this cause, and partly from the natural and artificial monopolies ... the inequalities of wages are generally in an opposite direction to the equitable principle of compensation erroneously represented by Adam Smith as the general law of the remuneration of labour (p. 383).

This constitutes an aspect of the linkage of macro- and micro-economics of the very first importance.

The reference to 'natural monopolies' involves the second point of difference. Here we note Mill's observation that only the first, third and fifth of Smith's 'circumstances' involve cases 'in which inequality of remuneration is necessary to produce equality of attractiveness, and are examples of the equalizing effect of free competition' (p. 385). Smith had erred regarding 'trust' by implying that the adoption of responsibility was burdensome; Mill urged rather that a monetary differential is paid as a monopoly not a compensatory payment: 'If all labourers were trustworthy, it would not be necessary to give extra pay to working goldsmiths on account of the trust. The degree of integrity required being supposed to be uncommon, those who can make it appear that they possess it are able to take advantage of the peculiarity, and obtain higher pay in proportion to its rarity'.

The case in point illustrated a much wider principle. Smith's allowances for educational costs went only some way to account for differentials between the remuneration of common and skilled labour; the skilled worker must indeed 'have a prospect of at last earning enough to pay the wages of all this past labour [training], with compensation for the delay of payment, and an indemnity for the expenses of his education' (p. 386). But this consideration (even when supplemented by allowance for legal restrictions on mobility) did not suffice to explain ruling differentials, for the costs even of a minimal education and of maintenance during the training period 'exclude the greater body of the labouring people' from exerting sufficient competitive pressure to reduce the monopoly return of the skilled. Here we touch on the concept of 'non-competing industrial groups' (a term coined by J. E. Cairnes, 1874, 96) to reflect the social and financial obstacles to upward mobility:

> So complete, indeed, has hitherto been the separation, so strongly marked the line of demarcation, between the different grades of labourers, as to be almost equivalent to an hereditary distinction of caste; each employment being chiefly recruited from the children of those already employed in it, or in employments of the same rank with it in social estimation, or from the children of persons who, if originally of a lower rank, have succeeded in raising themselves by their exertions.... Consequently the wages of each class have hitherto been regulated by the increase of its own population, rather than of the general population of the country (II, 387–8).

Two lines of development follow from the foregoing analysis, one relating to the population mechanism and the other to the theory of price. We shall consider them in turn.

Mill's chapter 'Of Wages' (Book II, xi) commences with the caution that the analysis would 'proceed in the first instance as if there were no other kind of labour than common unskilled labour, of the average degree of hardness and disagreeableness' (p. 337). The chapter on wage differentials reiterates the formal contrast between the wages of 'ordinary or average labour' determined by global wage fund and population principles, and the wage structure 'depending in some degrees on different laws' (p. 380). Mill failed to fulfil a promise given here to relate formally and explicitly the two analyses, but it is necessary for us to do so.

Characteristically for Mill, and contrasting with modern analysis, the discussion of the wage rate structure takes into account the population variable and is not limited to the allocation of a given work force. Expansion of the labour pool, in any sector, if relatively excessive will force down the wage below the due competitive level; conversely, a relatively restrained growth is required to maintain an excessive 'monopoly' return:

> If the professions are overstocked, it is because the class of society from which they have always mainly been supplied, has greatly increased in number, and because most of that class have numerous families, and bring up some at least of their sons to professions. If the wages of artizans remain so much higher than those of common labourers, it is because artizans are a more prudent class, and do not marry so early or so inconsiderately (p. 388).

The maintenance of excessive differentials evidently requires control of supply *internal* to the group, even in the absence of upward mobility and increase of supply from outside. Conversely, prudence on the part of the skilled will not suffice to maintain their excessive returns in the event of a disintegration of barriers. Here arises a pervasive consideration exercising Mill throughout his career – the danger that without prudential restraint on the part of the unskilled, there would emerge a wage structure weighed towards the lowest category, having in mind the breakdown of barriers with growing educational and other opportunities:

> The inequality of remuneration between the skilled and the unskilled is, without doubt, very much greater than is justifiable; but it is desirable that this should be corrected by raising the unskilled, not by lowering the skilled. If, however, the other changes taking place in society are not accompanied by a strengthening of the checks to population on the part of labourers generally, there will be a tendency to bring the lower grades of skilled labourers under the influence of a rate of increase regulated by a lower standard of living than their own, and thus to deteriorate their condition without raising that of the general mass; the stimulus given to the multiplication of the lowest class being sufficient to fill up without difficulty the additional space gained by them from those immediately above (p. 388).

Mill's population and wage structure analyses together thus imply that in the absence of non-competing groups, population growth rates across sectors cannot get out of line, and that a stable wage structure emerges. In the stationary state, and assuming mobility, there will be groups of workers earning more than the 'base' (subsistence) wage, and this excess will not stimulate expansion on their part. This dual condition of equalizing money wage differentials yet zero population growth in each sector must be modified for a growing system. A competitive wage structure will then emerge upon a 'base' (above subsistence) wage appropriate for a particular positive growth rate of population.

When, however, allowance is made for non-competing groups, wage differentials reflect independently operating population constraints, and it is no longer at all clear how meaningful the notion of an 'average' wage is. Mill's references, notwithstanding recognition of the non-competing group phenomenon, to an 'average' wage or to common unskilled labour as a first step in the analysis of wages, are troublesome. But we must not forget that he considered barriers to be in the course of disintegration thus widening the potential scope of the standard analysis rather than rendering it obsolete.

We turn next to the implications of the analysis of non-competing groups for the theory of value. Mill is clear that the excessive return to skilled labour is 'limited by the price which purchasers are willing to give for the commodity they produce'; whereas entry sufficing to reduce wages to the competitive level would entail a price for the commodity which reflects (*inter alia*) wage costs (p. 387) – a nice illustration of 'cost' envisaged in terms of alternative opportunities. Similarly, in cases of restrictions on entry because of apprenticeship laws or unions, wages may exceed 'their natural proportion to the wages of common labour...without any assignable limit, were it not that wages which exceed the usual rate require corresponding prices, and that there is a limit to the price at which even a restricted number of producers can dispose of all they produce' (p. 396). (Here we have illustrations of the notion of derived factor demand, a topic to be taken up in section 6.9 below.)

As in the case of population, in regarding value Mill also played down the implications of his allowance for non-competing groups. This cautious tone pervades the appropriate principles listed in the 'Summary of the Theory of Value' (Book III, vi):

> IV. The natural value of some things is a scarcity value; but most things naturally exchange for one another in the ratio of their cost of production, or at what may be termed their Cost Value.
> V. The things which are naturally and permanently at a scarcity value are those of which the supply cannot be increasd at all, or not sufficiently to satisfy the whole of the demand which would exist for them at their cost value.
> VI. A monopoly value means a scarcity value. Monopoly cannot give a value to anything except through a limitation of the supply...
> VIII. Cost of Production consists of several elements, some of which are constant and universal, others occasional. The universal elements of cost of production are, the wages of the labour, and the profits of the capital. The occasional elements are taxes, and any extra cost occasioned by a scarcity value of some of the requisites.
> IX. Rent is not an element in the cost of production of the commodity which yields it; except in the cases (rather conceivable than actually existing) in which it results from, and represents, a scarcity value...
> X. Omitting the occasional element; things which admit of indefinite increase, naturally and permanently exchange for each other according to the comparative amount of wages which must be paid for producing them, and the comparative amount of profits which must be obtained by the capitalists who pay those wages (III, 497–8).

Item IX refers to (one-use) land, demand for the product of which is sufficiently high to generate rent even at the 'margin' (see also item V). Even if one accepts that such cases are 'rather conceivable than actually existing', non-competing groups surely entail the same principle of 'scarcity' or 'monopoly' value. Yet Mill chose to include the phenomenon among 'occasional elements' and focused rather upon the propositions relating to cost, which turn, of course, on labour and capital which have alternative uses and are mobile between them. Again, this attitude may reflect his confidence in the breakdown of barriers.

6.9 Derived Demand

Ricardo's subscription to J. B. Say's embryonic notion of 'derived demand' has been dealt with earlier (pp. 93–4 above). Here I shall briefly demonstrate the presence in Mill's work of the same appreciation of derived demand, in the sense that the ultimate source of factor remuneration is in sales proceeds and the motive for factor employment in the added revenue product expected. The argument is not technically watertight because of the absence of a clear marginal principle; but it points to the close connection envisaged by the classicists between value and distribution at the micro-economic level of analysis.

A brief suggestion of the relationship is encountered in Mill's reference in the *Principles* to 'the present system of industrial life, in which employments are minutely subdivided, and all concerned in production depend for their remuneration on the price of a particular commodity...' (III, 455). The principle is elaborated in a chapter dealing with indirect inputs of labour in lengthy processes of production:

> All these persons ultimately derive the remuneration of their labour from the bread, or its price: the plough-maker as much as the rest; for since ploughs are of no use except for tilling the soil, no one would make or use ploughs for any other reason than because the increased returns, thereby obtained from the ground, afforded a source from which an adequate equivalent could be assigned for the labour of the plough-maker. If the produce is to be used or consumed in the form of bread, it is from the bread that this equivalent must come (II, 31).

In the case of materials which are 'destroyed as such by being once used, the whole of the labour required for their production, as well as the abstinence of the person who supplied the means of carrying it on, must be remunerated from the fruits of a single use' (p. 37). By contrast, labourers in the capital goods sector 'do not depend for their remuneration upon the bread made from the produce of a single harvest, but upon that made from the produce of all the harvests which are successively gathered until the plough, or the buildings and fences, are worn out' (p. 32).

Workers in transportation also derive their remuneration from the value of the ultimate product and so do those engaged in wholesale and retail activity: 'the produce so distributed, or its price, is the source from which the distributors are remunerated for their exertions, and for the abstinence which enabled them to advance the funds needful for the business of distribution' (p. 40). It is precisely because of the 'increased utility' afforded by these functions that the product 'could be sold at an increased price, proportioned to the labour expended in conferring it' (p. 48).

Although the 'distributive' functions are formally separated from the strictly 'productive', it is clear that the process of production in the capitalist exchange system only ends with sale to the final consumer. This applies also to wage goods. For Mill distinguished labourers' accommodation from industrial structures, on the grounds that the housing of workers is 'destined for their personal accommodation: these, like their food, supply actual wants, and must be counted in the remuneration of their labour' (p. 38). Similarly, coal may be employed 'not only in the process of industry, but in directly warming human beings. When so used, it is not a material of production, but is itself the ultimate product' (p. 35). That 'the finished products of many branches of industry are the materials of others' (p. 36) was thus an irrelevant consideration in the case of workers' consumables, which are treated on a par with all other final goods.

There is also in the *Principles* a passage of potential significance for Mill's intentions by his 'recantation' in 1869 of the wages fund doctrine (III, 474; see below, p. 222). It contains an observation drawn from Thomas De Quincey focusing upon the implications of the fact that input use is characterized by the properties of derived demand and joint demand. Again the perspective is one of micro-economics involving particular industries.

Mill's proposition that 'demand for commodities is not demand for labour' (see below, p. 210) has often been misunderstood as a denial of the role of final demand in employment decisions. This was the view of W. S. Jevons, who read Mill as asserting that capitalists 'maintain and pay for labour whether or not there is a demand for the commodities produced', and that 'production goes on independently of the use to which the produce is to be put' (1905, 127). The proposition is, in fact, unrelated to employment decisions by individual firms and refers to aggregate employment or earnings. There is certainly no conflict with the principle of derived demand.

6.10   International Values

At this point we digress to consider Mill's contribution to international trade theory. His appreciation of the 'law of demand' and its allocative role emerges with crystal clarity in this context.

Ricardo's presumption will be recalled that the terms of trade between two trading partners will settle half-way between the relative autarchic cost ratios (see above, p. 106). This Mill rejected. His analysis runs in terms of the 'law of exchangeable value' applied to the determination of the terms of trade between German linen and English cloth (the standard illustration), where international factor mobility is precluded: 'The principle, that value is proportional to cost of production being consequently inapplicable, we must revert to a principle anterior to that of cost of production, and from which this last flows as a consequence – namely, the principle of demand and supply' ('Of the Laws of Interchange Between Nations', IV, 237). Here Mill formulates, in a statement of general applicability, the negative slope of the demand curve and the process of adjustment whereby excess supplies (or demands) are corrected by price variation:

> It is well known that the quantity of any commodity which can be disposed of, varies with the price. The higher the price, the fewer will be the purchasers, and the smaller the quantity sold. The lower the price, the greater will in general be the number of purchasers, and the greater the quantity disposed of. This is true of almost all commodities whatever: though of some commodities, to diminish the consumption in any given degree would require a much greater rise of price than of others.
>
> Whatever be the commodity – the supply in any market being given – there is some price at which the whole of the supply exactly will find purchasers, and no more. That, whatever it be, is the price at which, by the effect of competition, the commodity will be sold. If the price be higher, the whole of the supply will not be disposed of, and the sellers, by their competition, will bring down the price. If the price be lower, there will be found purchasers for a larger supply, and the competition of these purchasers will raise the price.
>
> This, then, is what we mean, when we say that price, or exchangeable value, depends on demand and supply. We should express the principle more accurately, if we were to say, the price so regulates itself that the demand shall be exactly sufficient to carry off the supply (pp. 237–8).

It is noteworthy that the negative slope to the demand curve is here presented as a well-known property. Whatever may be said of Mill's minimization of the novelty of his own specific application – universally regarded as a brilliant achievement – there is every reason to accept his representation of received doctrine regarding the theory of demand itself.

A direct application is then made to the case at hand involving the German demand for English cloth at various 'linen' prices and the English demand for German linen at the equivalent 'cloth' prices (the analysis of reciprocal demand), the illustrative data yielding a unique equilibrium linen–cloth rate of exchange (lying between the limits imposed by the autarchic cost ratios): 'It may be considered...as established', Mill concluded, 'that when two countries trade together in two commodities, the exchangeable value of these commodities relatively to each other will adjust itself to the inclinations and circumstances of the consumers on both sides, in such manner that the quantities required by each country, of the article which it imports from its neighbour, shall be exactly sufficient to pay for one another' (pp. 239–40). Mill proceeds to establish the direction to follow in seeking a general formula by showing that in the limiting case of zero demand elasticity – for example of German demand for English cloth – the 'gain' falls entirely to Germany. In general, however, while 'there is no absurdity in the hypothesis, that of some given commodity a certain quantity is all that is wanted at any price – there will not be this extreme inequality in the degree in which the demand in the two countries varies with variations in the price' (pp. 240–1). In the *Principles*, the general proposition is nicely restated thus:

> The law which we have now illustrated, may be appropriately named, the Equation of International Demand. It may be concisely stated as follows. The produce of a country exchanges for the produce of other countries, at such values as are required in order that the whole of her exports may exactly pay for the whole of her imports. This law of International Values is but an extension of the more general law of Value, which we called the Equation of Supply and Demand [III, 466–8]. We have seen that the value of a commodity always so adjusts itself as to bring the demand to the exact level of the supply. But all trade, either between nations or individuals, is an interchange of commodities, in which the things that they respectively have to sell, constitute also their means of purchase: the supply brought by the one constitutes his demand for what is brought by the other. So that supply and demand are but another expression for reciprocal demand: and to say that value will adjust itself so as to equalize demand with supply, is in fact to say that it will adjust itself so as to equalize the demand on one side with the demand on the other (III, 604).

Mill further took account of the precise implications for the final equilibrium of alternative elasticity values, and extended the analysis to allow for multiple equilibria.

6.11   The Fundamental Theorem on Distribution and Allocation Theory

I return now to the main lines of my argument. Mill treated production, distribution and exchange in three consecutive books. In Book II the profit rate is related inversely to wages, in the sense of the 'cost of labour', understood by Mill as labour and past profit embodied in *per capita* wages but still identified, in Ricardian fashion, with labour's share in *per capita* output or the fraction of a man's labour time devoted to the production of his wages (II, 411ff). This analysis of profits was, however, provisional: 'It will come out in greater fulness and force when, having taken into consideration the theory of Value and Price, we shall be enabled to exhibit the law of profits in the concrete – in the complex entanglement of circumstances in which it actually works' (p. 415). The extended analysis of the impact of wage rate changes is undertaken in Book III, xxvi on 'Distribution, as affected by Exchange'. The initial discussion of distribution in Book II was thus provisional; in the chapter at hand the order is reversed and the problem of distribution is analysed in the light of the theory of exchange value. It would be an error to suppose that Mill's organization reflected a divorce of value theory from distribution.

When the distribution of national income occurs via the mechanism of exchange and money, the 'law of wages' remains unchanged in so far as the determination of commodity wages is concerned, for this depends upon 'the ratio of population and capital' (III, 695). Relevant from the perspective of the employer is not merely the commodity wage but the 'cost of labour', a cost that will be reflected by the *money* wages paid when money constitutes 'an invariable standard':

> Wages in the second sense [cost of labour], we may be permitted to call, for the present, money wages; assuming, as it is allowable to do, that money remains for the time an invariable standard, no alteration taking place in the conditions under which the circulating medium itself is produced or obtained. If money itself undergoes no variation in cost, the money price of labour is an exact measure of the Cost of Labour, and may be made use of as a convenient symbol to express it (p. 696).

Here we note that while Mill insisted, like Ricardo, upon the relativity of exchange value, and so rejected as illogical the notion of a general alteration in exchange value, he did accept the notion of a measure of value or cost of production:

> [Economists] have imagined a commodity invariably produced by the same quantity of labour; to which supposition it is necessary to add, that the fixed capital employed in the production must bear always the same proportion to the wages of the immediate labour, and must be always the same durability; in short, the same capital must be advanced for the same length of time, so that the element of value which consists of profits, as well as that which consists of wages, may be unchangeable (p. 579).

Missing here is Ricardo's condition that the metal be produced by mean factor proportions; but Mill may have been presuming uniform factor ratios. Now such a measure of cost 'though perfectly conceivable' would probably not be found in practice because of the high likelihood of changes in the production cost of any commodity chosen. Nevertheless, gold and silver were 'the least variable' and, if used, the results obtained must simply be 'corrected by the best allowance we can make for the intermediate changes in the cost of the production itself'.

Assuming money to be such an invariable measure, the rate of money wages will depend upon the commodity wage and the production costs (and accordingly the money prices) of wage goods, including agricultural produce, which vary with 'the productiveness of the least fertile land, or least productive agricultural capital' (p. 697). Since the cost of labour is equated with the proportionate share of the labour in *per capita* output, Mill fully subscribed to the Ricardian theorem on distribution involving a 'proportions-measuring' money in terms of which a rise of wages implies an increased share of the labourer in the 'value' of his output and a reduced profit share and rate of return:

> There is no mode in which capitalists can compensate themselves for a higher cost of labour, through any action on values or prices. If the labourers really get more, that is, get the produce of more labour, a smaller percentage must remain for profit. From this Law of Distribution, resting as it does on a law of arithmetic, there is no escape. The mechanism of Exchange and Price may hide it from us, but is quite powerless to alter it' (pp. 479–80).

The 'Marxian' flavour of this formulation may be reinforced by Mill's proposition that 'the cause of profit' can be traced to surplus labour time – the fact that labourers 'in addition to reproducing their own necessaries and instruments, have a portion of their time remaining, to work for the capitalist' (II, 411; first introduced in 4th edition of 1857). Mill's full case and its relation to Marx's position will be taken up in chapter 15.

I shall now show that for Mill the substantive prediction that an increase in wages ('cost of labour') is necessarily accompanied by a fall in the rate of return, holds good quite generally notwithstanding a failure of the measure of value to guarantee its theoretical suitability as an invariable standard. The issue pervades Mill's writings and stamps them as being fully in the Ricardian tradition.

The 'popular and widely spread opinion' which Mill set out to refute in his central chapter on the 'Ultimate Analysis of Cost of Production' (Book III, iv) was the Smithian view 'that high wages make high prices'. In the first place, the proposition implied that there could be 'no such thing as a real rise of wages; for if wages could not rise without a proportional rise of the price of everything, they could not, for any substantial purpose rise at all. This surely is a sufficient *reductio ad absurdam...*' (III, 479). Secondly, even were prices to rise following an increase in wages, producers would not benefit therefrom since all their expenses rise: 'It must be remembered too that general high prices, even supposing them to exist, can be of no use to a producer or dealer, considered as such; for if they increase his money returns, they increase in the same degree all his expenses'. These, however, are in the nature of formal or purely logical arguments. In correspondence, Mill drew on quantity-theory reasoning to assure the result that wage increases are non-inflationary:

> A general rise of prices, of anything like a permanent character, can only take place through a general increase of the money incomes of the purchasing community. Now a general rise of wages would not increase the aggregate money incomes, nor consequently the aggregate purchasing power of the community; it would only transfer part of that purchasing power from the employers to the labourers. Consequently a general rise of wages would not raise prices but would be taken out of the profits of the employers: always supposing that those profits were sufficient to bear the reduction (XVII, 1734–5).

Most important is the case in support of the inverse profit–wage relation based upon the principles of allocation economics. In contrast to an increase in wages affecting one sector where price will rise to assure equality of profit rates across the board, there exists no mechanism whereby prices would be forced upwards in the event of a general increase in wages, since all firms throughout the system are affected equally by the change:

> Expenses which affect all commodities equally, have no influence on prices. If the maker of broadcloth or cutlery, and nobody else, had to pay higher wages, the price of his commodity would rise, just as it would if he had to employ more labour; because otherwise he would gain less profit than other producers, and nobody would engage in the employment. But if everybody has to pay higher wages or everybody to employ more labour, the loss must be submitted to; as it affects everybody alike, no one can hope to get rid of it by a change of employment, each therefore resigns himself to a diminution of profits, and prices remain as they were....If wages fall, (meaning here by wages the cost of labour), why, on that account, should the producer lower his price? He will be forced, it may be said, by the competition of other capitalists who will crowd into his employment. But other capitalists are also paying lower wages, and by entering into competition with him they would gain nothing but what they are gaining already (III, 692).

A standard error that Mill here set out to refute relates to the reputed disadvantage under which a 'high-wage' economy operates in foreign markets; only wages in the export sector below the general domestic level would generate a real advantage by lessening the *comparative* cost of those articles relative to others: 'no . . . advantage is conferred by low wages when common to all branches of industry' (compare Ricardo on this same issue, above, pp. 95–6).

The Mill–Ricardo analysis of the inverse profit–wage relation thus involves a direct application of the principles of allocation. It is unlikely that Mill regarded his demonstration of the theorem in these terms to be in conflict with the demonstration in terms of the standard measure. That purely logical demonstration had no economic content, for nothing is said of the mechanism whereby the inverse profit variation is achieved. The theorem is in the nature of a macro-economic statement regarding proportionate shares in a net output of constant value, leaving open the causal explanation of the transition between equilibrium states in a competitive world. This explanation is provided by the analysis of the inverse relation in terms of the allocation mechanism.

The discussion thus far has implicitly presupposed a uniformity of capital–labour ratios across the board. But only where differentials in factor proportions exist between industries can the operation of the allocative mechanism be actually 'observed', the effects of a general increase of wages upon relative prices flowing from reactions by capitalists to a structure of profit rates disturbed by the differential impact upon costs. Specifically, immediately following the wage increase profits are reduced universally at the ruling prices; the allocative effects follow in consequence of the differential decline in the returns on capital, some industries expanding and others contracting depending upon their factor intensities, with inverse movements in their prices. Equality of profit rates throughout the system emerges at the new lower level along with the new pattern of outputs and new set of cost prices. All this Mill did not bother to trace out. We have seen in our discussion of cost price, however, that he did allow for the effect of a general change in wages upon relative prices; and the reader will recall the central role accorded relative rates of profit in governing the pattern of commodity supplies, and thus prices, following disturbances to costs (pp. 125–6 above). The process of transition between equilibrium states *must*, therefore, involve allocative effects set in motion by the disturbed structure of profit rates at the original outputs and prices; this approach to the inverse profit–wage relation is the only one consistent with Mill's theoretical framework.

Changes in distribution can play on the price structure. What of the reverse sequence? Can an alteration in the configuration of final demand play back upon distribution? While Mill did not directly address the impact of a change in tastes upon distribution, he did, following Ricardo, discuss the consequences for wages of exogenous alterations in technology which entail the 'conversion' of circulating into fixed capital (see below, p. 213). It is difficult to see why an alteration in the distribution of the capital stock brought about by a change in the pattern of tastes cannot be similarly investigated.

6.12 Concluding Note

In all key respects, Mill, as he himself insisted, was transmitting the Ricardian message on the fundamental theorem on distribution. This is not to suggest that he had nothing new to say. We have encountered his contribution to price analysis; and Stigler (1965a) has called attention to other impressive theoretical innovations. The point is that they fit into the broader Ricardian framework, and are not designed as part of an alternative theoretical structure. It should also be added that his applications of the theory – as for example to the question of union responsibility for upward wage pressure in the 1860s – were appropriate for his own age.

Suggested Reading

* Mill (1848), *Principles of Political Economy*, Book II: 'Distribution', especially chs iii, iv, xiv, xv, xvi; Book III: 'Exchange', especially chs i–vi, xxvi.
*'The Quarterly Review on Political Economy' (1825), in *Collected Works*, IV, 23–43.

Two contributions by Stigler, (1965a) and (1982a), dealing respectively with 'originality in scientific progress' and 'the scientific uses of scientific biography', provide particularly interesting background to Mill's status as economist touching, in part, on the topic of this chapter. From this general perspective see also Edgeworth (1910), Bladen (1965), Schwartz (1972) and de Marchi (1974).

A famous account of Mill's value theory by Marshall (1876) merits careful attention. Mill on allocation, trade and distribution, elaborating upon the present chapter, is discussed in Hollander (1985), ch. 5. Williams (1978), ch. 3, examines Mill and the theory of the firm. Chapter 5 of Bowley (1973), on market structure, is also pertinent.

For Mill on international trade see the suggestions under chapter 5.

7 Smith on Capital, Employment and Growth

7.1 Introduction

We turn now from classical micro-economics to classical macro-economics. The following three chapters dealing with capital, employment and growth may be read as a unit since the same general issues emerge throughout the entire classical period. My main concern will be to trace out the refinements of and modifications to the Smithian doctrine by the nineteenth-century writers, especially with respect to the trend paths of the factor returns, and specific problems such as the impact of 'machinery'.

Sections 7.2 and 7.3 are devoted to the Smithian national income accounts and the savings process respectively. The determinants of aggregate employment capacity are the subject matter of section 7.4. What was to become a primary classical preoccupation – the trend path of the factor returns based on the secular patterns of factor demand and supply – is taken up in sections 7.5 and 7.6. Various topics in economic development – technical progress, investment priorities, the place of agriculture and the role of money – are discussed in the four closing sections. (The reader might refer back to p. 61 for a caution regarding the order in which Smith himself proceeded in the *Wealth of Nations*.)

7.2 The National Income Accounts

Like his French contemporaries, Smith distinguished between capital (wealth) and income, and treated money as a relatively insignificant component of the former. The breakaway from the mercantilist perspective is clear.

Smith asserted in his chapter 'Of the Component Parts of the Price of Commodities' (Book I, vi) that all payments by the individual firm can be reduced to those made to land, labour and capital; depreciation was not a separate cost category, since 'the price of any instrument ... is itself made up of the three parts' (1776 [1937], 50).* This proposition is then extended to the national income:

> As the price or exchangeable value of every particular commodity, taken separately, resolves itself into some one or other, or all of those three parts; so that of all the commodities which compose the whole annual produce of the labour of every country, taken complexly, must resolve itself into the same three parts, and be parcelled out among different inhabitants of the country, either as the wages of their labour, the profits of their stock, or the rent of their land. ... Wages, profit, and rent, are the three original sources of all revenue as well as of all exchangeable value. All other revenue is ultimately derived from some one or other of these (p. 52).

The national accounts scheme in Book II 'Of the Nature, Accumulation, and Employment of Stock' does, however, distinguish *net* national income from *gross* national income, the latter allowing if not for depreciation than at least for maintenance. Thus 'machines and instruments of trade, &c. require a certain expence, first to erect them, and afterwards to support them, both which expences, though they make a part of the gross, are deductions from the neat revenue of the society' (p. 273); or again: 'The gross revenue of the society, the annual produce of their land and labour, is increased by the whole value which the labour of [additional] workmen adds to the materials upon which they are employed; and their neat revenue by what remains of this value, after deducting what is necessary for supporting the tools and instruments of their trade' (p. 279).

Unlike our own accounting practice, not only is the maintenance of fixed capital deducted from gross revenue to arrive at net revenue, but so also are the *additions* made in any period, the counterpart of the net revenue including only consumer goods. It is real goods not money which represent 'the community's periodical income', Smith the anti-mercantilist maintains. (Note that the accounts appear in a chapter 'Of Money', Book II, ii.) But these real goods he restricts to consumption items: 'Their real riches ... the real weekly or yearly revenue ... must always be great or small in proportion to the quantity of consumable goods which they can all of them purchase' (p. 275). Apparently then, wages, profit and rent generated in the capital goods industries are

---

*See above p. 61n.

excluded from net income. But this very restrictive view seems unlikely; Smith's intention may have been to define a special category within net national income covering only consumer goods.

A second characteristic of his accounts is (as with present-day practice) the exclusion of the existing stock of equipment from both the gross and net national product. Thus the fixed capital, both of the individual and society, 'makes no part either of the gross or of the neat revenue of either' (p. 273).

To arrive at net revenue Smith also deducts the maintenance of 'circulating capital' – inventories of food, raw materials and semi-manufactured materials, and finished manufactures in the business sector at wholesale or retail:

> The gross revenue of all the inhabitants of a great country, comprehends the whole annual produce of their land and labour; the neat revenue, what remains free to them after deducting the expence of maintaining; first, their fixed; and, secondly, their circulating capital; or what, without encroaching upon their capital, they can place in their stock for immediate consumption, or spend upon their subsistence, conveniences, and amusements. Their real wealth too is in proportion, not to their gross, but to their neat revenue (p. 271).

This notion, familiar to modern readers, that inventories of finished goods (even at retail) must be allowed for before calculating net product, is unfortunately clouded by a contrary statement that follows, namely that 'though the whole expence of maintaining the fixed capital is ... necessarily excluded from the net revenue of the society, it is not the same with that of maintaining the circulating capital':

> Of the four parts of which this latter capital is composed, money, provisions, materials and finished work, the three last, it has already been observed [p. 266], are regularly withdrawn from it, and placed either in the fixed capital of the society, or in their stock reserved for immediate consumption. Whatever portion of those consumable goods is not employed in maintaining the former, goes all to the latter, and makes a part of the neat revenue of the society. The maintenance of those three parts of the circulating capital, therefore, withdraws no portion of the annual produce from the neat revenue of the society, besides what is necessary for maintaining the fixed capital (p. 272).

Here a contrast is drawn between the individual and society. To the merchant his inventory of final goods constitutes part of capital, only his profit representing net income. These same goods, however, which cannot 'be placed in [the merchant's] own stock reserved for immediate consumption ... may in that of other people, who, from a revenue derived from other funds ... regularly replace their value to him, together with its profits, without occasioning any diminution either of his capital or of theirs' (p. 273).

This apparent contradiction regarding the treatment of inventories in the aggregate seems to reflect a confusion between the actual commodities constituting the inventory which do represent the real counterpart of net revenue when acquired by labourers, capitalists or landlords; and the inventory itself which does not. For until sale to final consumers the production process remains incomplete – retailers as well as factory workers are 'producers' – so that inventories of finished goods, like inventories of raw materials, must be maintained intact before calculating net national product. As we have seen, in some of his formulations Smith appreciated this fact, which is also confirmed by an important declaration:

> To maintain and augment the stock which may be reserved for immediate consumption, is the sole end and purpose both of the fixed and circulating capitals. It is this stock which feeds, clothes, and lodges the people. Their riches or poverty depends upon the abundant or sparing supplies which those two capitals can afford to the stock reserved for immediate consumption (p. 267).

Setting aside the complexities, we may summarize the main outcome thus far: Smith's primary concern in defining net national product was to capture the value of consumer goods alone, rather than (as with us) the total value of all goods produced and sold including investment goods net of depreciation; at the same time, he certainly did not neglect the latter. The classification rejects mercantilist precedent by treating the wages of labour on a par with rent and profit as part of net national income. And it differs also from that of his physiocratic contemporaries for whom agricultural activity alone generates society's net income.

Here we note two particular characteristics of the accounting scheme relating to wages. First, even the wages of labour engaged in maintaining fixed capital intact fall within net income: 'The price of that labour may indeed make a part of it; as the workmen so employed may place the whole value of their wages in their stock reserved for immediate consumption' (p. 271). Secondly, only the wages of 'productive' labour or labour in the business sector supported by capital with an eye to profit – as distinct from 'unproductive' labour which is hired for direct satisfaction out of income as a form of consumption – are included in net income. The wages of unproductive labour constitute a transfer payment not an original income: 'a great part of the revenue arising from both the rent of land and profits of stock, is annually distributed ... in the wages and maintenance of menial servants, and other unproductive labourers' (p. 838). The fact that only productive labour can add value while service labour 'adds to the value of nothing' constitutes the rationale for the unfortunate choice of terminology (p. 314).

It is taken for granted that the capitalist sector produces only material goods, that is, goods which have the character of capital – the ability to yield a stream of future utilities even if only over a short period – as distinct from pure services which leave behind no lasting source of enjoyment. For all that, Smith recognized that services do yield utility: 'The distinction between productive and unproductive workers had nothing to do with whether the work yielded utility, as some neo-classicists have scornfully but erroneously asserted' (Lewis, 1954, 146–7). And, of course, Smith's 'unproductive' sector is much reduced compared with the physiocratic 'sterile' sector.

In the first two chapters of Book II of the *Wealth of Nations*, with which we have been concerned here, Smith was writing as a national income statistician concerned largely with welfare, rather than with the 'production function' or physical input–output relations. But in other contexts, Smith did address the relationship between productive factors and output, and then a view of circulating capital including not merchant stocks of all kinds but specifically wage goods and raw materials comes into its own (see above, p. 75).

7.3 The Savings Process

According to Smith's formulation of the savings process in Book II, iii, 'Of the Accumulation of Capital', 'what is annually saved is as regularly consumed as what is annually spent, and nearly in the same time too; but it is consumed by a different set of people' (p. 321). This suggests that saving never leads to any actual change in the stock of capital goods, since it is not apparently the machinery and structures created by capital goods labour which is 'saved' but rather the food, clothing and lodging – the wages goods – consumed by them. Yet we must keep in mind that Smith was not here attempting to describe the actual *outcome* of a process of saving, but rather the process itself. As for his appreciation of real saving – an actual expansion of the capital stock – there can be no doubt at all: 'But whatever industry might acquire, if parsimony did not save and store up, the capital would never be the greater'. This conception is later elaborated in an index of national 'prosperity or decay' contrasting with the mercantilists' balance of trade, namely 'the balance of the annual produce and consumption':

> If the exchangeable value of the annual produce ... exceeds that of the annual consumption, the capital of the society must annually increase

in proportion to this excess.... If the exchangeable value of the annual produce, on the contrary, fall short of the annual consumption, the capital of the society must annually decay in proportion to this deficiency (p. 464).

In a discussion of contemporary British experience Smith maintained that but for wartime diversion of funds to 'unproductive' employment, the real national capital stock would have expanded: 'More houses would have been built, more lands would have been improved...more manufactures would have been established, and those which had been established before would have been more extended' (p. 328). Finally, we note a suggestive distinction within consumption expenditure between non-durables and durables:

> The revenue of an individual may be spent, either in things which are consumed immediately, and in which one day's expence can neither alleviate nor support that of another; or it may be spent in things more durable, which can therefore be accumulated, and in which every day's expence may, as he chuses, either alleviate or support and heighten the effect of that of the following day (p. 329).

The intial outlay is said to involve, in the one case, the employment of 'a great number of menial servants' and, in the other, 'the setting to work masons, carpenters, upholsterers, mechanics, &c.' (pp. 329, 331). There is an obvious parallel between the process whereby durable consumer goods are produced, and that of true savings where labour is currently maintained for the purpose of adding to the stock of capital goods.

To conclude, while the savings process certainly involves the maintenance of capital goods workers – part of the 'productive' labour force – the outcome of the process is an addition to the real capital stock including both fixed and circulating capital. The chapter on accumulation (II, iii) is concerned with the process, particularly the proposition that no leakage from the income stream, no gap between planned savings and investment, is involved (see below, p. 241), and for this purpose it was not essential to emphasize the outcome itself.

Yet there are conceptual difficulties impeding the account of the process of saving. The distinction between *stock* and *flow* was not always clearly enough drawn in the *Wealth of Nations*. The very title of the work refers to a stock concept whereas Smith's concern, as defined in the initial paragraph of the introduction, is annual income. (Similarly, the wages fund theory involves dealing with a flow in terms of the fund that determines it.) The failure to make a clear-cut distinction is not perhaps surprising, for the mercantilist writers never emphasized *income* and the Physiocrats never emphasized *labour* as the source of income.

7.4   Aggregate Employment Capacity

In his chapter 'Of Money' (Book II, ii) Smith relates employment capacity – the aggregate demand for (productive) labour – to aggregate 'circulating' capital, as in the following passage, which emphasizes the insignificance of money from an employment perspective:

> When we compute the quantity of industry which the circulating capital of any country can employ, we must always have regard to those parts of it only, which consist in provisions, materials, and finished work: the other, which consists in money, and serves only to circulate those three, must always be deducted. In order to put industry into motion, three things are requisite; materials to work upon, tools to work with, and the wages or recompence for the sake of which the work is done. Money is neither a material to work upon, nor a tool to work with; and though the wages of the workmen are commonly paid to him in money, his real revenue, like that of other men, consists, not in the money, but in the money's worth; not in the metal pieces, but in what can be got for them (pp. 279–80).

To discuss aggregate employment capacity without ambiguity, however, we need to assume a constant real wage. Even so, Smith's formulation is too general, since part of circulating capital consists of finished commodities in the business sector to be sold to landlords and capitalists not to labour; it is only the 'wage fund' element that is relevant. To be yet more precise, employment capacity – assuming a given real wage – depends only on the part of circulating capital that comprises wages and not materials. After all, technical progress which raises output per man will necessitate increased materials per man yet will not raise employment capacity. Even with technology given, increasing returns to scale will imply higher materials per man so that the materials component rises faster than the wages component. Smith could therefore only relate employment capacity to circulating capital by assuming technology constant and constant returns to scale.

With these restrictions the relationship is still imprecise, should the breakdown of total capital vary between sectors. To relate employment capacity to circulating capital alone is not to deny a role for fixed capital in the production function (see above, p. 76). Fixed capital serves as the vehicle for the embodiment of technology, and given the ruling pattern of demand cannot be dispensed with; it is quite irrelevant that labour can be set to work to produce something or other provided the means of feeding and clothing are available. Any statement linking employment to *total* capital would thus imply either that the wage fund components are identical in all industries, or, if not, that the structure of the economy remains unchanged.

A chapter on 'Different Employments of Capital' (Book II, v), distinguishes the employment-supporting capacities of alternative investments by sector: 'Though all capitals are destined for the maintenance of productive labour only, yet the quantity of that labour, which equal capitals are capable of putting into motion, varies extremely according to the diversity of their employment; as does likewise the value which that employment adds to the annual produce of the land and labour of the country' (p. 341). The categorization is based explicitly on the fraction of total capital devoted to wages as distinct from materials as well as fixed capital.

Unfortunately the formulation is riddled with difficulties. For each £100 invested the retailer will directly employ very little productive labour, his profits alone constituting value added, since the bulk of his investment outlay merely replaces the capital of wholesale merchants, with their profits, from whom he purchases inventory (p. 343). The wholesale merchant, per £100, directly employs sailors and carriers, and replaces the capitals of farmers and manufacturers with their profits, the value added in his case amounting to the wages of transportation workers as well as the wholesaler's own profits. An investment of £100 by the manufacturer will be allocated partly to fixed capital, replacing with its profits the capitals of the machine-makers; and partly to the purchase of raw materials, replacing with profit the capitals of farmers. But in contrast to wholesale and retail trade 'a great part of it is always, either annually, or in a much shorter period, distributed among the different workmen whom he employs' (p. 344). Value added includes wages, and profits on the stock of wages, materials and fixed capital. 'It puts immediately into motion, therefore, a much greater quantity of productive labour, and adds a much greater value to the annual produce of the land and labour of the society, than an equal capital in the hands of any wholesale merchant'.

In all this Smith has focused upon the vertical structure in given productive processes. But the final consumer purchases a manufactured product at retail and that purchase implies employment at all previous stages; accordingly, given the pattern of industrial organization, the comparative labour employed directly per £100 by the retailer, the wholesale merchant and the manufacturer is irrelevant. Only where the pattern of final demand shifts from one commodity to another will employment capacities per £100 come into play, assuming differentials exist at one or more 'rungs' on the two vertical ladders. At one point Smith observes (regarding the passage of a particular weight of flax through the process of manufacture) that the weaver requires more capital than the spinner since he must 'replace the capital' of the spinner (the earlier manufacturer) as well as pay his own employees (p. 51). This observation is neither economically nor technically interesting.

The problems in Smith's exposition are compounded when we consider what he has to say about agriculture. The employment-generating capacity of agriculture heads his list, for several extraordinary reasons. Asserting that 'not only...labouring servants, but...labouring cattle, are productive labourers', and that 'nature labours along with man', Smith proposes both that more 'labour' is directly employed per £100 than in any other sector, and that because of the utilization of land the value added by the investment is greater than in any other sector: 'The capital employed in agriculture...not only puts into motion a greater quantity of productive labour than any equal capital employed in manufactures, but in proportion too to the quantity of productive labour which it employs, it adds a much greater value to the annual produce' (p. 345). 'Of all the ways in which a capital can be employed', Smith concluded, 'it is by far the most advantageous to the society'.

The issues involved here are unsound. Smith treats land as an efficient machine which raises productivity in agriculture and in agriculture only. Land scarcity as a necessary condition for the appearance of rent is neglected. We are back in the world of Physiocracy! To treat labouring cattle as labour is also rather odd; Smith had elsewhere more correctly categorized labouring cattle as fixed capital (p. 263).

There are other problems. Marx was to attribute to 'variable' (wage fund) capital alone the ability to generate surplus value. 'Constant' capital (machinery and materials) is merely replaced in the process of production (below, p. 362). It will be that sector with the highest variable:constant capital ratio which will generate (per £100) the greatest surplus value. Smith's Book II, v also uses the same classification – the value added per pound of investment will be the greatest in those sectors with the highest labour:capital ratios. Now since he maintained that profits are proportional to value added – 'The produce of industry is what it adds to the subject or materials upon which it is employed. In proportion as the value of this produce is great or small, so will likewise be the profits of the employer' (p. 423) – and recognized that profits are generated 'upon the whole stock of wages, materials, and instruments of trade employed in the business' (p. 344), the Marxian problem of profit rate equilazation (see chapter 15) makes an appearance. Those sectors with a relatively high fraction of wages in a given capital should, in principle, have a relatively high profit rate; and we must then explain the process whereby profit rates are equalized across the board.

7.5   The Secular Pattern of Factor Demand and Supply

The foregoing discussion of aggregate employment capacity assumed a given real wage; we were concerned with one point on a (static) labour–demand function. We will consider next the more complex issue of the growth of labour demand and the determination of the average wage rate in a dynamic context. This requires that we attend also to the determinants of labour supply, especially population growth.

Smith accords the rate of capital accumulation the status of 'independent' variable governing the growth rate of labour demand (see the passage cited above, p. 83). This, of course, will be rigorously true only if the 'wage fund' component of circulating capital grows in proportion to total capital, a rather restrictive assumption. To each growth rate of labour demand, Smith explains in 'Of the Wages of Labour' (Book I, viii), there corresponds a long-run real wage rate which assures an equivalent rate of growth of population and the work force: 'The liberal reward of labour, by enabling them to provide better for their children, and consequently to bring up a greater number, naturally tends to widen and extend those limits [to population expansion]. It deserves to be remarked too, that it necessarily does this as nearly as possible in the proportion which the demand for labour requires' (p. 80). An increase in the (long-run) wage rate will follow a change in the rate of capital accumulation; a steady rate of increase of capital will not alter the wage, although the higher that rate of increase the higher will be the wage: 'It is not ... in the richest countries, but in the most thriving, or in those which are growing rich the fastest, that the wages of labour are highest' (p. 69). Competitive market pressures assure that a wage diverging from the secular trend will be corrected – a relatively low wage being forced upwards by a kind of 'Walrasian' competitive process with a subsequent effect upon the growth rate of population:

> If this [secular] demand is continually increasing, the reward of labour must necessarily encourage in such a manner the marriage and multiplication of labourers, as may enable them to supply that continually increasing demand by a continually increasing population. If the reward should at any time be less than what was requisite for this purpose, the deficiency of hands would soon raise it; and if it should at any time be more, their excessive multiplication would soon lower it to this necessary rate. The market would be so much under-stocked with labour in the one case, and so much over-stocked with labour in the other, as would soon force back its price to that proper rate which the circumstances of the society required (p. 80).

Smith compared the slow growth of European populations with the very rapid increase in the North American colonies where population was apt to double in a generation, some 25 years. The notion of a doubling of population in a single generation as evidence of its *maximum* physiological capacity can be found earlier in the literature, as in David Hume's writings, and was later taken up by Malthus (who, in his *Essay on Population*, paid tribute to Smith), Ricardo and John Stuart Mill. On Smith's reading of the North American case, the particularly high marriage and birth rates – in addition to low infantile and general death rates – reflected the very high earnings available which rendered 'the value of children...the greatest of all encouragements to marriage' (p. 71); labour was so well paid that 'a numerous family of children, instead of being a burthen is a source of opulence and prosperity to the parents'.

Also conspicuous is the notion, at the other extreme of elasticity values, of a 'subsistence' wage at which population growth ceases, a 'Malthusian' notion applying specifically to 'the inferior ranks':

> Every species of animals naturally multiplies in proportion to the means of their subsistence, and no species can ever multiply beyond it. But in civilized society it is only among the inferior ranks of people that the scantiness of subsistence can set limits to the further multiplication of the human species; and it can do so in no other way than by destroying a great part of the children which their fruitful marriages produce (p. 79).

Smith attributed the contemporary increase in population to above-subsistence, and rising, wages. This trend reflected an increasing growth rate of aggregate labour demand, the population reaction operating largely through a fall in the infant mortality rate. For a low wage ('poverty') does not check either the marriage or the birth rates – on the contrary; but 'is extremely unfavourable to the rearing of children....Though [the] marriages [of the poor] are generally more fruitful than those of people of fashion, a smaller proportion of their children arrive at maturity' (p. 79).

We have seen in chapter 4 that an increase in 'the price of provisions' influences the money wage, even when the real wage initially exceeds the 'subsistence' level, to assure against a reduction in the growth rate of population (p. 85; cited above, p. 83). The same applies for the indirect taxation of wages, in which context Smith distinguished between 'necessaries' and 'luxuries':

> Any rise in the average price of necessaries, unless it is compensated by a proportionable rise in the wages of labour, must necessarily diminish more or less the ability of the poor to bring up numerous families, and consequently to supply the demand for useful labour; whatever may be

the state of that demand, whether increasing, stationary, or declining; or such as requires an increasing, stationary, or declining popula- tion.... Taxes upon luxuries are finally paid by the consumers of the com- modities taxed, without any retribution. They fall indifferently upon every species of revenue, the wages of labour, the profits of stock, and the rent of land (p. 824).

The operational definition of a 'necessity' is thus any commodity the consumption of which affects the infantile death rate, that is, acts on 'the ability of the poor to bring up numerous families'; variation in the con- sumption of luxuries will have no effect upon population growth via the mortality rate and for that reason will not generate a compensatory rise in money wages. In a gloss on the theorem Smith observed that a luxury tax may actually *encourage* labour supply to the extent that workers are induced thereby to substitute in favour of relatively cheaper (and healthier) 'necessaries':

The high price of such commodities [as liquor] does not necessarily diminish the ability of the inferior ranks of people to bring up families. Upon the sober and industrious poor, taxes upon such commodities act as sumptuary laws, and dispose them either to moderate, or to refrain altogether from the use of superfluities which they can no longer easily afford. Their ability to bring up families, in consequence of this forced frugality, instead of being diminished, is frequently, perhaps, increased by the tax (p. 823).

This gloss implies that the entire population mechanism applies only to the productive work force ('the sober and industrious'), since unproduc- tive workers, who are considered 'dissolute and disorderly', are likely to spend any increase in their purchasing power on commodities (such as liquor), scarcely favourable to the well-being of mother and child. Accordingly, the taxation of 'luxuries' would have no impact on the growth rate of unproductive labourers. Smith retained a 'mercantilist' attitude towards service labour.

Formally, the category of 'necessaries' is said to extend beyond com- modities 'indispensably necessary for the support of life' to 'whatever the custom of the country renders it indecent for creditable people, even of the lowest order, to be without.... All other things I call luxuries' (pp. 821–2). And in his account of the rising real wage trend during the eighteenth century, Smith included in the budget calculation 'many agreeable and convenient pieces of household furniture', observ- ing 'that the labouring poor will not now be contented with the same food, cloathing and lodging which satisfied them in former times' (p. 78). But if the taxation of items like 'agreeable furniture' generates a compensatory rise in the money wage, it cannot be by way of the infantile death rate since physiological well-being (albeit culturally determined) is not at stake. It must be by an adverse effect upon the marriage rate, a single man postponing marriage because of the reduced prospect of maintaining a family at a 'creditable' level of comfort.

It follows logically, if we accept Smith's general analytical frame of reference for the study of secular wages, that it is only intra-marginal labourers, those whose decisions regarding the vital ratios are un-affected by real income variation, who may purchase both 'luxuries' and 'necessaries'. The (long-run) basket of marginal groups – the real counterpart of the minimum supply price for any given rate of popula-tion growth – is limited to necessaries alone by the terms of the (opera-tional) definition of the categories.

A word on short-run labour supply. In his *Lectures on Jurisprudence* of 1766, Smith implied a backward-bending labour supply curve in the 'commercial' sector ([1978], 540). This is no longer true in the *Wealth of Nations*, where it is positively denied that effort will be reduced upon a wage increase. On the contrary, 'The liberal reward of labour, as it encourages the propagation, so it increases the industry of the common people' (p. 81). Smith had abandoned the mercantilist perspective on labour – at least on 'productive' labour.

*   *   *

Next let us turn to labour demand. Since the rate of capital accumula-tion governs the aggregate demand for labour – more specifically for productive labour – we need to know more about its determinants.

Economists (such as Schumpeter, 1934) who maintain that there would exist even in full stationary equilibrium – the 'stationary state' – a *net* return to produced productive factors, need to explain why a sur-plus can exist over and above the value of the land and labour (the 'original' factors) contained in the product. The value of capital goods should in the very long run be precisely equal to the original factors used up in producing them. To say that at any time there exists a certain complex of capital goods, so that the return can be accounted for on productivity and scarcity grounds, does not suffice, for with expansion of capital any net return is competed away. That is the 'dilemma of interest'.

The nineteenth-century classical solution was to say that capital constitutes a third ultimate productive factor, and is *permanently* con-strained by the real or 'pain' cost of foregoing present consump-tion – Nassau Senior (1836) coined the term 'abstinence'. On this view, savers respond positively to movements in the interest rate, while in full long-run equilibrium prices must suffice to yield a net minimum return to the owners of capital goods, to prevent them from eating into capital. Interest is a necessary payment in the same way that wages are a neces-sary payment, a reduction of either leading to a fall in factor supply.

Smith took a different view. He allowed a minimum supply-price of loanable funds, that is some return to capital which is necessary for loanable funds to be forthcoming (p. 96); but he denied that if interest fell below that level, the rate of savings would necessarily be adversely affected. Capitalists might choose to employ their savings personally rather than lend to borrowers with all the risks that that entails. Indeed, Smith believed that a fall in the return on capital might even stimulate accumulation: 'The demand for labour increases with the increase of stock whatever be its profits; and after these are diminished, stock may not only continue to increase, but to increase much faster than before.... A great stock, though with small profits, generally increases faster than a small stock with great profits' (p. 93). This is consistent with a forceful contrast between the weak 'passion for present enjoyment' and the powerful passion 'which prompts to save' (p. 324).

It is clear then that interest was not regarded by Smith as a 'necessary payment' in the way that it was later regarded by Senior and by Ricardo and J. S. Mill. Smith's position is closer to that of Marx who, making merry at the expense of Lord Rothschild, maintained that there is no need for an interest payment to induce people to abstain from present consumption. Moreover the implication is that in the stationary state the return to capital will fall to zero.

From his conception of capital supply conditions Smith deduced that – at least in a closed system – interest, like rent, was taxable without any fear of adverse repercussions on the aggregate supply of capital:

> The interest of money seems at first sight to be a subject equally capable of being taxed directly as the rent of land. Like the rent of land, it is a neat produce which remains after completely compensating the whole risk and trouble of employing the stock. As a tax upon the rent of land cannot raise rents...so...a tax upon the interest of money could not raise the rate of interest; the quantity of stock or money in the country, like the quantity of land, being supposed to remain the same after the tax as before it (p. 799).

The identification of interest with rent as a genuine 'surplus' income at the aggregate level of conception – in the sense of an economic rent – is a vital proposition when considered in historical perspective.

As for aggregate land supply conditions, we have a famous statement in the *Wealth of Nations* that 'rent, considered as the price paid for the use of land, is naturally the highest which the tenant can afford to pay in the actual circumstances of the land'; it is 'naturally a monopoly price' (pp. 144–5). Now the renting out of land in fact satisfied all the conditions of competition, but Smith was using the term 'monopoly', as was to be common in the nineteenth-century literature, to reflect the fact of land scarcity as such – its inelasticity of aggregate supply. We shall shortly see what role was ascribed to land scarcity in the growth process.

7.6 The Trend Path of Factor Returns

David Hume and other eighteenth-century economists maintained that in the process of growth of capital and population, the return on capital tends downwards (see above, p. 34). This theorem is repeated by Smith at the outset of Book I, ix 'Of the Profits of Stock', in terms of an increase in 'competition of capitals':

> The increase of stock, which raises wages, tends to lower profit. When the stocks of many rich merchants are turned into the same trade, their mutual competition naturally tends to lower its profit; and when there is a like increase of stock in all the different trades carried on in the same society, the same competition must produce the same effect in them all (p. 87).

Smith's rationale is riddled with difficulties. In the first place, on his own showing increased wages can be passed on to consumers in the manufacturing sector and to landowners in agriculture (see above, pp. 83–4). If the capitalists can thus avoid the incidence of increasing wages, why should profits be squeezed by rising wages during the course of growth? Secondly, the proposition that prices tend to fall as the number of firms in a single industry increases cannot be extended to the economy as a whole. As Ricardo later insisted – and as Smith himself in other contexts was well aware – a general expansion of output implies higher aggregate incomes and this carries with it the power to purchase the increased output flow (see below, p. 195). From this 'law of markets' perspective (see chapter 10) there can be no 'increase in competition' in commodity markets.

A more satisfactory account of the tendency of the profit rate to fall, more in line with a productivity approach to distribution, occurs in Book II. It entails the notion of an increasing (technological) paucity of investment opportunities: 'As capitals increase in any country, the profits which can be made by employing them necessarily diminish. It becomes gradually more and more difficult to find within the country a profitable method of employing any new capital' (p. 336). It is precisely in consequence of this drying up of opportunities that competition between capitals increases, 'the owner of one endeavouring to get possession of that employment which is occupied by another ... by dealing upon more reasonable terms. He must not only sell what he deals in somewhat cheaper, but in order to get it to sell he must sometimes too buy it dearer'. The only example given of diminishing investment opportunities (and this in Book I) entails diminishing returns in the agricultural sector – an aspect of land scarcity:

> High wages of labour and high profits of stock, however, are things, perhaps, which scarce ever go together, except in the peculiar circumstances of new colonies. A new colony must always for some time be more under-stocked in proportion to the extent of its territory, and more under-peopled in proportion to the extent of its stock, than the greater part of other countries. They have more land than they have stock to cultivate. What they have, therefore, is applied to the cultivation only of what is most fertile and most favourably situated, the land near the sea shore, and along the banks of navigable rivers. Such land too is frequently purchased at a price below the value even of its natural produce. Stock employed in the purchase and improvement of such lands must yield a very large profit, and consequently afford to pay a very large interest. Its rapid accumulation in so profitable an employment enables the planter to increase the number of his hands faster than he can find them in a new settlement. Those whom he can find, therefore, are very liberally rewarded. As the colony increases, the profits of stock gradually diminish. When the most fertile and best situated lands have been all occupied, less profit can be made by the cultivation of what is inferior both in soil and situation, and less interest can be afforded for the stock which is so employed (pp. 92–3).

The profit rate thus declines with increasing manifestations of land scarcity. What of the wage rate? 'The wages of labourers do not sink with the profits of stock' Smith proceeds. For, as we have seen, labour demand rises proportionately with capital which, notwithstanding the profit rate decline, 'may not only continue to increase, but to increase much faster than before' (see above, p. 161). The wage rate, therefore, continues upwards even after the profit rate decline has set in. Smith's growth perspective thus entails an initial stage of small capital and population relative to land when both the commodity wage and the profit rate are high, and a stage entailing expansion of capital and population during which the rate of profit falls but, because of an acceleration of accumulation, real wages rise.

The story does not, however, end here. Smith also defined a stationary state in which both capital and population are constant. For there is some minimum return on capital at which net accumulation comes to a halt – strictly, the interest component of the return should have fallen to zero – and some minimum wage (the subsistence wage) at which population ceases to grow:

> In a country which had acquired that full complement of riches which the nature of its soil and climate, and its situation with respect to other countries, allowed it to acquire; which could, therefore, advance no further, and which was not going backwards, both the wages of labour

and the profits of stock would probably be very low. In a country fully peopled in proportion to what either its territory could maintain or its stock employ, the competition for employment would necessarily be so great as to reduce the wages of labour to what was barely sufficient to keep up the number of labourers, and, the country being already fully peopled, that number could never be augmented. In a country fully stocked in proportion to all the business it had to transact, as great a quantity of stock would be emloyed in every particular branch as the nature and extent of the trade would admit. The competition, therefore, would every-where be as great, and consequently the ordinary profit as low as possible (pp. 94–5).

Clearly Smith's account of the growth process is incomplete, for there is no explanation of the transition from an accelerating stage to a decelerating stage of accumulation with its limit in zero growth of capital. Such a transition must occur, however, unless one supposes a precipitous collapse in the rate of investment as the return on capital nears its minimum. Moreover, without a decelerating growth rate of capital there is no reason for the wage to fall, as it must do for the subsistence level to be reached.

These technical problems relating to the growth process were subsequently taken up by Malthus and Ricardo. It was their great achievement to demonstrate how, in consequence of land scarcity, both the profit and the commodity wage rates decline to their respective minima. But a first step, involving recognition of the role of land scarcity, following the line already suggested by Cantillon and Steuart but extended to the implications thereof for the profit and wage rates, had been taken by Smith.

Many commentators, including Ricardo, failed to note Smith's view of land scarcity as the force ultimately responsible for the fall in the profit rate. For this Smith is himself partly at fault, as can be shown by considering some of the 'disturbing causes' which counter the tendency towards a fall in the profit rate. For among those disturbances he included 'the acquisitions of new branches of trade' in addition to 'the acquisitions of new territory':

> The acquisition of new territory, or of new branches of trade, may sometimes raise the profits of stock, and with them the interest of money, even in a country which is fast advancing in the acquisition of riches. The stock of the country not being sufficient for the whole accession of business, which such acquisitions present to the different people among whom it is divided, is applied to those particular branches only which afford the greatest profit. Part of what had before been employed in other trades, is necessarily withdrawn from them, and turned into some of the new and more profitable ones. In all those old trades, therefore, the competition

comes to be less than before. The market comes to be less fully supplied with many different sorts of goods. Their price necessarily rises more or less, and yields a greater profit to those who deal in them, who can, therefore, afford to borrow at a higher interest (p. 93).

The acquisition of new territory as a potential check to the downward trend in the profit rate creates no problem for the argument in terms of land scarcity. But the introduction of new branches of trade flies in the face of the law of markets to which Smith subscribed, and also diverts attention from land scarcity. To this we may add that Smith confounded investment in land purchase and investment in land cultivation, and also failed to trace out the implications of diminishing returns for cereal prices, the splendid statement of the phenomenon that he did provide applying solely to the fisheries (see above, p. 73).

There remains a further complexity. Smith was concerned that a cessation of accumulation would entail a wage rate reduced to the minimum of subsistence. For when, in the course of development, the minimum rate of return has been reached and net investment reduced to zero, there exists no upward pressure on wages. But the reduction of wages to subsistence did not *necessarily* require an actual expansion of population, reflecting the end-point of the growth process – the stationary state. Should there occur a temporary period of zero growth, the wage might be reduced to the minimum independently of any population expansion. For in static conditions the competitive labour market process breaks down; employers' associations – difficult to maintain in circumstances of rising labour demand as masters 'voluntarily break through the natural combination...not to raise wages' – take on renewed vigour in conditions of stagnation and are able to impose low wages, although no amount of bargaining strength could for long force real wages *below* the subsistence level if the work force is to be maintained (pp. 67–8). In this context, it is to 'common humanity' that Smith has recourse to explain why wages will not be reduced below subsistence (p. 71), confirming that it is the decision of the monopsonistically organized employers – rather than the population mechanism – which assures a floor to the real wage rate. Any situation wherein wages are thus *artificially* reduced to subsistence would not, however, be a permanent one, in that renewed net accumulation out of artificially maintained profits is likely. A 'permanent' stationary state will set in only in circumstances which preclude the further effective exercise of monopsony power, that is when population size is such that wages are at subsistence in consequence of the preceding phase of operation of the competitive mechanism in the labour market, ruling out all scope for the regeneration of profits. Smith's account of contemporary China (p. 71) illustrates such a situation.

7.7 Economic Development: Technical Progress

The analysis of the downward paths of the wage and profit rates implicitly assumes the absence of technological change counteracting land scarcity. Yet Smith had much to say on the sources of new technology, and it is appropriate to deal with this matter here, in the context of economic growth, although the mechanisms involve 'micro-economic' decision-making.

Smith, who devoted his very first chapter to the division of labour, did not introduce the notion; the splitting up of occupations and the development of specialized crafts was much discussed in his day. His true originality lies in the attempt to account for sub-division of labour within plants in terms of plant size and also raw material and seasonal characteristics, and for the dispersion of processes between plants in terms of industry size. In these respects Smith made a significant advance over earlier treatments of the subject. Secondly, more than any other predecessor and contemporary, he represented division of labour as the crucial factor in economic progress, both innovation and invention being to a considerable extent induced by it. The role of division of labour is emphasized particularly in the manufacturing sector: 'The perfection of manufacturing industry, it must be remembered, depends altogether upon the division of labour; and the degree to which the division of labour can be introduced into any manufacture, is necessarily regulated, it has already been shown [Book I, ii], by the extent of the market' (p. 645). Seasonal characteristics limited specialization in agriculture (p. 6).

Economic growth in the *Wealth of Nations* involves the introduction by firms of improved organization and new techniques based on newly developed knowledge; and also the introduction of techniques or organizational methods only profitable, or financially possible, at a larger scale of operation. We should not, however, attribute to Smith a clear-cut distinction between technical change strictly defined and scale economies, either internal or external, since the development of new technology is itself frequently represented as hinging on scale, as in the 'Introduction' to Book II:

> The person who employs his stock in maintaining labour, necessarily wishes to employ it in such a manner as to produce as great a quantity of work as possible. He endeavours, therefore, both to make among his workmen the most proper distribution of employment, and to furnish them with the best machines which he can either invent or afford to purchase. His abilities in both these respects are generally in proportion to the extent of his stock, or to the number of people whom it can employ (p. 260).

To these formal technological efforts must be added the costless contributions originating on the floor of the plant with specialist operators, so that until processes had become finely subdivided – also a result of large scale – an important source of new knowledge was unavailable (p. 9).

The flow of improvements, in Smith's accounts, is taken for granted in almost the same way that one may forecast, in particular industries, cost reductions due simply to the overcoming of indivisibilities at large scale. To this extent the element of risk is scarcely discernible at either the inventive or the innovative stages. Similarly, the development of new knowledge (invention) is not carefully distinguished from its actual application (innovation). There is no recognition, for example, of the 'inventive genius' as distinct from the 'entrepreneurial spirit'. Smithian 'innovation' should not, therefore, be identified with the Schumpeterian variety, which reflects the operations of a minority of creative leaders who undertake radical changes in process at substantial risk. The Smithian process of improvement is summarized in his discussion of the effects of demand expansion upon costs, where technical progress was seen to be an almost automatic and assured process engendered by competition (see above, p. 74). Note also the considerable attention paid to 'small savings and small gains' (pp. 364, 385).

But the full picture is rather more complex. The significance of scale for technology manifests itself very broadly. Thus, novel techniques available to a firm originate partly with suppliers of equipment and with full-time inventors, both sources turning on growing opportunities for specialization created by economy-wide expansion:

> All the improvements in machinery, however, have by no means been the inventions of those who had occasion to use the machines. Many improvements have been made by the ingenuity of the makers of the machines, when to make them became the business of a peculiar trade; and some by that of those who are called philosophers or men of speculation, whose trade it is not to do any thing, but to observe every thing; and who, upon that account, are often capable of combining together the powers of the most distant and dissimilar objects (p. 10).

In fact, while Smith recognized limits to what can be expected from simple sub-division of labour at the plant level – 'The man whose whole life is spent in performing a few simple operations ... generally becomes as stupid and ignorant as it is possible for a human creature to become' (p. 734) – he did not fear the exhaustion of sources of new technology considering the role of specialist inventors and machine-makers.

Costly innovatory investment undertaken with the prospect of extraordinary returns in the face of risk is also discussed upon occasion (p. 115). And despite a minimization of the potentialities of joint-stock organization on grounds of the typical negligence of management divorced from control by the owners, Smith was prepared to make qualifications. Thus if the undertaking required particularly heavy conscription of capital, there might be a case for the establishment of a joint-stock company, as with banks, insurance companies, canals and waterworks. It is also conceded that a joint-stock trading company might with justification be formed in the case of a new, risky and expensive venture which, if successful, might even be accorded a (temporary) monopoly: 'It is the easiest and most natural way in which the state can recompense them for hazarding a dangerous and expensive experiment, of which the public is afterwards to reap the benefit' (p. 712). These same grounds are offered in justification of patent and copyright protection. In his treatment of agricultural development Smith also recognized expense and risk attached to inventive activity, writing of the new commercial landowner as a 'bold undertaker' willing to make large innovatory expenditures. At least a certain range of inventive and innovative activity required costly investment and entailed a significant element of risk.

In many cases the new processes discussed by Smith involve the adoption of increasingly capital-intensive techniques devoted to reducing unit (labour) costs: 'The intention of the fixed capital is to increase the productive powers of labour, or to enable the same number of labourers to perform a much greater quantity of work' (p. 271). Their introduction is not formally explained in terms of a response to variations in wage rates. Rather wage rates are rising and labour-saving methods are introduced simultaneously, the same general cause – economic growth – being responsible for both phenomena. In his discussion of the effects of 'improvement' on costs Smith is clear that the secular trend of real prices is downwards – which would not be the case were the new technologies merely a response to wage increases – the increase in productivity more than balancing any coincidental increase in wages:

> The increase in the wages of labour necessarily increases the price of many commodities, by increasing that part of it which resolves itself into wages, and so far tends to diminish their consumption both at home and abroad. The same cause, however, which raises the wages of labour, the increase of stock, tends to increase its productive powers, and to make a smaller quantity of labour produce a greater quantity of work.... There are many commodities, therefore, which, in consequence of these improvements, come to be produced by so much less labour than before, that the increase of its price is more than compensated by the diminution of its quantity (p. 86).

It is the natural effect of improvement, however, to diminish gradually the real price of almost all manufactures. That of the manufacturing workmanship diminishes, perhaps, in all of them without exception. In consequence of better machinery, of greater dexterity, and of a more proper division and distribution of work, all of which are the natural effects of improvement, a much smaller quantity of labour becomes requisite for executing any particular piece of work; and though, in consequence of the flourishing circumstances of the society, the real price of labour should rise very considerably, yet the great diminution of the quantity will generally much more than compensate the greatest rise which can happen in the price (pp. 242–3).

In all this Smith takes it for granted that output expansion is essential for unit cost reductions; the optimum size of the average productive unit rises with industry expansion and encourages adoption of machinery. The question of 'reabsorption' of labour displaced at the original level of output never arises, because the firm's entire labour force is required at the higher level of production. Essentially, for Smith technical change was designed to raise the output obtainable per man in response to growing demand.

Apart from technical change that entails an increase in the capital–labour ratio, there are instances also where new technology economizes on the use of fixed capital:

all such improvements in mechanics, as enable the same number of work-men to perform an equal quantity of work with cheaper and simpler machinery than had been usual before, are always regarded as advantageous to every society. A certain quantity of materials, and the labour of a certain number of workmen, which had before been employed in supporting a more complex and expensive machinery, can afterwards be applied to augment the quantity of work which that or any other machinery is useful only for performing (p. 272).

Maintenance labour is thus displaced in the first instance, but subsequently reabsorbed into the operating functions. Smith does not explain adequately the mechanism by which such re-employment will become profitable or even possible, but is satisfied with the assumption of increased 'circulating capital':

The whole capital of the undertaker of every work is necessarily divided between his fixed and his circulating capital. While his whole capital remains the same, the smaller the one part, the greater must necessarily be the other. It is the circulating capital which furnishes the materials and wages of labour, and puts industry into motion. Every saving, therefore, in the expence of maintaining the fixed capital, which does not diminish the productive powers of labour, must increase the fund which puts industry into motion, and consequently the annual produce of land and labour, the real revenue of every society (p. 276).

But to rely upon the maintenance of circulating capital to assure re-employment – rather in the manner of Steuart (see above, p. 32) – is inadequate without specifying the technological relationship between operating labour and fixed capital which must be satisfied under the new conditions. (Smith merely remarks loosely that output would be expanded from 'that [the new equipment] or any other machinery'.) Again, it is apparent that he is assuming general expansion of demand.

There is a further noteworthy matter, relating to the apparent assumption that the materials required per unit of output are constant even when allowance is made for changes in technology – that new techniques are directed specifically at the labour input (see above, p. 76). It is now clear that the constancy of the materials coefficient applies only to operating functions, for technological improvements that simplify fixed capital allow savings both of maintenance labour and materials. Moreover, the assumption applies to materials of a given kind; there might occur changes in the nature or quality of the raw materials utilized.

It is sometimes argued that Smith overlooked a technological revolution proceeding under his nose. We must recognize his neglect of certain conspicuous developments in the cotton industry; and there is, though with important qualifications, an emphasis upon progressive improvement rather than risky innovation. But we cannot conclude that he failed to anticipate the 'industrial revolution'. His attention to the determinants of plant and industry organization, fixed capital and its maintenance, the differential factor-saving effects of technical change and the contributions to knowledge of specialist inventors and machine-makers, shows remarkable prescience.

7.8 Economic Development: Investment Priorities and Policy

The establishment of a hierarchy of sectors with respect to the employment-generating capacities of alternative investments (section 7.4 above) seems to conflict with the famous argument of the first book of the *Wealth of Nations* according to which an optimum allocation of resources is achieved when profit rates – subject to risk and non-monetary differentials – are everywhere equalized; for, in terms of employment, there would be less than the 'optimum' amount of investment in agriculture and manufacturing, and more than the optimum amount in foreign trade. But this is only an apparent difficulty. Despite appearances, Smith's analysis of development rests squarely upon the principles of allocation economics, so that the optimum pattern of investment at any stage of a country's development is not to be determined *a priori* according to a pre-established schedule of priorities.

There is a related matter. David Ricardo devoted a chapter of his *Principles* to countering Smith's seeming mercantilist-like championship in the discussion of employment-generating capacities, of a large total national income derived from a large population. Ricardo himself insisted that 'provided its net real income, its rent and profits be the same, it is of no importance whether the nation consists of ten or of twelve millions of inhabitants' (1951, I, 348). J. R. McCulloch similarly objected that 'the prosperity of a country is to be measured by the rate of profit which her capital yields, or (for it is the same thing) by her capacity of employing capital and labour to advantage, and not by the actual amount of her capital, or the number of her people' (1863, 159n.). We shall also consider the validity of this objection.

It is a basic Smithian proposition in Book II, 'Of the National Progress of Opulence', that, but for institutional distortions, capitalists will not invest in manufactures designed 'for distant sale' as long as agricultural resources remain unused. So what assures that before agriculture is 'fully developed' there will in fact be investment therein rather than in any other branch of activity – that the agricultural profit rate exceeds the (potential) rate in manufactures? The only reason given by Smith runs in terms of factor endowments and relative factor prices:

> In our North American colonies, where uncultivated land is still to be had upon easy terms, no manufactures for distant sale have ever yet been established in any of their towns. When an artificer has acquired a little more stock than is necessary for carrying on his own business in supplying the neighbouring country, he does not, in North America, attempt to establish with it a manufacture for more distant sale, but employs it in the purchase and improvement of uncultivated land...
>
> In countries, on the contrary, where there is either no uncultivated land, or none that can be had upon easy terms, every artificer who has acquired more stock than he can employ in the occasional jobs of the neighbourhood, endeavours to prepare work for more distant sale. The smith erects some sort of iron, the weaver some sort of linen or woollen manufactory (p. 359).

It is the market process governing the relative price of land which assures that, whilst land remains cheap, the profit rate in agriculture will exceed that in industry, so that investors will prefer the former.

Consistent with this viewpoint is the position of Book I, vi on the components of price that the 'more refined' the commodity, the greater is the quantitative importance of the labour and capital, compared with the natural resource, content: 'As any particular commodity comes to be more manufactured, that part of the price which resolves itself into wages and profit, comes to be greater in proportion to that which resolves itself into rent' (p. 51). Smith pointed to British regulations forbidding the establishment in the colonies of steel furnaces and slit-mills, namely advanced stages in the manufacture of iron, while encouraging the production of pig and bar iron, the preliminary stages of manufacture (p. 548). These and similar restrictions, although unjust, were of little practical relevance, because 'refined or more advanced' products were in any event unprofitable:

> Land is still so cheap, and, consequently, labour so dear among them, that they can import from the mother country, almost all the more refined or more advanced manufactures cheaper than they could make them for themselves. Though they had not, therefore, been prohibited from establishing such manufactures, yet in their present state of improvement, a regard to their own interest would, probably, have prevented them from doing so (p. 549).

Here, it is the relatively high price of labour which renders investment in advanced manufactures uneconomic. It followed that even the colonies might at some stage find manufacturing profitable: 'In a more advanced state [the British regulations] might be really oppressive and insupportable'. The rate of profit in agriculture would evidently tend to fall *relative* to that in manufactures as the growth in population led, on the one hand, to a growing scarcity of land, and a consequent increase in rents, and, on the other, to reduced wages.

It is revealing to consider this line of argument with Smith's demonstration of how the value returns generated by a community's given resources can be maximized by way of foreign trade. It is assumed that the organizers of economic activity will seek out the most advantageous use of resources, which, Smith presumed, will entail specialization on those products in which the community has an absolute cost advantage – contrasting with the later nineteenth-century 'comparative cost' approach (pp. 424–6). Now in a new country the peculiar advantage would lie in the production of farm produce, because of the large supply of cheap available land, while the advantage for Europe lay with manufactured produce because of the relative cheapness of labour and high cost of land:

> It is rather for the manufactured than for the raw produce of Europe, that the colony trade opens a new market. Agriculture is the proper business of all new colonies; a business which the cheapness of land renders more advantageous than any other. They abound, therefore, in the rude produce of land, and instead of importing it from other countries, they have generally a large surplus to export. In new colonies, agriculture either draws hands from all other employments, or keeps them from going to any other employment. There are few hands to spare for the necessary, and none for the ornamental manufactures. The greater part of the manu-

factures of both kinds, they find it cheaper to purchase of other countries than to make for themselves (p. 575).

Smith thus defines each country's 'advantage' in terms of its specific factor endowment – early 'Heckscher–Ohlin type reasoning.

The nature of the labour supply function is also pertinent. The Ricardo–McCulloch critique of Smith referred to above implicitly attributes to his account the existence of surplus labour, for only then would a redirection of activity towards labour-intensive sectors act to raise employment. Yet there is little to suggest that the contemporary economy, in Smith's view, was suffering from unemployment. In fact, the immediate objective of policy was not employment as such, but the maximization of the national income derived from a given fully employed labour force; and this would be achieved, runs the argument, by market processes.

The general policy objective was designed to assure as large as possible a disposable surplus available for savings and therefore the future expansion of the productive sector:

> The capital of all the individuals of a nation is increased in the same manner as that of a single individual, by their continually accumulating and adding to it whatever they save out of their income. It is likely to increase the fastest, therefore, when it is employed in the way that affords the greatest revenue to all the inhabitants of the country, as they will thus be enabled to make the greatest savings. But the revenue of all the inhabitants of the country is necessarily in proportion to the value of the annual produce of their land and labour (p. 347).

An increasing rate of accumulation entails upward pressure on the wage rate; and expansion of national income will occur by way of population growth not through the absorption of unemployed workers. Similarly, tax capacity is defined in terms of the total annual revenue: 'The riches, and so far as power depends upon riches, the power of every country, must always be in proportion to the value of its annual produce, the fund from which all taxes must ultimately be paid' (p.352). The impression from such passages may be that the nation's savings and tax capacity increases in proportion with aggregate population and the productive labour force as total net national income – which includes the wages of productive labour – increases. But this is not so. The disposable surplus includes rent and profits but only that part of wages exceeding subsistence: 'It must always be remembered ... that it is the luxurious and not the necessary expence of the inferior ranks of people that ought ever to be taxed' (p. 839). The point is that given a fully employed work force it is immaterial whether one speaks of the desirability of maximizing current net national income or that part only in excess of subsistence wages. Smith on the whole followed the former practice, without representing a large national income achieved by way of mere expansion of numbers (living at subsistence) as a relevant objective of policy.

It was Smith's position that the maximization of income, given population, would be achieved in the absence of governmental intervention. During the course of a rejection of the infant industry case for protection (proposed amongst others by Josiah Tucker and Sir James Steuart), he conceded that protection might permit the more rapid development of particular industries, but it would be at the cost of capital accumulation in the aggregate because of a failure to maximize the current national income: 'the immediate effect of every such regulation is to diminish its revenue, and what diminishes its revenue is certainly not very likely to augment its capital faster than it would have augmented of its own accord, had both capital and industry been left to find out their natural employments' (p. 425). From this perspective we can also appreciate why, despite the emphasis upon the differential employment-generating capacities of alternative investments, Smith explicitly asserted that 'no regulation of commerce can increase the quantity of industry in any society beyond what its capital can maintain' (p. 421). He can only have intended to question the ability of government to increase the national income – the earnings derived from the productive sector – by redirecting capital towards peculiarly labour-intensive industries, since it is probable that the productive labour force could thereby be increased as menial service workers are drawn in. The point is that any such intervention would only tend to reduce the national income (or more specifically national income per head) – the value of the output added in consequence of intervention falling short of the value of output sacrificed – and thus would lower the disposable surplus.

Why then the formal emphasis upon the employment-generating capacities of alternative investments? I surmise that this emphasis reflects Smith's particular policy objective, which was the removal of those governmental regulations responsible for prematurely diverting resources from agriculture. Even in Europe, he wrote, 'much good land still remains uncultivated, and the greater part of what is cultivated, is far from being improved to the degree of which it is capable. Agriculture, therefore, is almost every-where capable of absorbing a much greater capital than has ever yet been employed in it' (p. 355). A reallocation according to the principle of profit rate equalization would allow the expansion of employment in the productive sector consistently with an increase of national income. This argument should not be interpreted as a general recommendation for the expansion of the productive labour force by all means. Assuming an initial allocation reflecting the equality of profit rates, an artificially induced reallocation of a given capital stock from less to more labour-intensive sectors would only diminish national income despite any increase in the employment of productive labour at the expense of menial services. Expansion of national income would be assured only by capital accumulation financed at each period from the 'surplus', or net income in excess of subsistence.

7.9 Economic Development: Agriculture

Statements in the *Wealth of Nations* which suggest that the advantage of agricultural investment over any other lies in its ability to 'reproduce' not only profits and wages but a rent as well, without reference to factor endowment (see above, p. 156), are physiocratic residues which, fortunately, do not have serious consequences for Smithian applied economics. Indeed, Smith warned against physiocratic-type interventions on the ground that there can be too much agricultural investment as well as too little. This emerges clearly in the chapter on Physiocracy itself ('Of the Agricultural Systems', Book IV, ix).

Our general conclusion here may be further supported by reference to the role accorded agriculture in the growth process. An analysis similar to that of Sir James Steuart (see above, p. 35), whereby an agricultural surplus exceeding maintenance requirements within the agricultural sector is essential for the development of a domestic manufacturing sector, is outlined in the *Wealth of Nations* (pp. 163–4, 356, 635). But international trade divorced growth from strict dependence upon the availability of productive domestic agricultural resources. Smith went so far as to emphasize the peculiar advantages enjoyed by an economy enabled by its endowment to devote its resources largely to manufacturing and foreign commerce – an argument which, oddly enough, has mercantilist overtones:

> The one [a manufacturing country] exports what can subsist and accommodate but a very few, and imports the subsistence and accommodation of a great number. The other [an agricultural economy] exports the accommodation and subsistence of a great number, and imports that of a very few only. The inhabitants of the one must always enjoy a much greater quantity of subsistence than what their own lands, in the actual state of their cultivation, can afford. The inhabitants of the other must always enjoy a much smaller quantity (p. 642).

Nevertheless, in Smith's view the economy that enjoys extensive agricultural resources does possess an advantage over the economy that lacks them. As we know, he recommended that a 'landed nation' should not attempt to industrialize by artificial means; for the essential precondition for successful growth was the generation of adequate capital supplies which would be forthcoming more readily by concentration on the production of those commodities for which the resource endowment created a cost advantage. When conditions became suitable – in terms of factor endowment – manufactures would be set up 'naturally', and would be able to compete against those of an already well-established manufacturing economy, initially in the domestic market only, but subsequently even in foreign markets. This is because any initial disadvantage in skills would be only temporary, and also because of the presumed availability of (relatively) cheap domestic raw materials and food supplies (p. 635). All economies in the 'natural' course of development would initially devote their growing capital and labour resources to agriculture alone, and subsequently introduce and extend manufactures, but the more substantial and productive is the agricultural base the sounder will be the ability to proceed ultimately to the successful development of a manufacturing sector.

Smith thus adopted an optimistic view of the ability of an agricultural economy to overcome any initial disadvantage in the way of industrialization. Yet his comparisons are between economies with differential agricultural bases. It is not so clear that of two similarly based agricultural economies the latecomer would be in so fortunate a position to proceed successfully. Indeed, at various junctures Smith implies that it may be rather difficult for a latecomer to catch up in terms of ability to compete. In this respect he was on the side of James Oswald and Josiah Tucker against Hume who, in his essay 'Of the Balance of Trade' (1752d), maintained that the advanced economy would ultimately lose its initial advantage. Contemporary Britain was an 'opulent' economy with a splendid agricultural base and industrial potential, and ahead in the race. But it is relevant to inquire how the recommended policy of non-intervention would be justified from the viewpoint either of an economy with poor natural resources, or one which, though plentifully endowed, had entered the race late compared with other 'landed' nations.

There was only one cloud on the horizon from the point of view of the opulent and growing economy, namely the state of stationariness wherein there is neither motive nor ability for further expansion (see above, p. 163). Smith failed to justify the implicit assumption that technical knowledge would ultimately cease to grow. But in any event the matter was scarcely of immediate relevance, for 'perhaps no country has ever yet arrived at this degree of opulence' when free of faulty laws and institutions (p. 95).

7.10   Economic Development: the Place of Money

Smith also differed from Hume regarding other aspects of the development process. It had been Hume's position in 'Of Money' (1752b) that a developing country would find its initial cost advantages continually diminishing in consequence of a rising level of money wages and prices. Smith rejected this view – the price level was more likely to decline: 'gold and silver will naturally exchange for a greater quantity of subsistence in a rich than in a poor country, in a country which abounds with subsistence, than in one which is but indifferently supplied with it' (p. 189; cf. pp. 323–4). Indeed, it was a falling price level that encouraged the import of the precious metals required to finance the expanding GNP (see above, p. 82). There were no monetary tendencies checking the on-going process of development.

Hume had also contended that, although the absolute quantity of money is immaterial, there are advantages to an economy while its money supply is actually increasing – that 'the good policy of the magistrate consists only in keeping [the quantity of money], if possible, still increasing; because, by that means he keeps alive a spirit of industry in the nation, and increases the stock of labour, in which consists all real power and riches' (1752b, 39–40). But these advantages presume initial unemployment; thus, for example, exporters who receive payment in gold and silver 'are enabled to employ more workmen than formally, who never dream of demanding higher wages, but are glad of employment from such good paymasters' (p. 38). Smith was unimpressed, possibly because he assumed full use of capacity; he complained in his *Lectures on Jurisprudence* of 1766 that Hume seemed 'to have gone a little into the notion that public opulence consists in money' ([1978], 507). None the less, he did note a relationship between the money supply and 'real' growth. In discussing the probable outcome of a relaxation by Spain and Portugal of their restrictions against the exportation of metals he reasoned that a proportion of the metal outflow would be exchanged abroad for capital goods rather than consumer goods, since in the first instance, real income, and therefore consumption, will be little affected: 'A part of the dead stock of the society would thus be turned into active stock, and would put into motion a greater quantity of industry than had been employed before' (1776 [1937], 480).

There remains to note Smith's denial – along with Hume and Turgot and against Locke, Law and Montesquieu – that the secular fall in the interest rate could be explained in monetary terms (see above, pp. 33–4). Loans at interest were indeed 'made in money', but 'what the borrower really wants, and what the lender supplies him with, is not the money, but the money's worth, or the goods which it can purchase' (p. 334); and the interest rate falls as the stock to be lent (real loanable funds) increases because of the increasing paucity of investment opportunities, independent of the quantity of money in circulation.

Suggested Reading

* Smith (1776 [1937]) *An Inquiry into the Nature and Causes of the Wealth of Nations*, Book I, chs i–iii; Book II.

Spengler (1959–60) in Wood (1984), item 84, Spengler (1976) in Wood (1984), item 107, and Eltis (1984), ch. 3, treat Smith's growth theory in general. Bowley (1973) considers aspects of Smithian wage and profit theory in a chapter (ch. 6) covering the period from Cantillon to Mill; and Tucker (1960) devotes chapter 4 of his book on progress and profits to Smith. Smith on growth, with special reference to capital accumulation, technical change and investment priorities, is discussed in Hollander (1973), chs 6, 7 and 10 respectively. Rosenberg (1965) deals effectively with the division of labour. Rosenberg (1968) treats consumer tastes and growth, and Richardson (1975) the related topic of consumption and increasing returns.

Samuelson's now famous canonical classical model, which finds in the *Wealth of Nations* a consistent growth theory based on land scarcity, should be consulted (1978). This article generated an exchange between Hollander (1980) and Samuelson (1980).

For Smith's treatment of international trade in a development context, see Myint (1977), in Wood (1984), item 117.

8 Ricardo on Capital, Employment and Growth

8.1 Introduction

This chapter continues the main themes of our story, namely the determinants of employment capacity and the secular path of the factor returns. Economic development as such, which so much preoccupied Adam Smith, is of secondary importance in Ricardo's *Principles*.

In sections 8.2 and 8.3 the nature of capital-supply conditions is again taken up, now from Ricardo's perspective. Sections 8.4, 8.5 and 8.6 deal with aggregate employment capacity; here we discuss the notion that 'demand for commodities is not demand for labour' – the phrase is due to J. S. Mill – and the problem of 'machinery'. Aggregate labour supply is the subject of section 8.7. We will then be in a position to consider Ricardo's version of the secular path of wage and profit rates – a central classical concern (8.8). T. R. Malthus's approach to the same issue, reflecting a concern to encourage 'prudential' population control, follows conveniently next. The chapter closes with a brief note on Ricardo's position regarding the class shares in national income.

8.2 Capital and Surplus

Like Smith, Ricardo included in 'capital' stocks of various kinds, plant and equipment, implying a production function approach to output and employment capacity: 'The whole business, which the whole community can carry on, depends on the quantity of its capital, that is, of its raw material, machinery, food, vessels, &c. employed in production'

(Ricardo, 1951, I, 365).* Ricardo objected that James Mill had minimized the role of fixed capital: '"Excepting only that part comparatively small which is fixed in durable machinery". Can this part be called justly comparatively small? It consists not only of durable machinery but of ships, canals, roads, bridges, workshops &c.' (IX, 128). Now a distinction has recently been drawn between 'capital' in the sense of *physical goods* and capital as a *fund* that is indeed embodied in physical goods in various ways but is none the less something other than the goods themselves (Hicks, 1974, 309–10). According to Sir John Hicks, the 'fundist' rather than the 'materialist' conception may be ascribed to the classical school as a whole. The fundist conception of capital, although typically characteristic of trading practice, was easily extended to agriculture and manufacturing as long as stocks and work in progress constituted the overwhelming portion of physical assets; the fund of capital is 'turned over' by being used in the purchase of materials and the services of labour and replenished from the sale of product. After 1870, however, 'most economists, in England and in America, went Materialist.... Anyone, indeed, who uses a Production Function, in which Product is shown as a function of labour, capital and technology, supposed separable, confesses himself to be (at least while he is using it) a Materialist'. It will be clear from our citations from Ricardo – and our earlier discussion of Smith – that the 'materialist' or 'production function' perspective emerges in classical literature far more conspicuously than implied above.

The Ricardian production function differs from the modern by its inclusion of wage goods, although this is not the invariable practice. (The profit rate in the chapter 'On Profits', for example, is calculated on the basis of a capital stock valued at replacement cost which excludes wages.) The inclusion of wage goods reflects Smith's approach towards consumption by 'productive' labour – labourers employed by profit-seeking capitalist entrepreneurs. In Ricardo's terms:

> It must be understood that all the productions of a country are consumed; but it makes the greatest difference imaginable whether they are consumed by those who reproduce, or by those who do not reproduce another value. When we say that revenue is saved, and added to capital, what we mean is, that the portion of revenue, so said to be added to capital, is consumed by productive instead of unproductive labourers (I, 151n.).

By contrast, service workers are employed out of revenue in a final consumption transaction: 'commodities consumed by unproductive con-

*See above p. 86n.

sumers [menials, etc.] are given to them, not sold for an equivalent' (II, 424–5).

To take a production function approach to employment capacity requires that wage goods capital be on a par with 'machinery' in its relation with labour, which is the case only if the real wage is constant. This Ricardo appreciated, adding in 1821 that 'if the price of labour should rise so high, that notwithstanding the increase of capital, no more could be employed, I should say that such increase of capital would be still unproductively consumed' (I, 151n.).

The wages of labour in the business sector may also be appropriately treated as a 'cost' item when the aggregate source of saving and taxation is in question (rather than welfare), provided they contain no element of disposable 'surplus'. Ricardo became increasingly conscious that part of the 'net' income of society is in fact earned by labourers; the assumption that only profits and rent can be drawn upon for taxes or for savings was, Ricardo added in the third edition of 1821, 'expressed too strongly, as more is generally allotted to the labourer under the name of wages, than the absolutely necessary expenses of production. In that case a part of the net produce of the country is received by the labourer, and may be saved or expended by him; or it may enable him to contribute to the defence of the country' (p. 348n.). He was, however, imprecise about the definition of 'absolutely necessary expenses'. A reference to a labourer's wage 'sufficient to prompt him to the necessary exertions of his powers' (IX, 17) implies maintenance of the worker alone; but in keeping with Ricardo's general position, we may fairly attribute to him a definition of 'subsistence' broad enough to cover maintenance both of the workers and his family such that his replacement in the work force is assured, namely the 'natural' wage which suffices 'to enable the labourers, one with another, to subsist and to perpetuate their race, without either increase or diminution' (I, 93). We shall see that even this broader classification proves inadequate once the full process of growth is under investigation.

There is also discernible, largely in the context of value theory, a 'fundist' conception of capital, the fund distinguished from the assets which it represents: 'the wheat bought by a farmer to sow is comparatively a fixed capital to the wheat purchased by a baker to make it into loaves. One leaves it in the ground, and can obtain no return for a year; the other can get it ground into flour, sell it as bread to his customers, and have his capital free to renew the same, or commence any other employment in a week' (p. 53n.). The reference to corn seed as 'comparatively a fixed capital' is significant. Formally the categories 'fixed' and 'circulating' capital are classified in terms of durability, 'according as capital is rapidly perishable, and requires to be frequently reproduced, or is of slow consumption' (p. 52). But Ricardo was dissatisfied, 'for there are almost infinite degrees in the durability of capital' (p. 150), and proposed in 1821 that questions of fixed capital be reduced to 'the relative times that must elapse before the result of ... labour can be brought to market' (VIII, 180). The materialist dimension fades away once *time* comes to the fore in this manner.

8.3   Capital Supply Conditions

The fundist perspective on capital accords well with Ricardo's further observation in 1821 that 'besides compensating for the labour, the price of the commodity, must also compensate for the length of time that must elapse before it can be brought to market. All the exceptions to the general [labour theory] rule come under this one of time' (I, 193). Profits thus constitute a necessary payment to ensure that time-consuming processes are undertaken, the time element causing deviations of value from labour quantity by restricting appropriately the supply of those products requiring capitals which turn over relatively slowly. J. R. McCulloch, Ricardo's contemporary, understands him as viewing profit as 'a compensation for time, or for our forebearance in not having consumed the capital immediately' (IX, 366) – implying a pain cost later to be labelled 'abstinence'. Alfred Marshall later observed, approvingly, that 'it seems difficult to imagine how [Ricardo] could more strongly have emphasized the fact that Time or Waiting as well as Labour is an element of cost of production than by occupying his first chapter with this discussion' (1920, 816).

There are numerous statements suggesting a regular positive dependency of savings upon the rate of return on capital. As early as 1814 Ricardo noted that 'the temptation to save from revenue to augment capital is always in proportion to the rate of profits, and if from accumulation of capital profits and interest should fall very low indeed, at that point accumulation would nearly stop, because it would be almost without an object' (VI, 121). Similarly in the *Principles*: '[The] motive for accumulation will diminish with every diminution of profit, and will cease altogether when [capitalists'] profits are so low as not to afford them an adequate compensation for their trouble, and the risk which they must necessarily encounter in employing their capital productively' (I, 122).

An increase in the rate of profit was not, however, envisaged as a necessary condition for an increase of savings. An increase in the 'ability' to save – in terms of the purchasing power of net income – was at least as significant a determinant of increased savings as a rise in the rate of profits. Chapter 26 'On Gross and Net Revenue' relates saving capacity to net income; more specifically, foreign trade is said to act as an incentive to saving, despite constancy of the rate of profit, by raising the purchasing power of net income (pp. 131–2); and the principle plays a central role in the chapter 'On Machinery', added in 1821: 'As, however, the power of saving from revenue to add to capital, must depend on the efficiency of the net revenue, to satisfy the wants of the capitalist, it could not fail to follow from the reduction in the price of commodities consequent on the introduction of machinery, that with the same wants he would have increased means of saving – increased facility of transferring revenue into capital' (p. 390). It is not merely the capacity to save that is raised but also actual saving, for we read of 'the stimulus to savings from revenue, which such an abundant net produce will afford' (p. 392).

While at an early stage of development the return on capital and total profit are envisaged as varying inversely, the impact on saving pulling in different directions, the rate of return and total profit tend to fall together in a mature economy: 'after capital has accumulated to a large amount, and profits have fallen, the further accumulation diminishes the aggregate of profits' (p. 123). References that relate accumulation simply to 'profits' are therefore consistent with both the motive and the ability to save.

The various classes of income recipients have differential savings propensities. The propensity to save of landlords is lower than that of capitalists (p. 270); a transfer of income from capitalists to landlords, such as occurs in the Ricardian growth model, would thus reduce the rate of saving. As for labour, while part of wage income may constitute net revenue, labourers fail on the whole to utilize their capacity to save. Only in new settlements where wages are 'enormous' and 'may be considered as part of the profits of stock' were they 'frequently the foundation of new capital' (VI, 147).

It should be noted that logically if profits are the *only* source of savings (investment) and are saved (invested) in their entirety, the rate of accumulation – investment relative to capital stock – will coincide with the profit rate – profit relative to capital stock. If a fixed proportion of profits are saved, the rate of accumulation will be strictly proportional to the rate of profit. These results are not, however, required by Ricardo's argument.

8.4 'Demand for Commodities is not Demand for Labour'

In the classical world, the aggregate demand for labour rises with accumulation, engendering a positive effect upon the real wage, or employment, or both, depending on labour supply conditions. Accumulation entails a reduction in 'unproductive expenditure' – consumer goods spending: 'if I have a revenue of £2,000 … in the expenditure of which I necessarily employ labour. If I turn this revenue into capital, I at first employ the same labour as before, but productively instead of unproductively. This labour may be employed in making a machine.... Or the labour may be employed on the land [in producing wages goods]' (II, 234–5). (The terms 'productive' and 'unproductive' are here used to designate employment in the capital goods and consumer goods sector respectively.) In the first instance, the savings process involves increased demand for capital goods which is satisfied by a switch of labour from the consumer goods sector. The demand for labour rises only when the capital goods are, as it were, in place. This perspective, much amplified, was later labelled by J. S. Mill 'demand for commodities is not demand for labour'.

The same proposition applies to an increase in outlays on menial services financed by reduced luxury spending:

> If my revenue were 10,000 *l.*, the same quantity nearly of productive labour would be employed, whether I realised it in fine clothes and costly furniture, &c. &c. or in a quantity of food and clothing of the same value. If, however, I realised my revenue in the first set of commodities, no more labour would be *consequently* employed: – I should enjoy my furniture and my clothes, and there would be an end of them; but if I realised my revenue in food and clothing, and my desire was to employ menial servants, all those whom I could so employ with my revenue of 10,000 *l.*, or with the food and clothing which it would purchase, would be to be added to the former demand for labourers, and this addition would take place only because I chose this mode of expending my revenue. As the labourers, then, are interested in the demand for labour, they must naturally desire that as much of the revenue as possible should be diverted from expenditure on luxuries, to be expended in the support of menial servants (I, 393).

The altered pattern of expenditure from commodities to services generates an expansion of the wage goods sector; labourers displaced in the consumer goods sector are not simply reabsorbed in the service sector but are reabsorbed in expanding wage goods production to meet the consumption requirements of the (additional) service labour.

The proposition, which describes the manner in which the aggregate demand for labour and thus the aggregate wage bill (reflecting either higher average earnings or higher employment or both) is expanded, in no way conflicts with derived factor demand which concerns the individual capitalist's motivation in offering employment. Jevons's complaint (see above, p. 140) that capitalists are presumed to 'maintain and pay for labour whether or not there is a demand for the commodities produced' is unwarranted.

8.5   Accumulation in Conditions of Labour Scarcity

Ricardo devoted considerable attention to accumulation given labour supply:

> It is very easy to perceive why, when the capital of a country increases irregularly, wages should rise, whilst the price of corn remains stationary, or rises in a less proportion...and why, when the capital of a country diminishes, wages should fall whilst corn remains stationary, or falls in a much less proportion, and this too for a considerable time; the reason is, because labour is a commodity which cannot be increased and diminished at pleasure...; you cannot increase their number in one or two years when there is an increase of capital, nor can you rapidly diminish their number when capital is in a retrograde state; and, therefore, the number of hands increasing or diminishing slowly, whilst the funds for the maintenance of labour increase or diminish rapidly, there must be a considerable interval before the price of labour is exactly regulated by the price of corn and necessaries (I, 165).

The reference at the commencement of the passage to an irregular increase in capital is not accidental. Ricardo has restricted the problem to the impact of a once-and-for-all increase in the demand for labour (probably assuming wages to be initially at 'subsistence'); in the case of a regular and constant growth rate of capital and corresponding population expansion, there would be no reason for the wage rate to increase, as we shall see presently. Insistence upon a slow population response is also deliberate. It again contrasts with the reverse assumption in a discussion of on-going growth. This is a matter of deliberate methodological procedure rather than self-contradiction; speed of reaction depends on the issue.

Ricardo did not subscribe to the 'wages fund' theory in his account of market wage determination, if by the term 'wages fund' is meant a given stock of wage goods (largely food) on hand – no more and no less – at the outset of the production period. There is no emphasis on a technical inability to vary the food component; but, in any event, the wage bill includes items other than food which are in elastic supply to the labourer who, upon a wage increase, will 'purchase any commodities that may contribute to his enjoyments' (VIII, 96); indeed, there might simply occur a diversion of goods hitherto available for capitalists. The composition of the wage basket is determined solely by the labourer's taste patterns. Our concern now is the case of a constant population, but we can easily appreciate Ricardo's objection to Malthus's identification of the food supply with the demand for labour (see above, p. 89). Should the workers' 'amended condition' increase the marriage and birth rates then only will the demand for food rise – in place of workers' demand for luxuries – and the supply increase in response:

> If Mr. Malthus had merely said that with the facility of providing food, population will rapidly increase, because food is one of the most important objects of consumption, it would be impossible to differ with him; but he invariably insists that the increase of population, does not depend on the means which we possess of providing for it, or rather which the people themselves have of providing for it, or rather which the people themselves have of providing for their offspring, but on the previous provision of food which is laid up for them (II, 111).

The conceptual framework of an annual agricultural cycle governing the demand for labour was more characteristic of James Mill (1773–1836) – John Stuart's father. Ricardo was unhappy with this conception, and explained the response that should be given to those who feared excess commodity supplies in consequence of accumulation, a response which Mill failed to give because of his agricultural frame of reference:

> If every man was intent on saving, more food and necessaries (the materials which are chiefly employed in procuring labour), would be produced than could be consumed. The supply above the demand would produce such a glut, that with the increased quantity you could command no more labour than before ... [But in fact] during the period of very high wages, food and necessaries would not be produced in such quantities as to occasion a glut, for it would be the interest of the producer to produce such things as were in demand, and suited to the tastes of those who had high wages to expend (IX, 131; cf. I, 292–3).

Some of Ricardo's formulations, it is true, involve pre-accumulation of wage goods in which context, moreover, workers do not themselves enter commodity markets to exercise their demand for final goods (see below, p. 188). Yet no specific deductions are drawn from such formulations. Capitalists are simply envisaged as acting as 'proxy' for their employees, whose taste patterns must be satisfied to assure against excess demands or supplies in particular markets; and assuming that capitalist employers accurately estimate their employees' requirements, the pattern of resource allocation which results will be identical to that which would exist if workers themselves entered the commodity market directly. It is a conception designed solely for expository convenience; the full analysis entails expenditure by labour upon commodities out of money wages in the manner of all income recipients.

The reversion to a notion of pre-accumulated stocks of commodities for disbursement to labour may originate also in a faulty interpretation of the term 'circulating capital'. As noted already on several occasions, circulating capital is not a wage fund, but rather the stocks of materials, semi-finished and finished goods or the goods in process which are needed to maintain production. Ricardo's usual formulations of the process of accumulation in the presence of labour scarcity, since they do not involve the literal pre-accumulation of the labourer's consumables, are consistent with this more accurate conception.

Even in terms of the more meaningful conception of 'circulating capital', however, employers may still, in one important sense, be envisaged as 'advancing' wages. For they postpone present consumption when undertaking accumulation, and make available to labourers the wherewithal to purchase commodities before the process on which these workers are currently engaged is completed. Ricardo appears to have this in mind by his formulations of the savings process, although it is easy to see how inviting becomes the simplification of an actual pre-accumulated stock and an advance in physical terms. Moreover, the smooth operation of the process requires appropriate resource allocation to reflect the pattern of labourers' demand. The 'pipelines' must be full not only in appropriate volume but in composition, and for this to be assured decisions must have been made at an earlier stage. Again the time-consuming nature of production remains pertinent.

8.6 Accumulation and Employment Capacity: the Problem of Machinery

We now turn to accumulation where there is no initial labour shortage, taking the limiting case of an infinitely elastic labour supply at some real wage rate. In this case reduced luxury expenditure out of profit income finances an expansion of real capital goods (as well as workers' consumables) to support additional workers.

In the event of strict technological complementarity between labour and fixed capital any expansion of the employed work force implies a proportionate expansion of fixed capital. Moreover, given the real wage, the aggregate wage bill also rises proportionately. Thus a doubling of employment under these conditions can only be accomplished if aggregate capital and both its constituents are doubled. But in fact Ricardo did not consistently assume strict factor complementarity. The possibility of substitution against labour is recognized in the secular context as a reaction to the rising real cost of producing wage goods:

> With every increase of capital and population, food will generally rise, on account of its being more difficult to produce. The consequence of a rise of food will be a rise of wages, and every rise of wages will have a tendency to determine the saved capital in a greater proportion than

before to the employment of machinery. Machinery and labour are in constant competition, and the former can frequently not be employed until labour rises.

In America and many other countries, where the food of man is easily provided, there is not nearly such great temptation to employ machinery as in England, where food is high, and costs much labour for its production. The same cause that raises labour, does not raise the value of machines, and, therefore, with every augmentation of capital, a greater proportion of it is employed on machinery (I, 395).

In consequence, 'the demand for labour will continue to increase with an increase of capital, but not in proportion to its increase; the ratio will necessarily be a diminishing ratio'. In this context 'the demand for labour' clearly refers to employment capacity at the going real wage. Allowing for substitution, the growth of employment capacity, and thus the wage bill, lags behind that of aggregate capital.

We are now in a position to appreciate Ricardo's repeated insistence in opposition to Malthus that it is impossible to conceive of a simultaneous excess of 'capital' and of labour: 'To say that I have a very abundant capital is to say that I have a great demand for labour. To say that there is a great abundance of labour, is to say that there is not an adequate capital to employ it' (II, 241). The point is the expansion of employment capacity with accumulation; redundancy of both capital and labour implies that employment potential is under-utilized despite the availability of labour, which Ricardo considered incomprehensible on grounds of the law of markets (see chapter 10).

*   *   *

That labour demand may not expand proportionately with capital is far less serious than would be an actual reduction in demand given the capital stock. The concept of exogenous (non-induced) technical change which reduces employment capacity constitutes the novelty of the chapter 'On Machinery' added in 1821. In a famous arithmetical example, which runs along wages fund lines, Ricardo considered a case where part of the work force hitherto engaged in the production of necessaries is directed to the production of a machine. Though aggregate capital remains unchanged, its distribution is altered to the detriment of the wages fund and employment capacity. (Steuart had touched on the problem earlier; while Adam Smith had envisaged the reverse case of economies in machine maintenance which permitted an increase in circulating capital; above pp. 169–70.) It must be stressed that the fall in employment capacity after installation of the new machinery is not the true problem. Ricardo's fundamental concern was that the conversion programme might be profitable – yielding, once the machinery is installed, a (roughly) unchanged net return on total capital – even though the gross yield declines, a possibility arising from the fact that machinery need not be entirely replaced in as short a period as circulating capital:

> My mistake arose from the exposition, that whenever the net income of a society increased, its gross income would also increase; I now, however, see reason to be satisfied that the one fund, from which landlords and capitalists derive their revenue, may increase, while the other, that upon which the labouring class mainly depend, may diminish, and therefore it follows, if I am right, that the same cause which may increase the net revenue of the country, may at the same time render the population redundant, and deteriorate the condition of the labourer...
>
> In this case, then, although the net produce will not be diminished in value, although its power of purchasing commodities may be greatly increased, the gross produce will have fallen from a value of 15,000 *l.* to a value of 7500 *l.*, and as the power of supporting a population, and employing labour, depends always on the gross produce of a nation, and not on its net produce, there will necessarily be a diminution in the demand for labour, population will become redundant, and the situation of the labouring classes will be that of distress and poverty (I, 388–90).

Table 8.1 Summary of Ricardo's illustrative data

	Wages fund (£)	Fixed capital (£)	Gross product (£)	Net product (£)
Original situation	13,000	0	15,000	2000
After conversion programme	5500	7500	7500	2000

The argument proceeds on the assumption of a constant real wage. But Ricardo was less concerned with technological unemployment than to show in general terms 'that the opinion entertained by the labouring class, that the employment of machinery is frequently detrimental to their interests, is not founded on prejudice and error, but is conformable to the correct principles of political economy' (p. 392). This objective would be satisfied even if the impact was upon wages rather than employment: 'Labour will fall because there will be a diminished demand for it', he explained in a letter (VIII, 399).

Unfortunately Ricardo made no concerted efforts to justify the supposition relating to 'output-reducing' technology. Because a lower output may suffice to cover costs in the machine-using process and yet yield the going rate of return, it is presumed that techniques actually do exist of this kind. More generally, there is no satisfactory account of how precisely the first introduction of the new technology occurs and spreads through the industry. This is particularly serious, since Ricardo takes for granted that the new process is cost- and (therefore) price-reducing, which implies the ultimate expansion of industry output.

That Ricardo was not satisfied with the basic model is suggested by his concession that it was only devised as a parable for pedagogic purposes: 'The case which I have supposed, is the most simple that I could select; but it would make no difference in the result, if we supposed that the machinery was applied to the trade of any manu-facturer, – that of a clothier, for example, or of a cotton manufacturer' (pp. 390–1). In this extension the fall in the wage fund is not a direct consequence of the conversion; rather, employment in cloth manufac-ture declines in consequence of 'output-reducing' machinery, and as a result, expenditure by workers on wage goods declines: 'the demand for labour would diminish, and the commodities necessary to the support of labour would not be produced in the same abundance'. Thus the level of agricultural activity is set by the pressure of labourers' con-sumption which in turn is governed by the level of employment. But this is still not quite the whole story. Agricultural capital is not left unused but is transferred to the cloth industry to satisfy the demand for cloth:

> the clothier would not want the food and clothing, having fewer men to employ and having less cloth to dispose of. The farmers and others, who only produced necessaries as means to an end, could no longer obtain cloth by such an application of their capitals, and, therefore, they would either themselves employ their capitals in producing cloth, or would lend them to others, in order that the commodity really wanted might be furnished; and that for which no one had the means of paying, or for which there was no demand [food], might cease to be produced.

It appears, therefore, that in the final analysis, allowing for an inflow of capital (and presumably labour) from agriculture to cloth-making, the output of cloth may rise (which would help explain the supposed reduc-tion in the price of cloth); it is employment capacity in the economy as a whole that has been reduced. Before the House of Commons Ricardo was careful to explain that his fears regarding machinery related to industry as a whole: 'his proposition was, not that the use of machinery was prejudicial to persons employed in one particular manufacture, but to the working classes generally. It was the means of throwing additional labour into the market, and thus the demand for labour, generally, was diminished' (V, 303).

Yet despite all the new attention given to the dangers of machinery, Ricardo was optimistic. He had painted the worst possible picture: 'To elucidate the principle, I have been supposing, that improved machinery is *suddenly* discovered, and extensively used; but the truth is, that these discoveries are gradual, and rather operate in determining the employment of the capital which is saved and accumulated, than in diverting capital from its actual employment' (I, 395). Even in the case involving absolute reduction in employment capacity, there would be some stimulus given to the employment of menial servants and to net accumulation by the rising purchasing power of unchanged nominal profits:

> As, however, the power of saving from revenue to add to capital, must depend on the efficiency of the net revenue, to satisfy the wants of the capitalist, it could not fail to follow from the reduction in the price of commodities consequent on the introduction of machinery, that with the same wants he would have increased means of saving – increased facility of transferring revenue into capital. But with every increase of capital he would employ more labourers; and, therefore, a portion of the people thrown out of work in the first instance, would be subsequently employed (p. 390).

Here we see that the fall in value (real costs) and prices due to new technology is an essential part of the story.

Of course, machinery need not be output-reducing. In that case, although labour would be initially displaced, total income would be unchanged, the net constituent rising appropriately. And here we may apply the proposition that 'demand for commodities is not demand for labour': if the increased net income (profit) is devoted to consumption, then resources will flow from the production of wage goods, the demand for which has fallen, to the luxury sector where the demand has increased, but the displaced labour remains unemployed at the going wage. If, however, capitalists chose to employ menial servants or to save out of their higher incomes, the displaced labour would be reabsorbed:

> if the increased production, in consequence of the employment of machinery, was so great as to afford, in the shape of net produce, as great a quantity of food and necessaries as existed before in the form of gross produce, there would be the same ability to employ the whole population, and, therefore, there would not necessarily be any redundancy of people.

8.7 Labour Supply Conditions

It is time to look more closely at labour supply conditions and set aside some of the restrictive assumptions – either a given population or a given wage rate – which were so convenient when considering labour demand alone. First we will consider the 'natural' or 'subsistence' wage rate.

The cultural determinants of the subsistence wage are much emphasized by Ricardo, as they had been by Smith, as is clear from a passage written under the influence of Robert Torrens:

> It is not to be understood that the natural price of labour, estimated even in food and necessaries, is absolutely fixed and constant. It varies at different times in the same country, and very materially differs in different countries. It essentially depends on the habits and customs of the people. An English labourer would consider his wages under their natural rate, and too scanty to support a family, if they enabled him to purchase no other food than potatoes, and to live in no better habitation than a mud cabin; yet these moderate demands of nature are often deemed sufficient in countries where 'man's life is cheap', and his wants easily satisfied. Many of the conveniences now enjoyed in an English cottage, would have been thought luxuries at an earlier period of our history (I, 96–7).

This passage alludes to the effects of below-subsistence earnings on the marriage rate, and in general Ricardo placed somewhat more emphasis than did Smith upon the marriage rate. This emerges in the accounts of the 'short-run' period during which real earnings exceed subsistence; for example: 'The amended condition of the labourer, in consequence of the increased value which is paid him, does not necessarily oblige him to marry and take upon himself the charge of a family... yet so great are the delights of domestic society, that in practice it is invariably found that an increase of population follows the amended condition of the labourer' (pp. 406–7). The decision relating to age of marriage hinges on the expectations of a single man regarding his ability to maintain a family at the customary 'adequate' living standard out of future wages earned as a married man, rather than on the ability to accumulate savings (or consumer durables) out of current earnings in preparation for marriage. That the adjustment also entails variations in the (infantile) death rate is implied in other contexts: 'It is when the market price exceeds its natural price, that the condition of the labourer is flourishing and happy, that he has it in his power to command a greater proportion of the necessaries and enjoyments of life, and therefore to rear a healthy and numerous family' (p. 94).

Ricardo's wage taxation theorems can be interpreted as applying to the case where the subsistence wage rules:

> A tax... on raw produce, and on the necessaries of the labourer, would... raise wages. From the effect of the principle of population on the increase of mankind, wages of the lowest kind never continue much above that rate which nature and habit demand for the support of the labourers. This class is never able to bear any considerable proportion of

taxation; and, consequently, if they had to pay 8 s. per quarter in addition for wheat and in some smaller proportion for other necessaries, they would not be able to subsist on the same wages as before, and to keep up the race of labourers. Wages would inevitably and necessarily rise; and in proportion as they rose, profits would fall (p. 159).

But, as with Smith, the wage taxation theorems do not stand or fall with the subsistence assumption. In discussing the impact on money wages of the taxation of necessaries, Ricardo specified carefully that the 'rate of progression' of labour demand is taken for granted, the analysis applying whether or not wages are at 'subsistence': 'Those who maintain that it is the price of necessaries which regulates the price of labour, always allowing for the particular state of progression in which the society may be, seem to have conceded too readily, that a rise or fall in the price of necessaries will be very slowly succeeded by a rise or fall of wages' (p. 161). Similarly, the chapter 'On Taxation of Wages' is based upon Smith's proposition that 'the demand for labour, according as it happens to be either increasing, stationary, or declining, or to require an increasing, stationary, or declining population, regulates the subsistence of the labourer, and determines in what degree it shall be either liberal, moderate, or scanty' (cited, p. 214).

That Ricardo should have proceeded in the chapter 'On Wages' and in other contexts on the assumption of a subsistence wage rate is not difficult to appreciate. It is another instance of simplification for pedagogic purposes. The broader application of the taxation theorems means simply that the mechanism of population adjustment to wages pushed below the 'subsistence' rate must now be applied to wage deviations from a labour supply curve relating the wage rate to the growth rate of population. Strictly speaking, it is only 'marginal' workers whose decisions affect the population growth rate and who consume 'necessaries' alone. (The latter category may still be defined as 'food, necessaries, and conveniences become essential from habit', but the magnitude of the wage basket must be specified anew for each growth rate of population.)

Ricardo's position, as outlined thus far, is precisely that of Smith (and Malthus). The rate of capital accumulation acts as an 'independent variable' which determines what the commodity wage rate must be to guarantee an equivalent growth rate of population. Any disturbance which raises the price of the wage goods consumed by 'marginal' groups of labourers necessitates an appropriate monetary compensation to assure that the growth rate of population is not impeded. The 'natural' wage, accordingly, corresponds to zero net accumulation, while to each positive growth rate of capital there will correspond a higher real-wage rate to assure the equivalent growth rate of labour supply. A 'high' rate of accumulation entails a 'high' wage rate; while an acceleration of the rate of accumulation generates an increase in the wage rate.

The basis for Ricardo's prediction of rising money wages in consequence of wage taxation lies in the proposition that at a reduced commodity wage the population growth rate falls behind the capital growth rate; money (and thus real) wages are pulled up by market pressures to check the deceleration of population growth. The process ends when the (net) wage is at its previous level and the population growth rate therefore restored. The full process is, however, sometimes short-circuited by Ricardo. Thus he sometimes reasoned as if employers forecast the impact of a fall in the net commodity wage on the growth rate of labour supply and short-circuit the otherwise lengthy adjustment process: 'The value of things', he wrote, 'I believe to be influenced not by immediate supply and demand only, but also by contingent [expected] supply and demand' (VIII, 196).

The assumption that the rate of capital accumulation is an independent variable – unaffected say by a reduction in profits corresponding to an increase in money wages – is no more than a first approximation. For a reduction in profits would probably have some effect on accumulation so that the compensatory increase in money wages in consequence of taxation would not entirely prevent a fall in real wages (I, 221–2). In this context we encounter a striking passage which identifies the final result of the taxation of profits and the taxation of wages. The direct or the indirect effect of profit taxation is to reduce the rate of accumulation so that the burden is shared:

> excepting in the immediate effects, I should think it of little importance whether the profits of stock, or the wages of labour, were taxed. By taxing the profits of stock, you would probably alter the rate at which the funds for the maintenance of labour increase, and wages would be disproportioned to the state of that fund, by being too high. By taxing wages, the reward paid to the labourer would also be disproportioned to the state of that fund, by being too low. In the one case by a fall, and in the other by a rise in money wages, the natural equilibrium between profits and wages would be restored (p. 226).

This reads much like Turgot (see above, pp. 54–5), although Turgot probably had in mind the limiting case of subsistence wages.

8.8   The Secular Pattern of the Wage and Profit Rates

We turn next to the secular paths of the wage and profit rates, perhaps Ricardo's primary analytical concern apart from the inverse wage–profit relation itself. The major weakness in Adam Smith's position on this issue, in so far as it turns on land scarcity, will be recalled (above, p. 164) – the failure to explain the downward path of wages from the above-subsistence (even rising) levels of a growing system, to the subsistence level which applies in the stationary state. There is no evidence that Ricardo saw the problem quite like this; he was in fact unaware of the role of diminishing returns in Smith's work. But looking backwards, and considering the problem technically, the matter can be represented in this light, as an instance of analytical progress.

Ricardo's procedure in the *Essay on Profits* (1815) is pertinent by way of introduction. In the construction of a famous table in this pamphlet Ricardo assumed a constant commodity wage (as well as unchanged technology) at an above-subsistence level. He explained why: 'We will...suppose that no improvements take place in agriculture, and that capital and population advance in the proper proportion, so that the real wages of labour, continue uniformly the same;...that we may know what peculiar effects are to be ascribed to the growth of capital, the increase of population, and the extension of cultivation, to the more remote, and less fertile land' (IV, 12). Ricardo thus consciously restricted the analysis of growth. He followed much the same practice in chapter 21 of the *Principles* on the 'Effects of Accumulation on Profits and Interest'. This chapter refutes Smith's increasing 'competition of capitals', which specified labour shortage and (by implication) inadequate aggregate demand as causal influences upon the profit rate (see above, p. 162). For Ricardo, labour shortage is not the issue in the growth context, while Say's Law ruled out downward pressure on commodity prices and profits. The profit rate falls rather because the real cost of a constant wage basket rises with land scarcity:

> From the account which has been given of the profits of stock, it will appear, that no accumulation of capital will permanently lower profits, unless there be some permanent cause for the rise of wages. If the funds for the maintenance of labour were doubled, trebled, or quadrupled, there would not long be any difficulty in procuring the requisite number of hands, to be employed by those funds.... If the necessaries of the workman could be constantly increased with the same facility, there could be no permanent alteration in the rate of profits or wages, to whatever amount capital might be accumulated....There cannot...be accumulated in a country any amount of capital which cannot be employed productively, until wages rise so high in consequence of the rise of necessaries, and so little consequently remains for the profits of stock, that the motive for accumulation ceases (I, 289–90).

The assumption of long-run constant commodity wages does *not*, however, represent Ricardo's full position. This becomes clear when we turn from the 'statement of principle' to the actual analysis of the growth process presumed to occur through historical time (subject, of course, to the assumption of unchanged technology) given in the chapter 'On Wages'. The outcome of the growth process is a downward path of wages and of the return on capital until the 'subsistence' level is reached where the growth rates of population and of capital are both reduced to zero – the stationary state. As we shall see, Ricardo also allows for the possibility of constant wages at early stages of development and even of an initial upward trend. This pattern does not accord with certain well-known interpretations which ascribe to Ricardo a constant growth path of wages at the 'natural' or subsistence level. It is worth mentioning also that this pattern is consistent with that of the earlier *Essay on Profits* where the declining profit rate in the full analysis is not dependent on constant corn wages.

The key features of Ricardo's fully fledged growth model are land scarcity manifested in diminishing agricultural returns, at least beyond a certain labour:land ratio; a positive relation between the return on capital (r) and the capital growth rate (g_k) – implying a negative relation between the commodity wage (w) and g_k; and a positive relation between the commodity wage and the population growth rate (g_L) up to some maximum capacity $(\bar{g}_L)$. The model lends itself to a simple geometric formulation.

For simplicity, we measure wages in commodity terms, and proceed *as if* wage goods are a single good. We neglect fixed capital. Panel A in the diagrams that follow portrays the marginal product curve generated by variable labour on given land (MM'). HH' depicts the maximum wage, w_{max}, that is obtainable when the minimum feasible return on capital (the return that reduces g_k to zero) rules. This minimum return we shall refer to as r^*; HH' is thus the marginal product curve 'discounted' by r^*.

In formal terms, the wage per worker, w, plus profits per worker, rw (in circulating capital models where wages are paid one period in advance of the sale of the product), exhausts the marginal product of labour, $F'(L)$, so that:

$$w + rw = F'(L)$$

and therefore:

$$w = \frac{F'(L)}{1 + r}$$

With w_{max} the wage such that $r = r^* > 0$, then:

$$w_{max} = \frac{F'(L)}{1 + r^*}$$

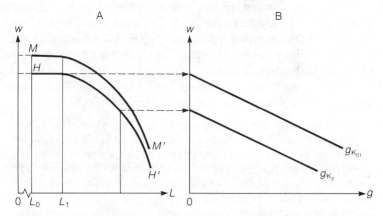

MM' represents the marginal product curve, F'(L); and HH' represents F'(L)/(1+r*).
Thus at population size such that F'(L)=10 units, the corresponding value on HH'
will be 9.70 assuming r*=3%; with F'(L)=1, the corresponding HH' value will be 0.97.
  For each L, read off the value on HH' to yield intercept in B such that $g_K=0$.
For each given MP value g_K rises as w falls. For each w in B the relevant g_K is read off
the family of curves, g_K falling as MP declines along MM'.

Figure 8.1   The derivation of g_k-w.

Panel B portrays the wage on the vertical axis and both g_k and g_L, the rates of growth of capital and labour, on the horizontal axis. The g_k-w relationship it depicts is derived from panel A in the following manner: (1) For any (absolute) labour supply, HH' indicates the wage (w_{max}) such that $r=r*$ and therefore $g_k=0$. A lower wage at that marginal product corresponding to the assumed labour supply will be associated with a higher r and therefore a higher g_k; for we know that Ricardo maintained that the rate of return on capital acts as a motive to accumulation (see above, p. 182). A positive g_k-r relation corresponds to a negative g_k-w relation, the curve emanating from the y axis at the appropriate level given by the height of HH'. (2) At the same time, at any given w (with labour supply increasing in A) a declining marginal product implies a decline in r and thus in g_k, and this effect of a declining marginal product at a given wage will be reflected by a continual inward shift of the g_k-w function in panel B.

So much for the framework of analysis. Now to the substance. Ricardo postulates an initial secular increase in the wage rate followed by a secular decline until $w=w_s$, the subsistence wage, when $g_L=0$. These movements are generated by deviations between g_k and constant g_L, with $g_k > \bar{g}_L$ to begin with and $g_k < \bar{g}_L$ subsequently. (The presumed constancy of g_L is subject to a qualification to be examined presently; it is not required by the logic of the argument.) There may be an intermediate period of 'steady-state' equilibrium with constant wages during which $g_k = \bar{g}_L$. These results follow from the assumptions made regarding agricultural productivity, which is said to be constant at early periods, diminishing returns setting in only after a particular labour:land ratio has been passed.

The upward wage trend over the range of constant marginal product is expressed in the following passage from chapter 5, 'On Wages':

> In different stages of society, the accumulation of capital, or of the means of employing labour, is more or less rapid, and must in all cases depend on the productive powers of labour. The productive powers of labour are generally greatest when there is an abundance of fertile land: at such periods accumulation is often so rapid, that labourers cannot be supplied with the same rapidity as capital.
>
> It has been calculated, that under favourable circumstances population may be doubled in twenty-five years; but under the same favourable circumstances, the whole capital of a country might possibly be doubled in a shorter period. In that case, wages during the whole period would have a tendency to rise, because the demand for labour would increase still faster than the supply (I, 98).

What can be said of the initial wage (w_0)? Assuming constant marginal product and given capital supply and labour supply conditions, there will be no motive force generating the upward wage movement if $g_k = g_L$ at w_0. It must be presumed, therefore, that $g_k > g_L$. As the wage rises so the deviation between g_L and g_k narrows until wage constancy is achieved (see figure 8.2). Once the equality of g_L and g_k has been achieved there will be no further motive for a change in the wage, which will proceed at a steady level above subsistence:

> Notwithstanding the tendency of wages to conform to their natural rate [the subsistence wage, w_s, at which $g_L = 0$], their market rate may, in an improving society, for an indefinite period, be constantly above it; for no sooner may the impulse, which an increased capital gives to a new demand for labour be obeyed, than another increase in capital may produce the same effect; and thus, if the increase in capital be gradual and constant, the demand for labour may give a continued stimulus to an increase of people (pp. 94–5).

It may be remarked – although Ricardo does not refer to the possibility – that an increasing wage trend will be generated even if $g_k = g_L$ at the initial position w_0, in the event of *increasing* returns. For a deviation between the growth rates will be continually recreated as population and productivity rise putting continuous upward pressure on g_k. Balanced factor growth is only achieved when increasing returns peter out (figure 8.3).

We turn finally to the downward stretch of wages, Ricardo's main concern (figure 8.4). He refers in the following passages to the role of

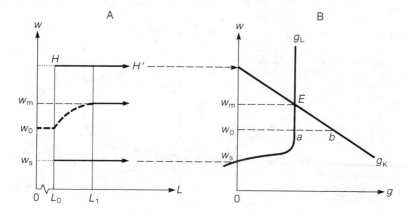

The intercept of g_K on y-axis is determined by the height of HH'; its slope reflects the inverse $w-r$ relation since $g_K = g(r)$ where

$$r = \frac{F'(L)}{w} - 1$$

At w_0, $g_K > \bar{g}_L$ generating upward pressure until w_m. Thereafter the wage remains steady at w_m.

Figure 8.2   Ricardo: the increasing wage trend: initial $g_k > g_L$.

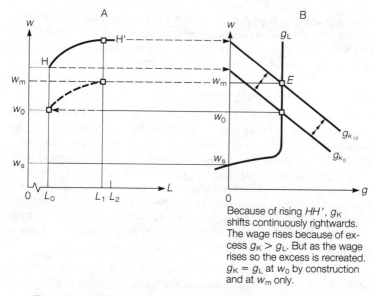

Because of rising HH', g_K shifts continuously rightwards. The wage rises because of excess $g_K > g_L$. But as the wage rises so the excess is recreated. $g_K = g_L$ at w_0 by construction and at w_m only.

Figure 8.3   Ricardo: the increasing wage trend: initial $g_k = g_L$.

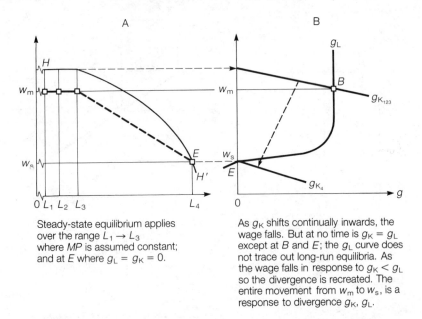

Steady-state equilibrium applies over the range $L_1 \to L_3$ where *MP* is assumed constant; and at *E* where $g_L = g_K = 0$.

As g_K shifts continually inwards, the wage falls. But at no time is $g_K = g_L$ except at *B* and *E*; the g_L curve does not trace out long-run equilibria. As the wage falls in response to $g_K < g_L$ so the divergence is recreated. The entire movement from w_m to w_s, is a response to divergence g_K, g_L.

Figure 8.4   Ricardo: the decreasing wage trend: initial $g_k = g_L$.

diminishing returns in depressing g_k, the constancy of g_L at $\bar{g}_L$ and the downward trend of wages as g_k falls steadily relative to $\bar{g}_L$:

> Although, then, it is probable, that under the most favourable circum-
> stances, the power of production is still greater than that of population, it
> will not long continue so; for the land being limited in quantity, and
> differing in quality, with every increased portion of capital employed on
> it, there will be a decreased rate of production, whilst the power of
> population continues always the same (p. 98).

> In the natural advance of society, the wages of labour will have a
> tendency to fall, as far as they are regulated by supply and demand; for
> the supply of labourers will continue to increase at the same rate, whilst
> the demand for them will increase at a slower rate. If, for instance, wages
> were regulated by a yearly increase of capital, at the rate of 2 per cent,
> they would fall when it accumulated only at the rate of $1\frac{1}{2}$ per cent. They
> would fall still lower when it increased only at the rate of 1, or $\frac{1}{2}$ per cent,
> and would continue to do so until the capital became stationary, when
> wages also would become stationary, and be only sufficient to keep up
> the numbers of the actual population (p. 101).

The notion that wages are 'regulated by [the] yearly increase of
capital' conflicts with the notion in the same paragraph that they are

'regulated by supply and demand' unless the labour growth rate is taken to be a constant. This indeed is Ricardo's presumption for much of the analysis. However, that 'the supply of labourers will continue to increase at the same rate' notwithstanding reduced wages, implies a precipitous fall in g_L from some positive constant to zero when the wage actually reaches subsistence. There is reason to believe that allowance was made for some response of g_L to wage reductions from levels above but close to subsistence, for Ricardo realized that otherwise the labourer 'would be soon totally deprived of subsistence' (p. 101), and saw some deceleration in the decline as realistic, a deceleration that can only be assured by a reduction in g_L. A generalized, positively sloping, g_L-w relationship might have been utilized throughout without changing the substance of the argument.

All that has been said may be translated into Ricardian 'money' terms (see above, p. 109). Commodity wages fall but the labour embodied therein, and thus the *money* wage which 'measures' labour embodiment, rises, forcing down the return on capital. The money wage rate, as we know, also reflects *proportional* wages, the profit rate changing inversely with the share of wages in the constant value of the marginal product per capita. That this is so can easily be seen by rewriting our basic expressions in 'money' terms thus:

$$w_m + rw_m = F'(L) \cdot p_c$$

or

$$r = \frac{F'(L) \cdot p_c}{w_m} - 1,$$

where w_m is the 'money' wage and p_c is the price of corn. Since the corn price is governed by marginal labour cost, $F'(L) \cdot p_c$ is a constant.

The burden imposed by diminishing returns is evidently shared by labour and capital. This is the essence of the matter. In terms of market pressures, if (initially) the money wage were to remain constant in the face of rising corn prices, there would result too rapid a decline in the population growth rate, thus correcting the imbalance. Conversely, if money wages were to rise to compensate labour fully so that real wages did not fall at all, there would follow too rapid a deceleration of the capital growth rate, again correcting the imbalance. Ricardo himself used the appropriate term 'equilibrium' in a similar context (above, p. 194).

The model outlined thus far assumes constant technology and a constant minimum profit rate (r^*). The reader might wish to trace out the implications of an improvement in technology, or of an increase in savings propensities which reduces the minimum return on capital at which net accumulation ceases.

8.9 Malthus and the Prudential Wage Path

In most respects Malthus's growth model is identical to Ricardo's. The common features are land scarcity manifested in diminishing agricultural returns, and the positive relation between the return on capital (r) and the rate of accumulation (g_k). There are only minor differences concerning labour growth; for Ricardo g_L is irresponsive to wage reductions except at levels close to subsistence, whereas Malthus allowed a regular (positive) g_L–w relationship. But this difference is not a substantive one, and for each the outcome of the growth process is a downward path of real wages to the subsistence level where both g_L and g_k have fallen to zero. A more substantive difference between the two is that for Ricardo wage movements result from deviations between the factor growth rates, while Malthus posits a declining wage path notwithstanding equality of the factor growth rates – his constitutes a 'dynamic equilibrium' path.

A clear statement will be found in Malthus's *Principles of Political Economy* (1820, 297ff; also in Ricardo, 1951, II, 255ff). There are four major propositions: (1) that in a system entailing population growth the real wage must exceed w_s; (2) that in consequence of land scarcity (diminishing returns) the excess $w > w_s$ must fall to zero; (3) that the profit rate declines steadily, as *proportional* wages rise, to r^*; and (4) that assuming $g_k = g_L$ at all times, this common growth rate must decline. Wage movements due to divergencies of g_L and g_k are distinctly contrasted with those reflecting balanced growth and treated in a separate section (1820, 326ff; in Ricardo, 1951, II, 285ff). Ricardo was impressed by Malthus's formulation and paid tribute to the analysis of a simultaneous decline in the rates of profit and wages.

Malthus presents the dynamic equilibrium path as a 'supposition', implying thereby a hypothetical reference path. And indeed this path cannot (assuming regular capital and labour supply growth functions) be achieved in a competitive world where capitalists and labourers act independently. For $r = [F'(L)/w] - 1$ (r moves inversely to proportional not absolute wages), as the economy expands, the initial impact of diminishing returns is to reduce r at the going wage, inducing a fall in g_k relative to g_L; the wage falls in consequence to correct the deviation, but the excess is continually reconstituted with the on-going decline in the marginal product. This was Ricardo's insight. The dynamic equilibrium path is, therefore, a construct of the mind derived by asking what the wage path would be if it is assumed that $g_L = g_k$ under conditions of diminishing returns. Evidently the return to the 'joint' factor declines; but the share of the incidence of declining productivity can be calculated by reference to the capital supply and labour supply growth functions. There is a unique wage rate for each marginal product which is consistent with balanced factor growth, as is illustrated by figure 8.5.

* * *

In the *Essay on Population* Malthus also investigated the implications for wages of 'prudence' – that check to population growth exercised by deliberate constraint designed to avoid the deterioration of living standards. That the population growth rate must in one way or the other decline is a necessary implication of land scarcity. Correspondingly, two categories of 'stationary state' are defined – the one entailing a 'low' corn wage and the other a 'high' corn wage:

> A diminished power of supporting children is an absolutely unavoidable consequence of the progress of a country towards the utmost limits of its population. If we allow that the power of a given quantity of territory to produce food has some limit, we must allow that as this limit is approached, and the increase of population becomes slower and slower, the power of supporting children will be less and less, till finally, when the

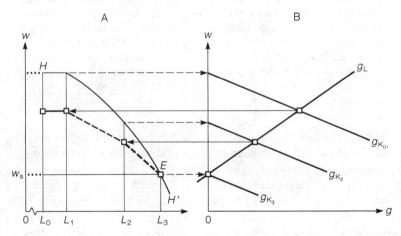

The wage corresponds to $g_K = g_L$ at all times. There is no competitive mechanism to assure this result so that the wage path is purely a reference path.

Figure 8.5 Malthus: the decreasing wage trend: $g_K = g_L$.

increase of produce stops, it becomes only sufficient to maintain, on an average, families of such a size as will not allow of a further addition of numbers. This state of things is generally accompanied by a fall in the *corn* price of labour; but should this effect be prevented by the prevalence of prudential habits among the lower classes of society, still the result just described must take place; and though, from the powerful operation of the preventive check to increase, the wages of labour estimated even in corn might not be low, yet it is obvious that, in this case, the power of supporting children would rather be nominal than real; and the moment this power began to be exercised to its apparent extent, it would cease to exist (1890, 420; first introduced in 1817).

An interesting application of the two versions was made to a proposal by Arthur Young to fix the wages of day labour at a peck of wheat a day. The proposal, Malthus pointed out, 'supposing no change of habits among the labouring classes', implied that 'under all circumstances, whether...resources in land were still great, or nearly exhausted...population ought to increase exactly at the same rate, – a conclusion which involves an impossibility' (1890, 583). Here we have an appeal to the 'standard' model – the corn wage path must fall to assure the appropriate deceleration in the population growth rate. But allow for prudence, and the picture is transformed:

> If however this adjustment, instead of being enforced by law, were produced by the increasing operation of the prudential check to marriage, the effect would be totally different, and in the highest degree beneficial to society. A gradual change in the habits of the labouring classes would then effect the necessary retardation in the rate of increase, and would proportion the supply of labour to the effective demand, as society continued to advance, not only without the pressure of a diminishing quantity of food, but under the enjoyment of an increased quantity of conveniences and comforts; and in the progress of cultivation and wealth the condition of the lower classes of society would be in a state of constant improvement.

In terms of our diagram, population control may be represented by inward shifts of the $g_L - w$ function generated by on-going educational or propaganda programmes. The outcome of Malthus's analysis is the possibility of constancy of the wage on the path to the stationary state (even increasing wages in principle), despite the pressure deriving from land scarcity. Unlike the 'standard' case where the path declines towards the given subsistence level (w_s), the subsistence level in effect 'rises' to meet the constant wage path at E, the 'stationary state' (see figure 8.6).

That Ricardo would have subscribed to this analysis is clear from a famous pronouncement that 'the friends of humanity cannot but wish that in all countries the labouring classes should have a taste for

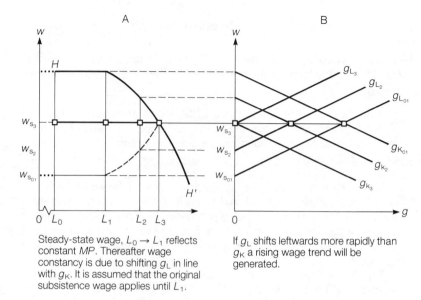

Steady-state wage, $L_0 \rightarrow L_1$ reflects constant *MP*. Thereafter wage constancy is due to shifting g_L in line with g_K. It is assumed that the original subsistence wage applies until L_1.

If g_L shifts leftwards more rapidly than g_K a rising wage trend will be generated.

Figure 8.6. Malthus: the constant wage trend.
(Source of figs 8.1–8.6: Hollander, 1984a.)

comforts and enjoyments…There cannot be a better security against a superabundant population' (I, 100). There is also the initial assumption of the early *Essay on Profits* that 'capital and population advance in the proper proportion, so that the real wages of labour, continue uniformly the same' (cited above, p. 195) which is fully consistent with the constant-wage growth model, as J. S. Mill was later to point out (see below, pp. 234–5).

It remains to add that at least one other economist of the period stated the options as Malthus had done and as Mill was to do, representing the cessation of growth in a light very different from Smith's 'dismal' state (1776 [1937], 81). I refer to Thomas Chalmers (like Malthus often misrepresented as a 'pessimist'), who summarized his position thus:

> That high wages are not necessarily confined to the period when the wealth of society is in a state of progressive increase; and neither does it follow, that, when this wealth has attained its maximum, and become stationary, the wages of labour must be low. That it remains in the collective power of labourers to sustain their wages at as high a level in the ultimate, as in the progressive stages of the wealth of a country (1832, 555).

8.10   The Secular Pattern of Class Distribution

In a much cited passage from the Preface of his *Principles* Ricardo formally stated an intention to account for the secular pattern of class distribution:

> The produce of the earth – all that is derived from its surface by the united application of labour, machinery, and capital, is divided among three classes of the community; namely, the proprietor of the land, the owner of the stock or capital necessary for its cultivation, and the labourers by whose industry it is cultivated.
>
> But in different stages of society, the proportions of the whole produce of the earth which will be alloted to each of these classes, under the names of rent, profit, and wages, will be essentially different; depending mainly on the actual fertility of the soil, on the accumulation of capital and population, and on the skill, ingenuity, and instruments employed in agriculture.
>
> To determine the laws which regulate this distribution, is the principle problem in Political Economy (I, 5).

Ricardo's primary discussion of the income shares will be found at the close of chapter 6, 'On Profits'. His 'predictions' include a rise in aggregate profits, but 'for a certain time' only (p. 123); for beyond a point the continuous decline in the rate of profits will depress the total profit income as the aggregate capital stock rises. Little is said about the *share* of profits in aggregate income, although it evidently must ultimately decline once total profits fall absolutely. Aggregate wages and aggregate rents both tend to increase continuously. The average wage in product terms, of course, declines, while 'the only real gainers would be the landlords' who 'receive higher rents, first, because produce would be of a higher value, and secondly, because they would have a greatly increased proportion of that produce' (p. 125).

Now, notwithstanding a tradition to the contrary, Ricardo forcefully denied ever having maintained that the rental share in output rises secularly; it was only the rental share of the original output prior to expansion which definitely tended to increase – 'a greatly increased proportion of that produce'. For expansion to less productive land assured a rise of the corn rent (at the expense of profit) yielded by intramarginal doses of capital and labour, so that the rental share of the total output on such doses necessarily increased. But no more could be said: 'Because the landlord had one-fourth of the gross produce, and has increased that proportion on all lands before cultivated, does it follow that I am bound to maintain that rents are also a larger proportion of the whole gross produce from all the lands in the country?' (II, 193). The rental share was left an open question.

The threefold class division was in fact of little import, for nothing turned upon it. Yet some aspects of the class distribution problem were central. For one thing, Ricardo was interested in the distribution of the output net of wages, since national savings depended on the distribution as well as the magnitude of 'net income'. Secondly, there is the distribution of the product less rent, upon which depended the rate of return on capital: 'Although a greater value is produced, a greater proportion of what remains of that value, after paying rent, is consumed by the producers, and it is this, and this alone, which regulates profits' (I, 125) – with all that implies for economic growth.

Suggested Reading

* Ricardo, *Principles of Political Economy,* in *Works and Correspondence* (1951), ed. P. Sraffa, chs 21, 26, 31.
* 'An Essay on the Influence of a Low Price of Corn on the Profits of Stocks' (1815), in *Works* (1951), IV, 1–41.
* Malthus, *Principles of Political Economy,* partial reprint of first (1820) edition, ch. 7 in *Works and Correspondence of David Ricardo* (1951), ed. P. Sraffa, II. (Book II, ch. 1 of second, 1836 [1964], edition.) The version in *Works* (1951) also contains Ricardo's *Notes on Malthus.*

On Ricardo's growth economics and an application to corn law policy see Hollander (1979), chs 7 and 11. The geometric wage-path analysis of this and the next chapter derives from Hollander (1984a) in Wood (1986), item 75. For other renditions of Ricardo's growth analysis, broadly in line with the foregoing, see Levy (1976), Eltis (1984), ch. 6, and Cararosa (1985). Tucker (1960), ch. 5, is very helpful.

The alternative formulations of the Ricardian growth model by Sraffa (1951), Kaldor (1960) and Pasinetti (1974), proceed on the assumption of a subsistence wage path, and thus differ from the present account. For a summary of these attributions, see Hollander (1979), appendix B.

For Ricardo on machinery, see Hollander (1979), 346–73; an exchange between Hicks (1971) and Beach (1971), in Wood (1985), items 35, 36; and Eltis (1984).

On Malthus and the population principle, see Flew (1970). Spengler (1945), in Wood (1986), item 35, and Eltis (1984), chs 4 and 5, examine the relation between Malthus on aggregate demand and population in a growth context. Tucker (1960), ch. 7, on Malthus and the principle of competition is important.

Helpful overviews of the analyses of growth undertaken during the period 1800–50 will be found in Tucker (1960), chs 5 and 8, and Eltis (1984), ch. 9.

9 Mill on Capital, Employment and Growth

9.1 Introduction

This chapter is concerned with J. S. Mill's treatment of the themes dealt with in the foregoing two chapters. The conceptual problem of capital, taken up in section 9.2, is followed in 9.3 and 9.4 by Mill's version of the Ricardian proposition 'demand for commodities is not demand for labour' and the Ricardian 'machinery' issue. The three following sections (9.5–9.7) deal with aspects of the 'wages fund' theory, including its relationship with economic organization and its formal abandonment by Mill in 1869.

The subsequent discussion deals with the secular path of the factor returns, setting the stage by a preliminary discussion of 'statics' and 'dynamics' (section 9.8). Mill's application of the growth model to contemporary conditions, including his approach to the 'stationary state', are dealt with in the two concluding sections.

9.2 On Capital and Capital Maintenance

J. S. Mill defined capital as 'a stock, previously accumulated, of the products of former labour', whose function in production is 'to afford the shelter, protection, tools and materials which the work requires, and to feed and otherwise maintain the labourers during the process. These are the services which present labour requires from past, and from the produce of past, labour' ([1965], II, 55).* This conception is summarized in the first of four propositions on capital (all part of standard Ricardian

---

*See above (p. 118n.).

theory when Mill wrote), namely that 'industry is limited by capital', which relates productive employment both to 'circulating capital' (wage goods and materials) and to 'fixed capital' or capital goods proper. This dual sense is nicely expressed thus:

> The only productive powers are those of labour and natural agents; or if any portion of capital can by a stretch of language be said to have a productive power of its own, it is only tools and machinery, which, like wind or water, may be said to co-operate with labour. The food of labourers and the materials of production have no productive power; but labour cannot exert its productive power unless provided with them (p. 63).

Similarly: 'In any large increase of capital a considerable portion will generally be...employed [as fixed capital], and will only co-operate with labourers, not maintain them' (p. 66).

But Mill also uses a conception of capital as a fluid fund distinct from the instruments of production, wage goods and materials in which the fund is embodied. The perpetual 'consumption' of capital according to degree of durability governs the distinction between the circulating and the fixed categories. Thus, 'circulating' capital is that component 'which, after being once used, exists no longer as capital' (p. 91). This category 'requires to be constantly renewed by the sale of the finished product, and when renewed is perpetually parted with in buying materials and paying wages'. This formulation suggests capital as a circulating money fund, but it is easy enough to transfer (as Mill sometimes does) from the fund to the inputs in which it is embodied.

'Fixed' capital comprises instruments of production 'of a more or less permanent character', whose 'function as productive instruments is prolonged through many repetitions of the production operation', and the return to which 'is spread over a period of corresponding duration' (p. 92). But even here the notion of a circulating money fund remains in focus, for capital goods undergo continual depreciation necessitating replacement: 'Most kinds of capital are not fitted by their nature to be long preserved.... Capital is kept in existence from age to age not by preservation, but by perpetual reproduction' (p. 74). This notion is encapsulated in Mill's third proposition on capital – that capital 'although saved, and the result of saving, is nevertheless consumed' (p. 70). By 'saving' is here intended the employment of productive labour or labour engaged with an eye to profit, in which venture structures and equipment (and, of course, wage goods and materials) are used up or 'consumed' more or less rapidly. What is involved in the maintenance of activity is well put by the observation that 'as this operation [of supporting productive labour] admits of being repeated indefinitely without any fresh act of saving, a saving once made becomes a fund to maintain a corresponding number of labourers in perpetuity, reproducing annually their own maintenance with a profit' (p. 71). For 'the saving person, during the whole time that the destruction [of capital goods, etc.] was going on, has had labourers at work repairing it; who are ultimately found to have replaced, with an increase, the equivalent of what has been consumed'.

The notion of a perpetual consumption and reproduction of capital implies a sum of values or a fund only temporarily embodied in specific assets. (The fundist approach is not much different from that of the early neo-classicists, who were to view interest as the return on 'capital' understood as a 'free' or 'floating' fund – to use Marshall's terms – independent of its specific forms.) Mill may have hoped to reconcile the empirical significance of plant and machinery with a fundist outlook on the grounds that 'most kinds of capital are not fitted by their nature to be long preserved'. For all that, he was sometimes emphatic in adopting a production-function perspective (as in the discussions of the source of profits and employment capacity).

In most instances capital goods undergo continual depreciation, necessitating replacement. But there were also 'permanent' investments which entail 'capital expended once for all, in the commencement of an undertaking, to prepare the way for subsequent operations' (p. 92) – land improvements in subsoil draining, soil mixtures and the like, the cutting of canals, the construction of roads and docks, the opening of mines. Such projects, while requiring regular or periodic repair, never require 'entire renewal'. Thus, land improvements 'produce an increase of return, which, after defraying all expenditure necessary for keeping them up, still leaves a surplus. This surplus forms the return to the capital sunk in the first instance, and that return does not, as in the case of machinery, terminate by the wearing out of the machine, but continues for ever' (p. 93). In the Ricardian tradition, the characteristic 'permanence' of land improvements and the like placed them in the same category as the natural properties of the soil, albeit that they are originally man-made: 'its productiveness is thenceforth indissolubly blended with that arising from the original qualities of the soil; and the remuneration for the use of it thenceforth depends, not upon the laws which govern the returns to labour and capital, but upon those which govern the recompense for natural agents'.

9.3 Net Investment: 'Demand for Commodities is not Demand for Labour'

We have understood 'saving' so far to imply the support and maintenance of labour in the production of material wealth in unchanged dimension: but the term is also used to indicate the creation of new capital goods. It is the subject matter of the second theorem on capital: 'all capital and especially all addition to capital, are the result of saving' (p. 69).

In the absence of an initially expended surplus in consequence of technical progress and assuming no idle resources, an increase in orders for capital goods implies reduced orders for 'luxuries'. And it is the product thus foregone that constitutes the ultimate cost of creating the new capital; conversely, an increase in 'luxury' spending necessarily implies a reduction in capital goods output: 'In proportion as any class is improvident or luxurious, the industry of the country takes the direction of producing luxuries for their use; while not only the employment for productive labour is diminished, but the subsistence and instruments which are the means of such employment do actually exist in smaller quantity' (p. 72). This is the sense in which we are to understand a celebrated declaration that 'saving . . . enriches, and spending impoverishes, the community, along with the individual'.

What precisely is involved in a net savings (investment) programme? Here we must have in mind Mill's famous fourth proposition on capital that 'the demand for commodities is not demand for labour' (p. 78) — a direct inference of the first. The proposition does not relate to the demand for particular kinds of labour or labour in particular industries, for Mill insisted repeatedly that a demand for a particular kind of commodity does give rise to a demand for labour to make that commodity (see above, pp. 139–40). The fourth proposition relates rather to aggregate employment or wages:

> if by the demand for labour be meant the demand by which wages are raised, or the number of labourers in employment increased, demand for commodities does not constitute demand for labour. I conceive that a person who buys commodities and consumes them himself, does no good to the labouring classes; and that it is only by what he abstains from consuming, and expends in direct payments to labourers in exchange for labour, that he benefits the labouring classes, or adds anything to the amount of their employment (p. 80).

Mill recognized that Ricardo (and J. B. Say) appreciated this position; and this is important since Ricardo also accepted Say's principle of imputation at the micro-economic level of analysis (above, pp. 93–4).

The fourth proposition thus states that net investment financed by reduced expenditure upon 'luxuries' generates an increase in the aggregate demand for productive labour. (Unproductive labour is maintained not by capital but by 'other funds'; p. 78.) Reduced expenditure on luxury consumption in favour of either investment or services (whether or not for commercial ends) entails the redirection of currently utilized resources towards the production of goods which will sooner or later be placed at the disposal of workers in the form of wages or technological capital. The employment of service labour in place of luxury consumption entails a net increase in labour demand for the same reason as does net saving, namely because the employer is assumed to 'postpone' the date of his own consumption of the results of labour. Should he delay his payment of wages, workers would have to draw on some other source for current maintenance by extracting the funds from elsewhere; and in such a case a transfer of expenditure from luxury consumption to services 'does not open a new employment for labour, but merely changes the course of an existing employment' (p. 81n.).

The fourth proposition implies that the configuration of demand is irrelevant to the distribution of the product between profit and wages: 'The demand for commodities determines in what particular branch of production the labour and capital shall be employed; it determines the *direction* of the labour; but not the more or less of the labour itself, or of the maintenance or payment of the labour' (p. 78). This assertion will only be valid if we assume that the proportions between capital and labour are equal in all industries. Yet the existence of differential factor proportions was conspicuous in the Ricardian formulations of value theory. It is, therefore, possible that Mill implicitly assumed uniform factor proportions in formulating his fourth proposition merely because the essential principle, designed to distinguish 'direct' expenditures on labour by capitalists and others from 'indirect' expenditures by final purchasers, did not require a more complex model differentiating between alternative forms of indirect outlay.

The fourth proposition applies to the long run. For the immediate result of an unexpected reduction in luxury consumption might merely be a piling up of stocks of goods which by their nature cannot be used in the 'support of labour' (p. 72). The appropriate assumption is that the supposed fall in demand for luxuries 'be gradual and foreseen, and ... attended with no waste of capital, the manufacture being discontinued by merely not replacing the machinery as it wears out, and not reinvesting the money as it comes in from the sale of the produce' (p. 79). 'The capital is thus ready for a new employment' (in our case in the capital goods sector). Mill's intentions might equally well be understood if instead of envisaging a change in the pattern of outlay from consumption to investment, we were to compare alternative equilibrium patterns; the higher the rate of investment per period the higher will be the rate of expansion of capacity, and thus the higher the rate of employment.

There is a second qualification. The fourth proposition presumed full use of existing capacity. In the event of available capacity a net expansion in demand for a particular commodity may stimulate an increase in employment and output in that sector which is not at the expense of activity elsewhere (pp. 57, 65, 87).

Mill neglected the need for technological capital in the employment of service workers, but took seriously its requirement in the productive sector. But, as in our discussion of Ricardo, we must exercise caution. In the polar extreme case of a given labour supply, an expansion of investment will simply mean that 'the whole of what was previously expended in luxuries, by capitalists and landlords, is distributed among the existing labourers, in the form of additional wages' (p. 68); in this case there will not even be required any transfer of resources from the 'luxury' sector. Only in the event of expanded employment does the requirement for technological capital arise.

In the limiting case of an available labour supply at constant wages, the positive effect of net investment upon employment can only manifest itself after the newly created (technological) capital goods have been installed. Mill should have explained that the programme is accomplished in two stages: first, a transfer of resources from 'luxury' industries to capital goods industries, which involves no net effect upon employment (and thus none on aggregate wages), and second, the operation of the capital goods by new entrants into the labour market. It is at this second stage that the aggregate wage bill rises, implying an expansion in the demand for wage goods on the part of the newly employed.

The expanded production of wage goods constitutes an aspect of the original decision to increase investment. The increased outflow of wage goods is thus at the expense of other categories of commodities (luxuries) and should not be confused with the net expansion of output resulting from the expanded capacity of the system. Mill seems to have confused the two. He attempts to prove that 'increase of capital gives increased employment to labour, without assignable bounds', since when capitalists abstain and 'turn their income into capital, they do not thereby annihilate their power of consumption; they do but transfer it from themselves to the labourers to whom they give employment', so that (in the case of available labour supply) 'the production of necessaries for the new population, takes the place of the production of luxuries for a portion of the old, and supplies exactly the amount of employment which has been lost' (pp. 67–8). This may be true, but it does not in itself explain the source of purchasing power for the net flow of output from the expanded national capacity once in place. That must be understood in terms of the Law of Markets.

9.4   On Machinery

The classical problem of 'machinery' or the conversion of circulating into fixed capital – Ricardo's 'output-reducing' technology (see above,

p. 189) – is discussed by Mill as an application of the first proposition (or its corollary, the fourth) generalized to 'all improvements by which capital is sunk; that is, rendered permanently incapable of being applied to the maintenance and remuneration of labour' (p. 94). Mill, like Ricardo, had in mind exogenous technological improvements, rather than the adoption of capital-intensive techniques in response to a preceding change in relative factor prices.

The problem arises, as for Ricardo, from the differential rates of depreciation of the two categories of capital. In the case of circulating capital 'the result of a single use must be a reproduction equal to the whole amount of the circulating capital used, and a profit besides'; but a machine need only yield sufficient per period to cover maintenance and depreciation 'with a surplus sufficient to yield the ordinary profit on the entire value of the machine' (p. 93). The matter is nicely summarized thus:

> By the adoption of machinery, a circulating capital, which was perpetually consumed and reproduced, has been converted into a fixed capital, requiring only a small annual expense to keep it up: and a much smaller produce will suffice for merely covering that expense, and replacing the remaining circulating capital of the producer. The machinery therefore might answer perfectly well to the manufacturer, and enable him to undersell his competitors, though the effect on the production of the country might be not an increase but a diminution (p. 134).

It is not immediately apparent why the original innovating entrepreneur should wish to undersell his competitors rather than take advantage of his reduced unit costs at the going price. We must not forget, however, that classical competition is not of the 'price-taking' variety. It is conceivable that the innovating firm – even assuming 'output-reducing' technology for a *given* capital stock – *expands* its capital stock (with an appreciable positive impact on total output) and that competitors react by following suit. Allowance should also be made for new entrants. In any event, Mill presumed that 'the extension of business which almost certainly follows in any department in which an improvement has been made, affords a strong inducement to those engaged in it to add to their capital' (p. 98); and he emphasized industry-wide expansion (implying of course a negatively sloped demand curve): 'the article will be sold cheaper, and therefore, of that single article there will probably be not a smaller, but a greater quantity sold' (p. 134). It thus emerges, as Ricardo had intimated (see above, p. 190), that a reduction in output does not occur in the industry where the output-reducing innovation is first introduced. It is a reduced wages fund in the economy as a whole that is at stake, employment possibly rising in the innovating sector: 'though that particular branch of industry may extend itself, it will be by replenishing its diminished circulating capital from that of the community generally; and if the labourers employed in that department escape loss of employment' – a result hinging obviously on the degree of demand elasticity for the product in question – 'it is because the loss will spread itself over the labouring people at large'.

Mill was sceptical regarding the empirical significance of the case. No examples at all are given from industry. As for agriculture 'the supposition, in the terms of which it has been stated, is purely ideal; or at most applicable only to such a case as that of the conversion of arable land into pasture, which though formerly a frequent practice, is regarded by modern agriculturalists as the reverse of an improvement' (p. 95); 'all the improvements due to modern science', he added in 1865, tend 'to increase, or at all events, not to diminish, the gross produce'.

The technologies under discussion thus far are labour-displacing for a given value of capital. But detrimental effects on labour might arise also from land improvements (or the construction of farm machinery), which permit an expansion of output from a given area but require retention of the original work force. Circulating capital is now diverted from the maintenance of operating labour to its support in undertaking the land improvement. In the standard case, a smaller crew suffices to operate the original (but improved) land area, the absolute yield therefrom possibly falling; in the alternative case, a smaller work crew can produce nothing, so that the entire original crew must be redirected to act as operating labour. Here the aggregate yield for the firm must expand if the innovation is to be viable. The problem that arises again reflects capital scarcity, but whereas in the first case the ratio of 'fixed' to 'circulating' capital rises within a *given* total, now the increase in the ratio requires a larger total capital and this implies transfers from other sectors – assuming capital in the economy as a whole to be unchanged (and, one should add, assuming full use of capacity):

> The improver will in that case require the same number of labourers as before, at the same wages. But where will he find the means of paying them? He has no longer his original capital of two thousand quarters disposable for the purpose. One thousand of them are lost and gone – consumed in making the improvement. If he is to employ as many labourers as before, and pay them as highly, he must borrow, or obtain from some other source, a thousand quarters to supply the deficit (p. 95).

Simple conversion thus involves labour displacement by firms of given size (in terms of capital value); complex conversion necessitates a higher capital by the firm but no labour displacement. But in both categories the net outcome is industry expansion, at least in the general case where the quantity demanded increases upon a fall in price, at the expense of activity elsewhere. Only if demand elasticity is very low will there be employment or wage contractions in the innovating sector itself. But Mill warned against drawing unjustifiably optimistic conclusions from observations of cost price reduction and industry expansion which characterize technologically progressive industries (p. 96). Attention must always be focused upon the ultimate source of any observed increase in funds for the maintenance of labour in a particular industry. Unless those funds emanate from net accumulation, expansion is necessarily at the expense of employment elsewhere. This amounts to a direct application of the first fundamental proposition on capital.

The formal statements of the conversion problem all entail a wage fund model involving literal pre-accumulations of wage goods. This is also true of Ricardo's analysis. But Ricardo had made clear that the 'real world' counterpart of the reduced wage fund takes the form of contractions in agricultural output in response to a lower demand for food on the part of those labourers adversely affected by the adoption of new technology (see above, p. 190). Mill, too, had earlier in this book rejected literal pre-accumulations of food (a matter amplified in section 9.5 below). His model was designed (like Ricardo's) as a convenient mental exercise to convey the essential forces at play rather than as a precise representation of the workings of an actual capitalist exchange system. It should also be repeated that global technological unemployment as such was not the concern. Rather it was 'injury' to labour in the broadest sense, even allowing for reabsorption as reduced wages. For the problem was to assure the employment of 'as many labourers as before, and pay them as highly' (p. 95).

Capital-absorbing innovation necessarily has a negative effect on the global 'wages fund' and, therefore, on either employment or *per capita* wages or both. This is the alpha and omega of the classical analysis of machinery. The whole problem will, however, be 'temporary' in the event of net savings sufficient to compensate for the shortfall in employment opportunities wherever created. As for the extent and rapidity of adoption of innovations relative to net accumulation, Mill was optimistic:

> It is not in poor or backward countries that great and costly improvements in production are made. To sink capital in land for a permanent return – to introduce expensive machinery – are acts involving immediate sacrifice for distant objects; and indicate, in the first place, tolerably complete security of property; in the second, considerable activity of industrial enterprise; and in the third, a high standard of what has been called the 'effective desire of accumulation:' which three things are the elements of a society rapidly progressive in its amount of capital. Although, therefore, the labouring classes must suffer, not only if the increase of fixed capital takes place at the expense of circulating, but even if it is so large and rapid as to retard that ordinary increase to which the

growth of population has habitually adapted itself; yet, in point of fact, this is very unlikely to happen, since there is probably no country whose fixed capital increases in a ratio more than proportional to its circulating (p. 97).

Further reason for optimism lay in the positive stimulus to savings engendered by the effects of new technology – effects on both the 'ability' and 'motive' to save. In all of this Mill was at one with Ricardo. Their empirical perspective contrasts sharply with Karl Marx's declining growth rate of labour demand due to an increase in the ratio of 'constant' to 'variable' capital (below, pp. 385–6).

9.5 The Wages Fund Theory and Economic Organization

We shall now take a closer look at Mill's wages fund approach to the determination of the 'average' wage in the short run, that is, given total capital and population. It will be convenient to have before us a strong version of the doctrine wherein a specific annual wage bill is 'destined' to be paid out to labour during the production period, upon which assumption is based a labour demand curve of unitary elasticity. This version was described by Mill in 1869 in a review article recanting the doctrine. In this review – of W. T. Thornton's *On Labour* (1869) – Mill maintained that the doctrine had been formulated in his own *Principles*:

> The demand for labour consists of the whole circulating capital of the country, including what is paid in wages for unproductive labour. The supply is the whole labouring population. If the supply is in excess of what the capital can at present employ, wages must fall. If the labourers are all employed, and there is a surplus of capital still unused, wages will rise....
> The theory rests on what may be called the doctrine of the wages fund. There is supposed to be, at any given instant, a sum of wealth, which is unconditionally devoted to the payment of wages of labour. This sum is not regarded as unalterable, for it is augmented by saving, and increases with the progress of wealth; but it is reasoned upon as at any given moment a predetermined amount. More than that amount it is assumed that the wages-receiving class cannot possibly divide among them; that amount, and no less, they cannot but obtain. So that, the sum to be divided being fixed, the wages of each depend solely on the divisor, the number of participants. In this doctrine it is by implication affirmed, that the demand for labour not only increases with the cheapness, but increases in exact proportion to it, the same aggregate sum being paid for labour whatever its price may be (V, 643–4).

The rationale for this conception of the labour market involves a form of discontinuous production – periodic 'rounds of business operations'.

But the argument runs in terms of 'the capitalists' pecuniary means', not in real terms:

> In the common theory, the order of ideas is this. The capitalist's pecuniary means consist of two parts – his capital, and his profits or income. His capital is what he starts with at the beginning of the year, or when he commences some round of business operations: his income he does not receive until the end of the year, or until the round of operations is completed. His capital, except such part as is fixed in buildings and machinery, or laid out in materials, is what he has got to pay wages with. He cannot pay them out of his income, for he has not yet received it. When he does receive it, he may lay by a portion to add to his capital, and as such it will become part of next year's wages-fund, but has nothing to do with this year's.

Strange as it may seem, the picture emerging in the *Principles* itself bears little resemblance to that portrayed in 1869. The most important statement relating to average wage rate determination appears in the chapter 'Of Wages' (Book II, xi):

> Wages, then, depend mainly upon the demand and supply of labour; or as it is often expressed, on the proportion between population and capital. By population is here meant the number only of the labouring class, or rather of those who work for hire; and by capital only circulating capital, and not even the whole of that, but the part which is expended in the direct purchase of labour. To this, however, must be added all funds which, without forming a part of capital, are paid in exchange for labour, such as the wages of soldiers, domestic servants, and all other unproductive labourers. There is unfortunately no mode of expressing by one familiar term, the aggregate of what has been called the wages-fund of a country: and as the wages of productive labour form nearly the whole of that fund, it is usual to overlook the smaller and less important part, and to say that wages depend on population and capital. It will be convenient to employ this expression, remembering, however, to consider it as elliptical, and not as a literal statement of the entire truth (II, 337–8).

This statement begs a host of questions. Most important, it fails to explain the breakdown of any given capital stock between its component parts and thus the determination of the size of the wages fund. But Mill evidently believed that the loose formulation sufficed for his purposes, basing upon it a barrage of conclusions regarding labour policy, primarily that every scheme for the benefit of the labouring class which does not act on the proportion between the wage fund and population is a 'delusion'. The larger part of the chapter 'Of Wages' actually focuses upon the implications of the Malthusian population doctrine – labour supply – rather than the nature of the demand for labour. A second formal statement of the doctrine in the following chapter dealing with the equilibrating function of wage movements is equally vague (p. 356), but it sufficed to counter popular remedies for low wages, particularly minimum wage legislation.

There is, however, one profoundly interesting theoretical insight in this context – Mill's somewhat grudging allowance for slack periods extending to the aggregate labour market:

> When there is what is called a stagnation...then work people are dismissed, and those who are retained must submit to a reduction of wages: though in these cases there is neither more nor less capital than before....If we suppose, what in strictness is not absolutely impossible, that one of these fits of briskness or of stagnation should affect all occupations at the same time, wages altogether might undergo a rise or a fall (pp. 338–9).

We have already encountered the allowance for excess capacity as a qualification to the fourth proposition on capital (see above, p. 212). Mill clearly intended to supplement the basic doctrine regarding aggregate employment by some function describing the state of aggregate demand for final goods (see also below, p. 259). But if variations in the aggregate demand for commodities can lead to variations in capacity usage, any notion of an aggregate sum of wealth unconditionally 'destined' for the payment of wages breaks down.

There is much else pointing to this conclusion. The less significant is the distinction between wage goods and luxury goods, of course, the greater the ease of expanding the former at the expense of the latter. Assuming a given work force, there may even be no need to alter the pattern of production to satisfy increased demand by labour upon expanded investment (see above, p. 213). More generally, Mill was careful to specify that stocks of various kinds, whose function it is to fulfil the tasks of 'maintaining' labour, need not actually take the form of wage goods:

> Food and clothing for his operatives, it is not the custom of the present age that [the capitalist] should directly provide...each capitalist has money, which he pays to his workpeople, and so enables them to supply themselves....What then is his capital? Precisely that part of his possessions, whatever it be, which is to constitute his fund for carrying on fresh production. It is of no consequence that a part, or even the whole of it, is in the form in which it cannot directly supply the wants of labourers (p. 56).

The reason for this position lies in the supposed flexibility of the system which permits, by exchange or by production, the easy and rapid transformation of commodities into a form suitable for workers' consumption. Increased food supplies might also be obtained immediately by importation. Otherwise it may take a 'season' for domestic food supplies to be expanded, but Mill played down any such delay, by concluding that:

> The distinction...between Capital and Non-capital does not lie in the kind of commodities, but in the mind of the capitalist – in his will to employ them for one purpose [investment] rather than another [consumption]; and all property, however ill adapted in itself for the use of labourers, is a part of capital, so soon as it, or the value to be received from it, is set apart for productive reinvestment. The sum of all the values so destined by their respective possessors, composes the capital of the country. Whether all those values are in a shape directly applicable to productive uses, makes no difference. Their shape, whatever it may be, is a temporary accident: but once destined for production, they do not fail to find a way of transforming themselves into things capable of being applied to it (p. 57).

Taking all this into account, there is clearly no emphasis on a rigid upper bound to the wages fund. The picture emerging of economic process in an advanced capitalist exchange system, like that drawn by Ricardo (see above p. 186), is not one of a primitive agricultural economy, for which the 1869 version of the wages fund theory seems most appropriate, in which workers consume a distinct class of commodities, produced in discrete annual bursts, and in which carry-over of supply from period to period is precluded. Like Ricardo, Mill in his *Principles* emphasized that workers are paid in money, not in kind, and enter the market to purchase commodities at retail like other consumers; there is no distinction in this regard between consumption by labour, by capitalists or by landlords. The 'wages fund', expressed in money, has a real counterpart in the flow of goods currently made available in the retail sector.

Of course, for current production to proceed smoothly at any particular rate it is necessary for the 'pipelines' to be of suitable dimension – the stock of technological capital and its distribution between sectors to correspond with the volume and the pattern of consumer demand must be appropriate. And while the production process only ends upon final sale – so that labourers, like all other consumers, buy goods currently produced – the bulk of activity on any batch of goods must have been undertaken in the past. Continuous or 'synchronized' activity does not deny that present production depends on past applications of inputs.

To presume that Mill's 'abstinence' approach to interest (see below, p. 230) necessarily entails discontinuous production, and the literal preaccumulation of stocks for advance to labour, would also be unjustified. As the fourth proposition on capital makes clear, when capitalist employers make an investment decision and abstain from current consumption, they do not directly provide wage goods to tide over additional labourers until the next season; rather, they abstain from using their own claim to purchase output currently forthcoming at retail outlets and place this purchasing power at the disposal of labourers with an eye to subsequent indemnification. In this limited sense it is legitimate to talk of 'advances' in Mill's system. It is, however, easy enough to confuse the latter conception with one entailing literal pre-accumulations of real wage goods by the immediate employer in a system involving discrete production periods. This is the trap into which Mill seems to have fallen in the 1869 review.

9.6 The Wages Fund Theory: the Recantation Interpreted

Mill's intentions by his rejection in 1869 of the wages fund doctrine constitute a most difficult problem in the history of economics. First, a word about W. T. Thornton's position, to which Mill had responded, will be appropriate.

Thornton (1813–80) had presented a general criticism of simple supply–demand equilibrium analysis turning upon complications created by the presence of completely inelastic schedules, discontinuities and the like. The argument was extended to the labour market on the grounds that both the labour demand and supply schedules were, at least over wide ranges, completely inelastic. Since employers' combinations were easily formed and workers were badly organized it followed that in practice the wage rate was determined by the employers' *dictat* unless counteracted by trade unions. The 'new view' led Thornton to reject the notion of a predetermined wages fund:

> Does any farmer or manufacturer or contractor ever say to himself, I can afford to pay so much for labour: therefore, for the labour I hire, whatever the quantity be, I will pay so much? Does he not rather say, *'So much labour I require,* so much is the utmost I can afford to pay for it, but I will see for how much less than the utmost I can afford to pay, I can get all the labour I require?' (1869, 84–5n.).

Wages are not a fixed cost to the individual employer, in which case, Thornton concluded, there could be no fixed aggregate wages fund.

As we know, Mill pleaded guilty to having maintained the notion of a predetermined wages fund. In the review he allowed for inelastic and apparently coincidental schedules of supply and demand. As for labour demand:

> Does the employer require more labour, or do fresh employers of labour make their appearance, merely because it can be bought cheaper?

Assuredly, no. Consumers desire more of an article, or fresh consumers are called forth, when the price has fallen: but the employer does not buy labour for the pleasure of consuming it; he buys it that he may profit from its productive powers, and he buys as much labour and no more as suffices to produce the quantity of his goods which he thinks he can sell to advantage. A fall of wages does not necessarily make him expect a larger sale for his commodity, nor, therefore, does it necessarily increase his demand for labour (V, 644).

Mill's new case thus relates to the *derived demand* for labour. Since a fall in wage costs does not 'necessarily' lead to expections of greater final sales for the product, it also does not 'necessarily' lead to an increase in demand for the factor.

At first sight this is an extraordinary statement. Thornton happened to believe that commodity markets are sometimes characterized by totally inelastic demand over significant ranges, but Mill certainly did not. Yet his position is not difficult to understand. In the *Principles* itself he had alluded to the properties of 'derived' and 'joint' demand with regard to input use. These characteristics were the source of technical rigidities in production and consumption which tended to delay any fall of price to new cost levels following an innovation:

Whether there will be a greater permanent supply of the commodity after its production has been cheapened, depends on quite another question, namely, on whether a greater quantity is wanted at the reduced value. Most commonly a greater quantity is wanted, but not necessarily. 'A man', says Mr De Quincey, 'buys an article of instant applicability to his own purposes the more readily and the more largely as it happens to be cheaper. Silk handkerchiefs having fallen to half-price, he will buy, perhaps, in threefold quantity; but he does not buy more steam-engines because the price is lowered. His demand for steam-engines is almost always predetermined by the circumstances of his situation. So far as he considers the cost at all, it is much more the cost of working this engine than the cost upon its purchase. But there are many articles for which the market is absolutely and merely limited by a pre-existing *system*, to which those articles are attached as subordinate parts or members. How could we force the dials or faces of timepieces by artificial cheapness to sell more plentifully than the inner works or movements of such timepieces? Could the sale of wine-vaults be increased without increasing the sale of wine? Or the tools of shipwrights find an enlarged market whilst ship-building was stationary?' (III, 474).

But such rigidities would ultimately be overcome: 'Nobody doubts, however, that the price and value of all these things would be eventually lowered by any diminution of their cost of production; and lowered through the apprehension entertained of new competitors, and an increased supply.' It is thus Mill's position that a reduction in the price of an input will generate an expansion of demand for the input provided sufficient time is allowed to overcome the various 'technical' rigidities in question, including that of assuring an expansion in final demand.

It seems probable, therefore, that when in the recantation Mill questioned whether a fall in wages will encourage an expansion of labour demand, he had in mind so short a period that an expansion of final sales is not taken seriously by employers, who accordingly refrain from immediately increasing their work force. This position does not, however, rule out expanded demand for labour when a longer period is allowed.

We are now in a position to draw the threads of the argument together. There are two distinct aspects to Mill's case. First, the argument that in the very short run firms may not respond to a change in the wage rate, because of low expectations of altered final sales; this is the only rationale offered for zero demand elasticity for an input. In the event of zero elasticity a variation in the wage rate entails a variation in the total industry wage bill – the wage bill is thus not predetermined. A second part of Mill's case – which also applies to the short-run period – urges that rapid alterations in the wage bill are indeed conceivable, since the received notion of a technical inability to vary its size was groundless: 'Exists there any fixed amount which, and neither more nor less than which, is destined to be expended in wages?' (V, 644). The wages bill 'cannot exceed the aggregate means of the employing classes' (after allowance for their personal maintenance), but 'short of this limit, it is not, in any sense of the word, a fixed amount'. For the capitalist is under no obligation to spend a specific sum upon labour; each employer (and therefore, Mill implies, *all* employers) can be obliged to spend more than expected on wages or may enjoy a windfall gain even during the brief period before old plans can be revised and new plans put into operation. The second aspect of the argument does not, however, in itself provide a rationale for zero demand elasticity for labour, and is supplementary to the primary intention of the review.

9.7 The Wages Fund as Equilibrium Solution

We still have not resolved the determination of the size of the wage bill (and the wage rate) in the case of a given work force. To say it depends on 'capital' only takes us part of the way, since the breakdown of capital between its components has to be accounted for. It will not do to assume simply that its magnitude is given technologically once aggregate capital is known; for this treats wage capital on a par with technological capital (structures, machinery, materials), a practice which only makes sense if the real wage is a constant so that a given stock of wage goods 'supports' a certain quantity of labour. In the event of variability of wages the 'dependency' of labour upon wages and its 'dependency' upon technological capital are quite distinct in nature.

There is to be found in the classical literature a treatment of the labour market which avoids placing wages on the same footing as technological capital. According to this approach, laid out by Robert Torrens (1780–1864) in 1834 and J. E. Cairnes (1823–75) in 1874, the wage bill is not a datum of the analysis but a dependent variable. On this view, to assure the employment of any given work force, a specific quantum of non-labour inputs (fixed capital and materials) must be provided. An increase in the capital stock therefore will take the form of wage payments entirely if the labour force is unchanged. The wages bill appears as the 'residual' portion of the capital stock, and is the equilibrium outcome in a model the data of which are aggregate capital and the factor proportions (which together generate the labour demand 'curve') and the working population, which, as usual, constitutes labour supply. Here the total of wage payments is not given independently of the size of the working population. An exogenous increase in the work force will actually lead to a smaller equilibrium wage bill since a larger fraction of total capital is required to take the form of fixed capital. The percentage decline in the wage rate thus exceeds the percentage increase in population; the demand curve for labour is relatively inelastic, in contrast to the supposed unitary elasticity of the 'standard' case.

We may formalize the Torrens–Cairnes version of the wages fund theory by means of simple equations. The quantity demanded of labour in aggregate (P), is dependent upon the aggregate capital stock (C), the technically determined ratio λ between labour and non-labour inputs or 'fixed capital', and the wage rate w, and may be written

$$P = \frac{C}{1/\lambda + w} \tag{1}$$

For total capital is made up of fixed capital (M) and wages capital (wP), that is $C = M + wP$. Replacing M by P/λ we obtain expression (1).

If the supply of labour (S) is given, equilibrium will be assured by the full-employment condition

$$P = S \tag{2}$$

and the wage rate may be obtained by inserting expression (1) into (2) since w is the only unknown to be determined. Thus

$$\frac{C}{1/\lambda + w} = S$$

and

$$w = C/S - 1/\lambda \tag{3}$$

Expression (3) may be compared with the 'standard' wages fund doctrine wherein

$$w = C'/S$$

C' referring to wage capital only, rather than aggregate capital.

The characteristic inelasticity of demand

$$-\frac{dp}{dw} \cdot \frac{w}{P} = \frac{1}{1/\lambda w + 1} < 1$$

is recognized only by Cairnes, who described it as 'an unexpected consequence, not, so far as I know, before adverted to' (1874, 173–4).

Cairnes's analysis is usually regarded as peculiar to him alone and atypical of classical doctrine. But Cairnes himself expressed surprise at Mill's statement in 1869 of received opinion because, in his view, Mill was mistaken in ascribing to the *Principles* the notion of a wages bill of unitary elasticity. Moreover he was justified in taking this position, as is clear from Mill's own discussion, following Ricardo, of the consequences for wages of increased investment; for, given population, the attempt by capitalists to expand the real capital stock is thwarted by lack of a sufficient labour supply, and competition for the given labour force drives up the wage until the additional investment outlays are entirely absorbed in payments to labour (see above, p. 213). The distribution of capital between its constituent elements is not a technological datum given independently of labour supply; and the wages bill is the outcome of an equilibration process.

Mill's concern in the above case was with the productive sector only. By contrast, in the *Fortnightly Review* he opened his attack with a formal statement of 'received doctrine' which includes a service sector. This contrast is not accidental. The Torrens–Mill–Cairnes version of the wages fund theory applies only to the productive sector because the use of technological capital (M) is irrelevant in the service sector.

A word now regarding the theoretical scope of the Torrens–Mill–Cairnes approach. In order to be assured of the competitive solution a labour demand curve of negative slope is required. To obtain such a demand curve when constant proportions between labour and fixed capital are the rule, as they are assumed to be, it is necessary to allow at least for hypothetical variations in the quantity of technological capital. For an excess demand for labour at the initial wage, which it must be supposed generates the upward pressure following an increase in investment, implies that employers are able to provide capital equipment in support of additional labour; in fact, the wage rate is forced upwards towards a new equilibrium position by the scarcity of labour services so that additional technological capital is not actually constructed, but the logic of the process requires that firms be able to make additions to their fixed capital stocks. Thus the analysis turns out to be applicable only to the Marshallian long run. Similarly, an experimental rise in the wage rate implies a reduction in the quantity of labour demand. This is because, for each demand 'curve', aggregate capital (C) is assumed unchanged so that the higher wage payment must be financed from that part of the stock hitherto reserved for fixed capital (M); given $M/P(= 1/\lambda)$, employment capacity falls. Again it is clear that the analysis logically applies to the long-run case since a potential variation of fixed capital must be accommodated. In the short run the demand for labour will be completely inelastic; and in fact, once the fixed capital is in place, there is no mechanism to assure that the 'residual' portion of the capital stock will be devoted to wage payments. These severe problems were not recognized by either Mill, Cairnes or Torrens.

The general approach serves better for the case of an expanding labour force. 'I do not mean to deny', Mill had written in his *Principles,* 'that capital, or part of it, may be so employed as not to support labourers, being fixed in machinery, buildings, improvements of land, and the like. In any large increase of capital, a considerable portion will be thus employed' (II, 66). This latter qualification can only refer to the case where population is rising and requires additional fixed capital. Here once more the division of total capital, and accordingly the size of the wages bill, depends upon the work force itself, and is not given independently. But in the simplest case of a constant real wage rate, and always assuming fixed proportions, an increase in aggregate capital will entail a proportionate expansion in the net demand for labour (employment capacity) allowing for the need to provide the expanded work force with 'machinery'. Labour supply is now given by $w = \bar{w}$ in place of equation (2); and, by equation (1), knowledge of the aggregate capital (C) and the machinery:labour ratio (λ) yields the quantity of labour demanded.

*   *   *

It may be helpful to contrast the foregoing approach to aggregate wages with the approach implied by the fundamental Ricardian theorem on distribution (above, p. 96).

According to the Torrens–Mill–Cairnes version of the wages fund theory – a more accurate version of classicism than the 'standard' version – an increase in the wage rate will, in the long run at least, bring about a reduction in the demand for labour. This is true despite the assumption of uniform factor proportions between industries implied by the presumed constancy of the overall labour–machinery ratio in the model. Yet in the same case the prediction generated by the inverse profit–wage relationship, in allocative terms, is very different. For assuming uniform factor proportions, the reduction in profits at going outputs and prices following the wage increase generates no allocative consequences and, accordingly, the overall quantity of labour demanded remains unchanged. This contrast reflects the fact that in the allocative model the wage increase is 'financed' by a reduction in profits rather than by a transfer of funds hitherto invested in fixed capital, which characterizes the wage fund approach. There occurs, as it were, a *forced* rise in aggregate capital (taking the form of the increased wage payments) which is not allowed for in the wages fund model.

In terms of the economic quality of the respective models the allocative analysis seems to have the advantage, for it is based upon the behaviour patterns of employers in the face of a wage change, whereas the wages fund model has no behavioural implications, and provides no explanation of the decision by employers to reduce their M quotas. Indeed, if factor ratios are everywhere identical, as is the supposition, no motive will exist to vary output or employment in any single industry and therefore in the economy as a whole. The conflicting outcomes of the two approaches to distribution can, however, be in part reconciled. For the fall in profits upon an increase in the wage rate allowed by the fundamental theorem is not the end of the story. Since the return on capital has fallen it is to be expected that the rate of accumulation will be adversely affected, in which event the 'forced' increase in capital will ultimately be, at least partially, cancelled.

We turn next to the case of differential factor ratios between industries. Formally, the wages fund model rules out differential factor ratios, but it is possible to accommodate the more complex case by tying the average machinery–labour ratio to the wage rate provided the pattern of demand curves in the system and the factor ratios in each industry are given. Making allowance for a variation in the (average) machinery–labour ratio, a wage increase will reduce the demand for labour more sharply than if λ is held constant.

The analysis in terms of allocation theory also generates a negatively sloped aggregate demand curve for labour by way of a change in activity to the detriment of labour-intensive industries. But the wages fund theory assumes given capital, while as already explained, no such constraint is imposed by the theory of allocation, since the wage increase will be financed from reduced profits. The elasticities of demand for labour derived by way of the two mechanisms will not therefore generally be the same.

9.8 'Statics' and 'Dynamics'

The trend paths of the wage and profit rates – the major theme in classical growth economics – are treated by Mill in Book IV of the *Principles* on 'The Influence of the Progress of Society on Production and Distribution'. Aspects of the growth model with its analysis of the trend path of wages and profits do appear in earlier parts; Book I covers the labour and capital supply functions and the determinants of productivity in agriculture and manufacturing. But all this is a setting of the stage. The formal growth model only comes in Book IV.

This Book is prefaced with an important distinction between 'Statics' and 'Dynamics':

> The three preceding Parts include as detailed a view as our limits permit, of what, by a happy generalization of a mathematical phrase, has been called the Statics of the subject. We have surveyed the field of economical facts, and have examined how they stand related to one another as causes and effects; what circumstances determine the amount of production, of employment for labour, of capital and population; what laws regulate rent, profits, and wages; under what conditions and in what proportions commodities are interchanged between individuals and between countries. We have thus obtained a collective view of the economical phenomena of society, considered as existing simultaneously. We have ascertained, to a certain extent, the principles of their interdependence; and when the state of some of the elements is known, we should be able to infer, in a general way, the contemporaneous state of most of the others. All this, however, has only put us in possession of the economical laws of a stationary and unchanging society. We have still to consider the economical condition of mankind as liable to change, and indeed (in the more advanced portions of the race, and in all regions to which their influence reaches) as at all times undergoing progressive changes. We have to consider what these changes are, what are their laws, and what their ultimate tendencies; thereby adding a theory of motion to our theory of equilibrium – the Dynamics of political economy to the Statics (III, 705).

This conceptual division suggests that the earlier discussion of long-run price formation turning on costs of production – satisfying, that is, the wage and profit rate uniformity conditions – applies to artificially imposed states of stationariness respecting capital, population and knowledge.

What is true of an artificial 'paralysis' of the forces of progress in regard to wage and profit rate uniformity holds also for the stationary state proper – the very long run:

When a country has carried production as far as in the existing state of knowledge it can be carried with an amount of return corresponding to the average strength of the effective desire of accumulation in that country, it has reached what is called the stationary state; the state in which no further addition will be made to capital, unless there takes place either some improvement in the arts of production, or an increase in the strength of the desire to accumulate (II, 169).

But it must be clarified whether the wage path during progress to the end-point position constitutes a locus of static states within each of which wage and profit rate uniformity ('long-run' equilibrium) is supposedly achieved; or whether, in the context of progress, we abandon the artificial 'static' construct and consider it pertinent only to the stationary state proper. In the first case, we can say nothing of the transfer between the points. In the second, the system is continually 'out of equilibrium' on the path to the stationary state, the non-uniformity of factor returns itself constituting an essential part of the driving mechanism of the growth process. The same question may be addressed to the growth models of the other major classicists.

The location of Mill's formal distinction between statics and dynamics might be said to imply that the progressive state was envisaged as a locus of static states; why else lay out the distinction precisely at the point of transfer to the problem of progress? But this presumption is not necessarily justified. There are broad ranges of problems that may best be treated by assuming constancy of aggregate capital, population size and knowledge. It is by no means an unreasonable procedure to provide a framework for study of such problems, before proceeding to the distributive and pricing implications of variable capital, population and knowledge – and without any presumption that the secular path of wages (and profits) is to be treated as a locus of static states.

More positively, Mill distinctly required 'a theory of motion' to supplement his 'theory of equilibrium'. This suggests that a stringing together of a series of equilibria would not have sufficed for his purposes. We have seen evidence in chapter 6 of Mill's 'Marshallian' perspective on the role of demand; and there are explicit references to the 'growing demand [for food] of so rapidly increasing a population as that of Great Britain' (III, 745). The wage path (the falling wage path) would then reflect extensions of cultivation under pressure of increasing demand for food; while the lesser pressure of demand for workers' 'conveniences' and 'luxuries' rules out profit rate uniformity until the stationary state is achieved. (There will also presumably be continuous changes in patterns of demand as income distribution alters.) In brief, market and natural prices coincide in stationary-state equilibrium alone.

This conclusion was, however, never drawn explicitly by Mill; and the same is true of our other economists.

It is sometimes argued that Mill's reflections on the potential merits of the stationary state influenced the whole structure of his work in that the investigation of equilibrium positions, for which static theory is appropriate, takes precedence over the 'path to equilibrium', this weighting indicating a concern for a desirable pattern of distribution as an end in itself. Mill's concern with desirable distribution is not in question; but it is going too far to conclude that he actually lost interest in the old growth economics. The stationary state was, of course, that much closer with population control than without. Yet Mill was thoroughly aware that both technological progress and increases in the propensity to save were in practice proceeding apace, so that stationariness was not in sight; indeed, in the Britain of his day steady wages accompanied by a *constant* secular return on capital were possible even without population control because of the extremely high rate of capital accumulation embodying new technology. We must be very careful how we understand a celebrated observation that the return on capital in contemporary Britain was 'within a hand's breadth of the minimum' (p. 738). In any event, Mill allows for technical change in his stationary state; even there 'growth' of sorts is not ruled out. The remainder of this chapter will be devoted to these matters.

9.9   Capital Supply and Labour Supply Conditions

My concern now is to isolate the building blocks required in Mill's growth model, and I shall start with capital supply.

The chapter treating the 'Law of the Increase of Capital' (Book I, xi) conceives the source of savings to be the surplus which defines the maximum ability to save, while the 'disposition' or motive to save governs the actual rate of savings: 'Since all capital is the product of saving, that is, of abstinence from present consumption for the sake of a future good, the increase of capital must depend upon two things – the amount of the fund from which saving can be made, and the strength of the dispositions which prompt to it' (II, 160). The surplus is carefully defined to include wage income exceeding subsistence: 'The capital of the employer forms the revenue of the labourers, and if this exceeds the necessaries of life, it gives them a surplus which they may either expend in enjoyments, or save. For every purpose for which there can be occasion to speak of the net produce of industry, this surplus ought to be included in it' (p. 161). The 'abstinence' involved in saving need not, however, literally entail 'privation'. Ricardo had insisted that additions to capital might be financed out of a surplus increased by technical change; as Mill put it: 'To consume less than is produced, is saving; and that is the process by which capital is increased; not necessarily by consuming less, absolutely' (p. 70).

Actual savings out of the maximum sum potentially available depends in part on prospective yield – 'the greater the profit that can be made from capital, the stronger is the motive to its accumulation' – but also on a variety of personal, sociological and institutional considerations, including the state of national security and life expectation, intellectual development and consciousness of the future, and the strength of other, as distinct from self-regarding, interests (pp. 161–2). In all this Mill relied heavily upon John Rae's important *New Principles* on political economy (1834).

It is not made absolutely clear whether an increase in the surplus during the course of development will generate an actual increased rate of savings despite a fall in the yield. This had been Adam Smith's view. But whatever the theoretical possibilities, Mill did insist – possibly assuming (like Ricardo) that a falling return coincided with a falling surplus available for accumulation – upon a regular positive relation. Thus, it is 'an almost infallible consequence of any reduction of profits' – a reference to the rate of return – 'to retard the rate of accumulation' (III, 843). At the same time, he also refers to the 'astonishingly' high rate of accumulation currently under way (II, 170), asserting that 'the desire of accumulation does not require, to make it effective, the copious returns which it requires in Asia, but is sufficiently called into action by a rate of profit so low, that instead of slackening, accumulation seems now to proceed more rapidly than ever' (p. 172). This is not to reverse the positive relation between rate of accumulation and return on capital; but rather to allow for shifts in the (upward sloping) function with secular increases in the 'effective desire to accumulate', a much-emphasized tendency in the discussion of 'social progress' in Book IV of the *Principles*. Allowing for changes in *ceteris paribus* conditions, at a return of approximately 3 per cent the rate of increase of capital was rising over time.

Let us now take a close look at the return to capital in the stationary state, albeit far from an immediate prospect. As a factual matter Mill took the minimum at which savings would cease to be approximately one per cent (V, 734). The question arises whether a positive interest rate was seen as a *necessary* feature of the full stationary state.

This issue should be seen in appropriate theoretical perspective. One view, associated with J. A. Schumpeter (1934), has it that in stationary-state equilibrium there can be no net return to produced capital goods, since their value falls to that of the ultimate factors of production required to produce them. To this argument it has been objected, as by Lord Robbins (1930), that a positive interest rate will be a feature of full stationariness since allowance must be made for the abstention from present consumption to maintain capital intact; if interest falls to zero the economy would no longer be stationary but contracting.

Mill apparently adhered to the Robbins rather than the Schumpeter view. That a positive interest rate is a necessary feature of the stationary state is implied by the definitions of interest given in the chapter 'Of Profits' (Book II, xv), as 'all that a person is enabled to get by merely abstaining from the immediate consumption of his capital, and allowing it to be used for productive purposes by others' (II, 400), or as 'an equivalent to the owner of the capital for forbearing to consume it' (p. 402). Mill seems very deliberately to be choosing his terms to indicate a positive return to assure against capital depletion. Equally suggestive is a formal justification given in the discussion 'Of Property' (Book II, i) for an interest payment out of the product of current labour, namely that while existing capital is not necessarily 'created' by the current owner, 'the abstinence at least must have been continued by each successive owner, down to the present' (II, 216). In the formal discussion of the stationary state, moreover, allowance seems to be made for a class of (interest-receiving) capitalists (III, 755).

* * *

Now let us turn to the secular conditions of labour supply. Mill nowhere much emphasized the possibility of drawing in labour from the unproductive into the productive sector at a constant wage – the basis for W. A. Lewis's celebrated attribution to the classicists of growth with 'unlimited supplies of labour' (1954). As was the case with the other principal classicists, Mill's interest was in population growth.

Mill approached the population variable by insisting upon the continued usefulness of the Malthusian conception of a maximum physiological capacity of a human population to double itself in approximately two decades, drawing for evidence upon 'the most favourable circumstances known to exist, which are those of a fertile region colonized from an industrious and civilized community' (II, 155). Under usual conditions this geometrical ratio was not, however, encountered and it was with the nature of the 'checks' that Mill was preoccupied in his chapter 'Of the Law of the Increase of Labour' (Book I, x): 'the unlimited extent of its natural powers of increase, and the causes owing to which so small a portion of that unlimited power is for the most part actually exercised' (p. 159).

Land scarcity was the essence of the matter. Malthus had not taught that the increase in population was limited by the power of increase of food, but rather 'by the limited quantity of the land on which [food] can be grown' which in the last resort constrained food supplies. Where (as in North America) land was not a limiting factor, the food supply was indeed forthcoming at 'the higher rate natural to it', permitting population also to expand at its maximum: 'When [the American critic] Mr Carey can show, not that turnips and cabbages, but that the soil itself, or the nutritive elements contained in it, tend naturally to multiply, and that too at a rate exceeding the most rapid possible increase of mankind, he will have said something to the purpose' (p. 156n.).

The check to the maximum population growth rate was not, however, necessarily imposed by the death rate (war and disease, and insufficiency of food), with the birth rate achieving the maximum level physiologically possible. Human reproduction was also to a greater or lesser degree 'restrained by the fear of want rather than by want itself', so that even where starvation was not an issue, many were yet influenced by 'the apprehension of losing what have come to be regarded as the decencies of their situation in life'; acting from motives of 'prudence' or the 'social affections' people married at such age and had that number of offspring 'consistent with maintaining themselves in the condition of life which they were born to, or were accustomed to consider as theirs' (p. 157).

The constraints on population growth by way of deaths and of prudential control on births designed to maintain living standards are said to be the sole forces 'hitherto…found strong enough, in the generality of mankind, to counteract the tendency to increase [at the maximum rate possible]'. Limitation of family size to the end of actually raising living standards is conceded amongst members of the middle class; but 'such a desire is rarely found, or rarely has that effect, in the labouring classes. If they can bring up a family as they were themselves brought up, even the prudent among them are usually satisfied'.

9.10 The Wage and Profit Paths

A formal contrast is made between circumstances where land scarcity is not yet manifest and where an increase in population at its 'maximum' potential rate can proceed with no downward pressure on wages, and those where (always given technology) this possibility is ruled out. The former include North America and the Australian colonies, which enjoyed advanced European technology and savings habits and were not subject to land scarcity, so that the rate of accumulation proceeded at least as rapidly as population at its maximum and the real wage was maintained above subsistence at a steady, perhaps increasing, level:

In countries like North America and the Australian colonies, where the knowledge and arts of civilized life, and a high effective desire of accumulation, co-exist with a boundless extent of unoccupied land, the growth of capital easily keeps pace with the utmost possible increase of population, and is chiefly retarded by the impracticability of obtaining labourers enough. All, therefore, who can possibly be born, can find employment without overstocking the market: every labouring family enjoys in abundance the necessaries, many of the comforts, and some of the luxuries of life (II, 343–4).

In the absence of this special confluence of circumstances and technology unchanged it would be impossible for population to expand at the maximum rate without downward pressure on wages, and this because of impediments to the rate of accumulation. These impediments might act directly:

> those circumstances of a country…in which population can with impunity increase at its utmost rate, are rare, and transitory. Very few are the countries presenting the needful union of conditions. Either the industrial arts are backward and stationary, and capital therefore increases slowly; or the effective desire of accumulation being low, the increase soon reaches its limit.

But even where these direct constraints on accumulation are absent, the effects of land scarcity – a falling marginal product – will bear upon the rate of accumulation: 'The increase of capital is checked, because there is not fresh land to be resorted to, of as good quality as that already occupied'.

The assumption of unrestricted population growth in this 'Ricardian' analysis, be it noted, is not required for the wage decline to occur. That is a limiting case only; and it is enough that there exists downward pressure on g_k for deviations between g_k and g_L to be generated, even if g_L is related positively to w (see above, p. 201).

I shall show in what follows that Mill also developed, in the Malthus–Chalmers mode (see above, pp. 203–5), a constant-wage growth model in the presence of land scarcity. In the central chapter on the distributive trends, 'Influence of the Progress of Industry and Population, on Rents, Profits, and Wages' (Book IV, iii), he spells out carefully that for the real wage to remain unchanged, under conditions of land scarcity, the growth rate of population must decline in line with that of capital: 'we shall suppose them…to increase with equal rapidity; the test of equality being, that each labourer obtains the same commodities as before, and the same quantity of those commodities' (III, 723). Mill then proceeds to trace out the consequence of a growth path entailing a given commodity wage:

Population having increased, without any falling off in the labourer's condition, there is of course a demand for more food. The arts of production being supposed stationary, this food must be produced at an increased cost. To compensate for this greater cost of the additional food, the price of agricultural produce must rise.... Rent will rise both in quantity of produce and in cost [labour embodied]; while wages, being supposed to be the same in quantity, will be greater in cost. The labourer obtaining the same amounts of necessaries, money wages have risen; and as the rise is common to all branches of production, the capitalist cannot indemnify himself by changing his employment, and the loss must be borne by profits.

Capital accumulation and population growth can thus proceed at the same rate, with the commodity wage constant at a level above 'subsistence' and the return on capital declining. But considering the accumulation–interest relationship always insisted upon (a fall in profits generates a decline in g_k), the common factor growth rate must, of course, also be decelerating.

It remains to note that Mill attributed a constant wage model to Ricardo. Unfortunately, his account of Ricardo's position is sometimes ambiguous, for he does not always make it crystal clear whether there occurs an *absolute* population reduction upon an increase in the price of corn – by way of an increased death rate should the wage be at a physiological minimum or a decreased birth rate should wages be at a psychological minimum – or a reduction in the population *growth rate* (II, 340). Only in the latter case would we have a true 'dynamic equilibrium' constant growth path of wages. Moreover, the extraordinary fact emerges of Mill's failure to recognize the *downward* secular path which, for us, appears to be Ricardo's main concern in devising his growth model:

This assumption [the constant-wage 'tendency'] contains sufficient truth to render it admissible for the purposes of abstract science; and the conclusion which Mr Ricardo draws from it, namely, that [money] wages in the long run rise and fall with the permanent price of food, is, like almost all his conclusions, true hypothetically, that is granting the suppositions from which he sets out. But in application to practice, it is necessary to consider that the minimum of which he speaks, especially when it is not a physical, but what may be termed a moral minimum, is itself liable to vary. If wages were previously so high that they could bear reduction, to which the obstacle was a high standard of comfort habitual among the labourers, a rise in the price of food, or any other disadvantageous change in their circumstances, may operate in two ways: it may correct itself by a rise of [money] wages brought about through a gradual effect on the prudential check to population; or it may permanently lower the standard of living of the class, in case their previous habits in respect of population prove stronger than their previous habits in respect of comfort. In that case the injury done to them will be permanent, and their deteriorated condition will become a new minimum, tending to perpetuate itself as the more ample minimum did before (p. 349).

It is regrettable that Mill failed to record Ricardo's full argument which recognizes conspicuously the falling-wage possibility, and he must be held partly responsible for thereby misleading commentators ever after.

*   *   *

The profit rate declines on either the 'standard' or the 'prudential' version of the growth model until the minimum is achieved; but this is a tendency only. Mill's chapter spelling out the path of profits (Book IV, iv) provides a splendid illustration of the sense of the notion 'tendency' to refer not to a necessarily observable trend but rather to one force amongst other and possibly conflicting forces acting on a particular variable:

> My meaning is, that it would require but a short time to reduce profits to the minimum, if capital continued to increase at its present rate, and no circumstances having a tendency to raise the rate of profit occurred in the meantime. The expansion of capital would soon reach its ultimate boundary, if the boundary itself did not continually open and leave more space (III, 739).

The conditions for a satisfactory test of the theory – 'to fulfil the conditions of the hypothesis' – include the cessation of capital exportation in foreign investment and of capital wastage in unproductive domestic ventures such as failing speculative investments; unchanged technology, whether involving new inventions or the adoption of already known superior processes; and also 'no increased production in foreign countries for the English market'. Given these conditions 'the fall in profits would be very rapid' (p. 740).

What assumption is being made here regarding population growth and the wage rate? A slower growth rate of population than capital would add to the downward pressure on the rate of profit given technology, and also given the distribution of productive and unproductive labour – yet a further item in the *ceteris paribus* basket: 'An augmentation of capital, much more rapid than that of population, must soon reach its extreme limit, unless accompanied by increased efficiency of labour (through inventions and discoveries, or improved mental and physical education), or unless some of the idle people, or of the unproductive labourers, became productive'. But, of course, even if population did increase in proportion to the increase of capital, the fall of profits would be inevitable because of the rising cost of agricultural produce; any such decline would only be 'retarded', not prevented, by a falling commodity wage.

9.11 Applications to Contemporary Conditions

Major net accumulation characterized contemporary British conditions. But the actual circumstances stood in sharp contrast with the theoretical in this respect – that while both capital and population were proceeding at a very rapid, roughly constant, pace, the profit rate remained unchanged over time and the wage rate was at worst unchanged and (Mill conceded in 1867) perhaps rising:

> [Rapid accumulation] is shown by the increasing productiveness of almost all taxes, by the continual growth of all the signs of national wealth, and by the rapid increase of population, while the condition of the labourers is certainly not declining, but on the whole improving [1867; till 1862: certainly is not on the whole declining]. These things prove ... that, invariably, room is either found or made for the profitable employment of a perpetually increasing capital, consistently with not forcing down profits to a lower level (p. 742).

All this was the result of a variety of 'counteracting circumstances' including pre-eminently new technology.

The foregoing account applied to the manufacturing sector. In manufacturing, 'prudential' behaviour was practised only by skilled workers (II, 346), so that the maintenance of above-subsistence wages at a steady level was only possible, despite uncontrolled population growth on the part of the unskilled, because of the high and steady rate of capital accumulation. The extraordinary rate of accumulation in the cotton-manufacturing centres – reflecting new technology – had not only maintained wages over several decades despite unchecked urban population growth, but had pulled up agricultural wages in areas near the cities (p. 344). (Because of the total absence of the 'prudential' motive – and presumably insufficient accumulation – the agricultural population was constrained by variation in the death rate alone (p. 346), and living conditions in the Southern counties were 'painful to contemplate' (p. 351).)

Mill, in a famous statement, played down 'schemes ... for making the labourers a very little better off. Things which only affect them a very little, make no permanent impression upon their habits and requirements, and they soon slide back into their former state' (p. 342). Major improvements were more likely to have the desired impact on behaviour; and drawing upon British and French experience, Mill alluded also to the consequences of changes in the minimum standard unrelated to the actual experience of higher wages:

> Every advance they make in education, civilization, and social improvement, tends to raise this standard; and there can be no doubt that it is gradually, though slowly, rising in the more advanced countries of Western Europe. Subsistence and employment in England have never increased more rapidly than in the last forty years, but every census since 1821 showed a smaller proportional increase of population than that of the period preceding (p. 159).

The recognition of a slackening in the growth rate of population relative to that of capital for some four decades comes as a surprise considering the other statements which assert that attempts to raise living standards are 'rarely found' in the labouring classes as a whole, and that the unskilled urban masses failed to practise prudential control. It is only in 1867 that Mill rather hesitatingly allowed formally that real wages were 'on the whole improving'.

What can explain Mill's failure to take fuller account, from the first edition in 1848, of his own allusions to the census results since 1821 which suggest the practice of prudential restraint quite generally, not only by the élite of the working class? Mill's generally pessimistic outlook may reflect his disappointment that the declining population growth rate was unimpressive compared to what could have been achieved; and since the high earnings of the unskilled town workers had not encouraged a really significant alteration in their conception of the minimum standard, a future slackening in the growth rate of capital would generate a collapse of wages to the level of the common farm labourer. This was the ever-present shadow. If this is indeed so, it is scarcely surprising that he minimized labour scarcity, sometimes writing as if the unskilled failed totally to exercise prudential control. Mill was quite clear that 'it is a much more difficult thing to raise, than to lower, the scale of living which the labourer will consider as more indispensable than marrying and having a family' (p. 342). The ideal opportunity that existed to elevate standards must not be lost. The falling-wage model had the strong prescriptive purpose of impressing on unskilled labourers the need to emulate the skilled whilst the going was good.

9.12   The Stationary State

The stationary state (Book IV, vii) was for Mill far from an immediate prospect: 'There is room in the world, no doubt, and even in old countries, for a great increase of population, supposing the arts of life to go on improving, and capital to increase' (III, 756) – with commodity

wages unchanged (or rising) since Mill focuses here only on the disadvantages of continued growth for amenity, including space. But he
does speculate on the stationary state – the 'high wage' variety of
course.

Starting from a position of zero net accumulation characterizing such
a state, an increase in the 'effective desire of accumulation' – a reduction in the minimum supply price of capital (our r^*, above p.
196) – would create the potential for new growth, as will technological
improvement; for the stationary state is one 'in which no further addition will be made to capital, unless there takes place either some
improvement in the arts of production, or an increase in the strength of
the desire to accumulate' (see above, p. 229). Recognition of a psychological supply price for capital (as for population) thus allows an infinite
diversity of stationary equilibria with wages and/or profits at different
levels; but the specific message of the chapter 'Of the Stationary State' is
that any new potential for expansion should ideally be taken out in
higher real wages, pre-eminently in the form of increased leisure:

> a stationary condition of capital and population implies no stationary
> state of human improvement.... Even the industrial arts might be as
> earnestly and as successfully cultivated, with this sole difference, that
> instead of serving no purpose but the increase of wealth, industrial
> improvements would produce their legitimate effect, that of abridging
> labour (p. 756).

The possibility of technological progress despite zero capital formation raises, incidentally, the shadow of 'conversion' with its potentially
adverse effects on labour (see above p. 213), but Mill is silent on that
issue. One would also expect that inventions would have an influence on
the supply of savings; but Mill (as noted) was presuming that any initial
increase in the return on capital will be absorbed by an upward shift of
the supply price of labour, preferably in the form of a shorter working
day. Appropriate population control would indeed be more easily
assured in a slowly growing or zero-growth economy:

> The same determination would be equally effectual to keep up their con-
> dition in the stationary state, and would be quite as likely to exist. Indeed,
> even now, the countries in which the greatest prudence is manifested in
> the regulating of population, are often those in which capital increases
> least rapidly. Where there is an indefinite prospect of employment for
> increased numbers, there is apt to appear less necessity for prudential
> restraint. If it were evident that a new hand could not obtain employment
> but by displacing, or succeeding to, one already employed, the combined
> influences of prudence and public opinion might in some measure be
> relied on for restricting the coming generation within the numbers
> necessary for replacing the present (p. 753).

It remains to add that in the absence of innovation even constant population could not be maintained permanently at constant wage and profit rates, and this because of exhaustibility of natural resources: 'The only products of industry, which, if population did not increase, would be liable to a real increase of cost of production, are those which, depending on a material which is not renewed, are either wholly or partially exhaustible; such as coal, and most if not all metals' (p. 712). In fact, Mill in 1866 proposed paying off the National Debt before Britain's coal reserves were exhausted (cf. I, 277). The fully fledged stationary state – constant technology, population and capital with unchanged wage and profit rates – could only be an approximation.

9.13 Concluding Note

Classical growth analysis elaborated in the foregoing three chapters turns out to be far more sophisticated than various modern renditions – which insist on a constant (subsistence) wage attribution – suggest. For Ricardo (and Smith) the secular wage was a variable; even for Mill, who indeed posited a constant-wage path, it was a wage rate *above* subsistence that applied. In either case the classicists were pointing out that given land scarcity the growth rate of population has to slacken until it falls to zero. It is worth repeating that Mill's perspective – pointing to zero population growth at 'high' wages – was not novel, but the discovery of Malthus; it would thus be historically inaccurate to think of his growth analysis as marking the transition to post-classical statics.

Suggested Reading

*Mill (1848), *Principles of Political Economy*, Book I: 'Production' and Book IV: 'Influence of the Progress of Society on Production and Distribution'.
*'Thornton on Labour and its Claims' (1869) in *Collected Works* (1967), V, 631–68.

Mill on economic development is discussed in Spengler (1960) and Hollander (1985), ch. 4. Hollander, ch. 6, treats Mill's formal growth theory; 'Mill and Malthusianism' is considered in the concluding chapter, 945–55. See also Bowley (1973), ch. 6, on aspects of wage and profit theory in a growth context from Cantillon to Mill; and Winch's 'Introduction' to Books IV and V of the *Principles* (1970). Tucker (1960), ch. 8, is particularly useful on the relation of trend and cycle, dealt with in my next chapter.

Mill's position on the wages fund theory and his recantation is elaborated in Taussig's still useful *Wages and Capital* (1896), chs 11 and 12. See too Hollander (1984b).

10 Money and Banking: I

10.1 Introduction

The early nineteenth-century formulators of the 'law of markets' – the key classical monetary concept – took off from the Smithian doctrine of savings, which eulogized capital accumulation, criticized luxury consumption and maintained that the process of savings entails no leakages from the income stream: 'Whatever a person saves from his revenue he adds to his capital, and either employs it himself in maintaining an additional number of productive hands, or enables some other person to do so, by lending it to him for an interest, that is, for a share of the profits' (1776 [1937], 321). The doctrine implies that no attempt is made to add to money balances from sales proceeds. Smith himself gave some explanation for such implied behaviour: 'In all countries where there is tolerable security, every man of common understanding will endeavour to employ whatever stock he can command, in procuring either present enjoyment or future profit....A man must be perfectly crazy who, where there is tolerable security, does not employ all the stock which he commands, whether it be his own or borrowed of other people, in some one or other of those ... ways' (p. 268).

Although the qualification regarding 'tolerable security' is potentially significant, nothing is said of excess demand for money in conditions of uncertainty. Furthermore, Smith did not explicitly formulate the proposition that there can (given tolerable security) be no general excess supply of commodities – the counterpart of the absence of net hoarding. It is this proposition and its rationalization which concern us in the following account of the nineteenth-century law of markets.

The notion that the money value of commodities supplied is identically equal to the money value of commodities demanded is referred to here as 'Say's Identity', and the very different notion that the two are equal only in conditions of equilibrium as 'Say's Equality', after J. B. Say (1767–1832). The former version may be interpreted to imply that money *per se* has no utility to recipients who, having no reason to hold it in the form of cash balances, attempt to disburse it immediately for goods. Under these conditions prices will be driven up to infinity given any positive money supply, which in fact implies the absence of money stocks, that is, a barter system wherein the price level has no relevance. This version of the law of markets is inconsistent with the 'quantity theory', which implies a determinate level of prices for every given money supply. By contrast, the weaker version of the law of markets avoids this inconsistency; on this version, 'supply creates its own demand' by way of changes in the price level. Thus, in the event of a reduction in the supply of money *ceteris paribus*, the resultant excess demand for money (and corresponding excess supply of commodities) will be corrected by way of a decline in the level of prices. The essence of the matter lies in the notion that the community wishes to hold a certain command over goods and services in the form of money balances; since the real value of any given stock varies with changes in general prices, the initial excess demand for money will be satisfied by a rise in the purchasing power of the (lower) money stock until a new equilibrium is achieved. In equilibrium no attempt is made to add to money balances out of sales proceeds.

On this second view, a doubling of both the money supply and the price level will leave relative prices unchanged. Relative prices thus appear to be determined solely in the 'real' sector of the economy while the level of prices depends on the supply of money. But in fact substitution of money for commodities and substitution between commodities occur in any transition between equilibrium states as just described. Relative prices may well be affected (temporarily) by changes originating in the money market.

In what follows I shall first consider the positions of J. B. Say and Ricardo on the law of markets (section 10.2) and then digress somewhat to discuss Malthus, who opposed the orthodox school (section 10.3). Returning to the main line, section 10.4 concentrates on J. S. Mill and the law of markets, with particular attention being given in 10.5 and 10.6 to the relation Mill defined between trade cycle and secular trend and to certain implications drawn from the analysis for macro-policy. Sections 10.7 and 10.8 deal with the analysis by Ricardo and Mill of the impact of money on prices, output and interest. The companion chapter (chapter 11) deals with banking issues.

10.2 J. B. Say and Ricardo and the Law of Markets

The first edition of J. B. Say's *Traité d'économie politique* (1803) contains a brief chapter entitled 'Des Débouchés', which asserts that the excess outputs of commodities over their producers' own requirements generate mutual outlets (*débouchés*) for each other. Say here implies that no attempt is made to add to money balances from sales proceeds, money serving merely as the medium of exchange (1803, I, 152ff). Sales opportunities thus depend upon the ability to purchase, which in turn is governed by production or real output. Money acts only as medium of exchange: 'L'argent ne remplit qu'un office passager.... Les échanges terminés, il se trouve qu'on a payé des produits avec des produits' (p. 154).

Say's general concern was evidently with problems of economic growth, for he corroborates the proposition that there always exists adequate purchasing power to absorb any volume of output from the secular record; were it otherwise, he asks, how could one explain that contemporary France absorbed several times the output produced in approximately 1400 (II, 179–80). Yet the possibility of (short-run) excess commodity supply, though not formally related to excess demand for money, is recognized. The proposed solution is to produce more of a second commodity to create a market for the one in excess: 'quand une nation a trop de produits dans un genre, le moyen de les écouler est d'en créer d'un autre genre' (I, 154). (General equilibrium also requires, of course, that the commodity mix reflects appropriately the pattern of demand for goods; cf. II, 178–9). The problem of excess supply is amplified by Say in later editions, where it is said to have its source in the burden of taxation. But in 1803 the emphasis is on those limits to output which are imposed by capacity; for in a freely operating system the consequence of expanded capacity will be a concomitant expansion of the market (II, 361–2). Moreover (as with Smith), the process of accumulation itself does not create problems since it implies consumption as much as does (unproductive) expenditure.

Having in mind that it is real production that generates the requisite purchasing power, Say took issue with Sir James Steuart (1767) for maintaining in characteristic mercantilist fashion that foreign trade is the *sine qua non* of expansion (I, 155n.). More generally, Say rejected the mercantilist concern with the adequacy of the money supply (pp. 179–80); and, since the level of expenditure depends upon the level of general activity, he charged the Physiocrats with confusing the order of causality by recommending high consumption as a means of encouraging production (II, 175, 358–9). But since Say also subscribed to Smith's notion of a falling return on capital with accumulation due to 'increasing competition' (p. 189), he laid himself open to Ricardo's charge of inconsistency, since the law of markets from the secular perspective precludes the Smithian notion (see above, p. 195).

But what of Say's references to money acting solely as a medium of exchange, and the implication of general expenditure being always at its limit? Did he not deliberately preclude *short-run* attempts to add to money balances from sales proceeds, or an excess demand for money to hold? Any such impression is belied by various explicit allowances for hoarding.

Under normal circumstances, it is true, hoarding was ruled out, for it implied irrational behaviour considering the loss of interest involved; nothing is said of 'precautionary' or other advantages of holding money stocks. But under circumstances of exceptional political instability, and of exceptional uncertainty regarding future prices (specifically expectations of general price reductions), the phenomenon took on great importance and was the source of, or at least was accompanied by, general depression (pp. 136–7). In this same context Say also considered the reverse circumstances where inflationary price expectations rule. Here the rapid disbursement of money funds reflects an effort to avoid a loss of purchasing power. Say gives a brilliant account of the construction of industrial plant, house repairs and the like undertaken during the *assignat* episode. But under 'normal' conditions, the case against the likelihood of hoarding was not the 'perishability' of the value of money, but the avoidance of a loss of interest.

In a much expanded chapter on 'Des Débouchés' in the second (1814) edition, Say repeats the proposition that it is 'la production qui ouvre des débouchés aux produits' (I, 145n.). Again money is said to act simply as a medium of exchange; but now a potentially important proposition is added, namely that 'un produit créé offre, *dés cet instant*, un débouché à d'autres produits pour tout le montant de sa valeur' (p. 147). Does the qualification 'dés cet instant' rule out excess commodity supply in the short run? Apparently not, for, as in 1803, Say recognized general depression – 'dans tout état où la production marche péniblement et ne remplace jamais la quantité des valeurs consommées, les demandes allant en déclinant, il y a toujours plus de marchandise offerte que de marchandise vendue; les profits, les salaires diminuent, l'emploi des capitaux devient hasardeux...' (p. 158). This phenomenon is again related to an inadequate output of 'counter-commodities', which deficiency is now formally identified with inadequate income and accordingly purchasing power: 'beaucoup de gens ont moins acheté, parce qu'ils ont moins gagné; et ils ont moins gagné, parce qu'ils ont trouvé des difficultés dans l'emploi de leurs moyens de production, ou bien parce que ces moyens leur ont manqué' (pp. 148–9). Say illustrated the phenomenon of general depression by reference to French experience in 1813:

> La France a pu se former une idée de cette situation pénible en 1813. L'industrie y était dans un tel état de souffrance, toute espèce d'entreprise industrielle y était tellement dangereuse, ou si peu lucrative, que les capitaux n'y trouvaient point d'emploi avec une sûreté, ils se prêtaient

moyennant un très-faible intérêt; et le bas intérêt des capitaux, qui est ordinairement une marque de prospérité, y était un signe de détresse (p. 159n.).

Unfortunately Say neglected to specify the conditions (such as rigid prices) which would bring such a disequilibrium about, though clearly he had in mind some artificial impediment to the normal working of the system, disturbing the smooth flow of expenditures in conditions of uncertainty (p. 164). There would be no problem of inadequate expenditure under normal conditions, Say rationalizing the rapid expenditure of sales proceeds, as in 1803, in terms of avoidance of loss of interest. Avoidance of loss of purchasing power as motive for rapid money flows, assuming inflationary expectations, is also discussed (p. 165) and much emphasized in the third edition of the *Traité* (1817).

In his *Letters to Malthus* (1821), Say sought to account for the contemporary phenomena of excess capacity and widespread unemployment: 'What is the cause of the general glut of all the markets in the world, to which merchandize is incessantly carried to be sold at a loss? What is the reason that in the interior of every state, notwithstanding a desire of action adapted to all the developments of industry, there exists universally a difficulty of finding lucrative employments?' (1821, 2). To set the stage, he explained again, following Adam Smith, that it is the income generated by production which provides the wherewithal to make purchases, while money serves only as medium of exchange. He sharpened the conception of circular flow in order to demonstrate that 'we have ... the means of consuming what we have the means of producing' (p. 10). The 'savings is spending' theorem is repeated and hoarding minimized (pp. 37–8). He complained to Malthus that

> you assume implicitly as fact, that a production saved is abstracted from every species of consumption; although in all these discussions, in all the writings you attack, in those of *Adam Smith*, of *Mr. Ricardo*, in mine, and even in your own, it is laid down that a production saved is so much subtracted from unproductive consumption to be added to capital, that is to say, to the value that is consumed reproductively (p. 39).

Say thus used the Smith–Turgot theorem within the context of a circular flow model to show that the income–expenditure flow is not broken at any point when 'savings' are made.

Amongst the principal deductions Say draws from his conceptualization of the economic process are the standard notions that 'we purchase commodities with productive services, and ... the more productive services we carry to market, the more we can buy in return' (p. 11); and that 'all the producers possess *collectively* the means of acquiring the whole of the productions' (p. 27). But there is also the old allowance 'that if certain goods remain unsold it is because other goods are not produced' (p. 3). Excess supply is thus allowed; and it is now traced to government interference by taxation which renders unprofitable the production of the necessary 'counter-commodities': 'To buy the super-abundant produce, it would be requisite to create other produce', whereas the benefit which a (potential) producer 'might derive from his production would not indemnify him for its expenses' (p. 48). Alternatively expressed, 'the utility of productions is no longer worth the productive services, at the rate at which we are compelled to pay for them' (p. 51); for 'taxes do not augment the profits [incomes] of the producers, although they increase the price of every production: the incomes of the producers become insufficient to purchase the produce, the moment its price is raised by the circumstances which I have just described' (p. 46). To the objection that tax revenues are ultimately spent by public functionaries, soldiers etc., Say merely asserted that such expenditures are 'entirely at the expense of the producers' (p. 48).

The notion of money as medium of exchange only was thus not applied universally by Say. Hoarding was a feature of the contemporary depression, as Say protested in a case against Ricardo, although not the causal feature – taxation being the culprit.

> Mr. Ricardo insists that, notwithstanding taxes and other charges, there is always as much industry as capital employed; and that all capital saved is always employed, because the interest is not suffered to be lost. On the contrary, many savings are not invested, when it is difficult to find employment for them, and many which are employed are dissipated in ill-calculated undertakings. Besides Mr. Ricardo is completely refuted, not only by what happened to us in 1813, when the errors of Government ruined all commerce, and when the interest of money fell very low, for want of good opportunities of employing it; and by our present circumstances, when capitals are quietly sleeping in the coffers of their proprietors (p. 49n.).

Before turning to Ricardo himself, a word on James Mill (1773–1836), who is often regarded as the originator of the classical law of markets. In point of fact, Say has priority, considering his statement of 1803. More important, for Mill 'the production of commodities creates ... a market for the commodities produced' (1808, 81), while for Say, as we have seen, a product once created affords a market for other products, a formulation allowing for excess capacity which will be corrected only if and when other products are brought into existence. Say also sought to rationalize the (normally) prompt expenditure of sales receipts in terms of the avoidance of any loss of interest, and the 'perishability' of the value of money; and he was prepared to specify exceptions to the rule. In Mill's case we find only a brief reference to the proposition that 'no man, if he can help it, will let any part of his

property lie useless and run to waste' (p. 71) and a formal recommendation to conceive of the system in barter terms which implies that money
holdings *per se* yield no utility (p. 82). The doctrinaire version of the
principle – Say's Identity – is due to James Mill, not to Say.

*   *   *

Ricardo's first allusion to the 'savings is spending' theorem occurs in a
Note (1810/11) on a manuscript by Jeremy Bentham where Ricardo
objected on Smithian grounds to a discussion therein of ways to raise
aggregate demand: 'Is not this assuming that what is not spent is
hoarded. The revenue is in all cases spent, but in one case the objects on
which it is expended are consumed, and nothing reproduced[;] in the
other those objects form a new capital tending to increased production'
(1951, III, 299).

In correspondence with Malthus of 1814, Ricardo also seems to
ascribe to the strict version of the law of markets. For Malthus had
taken issue with James Mill's formulation of the law of markets; he
readily conceded that production generates the purchasing power and
thus the 'power' to absorb any level of output, but denied that the 'will'
necessarily existed (VI, 131–2). Ricardo based a defence of Mill upon
the 'savings are consumed' theorem and the probability that purchasing
power will in fact be devoted either to accumulation or consumption
such that even if accumulation is adversely affected by falling profits
there would be compensatory consumption expenditures: 'I consider
the wants and tastes of mankind as unlimited. We all wish to add to our
enjoyments or to our power. Consumption adds to our enjoyments, – accumulation to our power, and they equally promote
demand' (pp. 134–5).

At the close of 1814 Ricardo alluded to the new edition of Say's
Traité that had just come into his hands, in support of the doctrine that
'demand is regulated by production' (pp. 163–4). Here he considered
the proposition that 'demand is always an exchange of one commodity
for another', so that 'whilst [the shoemaker] has shoes to offer in
exchange he will have an effective demand for other things'. The reference to Say was too casual, for in conceding the possibility that there
might be no market for shoes, Ricardo observed in James Mill fashion
that the error must be corrected by 'the manufacture of the commodity
required by the society' – a reallocation of resources – whereas Say had
asserted that when a commodity is produced in excess, the solution is an
insufficiency in the supply of counter-commodities requiring a net
expansion of output. But at least by 1820 Ricardo had come to recognize the nature of Say's position, as is clear from correspondence with
Malthus regarding Say's *Letters to Mr. Malthus* (1821):

[Say appears] to think that stagnation in commerce arises from a counter set of commodities not being produced with which the commodities on sale are to be purchased, and ... to infer that the evil will not be removed till such other commodities are in the market. But surely the true remedy is in regulating future production, – if there is a glut of one commodity produce less of that and more of another but do not let the glut continue till the purchaser chuses to produce the commodity which is more wanted (Ricardo, 1951, VIII, 227–8).

All of this seems to suggest that Ricardo adhered to James Mill's rigid version of the law of markets; but the evidence is mixed. There are explicit allowances for divergences between aggregate demand and supply in the short run: 'though for a short period capital and produce may diminish faster than demand, – yet in the long run effective demand cannot augment or continue stationary with a diminishing capital' (VI, 120). In his next letter Ricardo formally suggested that his differences with Malthus were essentially 'about the permanence of the effects' (p. 128). Ricardo may then be understood (like Say) as insisting not upon an *identity* of aggregate supply and demand but rather upon their *long-run or secular equality*. Certainly, his primary concern throughout the 1814 correspondence was to deny any downward secular pressures on the profit rate apart from rising 'real' wages.

Here it is appropriate to refer to two striking passages, the first from the correspondence of 1816 and the second from the *Principles*, which seem to confirm that it is indeed 'Say's Equality' to which Ricardo ascribed. The first passage relates to (temporary) excess demand for money reflecting an initial reduction in the money supply:

a reduction in the amount of the circulating medium should speedily operate on prices, but the resistance which is offered – the unwillingness that every man feels to sell his goods at a reduced price, induces him to borrow at a high interest and to have recourse to other shifts to postpone the necessity of selling. The effect is however certain at last, but the duration of the resistance depends on the degree of information, or the strength of the prejudices of those who offer it, and therefore it cannot be the subject of any thing like accurate calculation (VII, 67).

Here Ricardo goes beyond Say in introducing the condition – rigid prices – responsible for disequilibrium.

The second passage relates to the identification of an increase in the demand for money – the temporary postponement of expenditures during crisis conditions – and an increase in the supply of money as far as the temporary nature of their effects upon the interest rate is concerned:

The rate of interest, though ultimately and permanently governed by the rate of profit, is however subject to temporary variations from other causes. With every fluctuation in the quantity and value of money, the prices of commodities naturally vary.... When the market prices of goods fall...from a rise in the value of money, a manufacturer naturally accumulates an unusual quantity of finished goods, being unwilling to sell them at very depressed prices. To meet his ordinary payments, for which he used to depend on the sale of his goods, he now endeavours to borrow on credit, and is often obliged to give an increased rate of interest. This, however, is but of temporary duration; for either the manufacturer's expectations were well grounded, and the market price of his commodities rises, or he discovers that there is a permanently diminished demand, and he no longer resists the course of affairs: prices fall, and money and interest regain their real value. If by the discovery of a new mine, by the abuses of banking, or by any other cause, the quantity of money be greatly increased, its ultimate effect is to raise the prices of commodities in proportion to the increased quantity of money; but there is probably always an interval, during which some effect is produced on the rate of interest (I, 297–8).

This passage constitutes an embryonic formulation of J. S. Mill's famous essay 'Of the Influence of Consumption on Production' (see below, p. 255). Despite his frequent strong statements and his criticism of Say on the need for 'counter-commodities', Ricardo apparently adhered to that version of the law of markets labelled 'Say's Equality', which allows for temporary deviations between the money values of commodities supplied and demanded – temporary excess demand for money.

We are not, however, yet out of the woods. For Ricardo approached the post-war depression in terms of a model which incorporated the full-employment assumption and he insisted that an increase in government expenditure implies an equivalent reduction in private expenditure – in our century labelled the 'Treasury View' – despite awareness of severe unemployment and under-utilization of capacity over the years 1815–21. In Parliament, for example, he objected that 'when he heard honourable members talk of employing capital in the formation of roads and canals, they appeared to overlook the fact, that the capital thus employed must be withdrawn from some other quarter' (V, 32). He himself explained the depression by sluggish factor mobility in the post-war transition away from declining to potentially prosperous industries.

Ricardo's recognition of excess money demand should have led him, as it indeed led J. B. Say, to a more catholic interpretation of the post-war crisis. I would conjecture that he overstated his case in part because of the strength of his objections to those economists, including Smith, who implied the possibility of permanent stagnation quite independently of the depressing effects on the profit rate of high 'wages' – the inverse wage–profit relation. That the issue was on Ricardo's mind is certain. In the *Principles* he referred to an alternative account of the post-war difficulties that emphasized an actual reduction in aggregate capital; he admitted that the characteristics of crisis due to such a cause would be no different from those due simply to the frictions he had in mind, but since there was at hand a simple hypothesis, he felt it unnecessary to look further for an explanation:

> When, however, such distress immediately accompanies a change from war to peace, our knowledge of the existence of such a cause will make it reasonable to believe, that the funds for the maintenance of labour have rather been diverted from their usual channel, than materially impaired, and that after temporary suffering, the nation will again advance in prosperity (I, 265).

Ricardo's strong opposition to such notions may have led him to overstate his own position and disallow excess commodity supply as a relevant consideration in contemporary circumstances.

A second matter possibly played a part. Ricardo was perhaps afraid to play into the hands of crude inflationists by allowing much weight to short-period effects. For the long period might be considered as a succession of short periods, suggesting that a monetary stimulus called for in depression to satisfy excess demand for money to hold should be repeated once the first injection had been exhausted – with disastrous inflationary consequences.

10.3 Malthus and Aggregate Demand

The analysis of accumulation by Malthus in the *Principles of Political Economy* (1820; partly reprinted in Ricardo's *Works*, 1951, II) emphasizes an inherent danger that attempts to expand capacity may end in depression and unemployment.* His concern was that capitalists tended to respond too rapidly to high profits: 'Almost all merchants and manufacturers save, in prosperous times, much more rapidly than it would be possible for the national capital to increase, so as to keep up the value of the produce' (p. 465; *Works*, II, 423). The process of 'saving' involves a reduction in the demand for menial servants and a transfer of workers to the 'productive' sector – that sector involved in the production of (material) goods for sale with the objective of yielding profit, as distinct from unproductive or service labour, which is employed as a form of consumption (cf. pp. 32–3; *Works*, II, 15–16). The displaced labourers may be supported by wage goods which had hitherto maintained them

---

* The present account is based largely on *Principles*, 1820, pp. 32–3, 351–4, and 463–4; in *Works*, 1951, II, 15–16, 301–8, 347–8.

in their original occupation, but these wage goods now *in effect* act as 'capital goods' since workers maintained thereby are available to produce an increased quantity of material goods of the type seeking profitable markets. A problem arises, however, because of the failure of consumption to rise *pari passu* with the output forthcoming from the expanded capacity. For working class purchasing power in unchanged, despite the increase in aggregate output – there having occurred simply a transfer of labour between sectors – whereas capitalists' consumption is, by the initial assumption, reduced.

The result of the 'savings' process is therefore a reduction in commodity prices. But for Malthus, who typically presumed a degree of rigidity in money wages, it followed that savings 'must, by diminishing the effectual demand for produce, throw the labouring classes out of employment' (p. 369; *Works*, II, 325). (Effectual demand is 'a consumption by those who are able and willing to pay such a price for produce as will *effect* the continuation of its supply without a fall of profits not required by the state of the land'; 2nd edn, 1836 [1964], 411n.) The new situation is not a 'stable' one, characterized merely by low profits and an inability to continue the process of accumulation; and it is precisely this fact which distinguishes the result of Malthusian from Ricardian saving. Moreover the problem is not solved by a switch from saving to consumption; for the level of activity declines and both consumption and savings decline (1820, 466; *Works*, II, 424).

In the analysis by Ricardo (see above, p. 185), an increased savings process – in the case of a constant population – leads to a transfer of purchasing power to labour. Profits indeed fall as the wage rate paid to the fully employed labour force rises, but the 'final' situation is a stable one, wherein workers are in a position to purchase luxury goods. It is this transfer of purchasing power to labour that Ricardo relies on to assure the maintenance of expenditure. He, of course, expected population to expand ultimately, but the expansion would be in response to the state of high real wages paid to a fully employed work force. Apart from population increase, a second solution to the Ricardian case of depressed profits due to excess savings would be a reduction in the demand for labour as a result of a transfer from investment to consumption spending. Malthus's opinion regarding the empirical facts of money wage reactions is sharply rejected: 'I can seen no reason whatever why they should not fall before many labourers are thrown out of work…why should some agree to go without any wages while others were most liberally rewarded' (Letter to Malthus, in *Works*, 1951, IX, 25). The entire Ricardian position involves a straightforward application of the wages fund theory combined with the proposition that 'the demand for commodities is not demand for labour' (see above, p.

183). On the assumption of flexible wages there is no reason to expect unemployment upon variations in the demand or supply of labour. The following brief account contains the essence of Ricardo's ideas:

> If you [Malthus] had said, 'after arriving at a certain limit there will in the actual circumstances be no use to try to produce more – the end cannot be accomplished, and if it could instead of more less would belong to the class which provided the capital', I should have agreed with you – yet in that case I should say the real cause of this faulty distribution would be to be found in the inadequate quantity of labour in the market, and would be effectually cured by an additional supply of it.... I acknowledge there may not be adequate motives for production, and therefore things will not be produced, but I cannot allow, first that with these inadequate motives commodities will be produced, and secondly that, if their production is attended with loss to the producer, it is for any other reason than because too great a proportion is given to the labourers employed. Increase their number, and the evil is remedied. Let the employer consume more himself, and there will be no diminution of demand for labour [employment], but the pay of the labourer, which was before extravagently high, will be reduced (IX, 16).

One difference between Malthus and Ricardo lies in their alternative assumptions regarding the empirical facts of money wage flexibility. But in the great debate over accumulation each used logic relevant to his *own* vision of the accumulation process to counter the arguments of the other. In Malthus's analysis there occurs an expansion of output – even when population is constant – and no corresponding expansion of demand because of the transfer of labour out of the service sector; this expansion is absent in Ricardo's analysis. In the one case commodity prices fall (more rapidly than money wages) and in the other money wages rise (with commodity prices unchanged). The logic applicable to the one is not necessarily applicable to the other.

Malthus's general under-consumption or over-savings case is not easy to evaluate. There were contemporaries, pre-eminently Lord Lauderdale (1804), who condemned accumulation from the perspective of under-consumption – it has been well said that Lauderdale was the true anti-saver of the age. Malthus did not go so far; he after all maintained a formal Ricardo-like growth model which made no reference to the problem of under-consumption (see above, p. 202). For accumulation, he conceded, was essential for growth, and Lauderdale had 'gone as much too far in deprecating accumulation, as some other writers in recommending it' (1820, 352n.; *Works*, 1951, II, 301n.):

> It is certainly true that no permanent and continued increase in wealth can take place without a continued increase of capital; and I cannot agree with Lord Lauderdale in thinking that this increase can be effected in any

other way than by saving from the stock which might have been destined for immediate consumption, and adding it to that which is to yield a profit; or in other words, by the conversion of revenue into capital (1820, 351–2; *Works*, II, 301).

The problem was that in political economy 'so much depends upon proportions' (1836 [1964], 314n.). It is 'conversion of revenue into capital pushed *beyond a certain point* [that] must, by diminishing the effectual demand for produce, throw the labouring classes out of employment'; 'the adoption of parsimonious habits *in too great a degree*' was the problem (1820, 369; *Works*, II, 325, emphasis added). All this is already implied in the tendency of capitals to respond too rapidly 'in prosperous times' to high profits. But how to define the optimum rate of saving (investment) – for that seems to be the issue – he did not adequately clarify. Indeed, he was quite candid regarding this kind of issue: 'What the proportion is between the productive and unproductive classes of a society, which affords the greatest encouragement to the continued increase of wealth ... the resources of political economy are unequal to determine' (1820, 464; *Works*, II, 422).

*   *   *

The literature on the intellectual anticipation of Keynesian macro-economics by Malthus revolves around the function of saving in Malthus's theory of aggregate demand. Since Malthus usually meant by 'saving' real investment, his fears regarding excessive saving, whatever may be their precise origin, cannot be identified with those arising in the Keynesian system. This argument implies that oversaving (overinvestment) is, for Malthus, the only possible cause of depression. Yet the post-Napoleonic depression was not accounted for by Malthusian 'oversaving'; on the contrary, the account is consistent with Keynesian analysis.

The post-war depression, in Malthus's view, began with a disastrous reduction in corn prices, due to a series of excellent harvests in conditions of demand inelasticity. Demand for agricultural labour fell, since money wages were initially unchanged, and there resulted severe agricultural unemployment (1820, 444ff, in *Works*, II, 396ff; 1836 [1964], 386ff). Reduced farm incomes in turn led to reduced purchases of manufactured goods, resulting in widespread unemployment throughout the economy. (Ricardo also recognized the phenomenon of high demand inelasticity for agricultural produce and the post-war decline in corn prices and gross farm income; but he did not recognize the consequential reduction in expenditure by the agricultural community upon manufactured produce.) The situation was aggravated by a contraction in the money supply which reduced home demand further; and by a reduction in government expenditures accompanied by the increased 'savings' of those whose after-tax incomes rose, by which term Malthus, it seems, intended hoarding:

> The returned taxes, and the excess of individual gains above expenditure, which were so largely used as revenue during the war, are now in part, and probably in no inconsiderable part, saved....[This] contributes to explain the cause of the diminished demand for commodities, compared with their supply since the war. If some of the principal governments concerned spent the taxes which they raised in a manner to create a greater and more certain demand for labour and commodities, particularly the former, than the present owners of them, and if this difference of expenditure to be of a nature to last some time, we cannot be surprised at the duration of the effects arising from the transition from war to peace (1836 [1964], 421).

Further evidence of the recognition by Malthus of the contemporary significance of hoarding can be found in the exchange involving himself, Say and Ricardo. We have seen that Say, in his open letter to Malthus of 1820, condemned Ricardo's apparent refusal to recognize the phenomenon of leakages from income under any circumstances (see above, p. 246). Hoarding, Say pointed out, was an actual problem in France. For his part, Ricardo objected that Say 'concedes too much' (1951, VIII, 277–8). But Malthus was satisfied with the analysis, which he regarded as quite inconsistent with Say's general position and wrote as much to Ricardo:

> ...he fully concedes all that I ask for. He says 'qu'il y a beaucoup d'épargnes qui ne se placent pas lorsque les emplois sont difficiles, ou qui étant placées se dissipent dans une production mal calculé' – and this he illustrates by the present state of France. The present state of things indeed in England, America, Holland and Hamburgh still more than in France does appear in the most marked manner to contradict both his, and your theory. The fall in the interest of money and the difficulty of finding employment for capital are universally acknowledged, and this fact, none of your friends have ever accounted for in any tolerably satisfactory manner (p. 260).

Although in Malthus's account money wages at the outset of the depression were constant in the face of falling prices, money wages do ultimately decline: 'The fall in the price of labour which took place in 1815 and 1816 was occasioned solely by the diminution of demand [for labour], arising from the losses of the farmers' (1820, 242; *Works*, II, 225). But Malthus also wrote that unemployment was not thereby eradicated: 'Though labour is cheap, there is neither the power nor the will to employ it all;... owing to the diminished revenues of the country, the commodities which those labourers would produce are not in such request as to ensure tolerable profits to the reduced capital' (1836 [1964], 417). In essence, the price level remained too low even relative to the reduced level of money wages to assure increased profitability – the real wage rate was restrained at too high a level to permit full employment. It is certainly Malthus's view that real wages must be brought back at least to their original level, to achieve which the money wage rate has to fall appropriately. But, as Keynes was later to emphasize, this may not always be possible. The state of effectual demand which governs the price level thus plays an independent role, and there may be circumstances when the price level is such as to assure a real wage per man that does not permit full employment.

Malthus was quite pessimistic as to the measures that might be taken to counter the post-war depression. One of the few immediately effective partial solutions was public works. Support for public works is, of course, what might be expected from a 'Keynesian'. On the other hand, the reasoning is not Keynesian; public works were not supported because they represent a net injection of purchasing power into the economy which (together with multiplier effects) would lead to a higher level of activity. Malthus's argument, rather, is based upon the position that any transfer of funds from productive to unproductive expenditure will raise the level of effectual demand and, accordingly, the profit rate (1820, 511; *Works*, II, 446; 1836 [1964], 429–30). Essentially, he supported the first stage of the Treasury View argument to the effect that there will be a transfer of funds from one use to another, but objected to the second stage which maintained that accordingly there will be no purpose to the transfer. The argument behind Malthus's support for public works was based upon logic which has little in common with Keynes.

10.4   J. S. Mill and the Law of Markets

At this point we turn to a celebrated essay by J. S. Mill, 'Of the Influence of Consumption on Production' (written 1830–1). Mill commences his argument by referring to the importance attached to the stimulation of consumption from the perspective of economic growth, before Adam Smith had given economics its 'comparatively scientific character'. The true view, 'triumphantly established' in place of the 'palpable absurdities', amounted to the savings-is-spending theorem: 'The person who saves his income is no less a consumer than he who spends it: he consumes it in a different way; it supplies food and clothing to be consumed, tools and materials to be used, by productive labourers.' Attempts by government to encourage consumption merely diverted funds from 'reproductive' (investment) uses – an application of the Treasury View. The conclusion was unambiguous, that 'there will never... be a greater quantity produced, of commodities in general, than there are consumers for' (Mill, 1967, IV, 262–3).

Yet Mill then admitted to 'some strong appearance of evidence' which had misled those who maintained the 'palpable absurdities' regarding consumption. He proceeds to 'inquire into the nature of the appearances, which gave rise to the belief that a great demand, a brisk circulation, a rapid consumption (three equivalent expressions), are a cause of national prosperity', in order 'that no scattered particles of important truth are buried and lost in the ruins of exploded error' (p. 264). In the end he concluded that expanded aggregate consumption may indeed act as a stimulus.

The argument is twofold. The first part turns on the fact that advanced economies should never operate at full capacity in the literal sense, since inventories and money funds must be available at various stages of production to satisfy expected sales in the one case and make necessary purchases in the other. This is a 'technological' matter: if the turnover period were somehow reduced – the emphasis in this part of the argument is on inventory levels – hitherto idle 'capital' might be actively utilized in the expansion of physical plant, materials and wage goods. Mill, however, warned that the flexibility provided by inventories in a world of imperfect knowledge is essential to the smooth working of the system, and excess capacity of this nature can never safely be totally dispensed with (pp. 278–9). In short, he called for 'full employment at high wages' but not the maximum level of employment achievable in the short run. Lapses from full employment are associated with accumulations of stocks; but the carrying of normal stocks is no sign of a lapse.

The warning against unjustified increases in turnover rates is prologue to a discussion of cyclical variation in speculative mood:

> In the present state of the commercial world, mercantile transactions being carried on upon an immense scale, but the remote causes of fluctuations in prices being very little understood, so that unreasonable hopes and unreasonable fears alternately rule with tyrannical sway over the minds of a majority of the mercantile public; general eagerness to buy and general reluctance to buy, succeed one another in a manner more or less marked, at brief intervals. Except during short periods of transition, there is almost always either great briskness of business or great stagnation; either the principal producers of almost all the leading articles of industry have as many orders as they can possibly execute, or the dealers in almost all commodities have their warehouses full of unsold goods (p. 275).

These cyclical swings in speculative mood are, unfortunately, taken for granted and not further analysed. But they provide the backdrop for Mill's allowance of a short-run excess demand for money to hold of a speculative nature – one of the most important formulations in classical economics:

> There can never, it is said, be a want of buyers for all commodities; because whoever offers a commodity for sale, desires to obtain a commodity in exchange for it, and is therefore a buyer by the mere fact of his being a seller. The sellers and the buyers, for all commodities taken together, must, by the metaphysical necessity of the case, be an exact equipoise to each other; and if there be more sellers than buyers of one thing, there must be more buyers than sellers for another.
>
> This argument is evidently founded on the supposition of a state of barter; and, on that supposition, it is perfectly incontestable.... If, however, we suppose that money is used, these propositions cease to be exactly true.... [In] the case of barter, the selling and the buying are simultaneously confounded in one operation; you sell what you have, and buy what you want, by one indivisible act, and you cannot do the one without doing the other. Now the effect of the employment of money, and even the utility of it, is, that it enables this one act to interchange to be divided into two separate acts or operations; one of which may be performed now, and the other a year hence, or whenever it shall be most convenient.... The buying and selling being now separated, it may very well occur, that there may be, at some given time, a very general inclination to sell with as little delay as possible, accompanied with an equally general inclination to defer all purchases as long as possible. This is always actually the case, in those periods which are described as periods of general excess...(p. 276).

This argument stands apart from the allowance for unused 'capital' in the form of inventories as a necessary feature even at quiescent stages of the cycle.

Mill's essay thus provides a picture of temporary stagnation generated if people are inclined to sell without delay and disinclined to buy. But why is the stagnation only temporary? Mill suggests that the expectation of recovery encourages firms to delay sales wherever possible (pp. 276–7). Evidently then, at some stage during the crisis, the state of expectations must have reversed itself, for the original feature under analysis had been the general attempt to add to money balances from sales proceeds – a general anxiety to sell. The juxtaposition of this transition in mood with the emphasis upon the temporary nature of the crisis suggests that recovery is presumed to set in with expanded purchases in response to expected price increases. This, apparently, is as far as Mill went in explaining the presumption against a Keynes-like 'unemployment equilibrium'.

Mill insisted firmly that his recognition of excess demand for money to hold conceded nothing to the 'general glut' or 'overproduction' theorists (p. 272ff). Their view is, as usual, lambasted as absurd. Secondly, he claimed that no orthodox economist who subscribed to the law of markets would deny the possibility of an excess demand for money to hold (p. 276). His own account of excess money demand added nothing to what was known by 'the authors of the doctrine', who at most were sometimes 'inadvertant' in formulation and left the unfortunate impression that their doctrine contradicted 'well-known facts' (pp. 278–9). There is considerable justification for these assertions since Say generally (and Ricardo on significant occasions) did not insist upon the extreme version of the law of markets – Say's Identity. But they are unbecoming as far as Mill himself is concerned, since that version had governed his early perspective on monetary matters to the extent of blinding him to the very 'facts' (including unemployment) which now forced themselves upon his attention and with which he at last felt able to deal.

What emerges from the essays prior to the *Principles* in an allowance for crisis periods characterized by excess commodity supply, and excess capacity above and beyond the normal margin of quiescent periods. These crises are represented as part of a cyclical process involving swings in expectations of an endogenous order, swings which explain why 'unemployment equilibria' are not a feature of the argument. In two papers of 1826 and 1844 Mill links the state of expectations with the downward secular trend of the profit rate. Notwithstanding all this, the law of markets stands sentinel as firmly as ever, if by that term is meant the impossibility of overproduction as such, for *secular* expansion of output can never be checked by lack of purchasing power. On this matter Mill stood shoulder to shoulder with Ricardo.

Two chapters in Book III of the *Principles*, 'Of the Influence of Credit on Prices' (ch. xii), and 'Of Excess of Supply' (ch. xiv), deal with the same themes as the essay. In the latter Mill turns his attention to those such as Malthus, Chalmers and Sismondi who, on his reading, asserted that expansion of products in the aggregate is necessarily accompanied by a deficiency of purchasing power, thereby precluding sales at unchanged prices and profits (1848 [1965], III, 571).

The source of this 'overproduction error' was seen to lie in a misconceived appeal to 'mercantile facts'. The facts, Mill insisted, were better accountable in terms of his own conception of commercial crises. Here we find all the key elements of the earlier essay with its allowance for excess commodity supply:

> At such times there is really, an excess of all commodities above the money demand: in other words, there is an under-supply of money. From

the sudden annihilation of a great mass of credit, every one dislikes to part with ready money, and many are anxious to procure it at any sacrifice. Almost everybody therefore is a seller, and there are scarcely any buyers; so that there may really be, though only while the crisis lasts, an extreme depression of general prices, from what may be indiscriminately called a glut of commodities or a dearth of money. But it is a great error to suppose, with Sismondi, that a commercial crisis is the effect of a general excess of production. It is simply the consequence of an excess of speculative purchases. It is not a gradual advent of low prices, but a sudden recoil from prices extravagantly high: its immediate cause is a contraction of credit, and the remedy is, not a diminution of supply, but the restoration of confidence. It is also evident that this temporary derangement of markets is an evil only because it is temporary. The fall being solely of money prices, if prices did not rise again no dealer would lose, since the smaller price would be worth as much to him as the larger price was before (p. 574).

Mill is here presuming that the Malthus view alludes to secular trends, the growth process forcing down prices in consequence of inadequate purchasing power. As Mill viewed the matter, the facts of the case, as far as they concerned commercial crises, pointed only to temporary price and profit movements, the problem of profitability residing precisely in their non-permanent character. This objection is important from a methodological viewpoint, for appeal is made to facts which are convincingly shown to accord better with an alternative theoretical model.

Mill, in 1848, carries the analysis beyond the earlier essay by supplementing the inventory cycle by a cycle in fixed capital formation, and by extending the notion of excess supply to the labour market:

[During speculative periods,] mines are opened, railways or bridges made, and many other works of uncertain profit commenced, and in these enterprises much capital is sunk which yields either no return, or none adequate to the outlay. Factories are built and machinery erected beyond what the market requires, or can keep in employment.... Besides this, there is a great unproductive consumption of capital, during the stagnation which follows a period of general over-trading. Establishments are shut up, or kept working without any profit, hands are discharged, and numbers of persons in all ranks, being deprived of their income, and thrown for support on their savings, find themselves, after the crisis has passed away, in a condition of more or less impoverishment (p. 741).

The allowance for excess labour supply appears also in the discussion of the proposition 'industry is limited by capital', where Mill proposes that the doctrine regarding aggregate employment be supplemented by a function allowing for the state of aggregate demand for final goods (see above, p. 219).

J. M. Keynes cited Mill to illustrate an extreme 'classical' position on the law of markets (1936 [1973], 18). But he did so selectively, failing entirely to note the strong qualifications, and therefore seriously distorted the historical record (see also below, p. 275).

10.5   Trade Cycle, the Law of Markets and Secular Trend

An endogenous trade cycle, with phases merging one into another in semi-automatic fashion, was better developed by Mill than any earlier writer. Regularity of cyclical fluctuations was a matter already emphasized in Mill's 1836 paper: 'except during short periods of transition, there is almost always either great briskness of business or great stagnation' (above, p. 256). In the *Principles* Mill reiterates of speculative periods that 'all times are so, more or less' (1848 [1965], III, 512). But now more attention is paid to the 'quiescent' period itself and its place in the cycle (pp. 662–3).

During the quiescent state 'nothing [tends] to engender in any considerable portion of the mercantile public a desire to extend their operations. The producers produce and the dealers purchase only their usual stocks, having no expectation of a more than usually rapid vent for them'. Quiescence contrasts with the 'unusual extension' of the speculative state where there exists some exogenous stimulus – short crops, import restrictions, new foreign markets – which 'exciting more than usual hopes of profit, gives increased briskness to business'. At the same time, quiescence itself allows for expansion: 'Each person transacts his ordinary amount of business, and no more; or increases it only in correspondence with the increase of his capital or connexion, or with the gradual growth of the demand for his commodity, occasioned by the public prosperity'. That a quiescent period entails expansion in fact constitutes the necessary condition for the generation of cyclical fluctuations; for it is the downward 'tendency' of the profit rate with expansion that engenders speculation. Conversely, various capital losses associated with the cycle play back on the profit rate itself.

The notion that cyclical fluctuations are an outcome of the falling profit rate is elaborated in the chapter 'Of the Tendency of Profits to a Minimum' (Book IV, iv), with particular emphasis on the regular periodicity of cycles:

> that…revulsions are almost periodical, is a consequence of the very tendency of profits which we are considering. By the time a few years have passed over without a crisis, so much additional capital has been accumulated, that it is no longer possible to invest it at the accustomed profit: all public securities rise to a high price, the rate of interest on the

best mercantile security falls very low, and the complaint is general among persons in business that no money is to be made.... But the diminished scale of all safe gains, inclines people to give a ready ear to any projects which hold out, though at the risk of loss, the hope of a higher rate of profit; and speculations ensue, which, with the subsequent revulsions, destroy, or transfer to foreigners, a considerable amount of capital, produce a temporary rise of interest and profit, make room for fresh accumulations, and the same round is recommenced (p. 742).

The *ceteris paribus* conditions upon which the profit rate trend is predicated include constant technology and the absence of capital wastage of various kinds – unsustainable capital projects during speculative periods, and 'unproductive' consumption during the depressions which follow (see above, p. 259). A 'tendency' which itself encourages the counteracting force renders entirely questionable the designation of the latter as a 'disturbing cause', bearing as it does a connotation of independence. Similar issues are raised by capital exportation, which contributes to prevent profits 'from reaching the minimum' (p. 745). Whatever the methodological difficulties, it is apparently Mill's position that in the absence of various capital outflows, both domestic and abroad, the impact of technical progress would not suffice to balance that of land scarcity and allow 'a tolerably equal struggle against the downward tendency of profits' (p. 741); the net outcome of the various conflicting forces actually at work assured a constant trend path of the return on capital at about 3 per cent with fluctuations about it of a cyclical order.

Mill's allusions to technical change also create problems. For the most part he argues as if technical change constitutes a purely exogenous disturbance counteracting the downward profit rate trend. But allowance is sometimes made for induced technology:

> When the capital accumulated is so great and the rate of annual accumulation so rapid, that the country is only kept from attaining the stationary state by the emigration of capital, or by continual improvements in production; any circumstance [such as a profits tax] which virtually lowers the rate of profit cannot be without a decided influence on these phenomena. It may operate in different ways. The curtailment of profit, and the consequent increased difficulty in making a fortune or obtaining a subsistence by the employment of capital, may act as stimulus to inventions, and to the use of them when made. If improvements in production are much accelerated, and if these improvements cheapen, directly or indirectly, any of the things habitually consumed by the labourer, profits may rise, and rise sufficiently to make up for all that is taken from them by the tax (p. 827).

Mill's specific concern here happens to be with a tax on profits. But there is no reason why the secular decline itself should not similarly act as a stimulus to innovation, in which case to treat it as a 'disturbing cause' would be inappropriate. Indeed, Mill himself speaks of the profit–technology relation as a 'tendency', thus according it the same status, with all its implications, as he accords the pressure on profits of scarce land. We shall encounter a parallel difficulty in Marx's *Capital*.

10.6   Some New Implications for Policy

The implications of the analysis of the 'Consequences of the Tendency of Profits to a Minimum' are remarkable. In the absence of capital loss, the rate of accumulation would (on Mill's empirical estimate) be so high as to force down the return on capital, since technical progress would not suffice to counteract such heavy pressure on scarce land. It followed from the fact of so highly active a 'spirit of accumulation' that 'a sudden abstraction of capital, unless of inordinate amount', need not be feared, for 'after a few months or years, there would exist in the country just as much capital as if none had been taken away'. At most 'the abstraction, by raising profits and interest, would give a fresh stimulus to the accumulative principle, which would speedily fill up the vacuum', though more likely 'the only effect that would ensue, would be that for some time afterwards less capital would be exported, and less thrown away in hazardous speculation' (Mill, 1848 [1965], III, 747–8). Even the conversion of circulating into fixed capital took on a different colour:

> Since even the emigration of capital, or its unproductive expenditure, or its absolute waste, do not in such a country, if confined within any moderate bounds, at all diminish the aggregate amount of the wages fund still less can the mere conversion of a like sum into fixed capital, which continues to be productive, have that effect. It merely draws off at one orifice what was already flowing out at another; ... sums so applied [e.g. to railways] are mostly a mere appropriation of the annual overflowing which would otherwise have gone abroad, or been thrown away unprofitably, leaving neither a railway nor any other tangible result (pp. 749–50).

The conclusion altered entirely the perspective towards government expenditure, for the standard warnings by orthodox writers against measures that might reduce the rate of capital accumulation, were no longer pertinent (p. 748). Mill writes indeed as if capital is no longer to be treated as a scarce factor. The question immediately arises whether his support for expenditure of public money 'for really valuable, even though industrially unproductive purposes' has genuine Keynesian overtones. Was he advocating government spending of idle funds to offset a secular decline in the profit rate, casting doubt on Smith's doctrine of the unconditional benefits of parsimony, which he himself had so enthusiastically championed against the position of Malthus and Sismondi that capital might accumulate too fast? Clearly no issue can be of greater importance for an appreciation of classical macro-economics.

We would be faced with a remarkable situation were it the case that while formally insisting upon adherence to orthodoxy on matters of principle, Mill proceeded to reject that very orthodoxy in practice. But the main point to note is Mill's emphatic reiteration that the downward 'tendency' of the profit rate was to be *divorced* from any notion of lack of markets:

> The difficulty would not consist in any want of a market. If the new capital were duly shared amnong many varieties of employment, it would raise up a demand for its own produce, and there would be no cause why any part of that produce should remain longer on hand than formerly. What would really be, not merely difficult, but impossible, would be to employ this capital without submitting to a rapid reduction in the rate of profit (pp. 739–40).

The chapter on the downward trend in profits in fact opens with a severe criticism of the Smithian doctrine regarding 'competition of capitals' (p. 733). Moreover Mill's position on government spending is, in fact, quite consistent. The potential problem, as we have seen, was excessive capital accumulation forcing down the return on capital *in the Ricardian fashion* – excessive in the sense that the pressure on land exceeds the counteracting force of new technology. Such a decline, how-ever, was, in practice, temporary in consequence of capital losses. Those losses include poorly conceived 'speculative' additions to the real capital stock which prove untenable in quiescent periods – the specula-tion induced to some degree by the fall in the profit rate – and the draw-ing down of saved funds for consumption purposes in depression, the inevitable sequel to speculative periods. To this extent there is no question of leakages from the income stream by the non-investment of savings; savings are lost in the sense only of being unproductively used up. Mill's allowance for higher government spending thus amounts in effect to a proposal to tap the flow of savings, thereby preventing their excessive accumulation, the pressure on land and the fall in the return on capital – the Ricardian consequences – and also preventing the various cyclical consequences of that fall, which include wastage of capital. Mill was calling for opera houses in place of a superfluous network of railways and 'unproductive' private consumption. This is not a 'Keynesian' secular perspective.

That Mill recognized excess capacity and excess supplies of labour and commodities in depression we have demonstrated. But government expenditures were certainly not envisaged as counter-cyclical measures, for cyclical depression was seen to be self-corrective. So, from this perspective too, we are not in a Keynesian world. Only indirectly would government spending be effective, for by imposing a floor to the return on capital it checks the 'speculative fever' from which depression ultimately proceeds.

Apart from capital 'losses' of the order discussed thus far, attention is also given to genuine leakages from the expenditure stream in the form of capital exportation. Here it is essential to distinguish outflows due to a low domestic return relative to foreign return on capital, from those due to an actual decline in the domestic return. As for the latter, to the extent that government spending absorbs savings that would otherwise be invested in domestic ventures with a negative effect on profits – the reduction reflecting a rise in proportionate wages in the Ricardian manner – outflows abroad are actually discouraged. Government spending can be said to involve the absorption of funds otherwise leaking from the system only if capital export reflects a relatively low domestic level of profits and is 'actually' rather than 'potentially' under way. This is the full extent of Mill's abandonment of the Treasury View. Yet his formal adherence to the fully fledged law of markets – applied at the secular level – can easily be appreciated. For that doctrine applies, strictly speaking, to a closed economy. There is no reason to believe that Ricardo would have denied that, once allowance is made for international capital flows, a deviation between domestic and foreign rates of return might generate savings which are lost to the domestic economy.

At the same time, we must have in mind Mill's evaluation of contemporary conditions. Circumstances might be contemplated wherein capital exportation carried with it ominous implications. This would be so in a stationary state (as far as net domestic investment is concerned) should savings continue to be made only to flow abroad. But in contemporary Britain there was no question of the leakages abroad generating problems for the maintenance of activity of this kind. The rate of net domestic investment was positive and markedly so – capital export entailing not an absolute reduction in domestic employment but merely a restraint on its growth rate. Increased government spending was not conceived as absorbing otherwise unemployed resources. Its purpose was not the employment effect at all, but rather the creation of socially desirable public projects in buoyant circumstances which allowed a simultaneous expansion of the private sector.

Mill's 'failure' to investigate the full implications of capital exportation from a 'Keynesian' perspective can thus be largely appreciated as a reflection of a buoyant environment. He did, it is true, introduce a moderately concerned tone in discussing the implications of corn law repeal, for he questioned 'how far this resource [could] be counted upon, for making head during a very long period against the tendency of profits to decline as capital increases', assuming a population 'increasing at its present [rapid] rate' (p. 745). European agriculture was technologically backward; colonial and American agriculture had exhausted the latest advances; extension of agriculture in Europe would be a slow process; and America's own population growth equalled the rate of expansion of its agricultural produce: 'This limited source of supply', Mill concluded with reference to foreign imports, 'unless great improvements take place in agriculture, cannot be expected to keep pace with the growing demand of so rapidly increasing a population as that of Great Britain; and if our population and capital continue to increase with their present rapidity, the only mode in which food can continue to be supplied cheaply to the one, is by sending the other abroad to produce it'. But clearly any 'pessimism' on Mill's part regarding the future was strictly conditional: first, on a presumption of an unchanged population growth rate, whereas a central policy objective was to assure a reduction thereof by prudential checks and emigration; secondly, on a presumption of sluggish technological advance, whereas nothing in recent experience, as Mill himself evaluated the evidence, justified that presumption; and thirdly, on a neglect of the full implications of capital exportation whether to the colonies or elsewhere.

10.7 Money, Prices, Output and Interest: Ricardo

It is convenient for the discussion of the quantity theory which follows to have at hand a formulation provided by J. A. Schumpeter:

> For our present purpose we shall define it to mean: first, that the quantity of money is an independent variable – in particular, that it varies independently of prices and of physical volume of transactions; second, that velocity of circulation is an institutional datum that varies slowly or not at all, but in any case is independent of prices and volume of transactions; third, that transactions – or let us say, output – are unrelated to quantity of money, and it is only owing to chance that the two may move together; fourth, that variations in the quantity of money, unless they be absorbed by variations in output in the same direction, act mechanically on all prices, irrespective of how an increase in the quantity of money is used and on what sector of the economy it first impinges (who gets it) – and analogously for a decrease (1954, 703).

To what extent may the quantity theory in the foregoing sense be ascribed to Ricardo?

An early statement of the theory given in the 'Notes on Bentham' of 1810 relates the level of prices to the ratio MV/T: 'May we not...put the mass of commodities of all sorts on one side of the line, – and the amount of money multiplied by the rapidity of circulation on the other. Is not this in all cases the regulator of prices?' (Ricardo, 1951, III, 311). In the *Principles* the matter is expressed in terms of the demand and supply of money, quantity demanded varying inversely with respect to the 'value of money', that is, in direct proportion with the price level: 'The demand for money is regulated entirely by its value, and its value by its quantity. If gold were of double the value, half the quantity would perform the same functions in circulation, and if it were of half the value, double the quantity would be required....[For] money, the demand is exactly proportioned to its value' (I, 193). In this formulation, Ricardo presumed a given level of output and given velocity of circulation.

The notion of a demand for money of unitary elasticity with respect to its value was, however, by no means invariably taken for granted. In corespondence Ricardo in fact strongly denied this precise relationship, taking into account demand for the precious metals arising from non-monetary uses: 'I do not admit that if you were to double the medium of exchange it would fall to half its former value, not even if you were also to double the quantity of metal which was the standard of such medium. The consumption would increase in consequence of its diminished value...' (VI, 90). By this he meant that the demand for the metals is highly elastic for they 'are applicable to a great variety of *new* uses; – the fall of their price, in consequence of augmented quantity, would always be checked, not only by an increased demand for those purposes to which they had before been applied, but to the want of them for entirely new employments' (pp. 91–2). Yet this qualification is often neglected, a procedure which may be justified if paper currency constitutes the major component of the money supply, or if non-monetary uses of the metals are insignificant.

Let us consider now velocity of currency circulation. Velocity is related to population density such that 'the more dense the Population, the less, all other Circumstances being the same, will be the Amount of Circulating Medium required [to maintain any given price level]' (V, 421). Such considerations are consistent with Schumpeter's formulation. More significant, however, are allusions to the 'state of credit' by which is meant the availability of exchange media not formally included within the money supply, for 'Confidence and credit...are substitutes for currency' (p. 374). Thus: 'the Proportion [PT/M] must depend on the Economy in the Use of Money, which again must depend on the State of Credit at the Time' (p. 420). The easy availability of currency substitutes thus raises income velocity – reduces the demand for money to hold – so that the maintenance of any given level of prices requires a smaller volume of currency than otherwise would be the case. The point is made clearly in the *Proposals for an Economical and Secure Currency* of 1816:

> The value of money and the amount of payments remaining the same, the quantity of money required must depend on the degree of economy prac-tised in the use of it. If no payments were made by checks on bankers; by means of which money is merely written off one account and added to another, and that to the amount of millions daily, with few or no bank notes or coin passing; it is obvious that considerably more currency would be required, or, which is the same in its effects, the same money would pass at a greatly increased value, and would therefore be adequate to the additional amount of payments (IV, 58).

Ricardo thus recognized the effect on prices of 'non-monetary' exchange media, but formally attributed it to a change in the velocity of the money supply narrowly defined. Velocity in the latter sense cannot, therefore, be considered as 'an institutional datum that varies slowly or not at all'.

We turn next to evaluate whether in Ricardo's scheme increased money supplies act 'mechanically' on prices, irrespective of how the increase is used and in what sector of the economy it first impinges. Ricardo frequently implied a mechanical response of prices to changes in the money supply, simply reading off for each value of M the corre-sponding equilibrium P – a valid procedure in comparative-statics analysis. But this was not his invariable practice. In the first place, allow-ance is made for variations in the pattern of demand as a result of the altered income distribution characterizing a new state of equilibrium: 'By altering the distribution of property... an alteration would be made in the demand for some commodities; there would be a deficiency of supply to the new taste which came to the market, with the increase of property: and there would be too much for the taste whose resources had fallen' (V, 107–8). Secondly, increases in the money supply have implications for resource allocation in the presence of differential excise taxation:

> If a country were not taxed, and money should fall in value, its abundance in every market would produce similar effects in each... But this is no longer true when any of these commodities is taxed; if in that case they should all rise in proportion to the fall in the value of money, profits would be rendered unequal; in the case of the commodities taxed, profits would be raised above the general level, and capital would be removed from one employment to another, till an equilibrium of profits was

restored, which could only be, after the relative prices were altered (I, 209).

And thirdly, Ricardo allowed that 'the operations of an increased currency are not instantaneous, but require some interval of time to produce their full effect' (*The High Price of Bullion*, 1951, III, 118); and he gave some account of the transition between equilibrium states with reference both to the effects on commodity demand and the interest rate:

> I do not dispute, that if the Bank were to bring a large additional sum of notes into the market, and offer them on loan, but that they would for a time affect the rate of interest. The same effects would follow from the discovery of a hidden treasure of gold or silver coin. If the amount were large, the Bank, or the owner of the treasure, might not be able to lend the notes or the money at four, nor perhaps, above three per cent.; but having done so, neither the notes, nor the money, would be retained unemployed by the borrowers; they would be sent into every market, and would every where raise the prices of commodities, till they were absorbed in the general circulation. It is only during the interval of the issues of the Bank, and their effect on prices, that we should be sensible of an abundance of money; interest would, during that interval, be under its natural level; but as soon as the additional sum of notes or of money became absorbed in the general circulation, the rate of interest would be as high, and new loans would be demanded with as much eagerness as before the additional issues (p. 91; cf. also above p. 249 regarding I, 297–8).

The upward pressure on prices just alluded to occurs not automatically but by way of the generation of excess demands at the prices initially ruling, a process already clarified in the eighteenth-century literature (as by Hume and Cantillon) and by Henry Thornton (1760–1815; cf. 1802 [1939], 236ff). The proportionate impact on prices, allowance made for the generation of an excess demand for commodities (an excess supply of money), can be indicated diagrammatically. We set aside non-monetary uses of the metals in the case of a metallic currency, and also disregard distributional changes.

In figure 10.1, which plots the reciprocal of the price level against the money supply, it is assumed that part of a doubled money supply (from M_0 to $2M_0$) will be used to add to money balances, as indicated by the shift in the demand curve for money from D to D' at the original price level P_0. (This detail is necessary for the full logic of the argument, although Ricardo, like his contemporaries and predecessors, left it unstated.) At P_0 there now exists an excess supply of money to hold of UQ, with a counterpart in an excess demand for commodities; it is this excess that puts upward pressure on prices until their level has doubled and a new equilibrium is achieved at T. Points such as R and T consti-

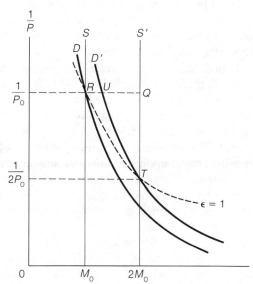

Figure 10.1
(Source: Patinkin, 1956, 42)

tute a locus of 'market equilibrium' positions which has unitary elasticity – a doubling in the price level corresponding to a doubling of the money supply *by way of* excess market demand for commodities rather than 'mechanically'.

Ricardo's allowance in *The High Price of Bullion* of a temporary impact on the interest rate of an increased money supply, just referred to, clarifies the interdependence between the commodity and the loan (bond) market in the manner of Hume and Thornton (1802 [1939], 255–6), and later of J. S. Mill (see below, p. 276). The initial injection of paper money adds to the supply of loanable funds, lowering the 'market' below the 'natural' rate of interest; but once prices have risen under pressure of excess demand for commodities – including capital goods – then 'new loans would be demanded with as much eagerness as before the additional issues', an obvious reference to a shift in the demand for loanable funds to cover the higher nominal cost of investment projects; a detail much elaborated by J. S. Mill.

Finally, let us consider the effect on the general level of activity of an increase in the money supply. David Hume, assuming an initial state of unemployment, had in the previous century developed an argument whereby a rising money supply has beneficial effects on output (see above, p. 177). This analysis Ricardo – taking Adam Smith's position – simply labelled 'an erroneous view' (1951, V, 524). In evidence given before the House of Lords committee on resumption in March 1819 he similarly maintained: 'on this Subject I differ from most other People. I do not think that any Stimulus is given to Production by the Use of fictitous Capital, as it is called' (p. 445). Henry Thornton had earlier noted that Hume's analysis assumed excess labour; to that extent there were 'bounds to the benefit which is to be derived from an augmentation of paper' (1802 [1939], 236).

It is appropriate to consider here the phenomenon of 'forced savings' – the positive effect upon the rate of accumulation reflecting an involuntary curtailment of real consumption on the part of groups whose money incomes lag behind the general rise in prices, and the consequent release of resources to the investment goods sector. An early formulation by Jeremy Bentham of such 'forced frugality' has the merit of specifying explicitly the assumption of full employment and emphasizing that all depends upon the precise place of injection of the increased money supply (1801–4 [1954], III, 344–5) Henry Thornton alluded to a forced 'defalcation of the revenue of the unproductive members of the society', and of labour, in consequence of excess note issues (1802 [1939], 238–9); and Malthus formulated the doctrine with emphasis upon the precise locus of the injection (1824 [1963], 95–7). An early reference thereto by Ricardo will be found in notes on a Bentham manuscript:

> That money is the cause of riches has been supported throughout the work and has in my view entirely spoiled it. There is but one way in which an increase of money no matter how it be introduced into the society, can augment riches, viz. at the expence of the wages of labour; till the wages of labour have found their level with the increased prices which the commodities will have experienced, there will be so much additional revenue to the manufacturer and farmer[;] they will obtain an increased price for their commodities, and can whilst wages do not increase employ an additional number of hands, so that the real riches of the country will be somewhat augmented. A productive labourer will produce something more than before relatively to his consumption, but this can be only of momentary duration (1951, III, 318–19).

Yet there was no guarantee that only low-saving groups would be adversely affected by inflation: 'there is a mere transfer of property, but no creation. Whether those who are enriched will employ their additional income more economically or more advantageously than those who before possessed it, must be matter of speculation only' (VI, 16). In this latter respect Ricardo did not differ much from Malthus or Bentham, who also considered forced savings as of small empirical importance. It should be emphasized that Ricardo and all orthodox economists condemned as totally immoral any programme of accelerated accumulation by inflationary means.

Ricardo's formal recognition of forced saving does not conflict with the assumption that output is unrelated to the quantity of money; the initial and direct effect of any monetary increase is upon prices, and thus the distribution of aggregate output, not its volume – this in contrast with the Hume analysis wherein increased money does act directly on total output. Ricardo's formulation of the forced savings doctrine has the merit of raising pertinent questions regarding the savings propensities of various groups of fixed or relatively fixed income recipients.

The 'quantity theory' has been approached thus far from the perspective of increases in the money supply. Considering Ricardo's denial of any positive effect on output along Hume's lines, it appears that initial full employment was a basic axiom, and a matter that should have been clarified as Bentham had done. For a full picture we must also consider monetary contraction. When we thus extend the canvas we find repeated allowances of a possible real deflationary impact on output and employment (see below, pp. 293–5). From this perspective even Schumpeter's third characteristic (see above, p. 265) does not apply to Ricardian monetary theory.

10.8   Money, Prices, Output and Interest: J. S. Mill

For J. S. Mill the value of money (like that of all other commodities) is determined 'temporarily by demand and supply, permanently and on the average by cost of production' (1848 [1965], III, 507; cf. 517). This unfortunate formulation has been misread to imply that changes in cost of production act on value independently of supply variation. The short-run value of money, its 'temporary' value, concerns us here. (Mill's basic money in the quantity theory context is metallic currency, but the same analysis can be applied to fiat notes.)

It is (as for Ricardo) by generating an excess demand for commodities that an injection of money acts on prices. Mill took great care to specify the experiment. Since 'money acts upon prices in no other way than by being tendered in exchange for commodities', changes in relative prices might occur, depending upon how precisely the increase impinges on the system (p. 539). More precisely:

> [It] is of course possible that the influx of money might take place through the medium of some new class of consumers, or in such a manner as to alter the proportions of different classes of consumers to one another, so

that a greater share of the national income than before would thenceforth
be expended in some articles, and a smaller in others; exactly as if a
change had taken place in the tastes and wants of the community (p. 510).

Such disturbances would, however, be temporary, lasting 'until production had accommodated itself to this change in the comparative demand
for different things...'. To rule out such disturbances and focus on the
main issue alone, Mill proposed as the experimental change that each
individual be supposed to find an extra pound added to each pound
already in his possession (for Hume's experiment of adding a guinea to
each individual's money stock would weight disproportionately the
impact on workers' outlays), following which – supposing tastes
unchanged – 'there would be an increased money demand, and consequently an increased money value, or price, for things of all sorts' (p.
511). All prices will then change in proportion to the change in money
supply, at least after the passage of sufficient time for the increase 'to
permeate all the channels of circulation'. Here lay a fundamental distinction between non-monetary commodities and money (albeit itself a
commodity), namely that the value of money 'varies inversely as its
quantity' (p. 512). For money is desired not for itself but 'as the means
of universal purchase, the demand [consisting] of everything which
people have to sell.... The whole of the goods being... exchanged for
the whole of the money which comes into the market to be laid out, they
will sell for less or more of it, exactly according as less or more is
brought'.

Allowance is, of course, made for velocity or the 'rapidity of circulation' of money. This Mill rephrased as 'the efficiency of money' to
avoid the irrelevant notion of 'the number of purchases made by each
piece of money in a given time', and to focus rather on 'the average
number of purchases made by each piece [in a given time] in order to
effect a given pecuniary amount of transactions [in that same time]' (pp.
513–14). The value of money can then be said to vary in direct proportion with the volume of transactions and inversely with the quantity of
money weighed by the velocity index.

What was said of Ricardo again applies. Mill's emphasis on the
impact of an increased money supply upon the demand for commodities supplemented by his observation that the injection of money
affects relative prices according to how and where it impinges, reflect
clear recognition that the causal relation between money and prices is
by no means a mechanical one. The argument as a whole constitutes an
impressive attempt to integrate monetary and value theory.

Mill's ultimate objective, however, was to bury not to praise simple-
minded applications of the quantity theory. An increase in the money

stock will not generate an increase in prices in the event that it does not raise the amount offered for sale against commodities:

> money hoarded does not act on prices. Money kept on reserve by individuals to meet contingencies which do not occur, does not act on prices. The money in the coffers of the Bank, or retained in a reserve by private bankers, does not act on prices until drawn out, nor even then unless drawn out to be expended in commodities (p. 515).

Both speculative and precautionary motives are listed (p. 539). An increase in the money supply which happens to coincide with a proportionate increase in these non-transactions components of demand – which disturbance might be formally treated as a reduction in velocity – will not generate an increase in the price level.

The analysis thus far pertains to an economy without credit:

> The proposition which we have laid down respecting the dependence of general prices upon the quantity of money in circulation, must be understood as applying only to a state of things in which money, that is, gold and silver, is the exclusive instrument of exchange, and actually passes from hand to hand at every purchase, credit in any of its shapes being unknown. When credit comes into play as a means of purchasing, distinct from money in hand, we shall hereafter find that the connexion between prices and the amount of the circulating medium is much less direct and intimate, and that such connexion as does exist, no longer admits of so simple a mode of expression (p. 514).

There were qualifications to the proposition that the value of the circulating medium varies inversely with its quantity, qualifications (Mill added in 1857) 'which, under a complex system of credit like that existing in England, render the proposition a totally incorrect expression of the fact' (p. 516).

Two chapters in Book III of the *Principles* are devoted to credit (chs xi, xii), the first of which constitutes a descriptive account of various 'substitutes for money', including bank notes, bills of exchange – on which topic Henry Thornton is cited at length (531ff) – promissory notes, including those issued by government, and 'deposits and cheques' (p. 536). To these written instruments must be added book or trade credit. 'Credit' creation is distinguished from 'capital' creation and represented as a means of transferring saved funds from owners to users (pp. 527–8). (This had also been Ricardo's position: '[Credit] does not create capital, it determines only by whom that capital should be employed'; 1951, IV, 436–7).

The implications of credit for interest rate determination are not here taken up, for Mill's primary concern is with credit as 'purchasing power', in which capacity it acts upon general prices:

In a state of commerce in which much credit is habitually given, general prices at any moment depend much more upon the state of credit than upon the quantity of money. For credit, though it is not productive power, is purchasing power; and a person who, having credit, avails himself of it in the purchase of goods, creates just as much demand for the goods, and tends quite as much to raise their price, as if he made an equal amount of purchases with ready money (1848 [1965], III, 530).

That general prices depend '*at any moment*' upon the state of credit more than upon the supply of money narrowly defined, is a crucial qualification that must not be lost sight of, since the '*permanent*' value of money was not the issue and not at all a disputed matter. 'Natural' value was 'determined by the cost of producing or of obtaining the precious metals' (p. 538). It is the level of 'immediate and temporary' prices that concerned Mill, and on that matter there was no 'general assent'.

As we know, Mill insisted that an injection even of metallic currency leaves prices unchanged if absorbed into 'hoards'. This proposition is prologue to an elaboration of the reverse relationship – that (always in the short run) expenditures playing on prices may be financed far beyond the means provided by the available money stock. It is credit *per se*, when drawn on, that acts on prices; and the impact on prices will occur even in the absence of any 'written instruments called substitutes for currency' (p. 540).

Whether or not bank notes are to be counted as 'money', Mill dismissed as a problem for those 'who seek to prove that bank notes and no other form of credit constitute "money" and act on prices; whereas in fact "money" and credit are...exactly on a par, in their effect on prices; and whether we choose to class bank notes with the one or the other, is in this respect entirely immaterial' (pp. 552–3). This approach seems to invite the expansion of the definition of 'money supply' to incorporate the full variety of credit forms, including book or trade credit, at least for purposes of analysis of the price level. Yet Mill did not follow this line. Possibly it is because trade credit (either its availability or the amount actually drawn on) – unlike written instruments acting as substitutes for currency and passing 'from hand to hand' – cannot be defined quantitatively, that it could not be included within the money supply. This raises serious problems for monetary policy, for if the 'money supply' in the broad sense cannot be quantitatively defined, its variations cannot be regulated – unless some proxy for it can be devised.

That the note issue was the basis of a 'superstructure of credit' and so might serve as proxy – a view attributed to the so-called 'currency school' (see below, p. 297) – Mill denied. Credit made available by dealers to a customer turned 'on their opinion of his solvency', not on the volume of notes or coins in circulation. As for the *use* of credit, that also turned on the 'expectation of gain', the fulfilment of which 'depends upon prices, but not especially upon the amount of bank notes' (pp. 554–5). Speculative periods involved 'circumstances calculated to lead to an unusually extended use of credit' (p. 546); while the collapse of credit characterizing the downturn of the cycle resulted from the collapse of confidence rather than the reverse.

The moral of all this is that direct control of trade credit – it is primarily use of credit that matters – is ruled out as a means of regulating prices. To regulate notes alone would certainly not suffice. These implications for policy are taken up in chapter 11.

*   *   *

We have next to consider Mill's analysis of the impact of a monetary increase upon the market rate of interest. Conspicuous here is the explicit relationship between the commodity and bond (loanable fund) markets. The following celebrated charge against the classics by J. M. Keynes, it will become clear, is completely misplaced:

> [It] has been usual to suppose that an increase in the quantity of money has a tendency to reduce the rate of interest, at any rate in the first instance and in the short period. Yet no reason has been given why a change in the quantity of money should affect either the investment demand-schedule or the readiness to save out of a given income. Thus the classical school had quite a different theory of the rate of interest in volume I dealing with the theory of value from what they had in volume II dealing with the theory of money. They have seemed undisturbed by the conflict and have made no attempt, so far as I know, to build a bridge between the two theories (1936 [1973], 182–3).

In Mill's *Principles* the interest rate is treated as the price of loanable funds in a splendid account of the process whereby quantities demanded and supplied come to be equalized (1848 [1965], III, 647ff). The interest rate is said to be more volatile than other prices, but, as in the standard theory of price,

> there must be…some rate which (in the language of Adam Smith and Ricardo) may be called the natural rate; some rate about which the market rate oscillates, and to which it always tends to return. This rate partly depends on the amount of accumulation going on in the hands of persons who cannot themselves attend to the employment of their savings, and partly on the comparative taste existing in the community for the active pursuits of industry, or for the leisure, ease, and independence of an annuitant (p. 648).

The emphasis throughout is on the demand and supply of loanable funds as a reflection of investment and savings decisions respectively, the rate of interest depending 'essentially and permanently on the comparative amount of real capital offered and demanded in the way of loan' (p. 657). Bankers are accorded a cloakroom function of lending out national savings – the 'general loan fund' (p. 650).

Our concern now is with the precise impact of a 'permanent' injection of money into a system. The monetary increase, assumed to enter the system by way of expanded loans, pushes the market rate of interest below the natural rate, creating a differential between expected profitability and cost of finance. This differential generates increased investment outlays and (assuming full employment) rising prices, including the prices of capital goods. But the higher cost of capital projects requires additional finance, that is, the demand for loanable funds shifts upward, so that in the final analysis there is a symmetrical impact on the demand and supply for loans (p. 655–6). There is no doubt of the same intimate linkage between the commodity and bond markets as recognized by Thornton and Ricardo (see above, p. 269). There can, however, also be no question in Mill's case of a certain unwillingness to emphasize the impact of changes in the money supply on the interest rate. Mill, especially before the 1865 edition of the *Principles*, seems to do his best to leave an impression of the irrelevance of money in interest rate determination by emphasizing the 'capital' rather than the monetary property of loanable funds. Doubtless his approach reflects a burning hostility towards mercantilist residues.

* * *

Mill's reaction to the old pre-Smithian notion of a monetary impact on real output and employment, which Smith had so strongly opposed, remains to be discussed. This sort of case was again made by Thomas Attwood (1783–1856), of the so-called Birmingham School, who supported expanded issues of an inconvertible paper money, in order to reduce the real pressure of debts and taxes and, by thus stimulating demand, act on employment and capital usage. As Mill paraphrased Attwood's argument: 'A large portion of the national capital, especially of that part which consists of buildings and machinery, is now, he affirms, lying idle, in default of a market for its productions; those various productions being, as he admits, the natural market for one another, but being unable to exchange for each other, for want of a more plentiful medium of exchange...' (1833; IV, 190). More generally, be it noted, Attwood gave as his ideal an inconvertible currency regulated to the end of creating 'full employment'.

Mill partly conceded Attwood's case, notwithstanding his horror of monetary unorthodoxy, though in a backhanded manner: 'an increase of production really takes place during the progress of depreciation' but only 'as long as the existence of depreciation is not suspected; and it is this which gives to the fallacies of ... Mr [Thomas] Attwood, all the little plausibility they possess' (1844; IV, 275). When the 'delusion' dissipates, these extended projects are proved unsustainable.

Attwood's conclusions, in so far as they implied the possibility of permanent real gains, Mill attributed to erroneous method – the appeal to 'practical experience' or an inductive logic, namely that because in 1825 general full employment had been achieved at a high level of prices, it would be desirable to return to that situation on the presumption that the former had been caused by the latter (IV, 190). Mill accepted that full capacity was achieved in 1825, and in fact that capacity was expanded, but attributed these facts to a 'state of insane delusion, in its very nature temporary' – the excessive pressure on capacity usage and unjustifiable additions to capacity during the upswing constituting 'partly the cause of their lying idle now' (p. 191). (Mill also warned, as we know, of the requirement, if steady growth is to be achieved, for some short-term flexibility; see above, p. 256.) In this respect a close resemblance can be discerned to the position of Friedrich von Hayek, who has cautioned of the inevitability of a crisis attending the adjustment of the economy after its over-extension, a crisis resulting in excess capacity and unemployment (1931).

In the *Principles* (Book III, xiii) Mill further insisted against Attwood that any stimulatory effects of a monetary expansion could only turn on expectations by each producer that his own output will sell at a higher *relative* price when it reaches the market (since an increase of *all* prices could evidently have no stimulatory effect); such expectations are inevitably disappointed, for it is inconceivable that people never discover the increase in their sales revenues to be purely nominal. Again only a *temporary* stimulus to output (involving upward price expectations fuelled by credit) – one likely to be reversed – could be allowed.

Mill's concern in the critique of Attwood was primarily to deny the possibility of a *secular* inflationary stimulus to output, capital and employment. And as Sir John Hicks has put it, 'the Classical Economists were quite right in refusing to look that way', for all that could be found along that route was a depreciated currency without (permanent) countervailing advantage; true, Hicks goes on, 'inflation does give a stimulus, but the stimulus is greatest when the inflation starts – when it starts from a condition that has been non-inflationary. If the inflation continues, people get adjusted to it. But when people are adjusted to it, when they *expect* rising prices, the mere occurrence of what they had expected is no longer stimulating ...' (1967, 163). Milton Friedman has made the same point: 'there is always a temporary trade-off between inflation and unemployment; there is no permanent trade-off. The temporary trade-off comes not from inflation *per se*, but from unantici-pated inflation, which generally means, from a rising rate of inflation' (1968, 11). This is precisely Mill's position in his rejection of Attwood.

Suggested Reading

*Smith (1776) *An Inquiry into the Nature and Causes of the Wealth of Nations*, Book II, ii.
*Ricardo, *Principles of Political Economy*, chs 19, 21, in *Works and Correspon-dence* (1951), ed. P. Sraffa.
*   'Notes on Malthus's Principles' (1820), in *Works* (1951), II, 297–452.
*Malthus, *Principles of Political Economy*, partial reprint of first (1820) edition, ch. 7, in *Works and Correspondence of David Ricardo* (1951), ed. P. Sraffa, II (Book II, ch. 1 of second, 1836 [1964] edition).
*Mill (1848), *Principles of Political Economy*, Book III, chs xiv, xxiii; Book IV, ch. v.
*   'Of the Influence of Consumption on Production' (1844), in *Collected Works* (1967), IV, 262–79.

Vickers (1975) and Laidler (1981) consider Smith as monetary theorist. See also Hollander (1973), 205–7 on the place accorded by Smith to money in accumulation.

On the nineteenth-century classicists' position on the law of markets see the splendid account by Baumol and Becker (1952) and also Corry (1962), especially chs 1–4, 7–9, and Sowell (1972). Hollander (1979), ch. 2, deals with James Mill and J. B. Say, and ch. 9, with Ricardo. Hollander (1985), ch. 7, 483–544, examines J. S. Mill's position on the law of markets along the lines of the present chapter.

Link (1959) is devoted to English theories of economic fluctuations 1815–48. This topic is also covered in Tucker (1960), ch. 8, and Corry (1962), chs 5 and 6.

Malthus's position on aggregate demand is treated in Hollander (1962, 1969). See also the references to Spengler, Tucker and Eltis regarding aggre-gate demand and growth, given in the suggestions for chapter 8 above.

On Thornton see references to chapter 11.

11 Money and Banking: II

11.1 Introduction

This chapter is concerned mainly with banking issues. Section 11.2 considers Smithian banking principles, which figured large in the nineteenth-century literature; this is prefaced by Smith's position on the international adjustment process, which also entered into the later discussions. It is followed by a demonstration in section 11.3 of the classical championship of the gold standard on grounds of price stability. Section 11.4 takes up the 'bullionist' debates regarding Bank of England policy 1797–1819 when Britain was off gold; while section 11.5 deals with Ricardo's qualification to his championship of a return to gold at the original par. Section 11.6 considers, with particular reference to J. S. Mill, the subsequent Banking–Currency School debate regarding Sir Robert Peel's 1844 Bank Act. Finally, Mill's position on counter-cyclical monetary policy is examined.

11.2 Smithian Banking Principles

In making his case against the mercantilist preoccupation with the adequacy of the national money supply (1776, Book IV, i), Adam Smith drew on Hume's specie-flow mechanism involving relative national price level adjustments. Thus an injection of the monetary metals in excess of the 'effectual demand' will generate an increase in the domestic price level, the process of equilibration involving a subsequent exportation of specie:

> on account of the small bulk and great value of those metals, no commodities can be more easily transported from one place to another, from the places where they are cheap, to those where they are dear, from the

place where they exceed, to those where they fall short of this effectual demand...

When the quantity of gold and silver imported into any country exceeds the effectual demand, no vigilance of government can prevent its exportation. All the sanguinary laws of Spain and Portugal are not able to keep their gold and silver at home. The continual importations from Peru and Brazil exceed the effectual demand of those countries, and sink the price of those metals there below that in the neighbouring countries (1776 [1937], 404).

Attempts to retain excessive supplies of the metals must fail:

The cheapness of gold and silver, or what is the same thing, the dearness of all commodities, which is the necessary effect of this redundancy of the precious metals, discourages both the agriculture and manufactures of Spain and Portugal, and enables foreign nations to supply them with many sorts of rude, and with almost all sorts of manufactured produce, for a smaller quantity of gold and silver than what they themselves can either raise or make them for at home (p. 479).

The various prohibitions

not only lower very much the value of the precious metals in Spain and Portugal, but by detaining there a certain quantity of those metals which would otherwise flow over other countries, they keep up their value in those other countries somewhat above what it otherwise would be, and thereby give those countries a double advantage in their commerce with Spain and Portugal. Open the flood-gates, and there will presently be less water above, and more below, the dam-head, and it will soon come to a level in both places.

(Here we have a nice illustration of the already standard mechanical analogy.) Conversely, if in any country the quantity of metals 'fell short of the effectual demand, so as to raise their price above that of the neighbouring countries, the government would have no occasion to take any pains to import them' (p. 404). A role for exchange rate variation in the process of international adjustment is also allowed, again in the Hume fashion (p. 402).

We turn now to Smith's observations on banking, particularly bank issues of paper currency. (The above adjustment mechanism applied to a wholly metallic system.) Three Smithian principles were to play a role during the early nineteenth-century monetary debates: the notion of 'needs of trade', the 'law of reflux' and the 'real bills' doctrine.

Throughout Smith's chapter 'Of Money' (Book II, ii) it is taken for granted that at any time there exists a requirement for a specific volume of means of payment. The dimensions of the 'channel of circulation' are determined by the magnitude of the real national income – 'the whole annual produce' (p. 277). In strict logic, of course, the notion makes little sense unless both the level of prices and the velocity of circulation are also specified, but the discussion here does not take these complications formally into account.

The total of (convertible) bank notes plus specie circulation, Smith maintained, cannot long exceed the amount of specie alone that would suffice to satisfy the 'needs of trade' in a fully metallic system. Either or both of two mechanisms assure this result in the event of an initial excess. That part of the excess circulation consisting of specie will be directly exported in exchange for goods; while that part of the excess consisting of notes will return to the banks for gold (thus reducing the reserves) which is then exported. In one illustration Smith assumed 'needs of trade' requiring a volume of £1 million and consisting initially entirely of specie. Banks are next assumed to issue a volume of notes amounting to £1 million against a gold reserve of £200,000. The net excess circulation of £800,000 is corrected by a direct outflow of specie, for paper money will not be accepted abroad: 'Gold and silver, therefore, to the amount of eight hundred thousand pounds will be sent abroad, and the channel of home circulation will remain filled with a million of paper, instead of the million of those metals which filled it before' (p. 278). In the event that, say, £1,100,000 of notes are issued, then even after the direct specie outflow of £800,000 the total money supply will still be excessive. But the excess note issue is envisaged as returning to the banks for specie – the 'law of reflux' – which is then exported.

Smith's illustration of the first mechanism represents an extreme case. It is more likely that there will be a demand for a minimum volume of specie, and in the event that the public requires £100,000 in this particular form, only £700,000 would flow out. The total circulation then amounts to £1,100,000 (assuming again an initial note issue of £1 million) which is excessive. But according to the second mechanism, £100,000 worth of notes will be returned to the banks in exchange for specie to be exported. Circulation will now amount to the required £1 million (£900,000 in notes and £100,000 in specie). The second mechanism, the 'reflux' of excess notes, is described in the following passage:

> The whole paper money of every kind which can easily circulate in any country never can exceed the value of the gold and silver, of which it supplies the place, or which (the commerce being supposed the same) would circulate there, if there was no paper money.... Should the circulating paper at any time exceed that sum, as the excess could neither be sent abroad nor be employed in the circulation of the country, it must immediately return upon the banks to be exchanged for gold and silver. Many people would immediately perceive that they had more of this paper than was necessary for transacting their business at home, and as

they could not send it abroad, they would immediately demand payment of it from the banks. When this superfluous paper was converted into gold and silver, they could easily find a use for it by sending it abroad.... There would immediately, therefore, be a run upon the banks to the whole extent of this superfluous paper, and, if they shewed any difficulty or backwardness in payment, to a much greater extent; the alarm, which this would occasion, necessarily increasing the run (pp. 284–5).

The outflow of specie – either directly or by way of a reduction in the reserves – is described by Smith without reference to the Hume-type specie-flow mechanism based on price level variation. Smith went so far as to reject the possibility of inflationary note issues because he could envisage no net increase in the money supply in consequence – each one pound of paper displacing an equivalent value of specie:

The increase of paper money, it has been said, by augmenting the quantity, and consequently diminishing the value of the whole currency, necessarily augments the money price of commodities. But as the quantity of gold and silver, which is taken from the currency, is always equal to the quantity of paper which is added to it, paper money does not necessarily increase the quantity of the whole currency (pp. 308–9).

The foregoing statement possibly rejects only long-term price increases in consequence of a paper issue, the logic for an unchanged aggregate money supply actually turning on short-run price increases which govern the outflow of specie. Ricardo was to interpret Smith in precisely this way (see below, p. 290); but Smith's silence regarding price movements in discussing a mixed currency in excess suggests that Ricardo's reading was perhaps too generous, as Henry Thornton (1802, 200) insisted.

It may be mentioned that Hume (who did apply his mechanism quite generally) objected to paper money on the grounds that it tended to drive up prices thereby stimulating an outflow of the precious metals. Any such outflow he believed would be regrettable considering the potential importance of metallic currency in foreign negotiations (1752b, 35; 1752d, 67–9, 71–2). Smith had no regrets regarding specie export, at least in so far as it results in the purchase of 'an additional stock of materials, tools, and provisions, in order to maintain and employ an additional number of industrious people' (1776 [1937], 278). As always, an expansion of capacity was a necessary precondition for increased output and employment. Yet there is an obvious limit to any deliberate programme of note issue designed to expand capacity, for Smith's support of paper money turns on the guarantee of convertibility. Hume, on the other hand, was able to recommend a policy of continual increase in the money supply, for the supposed stimulatory impact was unrelated to the circulation of paper currency specifically.

Smith also denied the possibility of a premium of bullion over (convertible) paper:

> A paper money consisting in bank notes, issued by people of undoubted credit, payable upon demand without any condition, and in fact always readily paid as soon as presented, is, in every respect, equal in value to gold and silver money; since gold and silver money can at any time be had for it. Whatever is either bought or sold for such paper, must necessarily be bought or sold as cheap as it could have been for gold and silver (p. 308).

The foregoing assurance is, however, no longer applicable in the case of conditionally convertible notes: 'Such a paper money would, no doubt, fall more or less below the value of gold and silver...' (p. 309). Even so, Smith insisted that the general level of gold prices remains unaffected by a discount on paper, for the gold price of commodities 'depends in all cases, not upon the nature or quantity of any particular paper money, which may be current in any particular country, but upon the richness or poverty of the mines, which happen at any particular time to supply the great market of the commercial world with those metals' (p. 313). Now the remark that the prices of commodities in terms of gold coin are independent of 'the quantity of any particular paper money' – not only its 'nature' – may have significant implications for the role of price-level movements in the process of correcting an excessive circulation; for it seems to imply that an increased note issue generates a rise in prices in terms of paper while the purchasing power of the coined currency remains unchanged. But we shall see (below, pp. 291–2) that the process of international adjustment to internal monetary expansion entailing price effects in the case of a mixed currency, does require variation in the purchasing power of the coins. From this perspective, too, we are led to conclude that Smith probably ruled out such adjustment.

A word now on the so-called 'real bills' doctrine. While the doctrine of 'needs of trade' assured, in the convertible case, that the total of means of payment would never for long be excessive, Smith recommended as a rule of thumb that bankers restrict their issues by discounting only 'real bills' or short-term bills based on goods in process, and avoid the finance of long-term capital projects or speculative ventures: 'When a bank discounts to a merchant a real bill of exchange drawn by a real creditor upon a real debtor, and which, as soon as it becomes due, is really paid by that debtor; it only advances to him a part of the value which he would otherwise be obliged to keep by him unemployed and in ready money for answering occasional demands' (p. 288). Paper currency thus issued by way of discount 'can never exceed the value of the gold and silver, which would necessarily circulate in the country if there was no paper money; it can never exceed the quantity which the circulation of the country can easily absorb and employ'. It would thus seem that Smith relied on the 'real bills' principle to prevent any excessive note issues. If the banking authorities neglected the rule and followed inappropriate discounting policies, the 'law of reflux' assured the almost immediate withdrawal of the excess.

Yet despite these principles, Smith allowed that the banks might generate an excessive money supply over an extended period by way of an on-going process of inappropriate discounting – as distinct from a once and for all injection of notes – should they neglect their own best interest. He illustrated the case of a circulation 'overstocked with paper money' by Bank of England notes, issued in 'too great a quantity' and this 'for many years together' (p. 286). Such possibilities would evidently be much increased in the case of inconvertible paper where the law of reflux is inapplicable.

11.3   The Gold Standard and Price Stability

In 1797 Britain abandoned the gold standard following serious losses from the reserves into private hoards and abroad. The fall in the value of the pound on foreign exchanges below the old par level and the discount on paper were particularly marked during the periods 1799–1803 and 1809–15. The great monetary controversy of the early nineteenth century – the so-called Bullionist Controversy – concerned the causes of the low value of the pound on foreign exchanges and the premium quoted on bullion over paper. The primary issue at stake was whether or not the paper pound had been over-issued, in the special sense of a volume of currency exceeding that which would have circulated had a metallic standard remained in force. 'Excess' thus referred not to an amount relative to some base period, but an amount relative to a hypothetical equilibrium, ruling out direct reference to money supply statistics for resolution of the disputed matters. According to the 'bullionist' critics of the Bank of England, the tests of excess were the premium on bullion over paper and an exchange rate below par.

Now Ricardo (one of the Bank's major critics) usually meant by the term 'depreciation' an excess of the market over the mint price of bullion rather than a fall in the general purchasing power of the pound. In the *Principles* he defined the term as 'a comparative difference between the value of money, and the standard by which by law it is regulated' (1951, I, 149). And while there might occur variations in the general purchasing power of the metals themselves, it is none the less a return to gold at the original parity of £3.17.10$\frac{1}{2}$ per fine ounce that is recommended:

To this standard we must conform till the law is changed, and till some other commodity is discovered, by the use of which we shall obtain a more perfect standard, than that which we have established. While gold is exclusively the standard in this country, money will be depreciated, when a pound sterling is not of equal value with 5 dwts. and 3 grs. of standard gold, and that, whether gold rises or falls in general value [purchasing power].

These formulations recall those of John Locke (1632–1704), and Ricardo spoke highly of Locke, who during the coinage controversy of the 1690s defended the standard when some were recommending temporary devaluation (1695). Moreover we find Ricardo recommending contraction of the money supply on the appearance of a discount of paper over bullion which is patently unrelated to note issues. Thus, for example, in a case where the money prices of commodities are constant but the purchasing power of gold rises, it would still be 'incumbent on the Bank to raise in an equal Degree the Value of their Paper, which could only be done by Reduction in Quantity' (1951, V, 425–6). This perspective has been called a 'City' view, whereby the primary concern in treating the 'value' of money is not with its general purchasing power but its value relative to the standard metal.

But there is much more to the matter. For the choice of metallic standard was itself justified in the first place in terms of the relative stability of purchasing power of the precious metals. This argument was used by Lord King, whose work on the bank restriction was much admired by Ricardo: 'Bullion is of all articles of commerce the least subject to variations of price; and though, in comparing distant times, its value is greatly affected by accumulation or the discovery of new mines, it may be considered as being stationary during short periods' (1803, 31). Any loss in purchasing power which reflected a fall in the value of the metals themselves simply had to be tolerated: 'The precious metals themselves, though the best practical standards of value, are far short of perfect truth and accuracy. In process of time, and during a course of years, they are subject to great variations' (p. 117).

Francis Horner, one of the authors of the *Bullion Report* of 1810 (Cannan, 1925) which took for granted that the proper value of the pound was that of $123\frac{1}{4}$ grains of gold, also argued in terms of relative constancy of general purchasing power in making a case for a metallic standard (1803 [1957], 81–2). The position of King and Horner is precisely that adopted by Ricardo in *The High Price of Bullion*:

Strictly speaking, there can be no permanent measure of value. A measure of value should itself be invariable; but this is not the case with either gold or silver, they being subject to fluctuations as well as other commodities. Experience has indeed taught us, that though the variations in the *value* of gold or silver may be considerable, on a comparison of distant periods, yet for short spaces of time their value is tolerably fixed. It is this property, among their other excellencies, which fits them better than any other commodity for the uses of money (1951, III, 65n.; cf. I, 149).

Ricardo denied that stability in the value of a currency divorced from the metals might be assured by regulating supply according to movements in general prices. Ignorance of, or dissatisfaction with, the notion of index numbers was one reason for rejecting an inconvertible paper currency regulated to assure constancy of general purchasing power. Equally important was a strong suspicion that the monetary authorities would not adhere to the test even if a strict measure of general purchasing power could be devised in practice (*Economical and Secure Currency* (1816), 1951, IV, 58ff). In general then, Ricardo maintained that 'to secure the public against any other variations in the value of the currency than those to which the standard itself is subject, and, at the same time, to carry on the circulation with a medium the least expensive, is to attain the most perfect state to which a currency can be brought...' (p. 66). Against such variations 'there is no possible remedy' (p. 62). Ricardo's 'City' interest in the money price of gold was proxy for a more basic concern with price stability.

Ricardo and his bullionist colleagues were evidently concerned with price inflation during the war period. The precise nature of their concern may be illustrated from the *Bullion Report*:

> The effect of such an augmentation of prices upon all money transactions for time; the unavoidable injury suffered by annuitants, and by creditors of every description, both private and public; the unintended advantage gained by Government and all other debtors; are consequences too obvious to require proof, and too repugnant to justice to be left without remedy. By far the most important portion of this effect appears to Your Committee to be that which is communicated to the wages of common country labour, the rate of which, it is well known, adapts itself more slowly to the changes which happen in the value of money, than the price of any other species of labour or commodity (Cannan, 1925, 67).

Ricardo, in *The High Price of Bullion*, drew on the *Wealth of Nations* to the same effect. He reproduced Smith's allusions in discussing debasement of the coinage to the erosion of real purchasing power suffered by 'the creditors of the public', and to the unfavourable distributional effects of inflation, namely that 'it occasions a general and most pernicious subversion of the fortunes of private people; enriching in most cases the idle and profuse debtor at the expence of the industrious and frugal creditor, and transporting a great part of the national capital from the hands which are likely to increase and improve it, to those which are likely to dissipate and destroy it' (1951, III, 97). Reference is also made to the larger taxation and borrowing requirements of government (p. 138).

The strong indictment of price inflation confirms that Ricardo's preoccupation with a stable price of gold reflects a more basic concern with stability of general purchasing power; a purely 'City' interest in a stable price of gold in the manner of Locke, should not be over-emphasized. The general objective might, in principle, be achieved for the future were cash payments resumed at a devalued rate of the pound. But in a *Morning Chronicle* article of 1809 Ricardo described such a proposal as a 'shocking injustice', for it would render permanent the unjust redistribution of the war years (1951, III, 25). Devaluation was also seen as an invitation to future irresponsibility (pp. 138–9). By the following year, however, Ricardo had become seriously preoccupied with the short-run deflationary implications of a return to gold at par (see below, p. 293).

When we turn to J. S. Mill we find the same general justification for a metallic standard as that maintained earlier in the century, namely the relatively stable 'value' (in the sense of general purchasing power) of the precious metals, and this a consequence of relative constancy in supply:

> They fluctuate less than almost any other things in their cost of production. And from their durability, the total quantity in existence is at all times so great in proportion to the annual supply, that the effect on value even of a change in the cost of production is not sudden: a very long time being required to diminish materially the quantity in existence, and even to increase it very greatly not being a rapid process (1848 [1965], III, 504).

In the great mid-century debate between the 'Banking' and 'Currency' Schools (see below, p. 297) inconvertibility was not at issue, since all the major parties maintained

> that the proper standard of currency is the precious metals, at an unaltered mint valuation; that a pound (precisely as stated by Sir Robert Peel) should mean a fixed quantity of gold of a given fineness; and that no one who has contracted to pay that given quantity, should be allowed on any pretext to discharge his debt by paying a smaller quantity, or making over paper equivalent to a smaller quantity ('The Currency Question' (1844), 1967, IV, 345).

As usual, the limitations of gold as a standard – its admittedly variable cost of production – are conceded; but gold approached closer to the ideal than any other commodity. In any event, 'if it were far more subject to fluctuation than it is, it would be less so than the policy of a government, – especially one which takes for its principle of guidance

"The wants of trade", which in this case simply means the convenience of debtors'. Mill thus maintained a strong line on the necessity for a standard, taking the Ricardian position in general, but going beyond Ricardo in refusing to countenance a devaluation of the pound in terms of gold 'on any pretext'. For him, 'the restoration of the ancient standard, and the payment, in the restored currency, of the interest of a debt contracted in a depreciated one, [had been] no injustice, but the simple performance of a plighted contract' ('The Currency Juggle' (1833), 1967, IV, 187); for lenders knew that the original restriction was temporary and that the standard would be restored at the original par. Indeed, instead of returning to gold six months after peace, as sanctioned by Parliament, the return to gold was delayed for years so that fundholders were actually paid interest in 'depreciated paper' although the nation was bound by contract to pay it in cash. In brief, 'we covenanted to pay in a metallic standard; we therefore are bound to do it. To deliberate on such a question is as if a private person were to deliberate whether he should pick a pocket' (p. 189).

Mill was incensed by those such as Thomas Attwood, the 'Birmingham' inflationist, who saw

> no harm in emancipating a paper currency from the restraint of convertibility, and from every definite principle of limitation, provided only that it is grounded on the security of actual property; forgetful that even the *assignats* were issued on no less a security than the principle portion of the soil of France, and that a paper so guaranteed is no more protected from depreciation, if issued in excess, than the land itself would be if offered for sale in unusual quantity (Mill, 1967, IV, 344).

What was at stake was a 'gigantic plan of confiscation [of private property] ... – a depreciation of the currency' (1967, IV, 184). Inconvertibility, moreover, permitted fraud in a manner which gave 'a set of bankers the power of taxing the community to an unlimited amount at their sole pleasure, by pouring forth paper which could only get into circulation by lowering the value of all the paper already issued' (p. 189). Mill predicted the end of pecuniary transactions, for 'no one in his senses would take money in exchange for anything, except he were sure of being able to lay it out before the next day'.

Mill's reaction to inconvertibility in the *Principles* is equally forceful. Mill rejected various proposals to regulate the value (purchasing power) of an inconvertible currency (1848 [1965], III, 556ff). The inevitable 'variations' in the value of the circulating medium would 'disturb existing contracts and expectations, and the liability to such changes renders every pecuniary engagement of long date entirely precarious' (p. 558).

11.4 Aspects of the 'Bullionist' Debates

The Bullion Committee, which reported to the House of Commons in June 1810, insisted that the Bank authorities must bear responsibility for the low exchange and the discount on paper. Adam Smith's 'real bills' rule, offered in defence by some witnesses, was admitted as a guarantee against over-issue in the case of convertibility alone; and in such a case alone would neglect of the rule entail a reflux:

> When Your Committee consider that this discretionary power, of supplying the Kingdom with circulating medium, has been exercised under an opinion that the paper could not be issued to excess if advanced in discounts to Merchants in good bills payable at stated periods, and likewise under an opinion that neither the price of Bullion nor the course of Exchanges need be adverted to, as affording any indication with respect to the sufficiency or excess of such paper, Your Committee cannot hesitate to say, that these opinions of the Bank must be regarded as in a great measure the operative cause of the continuance of the present state of things (Cannan, 1925, 53–4).

Paradoxically, while the defence by the authorities of its monetary policy was made on the Smithian grounds of 'real bills' discounting, the Committee itself drew on Smith's discussion of Scottish experience involving conditional convertibility (see above, p. 283) to illustrate the case of a premium of bullion over paper due to excess issue (1925, 37–8).

Ricardo, in his 'Reply to Bosanquet' (1811), similarly rejected the Smithian rule of thumb against excessive note issue:

> The refusal to discount any bills but those for *bona fide* transactions would be as little effectual in limiting the circulation; because, though the directors should have the means of distinguishing such bills, which can by no means be allowed, a greater portion of paper currency might be called into circulation, not that the wants of commerce could employ, but greater than what could remain in the channel of currency without depreciation (1951, III, 219).

In line with Henry Thornton, the great monetary economist, Ricardo pointed out that should the rate of profit exceed the interest on loans, there was no 'conceivable number of Bank Notes which may not be applied for', so that the argument in terms of '*bona fide*' loans (real bills) collapsed (p. 150–1). The only difference between the Bullion Committee and Ricardo is the latter's rejection of the rule in all circumstances and not only in the inconvertible case.

Despite the rejection of the real bills rule of thumb against initial excess note issue, Ricardo believed that his general case against the Bank authorities was consistent with the *Wealth of Nations*. He drew upon Smithian monetary principles to answer the question 'what is meant by an excessive issue?' to which current corn price increases were attributed by critics of the Bank of England (p. 147). He reproduced favourably Smith's account of the introduction into a purely metallic system of a convertible paper issue which, as we have seen, turns upon the notion of a requirement for a specific sum of money to circulate 'the whole annual produce' (pp. 148–9). Here we note Ricardo's (questionable) presumption that Smith's corrective outflow of metals turned upon the inflationary price effects of excessive note issues: 'The reason why gold was exported when paper was added to the circulation was not because both the paper and the gold could not be absorbed in the general mass of circulation', as Bentham had maintained of the Smith account, 'but because the diminished value of the currency here, whilst it retained its value abroad made it a profitable article of exportation' ('Notes on Bentham' (1810–11), 1951, III, 328). Henry Thornton (like Bentham) had thought otherwise:

> Dr. Smith does not . . . proceed sufficiently, as I conceive, on the practical principle of shewing how it is through the medium of prices (of the prices of goods in general, and of bullion in particular, compared with the price of the current circulating medium), that the operations of importing and exporting gold are brought about. He considers our coin as going abroad simply in consequence of our circulation at home being over full. Payment in coin, according to his doctrine, is demanded of every bank for as much of its paper as is excessive, because the excessive paper can neither be sent abroad nor turned to any use at home; whereas, when it is changed into coin, the coin may be transmitted to a foreign part, and may there be advantageously employed (1802 [1939], 203–4).

But Ricardo's acceptance of the Smithian 'law of reflux' (interpreted in Hume-like terms) applied solely to the case of convertible paper. It was inoperative under contemporary conditions; with an inconvertible currency there was no assurance against secular inflationary price movements of commodities and of bullion:

> [If], as is the case in this country, the Bank should be protected from paying its notes in specie, and should increase their issues to 1,200,000*l.*, I should call the 200,000*l.* excessive. It could not, as formerly, overflow and be exported, because every part of the currency consisted of paper, it must therefore either enlarge the channel of circulation, raising in the same proportion the prices of all commodities, not excepting gold and silver bullion, or it must, as is contended by the Bank Directors in their evidence before the Committee, return to them in the payment of bills

discounted, as no one would consent, they say, to pay interest for 200,000 *l*. which was superfluous and excessive. Here then the whole dispute rests...(1951, III, 149).

We turn next to the details of Ricardo's international adjustment mechanism. This analysis proves considerably more sophisticated than that of Smith, even allowing for generous interpretation of the *Wealth of Nations*. In what follows it is helpful to remember that by 1810 the actual currency was made up of inconvertible paper alone, coin no longer circulating; and that Ricardo, like the other monetary discussants, took for granted that the law which forbade the melting of (full-bodied) coin and its exportation was not obeyed.

Ricardo commenced the analysis of corrective metallic flows in *The High Price of Bullion* by reiterating Hume's doctrine regarding international monetary equilibrium in a *purely metallic world* with freedom of commodity and metal movement (III, 52). A universal increase in the money supply will raise general prices throughout the trading world but no gold movements would result, for 'excess of currency is but a relative term....The prices of commodities would every where rise, on account of the increase of currency, but there would be no exportation of money from either' (p. 56). By contrast, an exogenous increase in the money supply in any one country reduces the general purchasing power of the metal currency which will be exported in exchange for commodities until a new equilibrium is re-established. Conversely, a relative increase in activity in any one country will disturb the equilibrium, generating corrective flows.

Where both *inconvertible paper and coin* circulate, an expanded note issue will generate an increase in the money price (in terms of coin and notes) of bullion as well as regular commodities. But, allowing for the (illegal) melting of coin into bullion, 'the value of gold in coin, and the value of gold in bullion, would speedily approach a perfect equality' ('Reply to Bosanquet', III, 211); moreover, the purchasing power of bullion itself relative to commodities will be forced downwards as the domestic supply of bullion rises in consequence of the melting of coin. If this decline is sufficiently great, bullion will be exported (p. 212).

The rise in the supply of bullion and its fall in commodity value reflects the melting of coin withdrawn from circulation. The purchasing power of the remaining currency will therefore be rising continuously back towards its original level even before the export of metal, at the same time that the purchasing power of bullion over commodities is falling. The money price of bullion must therefore be falling even more rapidly than general prices from its initially increased level. The initial high price of bullion is thus being corrected while the falling purchasing power of bullion over commodities tends to encourage its exportation.

Ricardo was most helpful in making explicit the requirement that the purchasing power of bullion relative to commodities must fall before gold will be exported.

To summarize: a corrective process is at work even in the inconvertible case provided that coin constitutes part of the initial circulation:

> It will be readily admitted, that whilst there is any great portion of coin in circulation, every increase in bank-notes, though it will for a short time lower the value of the whole currency, paper as well as gold, yet that such depression will not be permanent, because the redundant and cheap currency will lower the exchange and will occasion the exportation of a portion of the coin, which will cease as soon as the remainder of the currency shall have regained its value, and restored the exchange to par. The increase of small notes, then, will ultimately be a substitution of one currency for another, of a paper for a metallic currency, and will not operate in the same way as an actual and permanent increase of circulation (*The High Price of Bullion*, 1951, III, 114).

Even inconvertibility thus had its safeguards provided coin circulates; because of the reduction of the coin in circulation, the currency cannot be permanently in excess in consequence of note issues.

A mixed currency, including inconvertible paper, circulated at the time Thornton published his *Paper Credit* in 1802. Thornton there defended the 1797 restriction, whereas in 1811 he strongly supported resumption. This contrast may perhaps be explained by the fact that in 1802 the gold standard had not yet been effectively abandoned in that gold coins still remained in circulation and were accepted on par with notes. The depreciation of money relative to the mint price of gold drew out coins from circulation, thus providing a new and acceptable export to fill the gap in the balance of payments and prevent a further fall in the exchange. The depreciation was not regarded as deplorable in those early years.

A mixed currency of *convertible notes and coin* can be treated in the same way. Again there is no danger of a permanent excess over the quantity appropriate in the case of a purely metallic currency. Commencing from a state of international equilibrium, an initial increase in the total currency due to note issues will be temporary only as the coin component is correspondingly reduced (Ricardo, 1951, III, 54–5). The immediate motive for the exportation of metal is a fall in its domestic purchasing power compared with its purchasing power abroad. But general prices, including that of the metal, rise proportionately in terms of the circulating media (coin and notes) upon the initial issue of additional paper; if bullion is to be exported, the price of the metal must fall relative to the prices of commodities. This brake on the relative rise in bullion results (as before) from the fact that the initial increase in its money price entails a premium of uncoined over coined metal, which by stimulating the melting of the coins adds to the supply of the metal for non-monetary domestic uses.

Where *convertible notes alone* circulate, an initial expansion above the 'equilibrium' quantity, will be returned to the Bank for specie which will be exported. The motive for the exportation of bullion is once again a fall in its purchasing power relative to commodities; for the initial increase in the note issue generates a rise in the paper price of commodities, including bullion; there is now a 'potential' divergence between the value of coined and uncoined metal which can be profitably exploited if notes are cashed in for coin. The newly issued coin is melted down adding to the supply of bullion in the market, thereby reducing its commodity value and stimulating its exportation. As far as the mechanism of bullion movement is concerned, the two cases of convertibility are analytically identical with the inconvertible case where a mixed currency circulates, for here too an addition to the note issue generates corrective outflows.

An *inconvertible paper circulation without gold coin* was, however, Ricardo's main concern, for such a case applied in 1810–11. In this circumstance an increase in the money supply raises the prices of bullion and commodities leaving their relative values unaffected, so that no motive is created for exportation of the metal:

> When the circulation consists wholly of [inconvertible] paper, any increase in its quantity will raise the [paper] *money* price of bullion without lowering its *value* [purchasing power], in the same manner, and in the same proportion, as it will raise the prices of other commodities, and for the same reason will lower the foreign exchanges; but this will only be a *nominal*, not a *real* fall, and will not occasion the exportation of bullion, because the real value of bullion will not be diminished, as there will be no increase in the quantity in the market (1951, III, 64n.).

Given the high money price of bullion, a return to cash payments at par would threaten the Bank with a severe outflow from its reserves. For with the renewed opportunity to exchange notes for coin the premium on bullion over paper now implies an exploitable premium of *uncoined* over *coined* metal. Notes will be cashed in and coins melted down for domestic use and ultimate exportation.

11.5 Ricardo and the Return to Gold

Ricardo went to considerable lengths to suggest ways to minimize the threat to output and employment implicit in monetary deflation. As the following passage from *The High Price of Bullion* indicates, he insisted upon slow reduction of the note issue before returning to gold:

> I am well aware that the total failure of paper credit would be attended with the most disastrous consequences to the trade and commerce of the country, and even its sudden limitation would occasion so much ruin and distress, that it would be highly inexpedient to have recourse to it as the means of restoring our currency to its just and equitable value.... Before therefore they can safely pay in specie, the excess of notes must be gradually withdrawn from circulation. If gradually done, little inconvenience would be felt; so that [if] the principle were fairly admitted, it would be for future consideration whether the object should be accomplished in one year or in five (1951, III, 94).

To the Prime Minister, Spencer Perceval, Ricardo formally recommended in 1811 a return to gold, to assure against further excessive note issues, but at an altered par – £4.15.0 instead of £3.17.10½ per ounce – for an unspecified period, during which interval the note issue would be slowly contracted and the mint price correspondingly reduced to the original standard. Ricardo himself clearly recognized the implication that his proposal amounted to effective devaluation for a time.

Similarly, before the House of Commons committee on resumption of 1819 (1951, V, 384ff) Ricardo did not insist on immediate resumption at par. He was satisfied with resumption at the going market rate of bullion followed by a gradual reduction in the Bank's selling price of the metal. During this interval the note issue would be slowly cut back by the Bank authorities to assure that the market price of gold did not exceed the ruling selling price and generate a loss of reserves. Moreover, an 'ingot' plan formulated in 1811 and 1816, according to which coins would not circulate, was designed to reduce deflationary pressure; and it was presumed that the Bank would avoid complicating matters by heavy purchases on world metal markets. For these reasons Ricardo made clear in his evidence that he expected only a small amount of general deflation from note contraction.

We come now to a fundamental qualification, made during the period of post-war deflation, to the entire question of the merits of a return to gold at par. The qualification amounts to a recognition that permanent devaluation might be a preferable alternative should the excess of the market over the mint price be of massive dimensions. 'I never should advise a government to restore a currency, which was depreciated 30 pcᵗ., to par', he wrote in September 1821;

> I should recommend ... that the currency ... should be fixed at the depreciated value by lowering the standard, and that no further deviations should take place. It was without any legislation that the currency from 1813 to 1819, became of an increased value, and within 5 pcᵗ. of the

value of gold, – it was in this state of things, and not with a currency depreciated 30 pc¹., that I advised a recurrence to the old standard (IX, 73–4).

The same allowance was made in Parliament in 1823:

> It was from seeing the immense power which the Bank, prior to 1819, possessed...that he had rejoiced, in 1819, in the prospect of a fixed currency. He had cared little, comparatively, what the standard established was – whether it continued at its then value, or went back to the old standard: his object had been, a fixed standard of some description or other (V, 310).

J. R. McCulloch referred to a proposal by William Lowndes in 1695 to alter the denomination of the coinage as 'this nefarious project' (1856b). But it is one also made by Ricardo – surprising as it may seem considering the uncompromising position on resumption usually attributed to him.

Ricardo's concern with the 'short run' in the context of resumption is reflected also in the general case made for a paper currency. One major argument relates to the greater flexibility of operation by the monetary authorities in dealing with short-run difficulties. In 1811, Ricardo rejected any policy of checking note issues by imposing formal quantitative limits precisely because of the need for flexibility:

> This might be done in a direct manner, by limiting the amount beyond which their paper should not be issued; but it has been plausibly urged against such a measure that occasions may arise in which sound policy may require a temporary augmentation of bank paper, and to deprive the Bank of the power of increasing their notes at such periods might be the cause of considerable distress and difficulty to the mercantile classes (1951, VI, 67).

He himself pointed out that 'this argument does not appear...to have as much weight as those who advance it imagine'; but it would be misleading to neglect it entirely. His proposal to return to gold at the devalued rate of £4.15.0 for a six-month period was designed to prevent further *excessive* issues, which were clearly distinguished from *legitimate* issues: 'if a greater circulation were required from the operation either of increased commerce, or of embarrassed credit, the bank might augment their issues without producing any effect whatever on the price of bullion, and consequently without exposing the Bank to any inconvenience, or depriving the merchants of that increased accommodation, which might be essential to their operations' (p. 68).

The concern with 'flexibility' is also apparent in the *Economical and Secure Currency* of 1816: 'Amongst the advantages of a paper over a metallic circulation, may be reckoned, as not the least, the facility with which it may be altered in quantity, as the wants of commerce and temporary circumstances may require' (1951, IV, 55). The advantage of credit elasticity in satisfying rapidly increases in the demand for liquidity – having in mind both fluctuations in 'confidence' which affect the acceptability of non-monetary media of exchange and the finance of expanding trade – is weighted very heavily in the pamphlet (p. 56ff). The distinction between legitimate and illegitimate accommodation even led Ricardo to describe the advantage of paper money in terms of the opportunity created for 'the judicious management of the quantity', thereby according a 'degree of uniformity, which is by no other means attainable... to the value of the circulating medium in which all payments are made' (pp. 57–8).

A Parliamentary intervention of 1822 confirms the foregoing perspective on Ricardo. He there objected to an assertion that note issues cannot be deficient in a convertible system, focusing specifically upon the short-run deflationary effects of a monetary contraction:

> His hon. friend had said, that whilst the Bank was obliged to pay its notes in gold, the public had no interest in interfering with the Bank respecting the amount of the paper circulation, for if it were too low, the deficiency would be supplied by the importation of gold, and if it were too high, it would be reduced by the exchange of paper for gold. In this opinion he did not entirely concur, because there might be an interval during which the country might sustain great inconvenience from an undue reduction of the Bank circulation. Let him put a case to elucidate his views on this subject. Suppose the Bank were to reduce the amount of their issues to five millions, what would be the consequence? The foreign exchanges would be turned in our favour, and large quantities of bullion would be imported. This bullion would be ultimately coined into money, and would replace the paper-money which had previously been withdrawn; but, before it was so coined, while all these operations were going on, the currency would be at a very low level, the prices of commodities would fall, and great distress would be suffered (Debate of 12 June 1822 on cash payments; 1951, V, 199–200).

The foregoing case was not offered as a theoretical example; 'something of this kind had, in fact, happened'. Circumstances were such as to require the Bank, had it operated 'correctly' during the period 1819–22, to increase its note issues rather than reduce them, as Ricardo believed it had done.

It is sometimes argued that one important distinction between Ricardo and Thornton (or later J. S. Mill) is that the former believed that if credit money would be made to behave like metallic money no further control would be required, while in the view of Thornton credit money must be managed. Now there are important differences in the degree of control envisaged as necessary by various classical authorities, but in so far as concerns Ricardo it should be clear by now that his insistence upon convertibility as an assurance against 'excess' note issues did not preclude recognition that some 'management' of credit money would be desirable. The authorities would still have to distinguish, presumably with an eye upon the exchanges, between legitimate and illegitimate accommodation, the former including note issues to counteract a reduction in alternative means of credit as well as to finance expanding activity. In some respects, as we shall see, Ricardo was more flexible in his allowance for Bank intervention than was J. S. Mill.

11.6 Mill and the Banking–Currency Debate

Supporters of Sir Robert Peel's 1844 Bank Act to regulate convertible note issues – Torrens, Norman, McCulloch and Loyd (Lord Overstone), who constituted the so-called Currency School – blamed fluctuations of the currency for the frequency and severity of commercial crises, and sought to remove the prime source of instability by control of the note issue. For Mill it was because speculative purchases are fuelled by expansion of credit in general that 'periods of general confidence, when large prospects of gain seem to be opening themselves, and when there is a disposition among dealers to employ not only all their money but all or much of their credit in enlarging their operations, are attended with so great a rise of general prices' – an outcome that would result 'if no such thing as a transferable acknowledgement of debt [in the form of notes] had ever been known in the country' ('The Currency Question' (1844), 1967, IV, 354).

The position of the Currency School is represented by Mill as involving the novel idea that an increase even of a convertible note issue will be destabilizing, since 'the check of convertibility' – although it assures against 'permanent depreciation' – 'acts too slowly, and admits of great mischief from excess of issues before it begins to operate' (p. 345). Peel's scheme had this problem in mind:

> To avert these evils, in the opinion of Colonel Torrens and Mr. Loyd, and we may now add of Sir Robert Peel, something more than convertibility is necessary. Their remedy is to place the issuers under a legal impossibility of ever increasing their issues (beyond a certain moderate minimum), except in exchange for bullion, which, if refused to them, would probably be sent to the mint and coined. By this contrivance the paper currency is prevented from being arbitrarily increased. It can only, under such a system, be extended, when, if the augmentation were not made, an equivalent increase would probably take place in the portion of the currency which consists of coin (p. 346).

Coupled with this would be a rule preventing the Bank from actively contracting its issues (as for example by sale of bank securities) in an effort to check an outflow of bullion during periods of falling prices, a practice which 'raises the rate of interest and increases the difficulty of obtaining loans,... thus heightening all the evils of a commercial revulsion' (pp. 346–7). The currency should not be diminished 'otherwise than by not re-issuing notes which are presented for payment':

> By the plan proposed, that of compelling the issuers to keep their securities at a fixed amount, and to let the currency contract or expand only by the exchange of gold for notes and of notes for gold, the paper will, according to this theory, be preserved exactly the same in quantity as the metallic money which would otherwise circulate in its place; this identity of quantity being, it is supposed, indispensable to secure identity of value.

In such a programme would supposedly be found the solution to cyclical instability.

All of this Mill denied outright, following Thomas Tooke (1774–1858). He summarized thus:

> That the proposed changes in the mode of regulating the currency will be attended with none of the advantages predicted; that, so far as intended to guard against the danger of over-issue, they are precautions against a chimerical evil; that the real evil of commercial vicissitudes, of 'cycles of excitement and depression', is not touched by them, nor by any regulations which can be adopted for bank notes or other mere instruments of credit; and that in what Mr. Tooke justly calls (next to solvency and convertibility) 'the main difference between one banking system and another', namely, 'the greater or less liability to abrupt changes in the rate of interest and in the state of commercial credit', [Tooke, 1844, *Inquiry into the Currency Principle*, 106] the present arrangements, under the condition of a larger bank reserve, have a decided advantage over the new system (pp. 360–1).

Thus, apart from the requirement for a larger reserve, Mill ruled out regulation either of the convertible note issue or of credit.

Yet one discerns some allowance by Mill for a positive impact on prices by the note issue. As background to this assertion, we must have in mind his insistence that increased note issues do not necessarily raise the money supply in circulation. Citing Tooke's *History of Prices* (1838), Mill observed that when the Bank buys securities in the market with its notes the interest rate indeed falls, but the seller might invest the funds abroad (as he would be encouraged to do by the fall in interest itself) rather than add to purchases domestically (1967, IV, 350–1). Similarly, the issue by country banks of notes to farmers (to allow them to hold stocks) may be counterbalanced by merchants who, finding no grain on the market, place their notes on deposit or repay outstanding loans.

Even when a net increase in notes does occur this need not entail an increase in general 'purchasing power'. To do so, it is necessary for the issues to impinge upon the production–income–expenditure process.

> The purchasing power which determines prices is of two kinds – *ultimate* purchasing power, which determines permanent prices; and the portion of that power which is in actual exercise at a given time; this determines the fluctuations of prices.
>
> The ultimate purchasing power of the community is, in the words of Mr. Tooke, 'the quantity of money constituting the revenues of the different orders of the state, under the head of rents, profits, salaries, and wages' [Tooke, 1844, 71]. We think he should rather have said their 'gross incomes', to include that portion of their receipts which is employed in replacing material, and in renewing machinery and buildings as they wear out. The whole of these incomes is destined to be, and is, expended in purchases, either for personal consumption or for reproduction. The aggregate of money incomes, compared with the whole annual produce of the country, determines general prices, as between the dealer and the consumer. If you add to the currency in a way which increases the aggregate of incomes, you raise prices; but this condition can be satisfied by nothing short of a permanent increase of the quantity of money in the country; either from an influx of the metals, caused by a diminution in the cost at which they can be produced and imported, or from increased issue of an inconvertible paper currency. We say inconvertible, because it is admitted that of that alone could any increase have the character of permanence (p. 352).

All of this reinforces what we already know of Mill's approach to general quantity theory reasoning, namely his refusal to adopt an 'automatist' approach in considering the impact of a change in money supply on the price level (see pp. 271–2).

It is clearly 'permanent prices' rather than their fluctuations that Mill has in mind when he maintains that 'nothing short of a permanent increase' of the money supply reflecting an influx of gold can be effective in raising prices. For there are two concessions relating to non-permanent increases in the note issue which are said to 'add to the aggregate of incomes' and evidently do entail at least temporary price increases:

> To be scientifically accurate, it must be admitted that if the increased issues were made in advances to employers of labour (for instance, in a loan to a manufacturer, who expends them in the direct payment of wages to his work-people), there would be, to that extent, as long as the expenditure was going on, an increase of the aggregate money income of the community, and hence a corresponding rise of prices. But this supposition is not applicable to our present currency, of which the smallest notes are of too high a denomination to be employed, in any extent worth considering, for the payment of wages.

> We may add, with Mr. Tooke [1844, 68ff], that the issues of a *Government* paper, even when not permanent, will raise prices; because Governments usually issue their paper in purchasing for consumption. If issued to pay off a portion of the national debt, we believe they would have no such effect (p. 352n.).

An important example of a note issue that would *not* act on prices is one injected in times of depression designed to satisfy a demand for liquidity ('Paper Currency and Commercial Distress' (1826), 1967, IV, 108–9). What of the effect on prices of increases in the note issue which occur during periods of speculation? Here Mill retreats to a line of defence prepared in 1826: increases in purchasing power due to net increases in note issue would have occurred even in their absence since increases in notes involve only one way amongst numerous others of drawing upon available credit (IV, 353–5). And as in 1826, the onus upon bankers' notes is further reduced by the observation (following Tooke) that the increased issues that do occur are a *passive* response to price increases not their cause, such increases – rather than other forms of credit – reflecting the particular institutional arrangements at play but not in any way essential to the process (pp. 355–6). Even so, there are concessions regarding the impact of note issues:

> It must be conceded, and Mr. Tooke does fully concede, that if bankers, urged by competition or caught by the contageous confidence of speculative times, make advances to persons who otherwise have *not* credit and cannot give good security, in that case the foregoing arguments do not apply. To that extent they do create a new purchasing power, a new demand, and, as its consequence, a rise of price (p. 355).

This concession Mill played down. For he proceeds to insist that it is not by notes 'as such' that an impact on prices occurs. There may be imprudent advances of all kinds by bankers; indeed, 'all extension of credit, legitimate or illegitimate, tends, in proportion as it is made use of, to a rise of price. And all contraction of credit produces an equivalent collapse'.

In his chapter 'On the Regulation of a Convertible Currency' in the *Principles* (Book III, xxiv), Mill repeated the Tooke position, also championed by John Fullarton, regarding the 'passivity' of the note issue under convertibility: 'bank issues, since they cannot be increased in amount unless there be an increased demand, cannot possibly raise prices; cannot encourage speculation, nor occasion a commercial crisis;... the attempt to guard against that evil by an artificial management of the issue of notes, is of no effect for the intended purpose' (1848 [1965], III, 662). Here the distinction between 'quiescent' and 'speculative' or 'expectant' states is critical. During the quiescent period there is no special demand for loans, and any (exogenous) increase in notes cannot remain in circulation to finance increased demand for commodities: 'In this case, therefore, there can be no addition at the discretion of the bankers, to the general circulating medium: any increase of their issues either comes back to them' – an application of the law of reflux – 'or remains idle in the hands of the public, and no rise takes place in prices' (p. 663). (Considering that the quiescent period is one of net investment, Mill's insistence upon the constancy of the note circulation is surprising.)

Attention is also given to the finance of the speculative transactions which characterize the 'expectant' state, 'when an impression prevails, whether well founded or groundless, that the supply of one or more great articles of commerce is likely to fall short of the ordinary consumption', and when traders are 'disposed to make a more than ordinary use of their credit' (p. 663). Mill allows that bankers often unduly administer to the increased demand for credit during the 'expectant state'. Although such expansions of the note issue are still regarded as the consequence not the cause of rising prices, the cause being largely simple book credit and cheques to a lesser extent, Mill's adherence to Tooke's position was subject to a qualification: 'I regard it as proved, both scientifically and historically, that during the ascending period of speculation, *and as long as it is confined to transactions between dealers*, the issues of bank notes are seldom materially increased, nor contribute anything to the speculative rise of prices' (p. 664; emphasis added). The notion of passivity collapsed when speculation touched the producers:

> Speculative orders given by merchants to manufacturers induce them to extend their operations, and to become applicants to bankers for increased advances, which if made in notes, are not paid away to persons who return them into deposit, but are partially expended in paying wages, and pass into the various channels of retail trade, where they become directly effective in producing a further rise of prices.

Thus although the initial note issues are the response to a preceding demand for increased advances, once they filter through into the labour market they take on an active life of their own in generating a kind of multiplier effect. (This qualification already appears in a note to 'The Currency Question' of 1844; see above, p. 299.)

A second qualification to the passivity of the note issue relates to the final stages of the speculative period when advances are requested by those unsuccessful speculators who, once the tide shows signs of turning, struggle to avoid selling in a falling market. In this case, an expanded note issue – while formally a passive response – 'tends to prolong the duration of the speculations', enabling 'the speculative prices to be kept up for some time after they would otherwise have collapsed' (1848 [1965], 665). For the extension of credit via note issues 'long after the recoil from over-speculation has commenced', prevents the increase in the interest rate which would otherwise have taken place in consequence of the demand for disposable capital and which would have obliged speculative holders 'to submit earlier to that loss by resale, which could not have been prevented from coming on them at last' (p. 668).

Serious consequences are in fact said to flow from the artificial maintenance of prices (and depression of the interest rate), namely an aggravated drain of the precious metals necessitating a more stringent contraction of notes than would otherwise be required, thereby worsening the subsequent deflation. For since the prolongation of the drain 'endanger[ed] the power of the banks to fulfil their engagement of paying their notes on demand, they are compelled to contract their credit more suddenly and severely than would have been necessary if they had been prevented from propping up speculation by increased advances, after the time when the recoil had become inevitable' (p. 665). The resultant increases in the interest rate, inflicted 'much greater loss and distress on individuals and destroy[ed] a much greater amount of the ordinary credit of the country, than any real necessity required' (p. 670).

It was Mill's repeatedly stated view that the rising prices of the speculative period were inconceivable without the support of a variety of credit forms, including book credits granted by manufacturers and importers to their clients. His opposition to expanded note issues after the 'recoil' from over-speculation had set in, was not to an increase in currency as such but to inappropriate extensions of credit (which happened to take the form of notes): 'Prices, having risen without any increase of bank notes, could well have fallen without a diminution of them; but having risen in consequence of an extension of credit, they could not fall without a contraction of it' (p. 669) – a contraction prevented by the supposed note issue. But this is a formal matter; the concessions themselves regarding the 'active' impact of notes on prices stood firm. This is especially so if we have in mind an allowance, on an analogy with simple velocity, for a differential impact on prices of alternative forms of credit, namely that 'credit transferable from hand to hand' is 'more potent, than credit which only performs one purchase' so that prices are likely to rise higher if (speculative) purchases are made with notes rather than with bills or book credits (p. 546).

11.7 Mill and Counter-cyclical Monetary Policy

Mill described the function of money in facilitating exchange as Adam Smith had done: 'There cannot...be intrinsically a more insignificant thing, in the economy of society, than money; except as a contrivance for sparing time and labour. It is a machine for doing quickly and commodiously, what would be done, though less quickly and commodiously, without it', to which Mill adds that 'like many other kinds of machinery, it only exerts a distinct and independent influence of its own when it gets out of order' (1848 [1965], III, 506). Again, 'money is to commerce only what oil is to machinery, or railways to locomotion – a contrivance to diminish friction' (p. 633). These observations have often been read to imply a rather restrictive view of the potentialities for monetary policy.

Similarly, Mill's championship of the gold standard has given the impression of a limited potential for an active monetary policy. This perspective has been very nicely put by Sir John Hicks:

> [Mill] makes it clear that it is confidence in the maintenance of a Gold Standard (in his days of full Gold Standard with gold coins in circulation) which is the basis of the required belief that in the long run prices cannot depart very far from normal. He is therefore opposed to the regulation of the Quantity of Money, however defined; the objective of monetary policy should be the maintenance of convertibility. That will not prevent fluctuations, nor could control of Quantity prevent fluctuations; for booms can start with an expansion of trade credit, without the banks themselves being, at that stage, much involved. As the boom develops, it requires to be fortified by more secure forms of credit, so the pressure is carried back from the circumference to the centre of the banking system. It is essential, at that point, that the centre should hold firm; it must protect itself, but only in order to be able to spread security around it. Booms are thus more dangerous than slumps; for a slump will cure itself, while in a boom there is a threat to the convertibility, on which the underlying stability is based. But once it is recognized that there is this threat, wise policy can ward it off (1983, 64; cf. 1967, 164–6).

We shall see now that the scope for a discretionary policy allowed by Mill was rather wider than appears at first sight. Notwithstanding his horror of monetary unorthodoxy of the Birmingham variety, he yet championed flexibility and intelligent judgement on the part of the central bank rather than the automaticity required by the Currency School, whose rules, designed to reduce central banking to the issue of gold certificates, were embodied in Peel's Act of 1844. To categorize his position on monetary policy as one of extreme *laissez-faire* is going much too far.

Mill appreciated that a primary concern of policy-makers must be the mitigation of the severity of the 'painful series' of 'commercial crises', a phenomenon peculiar to the nineteenth-century British economy, and that in part to this end the Bank Charter Act itself had been introduced (1848 [1965], III, 660). His opposition to the legislation reflected a rejection of the 'currency theory' which discerned in an arbitrary issue of notes the 'prime agent' of the initial price increases, generating a 'spirit of speculation in commodities' with its reaction in a 'commercial crisis'. To focus on the currency as the prime agent diverted attention from the real 'circumstances...influencing the expectation of supply' (p. 661). Yet the allowance (see above, pp. 301–2) of an active force to the note issue after the upper turning point implied a concession to the champions of the Act of 1844: 'I am compelled to think that the being restricted from increasing their issues, is a real impediment to their making those advances which arrest the tide at its turn, and make it rush like a torrent afterwards' (p. 670). Mill was thus prepared to make concessions to 'the more moderate' members of the Currency School – Overstone, Norman and Torrens. From this perspective the 'mitigation of commercial revulsions is the real, and only serious, purpose of the Act of 1844' (p. 665n.).

Notwithstanding these concessions, the balance of the case still rested with Tooke and Fullerton. What was required was a degree of flexibility on the part of the banking system deliberately precluded by the legislation of 1844:

> panegyrists of the system...boast[ed], that on the first appearance of a drain for exportation – whatever may be its cause, and whether, under a metallic currency, it would involve a contraction of credit or not – the Bank is at once obliged to curtail its advances. And this, be it remembered, when there has been no speculative rise of prices which it is indispensable to correct, no unusual extension of credit requiring contraction; but the demand for gold is solely occasioned by foreign payments on account of government, or large corn importations consequent on a bad harvest (p. 678).

This position, Mill maintained, presumed too hastily that in the case of a purely metallic currency a gold drain necessarily entailed a contraction of the internal circulation. A gold drain resulting from extraneous factors such as extraordinary foreign expenditures by government, private capital exports and the need for unusual imports because of poor harvests (and not from an increase in the price level generated by an undue expansion of currency or credit) would in all probability not be drawn from circulation, but from hoards – chiefly bankers' reserves (p. 673). Even a system designed to assure that the paper currency fluctuated in exact conformity to the variations of a metallic currency – supposedly the prime objective of the 1844 Act – required no contraction of the currency (or credit) in such cases. What, however, would be required was an adequate gold reserve to cover the drain (p. 677). Mill saw in the separation of the departments according to the 1844 legislation a measure dictating far larger reserves than would otherwise be required, and necessitating unnecessary upward pressure on the rate of discount. Accordingly, 'notwithstanding the beneficial operation of the Act of 1844 in the first stages of one kind of commercial crisis (that produced by over-speculation), it on the whole materially aggravates the severity of commercial revulsions. And not only are contractions of credit made more severe by the Act, they are also made greatly more frequent' (p. 682).

Flexibility was required also during periods of crisis. That notes should conform to the metallic standard as far as its 'permanent' value was concerned was not in question; Mill and the Banking School denied only that they should be required to vary in quantity in conformity with all the variations that would have occurred if metal alone circulated. For 'the fluctuations in the value of the currency are determined, not by its quantity, whether it consist of gold or of paper, but by the expansions and contractions of credit'; and a paper currency fluctuating in quantity according to the 1844 rules, in fact generated 'more violent revulsions of credit than one which is not held to this rigid conformity' and, therefore, destabilized the value of the currency (p. 667).

In taking this position Mill had in mind pre-eminently the desirability for an active role on the part of the Bank of England during depression, a role sufficiently important to outweigh even the disadvantages of too free a hand at the peak of the cycle:

> In the first place, a large extension of credit by bankers, though most hurtful when, credit being already in an inflated state, it can only serve to retard and aggravate the collapse, is most salutary when the collapse has come, and when credit instead of being in excess is in distressing deficiency, and increased advances by bankers, instead of being an addition to the ordinary amount of floating credit, serve to replace a mass of other credit which has been suddenly destroyed (p. 670).

Mill realized, of course, that the principles of 1844 allowed an expansion of notes when gold inflows occur, as they do when the general level of prices declines, but regarded such flows as occurring too late to prevent distress (p. 672).

As in 1826 (see above, p. 300), Mill still insisted that expanded note issues in depression were 'passive', since they did not result in increased expenditures on commodities (pp. 670–1). The same point recurs in evidence given in 1857:

> in the case of an internal panic ... there is no knowing how far the panic may reach; the longer it goes on the longer it is likely to go on, because panic creates panic. Any amount of issue of notes which the Bank could possibly make at such a time could not under any circumstances do any harm, because all that people would want them for would be to keep by them; they would never go into circulation (1967, V, 529).

In the absence of monetary expansion there must, however, occur – in consequence of the high rate of discount – general deflation of prices: 'the holders of goods, being unable to get money in any other way, are obliged to sell at a forced reduction of price' (p. 526). Mill's denial that a correction of excess commodity supply can be achieved by monetary means therefore applies only in the limited sense that there is no positive increase in purchases. But expansion of notes is seen to have the effect of checking forced sales and to this extent does alleviate the excess. The 'passivity' of note issue in this context turns out to be rather a formal matter.

We have seen also that Mill conceded to the 1844 Act the desirable consequence of requiring the Bank to reduce its note issues at or near the turning point of a 'speculative rise in prices', thereby allowing prices to decline and the gold drain (typical of such periods) to ease. His insistence that the Bank avoid such constraint where gold outflows originate in non-monetary circumstances implies the allowance of a degree of discretion to the Bank authority in distinguishing different categories of drain. Similarly, while the constraint required of the Bank at the upper turning point of a speculative cycle would avoid delaying the downturn, thus mitigating its intensity, the Bank had a positive responsibility to alleviate the crisis when it occurred though it was the (inevitable) outcome of a preceding speculation. What was appropriate at one period of the cycle was inappropriate at another. Discretion is of the essence. Mill indeed found Adam Smith at fault for neglecting the emergency borrowing requirements of generally 'prosperous mercantile firms' during periods of 'commercial difficulty' by his famous assertion that only 'prodigals and projectors' ever want to borrow at a rate of interest above the standard market rate (1848 [1965], III, 925).

There is little here to suggest that hesitancy to countenance a counter-cyclical monetary policy which is sometimes said to characterize Mill's position. Rejection of monetary unorthodoxy of the Attwood variety as an invitation to secular disaster did not imply that under convertibility (itself to be defended by the maintenance of adequate reserves) cyclical instability should not be assuaged by monetary means.

It had been Henry Thornton's position that a credit system required central-bank management which could not be reduced to a matter of mechanical rules (1802). And as Sir John Hicks has recognized, Mill '[is on] the same side as Thornton; he believes in monetary management' (1967, 166). Hicks, however, sees a lesser concern on Mill's part with the (direct) prevention of slumps; merely by avoiding over-expansion of credit in prosperous times, the disorganization caused by the crisis would be prevented and also the slump that emerges from such disorganization. But this is only part of the story, for it ignores Mill's very positive insistence upon credit expansion by the Bank of England during periods of depression to help satisfy the increased demand for liquidity of those periods.

The charge is sometimes also made that Mill neglected the problems of unemployment during the cycle, presumably because he thought the system reverted rapidly back to full employment. But Mill did not neglect the unemployment and excess capacity of the revulsion (see above, p. 259). And while there were forces at work generating ultimate recovery of expenditures and thus the correction of the excess demand for money, Mill did not wish to count on them alone, and precisely for that reason ascribed a positive role to the monetary authorities.

What is the source of the view that Mill opposed an active monetary policy? There are a number of possible explanations, in addition to the erroneous deductions drawn from his hostility towards inflationary proposals of the Attwood variety. His formal insistence upon the 'passivity' of the note issue is partly responsible. But this is a smoke screen: an injection of credit in depression may not generate increased expenditure, but it does check forced sales of commodities. It is true that Mill did not countenance counter-cyclical variation in public expenditure; various proposals for increased public expenditure were made with an eye to secular trends (though any prevention of the downward trend of the profit rate, as might be achieved by increased unproductive outlays, would act indirectly to check speculation and dampen fluctuations). But rejection of government spending of a cyclical variety must not be mistaken for a rejection of monetary intervention.

11.8 Concluding Note

There is a paradoxical flavour to the story of Mill on money and banking. He counted himself amongst the strongest defenders of the gold standard. In this he was, like other Banking School adherents, totally at one with the Currency School – a remarkable unanimity of opinion on policy. Moreover, his dismissal of the Currency School's concern with excess note issue under convertibility applied only to periods of 'quiescence', for he emphasized an 'active' impact of note issues at late speculative stages of the cycle. There was much then about which Mill agreed with the Currency School. On the other hand, he believed notes should not be treated as gold certificates in the manner of the Act of 1844: discretion was called for. Limitations of issue must be avoided in the case of gold drains unrelated to speculative price increases. It is this call for a discretionary insulation of the internal circulation from changes in the external position that appears self-contradictory from the perspective of so strong a champion of convertibility – convertibility without allowance for periodic devaluation.

The paradoxical tone to which I have alluded reflects Mill's standard quest for balance – in the present case his appreciation of the exquisitely difficult task of mitigating cyclical pressures, but yet avoiding secular depreciation of the currency. It is most unfortunate that his strong statements regarding a 'passive' note issue – statements that can perhaps be appreciated in terms of a taste for polemic – have clouded his true position. He gave the impression that money was unimportant, and thereby backed himself into a corner.

It remains to emphasize that the 'paradox' discernible in Mill's formulations is present also in those of Ricardo – that most stalwart champion of the gold standard. But in Ricardo's case we have found not only a recommendation for bank accommodation to satisfy the demand for liquidity in periods of 'want of confidence', but even – and here Ricardo totally surpasses Mill – a recommendation for devaluation of the currency if that is necessary to avoid severe deflation.

Suggested Reading

*Smith (1776) *An Inquiry into the Nature and Causes of the Wealth of Nations*, Book II, ch. ii; Book IV, ch. i.
*Ricardo, *Principles of Political Economy*, ch. 27, in *Works and Correspondence* (1951), ed. P. Sraffa.
*   *The High Price of Bullion* (1810–11), in *Works* (1951), III, 47–127.
*Mill (1848), *Principles of Political Economy*, Book III, ch. xxiv.
*   'The Currency Question' (1844), in *Collected Works* (1967), IV, 341–61.

Ricardo's views on the issues of this chapter are examined in Sayers (1953), in Wood (1985), item 92, and Hollander (1979), ch. 8. Pages 425–35 of the latter chapter cover Smith's banking principles and Ricardo's reaction thereto.

Thornton's *Paper Credit* (1802) is one of the finest contributions in the monetary literature to which Hayek has added an important 'Introduction' (1939). Hicks (1967), ch. 10, and Reisman (1971), which emphasize the 'unorthodox' features of Thornton's analysis, are recommended.

On the bullionist controversies see Cannan (1925) and Viner (1937), chs 3 and 4. Viner, ch. 5, Robbins (1958), chs 4 and 5, and Fetter (1965), ch. 6 provide excellent accounts of the later Banking–Currency School controversies. Tooke's position is examined by Laidler (1972), and Mill's position – along the lines of the present account – by Hollander (1985), ch. 7, 544–601. There is much on Mill and money and banking in Lord Robbins's 'Introduction' to the *Collected Works*, IV and V, reprinted in Robbins (1970), ch. 7.

The origins of the 1844 Bank Act are studied by Horsefield (1953) and Fetter (1965), ch. 6.

12   Smith on Method

12.1   Introduction

The next three chapters, which are concerned with methodology, draw upon the earlier discussions of value and distribution, growth and money. A methodological investigation will help place these specific contributions in broad perspective, by giving some idea of the classicists' view of the nature and scope of economic theory.

It has been well said that more than anyone Adam Smith directed English economics 'toward logically consistent synthesis of economic relationships, toward "system-building"', applying to economic phenomena 'the unifying concept of a co-ordinated and mutually interdependent system of cause and effect relationships' (Viner, 1958, 213–14). This chapter will place the methodology of Smith's economics – his system building – within a wider context relating to the methodology of the physical sciences (section 12.2). In the course of the discussion I will consider Smith's establishment and refinement of the 'self-interest' axiom based on observation from contemporary and historical data (section 12.3). Section 12.4 will show that on some conspicuous occasions Smith engaged in the irresponsible application to policy of complex models, against which practice Sir James Steuart had already warned in 1767 (see above, p. 38). The final section indicates some reactions to Smithian method during the period 1776–1816.

12.2   Scientific Method

The derivation of the axioms in systems of natural science and the verification of such systems are discussed by Smith in an *Essay on the History of Astronomy*, first published in 1795, with special reference to

Newton's principle of gravitation. The merits of the gravitation axiom are discussed in terms of an aesthetic dimension – its 'familiarity': 'the superior genius and sagacity of Sir Isaac Newton ... made ... the greatest and most admirable improvement that was ever made in philosophy, when he discovered, that he could join together, the movement of the Planets by so familiar a principle of connection [as gravitation], which completely removed all the difficulties the imagination had hitherto felt in attending to them' (1795 [1980], 98); the Newtonian system constituted 'the greatest discovery that ever was made by man, the discovery of an immense chain of the most important and sublime truths, all closely connected together by one capital fact, of the reality of which we have daily experience' (p. 105). In his *Lectures on Rhetoric* (delivered 1762–3) Smith wrote of the 'pleasure' which we see in 'the phaenomena which we reckoned the most unaccountable all deduced from some principle (commonly a wellknown one) and all united in one chain, far superior to what we feel from the unconnected method where everything is accounted for by itself, without any reference to the others' (1983, 146). The success in terms of general acceptance of any scientific system required that it be based upon simple, easily recognizable principles: 'no system, how well soever in other respects supported, 'has ever been able to gain any general credit in the world, whose connecting principles were not such as were familiar to all mankind' (1795 [1980], 46).

The general acceptability of basic principles is one matter. What of the way in which they are derived? Smith compared the process of discovery with someone attending a play who tries to imagine from his place in the audience what kind of machinery is at work behind the stage; Newton derived his gravitational principle by a process of logical deduction from the evidence, commencing with certain manifestations and seeking to explain them (pp. 42, 44). But the hypothesis still requires validation – for the principle is hypothetical, and might account for the data merely by accident: 'Having thus shown, that gravity might be the connecting principle which joined together the movement of the Planets, [Newton] endeavoured next to prove that it really was so' (p. 100). Smith here touched upon testing by prediction:

> [Newton's] principles, it must be acknowledged, have a degree of firmness and solidity that we should in vain look for in any other system. The most sceptical cannot avoid feeling this. They not only connect together most perfectly all the phaenomena of the Heavens, which had been observed before his time, but those also which the persevering industry and more perfect instruments of later Astronomers have made known to use; have been either easily and immediately explained by the application of his

principles, or have been explained in consequence of more laborious and accurate calculations from these principles, than had been instituted before (p. 105).

One 'prediction' confirmed by subsequent observation relates to the flattening of the globe at the poles; another, yet to be confirmed, predicted 'the returns of several [comets], particularly of one which is to make its appearance in 1758' – presumably Halley's comet (p. 103).

Smith retained these notions regarding scientific method throughout his later career. In his *The Theory of Moral Sentiments* (1759), he applied the analogy between a 'system' and a 'machine' to social studies: 'Human society, when we contemplate it in a certain abstract and philosophical light, appears like a great, an immense machine, whose regular and harmonious movements produce a thousand agreeable effects' (1759 [1976], 316). In the *Wealth of Nations*, in the context of moral philosophy, he described a transition from 'theory' to 'science', representing the latter in terms of system-building on a par with the natural sciences: 'The maxims of common life were arranged in some methodical order, and connected together by a few common principles, in the same manner as they had attempted to arrange and connect the phenomena of nature. The science which pretends to investigate and explain those connecting principles, is what is properly called moral philosophy' (1776 [1937], 724).

As for pure economics, perhaps the main objective of the *Wealth of Nations* was the formulation of a 'system' describing the optimum pattern of economic development. This system, turning on the self-interest axiom, demonstrates the non-chaotic nature of the competitive price mechanism in a *static* context but extends further to encompass the effects of changing factor proportions upon the pattern of activity *over time* (see above, p. 170). Smith's model of investment priorities was not devised for its own sake, though doubtless it satisfied an aesthetic taste for 'the beauty of a systematical arrangement'. It was intended rather to interpret observed differentials between patterns of resource allocation and growth rates in the North American colonies and in various European countries, pre-eminently Britain. It served to throw light on the probable future course of American development under alternative Imperial regulations. Its main function, however, was to provide an ideal pattern against which actual European and British progress could be measured, and the steps required to correct divergencies from the ideal discerned. The system was thus to serve as the basis for a reform programme. More precisely, by use of his model of investment priorities, Smith intended to demonstrate the adverse effects on economic development of allocative distortions created by government interventions and archaic institutions; at the same time, he also isolated contemporary institutions that had a favourable effect on growth.

12.3 History and the Self-Interest Axiom

In this latter exercise we can perceive one aspect of Smith's approach to history. To understand fully contemporary institutions, both outmoded and favourable, he believed required an appreciation of their origins, and Smith was a great economic historian. He engaged partly in a description of the historical record as he understood it – the long-term transition from an agicultural economy to a mixed economy, the former involving service obligation and the latter involving money; and he also attempted to interpret the transition. In approaching these secular trends he used themes and principles which were characteristic of the so-called Scottish Historical School, including (to use a Marxian term) a 'materialistic' conception of history – the view that customs and institutions (including legal systems) reflect productive relations or the way people make their living – and the notion of a temporal priority of agriculture over commerce during the course of normal development in a 'four-stages' sequence of development involving hunting, pasturage, agriculture and commerce. None the less, the historical part of the *Wealth of Nations* is limited largely to Book III and, to a lesser extent, Book V, and can be viewed as a digression from the perspective of the work as a whole. The actual recommendations for the reform of institutions and policy, the prime objective of the work, are based upon the analytical model of the progress of society applicable specifically to a competitive capitalist exchange system, the advanced stage of development. And this analysis stands on its feet independently of the Scottish procedures and the broad overview of progress and the origins of institutions. Smith was certainly fascinated by those matters, but as far as the reform programme is concerned, he was able to proceed without the superstructure. Smith based his reform programme on a model of development involving principles of allocation theory in a dynamic context – a perfect example of a hypothetico-deductive system crying out for mathematical formulation.

The model of investment priorities turns upon the fundamental assumption of profit-maximizing behaviour on the part of the capitalist ('the consideration of his own private profit'). In this context we find the most celebrated statement of the operation of economic man (and the consistency of private and public interests):

> Every individual is continually exerting himself to find out the most advantageous employment of whatever capital he can command. It is his

own advantage, indeed, and not that of the society, which he has in view. But the study of his own advantage naturally, or rather necessarily leads him to prefer that employment which is most advantageous to society....He generally, indeed, neither intends to promote the public interest, nor knows how much he is promoting it. By preferring the support of domestic to that of foreign industry, he intends only his own security; and by directing that industry in such a manner as its produce may be of the greatest value, he intends only his own gain, and he is in this, as in many other cases, led by an invisible hand to promote an end which was no part of his intention (1776 [1937], 421–3).

To say that self-interest is the governing motive in commercial activity – a world of anonymous or impersonal relationships – is, however, rather too vague. Smith went further and attempted to build up from contemporary and historical evidence the precise patterns of self-interested behaviour for which there is scope in the capitalistic exchange system. Here we discern a second major use for the historical materials of the *Wealth of Nations* – the fleshing our of self-interested behaviour in the contemporary world.

The basic behavioural motivation of the *Wealth of Nations* satisfies the scientific requirement that an axiom should be a 'familiar' notion. Indeed, recognition of the desire for profit as a controlling motive in economic behaviour has an ancient history. Both the mercantilist and the philosophic literatures refer to this assumption; and, as is clear from *The Theory of Moral Sentiments*, Smith had early on adopted this assumption as a central element in his conception of motivation, for amongst the elements which constitute human behaviour, 'prudence' (self-interest) plays a very large part:

> The qualities most useful to ourselves are, first of all, superior reason and understanding, by which we are capable of discerning the remote consequences of all our actions, and of foreseeing the advantage or detriment which is likely to result from them: and secondly, self-command, by which we are enabled to abstain from present pleasure or to endure present pain, in order to obtain a greater pleasure or to avoid a greater pain in some future time. In the union of those two qualities consists the virtue of prudence, of all the virtues that which is most useful to the individual (1759 [1976], 189).

Smith went out of his way to reject contemporary systems of thought which identified virtue with 'benevolence' rather than self-interest: 'The habits of economy, industry, discretion, attention, and application of thought, are generally supposed to be cultivated from self-interested motives, and at the same time are apprehended to be very praise-worthy qualities, which deserve the esteem and approbation of every body'; conversely, 'carelessness and want of oeconomy are universally disapproved of, not, however, as proceeding from a want of benevolence, but from a want of the proper attention to the objects of self-interest' (p. 304). That self-interest, which is said to be 'inherent in the very nature of our being', must in some circumstances give way to social interest, does not imply the exclusion of self-interest from good behaviour: 'Though the standard by which the casuists frequently determine what is right or wrong in human conduct, be its tendency to the welfare or disorder of society, it does not follow that a regard to the welfare of society should be the sole virtuous motive of action, but only that, in any competition, it ought to cast the balance against all other motives' (pp. 304–5). Benevolence 'is the sole principle of action in the Deity' alone.

The axiom of self-interest or prudence, of course, plays a key role in the *Wealth of Nations*: 'It is not from the benevolence of the butcher, the brewer, or the baker, that we expect our dinner, but from their regard to their own interest. We address ourselves, not to their humanity but to their self-love, and never talk to them of our own necessities but of their advantages' (1776 [1937], 14). It is possible that this assumption reflected a deliberate abstraction by Smith for analytical purposes. But it is more likely that he was representing what he thought to be the entire man within a specific environment, the anonymous environment of the market place where there is no place for the social sentiments such as benevolence or sympathy. For the end of self-interest fails in so far as one party in an economic transaction concerns himself with the welfare of the other party; and such interpersonal relationships are precluded within an anonymous commercial environment. The constrained environment of the *Wealth of Nations* carries us a long way in understanding the connection – the quite consistent connection – between that work and *The Theory of Moral Sentiments*, where interpersonal relations are of the essence.

That individuals within a commercial environment are motivated by self-interest is to some extent taken for granted without evidence – it is an 'axiom' in the literal sense of the term. But this property should not be exaggerated; there is an extensive empirical dimension to be taken into account. The contemporary world provided a good observer with broad spectra of institutions and stages of development to serve in comparative behaviour studies. At the most general level, Smith drew upon observation of his world to make the case that, compared with environmental circumstances, national character has little to do with behavioural patterns.

Whenever commerce is introduced into any country, probity and punctuality always accompany it. These virtues in a rude and barbarous country are almost unknown. Of all the nations in Europe, the Dutch, the most commercial, are the most faithful to their word. The English are more so than the Scotch, but much inferior to the Dutch, and in the remote parts of this country [Scotland] they [are] far less so than in the commercial parts of it. This is not at all to be imputed to national character, as some pretend. There is no natural reason why an Englishman or a Scotchman should not be as punctual in performing agreements as a Dutchman. It is far more reduceable to self interest, that general principle which regulates the actions of every man, and which leads men to act in a certain manner from views of advantage, and is as deeply implanted in an Englishman as a Dutchman (*Lectures on Jurisprudence*, 1766 [1978], 538).

To explain the behaviour differences between nations and over time by reference to national character rather than self-interest appeared to Smith to be forced.

The empirical dimension is yet more extensive. To exclude actions designed to promote the welfare of others still leaves an extremely broad range of 'self-interested' behaviour; we do indeed have a vantage point from which to interpret actual behaviour but it is not very precise. Smith proceeded to show how the socio-economic environment dictates particular kinds of self-interested behaviour.

The constraints imposed on types of self-interested behaviour by legal and institutional forms may be illustrated from the context of land tenure arrangements. Smith establishes that slavery is inefficient compared with the *metayer* system, but concludes that where slavery is legal and the profit margin large enough, masters were prepared to surrender some profitability for the psychic pleasures derived from domineering. For 'self-interest' includes both the love of money and the love of domineering so that marginal trade-offs have to be made between them: 'The pride of man makes him love to domineer, and nothing mortifies him so much as to be obliged to condescend to persuade his inferiors. Wherever the law allows it, and the nature of the work can afford it, he will generally prefer the service of slaves to that of freemen' (1776 [1937], 365). But the love of domineering – at least in one of its forms – is precluded once the law forbids slavery. Furthermore, the ability to adopt inefficient methods to some extent is due to the existence of monopoly, where there will be the greatest scope for very high profits. In a competitive environment the return on capital will be relatively low, reducing the scope for this form of self-interested behaviour (pp. 157–8).

Smith's interpretation of a resolution by the Quakers of Pennsylvania to free their slaves illustrates his typical procedure in approaching economical phenomena (p. 366). He observes first that production of corn in the English colonies as a whole was largely by free labour, and that of sugar and tobacco by slave labour. This contrast in itself pointed away from benevolence as a major motive on the part of the Quakers, and suggested some objective feature at play differentially in the two sets of markets to which self-interested masters responded. Tighter market conditions in the case of corn, Smith proposed, would have rendered the (supposedly) less efficient slave system unaffordable; and the decision by the Quakers could be explained in a more natural or unforced way in these terms:

> The planting of sugar and tobacco can afford the expence of slave culti-vation. The raising of corn, it seems, in the present times, cannot. In the English colonies, of which the principal produce is corn, the far greater part of the work is done by freemen. The late resolution of the Quakers in Pennsylvania to set at liberty all their negro slaves, may satisfy us that their number cannot be very great. Had they made any considerable part of their property, such a resolution could never have been agreed to.

Smith merely *asserts* that the resolution by the Quaker slave masters 'may satisfy us' that their slave holdings were small, the use of slaves having been rendered unprofitable; he would have done well to bring direct evidence of market conditions to avoid the possible charge of circular reasoning. However, the force of any such criticism is much reduced considering the presumptive case from the generally observed facts of free labour in corn and slave labour in sugar and tobacco pro-duction.

The savings propensity provides a second general case study. In common with other eighteenth-century economists, Smith did not believe that the interest rate was a payment needed to overcome a pain cost entailed by abstaining from present consumption. On the contrary, he gives pride of place to a very powerful savings propensity (see above, p. 161). Now this in-born behavioural characteristic, he proceeds to argue, is much strengthened by an appropriate legal framework: 'It is this effort, protected by law and allowed by liberty to exert itself in the manner that is most advantageous, which has maintained the progress of England towards opulence and improvement in almost all former times, and which it is to be hoped, will do so in all future times' (p. 329). But there is an exception to the general rule. The situation of the great landowner encouraged a desire for luxury consumption, a desire which reflects 'vain' behaviour pushed to the extreme: 'The situation of such a person naturally disposes him to attend rather to ornament which pleases his fancy, than to profit for which he has so little occasion. The elegance of his dress, of his equipage, of his house, and household furni-ture, are objects which from his infancy he has been accustomed to have some anxiety about' (p. 364). It is the small proprietor, who is 'generally of all improvers the most industrious, the most intelligent, and the most successful' (p. 392). Fortunately, in the modern capitalist exchange society, in contrast to feudal societies, this propensity to vanity is likely to be its own worst enemy, precisely because of the opportunities available to dissipate one's fortune in wasteful expenditure: 'In commercial countries... riches, in spite of the most violent regulations of law to prevent their dissipation, very seldom remain long in the same family' (p. 391). What is true of the great landowner is true also of capitalists enjoying very large fortunes: 'The high rate of profit seems every where to destroy that parsimony which in other circumstances is natural to the character of the merchant. When profits are high, that sober virtue seems to be superfluous, and expensive luxury to suit better the affluence of his situation' (p. 578). But again, competition tends to keep down profits, discouraging the propensity in question.

The foregoing comments on the spending propensity and disinterest in land improvement on the part of the great landed *rentiers* turn on actual comparisons between large estates and smaller commercial ones (p. 364). Similarly, for the maximizing habits of the merchant in contrast to those of the 'mere country gentlemen' Smith drew upon his own observations (pp. 384–5). At a more general level, the notion that the rate of accumulation is unaffected by the rate of interest is also based upon a reading of the historical and contemporary records (p. 326).

A most interesting instance of our theme that circumstances govern specific forms of self-interested behaviour is suggested by Smith's discussion of the supply of effort. In the *Lectures on Jurisprudence* given in 1766 crime and disorder are related to 'the corruption of men by dependency' and this in turn to the lower earnings of 'unproductive' labourers (menials) compared to those of 'productive' labourers:

> The establishment of commerce and manufactures, which brings about this independencey, is the best police for preventing crimes. The common people have better wages in this way than in any other, and in consequence of this a general probity of manners takes place thro' the whole country. No body will be so mad as to expose himself upon the highway, when he can make better bread in an honest and industrious manner (1766 [1978], 487).

Reference is made not only to the height of the wage, but to its greater steadiness in the capitalist sector, which also contributes to a less criminal type of behaviour. It is strongly implied by all this that an increase in the wage brings forth an increased supply of effort, the reverse of the mercantilists' presumption. Moreover this conception reappears in the *Wealth of Nations*, where the magnitude of the wage rate is said to govern the behaviour characteristics of the two broad classes of labourers:

The proportion between those different funds [supporting 'unproductive' and 'productive' labour] necessarily determines in every country the general character of the inhabitants as to industry or idleness. We are more industrious than our forefathers; because in the present times the funds destined for the maintenance of industry, are much greater in proportion to those which are likely to be employed in the maintenance of idleness, than they were two or three centuries ago. Our ancestors were idle for want of a sufficient encouragement to industry. It is better, says the proverb, to play for nothing, than to work for nothing (1776 [1937], 319).

Similarly, consumption behaviour differs between the two classes of workers, the elasticity of demand for luxury goods being much higher for productive workers. Thus in the case of 'the sober and industrious poor' excise taxes act as 'sumptuary laws, and dispose them either to moderate or to refrain altogether from the use of superfluities which they can no longer easily afford'; while 'the dissolute and disorderly might continue to indulge themselves in the use of such commodities after the rise in price in the same manner as before', a perfect example of an inelastic demand curve.

Smith recognized the possibility of dealing fruitfully with demographic trends in terms of conventional economic theory, explaining the rapid growth rate of population in North America compared to Europe in terms of both the relatively high earnings which rendered 'the value of children...the greatest of all encouragements to marriage', and the diminution of the infantile death rate with higher living standards (see above, p. 158). Now the distinction between the behavioural characteristics of the two categories of labourers proves central to this population mechanism. For whether, from the second perspective, population reacts positively to a rise in real earnings depends in part on the kind of goods upon which increased wages are expended; the health of mother and infant will scarcely be improved by a higher consumption of gin! Smith allowed, in fact, for the possibility of a fall in workers' real net income achieved by taxation of certain kinds of 'superfluities' which, by inducing substitutions in the pattern of consumption, permits an improvement in the standard of health and thus stimulates higher population growth. Again this economizing behaviour applies solely to the productive sector. Much of the picture drawn by Smith is derived from his own observations of 'mercantile and manufacturing' towns compared with towns having royal courts supporting immense retinues (p. 319).

It is clear then that for Smith environmental and institutional factors determined the range of relevant self-interested behaviour patterns. The self-interested man of Smith's economic theory within the capitalist exchange environment is a rather carefully specified individual. He has limited opportunities for indulging his taste for 'pride', which makes him love to domineer. 'Vain' behaviour is ultimately self-defeating. And as for the worker (at least the 'productive' worker), he has a rather elastic, positively sloped curve of effort. These specifications were not drawn from a hat but reflect Smith's own observations or the evidence of other observers.

12.4 The Uses of Economic Theory

Smith's respect for Newton extends beyond the insistence upon a sound axiomatic foundation for scientific systems to the championship of deductive theorizing itself. The essential point is his rejection of direct induction from the data as a means of discerning causal linkages. Because of their complexity, the appreciation of causal linkages was possible only with the aid of deductive theory.

An attempt to account for several centuries of corn price movements provides a nice example of the function of theory in the presence of *mutual cause–effect relationships* (where A causes B and B plays back on A). The raw data indicated an increasing money supply over long stretches of time, and also a downward trend in corn prices from the middle of the fourteenth century to the beginning of the sixteenth century, followed by an upward trend in the period 1570–1640. There were some people, Smith complained, who had even been led by the growth of the money supply to believe that corn prices could not have fallen, refusing to recognize the facts indicated by their own series of prices. While the quantity theory could account for upward price movements, Smith had at hand a theoretical relationship (an aspect of the Hume specie-flow mechanism) which reversed the order, and linked the level of corn prices as cause to the money supply as effect, such that a fall in the domestic price of corn attracted money from abroad (1776 [1937], 185, 188–9). The price data, which made little sense alone, were explicable in terms of the complex model.

Another example of the explanatory function of theory is provided by money wage movements. Here we have a problem of *multi-causality*, the money wage rate connected theoretically to corn price movements and to the state of demand for labour; given the rate of growth for labour demand and therefore the real wage, an increase in the price of corn will generate an increase in the money wage, while given the corn price, an increase in labour demand will generate an increase in the money wage (see above, pp. 82–3); but when both causal phenomena are at work simultaneously it is possible that the corn price increase will be accompanied by a fall in the money wage, should the growth rate of labour demand happen to fall off at the same time. On this Smith is very clear: 'Though the money price of labour...is sometimes high where the price of provisions is low, it would be still higher, the demand continuing the same, if the price of provisions was high' (p. 85). Empirically money wage movements and corn price movements were often and frequently in opposite directions, so to rely on the raw data would yield no worthwhile information. Theory alone permitted one to interpret the data.

Difficulties of a similar nature arise in the analysis of the effects of wage taxation. According to the model a tax on wages will generate a rise in the money wage rate, assuming that the real wage is given. But this assumption may not apply: 'If direct taxes upon the wages of labour have not always occasioned a proportionable rise in those wages, it is because they have generally occasioned a considerable fall in the demand for labour' (p. 817). Here the disturbance itself (the tax) generates a change in one of the *ceteris paribus* conditions that is taken for granted in stipulating the main principle.

Our general theme is that Smith viewed the direct (inductive) use of data as an impotent procedure. He was trying always to find hypotheses drawn from a model, or a subset thereof, to interpret the facts. In proceeding thus, be it noted, his concern was not with prediction but rather with interpretation or explanation to the end of giving advice to policy-makers. The analogy between Newtonian physics and economics breaks down in this respect, considering the evidently small confidence placed in clear-cut verification by specific prediction of economic (as distinct from physical) models.

The examples above suggest some of the problems in the way of making and refuting predictions. For a prediction requires that certain variables remain constant or that it be specified exactly how those variables are going to change. Of this Smith was perfectly aware; as we have seen he did not consider a failure of the money wage to respond in the 'expected' way to a corn price increase as a refutation. A further illustration is provided by the corn export bounty. This disturbance ought to cause the domestic price of corn to rise, as the home market is served less liberally. Smith knew that the average corn price had fallen considerably since the establishment of the bounty; but this, he insisted, 'must have happened in spite of the bounty, and cannot possibly have happened in consequence of it', for it could be shown from theory that the bounty in itself 'necessarily keeps up the price in the home market' (p. 474). He then suggests what might have prevented the 'expected' result – what disturbing causes were at play.

Are these irresponsible responses, reflecting a position that rules out any possibility of ever refuting a hypothesis? Provided that the *ceteris paribus* conditions are in fact stated formally at the outset, there is little to object to. But there are obvious dangers, to which we shall presently attend.

12.5 Some Reactions to Smithian Method

That Smith attempted to construct a co-ordinated and mutually inter-dependent system of cause and effect relationships cannot be doubted. He himself was aware of the danger inherent in the exercise – that of *excessive* attachment to system. Despite a largely favourable account of François Quesnay, he believed that Quesnay's status as 'a very specula-tive physician' had left its mark on his economics (1776 [1937], 638). In *The History of Astronomy* he remarked 'how easily the learned give up the evidence of their senses to preserve the coherence of the ideas of their imagination' (1795 [1980], 77); and in *The Theory of Moral Senti-ments* he complained of 'the man of system ... [who] is apt to be very wise in his own conceit' (1759 [1976], 233). For all that, opinion by con-temporaries and near contemporaries regarding his own performance was mixed, and some took him to task for the same deficiency that he had complained of in Quesnay.

Smith's editor, David Buchanan, observed that he had erred occasionally 'from too great a fondness for system' (1817 [1966], xi); Francis Horner, in a journal entry for 1800, phrased the complaint more sharply: 'Did not Adam Smith judge amiss, in his premature attempt to form a sort of system upon the wealth of nations, instead of presenting his valuable speculations to the world under the form of separate dissertations?' (1853, 126–7). It is revealing that James Mill – a 'man of system' *par excellence* and often regarded (mistakenly) as Ricardo's *éminence grise* – was very favourably disposed towards Smith, as a contrast made between Smith and Sir James Steuart indicates:

> To Sir James's eye the subject presented itself as a rude chaos; and he found himself unable to reduce it to light and order.... He explained some old errors, and established some new truths. But his opinions have no general bearing. The mind is bewildered in following Sir James's speculations. The general principles of Political Economy seem to become more obscure in his hands than they were before ... there is no combination of principles in his volumes which can be called a system at all.... Dr. Smith reared the study to the dignity of a science. He explained

the real sources of wealth, which till his time had been so grossly misunderstood; and conferred as great a benefit upon Political Economy, as
was conferred on Astronomy by those philosophers who first confuted
the perplexed doctrine of the cycles and epicycles, and established the
simple principles of the Copernican system (1806, 231–2).

Dugald Stewart also had warm praise for Smith's formulation of the
'system' relating to free trade and industry – 'the precision and perspi-
cuity with which [Smith] has stated it', and 'the scientific and luminous
manner in which he has deduced it from elementary principles' (1793
[1966], 65).

There is also the question of application – the use to which the
system is put. Here we are faced by a problem, the solution to which is
elusive. Smith was a sophisticated economist who, while appreciating
the positive role of theory in interpreting data, yet recognized the limitation of economic theory as a predictive engine. This maturity of position
would suggest the most responsible of applied economists who would
not dream of approaching a problem in policy without allowing for the
fact that every model is necessarily a simplification of reality, requiring
appropriate qualification in application. Yet it seems that Smith
neglected all the lessons that he himself had tried to expound when it
came to that aspect of his general model of value and distribution which
relates manufacturing prices to the price of corn (see above, pp. 84–5).
On the basis of the result that 'the money price of corn regulates that of
all other home-made commodities', Smith concluded that government
intervention designed to stimulate agriculture by encouraging an
increase in the domestic price of corn must be thwarted: 'The nature of
things has stamped upon corn a real value which cannot be altered by
merely altering its money price. No bounty upon exportation, no
monopoly of the home market can raise that value' (1776 [1937], 482).
To deny the possibility of raising the relative profitability of agriculture
by appropriate intervention is an extraordinary contention. Smith is
guilty of that very irresponsibility against which Sir James Steuart had
warned. Even if we accept the basic reasoning – and Ricardo brought to
light the logical defects – there is the neglect of frictions in the economic
system, especially the fact (which Smith himself recognized elsewhere)
that the money wage does not fluctuate from year to year with the
money price of corn. There are also lags between the rise in the price of
corn and the prices of other agricultural goods, including the raw
materials which enter into manufacturing costs. As Malthus was to
point out in his *Essay on the Principle of Population* (1803, 458ff), there
will therefore be at least a period during which agriculture can be stimulated, whereas Smith asserted an immediate and proportionate
response of manufacturing prices to the price of corn. I have stated this

here as a problem; it is not clear how Smith could be so irresponsible in the light of his apparent sophistication as an economic methodologist.

A further instance of irresponsible application of the conclusions drawn from an inappropriately constructed model is alluded to in an 'open letter' of 1776 from Thomas Pownall, a former Governor of Massachusetts. Here Pownall complains of Smith's treatment of government interference with the colony trade based upon a biological, specifically a blood-circulation, analogy (the same analogy used by Quesnay). The implications to be drawn from the apparent refutation of the model's predictions, Pownall further objected, were ignored by Smith who, after the event, apologetically sought out the disturbing causes which must have been at play:

> You think, that the unnatural spring applied to the colony-trade, has destroyed the natural ballance which would otherwise have taken place amongst all the different branches of British industry, and that the direction of it is thus thrown too much into one channel. The idea then of a blood vessel, artificially swelled beyond its natural dimensions, strikes your imagination, and you are brought under an apprehension of some terrible disorder. As this disorder did not seize Great Britain in the case you supposed, you then search out five unforeseen and unthought-of events...which fortunately occurred to prevent it. As I am no *malade imaginaire* in politicks, and have no fears of those 'convulsions, apoplexy, or death', which have been so often predicted, I know not how to go seriously, against fact, into reasoning upon them....[The] whole state of our trade as it stands in fact, and is found in effect, is to me a proof in point against your case in theory (1776 [1967], 44–5).

By resorting to 'unforeseen and unthought-of events', Smith had engaged in *ex post* apologetics to defend a model whose predictions had been refuted – in the modern parlance of Imre Lakatos (1970), Smith's was a 'degenerating research program'. James Anderson made a similar charge (1801, 16–17). J. S. Mill, as we shall see, later addressed himself to these complex issues, emphasizing the inevitable intervention of 'disturbing causes' which precludes positive prediction; but in his case, such intervention was welcomed as the source for model correction or improvement.

Suggested Reading

*Smith, *The History of Astronomy* (published posthumously 1795), in *Essays on Philosophical Subjects* (1980), 31–105.

On classical method as a whole, pertinent to this and the two following chapters, see Deane (1978), ch. 6, Blaug (1980), Part II, ch. 3, and Blaug (1985), ch.

17. On Adam Smith specifically, Skinner (1979), chs 2, 5 and 7, and Hollander (1979), 26–40 on the uses of economic theory and contemporary reactions to Smith's system building are suggested.

The historical dimension to the *Wealth of Nations* is discussed by Skinner (1979), ch. 4, and Hollander (1976); institutional aspects by Rosenberg (1960); and Smith's position on 'economic man' by Coase (1976) in Wood (1984), item 38, and by Hollander (1977a) in Wood (1984), item 47. Those interested in the philosophical background to the *Wealth of Nations* and the relation between that work and *The Theory of Moral Sentiments* might consult Morrow (1928), Viner (1928) and (1972), ch. 3, and Myers (1983), chs 8 and 9.

13 Ricardo on Method

13.1 Introduction

Smithian 'system building' was much commented on in early discussion of the *Wealth of Nations* and criticism of Smith for hasty applications of deductions drawn from incomprehensive models were quite common. Similar objections will also be found after the appearance in 1817 of Ricardo's *Principles*. Sir Edward West, for one, complained that Smith had given a faulty direction to economics:

> The opinion that the demand for labour is regulated solely by the amount of capital, has originated in a mode of reasoning very much used by Dr Smith, which frequently furnishes very beautiful illustrations, often gives a clue to important conclusions, and is always a very excellent test of the truth of our inductions, but which from an incautious use of it, has led perhaps to more false conclusions in the science than any other cause. I mean the reasoning from an assumed state of society and facts, and considering what the effects of the known or supposed principles of human nature would be in a state of society such as never existed (1826, 80).

Much post-1817 opinion, however, envisaged a sharp contrast between the Ricardian and Smithian approaches, neglecting Smith's systematizing propensity on the one hand, while exaggerating, on the other, the purely 'speculative' dimension of Ricardo's economics. Simonde de Sismondi compared Smith's view of political economy as '*une science d'éxperience*' with Ricardo's speculations (1827 [1951], I, 69–70); J. B. Say, in the sixth (1841) edition of the *Traité d'économie politique*, complained of the weak empirical foundation provided for Ricardo's logical abstractions which threatened to transport the subject back to a Scholastic age (pp. 15–16); and T. R. Malthus criticized the 'new' Ricardo school for altering Smith's theories upon mere speculation (1824 [1963], 172). He also apparently had the Ricardians in mind by a charge, in the second, posthumous, edition of his *Principles of Political Economy* of over-simplified theorizing and the avoidance of

Method: Ricardo

empirical testing, although he did not fail to denounce the other extreme:

> The principal cause of error, and of the differences which prevail at present among the scientific writers on political economy, appears to me to be a precipitate attempt to simplify and generalize. While their more practical opponents draw too hasty inferences from a frequent appeal to partial facts, these writers run into a contrary extreme, and do not sufficiently try their theories by a reference to that enlarged and comprehensive experience which, on so complicated a subject, can alone establish their truth and utility (1836 [1964], 4–6).

After Ricardo's death a concerted attack upon his method – or rather the method attributed to him, which was contrasted with that of the *Wealth of Nations* – was launched by the Cambridge inductivists led, in political economy, by Richard Jones. In this chapter I shall demonstrate that the charges against Ricardo – charges repeated to this day – are unfounded. Ricardo appreciated the limited scope of economics in general and economic theory in particular (section 13.2); his understanding of the historical relativity of the behavioural and technological axioms of his models is impressive (13.3); he rejected over-simplified models on empirical grounds, conceding only a pedagogical justification for 'strong case' assumptions (13.4). He was also greatly conscious of the clash between the short-run and long-run implications of policy proposals (13.5); and of the *ceteris paribus* conditions upon which his models were constructed, rendering them inappropriate as predictive engines or as unambiguous guides to policy (13.6).

13.2 The Scope of Economics

In a few brief remarks Ricardo made clear the limited scope of the whole subject matter of economics. Following J. B. Say, he took the position that 'it is not the province of the Political Economist to advise: – he is to tell you how you may become rich, but he is not to advise you to prefer riches to indolence, or indolence to riches' (1951, II, 338). Here we have the fundamental contrast between choice of ends and the effects of alternative means given the ends – the latter alone falling within the economist's competence.

This is not to say that Ricardo refused to engage in value judgement in his 'personal' capacity. He in fact brought into question the desirability of economic growth in contemporary 'underdeveloped' economies such as New Spain, having in mind the uncertain distribution of an expanded

GNP: 'Happiness is the object to be desired, and we cannot be quite sure that provided he is equally well fed, a man may not be happier in the enjoyment of the luxury of idleness than in the enjoyment of the luxuries of a neat cottage, and good clothes. And after all we do not know if these would fall to his share. His labour might only increase the enjoyments of his employer' (VII, 185). As for already advanced economies, he did not reject 'systems of quality' such as Robert Owen's, on grounds of impracticality, but rather because they implied growing numbers at low living standards, a blueprint scarcely conducive to increased 'happiness'; and he gave income stability greater weight than (average) magnitude from a welfare perspective: 'We cannot, I think, doubt, that the situation of mankind would be much happier if we could depend with as much certainty on a given quantity of capital and labour producing a certain quantity of food, as we can depend upon the same quantity of capital and labour producing a certain quantity of manufactured goods' (IX, 237).

Even the economist engaged in his legitimate domain is advised to be cautious. Here the distinction between *theory* or 'abstract speculation', and *practice* or 'application' is conspicuous. It is a distinction rejected by James Mill, subsequently insisted upon by J. S. Mill in a famous essay on method, and providing the key to an appreciation of many of Ricardo's procedures, including his adoption of the postulate of 'rational' decision-making.

The behavioural axiom is of course central to the *Principles*: 'Whilst every man is free to employ his capital where he pleases, he will naturally seek for it that employment which is most advantageous.... This restless desire on the part of all the employers of stock, to quit a less profitable for a more advantageous business, has a strong tendency to equalize the rate of profits of all ...' (I, 88).At the same time 'ignorance' in decision-making is allowed, though its place is in applied rather than theoretical economics, as Ricardo clarified in 1811:

I wish to prove that if nations truly understood their own interest they would never export money from one country to another but on account of comparative redundancy. I assume indeed that nations in their commercial transactions are so alive to their advantage and profit, particularly in the present improved state of the division of employments and abundance of Capital, that in point of fact money never does move but when it is advantageous both to the country which sends and the country that receives that it should do so. The first point to be considered is, what is the interest of countries in the case supposed? The second what is their practise? Now it is obvious that I need not be greatly solicitous about this latter point; it is sufficient for my purpose if I can clearly demonstrate that the interest of the public is as I have stated it. It would be no answer to me to say that men were ignorant of the best and cheapest mode of conducting their business and paying their debts, because that is a question of fact not of science, and might be urged against almost every proposition in Political Economy (VI, 63–4).

The maximization assumption might require modification in any specific application of theory but was the *sine qua non* of scientific investigation.

What though of the 'reality' of the behavioural assumption? The fact is that, for Ricardo, the assumption of maximization of money returns reflected an adequate first approximation to contemporary business reality, or else the theoretical exercise would be useless except as pure logic. The statement just cited from the *Principles* proceeds to describe the institutional arrangements characterizing advanced ('rich') economies whereby advantage may be taken of profit opportunities. Similarly, the early statement of 1811 refers to 'the present improved state' of society, and continues by implying that the institutional framework would have to be a very different one for an assumption other than maximization of net returns to be relevant. Ricardo's 'Reply to Bosanquet' in 1811 points in the same direction. Ricardo was troubled by Bosanquet's 'vulgar charge – which has lately been so often countenanced, and in places too high – against theorists' (III, 160); and he denounced the man 'who is all for fact and nothing for theory' (p. 181). His complaint was that without an initial framework of theory, apparent factual evidence might be quite misleading; for those who condemned theory 'can hardly ever sift their facts. They are credulous, and necessarily so, because they have no standard of reference'. Thus assuming the empirical validity of the income-maximizing assumption, it was inconceivable that Bosanquet could be correct in insisting upon differential exchange rates between major international centres lasting for some four years – for what was involved was 'a trade, the slightest fluctuations of which are watched by a class of men proverbial for their shrewdness, and in which competition is carried to the greatest extent'.

A sound empirical basis for the axioms assured that economic argument would not be a matter of pure logic. This position, we have seen, was yet further reinforced by the distinction between 'science' and 'fact', specifically the recognition of a place for 'ignorance' in applied investigations – even those relating to advanced capitalist economies. Ricardo also rejected universally valid axioms. Thus he was unhappy with James Mill's behavioural assumptions (the overwhelming quest for money and power) in the analysis of legislation (VII, 236–9); and as we shall see next, he was keenly aware that the appropriate assumptions even in the economic sphere varied geographically and temporally.

13.3 The Relativity of the Behavioural and Technological Axioms: Implications for Policy

Ricardo's consciousness of the institutional and sociological relativity of the behavioural and technological assumptions is strikingly clear in the context of alternative solutions to poverty. Here differential patterns of behaviour on the part of labourers provide the key. The policies appropriate for raising general standards differed entirely from case to case, revealing clearly the conditional character of the conclusions of political economy.

In the first (1817) edition of the *Principles* the problem of poverty in 'poor' countries – characterized by abundant fertile land – is said to derive from 'the ignorance, indolence, and barbarism of the inhabitants' (1951, I, 99). Because of the presence of plentiful land resources, the potential for substantial increase in labour productivity and in accumulation was excellent and exceeded by far any probable population growth. Not excessive population growth, but low productivity of labour and consequently a small surplus available for accumulation was the issue in 'poor' countries. All this in contrast with countries where the force of diminishing returns was such as to impose serious limits on the potential for accumulation relative to that of population, where the only solution was control over the growth rate of population. In fact population control in 'poor' countries – the edition of 1817 lists Poland, Ireland, the South Sea Islands, and parts of Asia – would be disastrous. For while average productivity was there extremely low, imposing a severe limit upon *per capita* wages, such economies nevertheless operated along a rising section of the average product curve, so that a reduced population would lower the product per man yet further. This phenomenon is ascribed to the reduction in effort per head induced by rising wages per unit of effort as the market is turned in favour of labour. In brief, Ricardo assumed the labour supply curve to be backward sloping in 'poor' countries (p. 100n.). The solution in the Irish case was to give to the labourer 'a taste for the comforts and enjoyments which habit has made essential to the English labourer, and he would then be content to devote a further part of his time to industry, that he might be enabled to obtain them'.

Ricardo explicitly distinguished British labourers from labourers of those countries where the problem of poverty largely derived from a low level of aspiration for goods. He insisted, for example, that accumulation in a modern capitalist economy does not imply a loss of purchasing power since any increase in labourers' real incomes will be spent if not on corn (assuming an initially unchanged population), then on luxuries. To an objection that characteristically 'the labourer is not a *consumer* of Conveniences', Ricardo replied: 'If he is not, must we not impute it to his poverty? Give him the means, and do you think he wants the inclination?' (VIII, 275). And against Malthus, he objected that the sociological characteristics of individuals in South American countries were 'little applicable to countries with a dense population abounding in capital, skill, commerce, and manufacturing industry, and with tastes for every enjoyment that nature, art or science will procure' (II, 340–1).

We cannot, however, deduce from Ricardo's exclusion of Britain from the category of 'poor' countries, its representation as a 'rich' country, that is one at or very close to a state of stationariness where the only solution to low standards is the positive 'reduction of people'. For this fails to take into account the highly optimistic evaluation of the actual and prospective growth rate of capital and of labour demand in contemporary circumstances. Although not a 'new' country, Britain retained all the features characteristic of an 'improving' country wherein future prospects for labour were satisfactory, assuming at least the eradication of institutional encouragements to population growth which prevented labourers from exercising 'prudential' restraint.

To some extent Ricardo's optimism reflects his evaluation of the empirical evidence regarding diminishing returns. He distinguished between the effects of accumulation in different countries; even with protection in the case of a small but fertile country – an obvious reference to Britain – there is little emphasis on a falling rate of return:

> However extensive a country may be where the land is of a poor quality, and where the importation of food is prohibited, the most moderate accumulations of capital will be attended with great reductions in the rate of profit, and a rapid rise in rent; and on the contrary a small but fertile country, particularly if it freely permits the importation of food, may accumulate a large stock of capital without any great diminution in the rate of profits, or any great increase in the rent of land (I, 126).

The weak force of diminishing returns in the British case is not even explained here by reference to the adoption of new technology. But a few pages earlier we do read that 'this tendency, this gravitation as it were of profits, is happily checked at repeated intervals by the improvements in machinery, connected with the production of necessaries, as well as by discoveries in the science of agriculture' (p. 120). These evaluations of technological conditions and prospects go far to explain the precise position adopted by Ricardo regarding corn law repeal (see below, pp. 335–6).

13.4 'Strong Cases' Justified and the Rejection of Over-simplified Models

The distinction between 'science' and 'fact' alluded to already is implied by Ricardo's own rationalization of his use of 'strong cases' in the *Principles*: 'Our differences', he wrote to Malthus, 'may in some respects, I think, be ascribed to your considering my book as more practical than I intended it to be. My object was to elucidate principles, and to do this I imagined strong cases that I might shew the operation of those principles' (1951, VIII, 184).

Ricardo's approach to wage theory can only be understood if we keep this in mind. Ricardo frequently utilized the assumption of a *constant* real wage (although not necessarily a constant wage at subsistence), not because he believed the assumption approximated 'factual' reality, but rather as a deliberate simplification for pedagogical purposes to be relaxed when appropriate, as for example in the examination of the growth process or taxation. This deliberate seeking for expositional simplicity may be illustrated from the *Essay of Profits*, at the outset of which he gave as his reason for assuming unchanged technology and a constant corn wage, 'that we may know what peculiar effects are to be ascribed to the growth of capital, the increase of population, and the extension of cultivation, to the more remote, and less fertile land' (IV, 12).

The illustration from wages entails the adoption of an extreme elasticity value in order to focus entirely on the implications for the profit rate of recourse to increasingly inferior land. Examples may also be given of the adoption for theoretical purposes of extreme values because the primary implications of the model are unaffected by more complex (albeit more realistic) assumptions. The problem of 'substitutability' provides an illustration.

Both factor and commodity substitution were recognized even in the first edition of the *Principles* (see above, pp. 187–8). Yet the basic model of distribution developed in the chapter 'On Profits' proceeds by assuming fixed factor proportions, uniform across all sectors. Possibly Ricardo proceeded thus because the neglect of substitutability had few practical consequences – a theoretical model which illustrated the effect on the rate of profits of rising wage costs may be satisfactory although its assumptions are known to be not totally 'realistic'. For the basic prediction is that increased wage costs must bring about a decline in the general profit rate. Now whatever the assumptions regarding substitution, capitalists must be worse off after a rise in 'real' wages; recognition of substitutability does not reverse the prediction. This is the significant fact, brought out by the model of distribution. Ricardo was perhaps prepared to proceed as if such complications were absent.

'Strong case' assumptions, needless to say, are the more justifiable the closer they reflect 'reality', although – as in the illustration from the labour market – they may none the less be justifiable on other grounds. In his discussion of the corn market, for example, Ricardo rejected the possibility of a numerically precise specification of the price–quantity relationship, but suggested that the extent of such small responsiveness as exists will depend in practice upon the 'wealth or poverty of the country, and on its means of holding over the superfluous quantity to a future season', and also 'on the opinions formed of the probability of the future supply being adequate or otherwise to the future demand' (IV, 220). There can be no doubt at all, therefore, that he was aware of the empirical responsiveness of quantity demanded to the price of corn. But what evidently struck him was the limited extent of the response, small enough to justify its neglect in the construction of theoretical models designed to capture the prime interrelationships – as distinct from applied studies of the corn market. Zero demand elasticity for corn constitutes a simplifying assumption comparable to that made in adopting a labour input account of relative price movements despite clear recognition of other sources of disturbance, on the grounds that variation in labour input is overwhelmingly the most significant quantitative determinant.

*   *   *

Ricardo justified his 'strong case' assumptions on pedagogic and sometimes on empirical grounds. But the degree of legitimate simplification in model construction must, of course, always be a matter of judgement, and Ricardo warned against adopting simplifications that yielded positively misleading conclusions. A number of illustrations follow.

As we know, Ricardo rejected the position that 'a demand for labour is the same thing as a supply of necessaries' on the grounds that food supplies are not advanced out of a 'wages fund' but increase along with growth of population in response to expanded demand (see above, pp. 185–6). In any event, the wage bill included items other than food which were certainly in elastic supply to the labourers. There is no better indication of his rejection of rigid wages fund theorizing than the denial of various standard results derived therewith, including Malthus's position that workers' combinations were 'irrational and ineffectual': 'A combination among the workmen would increase the amount of money to be divided amongst the labouring class' Ricardo objected, with resultant commodity wage increases at the expense of profits (VII, 203).

A second standard application was to poor law policy, and again Ricardo objected to Malthus's presumption that allowances merely raised the number of consumers without increasing available output (3, 202).

Other instances may be cited. Ricardo was disappointed with James Mill's failure, because of a limited agricultural frame of reference, to respond to 'general glut' theorists who feared excess commodity supplies in consequence of accumulation (see above, p. 186). He complained of James Mill's over-simplifications in the *Elements* regarding the demand for labour:

> You say... that the demand for labour and the power of employing it will be in proportion to the increase of capital – I believe I have said the same, and it may perhaps be right to say so in an elementary book, altho' it is not strictly correct. The power of employing labour depends on the increase of a particular part of capital, not on the increase of the whole capital. (See my Chapter on Machinery) (IX, 127).

Mill made no changes in the subsequent editions, leaving untouched an introductory reference to the 'universal' validity of his proposition. There is also a criticism that James Mill, in discussing accumulation, had neglected the impact of technical change: 'You do not speak of the two ways by which capital may be increased by saving; of one, the common and usual way, devoting more of the annual production to productive employments, you do speak, but you say nothing of the great increase which sometimes takes place in capital by the discovery of cheaper modes of production'. The issue also figured conspicuously in the foreign trade context, in that trade 'increases the amount and variety of the objects on which revenue may be expended, and affords, by the abundance and cheapness of commodities, incentives to saving, and to the accumulation of capital' (I, 133).

An excellent illustration of Ricardo's warnings against excessive simplification is provided by the theory of value. Commenting on Mill's formulation in the first edition of the *Elements* Ricardo noted: 'If a watch and a common Jack altered in relative value without any more or less labour being required for the production of either of them, could we say that the proposition "that quantity of labour determines exchangeable value" was universally true? What I call exceptions and modifications of the general rule you appear to me to say come under the general rule itself' (IX, 127). Similarly, Ricardo rejected J. S. Mill's juvenile efforts to retain the labour theory (p. 387).

As a final instance we recall the evidence indicating Ricardo's adherence to J. B. Say's version of their law of markets ('Say's Equality') rather than that of James Mill ('Say's Identity'). For he did not deny the possibility of excess commodity supply in the short run and warned strenuously against policies that entail sudden contractions of the supply of money (see above, pp. 293–5).

13.5 The Problem of the Short Run: the Policy Dilemma

It is doubtless true that Ricardo's *primary* interest lay in long-run analysis. Thus he wrote to Malthus:

> It appears to me that one great cause of our difference of opinion, on the subjects which we have so often discussed, is that you have always in your mind the immediate and temporary effects of particular changes – whereas I put these immediate and temporary effects quite aside, and fix my whole attention on the permanent state of things which will result from them. Perhaps you estimate these temporary effects too highly, whilst I am too much disposed to undervalue them. To manage the subject quite right they should be carefully distinguished and mentioned, and the due effects ascribed to each (1951, VII, 120).

It may well be because of this predilection that a tradition has developed according to which Ricardo was divorced in his intellectual interests from 'day-to-day' considerations, so that his recommendations lost much of their relevance. But this is going too far. The contrast in question must be understood at most in a comparative sense, for Ricardo was in fact also preoccupied with 'short-run' matters relating both to theory and policy, notwithstanding that qualifications reflecting a concern for the 'short run' diluted markedly the political effectiveness of policy proposals drawn from political economy.

Thus it is that Ricardo rejected corn law reform in time of depression because any liberalization – desirable in the long term – could only worsen immediate employment opportunities (VIII, 103). He only called for free trade legislation in 1821 after the return of prosperity in the manufacturing sector. Moreover, repeal – which was not to be total in any event – was to be brought about by gradual steps and after due warning, with allowance for compensation of those (other than landlords) adversely affected.

In the context of the poor law issue the clash between the desirability of abolition from a long-run perspective and the problems which may result therefrom in the more immediate future created a dilemma the solution to which eluded him:

> It is agreed by all who are most friendly to a repeal of these laws, that if it be desirable to prevent the most overwhelming distress to those for whose benefit they were erroneously enacted, their abolition should be effected by the most gradual steps.... No scheme for the amendment of the poor laws merits the least attention, which has not their abolition for

its ultimate object; and he is the best friend to the poor, and to the cause of humanity, who can point out how this end can be attained with the most security, and at the same time with the least violence (I, 106-7).

In correspondence he insisted that 'no man in his sober senses would wish for any sudden alteration of the present plan' (VII, 248). His own 'remedy' amounts to Malthus's solution, namely the refusal of all parish assistance to those born after a certain date, thus allowing for continued help to those of the present generation actually in need. Ricardo certainly did not countenance the immediate abandonment of the able-bodied paupers.

The resumption of cash payments provides a most important illustration of our theme. This matter has been considered in detail; we need do no more than recall that Ricardo did not advocate an immediate or very early return to cash payments at par, because of the potentially 'disastrous consequences to the trade and commerce of the country', and allowed that permanent devaluation of the currency would be preferable to severe deflation.

Ricardo's unearned reputation as an irresponsible applied economist evidently derives from a failure by readers to appreciate the nature of the *Principles*. The book has been considered from the beginning as 'more practical' than it was intended to be – as Ricardo himself pointed out to Malthus. For his applied economics we must turn to less formal forums – the pamphlets, correspondence, speeches. A *conscious* need to make appropriate qualifications to a model in practical applications, especially where policy was involved, becomes clear beyond doubt.

What has been said is relevant for an evaluation of Malthus's charge that Ricardo, by concentrating on the short-run distributional effects of corn law repeal and agricultural innovation – the negative effect on rents – was guilty of an uncharacteristic interest in the immediate implications of policy for political ends. Ricardo himself denied the charge (II, 117), and rightly so. This is not the only context where he carefully analysed the consequences of a disturbance prior to population expansion – the analysis of accumulation in conditions of labour scarcity is an obvious illustration. His general preoccupation with the immediate consequences of policy proposals fully justified his protest. Ricardo should not be identified with James Mill as far as concerns the attitude to landowners.

13.6 Historical Prediction and Theory Confirmation

That the charge of 'piling a heavy load of practical conclusions upon a tenuous groundwork' – the 'Ricardian Vice' as Schumpeter labelled it

(1954, 1171) – cannot fairly be applied to Ricardo as a general rule should by now be obvious. But the evidence pointing to this conclusion is yet more extensive. The corn law episode provides an illustration of Ricardo's refusal to use theory without honest qualification. The fact is that despite pressure from McCulloch, he felt unable to make his main case against agricultural protection in terms of the secular trend in the return on capital 'predicted' by the growth model. Ricardo allowed fully for the *ceteris paribus* conditions which must be fulfilled to justify any 'prediction' of a gradual vanishing of investment opportunities; past experience relating to technical change and future prospects could not justify an argument for repeal based upon the predictions flowing from his growth model which assumed unchanged technology. Corn law repeal, while certainly desirable – since the return on capital and the rate of accumulation would be higher at any point of time in an open than a closed economy – was none the less not the *sine qua non* for continuous rapid expansion into a foreseeable future, by which I mean a time span of concern to drafters of policy, even 'long-term' policy.

The corn law episode also illustrates the Ricardian approach to theory confirmation. Ricardo's primary objective in devising his growth model was to provide an analytical framework whereby to investigate the various factors that play upon the profit rate, rather than one designed to yield a specific prediction. This is clearly indicated by his early insistence (against Malthus) that the profit rate increase over the two decades 1793–1813, despite protection, in no way demonstrated the inadequacy of his theory considering the impact of technological change:

> I have little doubt however that for a long period, during the interval you mention, there has been an increased rate of profits, but it has been accompanied with such decided improvements of agriculture both here and abroad, – for the French revolution was exceedingly favourable to the increased production of food, that it is perfectly reconcileable to my theory. My conclusion is that there has been a rapid increase of Capital which has been prevented from shewing itself in a low rate of interest by new facilities in the production of food (1951, VI, 94–5).

He raised the same issue in response to Malthus's complaint in the *Principles* (1820) that he had 'never laid any *stress* upon the influence of permanent improvements in agriculture on the profits of stock, although it is one of the most important considerations in the whole compass of Political Economy': 'Once more I must say that I lay the very greatest stress upon the influence of permanent improvements in Agriculture. The passage quoted refers to a state of things when no improvements are taking place, and therefore the argument built upon it which supposes improvements has no foundation' (II, 293).

That Ricardo none the less adopted an analytical framework incorporating the principle of diminishing agricultural returns is partly explicable in terms of his concern to combat Smith's notion of a falling profit rate due to secularly increasing 'competition of capitals'. For that purpose there was no need to emphasize the intervention of technological change. Secondly, the conclusion that the rate of profit, and therefore capital accumulation, would be higher in an open than a closed economy held good independently of the actual course of new technology. But there is also a notion expressed in the *Essay on Profits* that since technological progress takes the form of *random* shocks it might be accorded secondary status compared to diminishing returns:

> The causes, which render the acquisition of an additional quantity of corn more difficult are, in progressive countries, in constant operation, whilst marked improvements in agriculture, or in the implements of husbandry are of less frequent occurrence. If these opposite causes acted with equal effect, corn would be subject only to accidental variation of price, arising from bad seasons, from greater or less real wages of labour, or from an alteration in the value of the precious metals, proceeding from their abundance or scarcity (IV, 19n.).

Ricardo's position on the foreign exchanges similarly illustrates his approach to theory confirmation. Neither he himself nor the Bullion Report contended that an increased note issue would *necessarily* lower the exchange, so that it would be premature to reject his theory on the grounds that increases in the note supply had sometimes been accompanied by a rising exchange rate. Correction was necessary for loss of coin, changes in the volume of transactions, in harvest conditions and in the relative values of gold and silver; and care had to be taken to allow for the time lag involved following an increased note issue (III, 114, 118). In evidence on resumption in 1819 Ricardo similarly insisted upon the principle of multi-causality: 'I am fully aware that there are other causes, besides the quantity of bank notes, which operate upon the exchanges...' (V, 372). When asked to account for the empirical fact that during the period 1817–19 an increase in the price of gold accompanied a reduced note issue, he replied: 'It does not in the least shake my confidence in the theory, being fully persuaded that such an effect [a reduced gold price] must have followed, if it had not been counteracted by some of those causes to which I have already adverted' (p. 376). He had in mind a variety of 'countervailing causes' such as an independent (world-wide) rise in the value of gold itself, and variations in 'credit' (substitutes for currency) and in country bank circulation; and, as in the corn law case, he argued that the disturbances in question were of a random nature: 'in commerce, it appears to me that a cause may operate for a certain time without our being warranted to expect that it should continue to operate for a much greater length of time' (p. 377). In all this Ricardo was following directly in Smith's footsteps, as will be clear from the previous chapter.

A general statement by Ricardo of the methodological issues involved in attempts at theory confirmation is applicable here:

> I should be more pleased [he wrote to Malthus] that we did not so materially differ. If I am too theoretical which I really believe is the case – you I think are too practical. There are so many combinations, – so many operating causes in Political Economy, that there is great danger in appealing to experience in favor of a particular doctrine, unless we are sure that all the causes of variation are seen and their effects duly estimated (VI, 295).

The foregoing statement, or at least the second sentence, is sometimes read as evidence that Ricardo and James Mill were at one regarding method, proposing the direct applicability of clear-cut principles. But it is difficult to see how the statement as a whole can be interpreted in this way; it is rather a balanced formulation of the problem of multi-causality and the impossibility of relying on appeals to 'experience' in theory confirmation. This is surely a characteristic inherent in all deductive theorizing, as Adam Smith had recognized. The same characteristic, of course, renders dangerous the use of theory in simple-minded policy applications, and we have seen that this was not Ricardo's general practice. In the corn law context it is Adam Smith who emerges as the guilty party.

Suggested Reading

For an elaboration of Ricardo and method, see Hollander (1985), 'The Methodological and Doctrinal Heritage', pp. 1–65. For a very different view see Hutchison (1978a), ch. 2. De Marchi (1970) in Wood (1985), item 19, treats the empirical content and longevity of Ricardian economics. Some of the suggestions given below for chapter 16 may prove useful.

14 Mill on Method

14.1 Introduction

This chapter demonstrates the extensive empirical dimension to political economy envisaged by J. S. Mill in his formal methodological writings – his essay 'On Definition and Method' of 1836 (1967, IV), and in the *System of Logic* of 1843 (VII–VIII).* It is inviting, but quite wrong, to represent Mill's 'economic man' as a deliberate abstraction, contrasting with Adam Smith's entire man situated in the anonymous market place wherein self-interested motivation alone is relevant. Mill was at one with his great predecessors Smith and Ricardo, and insisted upon the empirical accuracy of the behavioural axiom. His position on method reflects a confirmed hostility to any representation of the wealth-maximization assumption as of 'universal relevance'. In fact, his entire case for a specialized political economy is made on empirical grounds.

Although direct or 'inductive' evidence involving specific experience is useless in the face of complex causality ('composition of causes'), this source of evidence is essential for the derivation of the individual axioms used in deductive exercises. We must avoid any conception of 'induction' and 'deduction' as constituting opposing methodologies. The '*a priori*' or deductive method – the method appropriate for economics – is a 'mixed' method of induction and ratiocination (IV, 325); and 'although...all sciences tend to become more and more Deductive, they are not, therefore, the less Inductive', for there must be 'a direct induction as the basis of the whole;...the premises...must have been derived from induction' (VII, 218–19, 454).

I shall proceed as follows. The kingpin of J. S. Mill's case for a specialist economics – the empirical validity of the maximization axiom – is taken up in section 14.2. Section 14.3 treats the issue of 'veri-

* See above, p. 118n.

fication' and its role in model improvement; the testing of hypotheses is shown to be part of the scientific task. In section 14.4 the limitations imposed on the scope of economic science by empirical considerations – limitations which rule our 'prediction' – are discussed. Mill's assertion of the 'universality of the method' of political economy is explained, as is his celebrated distinction between 'the laws of Production and Distribution'. So much for formal method. The chapter closes with the empirical dimension to the *Principles of Political Economy*, (1848), having in mind specific applications of the more general propositions laid down in the formal statements (section 14.5); and with Mill's position on model improvement in the major work (section 14.6).

14.2 On Specialization

The famous essay on definition and method sought to explain the methodological procedures of the 'great masters' of economics. Here Mill drew an intimate connection between the wealth maximization hypothesis – 'the desire of obtaining the greatest quantity of wealth with the least labour and self-denial' – and the limited range of subject matter treated by economics, namely 'the production and distribution of wealth'. For there existed practical limits to the complexity of deductive models: 'the hypothetical combinations of circumstances on which we construct the general theorems of the science, cannot be made very complex, without so rapidly accumulating a liability to error as must soon deprive our conclusions of all value' (VIII, 900). The solution was a specialist treatment of wealth based upon a major behavioural trait. Specialization is thus represented as the most practical procedure in the light of causal complexity. It is readily conceded that the operations encompassed within 'the production and distribution of wealth' often result from a plurality of motives, but the science 'proceeds to investigate the laws which govern these several operations, under the supposition that man is a being who is determined, by the necessity of his nature, to prefer a greater portion of wealth to a smaller in all cases, without any other exception than that constituted by...two counter-motives' – namely 'aversion to labour, and desire of the present enjoyment of costly indulgences' (IV, 321–2). The approach is a strategic one:

> Not that any political economist was ever so absurd as to suppose that mankind are really thus constituted, but because this is the mode in which the science must necessarily proceed. When an effect depends upon a concurrence of causes, those causes must be studied one at a time, and their laws separately investigated, if we wish, through the causes, to obtain the power of either predicting or controlling the effect; since the

law of the effect is compounded of the laws of all the causes which determine it (p. 322).

Wealth maximization is not, however, regarded merely as one among roughly equal motives. It is the predominating influence governing a specific range of social phenomena:

> The manner in which [political economy] proceeds is that of treating the main and acknowledged end as if it were the sole end; which, of all hypotheses equally simple, is the nearest to the truth. The political economist inquires, what are the actions which would be produced by this desire, if, within the departments in question, it were unimpeded by any other. In this way a nearer approximation is obtained than would otherwise be practicable, to the real order of human affairs in those departments (p. 323).

The *System of Logic* contains a very helpful statement of the class of relevant social phenomena isolated for treatment by economists. It is that class

> in which the immediately determining causes are principally those which act through the desire of wealth; and which the psychological law mainly concerned is the familiar one, that a greater gain is preferred to a smaller. I mean, of course, that portion of the phenomena of society which emanate from the industrial, or productive, operations of mankind; and from those of their acts through which the distribution of the products of those industrial operations takes place, in so far as not affected by force, or modified by voluntary gift (VIII, 901).

The wealth maximization hypothesis entailed an abstraction by excluding other motivating forces acting upon wealth. But the assumption was correct 'as far as it goes' and differed from the truth 'as a part differs from the whole' (IV, 329). Precisely for this reason the results derived from ratiocination or logical deduction on the basis of the behavioural assumption constituted 'abstract truth'; only 'when completed by adding or subtracting the effect of the non-calculated circumstances' would they be rendered 'true in the concrete' and appropriate in application. Mill touches here upon the treatment of 'disturbing causes' – in the present case behavioural patterns left out of the formal account. The distinction between this category of causes and those causes formally incorporated into the model as axioms is governed entirely by empirical circumstances. What distinguishes the latter is their predominating influence, in the sense that the class of phenomena under investigation (the production and distribution of wealth, in our case) depends largely upon them, combined with their ubiquity – that they are causes 'common to the *whole class* of cases under consideration' (p. 326). In the *System of Logic*, Mill observed further that allowance for modifying circumstances at a subsequent stage of investigation was particularly desirable 'as certain fixed combinations of the former' – influences common to all cases – were 'apt to recur often, in conjunction with ever-varying circumstances of the latter class', namely the less important or less ubiquitous influences (VIII, 901). A review (1865) of Auguste Comte's *Cours de Philosophie Positive* contains a somewhat different though not inconsistent position:

> When an effect depends on several variable conditions, some of which change less, or more slowly, than others, we are often able to determine, either by reasoning or by experiment, what would be the law of variation of the effect if its changes depended only on some of the conditions, the remainder being supposed constant. The law so found will be sufficiently near the truth for all times and places in which the latter set of conditions do not vary greatly, and will be a basis to set out from when it becomes necessary to allow for the variations of those conditions also. Most of the conclusions of social science applicable to practical use are of this description (X, 309).

'Introspection' is one form of general experience to which Mill alluded in discussing the basis for the (individual) causal laws or premises. Deductive theorists based themselves on 'an observation of the tendencies which human nature has manifested in the variety of situations in which human beings have been placed, and especially observation of what passes in our own minds' (IV, 325). (Introspection must be distinguished from 'intuition'; Mill rejected any such source of knowledge as 'direct intuition'.) But evidence drawn from introspection varies with time and place and does not reflect some universal psychological propensity acting in a vacuum. This is made clear in behaviour patterns to be observed geographically; for example: 'those who know the habits of the Continent of Europe are aware how apparently small a motive often outweighs the desire of money-getting, even in the operations which have money-getting for their direct object' (VIII, 906). Mill also heaped scorn on historians who reasoned as if human behaviour was unchanged and unchangeable over time (p. 791). It is inconceivable that 'observation of what passes in our own mind' would turn out to be the same if the observer were an Englishman or a Frenchman.

The case for specialization in economics is based upon the presumption that different classes of social phenomena are dependent 'immediately and in the first resort, on different kinds of causes' (p. 900). This held good despite 'the universal *consensus* of the social phenomena, whereby nothing which takes place in any part of the operations of society is without its share of influence on every other part', and despite 'the paramount ascendancy which the general state of civilization and social progress in any given society must hence exercise over all the partial and subordinate phenomena'. Yet it is precisely these latter characteristics of social science which govern Mill's criticisms of the deductive procedures of Benthamite political scientists – including his father James Mill – who based themselves on the one comprehensive premise that 'any succession of persons, or the majority of any body of persons, will be governed in the bulk of their conduct by their personal interest' (p. 890). His criticism, at first glance, would seem also to apply to economics:

> There is little chance of making due amends in the superstructure of a theory for the want of sufficient breadth in its foundations. It is unphilosophical to construct a science out of a few of the agencies by which the phenomena are determined, and leave the rest to the routine of practice or the sagacity of conjecture. We either ought not to pretend to scientific forms, or we ought to study all the determining agencies equally, and endeavour, so far as it can be done, to include all of them within the pale of science; else we shall infallibly bestow a disproportionate attention upon those which our theory takes into account, while we mis-estimate the rest, and probably underrate their importance (p. 893).

The main complaint against the Benthamite 'interest philosophy' is its supposed predominance throughout time and space – its universality. Theoretical work of this order undertaken on a narrow behavioural basis, Mill protested, entailed

> a kind of error to which those are peculiarly liable whose views are the largest and most philosophical: for exactly in that ratio are their minds more accustomed to dwell upon those laws, qualities, and tendencies, which are common to large classes of cases, and which belong to all place and all time; while it often happens that circumstances almost peculiar to the particular case or era have a far greater share in governing that one case (IV, 333).

Qualifications and allowances in application for 'disturbing causes' woud not suffice. But this criticism of Benthamite political science did not apply to economics, envisaged as a science of relatively narrow scope rather than one designed to be of universal relevance. To repeat: the procedure of distinguishing between the wealth maximization and other behavioural patterns reflected a justified quest for practicality in the face of the problem of 'composition of causes', and was valid given the empirical 'relevance' of the wealth maximization hypothesis in that temporal and geographic environment for which the model was designed.

14.3 On 'Verification' and Model Improvement

'Disturbing causes' not known to the investigator when approaching a particular case are the 'only uncertainty' to which the social sciences are subject: 'here only it is that an element of uncertainty enters into the process – an uncertainty inherent in the nature of these complex phenomena, and arising from the impossibility of being quite sure that all the circumstances of the particular case are known to us sufficiently in detail, and that our attention is not unduly diverted from any of them' (IV, 330). Such disturbing causes were in principle discoverable by observation, in the sense of verification:

> we cannot ... too carefully endeavour to verify our theory, by comparing, in the particular cases to which we have access, the results which it would have led us to predict, with the most trustworthy accounts we can obtain of those which have been actually realized. The discrepancy between our anticipations and the actual fact is often the only circumstance which would have drawn our attention to some important disturbing cause which we had overlooked (p. 332).

Are we then to understand that the task of detailed empirical work is limited to the identification of unknown disturbing causes in particular cases leaving intact the basic model itself? Mill seems to presume just this in some of his formulations, implying that the model is impervious to criticism on grounds of inaccuracy of prediction. Thus, the *a posteriori* (inductive) method does not provide 'a means of discovering truth, but of verifying it, and reducing to the lowest point that uncertainty before alluded to as arising from the complexity of every particular case, and from the difficulty (not to say impossibility) of being assured *a priori* that we have taken into account all the material circumstances' (p. 331). In fact, 'to verify the hypothesis *a posteriori*, that is, to examine whether the facts of any actual case are in accordance with it, is no part of the business of science at all, but of the *application* of science' (p. 325).

But verification in fact amounted to much more than this. The testing procedure might yield new information of general relevance – rather than of particular relevance in a specific case, in which event it must have an impact on the model. Mill alluded to this possibility when he questioned the accuracy of the term 'disturbing' to describe causes at work which cannot be regarded as 'exceptions' (pp. 337–8). The discovery of a hitherto unknown disturbing cause of this order 'might always be brought within the pale of the abstract science' by 'inserting among its hypotheses a fresh and still more complex combination of circumstances' (p. 331). Indeed, verification often reveals 'that the data, from which we had reasoned, comprise only a part, and not always the most important part, of the circumstances by which the result is really determined' (p. 332). In short, verification might reveal the inadequacy of the axiomatic framework, even as a first approximation, and oblige a reformulation.

Mill also insisted that verification might show the logical 'ratiocinative' process to be defective. This allowance is made in the course of discussion of the conditions to be satisfied before a model can legitimately be used as the starting point for policy recommendation. Verification by reference to existing data (past and present) not only provided the sole means of assuring the reliability of a model in 'the guidance of practice', but also tested the quality of the 'abstract system' itself:

> [The political economist's] knowledge must at least enable him to explain and account for what *is*, or he is an insufficient judge of what ought to be. If a political economist, for instance, finds himself puzzled by any recent or present commercial phenomena; if there is any mystery to him in the late or present state of the productive industry of the country, which his knowledge of principle does not enable him to unriddle; he may be sure that something is wanting to render his system of opinions a safe guide in existing circumstances. Either some of the facts which influence the situation of the country and the course of events are not known to him; or, knowing them, he knows not what ought to be their effects. In the latter case his system is imperfect even as an abstract system; it does not enable him to trace correctly all the consequences even of assumed premises (p. 335).

The economist is obliged to seek the explanation for any failure 'conscientiously, not with the desire of finding his system complete, but of making it so....' And he is duty bound to carry out a verification 'upon every new combination of facts as it arises'. He must allow for 'the disturbing influence of unforeseen causes', but he also 'must carefully watch the result of every experiment, in order that any residuum of facts which his principles did not lead him to expect, and do not enable him to explain, may become the subject of a fresh analysis, and furnish the occasion for a consequent enlargement or correction of his general views' (pp. 335–6; cf. VII, 460–1; VIII, 909–10). Theorists must fight against the natural 'reluctance ... to admit the reality or relevancy of any facts which they have not previously either taken into, or left a place open for in, their systems'. Paul Samuelson was struck by Charles Darwin's advice to 'always study your residuals', in his case by writing down arguments *against* the theory of evolution (1965, 780); J. S. Mill is for us rather closer to home.

It is noteworthy for some methodological issues that Mill never refers to the actual abandonment of a theory in consequence of a failure to account adequately for past and present phenomena. But for us here the important point is that he does allow for alterations in the basic model in consequence of the procedure of verification – testing against specific experience: he allows for its 'improvement', 'correction', 'completion', 'enlargement'. Theory construction was thus portrayed as a continuous task turning crucially on verification against evidence. This constitutes the substance of a protest against contemporary critics for failing to appreciate that theoretical demonstration amounted only to conditional demonstration – 'a proof at all times liable to be set aside by the addition of a single new fact to the hypothesis' (IV, 334).

The statement that the verification of the hypothesis is 'no part of the business of science...but of the application of science', taken literally, is thus too loosely formulated; the model of political economy was, we know, constructed from its foundation to reflect empirical reality. The statement should rather be taken as a warning that even within the general environment of an advanced competitive capitalist system, for the analysis of which the model is designed (as a first approximation), other motives may be at play in special cases so that the applied economist must be ever on the alert. Furthermore, although verification may indeed contribute towards establishment of the axioms or correction of the logical process of deduction, it is not itself a device for the derivation of complex causal relations. That remains the function of 'ratiocination'. Verification contributes only indirectly by indicating the need for improvement in the axiomatic foundation or in the logical process.

14.4 The Scope of Economics

The term 'scientism' has been coined by F. A. Hayek to designate the belief that an extension of scientific and engineering techniques can legitimately be made to the study of society with the promise of similarly impressive results (1955). Hayek was incensed by the 'historicism' of the Saint-Simonians – their attribution to the social sciences of the task of discovering the 'natural laws' of the progress of civilization, supposedly as 'necessary' as that of gravitation, from which perspective derived their penchant for collectivist social engineering. For Hayek, the characteristic 'subjectivism' of the social sciences – the role of motive, knowledge, expectation and so forth – ruled out the parallel and precluded, above all, long-term historical prediction. It was Hayek's view that Mill had been early on infected by Saint-Simon and subsequently by Auguste Comte.

Yet this perspective on Mill's position does not ring true. There is a beautiful formulation in a letter of October 1829 of some of the special problems in social science which the Saint-Simonians had failed to appreciate. Here Mill emphasized that French procedure, by neglecting 'disturbing causes', distorted the operation even of those causes allowed for:

> They deduce politics like mathematics from a set of axioms & definitions, forgetting that in mathematics there is no danger of partial views: a

proposition is either true or it is not, & if it is true, we may safely apply it to every case which the proposition comprehends in its terms: but in politics & the social science, this is so far from being the case, that error seldom arises from our assuming premises which are not true, but generally from our overlooking other truths which limit, & modify the effect of the former (XII, 36).

In the essay on definition and method Mill denied the feasibility of predicting an 'actual result'; at most it is possible to predict 'a *tendency* to that result – a power acting with a certain intensity in that direction' (IV, 337). And in the *System of Logic* he concluded that social science, because it is 'insufficient for prediction', had to be distinguished from astronomy, the data of which are relatively few and stable. The problem was that of weighing the relative force of the numerous causal influences – supposedly known for the sake of argument – playing upon the condition and progress of society, influences

innumerable, and perpetually changing; and though they all change in obedience to causes, and therefore to laws, the multitude of the causes is so great as to defy our limited powers of calculation. Not to say that the impossibility of applying precise numbers to facts of such a description, would set an impassable limit to the possibility of calculating them beforehand, even if the powers of the human intellect were otherwise adequate to the task (VIII, 878).

Now Mill devoted attention in the *System of Logic* to what he called the 'Inverse Deductive' or 'Historical' Method (Book VI, x), and it is these chapters which most preoccupy those who charge him with 'scientism'. The problem there defined is to 'ascertain [the empirical laws of progress], and connect them with the laws of human nature, by deductions showing that such were the derivative laws naturally to be expected as the consequences of those ultimate ones' (p. 916). The exercise is designed to yield causal laws of progress extending beyond empirical generalizations, with which 'to predict the future with reasonable foresight' (p. 791).

This may have been the ideal, but in practical terms, all that could be hoped for was the isolation of secular tendencies extending beyond the limits of individual countries and periods, knowledge of which would permit policy-makers to exercise intelligent judgement. (He certainly intended tendencies in the simpler, specialist branches.) For the programme could scarcely proceed without development of the 'science of human character formation' (ethology) whereby to arrive at the 'ultimate' principles of human nature, and he was perfectly aware of the absence in his day of any such foundation (pp. 904–7, 914–15). For us the significance of the chapters on historical progress in fact lies in the caution that in the absence of genuine causal laws of a secular order there was a danger of attributing excessive predictive power to the specialist social sciences, such as economics, based as they are on locally relevant and impermanent axioms (p. 864).

Mill's warnings of the limited scope of economics bear repeating to this day. Yet he did not disparage the social sciences:

> an amount of knowledge quite insufficient for prediction, may be most valuable for guidance. The science of society would have attained a very high degree of perfection, if it enabled us, in any given condition of social affairs, in the condition for instance of Europe or any European country at the present time, to understand by what causes it had, in any and every particular, been made what it was; whether it was tending to any, and to what, changes; what effects each feature of its existing state was likely to produce in the future; and by what means any of those effects might be prevented, modified, or accelerated, or a different class of effects super-induced. There is nothing chimerical in the hope that general laws, sufficient to enable us to answer these various questions for any country or time with the individual circumstances of which we are well acquainted, do really admit of being ascertained (p. 878).

For social science to justify itself it was thus unnecessary 'to foresee infallibly the results of what we do' whether in social or private affairs: 'We must seek our objects by means which may perhaps be defeated, and take precautions against dangers which possibly may never be realized.' And here we arrive at the key classical moral:

> The aim of practical politics is to surround any given society with the greatest possible number of circumstances of which the tendencies are beneficial, and to remove or counteract, as far as practicable, those of which the tendencies are injurious. A knowledge of the tendencies only, though without the power of accurately predicting their conjunct result, gives us to a considerable extent this power (p. 898).

*   *   *

Economics is not to be disparaged for yet a further reason. Mill, in a review of 1834, took to task those English political economists who 'attempt to construct a permanent fabric out of transitory materials', and 'presuppose, in every one of their speculations, that the produce of industry is shared among three classes, altogether distinct from one another namely, labourers, capitalists, and landlords; and that all these are free agents, permitted in law and fact to set upon their labour, their capital, and their land, whatever price they are able to get for it' (IV, 225). At the same time he added a qualification which withdraws the barbs as far as concerns the method itself:

> It must not, however, be supposed that the science is so incomplete and unsatisfactory as this might seem to prove. Though many of its con-

clusions are only locally true, its method of investigation is applicable universally; and as he who has solved a certain number of algebraic equations, can without difficulty solve all others, so he who knows the political economy of England, or even of Yorkshire, knows that of all nations actual or possible: provided he have sense enough not to expect the same conclusion to issue from varying premises.

In the *System of Logic* Mill similarly pointed out that 'the deductive science of society will not lay down a theorem, asserting in an universal manner the effect of any cause; but will rather teach us how to frame the proper theorem for the circumstances of any given case. It will not give the laws of society in general, but the means of determining the phenomena of any given society from the particular elements or data of that society' (VIII, 899–900).

The claim regarding the universal applicability of the method of political economy seems to conflict with the position in the *Principles* that 'only through the principle of competition' – assuming the maximization axiom – 'has political economy any pretension to the character of a science [subject to] principles of broad generality and scientific precision' (above, p. 120). Moreover, Mill had questioned the universality of the principle of maximizing behaviour from at least 1830. Are we then obliged to charge him with a self-contradiction throughout the 1834 essay?

The formulation relating to the applicability of the method of economics to 'all nations actual or possible', is indeed far too strongly stated if understood literally. Fortunately Mill proceeded to elucidate his specific intentions by the expression:

> The conclusions of the science being all adapted to a society thus constituted, require to be revised whenever they are applied to any other. They are inapplicable where the only capitalists are the landlords, and the labourers are their property; as in the West Indies. They are inapplicable where the universal landlord is the State; as in India. They are inapplicable where the agricultural labourer is generally the owner both of the land itself and of the capital; as in France; or of the capital only, as in Ireland. We might greatly prolong this enumeration (IV, 226).

He was indeed pointing to the relevance of maximization principles for a very wide variety of specific institutional arrangements in addition to the capitalist exchange system. But there is little doubt that he stood by the position in the *Principles* that cases involving custom, or gift, or force were not generally amenable to economic analysis and would have to be dealt with by 'some other' science.

*   *   *

I return now to the essay on method. A specialist economics, with its basis in wealth maximization, was conceived only as part of the first stage of construction of a general theory of wealth – a first stage allowing for a variety of specialist treatments based on alternative axiomatic foundations – which would incorporate a wide range of behavioural patterns:

> The method of the practical philosopher consists,...of two processes; the one analytical, the other synthetical. He must *analyze* the existing state of society into its elements, not dropping and losing any of them by the way. After referring to the experience of individual man to learn the *law* of each of these elements, that is, to learn what are its natural effects, and how much of the effect follows from so much of the cause when not counteracted by any other cause, there remains an operation of *synthesis*; to put all these effects together, and, from what they are separately, to collect what would be the effect of all the causes acting at once (IV, 336).

That economics as such did not constitute the entire science of wealth comes to light very distinctly in the context of a celebrated contrast between the *malleable* 'laws of distribution' and the *immutable* 'laws of production' in Book II of the *Principles*.

By the latter, Mill intended the constraint imposed on industry by capital, the principle of diminishing returns, and the differential effects on wealth of productive and unproductive consumption (II, 199). But these 'laws' are explicitly defined with the states of physical energy, organization and knowledge given. What if allowance is made (let us say) for changing knowledge?

> We cannot [Mill conceded] foresee to what extent the modes of production may be altered, or the productiveness of labour increased, by future extensions of our knowledge of the laws of nature, suggesting new processes of industry of which we have at present no conception. But however we may succeed in making for ourselves more space within the limits set by the constitution of things, we know that there must be limits. We cannot alter the ultimate properties either of matter or mind, but can only employ those properties more or less successfully, to bring about the events in which we are interested (p. 199).

This conclusion is weak since 'the ultimate properties of matter or mind' are undefined and of no apparent interest to the economist. The only specific illustrations given of the 'immutable' laws of production presume unchanged knowledge.

The practical outcome of the formal categorization of laws is thus that political economy by itself can generate not even a tentative explanation of wealth differentials over space and trends over time, since it considers only the narrowest range of determinants – allocative efficiency and changing supplies of labour and capital in the presence of decreasing or increasing returns – relegating the 'qualitative' determinants, which include the state of knowledge, to the *ceteris paribus* pound as the subject matter of other sciences. This is, on reflection, a quite extraordinary position to take for one sensitive to the impact of new technology who sets out to write on the wealth of nations. I raise the issue here to emphasize Mill's consciousness of the limited scope of economics flowing from the limited applicability of the maximization axiom.

It turns out, however, that in practice Mill by no means adopted so narrow a perspective as the categorization itself implies. We revert to the 'Preliminary Remarks' of the *Principles* and the following statement on scope:

> In so far as the economic condition of nations turns upon the state of physical knowledge, it is a subject for the physical sciences, and the arts founded on them. But in so far as the causes are moral or psychological, dependent on institutions and social relations, or on the principles of human nature, their investigation belongs not to physical, but to moral and social science, and is the object of what is called Political Economy (pp. 20–1).

By the dependence of the 'economical condition of nations' upon 'institutions and social relations' Mill intended the impact on productivity of the joint-stock arrangement, of various systems of land tenure, of laws relating to inheritance and poor relief, and of civil protection. Here then we have obvious examples of the fact that production *is* 'malleable', and the implication that its 'malleability' (as far as it turns upon organization) *does* fall within the domain of the economist.

Now in fact much the same can be said of knowledge, as is apparent from a chapter on 'labour as an agent of production' (Book I, ii), where the scope of political economy is apparently widened to include activities not motivated by maximizing behaviour. For unlike the mental labour of invention, which is sometimes 'undergone...in the prospect of a remuneration from the produce', speculative activity in general is not undertaken with an eye to its 'material fruits' for which reason 'this ultimate influence [on wealth] does not, for most of the purposes of political economy require to be taken into consideration' (pp. 42–3). Mill, however, then proceeds to qualify himself:

> But when (as in political economy one should always be prepared to do) we shift our point of view, and consider not individual acts, and the motives by which they are determined, but national and universal results, intellectual speculation must be looked upon as a most influential part of the productive labour of society, and the portion of its resources employed in carrying on and in remunerating such labour, as a highly productive part of its expenditure.

The same distinction between the 'individual' and the 'national' points of view is made regarding elementary education and health expenditures.

In the course of his formal work on method, it will be recalled, Mill had allowed that where a 'disturbing cause' is encountered which acts through the same law of human nature as that reflected in the general behavioural axioms it might 'be brought within the pale of the abstract science [of political economy]' (see above, p. 344). What we have now, however, is the proposed incorporation of 'disturbing causes' governed specifically by something other than the wealth maximizing motive. For this too there was a precedent in the early essay of 1836 when Mill allowed that the analysis of population growth falls within the subject of economics despite a wide variety of non-maximization determinants, 'the strictness of purely scientific arrangement being thereby somewhat departed from, for the sake of practical utility' (IV, 323).

The presumption that wealth maximizing motivation is generally not at play in matters pertaining to 'intellectual speculation' is of the first importance; it is, therefore, regrettable that Mill failed to carry out an investigation of the topic as a whole – an analysis of the fraction of the community's resources devoted to knowledge creation (and also to health and education). The incorporation of the determinants of pure science was a mere 'proposal', albeit flowing from a realization that (even though maximization motivation was largely irrelevant) the subject was too close to home to be safely relegated to 'another science'.

14.5   The Empirical Dimension in the *Principles*: Some Case Studies

The roles accorded empirical analysis ('induction') in the derivation of individual axioms and in model improvement are central to the early (1836) essay, as we have seen. That essay Mill intended his readers to have at hand in 1848. It will be useful to take a brief overview of Mill's actual practice in the *Principles* from this perspective, with particular reference to the self-interest axiom.

We must first set aside an unnecessary terminological complexity, turning on the technical usage of 'wealth' to exclude services. This usage has led some commentators to assert that Mill's maximizing individuals concern themselves solely with material goods. In fact Mill had in mind nothing more than the rule that such individuals seek to sell goods and services at the highest price attainable and to buy at the lowest price attainable, and possess the knowledge to do so (III, 460). The consequence of such behaviour, combined with the assumptions relating to large numbers and free entry, is a single price for the same good (or service) in one market. These features characterize competition; and, as we have noted already (see above, p. 349), 'only through the principle of competition has political economy any pretension to the character of a science'.

That the maximizing man in the *Principles* refers to the real man in the market place rather than a psychological fiction comes clearly to light in Mill's restriction of price theory to the wholesale sector:

> The values and prices ... to which our conclusions apply, are mercantile values and prices; such prices as are quoted in price-currents; prices in the wholesale markets, in which buying as well as selling is a matter of business; in which the buyers take pains to know, and generally do know, the lowest price at which an article of a given quality can be obtained.... Our propositions will be true in a much more qualified sense, of retail prices; the prices paid in shops for articles of personal consumption (p. 460; see above, p. 121).

This restriction turns on the observation that buyers at retail outlets do not typically make their purchases 'on business principles' – a reflection of their indolence, carelessness, satisfaction derived from paying high prices, ignorance, defective judgement and coercion, all apart from high search costs. Equally conspicuous is the discussion of the motives governing employers of domestics (and of clerks) which explains why more is often paid than the 'competitive' wage in terms of 'ostentation' and a variety of 'more reasonable motives' all of which turn on the personal contact between employee and employer (II, 398–9). These case studies provide a very clear indication that the assumption of wealth maximization is pertinent to the anonymous market place where personal contacts are reduced to a minimum, precluding the range of considerations in question. Quite clearly Mill was at one with Smith and Ricardo regarding the supposed empirical accuracy of the maximising assumption in the capitalist exchange environment, and more specifically the limitations imposed by that environment on a range of 'self-interested' forms of behaviour.

Marshall maintained of Ricardo and his followers that they 'often spoke as though they regarded man as a constant quantity, and they never gave themselves enough trouble to study his variations' (1920, 762). While little harm was done in the contexts of money and trade they were 'led astray' particularly in that of distribution; they 'attributed to the forces of supply and demand a much more mechanical and regular action than is to be found in real life: and they laid down laws with regard to profits and wages that did not really hold even for England in their own time' (pp. 762–3). (This is rather harsh on Ricardo who had insisted on distinguishing British labour market conditions including behaviour from those of contemporary 'underdeveloped' economies; see above p. 329.) Marshall did not include the Mill of the *Principles* in this charge; it was rather Mill of the essay who was supposedly guilty, Marshall presuming (mistakenly) that it was written under the influence of James Mill (1920, 764–5n.). As for the *Principles*, Marshall was right in that Mill did not there apply the principles of supply and demand 'mechanically', either in the context of commodity or of service pricing. Yet he took great pains to avoid disparaging competitive pricing.

His course of action involves the matter of 'disturbing causes' so central to the formal discussion of method. Consider the declaration that while 'there is no proposition which meets us in the field of political economy more often than this – that there cannot be two prices in the same market...yet every one knows that there are, almost always, two prices in the same market' (Mill, II, 242). The solution adopted by Mill is in effect to treat non-maximizing behaviour in the retail sector as involving 'disturbing causes' in pricing – in principle the responsibility of 'some other science'. But this, it must be stressed, has an empirical justification, in so far as the primary force at work – that governing the determination of the underlying wholesale price – remained pecuniary maximization.

The latter procedure can be further illustrated by reference to the allowance in the essay that the 'perpetually antagonistic principles to the desire of wealth', namely 'aversion to labour, and desire of the present enjoyment of costly indulgences', are in practice taken into account by economics 'to a certain extent' precisely because of their empirical pervasiveness (IV, 321). This matter is much amplified in the *Principles*, where it is clarified that by desire of wealth is intended pecuniary maximization, and by the two antagonistic forces in question, a willingness to by-pass an opportunity to increase the return per hour or per unit of capital by movement between sectors, or to forego a bargain in commodity markets. Thus Mill observed regarding Continental Europe 'that prices and charges, of some or of all sorts, are much higher in some places than in others not far distant, without its being possible to assign any other cause than that it has always been so: the customers are used to it, and acquiesce in it' (II, 244). Similarly, 'an enterprising competitor, with sufficient capital, might force down the charges, and make his fortune during the process; but there are no enterprising competitors; those who have capital prefer to leave it where it is, or to make less profit by it in a more quiet way'. The same could be said of labour. Now in the British case too, where 'the spirit of competition' is the strongest, custom was still a 'powerful influence'; but in other environments people were 'content with smaller gains, and estimate their pecuniary interest at a lower rate when balanced against their ease or their pleasure'. Clearly Mill intended more than a quantitative difference between Britain and the Continent. In the latter kind of environment the force of the wealth maximization motive was swamped by the antagonistic motives so that little could be said of the response to a newly created wage or profit differential or to a reduction in price; havoc was wrought as far as concerns 'predictions' regarding labour and capital flows or rates of consumption with price change. In the British case, by contrast, there was a strong empirical presumption favouring the process of equalization of returns to labour and to capital, and also the negative slope to the demand curve and thus a tendency to stable equilibrium in competitive markets – at least up to the retail stage.

Thus it is that Mill appeals to the empirical accuracy of the behavioural axiom in his formal discussion of profit rate equalization: 'If the value of a commodity is such that it repays the cost of production not only with the customary, but with a higher rate of profit, capital rushes to share in this extra gain, and by increasing the supply of the article, reduces its value. This is not a mere supposition or surmise, but a fact familiar to those conversant with commercial operations' (III, 472). We recall too (above p. 127) the appeal to the real world of business and the complexity of entrepreneurial decision-making in the context of 'internal adjustment' to cost variation.

The same perspective emerges in Mill's general analysis of the wage structure with special reference to his allowance for 'non-competing' groups, a variety of features of the real world (conspicuously the impediments to mobility of a financial and social order) underlying his dissatisfaction with Smithian analysis (above, p. 134). It was his growing optimism regarding a breakdown of the impediments that ultimately led him to conclude that while 'there are few kinds of [skilled] labour of which the remuneration would not be lower than it is, if the employer took the full advantage of competition', yet competition 'must be regarded, in the present state of society, as the principal regulator of wages, and custom or individual character only as a modifying circumstance, and that in a comparatively slight degree' (II, 337).

Moreover, the existence of unusual cases is never denied. The most striking are instances of excessive entry, as in the literary professions (p. 392), generating negative returns even in equilibrium, in consequence of that 'principal of human nature' whereby the promise of a few great prizes stimulates miscalculation (p. 383). But this too was treated as a 'modifying circumstance' in going conditions.

That the primary behaviour axiom holds good as a first approximation is thus justified on purely empirical grounds as we were led to expect from the essay. But here we must note a fundamentally important caution regarding the allowances that have to be made in practice, a caution that appears upon recognition of possible cases of permanent inequalities in the return on capital:

> These observations must be received as a general correction to be applied whenever relevant, whether expressly mentioned or not, to the conclusions contained in the subsequent portions of this treatise. Our reasonings must, in general, proceed as if the known and natural effects of competition were actually produced by it, in all cases where it is not restrained by some positive obstacle. Where competition, though free to exist, does not exist, or where it exists, but has its natural consequences overruled by any other agency, the conclusions will fail more or less of being applicable. To escape error, we ought, in applying the conclusions of political economy to the actual affairs of life, to consider not only what will happen supposing the maximum of competition, but how far the result will be affected if competition falls short of the maximum (p. 244).

Again, this too reflects what is said in the essay on method, namely that verification of the hypothesis is 'no part of the business of science, but of the application of science' (above, p. 344); but this must be understood with all the qualifications previously outlined in the account of the earlier work.

14.6 Model Improvement

Always in line with the essay, Mill in the *Principles* allows the absorption into his economic models of market forms that do not fit the purely competitive case. Now what we have to say on this matter is pertinent to evaluation of the view that, from Mill's perspective, we never verify the 'validity' of theories, since the conclusions are necessarily true, based as they are on self-evident facts of human experience. That the notion of 'self-evident' facts is suspect we know already; but it further emerges that Mill attempts model improvement based upon testing against the record. Much more is involved in applied economics than an attempt to discover the disturbing causes at play, and thereby close the gap between the facts and the causal relationships specified by the model.

Model improvement as defined in the essay is the hoped-for consequence of the process of testing against the evidence (above, p. 344). In some instances a new disturbing cause might be discovered which in future use of theory would have to be kept in mind – as instanced by the obstacles to wage rate equalization which Mill's empirical studies brought to light. But model improvement in consequence of verification might be more substantive, taking the form of 'inserting among its hypotheses a fresh and still more complex combination of circumstances, and so adding *pro hâc vice* a supplementary chapter or appendix, or at least a supplementary theorem, to the abstract science' (IV, 331). Thus the exclusion of monopoly from the scientific domain and its treatment as a disturbing cause turns out to be purely a formal matter; in practice Mill admitted that it had 'always been allowed for by political economists' (II, 239), and he himself applied the tools of analysis to this case. He even allowed for the absorption of custom – again formally a 'disturbing cause' – where custom establishes prices yet competition acts to reduce profits to the economy wide rate by reducing market size – the 'monopolistic competition' model (above, p. 133). Here then we have two illustrations of the observation in the essay that 'a disturbing cause ... which operates through the same law of human nature out of which the general principles of the science arise ... might always be brought within the pale of the abstract science, if it were thought worthwhile' (IV, 331; see above, p. 344).

Mill's recognition of (short-run) excess demand for money to hold (see above, p. 257) illustrates model improvement, in this case a consequence of the anomaly of contemporaneous excess labour and capital which ultimately forced itself on his attention. And the idea of an endogenous trade cycle – clearly related to real-world events – is better developed by Mill than by any contemporary (above, p. 260).

14.7 Conclusion

Professor Phelps-Brown, amongst many others, has charged that the economics profession has contributed little by its sophisticated theoretical and econometric techniques to the most pressing economic problems of our age, and explained this discrepancy by the argument that our models are 'built upon assumptions about human behaviour that are plucked from the air', rather than drawn from observation – 'that the behaviour posited is not known to be what obtains in the actual economy' (1972, 3–4). This lament portrays the type of consequence against which J. S. Mill had sought to protect economics from 1830 onwards. His own council and also his practice justified a specialist economics but specifically on empirical grounds and thus provisionally; it implied a modest estimate of the subject's forecasting or predictive potential; it demanded model improvement by way of verification against factual evidence; it disdained any notion of the universal validity of economic principles; it focused attention upon the mechanics of pricing in the real world of business rather than some ideal world; and it invited consideration of how economic mechanisms might operate under a variety of alternative institutional arrangements. His position took a stand against professional arrogance and narrow-mindedness. In these respects Mill was following a line typical of all the major classical economists, as he himself always insisted.

Suggested Reading

*Mill, 'On the Definition of Political Economy; and on the Method of Philosophical Investigation in that Science' (1836), in *Collected Works* (1967) IV, 309–39.

The material in the present chapter is elaborated in Hollander (1985), ch. 2. Also pertinent are de Marchi (1974), Whitaker (1975), Hutchison (1978a), ch. 3, and Collini (1983).

15 Classical Features in Marxian Economics

15.1 Introduction

Investigation of the classical features that characterize Marxian economics provides an opportunity to summarize much of the allocation and growth theory covered in this work. We shall approach the allocation issue having in mind a central proposition of various 'Cambridge' accounts of Marxian economics – namely the priority of distribution over pricing: 'The nature of [Marx's] approach required him to start from the postulation of a certain rate of exploitation or of surplus-value (or profit–wage ratio in Ricardo's terms); since this was *prior* to the formation of exchange-values or prices and was not derived from them. In other words, this needed to be expressed in terms of production, *before* bringing in circulation or exchange' (Dobb, 1973, 148). The view of the economic system here implied is strikingly different from the general-equilibrium view and in line with the Cambridge interpretation of Ricardianism:

> It should be fairly clear ... that a system which determines distribution in terms of exchange and its emergent prices must, in one way or another, with possibility of varying emphasis, be cast in terms of supply and demand; but *au contraire*, the Ricardian system, which explains exchange in terms of distribution, and distribution itself in terms of productivity and conditions of production in one industry or sector of industry (given the real-wage), has no place for the relation of supply and demand – at least, until it comes to *movements* in relative prices, and in particular of Smithian market prices (pp. 118–19).

Here then we have a clear statement that general-equilibrium economics is supply–demand economics, whereas Ricardo–Marx economics is not. And, of course, if one takes this perspective there is discernible that supposed historiographic division about which I have spoken already several times: one line turning on allocation emanating from Smith, taken up by a number of dissenters from Ricardo, and by John Stuart Mill, and re-emerging with the 'Marginalists' and Marshall; and a second line, the Ricardo–Marx line, where distribution and pricing are divorced in some sense and demand–supply is reduced to a secondary role at best.

We know already that there is no justification for attributing to Ricardo (or Mill) a divorce of distribution and pricing and a relegation of demand–supply to the shadows. Changes in the pattern of demand for final goods (whether independent or brought about by prior changes in distribution) can play on the wage rate, and changes in the wage rate can affect relative prices by way of standard neo-classical supply adjustments. The Ricardian system, like the Smithian and the neo-classical systems, can only be understood in terms of supply and demand. This statement, I shall show, is true also of Marx.

It is possible to isolate the source of what appears to be a faulty interpretation of Ricado and Marx. The main reason for the erroneous interpretation turns upon the ascription to both Ricardo and Marx of a fix-wage model. We know that Ricardo often assumed constant wages, but that was for pedagogic clarity. His general model incorporated variable wages, opening the way for an impact on distribution of changes in final demand patterns. Marx was also a variable-wage theorist, and the same complication has to be recognized.

The ambiguous status of the fundamental theorem of distribution, the inverse profit–wage relationship, also plays a role. Ricardo sometimes considered the effect of a wage increase on profits by use of the measuring device, and applied the outcome to make predictions about pricing. Let us assume, he was in effect saying, that we have solved the problem of a measure and therefore have at hand a commodity in terms of which some second commodity's price will not vary upon a change in wages. Since the price of the latter is unchanged, it is a relatively simple matter to calculate the new profit rate corresponding to the higher wage rate for that industry; the outcome can then be applied to calculate the new set of cost prices throughout the economy. This way of working implies a solution to distribution before pricing. But here, as elsewhere, Ricardo was groping his way to a desirable exposition. In the full analysis of the mechanisms of adjustment, the increase in wages affects the whole structure of outputs in the system, with the new cost prices and the new general level of profits emerging together as a consequence of a reallocation of resources. And as mentioned, there is nothing in Ricardian logic to preclude a playback from the pattern of activity upon distribution, so that any 'forecast' of the final outcome requires knowledge of the entire set of final demand curves.

Now there is a parallel confusion generated by the manner in which Marx proceeds, which I shall examine in sections 15.2, 15.3 and 15.4. The complexity arises from the organization of *Capital* – the first two volumes based on a labour theory of value followed by a third based on 'prices of production' (cost prices including profits at the average rate). This procedure is an invitation to the presumption that distribution is 'solved' in terms of social and technical data, independently of pricing and allocation, with prices emerging only at a second stage.

What Marx intended by this procedure, however, as section 15.5 will show, was to develop and defend a particular interpretation of the source of non-wage income. He wished to lay out the problem in such a way that he could better defend the notion of profits as 'surplus' labour time – labour time not devoted to the production of workers' own goods. But this position in no way clashes with orthodox classical allocation theory; Marx's conception of the manner in which the capitalist exchange system operates is no different from that of John Stuart Mill, or Ricardo, or Smith. Moreover the notion of the source of profits in surplus labour time was already common coin when Marx published his first volume in 1867.

As for growth theory, section 15.7 documents Marx's adherence to a secular path of wages which tends to decline towards the 'subsistence' level defined in the orthodox manner as that wage at which population growth ceases. The underlying cause of the decline is a continually decelerating rate of growth in the demand for labour – though not for the orthodox reasons – in the face of on-going population expansion. The wage path thus entails the standard classical principle of population expansion in reaction to wages above 'subsistence' (section 15.8). And this notwithstanding Marx's condemnation of Malthus (set out in section 15.6). Marx's profit rate also has a 'tendency' to fall for reasons peculiar to his model.

Since the falling wage trend in industry is due to a deviation between the growth rates of labour demand and supply, the model has much in common with Ricardo's analysis. But there is a major difference. For Ricardo the falling wage and profit rates resulted from declining productivity in the agricultural sector (technology given); for Marx the declining growth rate in labour demand is the consequence of technological change – increasing rather than decreasing productivity is the rule.

The present chapter also deals with cyclical wage fluctuations and inter-sectoral labour movements (sections 15.9 and 15.10), and closes with a summary of Marx's formal objections to orthodox classicism.

15.2   Marxian Allocation Theory: the Transformation Problem

I begin with Marxian allocation theory. This has to be understood within the appropriate framework. According to Marx, the source of profits is excess labour time. Assume a ten-hour work day of which five hours are devoted to the production of the wage basket, and the remainder to commodities constituting profits, in the sense that five of the ten hours generate sufficient revenue to compensate the employer for his outlay on wages. The ratio of 'surplus' to 'necessary' labour, or s/v, is defined as the 'rate of exploitation' or the 'rate of surplus value', which in this instance amounts to 100 per cent (*Capital*, I, 216).* The various sectors of the economy are supposed to require different 'compositions of capital' or constant capital (machinery, structures, materials) relative to variable capital (wage goods), or c/v ratios. Since the ratio c/v is non-uniform between sectors (e.g., p. 307), but s/v is assumed to be uniform, it follows that if, as is the assumption throughout volume I of *Capital*, *commodities exchange in proportion to labour values* – which includes labour embodied in the net value added $(v + s)$ as well as in the constant capital used up during the process (c') – then the rate of profit or $s/(c + v)$, will also be non-uniform. For the same total capital $(c + v)$ in two industries yields differing s, and therefore, differing profit rates on the total, depending on the fraction of capital devoted to the maintenance of labour (v); the more 'labour-intensive' the industry (in modern parlance) the greater will be s and the greater accordingly will be the rate of profit. Note that only if wages *per capita* are constant will v – which represents the 'value' of (or labour embodied in) wage goods capital – vary with the current labour input; and even this will not suffice if technical progress should be reducing the labour cost of producing wage goods.

All this can easily be seen if the profit rate $s/(c + v)$ is written as

$$\frac{\left(\dfrac{s}{v}\right)}{\left(1 + \dfrac{c}{v}\right)}$$

Clearly a uniform s/v but differing c/v between industries implies differing profits rates.

---

* Extracts from *Capital* I (1867) and *Capital* III (1894) are from the Moscow 1965 and 1962 editions respectively. Throughout this chapter references to *Capital* will be given by volume and/or page number only.

Now non-uniform profit rates are atypical of competitive capitalism (p. 307). The next step (taken in the posthumously published volume III, chs 9 and 10) is *to allow cost prices to diverge from labour values in such a manner as to assure a common profit rate.* This Marx does by calculating the average profit rate (in the labour or volume I scheme) as the total of surplus values in all sectors relative to total capitals, and then adding this rate to production costs in each sector, namely to the used-up constant capital and variable capital. This yields 'prices-of-production' which now diverge from labour values, the deviations cancelling out to zero. The ratios of surplus (now in price terms) to variable capital also diverge from sector to sector, the labour-intensive industries subsidizing, so to speak, the capital-intensive industries. These conceptions are summarized in tables 15.1 and 15.2 (derived from *Capital*, III, 154–5).

Table 15.1

Organic composition of capital by industry	Order by v/c	Surplus value	Rate of surplus value (s/v) (%)	Used up capital (c') [arbitrary]	Cost price $(c' + v)$	Value $(c' + v + s)$	Rate of profit $(s/[c + v])$ (%)
$80c + 20v$	0.25(3)	20	100	50	70	90	20
$70c + 30v$	0.43(2)	30	100	51	81	111	30
$60c + 40v$	0.66(1)	40	100	51	91	131	40
$85c + 15v$	0.17(4)	15	100	40	55	70	15
$95c + 5v$	0.05(5)	5	100	10	15	20	5
$390c + 110v$		110					

Source: Marx, III, 154.

Table 15.2

Organic composition of capital by industry	Rate of profit[a]	Cost price[b]	Value[b]	'Price of production' $(c' + v + p)$	Deviation of price from value
$80c + 20v$	22	70	90	92	+2
$70c + 30v$	22	81	111	103	−8
$60c + 40v$	22	91	131	113	−18
$85c + 15v$	22	55	70	77	+7
$95c + 5v$	22	15	20	37	+17

[a] The rate of profit is calculated as $\Sigma s/\Sigma(c + v)$ in Table 15.1 = 110/500.
[b] From table 15.1.
Source: Marx, III, 155.

According to Marx's 'transformation' of values into prices, 'the sum of the profits in all spheres of production must equal the sum of the surplus-values, and the sum of the prices of production of the total social product equal the sum of its value' (III, 170); that is, total profits equal total surplus value, and the sum of all the prices equals the sum of all the values. (Note that it over-determines the transformation to require both conditions.) It is sometimes said that the foregoing identifications are meaningless since values are expressed in terms of *labour*, and prices and profits in terms of *money*. But this is an unjustified complaint, for surplus value is in fact expressed in terms of 'pounds' not labour units. This formal matter has to be established before we can proceed to more substantive issues.

Whether exchange rates reflect values or prices of production, these rates are expressed in money terms. Marx thought in terms of a fixed unit of currency to measure not only prices and profits but value and surplus value as well:

> If, *e.g.*, the necessary labour [required to produce wage goods] amounts to 6 hours daily, expressed in a quantum of gold = 3 shillings, then 3 s. is the daily value of one labour-power.... If, further, the rate of surplus-value be = 100%, this variable capital of 3 s. produces a mass of surplus-value of 3 s., or the labourer supplies daily a mass of surplus-labour equal to 6 hours (I, 303).

> If we are to assume all the time that £1 stands for the weekly wage of a labourer... and that the rate of surplus-value is 100%, then it is evident that the total value-product of one labourer in a week, is £2... [and] ten labourers cannot produce more surplus-value than £10 (III, 147).

A second preliminary point relates to the working assumption of constant 'value' (labour input, direct and indirect) in the case of the monetary commodity, and the insistence that where changes in the value do occur, the consequences are purely nominal (I, 319; III, 137).

It will now be shown that the transfer to prices of production from values – a set of money prices reflecting labour inputs – entails a changed distribution of resources between industries to assure that commodities indeed sell at money prices covering costs plus the average profit rate. The transformation in short implies an allocative readjustment of activity. It is precisely here that the adjustment mechanisms characterizing orthodox classical theory intrude.

Let us start, as in *Capital*, I, with a set of exchange values reflecting relative labour inputs, the degree of exploitation (s/v) assumed uniform across all sectors. As already explained, the rate of profit $s/(c+v)$ differs between sectors, considering the non-uniformity of organic compositions. Since the uniform profit rate condition is not satisfied, this initial set of prices (value prices) cannot be long-run equilibrium prices. Marx, to put the matter bluntly, did not (even in volume I) maintain a labour theory of value. His labour prices in the value scheme are disequilibrium prices.

The essential problem is set out clearly in the following extract, where Marx observes that a system of values – assuming a given *v per capita* and uniform s/v – apparently contradicts capitalistic 'experience', namely the competitive uniformity of profit rates:

> The law demonstrated above now, therefore, takes this form: the masses of value and of surplus-value produced by different capitals – the value of labour-power being given and its degree of exploitation being equal – vary directly as the amounts of the variable constituents of these capitals, *i.e.*, as their constituents transformed into living labour-power.
>
> This law contradicts all experience based on appearance. Everyone knows that a cotton spinner, who, reckoning the percentage on the whole of his applied capital, employs much constant and little variable capital, does not, on account of this, pocket less profit or surplus-value than a baker, who relatively sets in motion much variable and little constant capital. For the solution to this apparent contradiction, many intermediate terms are as yet wanted (I, 306–7).

The solution to this 'contradiction' is only given in the posthumous volume III. The key to the solution lies in the fact that the value scheme of volume I reflects Marx's deliberately imposed constraint on outputs to assure that prices indeed reflect labour values and not prices of production. The transition from the former to the latter occurs by allowing the process of competition to work effectively, so that the labour-intensive industries which in the value scheme have above-average profit rates will expand and their prices (and surpluses in price terms) fall; while conversely, capital-intensive industries will contract, their prices (and surpluses in price terms) rising, a process of adjustment which comes to an end when profit rate equality is achieved. It is the process of competition – the demand–supply process – which brings about that result.

The process is expounded by Marx in terms of money. The conditions are that money must itself be produced with constant labour input; and that the monetary commodity possesses the mean organic composition in the system as a whole. When, therefore, we relax the constraints imposed on commodity supplies, it will be found that no changes occur in the outputs and, accordingly, none in the prices (in terms of the monetary commodity), of any commodity also produced with a mean organic composition, since the profit rate in those sectors initially equalled the mean profit rate. The following two extracts contain the gist of Marx's argument:

> The capital invested in some spheres of production has a mean, or average composition, that is, it has the same or almost the same composition as the average social capital.
>
> In these spheres the price of production is exactly or almost the same as the value of the produced commodity expressed in money....Competition so distributes the social capital among the various spheres of production that the prices of production in each sphere take shape according to the model of the prices of production in these spheres of average composition, i.e., they $= k + kp'$ (cost-price plus the average rate of profit multiplied by the cost-price) (III, 170).

> [If] the commodities are sold at their values, then ... very different rates of profit arise in the various spheres of production, depending on the different organic composition of the masses of capital invested in them. But capital withdraws from a sphere with a low rate of profit and invades others, which yield a higher profit. Through this incessant outflow and inflow, or, briefly, through its distribution among the various spheres, which depends on how the rate of profit falls here and rises there, it creates such a ratio of supply to demand that the average profit in the various spheres of production becomes the same, and values are, therefore, converted into prices of production (p. 192).

It emerges very clearly from these passages that the adjustment entails a competitive process of reallocation from *disequilibrium* labour values to *equilibrium* 'prices of production'. These prices are nothing but standard classical (and neo-classical) costs of production or 'natural' prices. And as Marx himself explicitly states, it is the demand–supply mechanism that is at work. Indeed he provides a very detailed account, as did Ricardo and J. S. Mill, of the credit mechanism at play in a capitalist exchange system mediating the movement of resources between sectors (III, 192–3). Similar accounts are also to be found in Walras and Marshall. In all instances, the economists insist that it is a 'tendency' towards equilibrium that should be spoken of because the system is rarely in an equilibrium state.

In his famous *Theory of Capitalist Development*, Paul Sweezy has argued that 'it is perfectly legitimate to postulate a capitalist system in which organic compositions of capital are everywhere equal and hence the law of value does hold, and to examine the functioning of such a system', and then investigate the deviations from the rule required in practice (1942, 70). This procedure is attributed to Marx in his transformation. Marx in volume I is said to have assumed uniform organic composition, in which case the labour theory holds as an equilibrium statement; only in volume III did Marx consider deviations from the rule required in practice. But this interpretation will not do: Marx's labour values are not equilibrium values given the assumption of non-uniform organic composition. *A fortiori* the following statement cannot be accepted:

> We know that the assumption of equal organic composition of capital makes prices of production strictly proportional to values. Therefore, in spite of Marx having explicitly stated in various places of Volume I that sectors may differ from each other in composition of capital, we may consider that Marx tacitly assumed equal organic composition throughout the economy in those places where he did not distinguish prices from values (Morishima and Catephores, 1975, 327).

One cannot so easily dismiss Marx's own insistence upon non-uniformity of organic compositions.

For my interpretation I have relied upon Marx's verbal account. It is regrettable that tables 15.1 and 15.2 do not themselves indicate the output variations necessary to assure the transformation of values to prices; the magnitudes of the industries given in the first column of table 15.2 are the same as those of table 15.1. It is also regrettable that Marx's transformation is incomplete in that only the values of final outputs are transformed into prices, not the values of the constant and variable components of capital. We only have Marx's word for it that nothing is lost by this simplification (*Capital*, III, 203).

It remains to note that the strictly defined labour theory breaks down even with uniform factor ratios, once allowance is made for a structure of wage rates (even if constant). Marx allowed in the value of labour power for the costs of education and training (e.g., I, 172), but sought to avoid the inevitable conclusion.

15.3 The Inverse Wage–Profit Relation

We consider next the impact of an experimental change in the wage rate. Marx follows Ricardo step by step – i.e. Ricardo in the first chapter of his *Principles*. He assumes that there is a money commodity with average organic composition, and another commodity similarly produced. When the wage rate changes, there is no change in the money price of that commodity, so that (in the case of that commodity) it is very easy to observe the corresponding decline in the profit rate:

> Let the average composition of social capital be $80_c + 20_v$, and the profit 20%. The rate of surplus-value is then 100%. A general increase of wages, all else remaining the same, is tantamount to a reduction in the rate of surplus-value. In the case of average capital, profit and surplus-value are identical. Let wages rise 25%. Then the same quantity of labour, formerly set in motion with 20, will cost 25. We shall then have a

turnover value of $80_c + 25_v + 15_p$ instead of $80_c + 20_v + 20_p$. As before, the labour set in motion by the variable capital produces a value of 40. If v rises from 20 to 25, the surplus s, or p, will amount to only 15. The profit of 15 on a capital of 105 is 14 2/7% and this would be the new average rate of profit. Since the price of production of commodities produced by the average capital coincides with their value, the price of production of these commodities would have remained unchanged. A wage increase would therefore have caused a drop in profit, but no change in the value and price of the commodities (III, 196).

The lower profit rate of 14 2/7 per cent is next used to calculate the new prices of production throughout the system. In terms of Marx's illustration, profit rates decline in all industries at going prices following the supposed wage increase, but from 20 to 6 2/3 per cent in the case of a particular commodity produced by capital of below-average composition (the labour-intensive sectors), and from 20 to 17.6 per cent in the converse case (the capital-intensive sectors). But 'the new average rate of profit is 14 2/7%' and Marx proceeds to recalculate the new equilibrium prices on the basis of this figure.

In proceeding thus, Marx (like Ricardo) was taking an expository short cut. The new prices in fact emerge as a result of an allocative re-adjustment. And this must be so, for Marx (like Smith, Ricardo and Mill) never tired of insisting that capital reacts to differential profit rates, not to some pre-existing average profit rate. It is a disturbance to the structure of profit rates that is the key; when the wage increases at going prices, all profits are forced down, but more in some cases than others, and in response to the differentials there results reallocation of capital, outputs falling in some cases and increasing in others, prices rising and falling correspondingly.

To summarize the argument to this point, Marxian economics provides a picture of economic organization worked out and directed by price forces. As in the analyses of Ricardo (and Smith), demand and supply is the vehicle of determination of the system: 'The entire process of capitalist production is ... regulated by the prices of the products ... themselves in turn regulated by the equalization of the rate of profit and its corresponding distribution of capital among the various social spheres of production' (III, 860). It could not be clearer that Marx adhered to the standard classical allocative model, and that this model accounts for the inverse wage–profit relation in the Ricardian fashion.

15.4   The Rate of Surplus Value

The rate of surplus value or exploitation (s/v) and the rate of profit $(s/[c + v])$ are represented in many expositions of Marxian economics as *data* defined at the initial value stage and taken for granted as we move to prices. In fact, both are endogenous variables amenable to variation by disturbance to the pattern of demand for final goods.

The uniformity of the rate of surplus value across all sectors follows from the assumption of labour mobility and indifference on the part of labour to types of occupation. If labourers are thus indifferent and if they are paid the same commodity wage for a day's work, their competition assures that the length of the work day comes to equality, for workers will transfer away from occupations with relatively long work days. Now a common work day means that the 'value' generated per labourer is everywhere the same. And if from the value generated per head, the labour embodied in the worker's daily wage (which is the same for everybody) is deducted, there remains the same s. In short, the work day determines the magnitude of $(s + v)$ and is everywhere the same; and since v also is the same, s and s/v are similarly everywhere equal. Marx makes the point clearly, referring to 'competition among labourers and equalization [of the rate of exploitation] through their continual migration from one sphere of production to another' (III, 172).

The uniformity of the rate of exploitation is assured by labour mobility, whether or not values reflect prices. But there is another sense of the term 'rate of exploitation' – the profit–wage ratio. Now the profit–wage ratio will be the same as the rate of surplus value only in the value scheme. It is not the same in the price scheme where prices no longer reflect relative labour inputs. Consider a capitalist producer of cloth whose workers consume corn. At the end of the period of production the capitalist sells some of his cloth to buy enough corn to pay workers their wage. If corn and cloth exchange according to the labour theory one is equivalent to the other for any given amount of labour embodied, and we can proceed as above, deducting so much labour embodied in corn from the labour spent in producing cloth. But once the labour theory has been replaced by a regular cost of production theory, there is no longer a relationship of this order between these products; the cloth–corn exchange ratio diverges from labour inputs, and the simple reduction is no longer possible. In the value scheme, therefore, we may consider the uniform rate of exploitation either as a uniform s/v or a uniform profit–wage ratio. In the pricing scheme, s/v still remains uniform assuming labour mobility, but the profit–wage ratio, which is, of course, the only 'observable' ratio, will differ between sectors.

So much then for the uniformity of the rate of exploitation (s/v). Now to the common level itself. A given rate of surplus value implies both a given money wage (if the value of money is assumed constant) and a given commodity wage, ruling out technical progress in the wage goods sectors. And the rate of surplus value moves inversely to the wage: 'A general increase of wages, all else remaining the same, is tantamount to a reduction in the rate of surplus-value' (see above, p. 367). A fall in the length of the work day similarly implies a reduction in the rate of surplus value. The question we have now to address is whether the general level of wages is a datum of the analysis of pricing or not. That Marxian economics is not of the fix-wage variety emerges later in this chapter, when we discuss the trend paths of the factor returns. The wage rate, it there emerges, depends upon the relative growth rates of labour supply and of labour demand or the variable (wage fund) component of capital. Technical change, by altering the average c/v ratio, affects the rate of growth of labour demand and therefore the wage. But in principle, a change in tastes which alters the equilibrium pattern of economic activity, will also play upon the average c/v ratio. Marx himself dealt with alterations in the pattern of final tastes (I, 638), but whereas he normally insists on differential organic compositions between sectors, in this case he presumes an increase of demand for good A at the expense of good B under the implicit assumption that their organic compositions are the same, thereby precluding the effect on wages. In other words, he here proceeds just as Smith and Ricardo had done, despite his usual insistence upon differential organic compositions. By this simplification alone can the impact of changing demand patterns be avoided.

Marxian economics, it has been argued thus far, allows for the interdependence of distribution and pricing of two orders. First a change in the wage rate can affect relative prices by affecting the pattern of activity – on this Marx was quite explicit. Secondly, a change in the pattern of demand can affect the wage rate – a conclusion only avoided by the adoption of an atypical assumption. But nothing that has been said regarding the potential consequences of a change in the pattern of final demand for distribution gainsays Marx's profound and valid conviction that the factors regulating final demand are, as he put it, 'subject to the mutual relation of the different classes and their respective economic position' (III, 178); that it is insufficient merely to posit an exogenous change in tastes. Distribution of the national income is the major determinant upon which Marx quite rightly insisted: 'the factor which regulates the principle of demand, is essentially subject to the mutual relationship of the different classes and their respective economic position, notably therefore to, firstly, the ratio of total surplus-value to wages, and, secondly, to the relation of the various parts into which surplus-value is split up (profit, interest, ground-rent, taxes, etc.)'. 'Absolutely nothing', Marx concluded, 'can be explained by the relation of supply to demand before ascertaining the basis on which this relation rests'.

Marx, in fact, allowed a considerable degree of flexibility in patterns of demand as incomes (and prices) vary:

> It would seem, then, that there is on the side of demand a certain magnitude of definite social wants which require for their satisfaction a definite quantity of a commodity on the market. But quantitatively, the definite social wants are very elastic and changing. Their fixedness is only apparent. If the means of subsistence were cheaper, or money-wages higher, the labourers would buy more of them, and a greater 'social need' would arise for them, leaving aside the paupers, etc., whose 'demand' is even below the narrowest limits of their physical wants.... The limits within which the need for commodities in the *market*, the demand, differs quantitatively from the *actual social* need, naturally vary considerably for different commodities; what I mean is the difference between the demanded quantity of commodities and the quantity which would have been in demand at other money-prices or other money or living conditions of the buyers (p. 185).

Considering this insight into the impact of changing distribution on final demand, it is all the more important to take into account the possibility of a mutual relationship whereby an alteration in demand patterns plays back on distribution by way of the labour market.

15.5 The 'Scientific' Problem: Marx's Strategy

We come now to Marx's strategy, the reasons why he chose to present to the public a first volume turning on non-equilibrium exchange rates proportionate to labour inputs and differing profit rates, although he was in possession of a body of price theory of the 'orthodox' classical variety. As he explained in his chapter on the 'trinity formula' (III, ch. 48), his purpose was to combat any conception of factor returns suggesting that they 'grow out of the role played by the land, produced means of production, and labour'; that profit and rent 'arise from sources of their own, which are specifically different and independent of labour ... from the participating elements of production, to the share of whose owners they fall' (p. 805). In Marx's view, very graphically expressed, 'capital is a perennial pumping-machine of surplus-labour for the capitalist, land a perennial magnet for the landlord, attracting a portion of the surplus-value pumped out by capital, and finally, labour the constantly self-renewing condition and ever-renewing means of acquiring under the title of wages a portion of the value created by the labourer ...' (pp. 801–2).

But there were severe problems of proof. In general terms Marx operated on the methodological rule that 'all science would be superfluous if the outward appearance and the essence of things directly coincided' (p. 797). Unfortunately, Marx conceded, the 'outward appearance' of the competitive world of production and exchange favoured the 'erroneous' rather than his own view:

> The conversion of surplus-value into profit...is determined as much by the process of circulation as by the process of production. Surplus-value, in the form of profit, is no longer related back to that portion of capital invested in labour from which it arises, but to the total capital....A complicated social process intervenes here, the equalization process of capitals, which divorces the relative average prices of the commodities from their values, as well as the average profits in the various spheres of production...from the actual exploitation of labour by the particular capitals. Not only does it appear so, but it is true in fact that the average price of commodities differs from their value, thus from the labour realized in them, and the average profit of a particular capital differs from the surplus-value which this capital has extracted from the labourers employed by it....Normal average profits themselves seem immanent in capital and independent of exploitation (pp. 807–8).

Already in *Capital* I, Marx explains his procedure in precisely the same way. He starts from the assumption that labour is the source of surplus value:

> The labour which is set in motion by the total capital of the society, day in, day out, may be regarded as a single collective working-day. If, *e.g.*, the number of workers is a million and the average working-day of a labourer is 10 hours, the social working-day consists of ten million hours. With a given length of this working-day...the mass of surplus-value can only be increased by increasing the number of labourers, *i.e.*, of the labouring population. The growth of population here forms the mathematical limit to the production of surplus-value by the total social capital. On the contrary, with a given amount of population, the limit is formed by the possible lengthening of the working-day (I, 307).

But given this assumption regarding the generation of surplus by living labour, it ought to be the case that commodities in equilibrium exchange according to their labour input in order to assure the appropriate generation of surplus value; the higher the labour input relative to the machinery input, the higher should be the price in order to generate a higher surplus value, since surplus value is generated by living labour. But, as Marx recognized, such an outcome 'clearly contradicts all experience based upon appearance'. A baker earns no more profit per £100 invested in his business than a cotton manufacturer although more labour is employed per £100 investment. On this point Marx was adamant: 'There is no doubt...that aside from unessential, incidental and mutually compensating distinctions, differences in the average rate of profits in the various branches of industry do not exist in reality, and could not exist without abolishing the entire system of capitalist production' (III, 151).

Also relevant is a chapter entitled 'illusions created by competition' (III, ch. 50), where Marx focuses on the constancy of the value of the net product, his second identity. Here he sought again to counter the view suggested by too casual observation that wages, profits and rent represent 'the constituent elements which... are the source of the regulating price (natural price, *prix nécessaire*) of the commodities themselves', or that wages, profit and rent are 'three independent magnitudes of value, whose total magnitude produces, limits and determines the magnitude of the commodity-value' (p. 841). It is the Smithian view – the view that since natural price equals the sum of wages, profit and rent per unit, an increase in any constituent implies an increase in the whole price – to which he objected. For Marx, as for Ricardo, when wages rise, profits must fall because the total to be divided is constrained.

Following his general methodological rule regarding science, Marx sought to prove that rejection of labour as the source of profits by reference to the 'facts' of profit rate uniformity and disproportionality between equilibrium prices and labour inputs, would be illegitimate; exchange rates proportionate to prices rather than values, and surplus in each industry proportionate to total capital (not variable capital) – the 'observed' data – do not constitute proof against his interpretation of the source of profits. If the sum of profits in all sectors equals the sum of surplus values in all sectors, and if aggregate product in value terms equals aggregate product in price terms, then it could be maintained that the source of profits in the aggregate, despite market appearances, lay in surplus labour time.

The identity of aggregate surplus value and aggregate profits is, in fact, built into the transformation. The total amount of surplus available in the system – proportioned to the direct labour input by construction – is distributed as profit amongst all the capitalists in the system to secure profit rate equality. Surpluses generated in a particular sector do not (necessarily) remain to be enjoyed by that sector's capitalists. The relatively labour-intensive sectors subsidize the less labour-intensive sectors – the baker subsidizes the cotton manufacturer:

> Thus, although in selling their commodities the capitalists of the various spheres of production recover the value of the capital consumed in their production, they do not secure the surplus-value, and consequently the profit, created in their own sphere by the production of these commodities. What they secure is only as much surplus-value, and hence profit, as falls, when uniformly distributed, to the share of every aliquot part of the total social capital from the total social surplus-value, or profit, produced in a given time by the social capital in all spheres of production (p. 156).

Marx's strategy, designed to defend his approach to the source of profits, suggests that a mass of surplus value exists *prior to* the formation of prices, and is available for allocation among the various industries to assure profit rate equality. It would appear that distribution is settled in the 'value' scheme, and the results then utilized to derive prices in a causal sense. But this is in fact a misleading impression. Nothing in the way Marx laid out the scheme has any relevance to actual process analysis; certainly it is not true that prices are in some causal sense derived from values. Equally important, aggregate surplus value turns on the rate of exploitation, which is a variable partly dependent upon the pattern of demand, itself a function of distribution.

The identity between net income in the price and in the value schemes was utilized to investigate the inverse wage–profit relation, Marx reproducing Ricardo's construct of a product of constant value to be distributed between labour and capital (see above, p. 367). Nothing is added to the Ricardian analysis. Moreover, Ricardo's formulation had become standard doctrine by the time Marx was writing, and is to be found in the major orthodox texts. Here is a citation, for example, from the first edition of J. R. McCulloch's *Principles*:

> Though fluctuations in the rate of wages occasion some variation in the exchangeable value of particular commodities, they neither add not take from the *total value* of the entire mass of commodities. If they increase the value of those produced by the least durable capitals, they equally diminish the value of those produced by the more durable capitals. Their aggregate value continues, therefore, always the same. And though it may not be strictly true of a particular commodity, that its exchangeable value is directly as its *real* value, or as the quantity of labour required to produce it and bring it to market, it is most true to affirm this of the mass of commodities taken together (1825, 312–13).

McCulloch, long before Marx, was saying in very explicit terms that deviations of prices of production from values cancel out; and that it is this that counted for the derivation of the inverse profit–wage relationship.

John Stuart Mill's *Principles* had also reproduced the fundamental theorem on distribution and its derivation in terms of the standard measure; the category of wage increases that reduce profits is that entailing proportionate changes in distribution (see above, p. 144). Mill had also warned against drawing false conclusions from 'the outside surface of the economical machinery of society' (1848 [1965], II, 410), specifically the notion that profits somehow depend on prices when in fact their source is in surplus labour time:

> the reason why capital yields a profit, is because food, clothing, materials, and tools, last longer than the time which was required to produce them; so that if a capitalist supplies a party of labourers with these things, on condition of receiving all they produce, they will, in addition to repro-

ducing their own necessaries and instruments, have a portion of their time remaining, to work for the capitalist. We thus see that profit arises, not from the incident of exchange, but from the productive power of labour; and the general profit of the country is always what the productive power of labour makes it, whether any exchange takes place or not. If there were no division of employments, there would be no buying or selling, but there would still be profit. If the labourers of the country collectively produce twenty per cent more than their wages, profits will be twenty per cent, whatever prices may or may not be. The accidents of price may for a time make one set of producers get more than the twenty per cent, and another less, the one commodity being rated above the natural value in relation to other commodities, and the other below, until prices have again adjusted themselves; but there will always be just twenty per cent divided among them all (II, 411; the passage was first introduced into the 4th edition of 1857).

Despite all this, in his chapters on the 'trinity formula' and 'illusions created by competition' Marx gives the Ricardians at most backhanded compliments, ascribing to them an inevitable if unconscious bourgeois bias: 'even the best spokesmen of classical economy remain more or less in the grip of the world of illusion which their criticism had dissolved, as cannot be otherwise from a bourgeois standpoint, and thus they all fall more or less into inconsistencies, half-truths and unsolved contradictions' (*Capital*, III, 809). Even Ricardo, whom Marx much admired, does not escape. Ricardo, Marx asserted quite unfairly, 'naturally proceeds differently from us, since he did not understand the levelling of values to prices of production' (199n.). In fact, 'Ricardo never concerns himself about the origin of surplus-value. He treats it as a thing inherent in the capitalist mode of production, which mode, in his eyes, is the natural form of social production. Whenever he discusses the productiveness of labour, he seeks in it, not the cause of surplus-value, but the cause that determines the magnitude of that value' (I, 515–16). If this is true of Ricardo, who indeed did not *formally* address the issue of the source of profits – though it is implied unquestionably in his formulations – it is positively not true of Mill, who did so in the passage added in 1857. Yet Marx had this to say of Mill:

[Ricardo's] school has openly proclaimed the productiveness of labour to be the originating cause of profit (read: surplus-value). This at all events is a progress as against the mercantilists who, on their side, derived the excess of the price over the cost of production of the product, from the act of exchange, from the product being sold above its value. Nevertheless, Ricardo's school simply shirked the problem, they did not solve it. In fact these bourgeois economists instinctively saw, and rightly so, that it is very dangerous to stir too deeply the burning question of the origin of surplus-value. But what are we to think of John Stuart Mill, who, half a century after Ricardo, solemnly claims superiority over the mercantilists, by clumsily repeating the wretched evasions of Ricardo's earliest vulgarizers? (p. 516).

Marx's reaction to J. S. Mill was the subject of a sharp objection by L. von Bortkiewicz in 1907, which is worth reproducing:

> Marx comments on this passage [of 1857] that 'Mill here confuses the duration of the working-time with the duration of its products' [I, 516]. In doing so, Marx suppresses the second half of the quotation, which removes any doubt of the fact that Mill deduces profit from surplus value, just as Marx does. Mill goes on to show that profit is conditioned, not by exchange, but by the productive power of labour. Were there no division of labour, says Mill, there would be neither selling nor buying, but profit would continue to exist. One would think that at least with this assertion, Mill would draw a word of approval from his severe critic. But no! Marx pretends to be shocked: 'Here', says he, 'exchange, sale and purchase, the general conditions of capitalist production are thus sheer accessories, and yet there still subsists profit without the sale or purchase of labour power!' [I, 516]. It is, however, clear that Mill did not mean the buying and selling of labour power, but merely the buying and selling of products. One will not go wrong if one connects the ill will which Marx displays towards Mill, with the circumstance that Mill had, basically, anticipated Marx's theory of surplus value (1907 [1952], 52–3n.).

But can one go beyond 'ill will'? What appears to have irked Marx is the failure of Mill, as he read him, to get to grips with the institutional circumstances which defined capitalist organization. Without question surplus labour time was a *necessary condition* for capitalism as for all other forms of exploitation – that was not at issue:

> If the labourer wants all his time to produce the necessary means of subsistence for himself and his race, he has no time left in which to work gratis for others. Without a certain degree of productiveness in his labour, he has no such superfluous time at his disposal; without such superfluous time, no surplus-labour, and therefore no capitalists, no slave-owners, no feudal lords, in one word, no class of large proprietors (*Capital*, I, 511).

But the generation of *surplus value* or profit (as distinct from the general categories surplus labour and surplus product) characterized a capitalist market economy alone; and for this to arise, specific institutional conditions had to be satisfied, particularly those allowing the purchase and sale of labour power. Mill had hit upon a necessary condition but had failed to carry the investigation far enough to arrive at the sufficient conditions. That, at least, was the charge, and it is implied that Mill deliberately evaded this aspect of the source of profits for ideological reasons – a charge which scarcely seems justified when levelled at Mill of all people.

A second but related objection to Mill is also apparent. The year 1830 constituted for Marx the dividing line between 'scientific' and 'apologetic' economics. This reading of the literature appears, for example, in early draft notes (the *Grundrisse*) written in 1857:

> The history of modern political economy ends with Ricardo and Sismondi.... Subsequent political-economic literature loses its way, moving either toward eclectic, syncretistic compendia, such as e.g., the work of J. St. Mill, or into deeper elaboration of individual branches... or the reproduction of old economic disputes for a wider public, and the practical solution of questions of the day... – or, finally, into tendentious exaggerations of the classical tendencies ([1973], 883).

An illustration of Mill's 'eclectic syncretism' is that he 'accepts on the one hand Ricardo's theory of profit, and annexes on the other hand Senior's "remuneration of abstinence". He is as much at home in absurd contradictions, as he feels at sea in the Hegelian contradiction, the source of all dialectic' (*Capital*, I, 596n.). Similarly, in *Theories of Surplus Value*:

> It is incomprehensible how economists like John Stuart Mill, who are Ricardians and even express the principle that profit is equal to surplus-value, surplus labour, in the form that the rate of profit and wages stand in inverse ratio to one another and that the rate of wages determines the rate of profit (which is incorrect when put in this form), suddenly convert industrial profit into the individual labour of the capitalist instead of into the surplus labour of the worker, unless the function of exploitation of other people's labour is called labour by them (1862–3 [1971], III, 506).

Now there does not appear, in fact, to be good reason to avoid the simultaneous adoption of a concept of profit envisaged as a residual arising from surplus labour time, and the abstinence theory; the one is the basis for investment demand, while the other relates to capital supply conditions and contributes therefore to the actual determination of surplus labour time. For the wage rate is a variable partly governed by capital supply conditions; the 'necessary' part of the work day is as much a consequence as a determinant of the 'surplus' part. To isolate the source of profit in surplus labour time does not rule out the conception of interest as a necessary reward. Marx did not make out a valid case against Mill.

15.6   Marx and Malthusianism

Our next general topic concerns the trend paths of the wage and profit rates, and here it is necessary to prepare the ground by reference to Marx's attitude towards Malthus.

Marx identified the 'Malthusian' doctrine with the 'iron law of wages', and read it as precluding improvement under any form of institutional arrangements, whether capitalist or socialist. This is clear from his reaction in 1875 to Ferdinand Lassalle's proposal that 'the German Workers' Party strives...for...the abolition of the wage system together with the iron law of wages':

> if [the Malthusian theory] is correct, then again I *cannot* abolish the law even if I abolish wage labour a hundred times over, because the law then governs not only the system of wage labour but *every* social system. Basing themselves directly on this, the economists have been proving for fifty years and more that socialism cannot abolish poverty, *which has its basis in nature*, but can only make it *general*, distribute it simultaneously over the whole surface of society! (Marx–Engels, 1958, II, 28–9).

In fact, as Marx insisted in *Capital*, 'every special historic mode of production has its own special laws of population, historically valid within its limits alone. An abstract law of population exists for plants and animals only, and only in so far as man has not interfered with them' (I, 632). The success of Malthus's *Essay on Population* is said to have been due 'to party interest' (p. 616n.); the principle of population had been 'greeted with jubilance by the English oligarchy as the great destroyer of all hankerings after human development'. Marx's vituperations reach new heights in *Theories of Surplus Value*:

> The parson Malthus...reduces the worker to a beast of burden for the sake of production and even condemns him to death from starvation, and to celibacy....The scientific conclusions of Malthus are '*considerate*' towards the ruling classes...he *falsifies* science for these interests. But his conclusions are *ruthless*; he *affects* ruthlessness; he takes a cynical pleasure in it and *exaggerates* his conclusions in so far as they are directed against the poor wretches, even *beyond* the point which would be scientifically justified from his point of view (1862–3 [1968], II, 119–20).

As a representation of Malthus's position, and that of the mainstream of British classical orthodoxy, Marx's account is a travesty. It was a central theme of J. S. Mill's social philosophy that Malthusianism, as understood by the Philosophical Radicals, was a *reformist* doctrine indicating the means for 'securing full employment at high wages to the whole labouring population' (1981, I, 107). In fact, Mill ascribed anti-Malthusianism to apologetic class interests – an upper-class attempt to placate labour and avoid revolution: 'I never remember a time', he wrote in 1844, 'when any suggestion of anti-population doctrine or of forethought and self-command on the part of the poor was so contemptuously scouted as it is now. The "Times" is at the head of this movement, and has contributed very much to set it going' (1963, XIII, 641).

'Malthusianism', as understood by the classical economists including Malthus, was clearly not a universalist doctrine regarding the non-improvability of mankind as Marx maintained. The 'prudential wage' growth model (see above, pp. 203–4) is evidence of that.

On the other hand, radical institutional change would not, on the classical view, in itself provide the answer to low standards of living, for excessive population growth would still have to be avoided. It is in these terms that Mill weighed the relative advantages of alternative regimes. For Mill the outcome was still unclear: 'We are too ignorant either of what individual agency in its best form, or Socialism in its best form, can accomplish, to be qualified to decide which of the two will be the ultimate form of human society' (1848 [1965], II, 208). Friedrich Engels by contrast (and presumably Marx) already had the answer – population control would be possible only under Communism: 'if at some stage communist society finds itself obliged to regulate the production of human beings ... it will be precisely this society, and this society alone, which can carry this out without difficulty' (Engels to Kautsky, 1 February 1881; in Meek, 1971, 120).

While Mill was uncertain of the balance of prospects in any comparison between alternative regimes, he was not prepared to accept the prediction, as by Louis Blanc, of an actually falling wage trend in contemporary circumstances. This prediction, he maintained in his 'Chapters on Socialism' (1869), was based on an 'ignorance of economic facts, and of the causes by which the economic phenomena of society as it is are actually determined' (Mill, 1967, V, 727). As to the facts regarding earnings, even population pressure was no longer an 'irrepressible tendency' and an 'increasing evil' considering the rapid acceleration of capital accumulation, easier emigration (due to transportation advances and improved knowledge) and increased 'prudence' (p. 728). By contrast, Engel's comment suggests that excessive population growth was inevitable under capitalism; and that this was indeed the Marxist position will be documented below with special reference to the falling trend in real wages.

15.7 The Falling Wage Trend

There is a singular unwillingness on the part of many commentators to recognize Marx's pronouncements regarding the tendency of the commodity wage to decline (the law of immiseration under capitalism). Some Marxologists admit a secular decline in the value of labour power, but they insist it reflects increasing productivity cheapening the costs of wage goods (such decline being consistent even with rising commodity wages); or they allow only a relative decline in real wages compared with the return to property.

In a talk of 1865 to a working class audience ('Wages, Price and Profit'), Marx is absolutely clear that the commodity wages of the employed work force tend downwards. He refers to the 'continuous struggle between capital and labour, the capitalist constantly tending to reduce wages to their physical minimum, and to extend the working day to its physical maximum, while the working man constantly presses in the opposite direction' (Marx–Engels, 1958, I, 443). 'The very development of modern industry', he continues, 'must progressively turn the scale in favour of the capitalist against the working man, and that consequently the general tendency of capitalistic production is not to raise, but to sink the average standard of wages, or to push the *value of labour* more or less to its *minimum limit*' (p. 446). He warns that were the labourers to 'abandon their attempts at making the best of the occasional chances for their temporary improvement ... they would be degraded to one level mass of broken wretches past salvation'; yet they cannot by union activity reverse or even prevent the downward trend: 'the working class ought not to exaggerate to themselves the ultimate working of these everyday struggles. They ought not to forget that they are fighting with effects, but not with the causes of those effects; that they are retarding the downward movement, but not changing its direction; that they are applying palliatives, not curing the malady'. There can be no doubt that this discussion refers to the commodity wage.

In *Capital*, Marx declaimed regarding the labourer's worsening condition in consequence of technological advance, 'the higher the productiveness of labour, the greater is the pressure of the labourers on the means of employment, the more precarious, therefore, becomes their condition of existence, viz., the sale of their own labour-power for the increasing of another's wealth' (I, 645). Consider also the account of 'the material conditions' of factory labour which should certainly be included in any measure of the commodity wage:

> Economy of the social means of production, matured and forced as in a hothouse by the factory system, is turned, in the hands of capital, into systematic robbery of what is necessary for the life of the workman while he is at work, robbery of space, light, air, and of protection to his person against the dangerous and unwholesome accompaniments of the productive process, not to mention the robbery of appliances for the comfort of the workman (pp. 426–7).

The falling commodity wage is a refrain repeatedly heard. Marx cites Ricardo: 'The same cause which may increase the revenue of the country [rent and profit], may at the same time render the population redundant and deteriorate the condition of the labourer' (p. 432n.).

Andrew Ure is cited to similar effect regarding the impact of improvement of machinery within 'Modern Industry'. 'The effect of improvements in machinery, not merely in superseding the necessity for the employment of the same quantity of adult labour as before, in order to produce a given result, but in substituting one description of human labour for another, the less skilled for the more skilled, juvenile for adult, female for male, causes a fresh disturbance in the rate of wages' (p. 433). Declining commodity wages is a key feature of the account of the cotton industry during the 1860s: 'the inventive spirit of the master never stood still, but was exercised in making deductions from wages', a trend supplemented by a deterioration in work conditions (p. 457). The net outcome of cyclical periods of crisis and depression was a 'general reduction of wages', the period 1815–63 including 'only 20 years of revival and prosperity against 28 of depression and stagnation' (p. 458). Finally, whereas Marx accepted Gladstone's reference in 1843 to the 'decrease in the consuming powers of the people', he rejected his assertion in 1863 that the poor 'have been growing less poor' (p. 651).

Some confusion has been created in the secondary literature by a famous statement that 'in proportion as capital accumulates, the lot of the labourer, be his payment high or low, must grow worse' (p. 645). It is sometimes said that this formulation allows one to conceive of increasing 'immiseration' despite rising real wages, the 'worsening payment' understood as relative to property income. But given our evidence of declining commodity wages it is much more likely that Marx intended a decline in the general rate which affects all classes of labourers – those high on the wage scale as well as those at a lower level. (On sectoral differentials, cf. pp. 653, 659, 667ff).

15.8 Labour Market Conditions and the Role of Population Pressure

To clarify the Marxian growth path of wages the relation between the orthodox 'subsistence' wage and Marx's 'value of labour power' must be defined. In his speech on 'Wages, Price and Profit' of 1865, market wages are said to tend towards equality with 'the value of labour power'. This latter comprises both a 'physical element' (corresponding to 'the necessaries absolutely indispensable for living and multiplying') which forms the minimum limit to the wage defined as an (apparently unchangeable) physiological quantum, and a cultural element reflecting the 'traditional standard of life', which is represented as variable (Marx–Engels, 1958, I, 441–2). Thus, 'by comparing the standard wages or values of labour in different countries, and by comparing them in different historical epochs of the same country, you will find that the *value of labour* itself is not a fixed but a variable magnitude, even supposing the values of all other commodities to remain constant' (p. 443). For the present we may, therefore, assume that the value of labour power reflects variations in the magnitude of the wage basket rather than variations in the cost of producing a given basket.

Wages reflecting the 'physical element' permit labour merely 'to perpetuate its physical existence'; at the physical limit the wage is just equal to an amount 'necessary for the physical perpetuation of the race' (pp. 442–3). The 'ultimate limit' to the wage corresponds therefore to the orthodox subsistence wage, or that wage assuring zero population growth. But a wage equal to the value of labour power is consistent with net population growth when allowance is made therein for the cultural element. (Here is a source of confusion, since for the orthodox economists the zero growth wage itself contained a cultural element.) In *Capital* too will be found the minimum wage defined with reference to constancy of population:

> The labour-power withdrawn from the market by wear and tear and death, must be continually replaced by, at the very least, an equal amount of fresh labour-power. Hence the sum of the means of subsistence necessary for the production of labour-power must include the means necessary for the labourer's substitutes, *i.e.*, his children, in order that this race of peculiar commodity-owners may perpetuate its appearance in the market (I, 172).

In this particular context Marx stressed the constancy, at any particular stage of historical development, of the 'value of labour power', by which expression he intended not merely the minimum wage but the minimum supplemented by the cultural element – the labourer's 'necessary' in addition to his 'natural' wants – an element governed by the habits under which 'the class of free labourers has been formed', in contrast to the 'natural' element which varies 'according to the climatic and other physical conditions of the country' (p. 171). We shall see presently that in the full analysis of the growth process the value of labour power is treated in *Capital* (as in the speech of 1865) as a variable – this is, in fact, what the falling wage trend entails. At this point it is the Marxian position that a wage equal to the supposedly known value of labour power is consistent with population growth that I wish to establish.

On this Marx is quite clear in a passage which also nicely encapsulates the meaning of real investment. In a growing system the long-run wage rate, while equal to the value of labour power, exceeds the 'subsistence' rate at which population growth ceases; population growth is, as it were, built into the value of labour power:

To accumulate it is necessary to convert a portion of the surplus-product into capital. But we cannot...convert into capital anything but such articles as can be employed in the labour process (*i.e.*, means of production), and such further articles as are suitable for the sustenance of the labourer (*i.e.*, means of subsistence)....

Now in order to allow of these elements actually functioning as capital, the capitalist class requires additional labour. If the exploitation of the labourers already employed do not increase, either extensively or intensively, then additional labour-power must be found. For this the mechanism of capitalist production provides beforehand, by converting the working-class into a class dependent on wages, a class whose ordinary wages suffice, not only for its maintenance, but for its increase. It is only necessary for capital to incorporate this additional labour-power, annually supplied by the working-class in the shape of labourers of all ages, with the surplus means of production comprised in the annual produce, and the conversion of surplus-value into capital is complete (I, 580–1).

The working-class must find at least the same quantity of necessities on hand if it is to continue living in its accustomed average way....Moreover, there must be an additional quantity to allow for the annual increase of population (III, 184–5).

Let us now consider more closely the labour supply function. Labourers engaged in the centres of modern industry – 'factories, manufactures, iron works, mines, &c.' as distinct from 'domestic industry' – constitute a category with a particularly high death rate and extremely short life span: 'The consumption of labour-power by capital is...so rapid that the labourer, half-way through his life, has already more or less completely lived himself out....It is precisely among the workpeople of modern industry that we meet with the shortest duration of life' (I, 641). Marx, taking for granted net population growth as an aspect of the general process of capitalist development, points to peculiarly high marriage and birth rates to assure such growth notwithstanding the high death rate:

In order to conform to these circumstances [physical disability and high mortality], the absolute increase of this section of the proletariat must take place under conditions that shall swell their numbers, although the individual elements are used up rapidly. Hence, rapid renewal of the generations of labourers (this law does not hold for the other classes of the population). This social need is met by early marriages, a necessary consequence of the conditions in which the labourers of modern industry live, and by the premium that the exploitation of children sets on their production (p. 642).

The net increase in labour supply in the modern industrial sector is thus a consequence of population growth internal to that sector.

In some contexts Marx allows explicitly for population response to the level of wages. An important instance is encountered in a discussion of upward pressure on wages exerted by particularly rapid accumulation: 'Prosperity would have led to more marriages among labourers and reduced the decimation of offspring' (III, 249); 'a momentary excess of surplus-capital over the working population it has commandeered, would ... by raising wages, mitigate the adverse conditions which decimate the offspring of the labourers and would make marriages easier among them, so as to gradually increase the population' (p. 214). Yet, conversely, we also read that a fall in wages would 'be a breeding ground for a really swift propagation of the population, since under capitalist production misery produces population' (p. 214). Similarly, in volume I:

> not only the number of births and deaths, but the absolute size of the families stand in inverse proportion to the height of wages, and therefore to the amount of means of subsistence of which the different categories of labourers dispose. This law of capitalist society would sound absurd to savages, or even civilised colonists. It calls to mind the boundless reproduction of animals individually weak and constantly hunted down (I, 643).

There is no paradox in the proposition that both wage increases and wage decreases are consistent with an increased rate of population growth. Any given standard of life reflects a specific level of the 'value of labour power'; a wage increase, given the standard, will stimulate an increased population growth rate, and a wage decrease a decline. This much for fluctuations of the wage about a given standard: but should the fall in the wage entail a fall in the standard itself (in the value of labour power), matters are very different – at the lower standard the population growth rate may remain constant, or indeed may even rise compared to the original level if the degradation is sufficiently marked. This latter possibility was to play a role in the full account of the downward wage path.

*   *   *

We turn next to labour demand. In the earliest stages of capitalism, accumulation proceeds with (average) organic composition unchanged, the demand for labour rising (at any given wage) in proportion to the rate of accumulation. Following Adam Smith, Marx maintains that the wage will be higher the higher the rate of capital accumulation: 'According to the economists themselves, it is neither the actual extent of social wealth, nor the magnitude of the capital already functioning, that lead to a rise of wages, but only the constant growth of accumulation and the degree of rapidity of that growth (Adam Smith, Book I, chapter 8)' (*Capital*, I, 621).

At the outset of the chapter under consideration Marx postulates conditions generating a 'sudden' extension in 'the scale of accumulation' which forces wages upwards in so far as 'the requirements of accumulating capital ... exceed the increase of labour-power or of the number of labourers.... For since in each year more labourers are employed than in its predecessor, sooner or later a point must be reached, at which the requirements of accumulation begin to surpass the customary supply of labour, and, therefore, a rise of wages takes place' (p. 613). It is thus to deviations between the growth rates of labour demand and supply that Marx attributes the wage movement.

Given labour productivity, rising wages imply, of course, a corresponding reduction in the profit rate. Smith is cited to the effect that any such reduction has no depressing effect on accumulation since 'a great stock, though with small profits, generally increases faster than a small stock with great profits' (p. 619); but Marx did not quite commit himself for he allowed also for the possibility of a slowdown in accumulation, since the 'stimulus of gain is blunted', such slowdown acting as a corrective with the result that 'the price of labour falls again to a level corresponding with the needs of the self-expansion of capital, whether the level be below, the same as, or above the one which was normal before the rise of wages took place'. This is problematic for there is no patent reason why a deceleration in accumulation due to the rise in wages should be able to force wages back to, and even below, its initial level. But Marx does later make the more reasonable allowance that the correction reduces the wage but to a level somewhat higher than at the start, thus allowing for an upward trend in wages (p. 621).

In all this nothing is said of the effect of the higher wage on the growth rate of labour supply. The reference to 'the customary supply of labour' suggests, in fact, a given growth rate. But there is in principle no reason to exclude a positive effect due to the wage increase, thus adding a second corrective – unless it is supposed that the standard itself, which reflects the value of labour power, shifts upwards.

We now introduce the complexity of a changing organic composition of capital – the source of the so-called Industrial Reserve Army and of falling secular wages – 'that change in the technical composition of capital by which the variable constituent becomes always smaller and smaller as compared with the constant' (p. 624). Exogenous technical change takes precedence by far over wage-induced substitution against labour, Marx drawing *inter alia* upon Ricardo and John Barton (p. 631n.; Marx–Engels, 1958, I, 445).

First we note that it is not merely the additions to capital which embody the new technologies that entail altered composition; the entire capital stock ultimately comes to be transformed:

> The additional capitals formed in the normal course of accumulation ... serve particularly as vehicles for the exploitation of new inventions and discoveries, and industrial improvements in general. But in time the old capital also reaches the moment of renewal from top to toe, when it sheds its skin and is reborn like the others in perfected technical form, in which a smaller quantity of labour will suffice to set in motion a larger quantity of machinery and raw materials....
>
> On the one hand, therefore, the additional capital formed in the course of accumulation, attracts fewer and fewer labourers in proportion to its magnitude. On the other hand, the old capital periodically reproduced with change of composition, repels more and more of the labourers formerly employed by it (*Capital*, I, 628).

Now an absolute fall in the demand for labour in consequence of the altered composition is not what Marx had in mind in the advanced industrial sector. The net outcome of an expanding aggregate capital stock and altering capital composition is said to be expanded demand for labour, though at a decelerating rate:

> Since the demand for labour is determined not by the amount of capital as a whole, but by its variable constituent alone, that demand falls progressively with the increase of total capital, instead of, as previously assumed, rising in proportion to it. It falls relatively to the magnitude of the total capital, and at an accelerated rate, as this magnitude increases. With the growth of the total capital, its variable constituent or the labour incorporated in it, also does increase, but in a constantly diminishing proportion (p. 629).

An absolute expansion of labour demand is frequently reiterated: 'In the centres of modern industry ... the labourers are sometimes repelled, sometimes attracted again in greater masses, the number of those employed increasing on the whole, although in a constantly decreasing proportion to the scale of production' (p. 641). In one of the most remarkable pronouncements in his supposedly revolutionary tract, Marx asserts that 'a development of productive forces which would diminish the absolute number of labourers, i.e., enable the entire nation to accomplish its total production in a shorter time span, would cause a revolution, because it would put the bulk of the population out of the running' (III, 258).

*   *   *

Labour demand therefore is increasing. What then is the problem? Why the creation of excess labour supply with downward pressure on the wage? The answer evidently lies in the assumption of on-going population growth – the 'additional labour-power, annually supplied by the working-class in the shape of labourers of all ages' (see above, p. 383). It follows that 'what are set free [by technical progress] are not only the labourers immediately turned out by the machines, but also their future substitutes in the rising generation, and the additional contingent, that with the usual extension of trade on the old basis would be regularly absorbed' (I, 639). And the consequence of the deviation between the growth rates of labour demand and supply is a reduction in real wages:

> The first word of this adaptation [of variable into constant capital] is the creation of a relative surplus-population, or industrial reserve army. Its last word is the misery of constantly extending strata of the active army of labour, and the dead weight of pauperism.... [The] higher the productiveness of labour, the greater is the pressure of the labourers on the means of employment, the more precarious, therefore, becomes their condition of existence, viz., the sale of their own labour-power for the increasing of another's wealth, or for the self-expansion of capital (pp. 664–5).

This picture should be contrasted with that in the colonies (pp. 769–70), or with early capitalism, with their upward wage trends due to deviations in factor growth rates favouring labour.

The problem is summarized in a passage which appears at first sight rather mysterious, since reference is made to 'an *apparently* absolute increase of the labouring population' (my emphasis) when we know that Marx has presumed throughout an *actual* absolute increase in population (even in employment, considering the net expansion of labour demand):

> [The] accelerated relative diminution of the variable constituent, that goes along with the accelerated increase of the total capital, and moves more rapidly than this increase, takes the inverse form, at the other pole, of an apparently absolute increase of the labouring population, an increase always moving more rapidly than that of the variable capital or the means of employment. But in fact, it is capitalistic accumulation itself that constantly produces, and produces in the direct ratio of its own energy and extent, a relatively redundant population of labourers, *i.e.*, a population of greater extent than suffices for the average needs of the self-expansion of capital, and therefore a surplus-population (p. 630; cf. 633).

The mystery is resolved if we understand Marx's intention to be the denial that the problem of excess labour supply was 'due to' population growth as the active cause. That on-going population growth occurs is not in doubt; but the problem of excess labour supply has its immediate source in a falling rate of growth of labour demand.

Marx's seeming denial of an absolute increase in population emerges also during the course of a formal critique of Malthus, the complaint that while Malthus had recognized 'over-population as a necessity of modern industry' he had 'after his narrow fashion' explained it 'by the absolute over-growth of the labouring population, not by their becoming relatively supernumerary' (p. 634). But Marx's position here may be appreciated as a denial of any problem of absolute population growth relative to land and manifested in diminishing agricultural productivity; increasing productivity – new technology – is the key. This is how the matter is summarized in volume III, in passages unambiguously allowing for on-going population expansion:

> ...the possibility of a relative surplus of labouring people develops proportionately to the advances made by capitalist production not because the productiveness of social labour *decreases*, but because it *increases*. It does not therefore arise out of an absolute disproportion between labour and the means of subsistence, or the means for the production of these means of subsistence, but out of a disproportion occasioned by capitalist exploitation of labour, a disproportion between the progressive growth of capital and *its relatively shrinking need for an increasing population*....[As] the capitalist mode of production develops, an ever larger quantity of capital is required to employ the same, *let alone an increased*, amount of labour-power. Thus, on a capitalist foundation, the increasing productiveness of labour necessarily and permanently creates a seeming over-population of labouring people (III, 217–19; emphasis added).

The fact of on-going population growth is thus beyond doubt, as is the relatively slower growth of labour demand. And, to repeat (in terms of the speech of 1865) the consequence is a reduction in the value of labour power 'to its minimum limit'. The major forces at work are portrayed in figure 15.1.

The downward wage trend could not be avoided by trade union counter-pressure: 'The matter resolves itself into a question of the respective powers of the combatants', but the advantage lay with the employers (Marx–Engels, 1958, I, 443). This evaluation in fact plays a key part in Marx's general political strategy – his call for a 'reconstruction of society'; for the working class can at best only retard the downward movement of wages but not change its direction:

> They ought, therefore, not to be exclusively absorbed in these unavoidable guerilla fights incessantly springing up from the never-ceasing encroachments of capital or changes in the market. They ought to understand that with all the miseries it imposes upon them, the present system

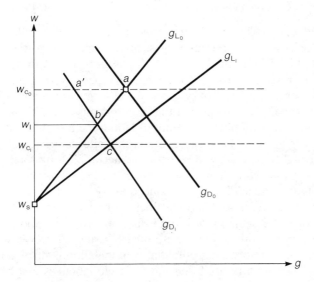

w_s represents the physiological subsistence minimum at which the growth rate of labour supply has fallen to zero, and w_{c_0} the culturally determined 'value of labour power'. The negative slope to g_D implies an allowance for a degree of substitution in favour of labour-intensive products and processes upon wage reductions. The positive slope to g_L reflects positive responses of population growth upon wage variations from w_c.

A fall in the growth rate of labour demand from g_{D_0} to g_{D_1} will generate a reduced wage rate until $w_1 < w_{c_0}$, i.e., a wage *below* the 'value of labour power' (at b). But the existence of the cultural 'minimum' indicates that if growth of labour demand remains stable at g_{D_1} long enough, there will be a reduction in population growth raising the wage back towards w_{c_0} (at a').

A reduction in the value of labour power itself is tantamount to a fall in standards from w_{c_0}. Assume that this takes the value w_{c_1}. At w_1 the growth rate of labour supply will now exceed $w_1 b$ forcing the wage rate to its new cultural 'minimum', with $g_L = g_D$ at c.

Through c, there passes a 'short-run' g_L curve describing population growth reactions to changes in the wage about w_{c_1}. This curve (g_{L_1}) lies to the right of g_{L_0} reflecting Marx's dictum that 'misery produces population'. Marx's account of capitalist development involves *continuous* inward shifts of g_D accompanied by downward shifts of w_c (and thus outward pivots of g_L). So that there is continuous downward pressure on the wage toward w_s.

We neglect for simplicity reductions in the value of labour power reflecting technical progress in wage-goods production.

Figure 15.1   Marx: labour market trends.

simultaneously engenders the *material conditions* and the *social forms* necessary for an economical reconstruction of society (p. 446).

Doubtless population pressure relative to labour demand is not the only force at work depressing wages. Marx's reference to the employment of child labour made possible by 'improvements in machinery' causing a 'fresh disturbance to the rate of wages' (see above, p. 381) implies a force supplementary to those we have been elaborating. On the other hand, a statement that the requirements of capital accumulation entail 'larger numbers of youthful labourers, a smaller number of adults' (*Capital*, I, 641), suggests a possible alternative reading of the inconceivability that the 'entire nation...accomplish its total production in a shorter time span' (see above, p. 386). For this raises the possibility that the adult wage is reduced in consequence of an *absolute fall* in the demand for adult labour, albeit more than compensated for by an *increase* in the demand for juvenile labour. (Women's labour and displacement by unskilled labour raise further issues.) Yet even were this the case, the countervailing potential of population control cannot be neglected; for the increased demand for child labour is met by a high birth rate, a reduction of which would surely reduce the attractiveness of this source of supply and lessen the downward pressure on the adult wage. In any event, we must not forget Marx's reference to population increase 'in the shape of labourers of all ages' alluded to already.

15.9 The Industrial Reserve Army and Cyclical Wage Fluctuations

The falling secular wage does not act as a corrective to excess labour supply in so far as the population growth rate is concerned – on the contrary, the fall in standards may be such that the rate of growth of population even accelerates. On the other hand, workers displaced are to some extent reabsorbed at lower wages into labour-intensive sectors (*Capital*, III, 232). Yet any stimulation to labour demand could at best act as a partial corrective, for the conversion of variable into constant capital is an on-going process, proceeding at an ever-faster rate, which – bearing in mind steady and possibly accelerating population growth – continually reconstitutes the excess labour supply and assures continuous downward pressure on the wage.

But while the trend path of wages is certainly downward, allowance must be made for cyclical fluctuations about the trend, and the possibility even of periods of constant wages. These short-term plateaux must not be mistaken for the secular trend itself, as may be easy to do. I touch here on the role of the 'Reserve Army of Unemployed' in providing a source of available labour to satisfy cyclical bursts of activity:

> But if a surplus labouring population is a necessary product of accumulation or of the development of wealth on a capitalist basis, this surplus-population becomes, conversely, the lever of capitalistic accumulation, nay, a condition of existence of the capitalist mode of production. It forms a disposable industrial reserve army, that belongs to capital quite as absolutely as if the latter had bred it at its own cost. Independently of the limits of the actual increase of population, it creates, for the changing needs of the self-expansion of capital, a mass of human material always ready for exploitation. With accumulation, and the development of the productiveness of labour that accompanies it, the power of sudden expansion of capital grows also; ... there must be the possibility of throwing great masses of men suddenly on the decisive points without injury to the scale of production in other spheres. Over-population supplies these means. The course characteristic of modern industry, viz. a decennial cycle (interrupted by smaller oscillations), of periods of average activity, production at high pressure, crisis and stagnation, depends on the constant formation, the greater or less absorption, and the re-formation of the industrial reserve army or surplus-population (I, 632–3).

This pattern stands in sharp contrast to early capitalist experience where net accumulation, and the corresponding net increase in labour demand, although of slow growth, 'found a check in the natural limits of the exploitable labouring population'. What was now occurring was 'expansion by fits and starts of the scale of production', calling for 'an increase in the number of labourers independently of the absolute growth of the population'.

The argument to this point implies that cyclical variations in employment can occur without pressure on wages. Yet this requires qualification. Wages may yet fluctuate (within limits) governed by the extent of the excess labour supply:

> Taking them as a whole, the general movement of wages are exclusively regulated by the expansion and contraction of the industrial reserve army, and these again correspond to the periodic changes of the industrial cycle. They are, therefore, not determined by the variations in the absolute number of the working population, but by the varying proportions in which the working-class is divided into active and reserve army, by the increase or diminution in the relative amount of the surplus-population, by the extent to which it is now absorbed, now set free. For Modern Industry with its decennial cycles and periodic phases, which, moreover, as accumulation advances, are complicated by irregular oscillations following each other more and more quickly, that would indeed be a beautiful law, which pretends to make the action of capital dependent on the absolute variation of the population, instead of regulat-

ing the demand and supply of labour by the alternate expansion and contraction of capital, the labour-market now appearing relatively under-full, because capital is expanding, now again over-full, because it is contracting (p. 637).

'Thus the law of supply and demand of labour is kept in the right rut, the oscillation of wages is penned within limits satisfactory to capitalist exploitation . . .' (p. 769).

15.10   Inter-Sectoral Labour Movements

We return to the downward secular trend in the real wage. This trend was particularly marked in the agricultural sector and had there been under way since the late eighteenth century (*Capital*, I, 673). Indeed, Marx maintained that wages had there actually fallen 'to the minimum', the agricultural labourer standing 'with one foot already in the swamp of pauperism' in consequence of absolute reduction in labour demand (p. 642). Can the wage decline in the advanced industrial sector be explained by an inflow from agriculture (cf. p. 708)? It seems not. Consider again Marx's declaration that 'a development of productive forces which would diminish the absolute number of labourers . . . would cause a revolution, because it would put the bulk of the population out of the running' (see above, p. 386). This appears to mean that the net increase in labour demand in the advanced industrial sector exceeds the net decrease in agriculture and elsewhere. Under such conditions even were the entire displaced agricultural labour force to flow into the modern industrial sector there should be no downward pressure on the real wage – unless there is some further source supplementing net labour supply.

But there is a further matter. Marx seems to reason as if such transfers as occur are largely the response to cyclical peaks of industrial activity. If this is so then a flow from agriculture at the most puts a damper on the extent industrial wages can rise cyclically. We have seen that the function of the Industrial Reserve Army is to provide 'the possibility of throwing great masses of men suddenly on the decisive points without injury to the scale of production in other spheres'. Agricultural labour would doubtless provide one source (cf. pp. 662–3). Moreover, part of the outflow from agriculture is to non-industrial urban occupations – in which case it would have little if any effect on industrial wages. These propositions are supported by the following text:

> As soon as capitalist production takes possession of agriculture, and in proportion to the extent to which it does so, the demand for an agri-

cultural labouring population falls absolutely, while the accumulation of capital employed in agriculture advances, without this repulsion being, as in non-agricultural industries, compensated by a greater attraction. Part of the agricultural population is therefore constantly on the point of passing over into an urban or manufacturing proletariat, and *on the look-out for circumstances favourable to this transformation.* (Manufacture is used here in the sense of all non-agricultural industries.) This source of relative surplus-population is thus constantly flowing. But the constant flow towards the towns presupposes, in the country itself, a constant latent surplus-population, the extent of which becomes evident only when its channels of outlet open to *exceptional width* (p. 642; emphasis added).

Marx also goes out of his way to emphasize the attraction provided by the non-industrial urban sector, and the likely destiny of the agricultural emigrant within the town's 'pauper' population.

There is yet to consider the 'domestic industry' segment of the urban population, which provides capital with 'an inexhaustible reservoir of disposable labour-power' (p. 643). For 'its conditions of life sink below the average normal level of the working-class; this makes it at once the broad basis of special branches of capitalist exploitation. It is characterised by maximum of working-time, and minimum of wages.' Again, Marx gives the impression that, at most, the advanced industrial sector draws upon this sector for its exceptional needs – otherwise it is incomprehensible that the wage differential should not be eradicated. As for secular trends, it is helpful to think of the non-industrial urban sector as impinged upon by tendencies in the advanced industrial sector (and in agriculture) rather than the reverse: 'It recruits itself constantly from the supernumerary forces of modern industry and agriculture, and specially from those decaying branches of industry where handicraft is yielding to manufacture, manufacture to machinery. Its extent grows, as with the extent and energy of accumulation, the creation of a surplus-population advances'.

It remains to add that net population growth is actually a feature not only of the advanced industrial sector, but of agriculture too – over the decade 1851–61 the rural growth rate was recorded by the Census as 6.5 per cent, the difference with the 17.3 per cent of the towns ascribed to migration from the country (p. 642n.). The 'domestic industry' segment of the urban population is also said to be 'a self-reproducing and self-perpetuating element of the working-class, taking a proportionally greater part in the general increases of that class than the other elements' (p. 643). It is in this context (though possibly not restricted thereto) that we encounter the declaration regarding the inverse relation between population growth and earnings (see above, p. 384). Adam Smith's belief that 'poverty seems favourable to generation' is then cited, as is Samuel Laing's to the effect that 'misery up to the extreme point of famine and pestilence, instead of checking, tends to increase population'. Thus even were it the case that Marx's downward wage trend in the advanced industrial sector turned on an inflow from other sectors, it would still be impossible to ignore the demographic component of the analysis.

15.11 Marx's Objections to Orthodox Classicism Summarized

For Ricardo, Malthus and Mill on the one hand, and Marx on the other, the growth of labour demand tends to decline secularly, though for very different reasons, since for Marx land scarcity is not the issue. My concern now is Marx's presumption, in contrast to the orthodox classicists, of a *necessarily* excessive growth rate of labour supply forcing wages downwards. His purpose was not, of course, the formulation of a reform programme to improve the living standards of the masses under capitalism. None the less, since his forecast of falling real wages hinged upon excessive population pressure, we are obliged to look more closely into his neglect of the 'Malthusian' solution. Here two issues must be distinguished: first, prospects for birth control under capitalism; and second, the probable effectiveness of population restraint (assuming it to be feasible).

For the first issue there is very little to go on. We have Engels' assertion in 1881 that only a communist society could undertake population control 'without difficulty' (above, p. 379). The implied difficulties facing population control under capitalism and the form control would take under communism are unfortunately not clarified. But Marx himself pointed to the steady decline in the rate of population growth over the years – the fact that 'although the absolute increase of the English population in the last half century was very great, the relative increase or rate of growth fell constantly' (*Capital*, I, 648). And, citing the Registrar General, 'rapidly as the population has increased, it has not kept pace with the progress of industry and wealth' (p. 651). Notwithstanding, he supposed the living standards of the masses were falling. To ascribe the presumed deterioration in real wages to a greater proportional decline in the growth rate of labour demand than supply (as Marx must have done) is open to the objection that, with no check at all to the population growth rate, the deterioration would have been sharper still; while conversely, a determined programme of birth control might have been more effective in checking and perhaps halting the deterioration.

Marx in fact condemned 'the economic wisdom that preaches to the labourers the accommodation of their number to the requirements of capital', on the grounds that 'the mechanism of capitalist production and accumulation constantly affects this adjustment' (p. 644). This is not a convincing position. The decelerating growth rate of labour demand is an on-going process, reflecting exogenous technical progress (the general context of the foregoing comment). A simultaneous programme of continuous population control acting on the growth rate of labour supply must tend at the least to ease the downward pressure on real wages.

Marx's case against orthodoxy was reinforced by allusion to Ireland 1840–60, where, notwithstanding absolute population decline, real wages had failed to improve and indeed had fallen:

> Here, then, under our own eyes and on a large scale, a process is revealed, than which nothing more excellent could be wished for by orthodox economy for the support of its dogma: that misery springs from absolute surplus-population, and that equilibrium is re-established by depopulation....
>
> What were the consequences for the Irish labourers left behind and freed from the surplus-population? That the relative surplus-population is today as great as before 1846; that wages are just as low, that the oppression of the labourers has increased, that misery is forcing the country towards a new crisis. The facts are simple. The revolution in agri-culture has kept pace with emigration. The production of relative surplus-population has more than kept pace with the absolute depopula-tion (pp. 703–4).

But this too is unconvincing, for orthodox classical economics did not constitute a predictive engine allowing a forecast of the course of wages. The intervention of 'disturbing causes', in the present case the agri-cultural revolution involving consolidation of farms, conversion of arable into pasture and use of machinery, does not contradict the general principle that control of population growth would contribute to the maintenance of wages. Population control was considered a neces-sary but not always a sufficient condition to assure against falling wages.

An objection to population control as an effective means for posi-tively raising wages is stated in *Theories of Surplus Value* in terms of substitution against labour:

> Essentially... the whole of the absurd theory of population was thus overthrown, in particular also the claptrap of the vulgar economists, that the workers must strive to keep their multiplication below the standard of the accumulation of capital. The opposite follows from Barton's and Ricardo's presentation, namely that to keep down the labouring popula-tion, thus diminishing the supply of labour, and, consequently, raising its price, would only *accelerate* the application of machinery, the conversion

of circulating into fixed capital, and, hence, make the population artificially 'redundant'...(1862–3 [1968], II, 578).

This same argument is applied also in *Capital*, to the increase in real
wages in English agricultural districts following a sudden and unusual
fall in local labour supplies (1849–59):

> What did the farmers do now? Did they wait until, in consequence of this
> brilliant remuneration, the agricultural labourers had so increased and
> multiplied that their wages must fall again, as prescribed by the dogmatic
> economic brain? They introduced more machinery, and in a moment the
> labourers were redundant again in a proportion satisfactory even to the
> farmers. There was now 'more capital' laid out in agriculture than before,
> and in a more productive form. With this the demand for labour fell, not
> only relatively, but absolutely (I, 638).

Two points must here be made. Substitution against labour in the
event of an absolute fall in labour supply of the foregoing kind could
only limit the resultant wage increase, there being no reason to expect
the creation of an excess labour supply with downward pressure on the
wage. The simple point is that substitution against labour is already reflected in the negative slope of the demand curve. This principle,
applied to the dynamic context, implies that there is no reason why a
reduced population growth rate cannot retard the falling wage trend
even if some substitution against labour, with an impact on the labour-
demand growth rate, is induced.

I close with a look at an anomaly in Marxian economics – the falling
profit rate. For Ricardo, Malthus and Mill the profit rate tends to
decline given technology, notwithstanding falling real wages. This is
quite logically accounted for by the fact that the 'value' of (labour
embodied in) the smaller wage basket is rising due to diminishing agricultural returns. Now for Marx too we have a 'tendency' of the profit
rate to fall. In his case this reflects the changing organic composition of
capital, for if the organic composition of capital (c/v) increases secularly,
then a constant s/v necessarily implies a declining $s/(c + v)$ (*Capital*, III,
207ff). This formal argument is riddled with difficulty, for s/v is not
constant – its trend is upward not only because the commodity wage
tends downwards, but also because the labour required per unit of wage
goods is likely to fall with new technology. Now it is legitimate for the
orthodox school to treat technical progress as a 'disturbing cause'
counteracting the falling profit rate trend; but it is not legitimate for
Marx to do so since technical progress is supposed to be the kingpin of
his main system. If it is central to the higher c/v and reduced rate of
growth of labour demand, it is equally central to a rising s/v.

Let us, however, presume with Marx a declining profit rate trend.
What are the implications for accumulation? Marx cited Richard Jones

to the effect that 'in spite of the falling rate of profit the inducements and faculties to accumulate are augmented' (260). The curve relating the profit rate and accumulation – whatever its slope – is continually shifting outward because of an increase in the purchasing power of aggregate profits, because 'the wants and greeds for wealth increase', and because of various institutional changes which ease the savings-investment process. Marx also alludes to the impact on savings of 'growing relative over-population', – the generation of excess labour supply. But this is reasoning in circles. With capital growing so rapidly, the notion of a supposedly falling growth rate of labour demand comes into question; for whether or not it declines is an empirical matter and the negative impact of conversion might well be outweighed by the positive impact of rapid accumulation. If, moreover, we were to allow for prudential population control the outcome would be as Mill had portrayed it (above, p. 237) rather than one of 'growing relative over-population'. But too rosy a picture of capitalistic development would not, presumably, have appealed to Marx.

Suggested Reading

*Marx (1867, 1894) *Capital*, vol. I, Parts III, V, VI and VII; vol. III, Parts II, III and VII.
*   (1865), 'Wages, Price and Profit', in Marx–Engels, *Selected Works* (1958), Moscow, I, 398–447.

A useful 'guide' to Marx's *Capital* is provided by Brewer (1984). For a 'Marxian' perspective on Marx's value theory, see Dobb (1973), ch. 6, Meek (1956) chs 4 and 5, and Meek (1974). Gordon's 1959 paper 'What was the labour theory of value?' is again relevant. On the 'transformation' issue in particular see Samuelson (1971), an exchange between Baumol (1974) and Samuelson (1974), and Meek (1977), chs 5 and 6. The issue as discussed in the present chapter is elaborated in Hollander (1981).

Marx's economic predictions are analysed by Gottheil (1966). On the population problem as discussed above, see Hollander (1984c).

For the Marx–Engels theoretical relationship see Hutchison (1978b). Balassa (1959) treats the relation between Marx and Mill. Schumpeter (1954), 590–8, 651–4, Blaug (1958), Appendix A, and Tucker (1961) consider that between Marx and Ricardo. Meek (1977), devotes chapter 1 to the relation between Marx and Smith, and chapter 9 to marginalism and Marxism.

16 Some Intellectual Linkages

16.1 Introduction

This chapter traces certain major intellectual linkages. Despite appearances, the Ricardian approach to value and the inverse wage–profit relationship based on the standard measure of value left a positive impression on the work of a number of authors traditionally regarded as 'dissenters', including T. R. Malthus, Samuel Bailey (1791–1870), Robert Torrens (1790–1864) and Mountifort Longfield (1802–84). A demonstration of the resilience in their works of the Ricardian distribution theorem points away from a dual development in the course of nineteenth-century economic analysis (see above, p. 6). These doubts are reinforced by the fact that in many cases the criticisms constitute a misunderstanding of Ricardo's position, while in others the contributions of the dissenters would not have been considered objectionable by Ricardo (section 16.2 and 16.3). Section 16.4 touches on post-Ricardian opinion on the secular trends, and section 16.5 on opinion regarding methodology.

The relation between economics and ideology is taken up in section 16.6 where the notion that the roots of British socialism can be traced to Ricardo is questioned. It becomes clear that no obvious link between a body of economic theory and the social attitudes of the economist subscribing to it can be defined.

We return to the longevity of Ricardianism in section 16.7 dealing with J. S. Mill. His response in 1848 to the literature of the preceding quarter-century is there shown to be objective and fair. A problem involving Mill's relation with the 'inductivist' critics is taken up in section 16.8.

16.2 Post-Ricardian Opinion on Value Theory

Many post-Ricardian 'dissenting' critics misunderstood Ricardo on value. Malthus, for one conspicuous example, believed that Ricardo maintained his cost theory of exchange value as an alternative to demand–supply theory (1820). Samuel Bailey implied that Ricardo failed to appreciate the relativity dimension of exchange value (1825). Nassau Senior (1790–1864) objected that to say 'it is the price of [the] last portion of corn, which governs that of the remainder, is to mistake the effect for the cause' and his adoption of a demand–supply or 'monopoly' explanation of rent (1836) falls into the same category. The fact is that the Ricardians – in some conspicuous cases Ricardo himself – accepted much of the substantive argument of the 'critics'.

Schumpeter gave pride of place to Samuel Bailey amongst those who reacted against orthodoxy (1954, 486). But this will not do. While Bailey maintained in his *Critical Dissertation on... Value* that the notion of an invariable standard 'amidst universal fluctuations' involves an inherent contradiction, it is quite clear that this follows from his own definition of value as price, or exchange value:

> The specific error of Mr. Ricardo on the subject of invariable value consists ... in supposing, that if the causes of value affecting one commodity remained the same, the value of that commodity could not vary, overlooking the circumstance, that value denotes a relation between two objects, which must necessarily alter with an alteration in the causes affecting either of them. He incessantly identifies constancy in the quantity of producing labour with constancy of value. Hence he maintains, that if we could find any commodity invariable in the circumstances of its production, it would be in the first place invariable in value; and, secondly, it would indicate, or would enable us to ascertain, the variations in value of other commodities (1825, 120–1).

Bailey's case turns out to be a purely terminological one, as was well appreciated by a *Westminster Review* contributor, possibly James Mill, who made the point that Bailey 'makes profession, or rather ostentation and parade, of being [in] controversy with Mr. Ricardo' (1826, 157) on the relativity dimension of exchange value. That this would have been Ricardo's view is clear from his reaction to an anonymous work, *Verbal Disputes* (1821), which in its essentials was so similar to the *Critical Dissertation* that Bailey feared he might be accused of plagiarism (see Ricardo, 1951, IX, 27n., 38). Bailey, who formally championed greater 'generality' in price theory than he found among the Ricardians – the key lying in scarcity – himself reluctantly conceded that Ricardo had recognized elements of 'scarcity' or 'partial monopoly' in the long-run, increasing-cost case (1825, 194–5, 227–9). He generalized the conception of differential rent to apply to labour, and this is important; but he also maintained that rent is not a 'cause' of value (p. 197). His insistence that rent may be generated even in the absence of differential land qualities by dint of land scarcity had been allowed by Ricardo (see above, pp. 98–9). He forcefully rejected statements of the labour theory by James Mill, De Quincey and McCulloch, but was less harsh with respect to Ricardo himself who had recognized that a wage variation will influence relative prices in the event of differing factor proportions (pp. 207–8; 213–14).

J. S. Mill probably had in mind objections by Senior (1821) to Ricardo's rent theory when he criticized those 'who affect to suppose that Sir Edward West, Mr. Malthus, and Mr. Ricardo, considered the cultivation of inferior land as the *cause* of a high price of corn' (see above, p. 132). Mill's reaction was justified. Ricardo himself had said of Senior's article: 'I am glad I have got so good an ally, for what I think the correct principles' (1951, IX, 122). Ricardo had indeed appreciated that differential rent is but a special case of land scarcity; and also that rent may be generated even in the absence of diminishing returns in the face of an absolute constraint upon output expansion in the face of rising demand.

We turn next to the Ricardian response to Malthus. In an *Encyclopaedia Britannica* contribution of 1823, commenting upon Malthus's *Principles* of 1820, J. R. McCulloch observed that 'Mr. Malthus does not attempt to invalidate the leading principles established by Mr. Ricardo' (1823 [1966], 135). That this is so is revealed by Malthus's adoption of the Ricardian inverse profit–wage relationship and common ground regarding much else in distribution theory (see below, p. 403). Ricardo also saw eye-to-eye with Malthus regarding the effects of changes in distribution upon prices. On reading of Malthus's acceptance of the proposition that a fall profits (increase in wages) will generate a decline in the prices of capital-intensive goods, Ricardo expressed surprise, 'because in some of his works he has maintained [Smith's view] that a rise in the price of corn will be followed by an equal rise in the price of labour, and by an equal rise in the price of *all* commodities' (1951, II, 60–1). In fact, Ricardo saw his position as closer to Malthus's than to that of the arch-Ricardian McCulloch, considering the latter's extreme position on the labour theory: 'You go a little further than I go in estimating the value of commodities by the quantity of labour required to produce them: you appear to admit of no exception or qualification whatever, whereas I am always willing to allow that some of the variations in the relative value of commodities may be referred to causes distinct from the quantity of labour necessary to produce them' (1951, IX, 178). Ricardo had in mind the effects of changing wages: 'To this second cause I do not attach near so much importance as Mr. Malthus and others but I cannot wholly shut my eyes to it.'

As for Malthus's contention in the *Quarterly Review* of 1824 that Ricardo's New School (unlike Adam Smith) rejected demand and supply in accounting for competitive long-run price, we have J. S. Mill's valid insistence that the very opposite was the case (see above, p. 124). All influences upon price operated by way of demand and supply, and the cost theory was dependent thereupon, as Ricardo had maintained: 'Mr. Malthus mistakes the question', Ricardo protested on reading Malthus's *Principles*. 'I do not say that the value of a commodity will always conform to its natural price without an additional supply, but I say that the cost of production regulates the supply, and therefore regulates the price' (1951, II, 48–9).

Mountifort Longfield represents the most original of that group of writers known variously as 'the Dissenters', 'the Men who Wrote above Their Time', and 'Voices in the Wilderness' and in *Lectures on Political Economy* (1834) developed (possibly drawing on Malthus) the notion of marginal demand price ([1971] 113 ff). But again, Ricardo, whose economics hinged upon demand–supply analysis, would not have objected to an elaboration of the law of demand. (Longfield himself, like Ricardo, rejected the 'indefinite and vague' expression 'proportion between the demand and supply' as unhelpful (p. 247).) The same may be said of Nassau Senior's brief statement of diminishing utility (1836, 11–12) or W. F. Lloyd's more extensive analysis of marginal utility (1834).

J. S. Mill's reaction to the few critical remarks by Thomas De Quincey (1785–1859) is pertinent here. Mill denied that various observations in De Quincey's *Logic of Political Economy* (1844) on the relation between value-in-use and value-in-exchange had 'all the originality which he ascribed to them', for he had merely brought 'into full theoretical explicitness what was known to all clear thinkers' (Mill, 1967, IV, 395–6). De Quincey had not given due credit to received doctrine:

> Have not all political economists distinguished between articles which can be multiplied to an indefinite extent by labour, and articles naturally or artificially limited to a quantity short of demand; and have they not all, from Ricardo downwards, affirmed that in the former, and more common case, the value conforms on an average to the cost of production, while in the latter there are no limits to the value except the necessities or desires of the purchaser? (p. 398).

But considering the work as a whole, Mill found little to object to, approving of De Quincey's basic allegiance to Ricardo: 'One of [De Quincey's] merits is his early and consistent appreciation of Ricardo, the true founder of the abstract science of political economy, and whose writings are still, after all that has been since written, its purest source' (p. 394).

That the Ricardians were thus able to see eye-to-eye with much of the apparently critical work on value is not surprising. For Ricardo had never envisaged his cost of production theory as an alternative to supply–demand analysis. But conversely, many 'dissenters' continued to emphasize the cost determination of price. A comment by C. F. Cotterill in 1831 that there are 'some Ricardians still remaining' led Professor Schumpeter to conclude that 'the decay of the Ricardian school must have become patent' shortly after Bailey's contribution and that 'Ricardianism was then no longer a living force' (1954, 478). But Cotterill refers to variations of exchange value proportionate to alterna-tions in relative labour input as a proposition which 'most economists maintain' – in contrast to Adam Smith's position relating increases in prices 'to the rise in wages' (1831, 107). And he regarded production costs as the main consideration in price determination, excluding rent from costs in Ricardian fashion. Similarly G. Poulett Scrope (1797–1876), who praised the inductivist critic Richard Jones, none the less rejected the 'vulgar opinion' that rent affects price (1831, 35). Samuel Read adopted a cost theory, and objected to Bailey in strong terms:

> I find occasion to differ from him very widely in his main positions in the 'Critical Dissertation'. It appears to me that the fundamental error in that work, and that from which all the others to be found in it flow, consists in his treating of value as if it were *a mere relation of commodities between themselves*; whereas it appears to me that the idea of value in commodi-ties *cannot even be conceived* without being mingled with the idea that their relation to mankind and to human labour, of which *some portion* must always be employed in producing or procuring them originally (1829, viiin.).

Much weight is sometimes placed on criticism by Richard Whately (1787–1863) of the labour theory: 'It is not that pearls fetch a high price *because* men have dived for them; but on the contrary, men dive for them because they fetch a high price' (1832 [1855], 167). But his criti-cism explicitly relates to the case of given supplies, and is not inconsis-tent with a labour or cost explanation of long-run value; indeed, Whately himself conceded that 'valuable articles are, in *almost* all instances, obtained by Labour'. As for Longfield, at the commencement of Lecture VI, where the fullest treatment of demand is undertaken, the main Ricardo-like propositions regarding value are re-stated, including the emphasis on long-run costs. Thus labour is justified as providing a suitable measure: 'as most of the commodities in which the wealth of a country consists are produced by labour, political economists make use of it as a measure of value' (1834, [1971], 109). And in Lecture VIII we read that 'all the commodities which men consume, and which can be made the subject of exchanges, owe their existence and their value to labour. The exceptions to this are very trifling, and are of such a nature that they do not vitiate any of the conclusions drawn from it' (p. 164). Finally, W. F. Lloyd's marginal utility analysis is not inconsistent with a cost or even a labour theory, and was not so envisaged by Lloyd (1795–1852) himself: 'if labour becomes more effective, so that commodities of all kinds shall be produced in a degree of abundance greater in proportion to the wants of mankind, all sorts of commodities, though exchangeable in the same proportions as before for each other, could be said to have become less valuable' (1834, 28). This statement is quite consistent with a labour theory of exchange value.

16.3 Post-Ricardian Opinion on Distribution Theory

Despite appearance, Ricardo's inverse wage–profit relationship derived on the basis of the measure of value was alive and well in the 1830s and 1840s. J. S. Mill was not engaged in the resuscitation of a corpse.

Malthus himself, formally a severe critic of Ricardo, accepted much of its substance: 'Of all the truths which Mr. Ricardo has established, one of the most useful and important is, that profits are determined by the proportion of the whole produce which goes to labour. It is, indeed, a direct corollary from the proposition, that the value of commodities is resolvable into wages and profits; but its simplicity and apparent obviousness do not detract from its utility' (1824 [1963], 189). His only substantive criticism is of the unsatisfactory manner in which, he believed, the division between wages and profits was actually determined by Ricardo. The inverse profit–wage relationship was 'only one important step in the theory of profits, which of course cannot be complete till we have ascertained the cause which, under all circumstances, regulates this proportion of the whole produce which goes to labour immediate and accumulated'. Malthus also believed that his own doctrine relating to the role of aggregate demand was required to account for the presumed historical decline in the profit rate, but he conceded readily that the evidence accorded 'most perfectly with the more general proposition of Mr. Ricardo respecting profits, namely, that they are determined by the proportion of the whole produce which goes to labour' (p. 198).

That Malthus accepted the substance of Ricardo's position is also confirmed by an important note attached to his *Measure of Value* (1823). Malthus had observed in the text that 'it may be laid down...as a general proposition, liable to no exception, that when the value of any produce can be resolved into labour and profits, then as the *proportion* of such produce which goes to labour increases, the proportion which goes to profits must decrease in the same degree' (p. 28). To this he added:

> This proposition is essentially the same as that which is very clearly and ably expressed by Mr. Ricardo in his chapter On Profits in the following terms: 'in all countries and at all times profits depend on the quantity of labour requisite to provide necessaries for the labourers on that land, or with that capital which yields no rent;' a proposition which though incomplete in reference to the ultimate causes of the variations of profits, contains a most important truth. From this truth the legitimate deduction appears to me to be, the constant value of labour; but Mr. Ricardo has formed his system on a deduction exactly opposite to it. He has, however, in my opinion, amply compensated for the errors into which he may have fallen, by furnishing us, at the same time, not only with the means of their refutation, but the means of improving the science of Political Economy (p. 29n).

The criticisms alluded to here relate to Ricardo's supposed failure to deal satisfactorily with commodity wage determination and to the tortuous issue of the measure of value. As for the former, Malthus was simply mistaken in asserting that, for Ricardo, the sole cause of falling profits was diminishing returns; variable commodity wages will have an impact on profits. As for the measure of value, communications broke down. But one fact remains – Malthus's insistence that by the relationship which he envisaged between the constancy of the value of a given 'command over labour' (his chosen measure) and the proportionate shares, he was attempting to get across precisely the same conception of things as Ricardo himself.

How did Ricardo himself view Malthus's position on distribution? The treatment of profits in his *Principles* met with his approval; he commented favourably on Malthus's analysis of the adverse effects upon the profit rate generated by increased difficulty of producing wage goods, and by increased commodity wages, and concluded:

> These two causes may both be classed under the name of high or low wages. Profits in fact depend on high or low wages, and on nothing else....In all this Mr. Malthus and I appear to concur. Whenever the difficulty of production on the land is such that a greater proportion of the value of the whole produce is employed in supporting labour, I call wages high, for I measure value by these proportions; and from Mr. Malthus's

language here, everybody would think he agreed with me... (1951, II, 252).

His great complaint was Malthus's charge that he had neglected the effect of commodity wage variation upon the profit rate:

> I have invariably insisted that high or low profits depended on low and high wages, how then can it be justly said of me that the only cause which I have recognized of high or low profits is the facility or difficulty of providing food for the labourer. I contend that I have also recognized the other cause, the relative amount of population to capital, which is another of the great regulators of wages (pp. 264–5).

Longfield was to repeat Malthus's misreading (see below, p. 407).

As for Bailey, this 'dissenter' *par excellence* conceded to Ricardo that a commodity produced with constant labour input would enable one to establish in which commodity observed fluctuations in relative value 'had originated' (1825, 121), and also that wages expressed in money of constant value – again, using the term 'value' in Ricardo's sense of labour embodied – would indeed reflect proportionate wages:

> Mr. Ricardo's inference is a legitimate deduction from his premises, if we concede certain postulates. Grant him the kind of value called *real*, which has no relation to the quantity of commodities commanded, but solely to the quantity of producing labour, and it inevitably follows, that there could be no alteration in the *real* value of labour, but from an alteration in the proportion of the product which went to the labourer. Neither, if money were always produced by a uniform quantity of labour, could there be any other alteration in the money-value of labour (p. 58n.).

Bailey's recognition that the profit rate falls when commodity wages rise (given labour productivity) runs along strictly Ricardian lines, involving as it does the proposition – against Adam Smith – that capitalists cannot pass on higher wage costs to consumers since the prices, or exchange values, of all commodities cannot logically be simultaneously raised:

> If labour rises while [its] productive powers remain the same, profits will inevitably fall.... It will be said, perhaps, that [the capitalist] may raise the value of his goods, that is, he may require a greater quantity of other commodities than before, in exchange for his own. But the capitalist who produces these other commodities is in the same predicament, and they cannot both raise their goods... [It] is a contradiction to maintain, that a universal rise in the value of labour can increase the value of commodities (pp. 64–5).

The entire Bailey episode has been overdone as an indication of revolt against Ricardo.

C. F. Cotterill is another so-called 'dissenter' who recognized the need for an 'invariable standard', and believed in the possibility of its construction, refuting 'the erroneous doctrine that the supposition of such a standard involves contradictory conditions' (1831, v), and illustrating the 'correct' procedure to guarantee that aggregate money value remains unchanged in the face of an alteration in distribution (p. 76). He candidly recognized Ricardo's contribution to the proposed solution: 'The conditions, however, essential to an invariable standard, do appear to me so very obvious, especially upon Mr. Ricardo's own principles in opposition to Adam Smith' (p. 75n).

Turning next to Longfield, the differential rent theory served for him the same function as for Ricardo, namely to permit the focus of attention upon the wage–profit relationship: 'This analysis I shall enter upon, merely for the purpose... of rendering questions concerning wages and profits more simple' (1834 [1971], 116). He insisted, as Ricardo had done, that differential land fertility as such was not the 'cause' of rent, since 'whatever is useful, and is limited in quantity, is capable of possessing value, if it can be made the subject of exchange' (p. 134); and he rejected the Smithian notion that the multifold use of land renders rent a cost in any single use: 'I... cannot agree with Mr. Malthus, in supposing that the rent which the worst land could pay, as pasture land, should be deemed part of the cost of production of corn' (p. 148).

Longfield, who defined profits as a 'discount which the labourer pays for prompt payment' (p. 170) or a sort of 'sacrifice of the present to the future' by the capitalist, defended Ricardo's inverse wage–profit theorem against Robert Torrens's position that the theorem 'is equally untenable, whether the terms alteration of wages, alteration of profits, are employed with a reference to proportions, or whether they are used in relation to quantities' (Torrens, 1826, xv-xvi). According to Longfield, the profit rate 'depends upon the proportion of the shares of the final value received by the labourer and the capitalist' (1834 [1971], 175). Ricardo's conditions to assure that changes in money wages will reflect changes in proportionate wages are also defended:

> Mr. Ricardo frequently asserts that wages and profits together are always of the same value, and that nothing but a rise in one can produce a fall of the other. He uses the term '*wages*', sometimes to signify the absolute wages which the labourer receives, and sometimes as the proportional wages. This did not arise from an abuse of words or a confusion of ideas, it was the natural and necessary consequence of a hypothesis, which for simplicity of illustration, he laid down at the commencement of his work. He assumes that any given quantity of gold, or the metal of which money is made, is always produced by the same quantity of labour, with the same quantity of fixed and circulating capital employed at the same interval of time before its production. On this hypothesis, if gold is raised from

mines within the kingdom, absolute money wages will be identical with, and be measured by, proportional wages, and a rise of wages, that is of money wages, will always be accompanied by a fall of profits (pp. 266–7).

The *Lectures* in fact elicited a formal retraction from Torrens of his earlier objections. There exists no clearer statement of the inverse wage–profit theorem involving the proportions-measuring 'gold' than that presented, favourably, in Torrens's *Colonization of Southern Australia* (1835, 22–35); similarly, in *The Budget* he candidly withdrew his earlier objections (1844 [1970], xxxvi).

Longfield's discussion thus far has merely provided a definition of profits and a statement of how the rate of profits is to be calculated. In a lecture devoted to the 'laws which determine their actual amount', he applied the marginal principle to distribution in a short-run context, in the specific sense of *given population* but allowance made for capital accumulation. This brilliant piece of analysis turns on the efficiency of capital (envisaged as 'machinery') in its least productive application, all placed within a demand–supply framework (1834 [1971], 186ff). This approach, I repeat, was not seen as a rejection of the inverse profit–wage relationship.

One Irish writer (Isaac Butt, 1838) combined the utility teaching of Say with Longfield's approach to distribution to arrive at the marginal utility theory of imputation. Since Ricardo himself accepted Say's micro-economic approach, it is not self-evident that he would necessarily have objected on principle to this kind of development. Like Malthus, Longfield was seriously mistaken when he asserted that the Ricardians 'maintain, that the increase of capital in any country, unaccompanied by an increase in population, has not even any tendency to reduce the profits of capital' (1834 [1971], 184), and it is precisely this supposed defect in Ricardian economics that had provided his rationale for seeking an alternative approach. Still, it is true that Ricardo's analysis of capital accumulation given population ran on over-simplified wage fund lines and Longfield's innovations would have strengthened the analysis.

*　　*　　*

To what extent must the conception of interest as a return to 'abstinence' developed by Senior, Scrope, Read and Longfield be interpreted as a sharp break with Ricardian procedures? The fact is that Ricardo's conception of profits as residual reflects nothing more than an implicit presumption that the only contractual payment is that to labour. Ricardo recognized the 'necessity' of interest payments, taking into account the effect of a declining profit rate on accumulation, which he related to abstinence without coining the term. J. S. Mill, in his turn, found no difficulty in subscribing at one and the same time to the inverse wage–profit relationship and to a fully articulated abstinence conception (see above, p. 377).

What finally of the widespread application of market demand–supply analysis to long-run wage determination, as for example by Malthus, Longfield, Torrens, Read, Scrope and Senior? Here too there occurred no breakaway. The story would be a different one were it the case that the subsistence wage played a key role in Ricardo's growth model. But Ricardo's was a growth model in the true sense, with wages and profits above their respective minima which become relevant only in the stationary state. It is significant that Longfield did not attribute to Ricardo a subsistence theory of wages; he recognized that Ricardo subscribed to a growth model entailing secularly falling wages. He objected that there is no reason why wages cannot bear the full brunt of secularly rising food prices (1834 [1971], 185); but this is very poorly grounded, since Ricardo (and Malthus) had fully justified the secular decline in the rate of profit, declining commodity wages notwithstanding.

16.4   Post-Ricardian Opinion on Secular Trends

The frame of reference designed by Ricardo to deal with the secular paths of wages and profits, with its underpinning in the law of diminishing returns, dominated economic thinking throughout the post-Ricardian period. Nevertheless, a degree of scepticism on the part of various economists (including Read, Scrope, Senior, McCulloch, Torrens and Longfield) regarding the 'prediction' of secularly declining commodity wages deriving from population pressure is apparent. The picture is not totally one-sided (compare the positions of Herman Merivale and William Forster Lloyd). More important, what would a general decline in adherence to 'Malthusianism' in the sense of pessimistic predictions regarding living standards imply for the fortunes of Ricardian economics? Ricardo himself had no intention of using his model to make definite predications, appealing as he did for the more extensive practice of moral restraint as a means of raising the 'subsistence' level. Particularly pertinent is Richard Whately's insistence on a distinction between the notion of 'a "tendency" towards a certain result' in the sense of 'the existence of a cause which, if *operating unimpeded,* should produce that result', and in the sense of 'the existence of such a state of things that that result *may be expected to take place*'. There may be a 'tendency' in population to grow faster than the means of subsistence in the first sense, while, as was evident from the historical experience of several hundred years, there was no such tendency in the second sense. To 'inaccuracies of this kind', Whately ascribed the 'discrepancies and occasional absurdities from which some persons infer that Political Economy is throughout a chimaera' (1832 [1855], 164–5). He made no adverse mention of Ricardo in this regard, and also denied that Malthus was responsible for the pessimistic predictions regarding long-term prospects which had 'obtained considerable currency' on his supposed authority; in Malthus's work 'I have never myself been able to find this doctrine' (p. 120). It was not Whately's view that the empirical evidence constituted a refutation of the orthodox analysis of trend patterns under *ceteris paribus* conditions and in the absence of 'disturbing causes'. Whately's distinction was formally adopted by J. S. Mill, and by Senior in the population context (1836, 47).

De Quincey denied the validity of 'an immutable law of declension' of the profit rate (which he mistakenly ascribed to Ricardo), since this prediction did not allow for the 'eternal counter-movement which tends...to redress the disturbed balance' (1844 [1897], 249). Yet he fully adhered to Ricardo's distribution analysis. And Longfield, who in his discussion of future prospects did not emphasize an historical upward trend in agricultural prices, yet placed diminishing returns and differential rent in the centre of the analytic stage:

> I attempted to give an explanation of the manner in which, as population increases, inferior soils must be brought into cultivation, and the soils already cultivated must be forced, at a greater proportional expense, to yield a greater produce. I have shewn that rent has therefore a tendency to increase as population increases, and that the natural price of corn, or its cost of production, may be measured independently of rent; that it will be equal to the cost of raising it on that land which pays no rent, or to the cost of production of that portion which is raised under the most naturally disadvantageous circumstances (1834 [1971], 132).

Longfield found the conceptions of diminishing agricultural returns and differential rent to be valuable analytical devices, despite awareness not only of the potentialities of new technology but also – in the case of Ireland – of the existence of a body of yet unapplied knowledge available for adoption in support of a rising population. The historical fact, as he read it, that 'corn is not constantly and rapidly increasing in price' was not seen as negating the validity and function of the analytical conceptions.

16.5 The Inductivist Critics

According to the 'Cambridge' inductivists, led by Richard Jones (1790–1855) and William Whewell (1794–1866), Ricardo's procedure (as distinct from Smith's) entailed hasty and illegitimate generalizations from axioms which, while supposedly universal, were in fact based on casual observation and even introspection. The defective approach and the proposed legitimate (inductive) procedures are described in the following characteristic passage by Jones:

> It wants no great deal of logical acuteness to perceive, that in political economy, maxims which profess to be universal, can only be founded on the most comprehensive views of society. The principles which determine the position and progress, and govern the conduct, of large bodies of the human race, placed under different circumstances, can be learnt only by an appeal to experience. He must, indeed, be a shallow reasoner, who by mere efforts of consciousness, by consulting his own views, feelings and motives, and the narrow sphere of his personal observation, and reasoning *a priori* from them expects that he shall be able to anticipate the conduct, progress and fortunes of large bodies of men, differing from himself in moral or physical temperament, and influenced by differences, varying in extent and variously combined, in climate, soil, religion, education and government (1831, xv).

The object of the exercise for Jones is the derivation of 'universal maxims', which required 'the most comprehensive views of society' based upon 'appeal to experience'. As he further maintained, 'a comprehensive and laborious appeal to experience' was required since 'the mixt causes which concur in producing the various phenomena with which the subject is conversant, can only be separated, examined, and thoroughly understood by repeated observation of events as they occur, or have occurred, in the history of nations; and can never be submitted (except in cases extremely rare) to premeditated experiment' (pp. xix–xx).

Jones objected primarily to Ricardo's theory of rent interpreted as the proposition that 'a difference in the natural fertility of soils is the sole origin of rent' (p. 206). His conclusion, from an investigation of pre-capitalist and non-capitalist (largely peasant) societies, was that the institutional forms adopted by the Ricardians in their analysis of rent were relevant to scarcely 'one-hundredth part of the cultivated surface of the habitable globe' (p. 14). Jones accepted a version of the principle of diminishing returns as an exception to the general theory of the subject, but still denied its contemporary relevance in the light of technological progress (pp. 199–200). Even granting for the sake of argument the orthodox position regarding the 'sole cause of rent', Ricardo was none the less mistaken in the assertion that rents can *only* rise in consequence of a rise in the magnitude of the differential. Jones's argument (pp. 203–8) is based on arbitrarily constructed counter-examples which have no economic content whatsoever.

Jones's work was devoted to rent but the Preface contains an observation relating to accumulation. Any relationship between high profit rates and rapid accumulation, he maintained, was the exception rather than the rule, as was maintained by orthodox doctrine. The belief to the contrary reflected 'an almost wilful disregard of experience, and of the testimony which the history and statistical position of every country in the world bear to the laws really determining the varying powers of communities to accumulate capital' (p. xxxii). No empirical evidence for the assertions is provided – although this was supposedly to follow.

The kind of argument addressed at the Ricardian deductivists by the Cambridge school was not restricted to that group. Interest in a broad range of institutional arrangements was expressed by several of the 'Ricardian Socialists', and also by Mathias Attwood, who listed rights of proprietorship and fuedal tenure amongst the key considerations determining land use (cf. Ricardo, 1951, V, 162).

The inductivist challenge was totally misconceived. For Ricardo had never proposed 'maxims which profess to be universal', that is applicable to all periods and circumstances, based upon axioms derived from 'mere efforts of consciousness...and the narrow sphere of personal observation'. He had also not neglected technical progress. All of this soon came to light.

Jones himself excluded not only Smith but Malthus from his general indictment of the economists. He would doubtless have been surprised by the fact that Malthus, the insistent realist, refused to condone his effort to discredit deductive methodology. For Malthus insisted in correspondence on quite a wide role for definitions as starting hypotheses in economics and he defended the principle of diminishing returns as an explanation of rent, charging that Jones had neglected 'the most important parts of the subject', namely 'the progress of rent in new colonies' and the (Ricardian) case of 'farmers' rents in the more improved states of Europe'. Furthermore, Jones was in error in denying the 'tendency' of continued accumulation and population growth to lower the rates of profits and corn wages on the land (de Marchi and Sturges, 1973). In the *Principles* he refers to the 'more practical opponents' of the deductivists who 'draw too hasty inferences from a frequent appeal to partial facts' (2nd edn, 1836 [1964], 4).

Mountifort Longfield, too, defended Ricardian rent theory:

[This] theory of rent is brought forward only to explain the causes which determine farmers' rents on the system in which they are demanded in these countries, where the land is let to the tenant as the result of a contract which either party may enter into as he thinks proper, and where the amount of rent is a fixed sum, not dependent upon the success of the

> tenant in raising great or scanty crops. Hence no objections to this theory can be drawn from the examples of those countries where contracts of this nature are not freely made (1834 [1971], 141–2).

All tests of the theory drawn from the 'experience' of early states of society or alternative contemporary institutions were, therefore, irrelevant. Longfield rejected the objection that there in fact existed no rent-free land. In some cases the contractual rent constitutes merely interest on the land-owner's investment rather than an 'annual sum paid for the use of the original inherent powers of the soil'; while in any event, the theory depended less 'upon the varying fertility of different soils, as upon the continually decreasing returns which land will give to successive equal applications of labour and capital' (pp. 147–8).

Robert Torrens, upon reading J. S. Mill's *System of Logic* (1843), came to the defence of Ricardo's differential rent theory. He took Jones – indeed his own earlier work – to task for rejecting Ricardo's conclusions 'not because they are incorrectly deduced from his premises, but because they do not coincide with other conclusions deduced from other premises' (Torrens, 1844, xiv). On the effects of technological change on rent, Torrens insisted on the necessity of distinguishing the immediate and long-term effects, in which case 'Ricardo was ... perfectly correct in affirming the abstract proposition, that the effect of improvements in agriculture, *other things remaining the same*, is to diminish rent' (pp. xiv–xv). This answer would apply equally to various strictures directed against Ricardo by Scrope in the *Quarterly Review* (1831). But even Scrope, who accused some theorists of 'generalising hastily from insufficient facts' (1833, 35), directed his criticisms only at the 'hyper-economists'; his appeal was for balance, for he also pointed to 'the most pernicious fallacies and absurd paradoxes ... current among those who pride themselves on being "practical" men, and on despising theory' (p. 37).

Richard Whately came to the defence of deductive economics against those who appealed to 'the experience of practical men', or 'common sense', on the grounds that no progress is possible without 'fixed principles by which to regulate their judgement on each point' (1832 [1855], 49). He took issue with those who championed 'fact collection', arguing that political economy, although 'a science which is founded on facts, and which has a practical application in reference to facts ... yet requires for the establishment of its fundamental principles very little information beyond what is almost unconsciously, and indeed unavoidably, acquired by every one' (p. 149) – here taking a position much narrower than Ricardo's or Mill's. His defence of theoretical economics is expressed in the following passage:

... the prominant part, and that which demands the principal share of our attention, in Political Economy, strictly so called (*i.e.*, considered as to the *principles* of the science), must be the Reasoning process; – the accurate and dexterous application of Logical principles, in combining, and drawing inferences from, those few and simple data from which we set out; – in short, the Logical, not the Physical investigation (p. 158).

Opponents of Ricardianism writing from an inductivist or historical point of view would scarcely have read Whately's work as an attack on Ricardian procedures, as it is sometimes taken to be. Whately's interpretation of the notion 'tendency' also implies support for the Ricardians (see above, p. 408). Finally, his suggestion to rename political economy 'CATALLACTICS, or the "Science of Exchanges"' carries no anti-Ricardian implications (p. 4). This nomenclature was not proposed to deflect classical economics from its primary preoccupations to an emphasis upon the sphere of circulation. Its purpose was to assure that a study of the wealth of nations should be limited to exchangeable commodities and exclude, for example, the analysis of problems relating to a Robinson Crusoe type economy. Whately remained concerned with 'the nature, production, and distribution of wealth' (p. 16).

A single adverse comment by Herman Merivale on Ricardian rent theory – 'a lapsis offensionis, startling and offending many' (1837, 96) – cannot safely be regarded as indicative of a generally hostile position, as has been maintained. On the contrary, Merivale supported the method of the 'modern English school': 'Mr Ricardo investigated the fundamental truths of the science with singular profoundness; his theories, while they have led many followers astray, have nevertheless penetrated thoroughly into all subsequent lucubrations on the subject and he may be regarded, more justly than any other, as the real founder of the school which at present exists in England' (1840, 429).

Broadly speaking, therefore, Jones failed to make a favourable impression on his contemporaries. And with the passage of time – partly in consequence of J. S. Mill – any positive influence it might have had was further diminished. A split on matters of principle between Jones and William Whewell in the 1830s further weakened the force of the inductivist case against Ricardo. For Whewell had growing doubts about the inductivist programme for political economy championed by Jones. 'I am quite satisfied', he had written in 1827, 'of the truth of Jones's general views, and also that they possess the great property of being proved at any step of their induction between the most general and the most particular' (Todhunter, 1876, 86n.). But by 1831 we find him warning against 'vapour[ing] about the successive steps of generalization' and 'declaiming ... about generalization' when what was required were positive examples 'to guide and substantiate' the inductive procedure (pp. 115–16).

One of Whewell's problems was the difficulty of conceiving of induction from the facts independently of some preliminary theoretical framework: '*conceptions* must exist in the mind in order to get by induction a law from the collection of facts' because of 'the impossibility of inducting or even of collecting without this' (p. 141n.). Indeed, in private correspondence he expressed the hope that he would not be misunderstood as taking too 'heterodox' a position regarding the need for *theory* in statistical studies, since 'unconnected facts are of comparatively small value' (pp. 228–9). Whewell had himself in 1829 and 1831 published mathematical versions of Ricardian economics and had been clear enough about the positive role of deduction, provided it was based on an adequate axiomatic basis.

### 16.6	Economics and Ideology

That the roots of early British socialism can be traced to Ricardo is an important theme in Marxian historiography. The writings of Piercy Ravenstone (pseudonym of Richard Puller) and Thomas Hodgskin (1787–1869), among other opponents of 'bourgeois' political economy, were said by Marx to 'derive from the Ricardian form', and Marx refers to the 'opposition evoked by the Ricardian theory' (*Theories of Surplus Value*, 1862–3 [1971], III, 238, 258). The derivation in question was a complex one, entailing adoption and development of Ricardian value theory rid, however, of any allowances for the independent productivity of capital. The champions of the proletariat

> seize[d] on this contradiction, for which they found the theoretical ground already prepared. Labour is the sole source of exchange value and the only active creater of use-value. This is what you [the Ricardians] say. On the other hand, you say that *capital* is everything, and the worker is nothing or a mere production cost of capital. You have refuted yourselves. Capital is *nothing* but defrauding of the worker. *Labour* is *everything*. This, in fact, is the ultimate meaning of all the writings which defend the interests of the proletariat from the Ricardian stand-point basing themselves on his assumptions (p. 260).

As one example, Thomas Hodgskin's insistence upon the non-productivity of capital was the 'inevitable consequence of Ricardo's presentation' (p. 266). What was involved, according to Marx, is a kind of 'inversion' of the Ricardian analysis.

It is a second feature of Marx's reading of the record that the bourgeois dissension from Ricardo of the 1820s and 1830s must be understood as a reaction to the use made of Ricardian doctrine by the labour writers. What is referred to as 'vulgar' political economy 'only becomes widespread', Marx wrote,

> when political economy itself has, as a result of its analysis, undermined and impaired its own premises and consequently the opposition to political economy has come into being in more or less economic, utopian, critical and revolutionary forms. ... *Ricardo* and the further advance of political economy caused by him provide new nourishment for the vulgar economist ... the more economic theory is perfected, that is, the deeper it penetrates its subject-matter and the more it develops as a contradictory system, the more is it confronted by its own, increasingly independent, vulgar element, enriched with material which it dresses up in its own way until finally it finds its most apt expression in academically syncretic and unprincipled eclectic compilations (p. 501).

Furthermore, 'vulgar political economy deliberately becomes increasingly *apologetic* and makes strenuous attempts to talk out of existence the ideas which contain the contradictions' – contradictions, which were 'in the process of being worked out in socialism and the struggles of the time'. This reading of the historical record reappears in a famous 'Afterword' to the second German edition of *Capital*, where Ricardo (and Sismondi in France) is portrayed as the 'last great representative of political economy', and the year 1830 as the watershed between 'scientific' and 'apologetic' economics:

> In France and in England the bourgeoisie had conquered political power. Thenceforth, the class-struggle, practically as well as theoretically, took on more and more outspoken and threatening forms. It sounded the knell of scientific bourgeois economy. It was thenceforth no longer a question, whether this theorem or that was true, but whether it was useful to capital or harmful, expedient or inexpedient, politically dangerous or not. In place of disinterested inquiries, there were hired prize-fighters; in place of genuine scientific research, the bad conscience and evil intent of apologetic (1965, I, 15).

The record in fact suggests that no use was made of Ricardo's labour theory by Thomas Hodgskin, the best known labour writer (1825, 1827, 1832); this is true also of Piercy Ravenstone (1821) and William Thompson (1824, 1827). As Marx himself pointed out, the labour writers criticized the positive role attributed to capital by Ricardo, but he vastly understated the strength of their objection. It is difficult to imagine a stronger critic of Ricardo than Hodgskin, who condemned his economics as an apologia for the institutional *status quo*. The true impetus to early nineteenth-century British socialism deriving from the conception of profits and rent as 'deductions from the whole produce of labour' came rather from the *Wealth of Nations* (see above, pp. 74–5).

The vehement anti-Ricardianism of the labour writers makes it difficult to believe that the dissenters reacted against a dangerous use of the orthodox doctrine for socialistic ends. They may have believed that Ricardo's analysis of value (especially as interpreted by McCulloch and James Mill) justified the notion of interest as an 'exploitation' income, but their objections did not follow from any dangerous use which they believed the socialists were making of Ricardian theory.

One economist did complain bitterly of the ammunition provided (inadvertently) by Ricardo for the socialists, but this individual was not one of the 'dissenters'. He was Thomas De Quincey, one of Ricardo's most faithful followers, who focused on Ricardo's minimization of technological progress and the consequent emphasis upon continuously rising rent:

> And it happens (though certainly not with any intentional sanction from so upright a man as David Ricardo) that in no instance has the policy of gloomy disorganising Jacobinism, fitfully reviving from age to age, received any essential aid from science, excepting in this one painful corollary from Ricardo's triad of chapters on Rent, Profit and Wages.... The class of landlords, they urge, is the merest realisation of a scriptural idea – *unjust men reaping where they have not sown*. They prosper... *by* the ruin of the fraternal classes associated with themselves on the land.... [The] noblest order of men amongst us, our landed aristocracy, is treated as the essential scourge of all orders beside (1844 [1897], 250–1).

The notion of class hostility, supposedly engendered by Ricardo's distribution theory, providing a handle for the anarchists, did not lead De Quincey to seek for an alternative structure. J. S. Mill in a review in fact complained of De Quincey's 'ultra-Tory prejudices', which deformed his otherwise excellent work as an economic theorist (1967, IV, 403–4).

We should also keep in mind James Mill, whose hysterical response to Hodgskin is sharper than that of any of the dissenters. Mill evidently saw nothing in the standard Ricardian position – even in the labour theory as interpreted by himself – which served the purposes of the socialists. The episode commences with Mill's complaint to Francis Place about a working class deputation to the editor of the *Morning Chronicle*: 'Their notions about property look ugly;... they seem to think that it should not exist, and that the existence of it is an evil to them. Rascals, I have no doubt, are at work among them.... The fools, not to see that what they madly desire would be such a calamity to them as no hands but their own could bring upon them' (cited in Wallas, 1925, 274n.). It was Hodgskin's *Labour Defended* which the labourers were preaching. In the following year Mill wrote that 'The nonsense... about the rights of the labourer to the whole produce of the country, wages, profits and rent, all included, is the mad nonsense of our friend Hodgskin which he has published as a system, and propagates with the zeal of perfect fanaticism.... These opinions, if they were to spread, would be the subversion of civilized society; worse than the revolutionary deluge of Huns and Tartars'.

A further feature – inexplicable from a Marxian perspective – is that Scrope, perhaps the first of the 'abstinence' writers (1831, 18; 1833, 146), opposed Ricardianism because the doctrine, by neglecting the implications for social welfare of unequal distribution, lent itself to social apologetics. Scrope was a reformer who saw in orthodoxy a rock against which proposals for social improvement must inevitably be destroyed. (By contrast, Hodgskin accorded no role whatsoever to government – the standard anarchist position.) The parallels between Scrope and, for example, William Thompson regarding their attitudes to Ricardo in this respect are quite remarkable. In Longfield's case it is more accurate to say that he made much positive use of Ricardian theory in formulating a reply to Hodgskin, fitting his own theoretical modifications into the existing framework, appropriately interpreted, and thereby avoiding what he envisaged to be negative implications for interclass relationships. But he too was certainly no apologist; like Scrope, he presented an impressively advanced programme of social reform. Marx's interpretation seems to be the exact reverse of the actual course of events.

An alternative interpretation of the bourgeois dissent subtly different from that which turns on the positive use supposedly made of Ricardo's theory by the labour writers has rather more merit. It is the argument that the bourgeois economists found the Ricardian doctrine unable to serve as a convincing reply – an apologetic reply – to the labour writers. Several dissenters expressed their dissatisfaction with the (supposed) implications of Ricardianism for class conflict and with its (supposed) 'pessimism'. But we must ask to what end did the dissenters seek to reply to the labour writers? It was positively not that of justifying contemporary capitalism, as is implied by the hypothesis. It is true also that economists sometimes had to prove their moral and religious *bona fides* and reconcile economics with Christianity in order to gain entry into the universities. But the fact is that the labour writers frequently expressed themselves in much the same language. Rejecting the Malthusian principle, Hodgskin proclaimed that 'moral feelings and scientific truth must always be in harmony with each other' (1827, xxi–xxii): 'The science of Political Economy... will be found when perfectly known... to – "Justify the ways of God to man"' (p. 268). And Piercy Ravenstone rejected Malthusianism because it weakened the 'veneration for the divine nature' (1821, 17).

Clearly there is no self-evident relationship in the post-Ricardian literature between a body of economic theory and the social attitudes of the economist subscribing to it. The positive contributions by some of the labour writers point in the same direction. Thompson's discussion of value includes the conceptions of differential land use, alternative cost and scarcity value. He defined and utilized the principle of diminishing marginal utility together with the principle of increasing marginal disutility of effort in an attempt to define an equilibrium wage rate, and also to calculate the effects of income redistribution (1824, 71–3). He expressed the significance of free exchange in utility terms: 'All voluntary exchanges of the articles of wealth, implying a preference, on both sides, of the things received to the thing given, tend to increase the happiness from wealth, and thence to increase the motives to its production' (p. 45). And while labour was said to be the best measure of value, it was not an accurate measure considering changes in preference patterns over time, so that to seek an accurate measure was 'to hunt after a shadow' (p. 15) – as clear-cut a criticism as any by Bailey. In Hodgskin's case, what stands out is his emphasis upon synchronized activity, elaborated in an *Economist* review of 1854 in terms of the mutual exchange of valuable services. It is precisely conceptions such as these which, when found in the 'dissenting' literature, are said to indicate a developing hostility to Ricardianism and a justification of unregulated capitalism.

16.7 Ricardo and J. S. Mill

Early in 1848 John Stuart Mill proclaimed his *Principles of Political Economy* to be Ricardian: 'I doubt if there will be a single opinion (on pure political economy) in the book, which may not be exhibited as a corollary from his doctrines' (1963, XIII, 731). Some commentators believe that this self-proclaimed adherence to Ricardo was fanciful and superficial – that in some objective sense he ought to have achieved independence. Schumpeter is quite explicit on this matter:

> the economics of [Mill's] *Principles* are no longer Ricardian. This is obscured by filial respect and also, independently of this, by J. S. Mill's own belief that he was only qualifying Ricardian doctrine. But this belief was erroneous. His qualifications affect essentials of theory and, still more, of course, of social outlook. . . . From Marshall's *Principles,* Ricardianism can be removed without being missed at all. From Mill's *Principles,* it could be dropped without being missed very greatly (1954, 529).

The same position has been reiterated more recently:

> A silent revolution in the direction of the marginalist supply-and-demand theory was brought about [by Marshall] in the course of adopting, extending and transforming some ideas in Mill. As Mill himself had departed considerably from Ricardo, Marshall was thus moving even further from the Ricardian source (Bharadwaj, 1978, 254).

> It was precisely the beginnings in Mill of considerable deviations from Ricardo's theory of value and distribution that called for and received at Marshall's hands...extensions and refinement; so that Marshall's deliberations on value and distribution departed systematically from the questions Ricardo posed and the framework of analysis he employed.... What [Gerald] Shove regarded as extensions and generalizations of Ricardo in Marshall's *Principles* (the introduction of the demand side, the functional relation between costs and output, the supply and demand determination of wages and profits) are radical departures from the Ricardian standpoint (p. 269; for the reference to Shove, see below, pp. 429–30).

A further conundrum has indeed been discerned by students of the economics of J. S. Mill: 'it seems remarkable how, with his broad intellectual sympathies and extensive understanding, he was prepared to lend his immense influence and prestige' to the 'non-historical and non-historiate' economics of Ricardo (Hutchison, 1978a, 220). Allusion has been made to Mill's 'remarkable ingenuity in admitting evidence adverse to Ricardo's predictions while preserving the essential position embodied in the theory', and to his 'delicate balancing act' of 'reaffirming and expanding new ideas and taking account of evidence which others considered to be antagonistic or damaging to the Ricardian system' (Winch, 1970, 28–9). And it is to the psychiatrist's couch that some would send Mill: 'The key to this continuing servitude no doubt lies in Mill's psyche', in 'a profound imbalance in the emotional side of his nature' (Schwartz, 1972, 49–50).

Mill's self-proclaimed identification with Ricardo can easily be accounted for without recourse to psychiatry. Mill insisted (and rightly so) that Ricardian method had wide applicability, extending far beyond the specific frame of reference pertinent to a capitalist exchange system; there was therefore nothing 'non-historiate' about the method as such. In any event, in Mill's estimate, the axiomatic framework of Ricardian theory retained its empirical relevance in contemporary circumstances; it is not difficult to demonstrate his limited vision of early prospects for significant institutional change. Above all, the key theorem derived on the basis of the Ricardian axiomatic framework – the inverse wage-profit relation – retained its relevance, and served as a potent reply to critics of union activity during the 1860s who argued on Smithian grounds that wage increases are inflationary. Ricardianism provided Mill with a powerful weapon in the battle for social reform, and there is no cause for wonderment at his fidelity from this perspective.

Mill, furthermore, did not, when composing his *Principles,* ignore the various criticisms of the preceding quarter-century directed against Ricardo's 'New Political Economy'. The point is that he (quite rightly) did not believe them to be destructive of the fundamental theoretical structure: 'these new views have been too frequently promulgated as contradictions of the doctrines previously received as fundamental; instead of being, as they almost always are, *developments* of them; corollaries flowing from these fundamental principles, certain conditions of fact being supposed' (1967, IV, 394). As we know, many of the criticisms of Ricardo indeed turn out to be in accord with Ricardian theory.

We should add that any charge against Mill of inconsistency for allowing both 'Ricardian' and 'neo-classical' conceptions of value and distribution would be misconceived. The demand side, the functional relation between cost and output, the supply and demand determination of wages and profits are central not only to Marshall but also to Ricardo, without which his cost theory of price and the inverse wage–profit relation cannot be understood. Our perspective thus avoids the difficult psychological problems posed by interpretations that refuse to accept at face value Mill's own insistence that he was elaborating upon Ricardian themes; or Marshall's own statements of his relationship with his classical forebears (see below, p. 429). Some of the broader issues involved here will be taken up in section 16.8.

16.8　Mill and the Inductivists

I go on now to lay out a problem relating to Mill's essay on definition and method (see above, p. 339). The problem concerns the relationship between the essay and John Frederick William Herschel's *Preliminary Discourse on the Study of Natural Philosophy* (1830) reviewed by Mill himself in the *Examiner,* and William Whewell's papers on mathematical economics and economic method (first published in 1829 and 1831) and review for the *British Critic* (1831) of Richard Jones's *Essay on the Distribution of Wealth.* It is difficult to appreciate the absence of any positive reference by Mill to the Cambridge scientists (especially Herschel), despite the fact that on matters of methodological principle and even of detailed formulation there is so much common ground between them. In effect, Mill – and here he was at one with

Ricardo – stood side by side with the inductivists against the championship of Nassau Senior (1827) of an axiomatic foundation of '*universal*' relevance, particularly in so far as the behavioural axiom is concerned. It is Mill (rather than Senior) who, in line with Ricardo, championed a '*positivistic*' in place of an '*hypothetical*' axiomatic foundation for political economy.

The extent of agreement between Mill and the Cambridge scientists has been unfortunately clouded by the erroneous tradition that Mill's essay makes out an extreme case for *a priori* procedure in economics, a procedure designed to yield universally applicable generalizations based on unobservable behavioural motivation, when in fact it champions 'a *mixed* method of induction and ratiocination' – direct induction being essential for the establishment of individual axioms. This latter perspective figures large in Herschel's appeal for a judicious blend of induction and deduction in scientific method – the former a process of 'reasoning upwards' from specific instances to general principle, and the latter a process of 'reasoning downwards' from general principle to particular application; in the role he accorded 'verification' of theory in the establishment of axioms and in their improvement; and in the attention he paid to the problem of 'disturbing causes' – causal forces excluded from formal consideration within a model but dealt with at the stage of application. Herschel, it may be added, had no complaints about contemporary political economy on matters of method.

Whewell's papers on Ricardian theory (1829, 1831a) and his review of Jones on rent (1831b) also insist upon a firm inductive basis for deductive reasoning and charge Ricardian economists for attempting to 'reason downwards' from axioms supposedly universal although at best of local relevance only. In some statements he implied that the immediate task at hand in political economy – the construction of generally applicable axioms by careful induction – was so immense that the process of 'downward reasoning' was for the distant future. But the positive role accorded deduction is apparent, provided *premature* deduction based on an inadequate axiomatic foundation is avoided. The positions of Mill and Whewell have much in common.

To approach a solution to this problem – especially the absence of any mention of the extensive and unambiguous common ground with Herschel – it is helpful to place the issue in perspective. The Cambridge 'inductivist' group as a whole included leading churchmen and professors opposed to Ricardianism, at least their conception of Ricardianism, particularly the population and rent principles. To render the tone of their hostility, we may refer to Richard Jones's bitter denunciation of the birth control notions said to be implicit in the former doctrine – 'vile', 'miserable', 'degrading' (1831, xiii–xiv, x–xi) – and of the proposition that the interests of the landlord are opposed to those of society as a whole (xxxi–xxxii). Now Mill, writing in 1835, attacked the old universities as second rate and blamed them for the low cultural state of the community: 'All is right so long as no one speaks of taking away their endowments, or encroaching upon their monopoly' (1969, X, 35). His neglect of Whewell's economics can perhaps be accounted for by his profound hostility towards the general *Weltanschauung* of the Cambridge inductivists. If, moreover, he included Herschel in the same category, we would better appreciate his failure to specify the common ground between them.

There is also the more specific and concerted attempt by Jones to disparage orthodox economics (see above, p. 410). Whewell's increasing doubts about Jones's inductivist programme may not have been known to Mill who perhaps read him as being opposed to deduction as a matter of principle. This latter would not, however, explain the neglect of Herschel, whose championship of a mixed method is unambiguous.

16.9 Conclusion

In this chapter I have demonstrated the longevity of Ricardian economics regarding substantive theory relating to value and distribution and economic growth. The demonstration supports a major theme of this text, that the story of nineteenth-century economics is not one of dual or parallel paradigms – Ricardian and embryonic neo-classical. Secondly, it shows that on the matter of method, the misconceived attacks by the 'inductivist' critics failed to leave a mark. Thirdly, the notion that the history of post-1830 theory can be interpreted in ideological terms is proved to be wanting.

Suggested Reading

On post-Ricardian opinion – the reception of Ricardian economics – and on the ideological dimension to the so-called 'dissension' as discussed above, see Hollander (1977b) and (1980) respectively. The propagation and fortunes of Ricardian economics are also analysed by Checkland (1949), Blaug (1958), particularly ch. 22 and 'Conclusion', Fetter (1969), and de Marchi (1970). Meek (1967), 51–74, and Dobb (1973), ch. 4, emphasize the role of ideology in the post-Ricardo period. Hicks (1983), ch. 5, gives his views on Mill's role in the transition 'from Classical to Post-classical'.

On the 'Ricardian Socialists', see again Hollander (1980), and also King (1983). The Cambridge 'inductivist' critics of Ricardo are treated in Hollander (1895), 149–58; 'Mill, Ricardianism and the Historical School' is also discussed, 913–28.

The 'marginal revolution' is the subject matter of a collection edited by Black, Coats and Goodwin (1973). Jaffé (1983), ch. 17, insists that Jevons, Walras and Menger be 'de-homogenized'. On marginalism, see Schumpeter (1954), 825–40, 909–20. Bowley (1972), argues convincingly against the notion of a marginal utility revolution. Meek (1977), ch. 9, on marginalism and Marxism, is again pertinent.

17 Conclusion: the Classicists and After

17.1 Introduction

The foregoing chapters will contribute to the on-going debate on the nature of the neo-classical developments of the 1870s, particularly the legitimacy of the term 'revolution', with its implication of analytical discontinuity, as a valid description of those developments. This representation has become particularly topical since the notion of a modern marginalist economics, with its roots in the contributions of the 1870s and contrasting sharply in analytical essentials with Ricardian classicism, constitutes a central theme of the historiography of the modern Cambridge (UK) School. The first two sections below (17.2 and 17.3) question the usefulness of the term 'marginal revolution' in the light of the version of classicism established in this book and indicate the presence in Walras and Marshall of certain key classical features relating to long-run resource allocation and to growth.

The 'Cambridge' economists find little merit in general-equilibrium procedure, and champion rather an approach involving the treatment of prices, production levels and distributions by means of separate models with an eye upon the isolation of 'one-way-direction' relationships or the 'causal ordering' of variables (see above, pp. 4–5 and appendix 1). This is a method commonly attributed to Ricardo, Marx and Sraffa (as well as to Keynes). The conclusion of this book, stated in section 17.4, is that Ricardo's method has much more in common with that of the general-equilibrium theorists.

17.2 A Marginal 'Revolution'?

A word first on the 'marginalists' themselves. Distribution was envisaged by W. S. Jevons as (ideally) a matter of service pricing, 'entirely subject to the principles of value and the laws of supply and demand' (1924, xlvi), with input prices 'the effect not the cause of the value of the produce' (p. 1) – 'I hold labour to be *essentially variable, so that its value must be determined by the value of the produce, not the value of the produce by that of the labour*' (p. 166); and cost of production as a reflection of opportunities foregone (pp. xlviii–l). He accordingly directed his criticisms at the wage fund and subsistence approaches to wage rate determination and the cost approach to value – as he understood them – paying tribute to the French tradition of J. B. Say and others: 'the only hope of attaining a true system of Economics is to fling aside, once and for ever, the mazy and preposterous assumptions of the Ricardian School. Our English Economists have been living in a fool's paradise. The truth is with the French School' (pp. xliv–v). Jevons recognized elements of the 'correct' position in Mill's *Principles* – that rent enters into cost where land has alternative uses, that all inequalities (whether natural or artificial) generate economic rents and the representation of demand and supply as a law 'anterior' to costs (pp. xlviii, li, 198) – but could not resist remarking on Mill's 'philosophic character', namely his inconsistency (p. li). Jevons's view of the history of economics reflects the foregoing perspective:

> When at length a true system of Economics comes to be established, it will be seen that that able but wrong-headed man, David Ricardo, shunted the car of Economic science on to a wrong line – a line, however, on which it was further urged towards confusion by his equally able and wrong-headed admirer, John Stuart Mill. There were Economists, such as Malthus and Senior, who had a far better comprehension of the true doctrines (though not free from the Ricardian errors), but they were driven out of the field by the unity and influence of the Ricardo–Mill school (p. li).

Léon Walras, whose intellectual origins include J. B. Say, similarly objected to the classical pricing and distribution model (as he understood it), particularly the cost orientation and the natural wage approach. By neglecting a final demand dimension and accordingly derived demand, so he charged, the English had constructed an underdetermined system:

> Let P be the aggregate price received for the products of an enterprise; let S, I and F be respectively the wages, interest charges and rent laid out by the entrepreneurs, in the course of production, to pay for the services of personal faculties, capital and land. Let us recall now that, according to the English School, the selling price of products is determined by their costs of production, that is to say, it is equal to the cost of the productive services employed. Thus we have the equation
>
> $$P = S + I + F,$$

and *P* is determined for us. It remains to determine *S*, *I*, and *F*. Surely, if it is not the price of the products that determines the price of productive services, but the price of productive services that determines the price of the products, we must be told what determines the price of the services. This is precisely what the English economists try to do. To this end, they construct a theory of rent according to which rent is not included in the expenses of production, thus changing the above equation to

$$P = S + I.$$

Having done this, they determine S directly by the [subsistence] theory of wages. Then, finally, they tell us that 'the amount of interest or profit is the excess of the aggregate price received for the products over the wages expended on their production', in other words, that it is determined by the equation,

$$I = P - S.$$

It is clear now that the English economists are completely baffled by the problem of price determination; for it is impossible for *I* to determine *P* at the same time that *P* determines *I*. In the language of mathematics one equation cannot be used to determine two unknowns (1874 [1954], 424–5).

In more recent times we have a famous criticism of classicism along similar lines by Professor Frank Knight (1956). For Knight, prices depend on the relative subjective appeal to consumers, the flow of goods and thus their marginal utilities governed by cost consideration, where 'costs' reflect alternatives surrendered rather than 'pain' in the sense of labour or abstinence. On this view, the economizing principle involves maximizing the total return from any resource by equalizing the increments of return at the margin to the scarce resource in alternative uses. The severity of Knight's charges against Ricardo for failing to recognize the economizing principle must be read to be believed.

For Knight the developments of the 1870s were, obviously, 'revolutionary'. But for a pristine formulation of the supposedly revolutionary status of the developments of the 1870s – especially respecting the role of final demand – the following statement is difficult to improve upon:

The classical theory of value – as we find it streamlined in Stuart Mill – was essentially a theory of production costs based on the thinking of the private entrepreneur. The entrepreneur will think as follows: 'If I could only cut my selling price I would be able to draw the customers to me [']. This, however, is also the way [his] competitors think. So, there emerges a sort of gravitational force that pulls prices down. The cost of production is so to speak the solid base on to which the prices fall down and remain. Hence the cost of production is the 'cause' of prices. This general viewpoint the classical economists applied with great sagacity to a whole range of commodities, to the relation between wages and profits, and to the theory of international prices.

This theory contains, of course, an irrefutable element of truth. But it is too simple to give even a crude presentation of the forces at play. The economic process is an *equilibrium affair* where both technological and subjective forces are at play. The subjective element was nearly left out by the classicists.

On this point economic theory was completely renewed, in the years between 1870 and 1890 when a number of Austrian economists headed by Carl Menger (1840–1921) undertook a systematic study of the *human wants* and their place in a theory of prices. Similar thoughts were expressed also by the Swiss Léon Walras (1834–1910) and the Englishman Stanley Jevons (1835–1882). This was the first break-through since Stuart Mill.

The Englishman, Alfred Marshall (1842–1924) subsequently did much to combine the subjective viewpoint and the cost of production viewpoint. This led to what we now speak of as the neo-classical theory (Frisch, 1981, 5).

It has also been suggested (Arrow and Starrett, 1973, 132–3) that Mill's recognition of non-competing groups implied a multiplicity of primary factors which 'required a new theory'. The founders of the neo-classical school 'understood the glaring omission of demand from the classical model'. Classical theory, runs the argument, could not solve the logical problem of explaining the relative wages of heterogeneous types of labour. The same theme of a revolutionary break by the general-equilibrium economists from classicism is also a feature of modern 'Cambridge' historiography.

                              *   *   *

The evidence discussed in this book points away from the foregoing interpretations. It suggests how useful, in the present context, is the notion of altered 'concentrations of attention' (see above, p. 1), which avoids any revolutionary connotation. For what seems to have occurred after 1870 was a sharpening of theoretical tools, particularly those relating to consumer choice (the marginal utility approach); the algebraic formulation of general-equilibrium relationships; and a narrowing of focus, specifically a greater concern with exchange and allocation in their own right rather than within a growth context, the neo-classicals taking as their expository point of departure the model of pure exchange. These are developments that could have been absorbed by the traditional corpus of analysis, whereas the impatience of the marginalists and their apparent wish to wipe the slate clean meant that much of great import in classical theory for their own chosen and relatively narrow sphere of discourse was not recognized, and spurious analytical distinctions were artificially reinforced. For, as will by now be clear, the economics of Ricardo and J. S. Mill comprises in its essentials an exchange system consistent with the marginalist elaborations. Its cost price analysis is pre-eminently an analysis of the allocation of scarce resources, proceeding in terms of general equilibrium, with allowance for final demand and the interdependence of factor and commodity markets. A role is accorded opportunity cost and derived factor demand, reflecting a simultaneous and consistent attachment to cost theories of value and to the general-equilibrium conception of economic organization as formulated by J. B. Say and much admired by Walras. The classical notions of wages and interest as compensation for effort and abstinence are pertinent only at the macro-economic level, where the determinants of aggregate factor supplies are under investigation and not in the micro-economic context where cost refer to foregone opportunities in the sense of foregone products. Even in their own domain of price-theory, the marginalists failed to build on their predecessors.

The marginal productivity principle, adopted a generation after the so-called 'marginal revolution' itself, added to the understanding of factor demand in particular uses. But this elaboration was required as much by Say as by Ricardo and Mill. To assert that recognition of a multiplicity of primary factors required a new theory based upon the principles of demand, or that classical theory could not explain the relative wages of heterogeneous types of labour is historically unjustified. Since Smith's time and before the wage structure had been analysed in terms of demand–supply. Smith and his successors had all recognized a productivity dimension on the demand side of the labour market, although in dealing with the wage structure the classicists typically chose to focus on the supply side; and while value productivity is more conspicuous the more specialized to a particular use are individual factors, those same considerations are equally relevant when allowance is made for factor mobility between uses, although now strict limits are placed on the extent to which returns in different uses can diverge. In any event, although short-run factor specificity was indeed a neoclassical preoccupation, both Ricardo and Mill carried this very matter far in their generalizations of the rent doctrine. Furthermore, if we take into account the matter of foreign trade and classical analysis in that case – the conspicuous role accorded demand considerations where the factor mobility axioms are abandoned – it becomes yet clearer that the notion of a paradigmatic transformation in the 1870s is unhelpful.

By adopting the assumption of single-use land Ricardo certainly indicated a preoccupation with the macro dimension. Yet the 'class' relationship that concerned him, pre-eminently the inverse wage–profit relationship, could not be understood except in terms of allocation theory; like Mill, he insisted upon a micro-foundation for macro-analysis, which seems eminently sensible if capitalist exchange institutions are taken seriously. To trace through the consequences of a variation in the general wage in the case where (marginal) cost price incorporates land rent in the Smith–Say manner would have been technically impossible given the state of the science. (It is doubtful whether a specific outcome could be generated in the present day and age, for which reason so much analysis proceeds on the basis of two-factors and two-products.) For all that, any problems created for Ricardo's theorem by allowance for multi-use land derive from an analytical model (the allocative model) with which Ricardo himself was familiar.

Our perspective suggests how justified was Alfred Marshall's insistence, against the marginalists, upon the essential continuity of nineteenth-century doctrine: 'under the honest belief that Ricardo and his followers had rendered their account of the causes that determine value hopelessly wrong by omitting to lay stress on the law of satiable wants [diminishing marginal utility], [Jevons] led many to think he was correcting great errors; whereas he was really only adding very important explanations' (1920, 101n.). We have seen how the classicists were perfectly capable of dealing with the issue of scarcity without explicitly referring to the margin; making that notion explicit was certainly a step forward, but it did not amount to a revolutionary change. Indeed, Marshall found Ricardo's formulations to be 'more philosophic [scientific] in principle and closer to the actual facts of life' (p. 819), for Jevons had substituted 'a catena of causes for mutual causation' – a reference to his sequence:

> Cost of production determines supply;
> Supply determines final degree of utility;
> Final degree of utility determines value (1871 [1924], 165).

Jevons had 'achieved some apparently unfair dialectical triumphs, by assuming that Ricardo thought of value as governed by cost of production without reference to demand' (p. 821n.). We conclude that an estimate by Gerald Shove regarding the place of Marshall – diametrically opposed to that by Frisch (cited above, pp. 426–7) – stands the test of time:

> the analytical backbone of Marshall's *Principles* is nothing more or less than a completion and generalization, by means of a mathematical apparatus, of Ricardo's theory of value and distribution as expounded by J. S. Mill. It is not, as many have supposed, a conflation of Ricardian notions with those of the 'marginal utility' school. Nor is it an attempt to

substitute for Ricardian doctrine a new system of ideas arrived at by a
different line of approach.... [So] far as its strictly analytical content is
concerned, the *Principles* is in the direct line of descent through Mill from
Ricardo, and through Ricardo from Adam Smith (1942 [1960], 712).

But even Shove did not go quite far enough. For he still believed that
'the process of completion and generalization involved a transformation
more thoroughgoing than Marshall himself was disposed to admit'.

17.3 Classical Features in Walrasian Economics

We now consider the reverse side of the coin – classical features in
Léon Walras's neo-classical economics. From this perspective too it is
clear that the term 'revolution' would be inappropriate as a description
of the transition.

In his criticisms of Ricardo and Mill, Walras wrote that 'it is not the
cost of the productive services that determines the selling price of the
product, but rather the other way round' (1874 [1954], 400). He praised
Jevons's statement of the ideal procedure according to which 'the
formula of the English School, in any case the school of Ricardo and
Mill, must be reversed, for the prices of productive services are determined by the prices of the products, and not the other way round' (p.
45). This does not, in fact, constitute a picture of mutual interdependence between factor and product markets; it is rather a statement that emphasizes what the classics had supposedly omitted, and
does so by implicitly adopting a short-run perspective where factor supplies in each sector are given. Nevertheless, Walras accepted the
'classical' conception of long-run cost prices – 'costs' incorporating
profits at a uniform rate on the supply prices of capital goods. And he
was not inconsistent by so doing; for he insisted upon profit rate
uniformity, as Ricardo had done and as Marshall was to do, only if sufficient time is allowed to change the outputs of the different types of
capital goods. (The same applies to labour.) Walras adhered to classical
cost price analysis given the appropriate long-run assumptions and, like
Ricardo and Marshall, distinguished between maximising decisions
regarding new investments and the actual return on capital goods once
constructed.

Walras's subscription to a cost price analysis of the classical order is
quite explicit:

> under free competition, if the selling price of a product exceeds the cost
> of the productive services for certain firms and a *profit* results, entrepre-
> neurs will flow towards his branch of production or expand their out-
> put, so that the quantity of the product [on the market] will increase, its

price will fall, and the difference between price and cost will be reduced; and, if [on the contrary], the cost of the productive services exceeds the selling price for certain firms, so that *a loss* results, entrepreneurs will leave this branch of production, or curtail their output, so that the quantity of the product [on the market] will decrease, its price will rise and the difference between price and cost will again be reduced (p. 225).

Because of changes in technology or demand patterns the market is 'perpetually tending towards equilibrium without ever reaching it' (p. 380). In fact,

> there never is a day when the effective demand for products and services equals their effective supply and when the selling price of products and services equals the cost of the productive services used in making them. The diversion of productive services from enterprises that are losing money to profitable enterprises takes place in various ways, the most important being through credit operations, but at best these ways are slow.

Involved in the adjustment process are variations in factor supplies, and not merely transfer of services between sectors without alteration in the supplies of the factors from which they derive, for such transfers would be almost instantaneous, whereas Walras emphasized the slowness of adjustment following a disturbance. Thus alteration in the types of 'personal capital' in response to market pressures requires retraining of the labour force (or even perhaps the renewal of the population stock) (p. 401). There is, in brief, a long-run 'tendency' towards wage rate equalization, contingent upon training and education, very much like that of Adam Smith. The same conception is applied to the capital factor in general (p. 380).

In Walras's formal theory of capital, net savings (incomes exceeding consumption and allowance for depreciation) are exchanged for new additions to the stock of capital goods, the quantities of the different types of capital goods satisfying the condition of equality between their demand and supply prices (pp. 269–70). But this condition also reflects the principle of uniformity of net return on the new investments, for if the condition of uniformity 'is not fulfilled with respect to any two capital goods, it will be advantageous to produce less of the capital good for which the ratio is smaller, and more of the capital good for which this ratio is larger' (p. 276; cf. p. 305). The emphasis is thus upon uniformity of return on *new* investments; but evidently a change in the structure of final demand patterns or in technology, such as Walras emphasizes, might lower the rentals on certain types of existing capital goods and thus require a contraction in their quantities by the non-investment of available depreciation allowances. The principle of uniformity of the return on capital extends to investment decisions in general – to replacement demand as well as the net demand for new capital goods – although at any particular moment of time it is unlikely that uniformity across-the-board will be satisfied considering the disturbances in question: 'In an economy like the one we have imagined, which establishes its economic equilibrium *ab ovo*, it is probable that there would be no equality of rates of net income. Nor would such an equality be likely to exist in an economy which had just been disrupted by a war, a revolution or a business crisis' (p. 308). As explained, we are dealing with a 'tendency' to uniformity on capital in general.

It is clear that equality of net interest is treated by Walras as a 'point of reference' only. It is in the course of adding to and replacing capital goods that decisions are made with an eye on prospective earnings, but expectations are continually disappointed so that actual yields diverge from those expected when the investments are undertaken. This was also true of Marshall who maintained that interest is earned on 'free' or 'floating' capital, and the phrase 'rate of interest is applicable to old investments of capital only in a very limited sense'; given complexes earn quasi-rents, and in the polar extreme case of permanent investments the term 'interest on capital' is totally inapplicable (1920, pp. 592–3; also pp. 411–12, 418–19, 533). None the less, the 'tendency' to equalization is continually at play to the extent that complexes do wear out more or less rapidly. Indeed, Marshall estimated that as much as 25 per cent of existing capital goods is replaced annually 'even in a country in which the prevailing forms of capital are as durable as in England', and he was prepared for some analytical purposes (particularly in the context of accumulation) to assume 'that the owners of capital in general have been able in the main to adapt its forms to the normal conditions of the time, so as to derive as good a *net* income from their investments in one way as another' (p. 592).

Uniformity of the rate of profits on 'free capital' entails not the across-the-board uniformity appropriate for true long-run equilibrium analysis, in a stationary state sense, but a pseudo long-run equilibrium involving new capital gradually flowing towards sectors where quasi-rents are highest. This conception has been termed a 'sort of development of Walrasian theory' (Harcourt, 1975, 351). In fact, it is the *Walras–Marshall* line itself, and this line is fully in the classical tradition. For some analytical purposes Ricardo (like Marshall) presumed across-the-board equality of the return on capital. Thus, to investigate the consequences of a change in demand patterns or in technology he would set off from an assumed state of equilibrium in the sense that we 'suppose that all commodities are at their natural price, and consequently that the profits of capital in all employments are exactly at the same rate' (Ricardo, 1951, I, 90). But he was perfectly well aware, first, that what

matters in the (practical) profitability calculations which govern allocation is the return on *new* investments, for once investments are
embodied in an actual capital structure we are dealing with rentals; and
secondly, that in the polar case of permanent embodiments it is no
longer pertinent to talk of a return on *capital* at all (see above, p. 99).
And, like both Walras and Marshall, Ricardo appreciated that adjustments are never instantaneous even where the 'withdrawal of capital' is
physically possible: 'it always becomes a matter of calculation, whether
these [capital goods] shall continue to be employed on the land, notwithstanding the low [the unexpectedly low] price of corn, or whether they
shall be sold, and their value transferred to another employment' (p.
269) – a calculation characterized by 'the prejudices and obstinacy with
which men persevere in their old employments, – they expect daily a
change for the better, and therefore continue to produce commodities
for which there is no adequate demand' (1951, VIII, 277).

The classical and late nineteenth-century economists were concerned
with both growth and allocation, although the weighting of their preoccupations differed. Depending upon the context, it was appropriate to
emphasize factor 'scarcity' or factor 'reproducibility' or various combinations. Thus Ricardo frequently dealt with disturbances (demand
changes, innovation, taxation) within a static framework, although there
is no question of a predominant concern with analytical issues relating
to the growth process, the aggregate factors (capital and labour) treated
as variables. Conversely, Walras extended his own static analysis in the
Elements to deal with growth.

His growing economy is specified in terms of classes – consisting of
workers, landowners, capitalists and entrepreneurs – not merely firms
and householders. The source of accumulation is isolated in the 'excess
of income over consumption in the aggregate' (1874 [1954], 264),
allowance made for differential savings propensities by class. Part VII
of the *Elements* is devoted entirely to the 'Conditions and Consequences of Economic Progress', dealing with the distributional implications of growth in labour and capital supplies (given land): 'What does
need to be discussed . . . in view of its extremely weighty consequences,
is the fact . . . that the quantity of land cannot possibly increase though it
is possible to increase the number of persons and the quantity of capital
goods proper in an economy that saves and converts its savings into
capital' (p. 382). In this part, his expanded system of equations – which
allow for choice between alternative techniques depending on relative
factor prices – is shown to generate 'the *laws of the variation of prices in
a progressive economy*'. These include the proposition that '*In a progressive economy, the price of labour (wages) remaining substantially
unchanged, the price of land-services (rent) will rise appreciably and the*

price of capital-services (the interest charge) will fall appreciably' (pp. 390–1). With his constant wage, Walras out-Ricardos Ricardo! Secondly, a decline in the interest charge relative to a roughly constant cost price of capital goods implies that *'In a progressive economy the rate of net income'* – and therefore the profit rate – *'will fall appreciably'*.

Technical difficulties with the extended analysis exist, although modern technique has gone some way in their resolution (Morishima, 1977, 1980). But clearly the central themes of the classical growth model (and several of the conclusions) were not superannuated in the 1870s.

17.4 On the Cambridge ('Neo-Ricardian') Version of Classicism

In the so-called 'Cambridge' account, the 'analytical core' of marginalism or neo-classicism is

> the model of pure exchange, whereby perfect competition is depicted as the solution to the problem of the optimal allocation of scarce resources. Prices are interpreted as indexes of resource scarcity relative to wants, income distribution comes out as a by-product of price-determination, distributive variables being but the prices for the services of the so-called 'factors of production'. Production processes are only an intermediate stage connecting consumers' tastes to the initial endowments of scarce original resources (Roncaglia, 1985, 108)

'Classicism', by contrast, is represented as a reproductive process involving the 'production of commodities by means of commodities'. At the beginning of each production period, specific quantities of various commodities are advanced, as means of production and as subsistence for labour at an exogenously determined wage rate. The utilization of the advanced commodities yields a (physical) surplus consisting of a heterogeneous set of commodities; and relative prices are such as to assure a profit inducement to repeat the production process at a uniform rate of profit. The average profit rate is determined solely by the exogenously given wage rate and technology – 'technology' including the technique or factor ratios required, and also the structure of production or output levels.

The contrast envisaged between paradigms has been well stated thus:

> this *separate* determination of real wage and social product entails a structuring of the analysis which is radically different from that of the theories which were to become dominant later. The surplus theories have, so to speak, a *core* which is isolated from the rest of the analysis because the wage, the social product and the technical conditions of pro-

duction appear there as already determined. It is in this 'core' that we find the determination of the shares other than wages as a residual: a determination which ... will also entail the determination of the relative prices of commodities (Garegnani, 1984, 296).

The factors influencing the 'independent' variables, such as the wage and the social product (and its breakdown between sectors), are matters falling outside the 'core'. Allowances for playbacks from the dependent variables (particularly the profit rate) on the wage by way of the speed of accumulation are also left to be studied outside the core, such playbacks not being subject to any general rule: 'The multiplicity of these influences and their variability according to circumstances was in fact understood to make it impossible to reconduct [sic] them to *necessary* quantitative relations like those, studied in the 'core', between distributive variables and relative prices and between outputs or techniques and the dependent distributive variables and prices' (p. 297). By contrast are the 'marginalist' theories:

> In these, the determination of the wage is in fact inseparable from, and symmetrical to, that of the other shares of the product. Moreover, the demand-and-supply mechanism used in that determination implies that real wages and the other distributive variables (and hence relative values) can only be determined *simultaneously*, and simultaneously with the volume and composition of the product. Indeed, in later theory, distribution, outputs and relative values of commodities are all determined simultaneously taking as data the tastes of consumers, the endowments of 'factors of production' and the technical conditions of production.

On the Cambridge view of classicism output levels are given to the 'core'. Values (prices) and output levels are not determined simultaneously by the forces of demand and supply. The classicists ruled out functional relations between price and quantity (as between the wage and labour demand or labour supply), for such relations were too complex and too variable to be specified with precision. Figure 17.1 contrasts the notion of demand attributed to the classicists (A) with that of the neo-classical school (B). On this interpretation of classicism prices corresponding to quantities below the normal quantity (q_n) are determinate only in that they exceed (to an indeterminate extent) the normal price (p_n) falling somewhere within the northwest quadrant (1) in the figure. Positions in that quadrant (or in the southeast quadrant, 2, in the event $q > q_n$) are, as it were, 'accidental', there being no theory of demand which would allow them to be envisaged as lying on a demand curve in the neo-classical fashion. In short, only the 'natural' or 'normal' price–quantity relation is a determinate one. The Cambridge view allows only that the accidental market prices will 'gravitate' towards the natural price, and output to the normal level, but denies that this entails

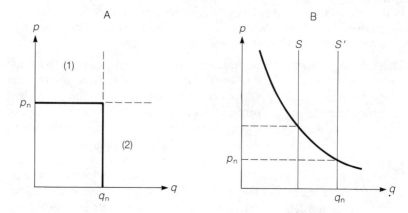

Figure 17.1   A, the classical notion of demand and B, demand curve attribut-
able only to neo-classicists, according to Garegnani (1983).

movements along a given demand curve. (What is said of commodity
markets is applied also to factor markets. In particular, there is a normal
wage to which the market wage will 'gravitate' but there is no sense to a
labour demand function.)

Now to divorce value and output levels is in fact to imply the divorce
of prices and distribution. Assume, for example, a change in consumer
tastes in favour of a labour-intensive good – a shift in the demand curve.
Neo-classicists would argue that the change in output levels will affect
relative factor scarcity, in this case exerting increased competition for
labour and forcing the real wage upwards. That the expansion of output
renders more costly the factor used in a relatively high proportion
means in turn an increase in the relative price of the commodity in question; this impact can be thought of as introducing an upward slope to
the supply schedule such that, in the new long-run equilibrium, cost
price is higher than initially (cf. Garegnani, 1983, 310). (Note that the
upward slope is generated even in the absence of 'diminishing returns'.)
By contrast, on the Cambridge view of classicism the real wage is given
'institutionally' before and independently of the determination of relative prices, thus precluding the foregoing interdependence; with this
restriction relative prices and the profit rate are determined independently of demand functions (p. 311). Indeed, as explained already, the
very notion of a demand function is suspect in Cambridge. The essence
of the matter is that 'the procedure of the classical economists
renounces what was attempted by later theory, a simultaneous treatment of the interrelations between most economic phenomena' (p. 312).

In all this Garegnani follows Piero Sraffa in his interpretation of the classicists. Sraffa's *Production of Commodities by Means of Commodities* (1960) studies the relationship between the wage and profit rates and between these distributive variables and relative prices. It is a characteristic of the approach that 'no changes in output and...no changes in the proportions in which different means of production are used by an industry are considered, so that no question arises as to the variation or constancy of returns' (1960, v). The assumption of unchanged output is said to be that 'of the old classical economists from Adam Smith to Ricardo', which 'has been submerged and forgotten since the advent of the "marginal method"' with its characteristic emphasis on change in scale of industry and in factor proportions. On this basis, Sraffa proceeds to demonstrate that given any one of the two distributive variables it is possible to derive values for the other and for a set of relative prices consistently with the condition that a uniform rate of profit rules throughout the system. The analysis makes no use of demand theory and there is, by implication, no assurance that the prices derived will be 'equilibrium' prices in the dual senses of equality of quantity demanded and quantity supplied and equality of market price and cost price. As has recently been suggested: 'Sraffa leaves us to find out what his prices are, but I doubt if they are equilibrium prices. They seem to be prices which are set upon products, by their producers, according to some [conventional] rule...; the uniformity of the rate of profit throughout this system...is just a uniformity of convention' (Hicks, 1985, 306).

Our interpretation of Ricardo – and this applies to Mill and Marx – points directly away from the Sraffa–Garegnani perspective. In the first place, re-establishment of a system of relative prices, following (for example) a variation in wages, occurs by way of changes in output allowing for the condition of equality between quantities demanded and supplied in commodity markets. There is no justification for attributing to the classicists the assumption of constant outputs in the analysis of the effects of given variations in the wage rate, and none for the belief that they rejected demand–supply analysis, demand and supply understood as 'schedules' or 'functions'. Full equilibrium entails equality in the returns on capital throughout the system – market equal to cost prices and equality of demand and supply – conditions already well established in the *Wealth of Nations*. Thus, whereas in Sraffa's model there is no process analysis to ensure profit rate equality following a disturbance, for Ricardo (who accepted Smithian process analysis) re-establishment of equilibrium entails reactions by capitalists to profit rate differentials which manifest themselves in expansions or contractions of the various industries with inverse movements in prices. It is an historical anachronism to attribute the Sraffian procedure to Ricardo.

This takes us to a further fundamental difference between the two structures. Sraffa does not provide a theory of distribution; as explained earlier, one of the distributive variables must be given exogenously. By contrast, neither the profit rate nor the wage rate appears as data in Ricardo's growth analysis. The wage rate is a variable determined by the general system of demand and supply relationships in the labour market while the profit rate is merely a formal residual, there being a mutual dependency of the one upon the other. Ricardo's model uses something akin to the 'equilibrium' (his word) conception of marginalist theory.

The neo-classicists were largely – but certainly not wholly – concerned with distribution *given* factor supplies; the marginal productivity approach to distribution was devised to deal better with the conditions of factor demand. For the classicists were (with an exception made for Longfield) constrained within an alternative frame of reference – the wage fund approach. The average wage was still a determinate one governed by market conditions; and they were right to take this view in the circulating capital model. But where the existence of fixed capital is taken seriously, a problem of indeterminacy arises as we have seen (above, pp. 225–6). Yet interestingly enough, dissatisfaction was later expressed on similar grounds with the neo-classical concept of a short-period marginal product – the additional product due to a small increase in the quantity of labour when the quantity of cooperating capital is unchanged. For the theory requires that technical methods should be freely variable; only then can the number of units of a factor used together with given amounts of other factors be reduced without rendering a part of the supply of the fixed factors completely useless, or be increased with a yield of some positive product. Should these variations be technically ruled out, the reduction in output in the first case would far exceed the amount that can be attributed to that factor; and in the second case the contribution to output would be zero.

It is in the long-run case (allowing for growth of capital and change in its form) that classical market analysis comes fully into its own, the data of the system including the functional relations tying accumulation and population growth to the return on capital and the wage respectively. The classical practice is frequently to ask: 'what will be the impact on profits and prices of a given change in the wage?' But this is not because the wage is determined exogenously or 'outside the core', but rather because analysis requires just this – analysis followed by synthesis. Ricardo (and this applies also to J. S. Mill) was concerned with the trend paths of the distributive variables in a growth context. On his view the commodity wage tends downwards. Because the real (labour) cost of producing the smaller wage basket increases, and thus the proportionate share of labour in the value of the product rises, the profit rate must fall also. The inverse wage–profit theorem – the impact of a given wage change on profits – has to be fitted into this growth investigation, for the wage is subject to continuous market pressures. This is true too of Marx, though the precise rationale for the real wage movement differs.

Now aggregate labour demand depends partly on the rate of capital accumulation and therefore (for Ricardo and Mill, though not for Marx) on the profit rate, and, of course, inversely on the wage rate. For all three economists, labour demand also varies with the organic composition of capital. This latter, however, is not solely a technological matter, depending as it does on the pattern of economic activity once allowance is made for differential labour–capital ratios between industries. Given these differentials, it should follow that output patterns will be influenced by a wage change either directly in consequence of changing expenditure patterns, assuming they differ between classes, or indirectly, in that the wage change has a differential impact on relative profit rates in the different industries, bringing about alterations in outputs depending on the demand conditions in each industry.

How much of this is *explicit* in classical theory? Apart from the competitive labour market analysis which is unquestionably present, classical economics also allows conspicuously for factor substitution in response to wage variations by way of industry contraction and expansion – their analysis presuming alternative uses of resources between industries and a resultant process of supply–demand adjustment to assure profit rate equalization. The classicists failed to make explicit the further complexity that a wage change can, by influencing output levels in the various industries, *play back* on the wage itself. (Even the impact of exogenous shifts in demand patterns on distribution was frequently bypassed.) But there is no reason why any of them would have objected to this *mutual* interdependence of pricing and distribution. Thus, for example, Marx appreciated that the rate of surplus value is not a *datum* given in the value scheme, but varies with the wage; and he made much of the dependency of the pattern of demand on distribution (see above, pp. 370–1). Ricardo made the same point (see above, p. 97). There would be nothing 'anti-classical' in adding that changes in the structure of industry – possibly induced by a wage change – may play back on the wage by influencing labour market conditions in so far as such changes affect the breakdown between constant and variable capital.

Only by artificially imposing narrow frontiers around a so-called 'classical core' can such interconnections be precluded. This misleading strategy has been correspondingly applied to accounts of neo-classicism (general equilibrium), thereby reinforcing the distortion. It may be allowed that the neo-classicists, particularly Walras, took as the point of departure the model of pure exchange, with factor supplies amongst the data of the system. But there is no warrant to take this starting point as constituting the 'core' of neo-classicism. For this perspective neglects entirely the extensions of general-equilibrium theorizing to the problem of 'progress' – extensions which yielded remarkably classical results relating to wage and profit trends in an expanding system subject to land scarcity.

Suggested Reading

The first three sections above draw on Hollander (1982). For recent appreciations of the growth dimension to Walras's economics see Collard (1973) and Morishima (1977, 1980). A brief account, in historical context, of the technical difficulties entailed by attempts to determine the general rate of return in terms of demand and supply is given by Milgate (1979). These difficulties first came to light only in the late 1920s and early 1930s, and led on to what is now referred to as the 'neo-neoclassical' concern with 'inter-temporal equilibrium', which abandons the entire concept of 'the rate of profit'.

The 'Italo-Cambridge' interpretation of the classicists on value and distribution, is developed by Garegnani (1983, 1984, 1985), and Roncaglia (1985). On the interpretation of the beginnings of neo-classicism from a Cambridge perspective, see Bharadwaj (1978). On the recent 'revival of classicism' as understood in Cambridge, see Harcourt (1975). This article is followed by comments from Hahn, Hicks and Dobb and Harcourt's response.

For an obituary article on Sraffa, see Porta (1984). Excellent summaries of Sraffa's 1960 book are by Harcourt (1972), 177–204, and Meek (1967), 161–78.

Appendix 1 The Sraffa Model

1 Introduction

Piero Sraffa's vision of economic process as outlined in *Production of Commodities by Means of Commodities* (1960) has been referred to on various occasions throughout this book. But it has appeared as a ghost flitting through the pages. It is time to give an outline of Sraffa's contribution, which was intended to by-pass the marginalist or demand–supply tradition, and above all to avoid the relationship between income payments and productivity characteristic of much of contemporary orthodoxy. Appropriately, Sraffa sub-titled his work 'Prelude to a Critique of Economic Theory'.

In the Preface to the work this perspective is briefly elaborated (v–vi). Sraffa's scheme is founded on the assumption that no changes occur in outputs and in proportions between means of production: 'The investigation is concerned exclusively with such properties of an economic system as do not depend on changes in the scale of production or in the proportions of "factors"'. And since there are no changes in scale or proportion, there can be neither marginal product or marginal cost, nor any question of variation or constancy of returns to scale. Sraffa draws a parallel between his own perspective and that of Quesnay's *tableau économique* with its system of production and circularity of process, contrasting with the 'modern' view of a 'one-way avenue' that leads from given endowments of 'Factors of production' to 'Consumption goods' (p. 93). (We have seen that the latter representation would scarcely apply to the original 'neo-classical' writers who allowed for economic 'progress' and expanding factor supplies.)

2. The Subsistence Case

Two products, wheat (in quarters) and iron (in tons), are both used to maintain labour and as means of production in an annual production process. We tabulate a year's operations, which define '*the methods of production*' such that:

TOTAL OUTPUT

280 qr wheat + 12 t. iron → 400 qr wheat

120 qr wheat + 8 t. iron → 20 t. iron

TOTAL INPUT 400 qr wheat 20 t. iron

Here 400 qr of wheat and 20 t. of iron are annually used up to produce 400 qr wheat and 20 t. iron, without 'surplus' at the end of the production period.

For the next round of activity to proceed the producer of wheat must retain 280 qr out of his 400 and sell the remaining 120 such that he can acquire 12 t. iron; similarly the producer of iron must retain 8 t. iron for the next round and sell the remaining 12 t. at a rate allowing him to acquire 120 qr wheat. A rate of exchange of 10 wheat to 1 iron satisfies these conditions: 'there is a unique set of exchange-values which if adopted by the market restores the original distribution of the products and makes it possible for the process to be repeated; such values spring directly from the methods of production' (1960, 3). Note that beyond this cryptic reference to the market nothing is said about *how* precisely the exchange rate is arrived at.

The principle can be generalized to any number of commodities, $a, b, \ldots, k$. Let A be the annual output of a, B of b, etc; $A_a, B_a, \ldots, K_a$ the quantities of a, $b, \ldots, k$ used up in producing A, and $A_b, B_b, \ldots, K_b$ the quantities of $a, b, \ldots, k$ used up in producing B, etc. These input coefficients and the total outputs are *data*. The unknowns are the prices $p_a, p_b, \ldots, p_k$ required to allow the process to be repeated. The general system can be stated as

$$A_a p_a \qquad + B_a p_b \qquad + \ldots + \ K_a p_k \qquad = A p_a$$
$$A_b p_a \qquad + B_b p_b \qquad + \ldots + \ K_b p_k \qquad = B p_b$$
$$\cdots\cdots\cdots\cdots\cdots\cdots\cdots\cdots\cdots\cdots\cdots\cdots\cdots\cdots\cdots\cdots\cdots\cdots$$
$$A_k p_a \qquad + B_k p_b \qquad + \ldots + \ K_k p_k \qquad = K p_k$$

$$(A_a + A_b + \ldots + A_k) \quad (B_a + B_b + \ldots + B_k) \qquad (K_a + K_b + \ldots + K_k)$$

The absence of surplus implies that

$$A_a + A_b + \ldots + A_k = A; \ B_a + B_b + \ldots + B_k = B \text{ etc.}$$

As noted, the prices (p) are the unknowns. But if one commodity is taken as standard of value and its price made equal to unity we have only $(k-1)$ unknowns. There are k equations, but only $(k-1)$ *independent* equations since the same aggregate quantities appear as inputs and as outputs, so that any one equation can be inferred from satisfaction of the others.

3. Production with a Surplus

Consider next a modification to allow for an excess of one or more commodities over the amount used up as input. For example, let the output of wheat now be 575 rather than 400 qr, all else remaining the same:

TOTAL OUTPUT
280 qr wheat + 12 t. iron → 575 qr wheat
120 qr wheat + 8 t. iron → 20 t. iron

TOTAL INPUT   400 qr wheat   20 t. iron

Assume also that the surplus (rather its value) is to be distributed equally between the 'owners' of both industries, in the sense that the rate of profit is to be uniform. Note that profit rate uniformity is an axiom of the analysis (1960, 6); *how* it is achieved is not entered into. Prices must then be such as to allow the process to continue at the above dimensions (that is, the inputs must be replaced) and a uniform profit rate yielded.

In this slightly more complex case there are *two* independent equations to solve for the two unknowns, namely the price of iron in terms of wheat and *r*:

$$(280 + 12p_i)(1 + r) = 575$$

$$(120 + 8p_i)(1 + r) = 20p_i$$

yielding $p_i = 15$, $r = 25$ per cent. Thus in the iron sector: of the 20 tons produced, 8 are required as input leaving 12 to be sold for wheat. At a rate of 15:1 the iron producer receives 12×15 or 180 qr, of which 120 are needed in production leaving 60 qr as profit. On a total input in wheat terms of 240 qr – i.e., 120 qr + (8 t. iron × 15) – this amounts to 25 per cent. Similarly for the corn producer: 280 qr are required as input leaving 295 qr of which 180 qr will exchange (at 15:1) for the 12 t. iron needed in production, leaving 115 as profit on an input in wheat terms of 460 qr – i.e., 280 qr + (12 t. iron × 15) – again 25 per cent.

Generalizing, we have a system described as follows:

$$(A_a p_a + B_a p_b + \ldots + K_a p_k)(1 + r) = A p_a$$
$$(A_b p_a + B_b p_b + \ldots + K_b p_k)(1 + r) = B p_b$$
$$\cdots\cdots\cdots\cdots\cdots\cdots\cdots\cdots\cdots\cdots$$
$$(A_k p_a + B_k p_b + \ldots + K_k p_k)(1 + r) = K p_k$$

such that $A_a + A_b + \ldots + A_k \leqslant A$; $B_a + B_b + \ldots + B_k \leqslant B$ etc.

Here there are *k* independent equations (rather than $k - 1$) since the same aggregate quantities no longer appear as inputs and outputs, and also *k* unknowns, namely $k - 1$ prices and the profit rate.

The profit rate is determined 'through the same mechanism and at the same time as the prices of commodities' (p. 6). For to distribute the surplus so as to assure a uniform profit rate requires knowledge of the prices in order to calculate the value of the means of production (which are heterogeneous products); conversely, to calculate the prices implies knowledge of *r* – a fundamental Sraffian characteristic which will be elaborated presently. Again, nowhere does Sraffa explain by *which* 'mechanism' prices and the profit rate are determined, except in the sense of 'determined' by the solution to a set of simultaneous equations.

4   On 'Basics' and 'Non-Basics'

In a system involving simple reproduction – our first case – the quantity of each commodity produced exactly equals the amount used up as input. Here each commodity appears on both sides of the production process among the products *and* the means of production. It is possible that a commodity might not enter directly into the production of some other commodity, or of itself, but it will at least enter indirectly. Such a system is said to include only 'basic' commodities – commodities that serve, either directly or indirectly, as means of production of *every* commodity (pp. 7–8). Alternatively expressed, a basic commodity is one technically necessary for the production of itself and all other commodities.

'Non-basic' commodities are commodities that do *not* enter (directly or indirectly) into the production of every commodity. The existence of a 'non-basic' indicates that the situation cannot be one of simple reproduction, since this product is not itself absorbed as input. (In the simple case, all commodities are absorbed exactly as means of production.) Thus non-basics can only appear on the scene when allowance is made for a surplus.

In the equational system, to eliminate an equation describing the cost conditions of a non-basic commodity eliminates at the same time one unknown (its price), while the rest of the system remains unaffected. By contrast, to eliminate an equation relating to a basic does not simultaneously eliminate an unknown since the basic appears in the other equations, so that the system would become indeterminate. This implies that the cost conditions of non-basics, unlike those of basics, do not play a part in determining general prices and the profit rate. Thus, a reduction in the costs of such a commodity will entail a fall in its price, but will leave unaffected the prices of basics and the profit rate; whereas a reduction in costs of a basic good will alter the entire structure of prices and the profit rate.

Sraffa is careful to insist that, strictly speaking, the term 'costs of production' is not suitable in the case of basics. The price of a non-basic indeed reflects costs in a one-way relation; but that of a basic, dependent as it is on the general system of equations, turns as much on its own use as an input in other basics as on the reverse, with the prices of the means of production it requires itself depending partly on its own price (but see below, p. 450).

5   The Treatment of Labour

The foregoing distinction between basics and non-basics emerges conspicuously in Sraffa's treatment of labour. Thus far (in sections 2 and 3) the payment of wages had been implicitly treated on the input side in the form of articles of subsistence, an appropriate procedure if labour is paid a given subsistence wage on a par with the feed of cattle. And as such, necessaries of consumption appear as output and also (since labour is required by all products) as input or means of production in all equations. Necessaries are thus *basic* commodities. But if we allow labour to share in the surplus and receive a variable wage, and wish to stay with the usual notion of a single (and variable) wage payment, rather than conceive the wage in two segments – a fixed subsistence element and a variable element – the procedure requires modification. Sraffa proposes to treat labour explicitly as a separate input in the system of equations.

Proceeding thus means relegating necessaries to the *non-basic* category since they no longer appear as means of production in the equations. As explained in section 4, a fall in the cost of producing a non-basic reduces its price, and only its price, leaving other prices and the profit rate unaffected. Yet this procedure is not quite satisfactory. As Sraffa puts it, we think of necessaries as 'essentially basic' (p. 10); a fall in the price of, let us say, corn, should (intuitively) have a general impact. Now such an impact will indeed occur if the magnitude of the wage is affected, as Ricardo had emphasised. Unfortunately, nowhere is the matter of wage determination analysed by Sraffa.

Differences in quality amongst labourers are allowed, but assumed 'to have been previously reduced to equivalent differences in quantity so that each unit of labour receives the same wage' (p. 10). There seems to be a market process at play, but (as one comes to expect) Sraffa is silent on the *mechanism* of 'labour reduction'.

The payment of wages is assumed to be *ex post*, capitalists earning profits on means of production excluding wage payments, a rather non-classical perspective. Treating labour explicitly as a separate input (and w as the wage per unit of labour paid *ex post*) our system of equations becomes,

$$(A_a p_a + B_a p_b + \ldots + K_a p_k)(1 + r) + L_a w = A p_a$$
$$(A_b p_a + B_b p_b + \ldots + K_b p_k)(1 + r) + L_b w = B p_b$$
$$\cdots\cdots\cdots\cdots\cdots\cdots\cdots\cdots\cdots\cdots\cdots\cdots\cdots\cdots$$
$$(A_k p_a + B_k p_b + \ldots + K_k p_k)(1 + r) + L_k w = K p_k$$

where as before $A_a + A_b + \ldots + A_k \leqslant A$ etc. But now we have added w to the k variables to be determined – $(k - 1)$ prices and r – with only k independent equations. 'The result of adding the wage as one of the variables is that the number of these now exceeds the number of equations by one and the system can move with one degree of freedom; and if one of the variables is fixed the others will be fixed too' (p. 11). Here we have the fundamental Sraffian notion that *given the wage (or the profit rate) – in addition to the structure of production, i.e., the production coefficients and the output quantities – the profit rate (or the wage) and the set of relative prices can be determined.* Again, be it noted, determined 'mathematically' not 'economically'.

In actuality, Sraffa's account is slightly modified from that just described. Rather than proceed with prices expressed in terms of some arbitrarily chosen commodity, he takes as his unit the value of the composite commodity which forms the (net) national income or surplus, namely the excess (in value terms) of

A output over the *A* absorbed in production *plus* the excess of *B* output over the *B* absorbed in production etc., which sum he sets equal to unity:

$$[A - (A_a + \ldots + A_k)]P_a + [B - (B_a + \ldots + B_k)]P_b$$
$$+ [K - (K_a + \ldots + K_k)]P_k = 1.$$

But we still have an excess of variables over equations: $k + 2$ unknowns, namely k prices, w and r; and $k + 1$ equations so that the main outcome still holds good – we can move with one degree of freedom. (Subsequently Sraffa proposes a yet more complex numeraire.)

6   The Impact of Changes in the Wage on Prices

Sraffa next takes the wage to be an exogenous variable, giving it various values – in the sense of *proportions* of the net product rather than the wage per labour unit – from 1 (the case of a *zero* profit rate) to zero (the *maximum* profit rate). At the first limit with $r = 0$ all the national income goes to labour and relative commodity prices will be proportionate to labour costs – direct and indirect labour input (p. 12). The economic rationale apparently reflects the circumstance that with $r = 0$ the sole scarce factor is effectively labour; commodities which appear as inputs are themselves produced by labour at one or more remove. If this is indeed so, we are back to a very 'neo-classical' world of original factors. The 'production of commodities by means of commodities' is not so different a product from what we are accustomed to after all.

Prices proportionate to labour input may also apply if we take a lower wage and allow $r > 0$, 'capital' now becoming a scarce factor that requires payment, though this is certainly not how Sraffa phrases it. Provided that the ratio of (direct) labour to (the value of) the aggregate means of production is the same from industry to industry, the labour theory will apply.

In the case of uniform ratios a fall in the wage frees equal amounts of net income in each sector, allowing at the original prices positive profits to be paid at a uniform rate on the value of means of production. But in cases of differential ratios of labour to the aggregate value of means of production the matter is much more complex. At the original prices, the savings of net revenue yielded at the lower wage will differ according to the direct labour employed, while the amounts needed to allow positive profits at a uniform rate will depend on the aggregate value of the means of production. More specifically, some industries will save too little in wage payments to allow payment of profits at a uniform rate – 'deficit' industries Sraffa labels them; and conversely in other cases. (At this stage the actual level of the profit rate is not at issue; we assume only $r > 0$ at some level.) Only in the case of an industry with the mean ratio ('balancing proportions' in Sraffa's terminology) will savings from the given wage reduction, at the original prices, suffice exactly to pay profits at the general rate. Complex price movements will be required to reduce the 'deficits' and 'surpluses'. The complexity arises from differences in the 'proportions' between labour and the means of production at the different stages of production in the vertical production process, although 'however complex the pattern of the price-variations arising from a change in distribution, their net result, and their complete justification, remains the simple one of redressing the balance in each industry' (p. 15).

Here we note an important theoretical advance over Ricardo's analysis (see above, p. 88). Ricardo had assumed that upon a wage decrease the prices of goods produced with high labour/means of production would fall relatively to those of goods produced with a low ratio, taking for granted that the price of 'machinery' remains constant. But this neglects the possibility that machinery (the means of production) is in the first group, itself produced with a process entailing a relatively *low* ratio; and conversely in the latter case. What Sraffa shows is that 'the relative price of two products may move with the fall of wages, in the opposite direction to what we might have expected...' (p. 15), there being no clear-cut definition possible of a more-or-less ' labour-intensive' process (see above, p. 5).

7 The Standard Commodity and Distribution

Let us here recall Ricardo's concern with a measure of value (see above, p. 106). His problem was that even if the technical coefficients in 'gold' production should be constant, a change in distribution affects the gold price of commodities produced with different factor proportions than gold itself, thus disqualifying gold as a perfect measure of the 'real' cost – the labour input – of producing other commodities. Sraffa now shows it to be theoretically possible to construct a measure which has the property that it is *itself* invariable to a change in distribution. True enough, a change in distribution will alter its rate of exchange against other commodities produced under different technical conditions, but the variation can be said not to 'originate' in the measure itelf. As Ricardo put it, the ideal measure 'should itself be subject to none of the fluctuations to which other commodities are exposed' (see above, p. 107).

It is intuitively apparent that the commodity whose price remains unchanged with a change in distribution will be one produced with the 'balancing input proportion' recurring at all stages in the vertical production process (p. 16). Sraffa sought to identify the commodity satisfying these conditions. In this exercise he abandoned as index of input proportions the ratio of labour to the value of the means of production – a hybrid ratio – in favour of the ratio of net product to means of production both numerator and denominator measured in value terms. It is this ratio that is to remain constant with changes in distribution.

Although no individual commodity is likely to have the requisite characteristics, Sraffa demonstrates that a 'composite' commodity can be constructed which does. Such a commodity has the property that the commodity-mix of the aggregate (gross) product is identical with the commodity-mix of the aggregate means of production. Sraffa explains the derivation of the composite commodity – a weighted average of 'actual' commodities which includes all basics and only basics (pp. 23–25); and proves (p. 26ff) first, that any 'actual' system can be reduced to a 'Standard system' which describes the input–output relations relating to the sought-after composite commodity, and secondly, that only one such miniature system will apply. These proofs will not concern us here.

Sraffa illustrates the structure in terms of an actual system described by the following equations with a net product yielded in coal and wheat only:

TOTAL OUTPUT
90 t. iron + 120 t. coal +   60 qr wheat + 3/16 labour → 180 t. iron
50 t. iron + 125 t. coal + 150 qr wheat + 5/16 labour → 450 t. coal
40 t. iron +   40 t. coal + 200 qr wheat + 8/16 labour → 480 qr wheat

TOTAL
INPUT   180 t. iron   285 t. coal   410 qr wheat   1   labour

We now seek a composite commodity (the Standard commodity) such that the commodity-mix comprising the (gross) output equals that of the means of production. This is satisfied if with the whole iron industry we take 3/5 of the coal and 3/4 of the wheat industry. (As mentioned, how these specific multipliers are derived we leave open.) We now have the reduced-scale or Standard system:

TOTAL OUTPUT
90 t. iron + 120 t. coal +   60 qr wheat + 3/16 labour → 180 t. iron
30 t. iron +   75 t. coal +   90 qr wheat + 3/16 labour → 270 t. coal
30 t. iron +   30 t. coal + 150 qr wheat + 6/16 labour → 360 qr wheat

TOTAL
INPUT   150 t. iron   225 t. coal   300 qr wheat   12/16 labour

Here the commodity mix of (gross) output (180:270:360) is exactly equal to that of the (aggregate) means of production (150:225:300) – the proportions $1:1\frac{1}{2}:2$.

Now in the Standard system the excess of gross output over means of production – that is, the ratio of net output to means of production – is the same for all commodities, amounting in the above example to 20 per cent:

$150 (1 + 20/100) = 180$ t. iron
$225 (1 + 20/100) = 270$ t. coal
$300 (1 + 20/100) = 360$ qr wheat

or generalizing:

$$\frac{A}{A_a + \ldots + A_k} = \ldots = \frac{K}{K_a + \ldots + K_k} = 1 + R$$

This rate of 20 per cent – the Standard ratio – applies also to the excess of the *aggregate* output relative to the *aggregate* means of production and can be specified independently of prices since effectively we have the *same* 'physical' commodity in the denominator and numerator of the expression – the proportionate mix of commodities being the same for both. (A simplified variant of this notion, with wheat alone entering as output and input, was tentatively attributed by Sraffa to Ricardo in correspondence of 1814 and in his *Essay on Profits* of 1815 (Ricardo, 1951, I, xxxi–xxxii).)

And now to the major uses of the device. First and foremost, changes in the division of the net product between wages and profits may affect relative prices in terms of the measure, but the ratio (R) of the net product to means of production in the Standard system will be unaffected. In this sense, although relative prices in terms of the standard will vary with distribution changes, the conditions of production of the standard allow us to say that the 'origination' of the disturbance lies in the commodities being measured.

Secondly, if the net product is divided between wages and profits – these shares as well as the total consisting of Standard commodity – then the rate of profit will equal the profit share times the Standard ratio. Thus, with a Standard ratio of 20 per cent and a profit share of 1/4, the rate of profit will equal 5 per cent. Should profits absorb the entire net product $(w = 0)$ the profit rate will amount to 20 per cent, coinciding with the Standard ratio. Like the Standard ratio itself, the rate of profit in the Standard system is effectively a ratio between quantities of commodities and is therefore unaffected by movements in relative prices (Sraffa, 1960, 22).

These results may be expressed simply as

$$r = R(1 - w)$$

where r is the profit rate, w the share of wages in the net product, R the Standard ratio (or the maximum rate of profit). Variations of (proportionate) wages from 1 to 0 entail inverse variations in r in direct proportion, generating a *straight-line inverse relation*.

We have thus reached the Ricardian proposition that the profit rate varies inversely with the proportion of net revenue going to wages, to demonstrate which Ricardo had sought a measure of value in terms of which the net revenue remains constant with changing distribution notwithstanding any induced variations in relative prices. At first sight it appears that Sraffa's demonstration is restricted entirely to the Standard system as distinct from the 'actual economic system of observation' (p. 22). However, the straight line relation in fact holds quite generally provided that the wage is *expressed* in terms of the Standard product (p. 23). (This does not mean that workers buy units of Standard commodity, but rather that the physical goods bought will equal in value, at going prices, the value of the amount of Standard product making up the wage.)

This is surprising. In the Standard system with wages paid in Standard commodity units the residual profit is also a quantity of that commodity, of the same mix precisely as the means of production. The profit rate is thus yielded as a physical ratio independent of relative prices – and a wage increase implies a directly proportional fall in the profit rate. In the actual system, by contrast, the value of what remains for profit (after the value equivalent of the Standard commodity has been paid in wages) need not, it would seem, be in the same ratio to the value of means of production as in the Standard system. But this latter presumption. Sraffa explains, is fallacious. For the equations of the actual system are identical to those in the Standard system except in their proportions. Given the wage in terms of Standard commodity, the profit rate is determined in both systems. Again consider the above illustration. The ratio of net product to means of production, the Standard ratio R, is 20 per cent. If now the wage is fixed in terms of the Standard net product at a level absorbing 3/4 of R, then $r = R(1 - w) = 1/4(20)$ or 5 per cent. This rate applies also in the actual system wherein prices must be such as to make the value of what goes to profit equal to 5 per cent of the value of the actual means of production.

As Sraffa nicely puts it, the role of the Standard system is to 'give transparency to an [actual] system and render visible what was hidden' (p. 23). Shades of Marx and Mill on the role of science! Similarly: '[We] are at last able "to see", as it were, the alternative possible distributions of the net national income between wages and profits in ideal conditions, free from any interference due to price changes specific to the commodity used as the unit of measurement' (Pasinetti, 1977, 120).

8   The Choice of Independent Distributive Variable

We come next to Sraffa's renunciation of the wage as independent variable in favour of the profit rate (p. 33). The merit of taking the wage as an exogenous variable is high so long as it is definable in physiological-social terms independent of prices. Once labour is allowed to share in the surplus, however, this is no longer so; and when the wage is given in terms of an *abstract* standard which only has real-world meaning after prices are determined, it is even less appropriate. Now it becomes preferable to take the profit rate as independent variable. Sraffa proceeds with the profit rate determined outside the system by the level of money rates of interest.

9   Reduction to Dated Labour

We turn briefly to a variety of elaborations. Sraffa extends his horizon from a timeless world to one where time is explicitly brought into the picture. Early in his book he was very careful to avoid the term 'cost of production' when discussing basic goods, for the prices of means of production entering into any given commodity are not data, as they are to non-basics, but depend partly on their own price (see above, p. 444). Yet he introduces a chapter on 'Reduction to Dated Quantities of Labour' in which 'prices are considered from their cost-of-production aspect, and the way in which they "resolve themselves" into wages and profits is examined' (p. 34). So surprising is this apparent turnabout that some commentators have been led to believe that we are being offered an 'alternative approach' to price formation (Harrod, 1961, 785).

Consider the equation for a commodity a, with w and r expressed in Standard commodity units:

$$(A_a p_a + B_a p_b + \ldots + K_a p_k)(1 + r) + L_a w = A p_a$$

Replace the commodities constituting the means of production of A with *their* means of production and labour input, which were applied a year earlier. To the means of production we apply a compound profit factor of $(1 + r)^2$ and to the labour (paid *ex post* by assumption rather than *ex ante*) a profit factor of $(1 + r)$.

We treat similarly the means of production entering into the second rank of means of production, applying the appropriate profit factor of $(1 + r)^3$, and of $(1 + r)^2$ to the labour input. We thus proceed backwards so that the cost of a can be expressed as an infinite series containing only wages and profits:

$$L_a w + L_{a_1} w(1 + r) + \ldots + L_{a_n} w(1 + r)^n + \ldots = A p_a$$

where L_a is the direct labour embodied in a and $L_{a_1} \ldots L_{a_n}$ the indirect labour inputs applied at earlier stages.

What though has happened to the notion of production of commodities by means of commodities? Depending upon how far back we go in the series there will be a more or less important 'commodity residue', but this can be made a negligible quantity by extending the series. (Only with $w = 0$, or $r = R$, will costs reflect this commodity residue since the labour elements fall out.) We seem to be back in a very familiar world of wages and profit costs.

Replacing each term involving w by $(1 - [r/R])$, which is permissible if the wage is expressed in terms of Standard commodity (see above, p. 449), we obtain labour terms in the form:

$$L_{a_n} \left(1 - \frac{r}{R}\right) (1 + r)^n$$

and Sraffa proceeds to show how variations in the profit rate – the profit constituting his exogenous variable – give rise to possibly complex cost price movements, including 'reversals' in the direction of the movement of relative prices. These complexities make it impossible to define a *quantity of capital* in terms of the so-called 'period of production' (p. 38), a circumstance reinforcing an earlier demonstration that capital cannot be unambiguously defined independently of the return to capital itself (p. 9: see above, pp. 5–6).

10   Land Rent

Sraffa's general equations may be extended to allow for the fact that scarce land – land in 'short supply' (p. 74) – yields a rent. Given the profit rate, then the prices of all commodities, the wage and the rents will be determinate. Consider n qualities of land in use, with corn the only land-using product. To each corresponds a different 'method' of producing corn yielding n production-equations, and n unknowns, namely $(n - 1)$ rents, for the nth land is 'no-rent' land, and the corn price. Note that land is a non-produced means of production, which like produced commodities that do not serve as means of production, the non-basics, must be excluded from the Standard product.

Should land be all of one quality, though in 'short supply', it becomes possible for two processes with differing labour:land ratios to be used side by side determining a common rent per acre. One method, however, will produce more corn at a higher unit cost per unit than the other. Here Sraffa introduces an interpretation of expansion of output, the only instance in his book where he explicitly extends his vision beyond constancy of output. Expansions of corn output are seen as occurring by way of the 'spread' of the technique producing more corn at a higher unit cost at the expense of the alternative. Once the entire area is subject to the former method, the rent rises to allow a third method to be introduced: 'In this way the output may increase continually, although the methods of production are changed spasmodically' (p. 76). It might appear that we are close to a notion of the intensive margin if there should be a sufficiently large number of techniques, but Sraffa does not point his reader in this direction.

With allowance for scarce land – a non-produced means of production – it appears also that the notion of original factors has made an appearance, notwithstanding Sraffa's disclaimers. The fact that the price of homogeneous land varies with its quantity, implies that a productive process 'unprofitable' at a high land price, may become profitable at a lower land price (Reder, 1961, 695). And should the product in question be a basic, then the system of Standard equations and the structure of the Standard commodity is affected.

The same should apply to labour. After all, labour too is treated as a non-produced means of production (see above, p. 445). From a production perspective there seems no reason to distinguish land and labour (although in the treatment of labour, reduction to a common unit is presumed somehow to be already accomplished). This is especially so if we recall the process of reduction to dated labour in which commodity inputs disappear entirely from the scene so that costs reduce to wages and profits.

11 Tastes, Techniques and the Inverse Relation

The prices of commodities have been shown to depend solely on the technical conditions of production. There may doubtless occur exogenous changes in taste patterns and thus in the make-up of the net product; and such alterations will require that we set up a new general system of equations from which would be derived a new Standard system and Standard measure. Given the taste patterns we are apparently safe; and given outputs is indeed an axiom of the system. But should the set of outputs be treated as variable, particularly as a function of the ratio of wages to profits, it becomes impossible to define a unique measure of value invariant to changes in distribution.

Problems of a similar order arise when allowance is made for a variety of techniques for each of our (single-product) industries. Here the relative cost advantage of each process will depend on the wage–profit relation (Sraffa, 1960, 81ff), and each change in method of production will entail a new Standard system and Standard measure. Without some very special restrictive assumptions it again becomes impossible to define a measure of value independently of distribution (Reder, 1961, 695).

Ricardo's quest for an invariable measure is after all insoluble – there is no unique 'composite' commodity of the kind constructed earlier. None the less, we need not throw in the towel. Ricado did not make his inverse wage–profit relation hinge on a unique standard. And in fact, although Sraffa's measure will change with a change in outputs or technique so that the wage–profit frontier shifts, we can still be sure of the inverse relation. For that holds good in terms of any commodity, indeed even if a change is made from one to another (Sraffa, 1960, 85–6). In short, by adopting the composite commodity as Standard of wages and prices, we obtain a *straight-line* inverse wage–profit relation; but it is still true that given the wage expressed in terms even of an arbitrarily selected commodity the profit rate and the set of relative prices yielding uniform returns emerges and a general inverse wage–profit rate applies. (This latter requires qualification. It only holds good for single-product industries. In the case of multiple-product industries – joint production – the generalization that a fall of the wage in *any* standard involves a rise in the rate of profits breaks down; 1960, 61–2.)

12   Concluding Note

Sraffa's brilliant monograph purports to be an introduction to a critique of modern (read demand–supply orientated) economic analysis. That it yields deep insights into particular technical issues is certain. Unfortunately, it suffers from a failure to indicate adequately its intended status or scope, and its precise relationship to traditional structures. It is also inherently static and of little use in treating the growth-orientated classical problems. There is a close parallel here with the characteristic stationariness of the *tableau économique* (see above, p. 42).

The assumption of uniform profit rates but refusal to accept that all markets must be cleared if the system is to repeat itself period by period is a source of much confusion. We have encountered the position that 'where supply and demand rule, there is no room for uniform levels of wages and the rate of profit' (cf. above, p. 69). But it is not clear why this holds good if the Sraffian structure is intended to portray a long-run equilibrium situation. If it is not, then the profit uniformity axiom requires justification. This is particularly so since we have seen that the operation of the market and even the notion of original factors do, after all, make an appearance in the Sraffian analysis, though through a glass darkly. One recalls Quesnay's formal emphasis on physical surplus, yet inability to avoid allusion to the scarcity dimension.

There remains one final issue. The Sraffian system proceeds with one degree of freedom; either the wage rate or the profit rate must be given exogenously. (Indeed, the price of any commodity can be fixed to close the model.) But which is it to be? Most Sraffians chose the wage; Sraffa himself chose the profit rate. A non-committed economist will be confused by so cavalier an approach to what is to be allowed into the 'core' of economics and what is to be kept out.

Appendix 2 *Dramatis Personae*

Adam Smith

Baptised 5 June 1723 in Kirkcaldy, Scotland; died 17 July 1790 in Edinburgh. Smith studied at the University of Glasgow with Francis Hutcheson, the Professor of Moral Philosophy, and at Balliol College, Oxford. He gave a series of public lectures on literary criticism and jurisprudence in Edinburgh 1748–51, and subsequently held the Chair of Logic (1751–2), and the Chair of Moral Philosophy (1752–64) at the University of Glagow. His teaching covered logic and metaphysics, rhetoric and *belles-lettres*, and moral philosophy – including theology, ethics, law, government and economics, the latter as part of the history of law and society under 'jurisprudence'. Smith resigned his Chair to accompany the Duke of Buccleuch on a continental tour, 1764–6, during which he encountered Quesnay. Following his return to Britain, Smith worked on the *Wealth of Nations* in Kirkcaldy and London. He was appointed Commissioner of Customs in Edinburgh in 1778.

For Smith's life and general overviews of his work, see Rae (1895), reprinted (1965) with additional material by Viner; Scott (1937); Mossner (1969); Campbell and Skinner (1982); Stigler (1982b), chapter 13; and Raphael (1985). Smith's *Correspondence* (1977) is instructive and sometimes amusing.

T. R. Malthus

Born 14 February 1766 near Dorking, Surrey; died 29 December 1834. Malthus entered Jesus College, Cambridge in 1784, graduating in mathematics as Ninth Wrangler four years later. He became a Fellow of Jesus in 1793, forfeiting the Fellowship upon marriage in 1804. He took Holy Orders after graduation, serving for several years as curate in Surrey. He was appointed Professor of History and Political Economy in 1805 in the newly founded East India College, Haileybury.

For Malthus's life and work, see Otter (1836); Bonar (1924); Keynes (1933); Grampp (1974); James (1979); and Pullen (1986).

David Ricardo

Born London 18 April 1772; died 11 September 1823. Ricardo was educated privately, and first employed in the Stock Exchange at the age of 14. 'It was not till Mr. Ricardo was somewhat advanced in life that he turned his attention to the subject of political economy. While on a visit to Bath [in 1799], where he was staying for the benefit of Mrs. Ricardo's health, he took up and read the work of Adam Smith. It pleased him; and it is probable that the subject from that time occupied, with the other objects of his curiosity, a share of his thoughts, though it was not till some years after that he appeared to have fixed upon it much of his attention' (from a memoir ascribed to his brother, Moses Ricardo; see Ricardo, 1951, X, 7). Ricardo progressively withdrew from his Stock Exchange business during 1814–16, and retired to his country estate, Gatcomb Park, Gloucestershire. He entered the House of Commons in 1819 as member for Portarlington.

For Ricardo's life and work see J. H. Hollander (1910); the 1951 *Works and Correspondence*, vol. X, edited by Sraffa; Heertje (1975); and Weatherall (1976). The *Works* contains four volumes of Ricardo's correspondence.

John Stuart Mill

Born 20 May 1806 to James and Harriet (Burrow) Mill in Pentonville, London; died 7 May 1873 in Avignon. Mill was educated privately by his father on 'Benthamite' pedagogic principles. At 17 he joined his father at the East India Company as junior clerk; he retired as Chief Examiner in 1858. In 1824 there appeared the first of many contributions to the *Westminster Review*. Mill married Harriet Taylor (1807–58) in 1851 after an extended but platonic liaison. He directed the *London Review* (*London and Westminster Review* 1836) from 1834 till 1840. He sat as MP for Westminster from 1865 to 1868.

For Mill's life and work see Bain (1882); Courtney (1889); Hayek (1951); Packe (1954); and Robson (1968). Mill's own *Autobiography*, vol. I of the *Collected Works* (1981), 1–290 is a fascinating document. The *Collected Works* includes six volumes of Mill's correspondence.

Karl Marx

Born 5 May 1818 in Trier, Prussia; died 14 March 1883 in London. Marx studied law, philosophy and history at the Universities of Bonn (1836–7) and Berlin (1837–41). He submitted his doctoral thesis to the University of Jena, earning his degree in 1841. He thereafter engaged in radical journalism, private study and political activity in Cologne, Brussels and Paris, beginning his lifelong collaboration with Friedrich Engels (1820–95) in 1844. He emigrated to London in 1849 after his Cologne paper was suppressed. Marx derived his income from Engel's cotton enterprise in Manchester, journalism and various legacies. He was elected to the General Council of the First International in 1864. The first volume of *Capital* was published in German in 1867; volumes II and III were published posthumously by Engels.

For Marx's life and work, see Mehring (1957); McLellan (1974); Rubel (1980); and Wolfson (1982). Selected correspondence will be found in Padover (1979).

Bibliography

Primary

Anderson, James (1801) *A Calm Investigation of the Circumstances that have led to the Present Scarcity of Grain in Britain.* London.

[Anon.] (1821) *On Certain Verbal Disputes in Political Economy.* London.

Aquinas, Thomas (1964) *Commentary on the Nichomachean Ethics.* Chicago.

— — (1924) *Summa Theologica*, Questions 77–78. In A. E. Monroe (ed.), *Early Economic Thought*, Cambridge, Mass., 51–77.

Attwood, Thomas (1831–2) 'Evidence Taken Before the Committee of Secrecy on the Bank of England's Charter', *Parliamentary Papers*, VI, 452–68.

Bailey, Samuel (1825) *A Critical Dissertation on the Nature, Measures, and Causes of Value.* London.

Bentham, Jeremy (1801–4) 'The Institute of Political Economy'. In W. Stark (ed.), *Jeremy Bentham's Economic Writings*, III, London, 1954, 303–80.

Buchanan, David (1817) *Observations on the Subjects Treated in Dr Smith's Inquiry*, 2nd edn. New York, 1966.

Bullion Report (1810). See Cannan, E.

Butt, Isaac (1838) *Rent, Profits, and Labour.* Dublin.

Cairnes, J. E. (1874) *Some Leading Principles of Political Economy.* London, 1883.

Cannan, E. (ed.) (1925) *The Paper Pound of 1797–1821: a Reprint of the Bullion Report* (1810). London.

Cantillon, Richard (1755) *Essai sur la Nature du Commerce en Général*, ed. H. Higgs. London, 1931.

Chalmers, Thomas (1832) *On Political Economy in Connexion with the Moral State and Moral Prospects of Society*, 2nd edn. Glasgow.

Comte, Auguste (1864) *Cours de Philosophie Positive*, 2nd edn (6 vols). Paris.

Cotterill, C. F. (1831) *An Examination of the Doctrines of Value.* London.

Daire, E. (ed.) (1846) *Les Physiocrates.* Paris.

Davenant, Charles (1699) *An Essay Upon the Probable Methods of Making a People Gainers in the Balance of Trade.* In Sir Charles Whitworth (ed.), *The Political and Commercial Works of . . . Charles D'Avenant*, II, London, 1771, 163–382.

De Quincey, Thomas (1844) *The Logic of Political Economy*. In D. Masson (ed.), *Political Economy and Politics*, vol. X *Collected Works of Thomas De Quincey*, New York, 1897.

Gervaise, Isaac (1720) *The System or Theory of the Trade of the World*, ed. J. M. Letiche. Baltimore, 1954.

Hales, John (1549) *A Discourse of the Common Weal of This Realm of England*. London.

Herschel, J. F. W. (1830) *A Preliminary Discourse on the Study of Natural Philosophy*. London.

Hodgskin, Thomas (1825) *Labour Defended Against the Claims of Capital*. London, 1922.

— — (1827) *Popular Political Economy*. London.

— — (1832) *Natural and Artificial Rights of Property*. London.

Horner, Francis (1803) 'Lord King's Thoughts on the Restriction of Payments in Specie at the Banks of England and Ireland', *Edinburgh Review*, II, no. IV, July, 402–21. In F. W. Fetter (ed.), *The Economic Writings of Francis Horner in the Edinburgh Review*, New York, 1957, 77–95.

— — (1853) *Memoirs and Correspondence of Francis Horner*, ed. Leonard Horner. London.

Hume, David (1752a) 'Of Commerce'. In E. Rotwein (ed.), *Writings on Economics*, London, 1955, 3–18.

— — (1752b) 'Of Money'. ibid., 33–46.

— — (1752c) 'Of Interest'. ibid., 47–59.

— — (1752d) 'Of the Balance of Trade'. ibid., 60–77.

— — (1752e) 'Of Public Credit'. ibid., 90–107.

— — (1932) *The Letters of David Hume*, ed. J. Y. T. Greig. Oxford.

Jevons, W. S. (1871) *The Theory of Political Economy*, 4th edn. London, 1924.

— — (1905) *The Principles of Economics*, rev. edn. London.

Jones, Richard (1831) *An Essay on the Distribution of Wealth and on the Sources of Taxation: Part I – Rent*. London.

Keynes, J. M. (1936) *The General Theory of Employment, Interest and Money*. In D. Moggridge (ed.), *Collected Writings*, VII, London, 1973.

— — (1946). 'The Balance of Payments of the US', ibid., XXVII, London, 1980, 422–46.

King, Lord (1803) *Thoughts on the Restriction of Payments in Specie at the Banks of England and Ireland*. London.

Lauderdale, Lord (1804) *An Inquiry into the Nature and Origin of Public Wealth*. New York, 1962.

Law, John (1705) *Money and Trade Considered*. Edinburgh.

Lee, Joseph (1656) *A Vindication of a Regulated Enclosure*. London.

Lloyd, W. F. (1834) *A Lecture on the Notion of Value*. London.

Locke, John (1691) *Some Considerations of the Consequences of the Lowering of Interest, and Raising the Value of Money*. New York, 1968.

— — (1695) *Further Considerations Concerning Raising the Value of Money*. London.

Longfield, Mountifort (1834) 'Lectures on Political Economy'. In *The Economic Writings of Mountifort Longfield*, New York, 1971.

McCulloch, J. R. (1823) 'Political Economy), contribution to Encyclopaedia Britannica. In John McVickar (ed.),, *Outlines of Political Economy* (1825), New York, 1966.

— — (1825) *Principles of Political Economy*, 1st edn. London.

— — (ed.) (1856a) *A Select Collection of Early English Tracts on Commerce*. London.

— — (ed.) (1856b) *A Select Collection of Scarce and Valuable Tracts on Money*. London.

— — (ed.) (1863) *Adam Smith's An Inquiry into the Nature and Causes of the Wealth of Nations*. Edinburgh and London.

Malthus, T. R. (1798) *An Essay on the Principle of Population*. London.

— — (1803 *An Essay on the Principle of Population*, 2nd edn. London.

— — (1820) *Principles of Political Economy*. London (partly reprinted in P. Sraffa ed., *Works and Correspondence of David Ricardo*, II, Cambridge, 1951); second (posthumous) edn (1836), New York, 1964.

— — (1823) *The Measure of Value Stated and Illustrated*. New York, 1957.

— — (1824) 'Political Economy', *Quarterly Review*, XXX, no. LX, 297–334. In B. Semmel (ed.), *Occasional Papers*, New York, 1963, 171–208.

— — (1890) *An Essay on the Principle of Population*, reprinted from last edn, revised by author (1826). London.

de Malynes, Gerard (1601) *The Canker of England's Common Wealth*, London.

Mandeville, Bernard (1714) *The Fable of the Bees; or Private Vices, Publick Benefits*, ed. F. B. Kaye from 6th edn (1732). Oxford, 1924.

Marshall, A. (1876) 'Mr Mill's Theory of Value'. In A. C. Pigou (ed.), *Memorials*, London, 1925, 119–33.

— — (1890) *Principles of Economics*, 8th edn. London, 1920.

Marx, Karl (1857–8) *Grundrisse: Foundations of the Critique of Political Economy*. Harmondsworth, 1973.

— — (1862–3) *Theories of Surplus Value*. Moscow, I, 1954; II, 1968; III, 1971.

— — (1865) 'Wages, Price and Profit'. In Marx–Engels, *Selected Works*, Moscow, 1958, I, 398–447.

— — (1867) *Capital* I, Moscow, 1965; (1894) *Capital* III, Moscow, 1962.

— — (1875) 'Critique of the Gotha Programme' (and related documents). In Marx–Engels, *Selected Works*, Moscow, 1958, II, 13–48.

— — (1979) *The Letters*, ed. S. K. Padover. Englewood Cliffs, NJ.

Marx (Karl)–Engels (Friedrich) (1958) *Selected Works*. Moscow, 1958.

Menger, Carl (1871) *Principles of Economics* (1st German edn), trans. and ed. B. F. Hoselitz and J. Dingwall. Glencoe, Ill., 1950.

Merivale, Herman (1837) 'Senior on Political Economy', *Edinburgh Review*, no. 133, October, 73–102.

— — (1840), 'McCulloch's edition of the Wealth of Nations', *Edinburgh Review*, no. 142, January, 426–45.

Mill, James (1806) 'Sir James Steuart's "Collected Works"', *Literary Journal*, I, 2nd ser., March, 225–35.

— — (1808) *Commerce Defended*. London.

Mill, John Stuart *Autobiography and Literary Essays*. In J. M. Robson (ed.),

Collected Works of John Stuart Mill, I, Toronto, 1981.

— — (1848) *Principles of Political Economy with Some of their Application to Social Philosophy*, last (7th) edn by Mill (1871). ibid., II–III, Toronto, 1965.

— — *Essays on Economics and Society.* ibid., IV–V, Toronto, 1967.

— — (1843) *A System of Logic Ratiocinative and Inductive*, last (8th) edn by Mill (1872). ibid., VII–VIII, Toronto, 1973.

— — *Essays on Ethics, Religion and Society.* ibid., X, Toronto, 1969.

— — *The Earlier Letters*, 1812–1848. ibid., XII–XIII, Toronto, 1963.

— — *The Later Letters*, 1849–1873. ibid., XIV–XVII, Toronto, 1972.

— — *Essays on Politics and Society.* ibid., XVIII–XIX, Toronto, 1977.

Mun, Thomas (1664) *England's Treasure by Forraign Trade* (written *c.* 1630). Oxford, 1959.

North, Dudley (1691) *Discourse Upon Trade.* In McCulloch (ed.) (1856a), 505–40.

Otter, William (1836) 'Memoir of Robert Malthus', Introduction to 2nd edn of Malthus's *Principles.* London.

Petty, Sir William (1899) *The Economic Writings of Sir William Petty*, ed. C. H. Hull. Cambridge.

Petyt, William (1680) *Britannia Languens.* In McCulloch (ed.) (1856a), 275–504.

Pownall, Thomas (1776) *A Letter from Governor Pownall to Adam Smith.* New York, 1967. Also in Smith (1977), appendix A.

Pufendorf, Samuel (1672) *'On the Law of Nature and of Nations'.* In *The Classics of International Law*, no. 17, vol. II, Oxford, 1934.

Quesnay, François (1766) *Analyse du tableau économique.* In Daire (ed.) (1846).

— — (1958) 'Textes annotés. In *François Quesnay et la Physiocratie*, II. L'institut national d'etudes demographiques, Paris.

— — (1972) *Quesnay's Tableau Economique*, ed. M. Kuczynski and R. L. Meek. London.

Rae, John (1834) *Statement of Some New Principles on the Subject of Political Economy.* Toronto, 1965.

Ravenstone, Piercy [Richard Puller] (1821) *A Few Doubts as to the Correctness of Some Opinions Generally Entertained on the Subjects of Population and Political Economy.* London.

Read, Samuel (1829) *Political Economy.* Edinburgh.

Ricardo, David (1951) *Works and Correspondence*, ed. P. Sraffa, vols. I–XI. Cambridge.

Sauvy, A. (ed.) *François Quesnay et la Physiocratie*, Paris.

Say, J. B. (1803) *Traité d'économie politique*; 2nd edn, 1814; 3rd edn, 1817; 4th edn, 1819; 6th edn, 1841. Paris.

— — (1821) *Letters to Mr Malthus on Several Subjects of Political Economy and on the Cause of Stagnation of Commerce*, London.

Scrope, G. Poulett (1831) 'The Political Economists', *Quarterly Review*, XLIV, no. LXXXVII, January, 1–52.

— — (1833) *Principles of Political Economy*, London.

Senior, Nassau (1821) 'Report on the State of Agriculture', *Quarterly Review*, XXV, no. L, July, 466–504.

— — (1827) *An Introductory Lecture on Political Economy*. In *Selected Writings on Economics*, New York, 1966.

— — (1836) *An Outline of the Science of Political Economy*. London.

de Sismondi, J. C. L. Simonde (1827) *Nouveaux principes d'économie politique*, ed. G. Sotiroff. Geneva, 1951.

Smith, Adam (1759) *The Theory of Moral Sentiments*, 6th edn (1790), eds D. D. Raphael and A. L. Macfie. Oxford, 1976.

— — *Lectures on Rhetoric and Belles Lettres* (delivered 1762–3), ed. J. C. Bryce. Oxford, 1983.

— — (1766) *Lectures on Jurisprudence*, eds R. L. Meek, D. D. Raphael and P. G. Stein. Oxford, 1978.

— — (1776) *An Inquiry into the Nature and Causes of the Wealth of Nations*, 5th edn (1789), ed. E. Cannan, New York, 1937; eds R. H. Campbell, A. S. Skinner, W. B. Todd, Oxford, 1976.

— — (1795; written *c.* 1750) *The History of Astronomy*. In W. P. D. Wightman, J. C. Bryce and I. S. Ross (eds), *Essays on Philosophical Subjects*, Oxford, 1980, 31–105.

— — (1977) *The Correspondence*, eds E. C. Mossner and I. S. Ross. Oxford.

Spence, William (1807) *Britain Independent of Commerce*. London.

Steuart, Sir James (1767) *An Inquiry into the Principles of Political Economy*, ed. A. S. Skinner. Chicago, 1966.

Stewart, Dugald (1793) *Biographical Memoir of Adam Smith*, ed. Sir W. Hamilton (1858). New York, 1966.

Temple, Sir William (1673) *Observations upon the United Provinces of the Netherlands*, 2nd edn. London.

Thompson, William (1824) *Inquiry into the Principles of Distribution of Wealth*. London.

— — (1827) *Labor Rewarded: the Claims of Labor and Capital Conciliated*. London.

Thornton, Henry (1802) *An Enquiry into the Nature and Effects of the Paper Credit of Great Britain*, ed. F. A. Hayek. London, 1939.

Thornton, W. T. (1869) *On Labour*. London.

Todhunter, I. (1876) *William Whewell, D. D.: an Account of His Writings with Selections from his Literary and Scientific Correspondence*. London.

Tooke, Thomas (1838) *A History of Prices*, 2nd edn. 1840. London.

— — (1844) *An Inquiry into the Currency Principle*, 2nd edn. London.

Torrens, Robert (1822) *Three Editorial Notes on Value Contributed to The Traveller*. In J. H. Hollander (ed.), *Two Letters on the Measure of Value by John Stuart Mill*. Baltimore, Md, 1935.

— — (1826) *An Essay on the External Corn Trade*, 3rd edn. London.

— — (1834) *On Wages and Combination*. London.

— — (1835) *Colonization of South Australia*. London.

— — (1844) *The Budget: On Commercial and Colonial Policy*. New York, 1970.

Tucker, Josiah (1757) *Instructions for Travellers*. In R. L. Schuyler (ed.), *A*

Selection of Tucker's Economic and Political Writings, New York, 1931.
— — (1774) *Four Tracts with Two Sermons on Political and Commercial Subjects*. Gloucester.
Turgot, A. R. J. (1767) 'Observations sur le mémoire de M. de Saint-Péravy'. In E. Daire and H. Dussard (eds), *Oeuvres de Turgot*, Paris, 1844, I, 418–33.
— — (1770; written 1766) *Reflections on the Formation and Distribution of Riches*. New York, 1963. Also in R. L. Meek, *Turgot on Progress, Sociology and Economics*, Cambridge, 1973, 119–82.
Walras, Léon (1874) *Elements of Pure Economics*, ed. W. Jaffé, 4th definitive edn. London, 1954.
West, Sir Edward (1826) *Price of Corn and Wages of Labour with Observations upon Mr Ricardo's and Mr Malthus's Doctrines upon These Subjects.* London.
Westminster Review [James Mill?] (1826) 'On the Nature, Measures, and Causes of Value', V, no. IX, January, 157–72.
Whately, Richard (1832) *Introductory Lectures on Political Economy*, 4th edn 1855. London.
Whewell, William (1829) *Mathematical Exposition of Some Doctrines of Political Economy*. New York, 1971.
— — (1831a) *Mathematical Exposition of Some of the Leading Doctrines in Mr Ricardo's 'Principles of Political Economy'*. New York, 1971.
— — (1831b) 'Jones – On the Distribution of Wealth', *British Critic*, X, July, 41–61.

Secondary

Allen, W. R. (1965) *International Trade Theory: Hume to Ohlin*. New York.
— — (1970) 'Modern Defenders of Mercantilist Theory', *History of Political Economy*, 2, 381–97.
Appleby, J. (1978) *Economic Thought and Ideology in Seventeenth Century England*. Princeton, NJ.
Arrow, K. J. and D. A. Starrett (1973) 'Cost- and Demand-Theoretical Approaches to the Theory of Price Determination'. In J. R. Hicks and W. Weber (eds), *Carl Menger and the Austrian School of Economics*, Oxford, 129–48.
Ashton, T. S. and R. S. Sayers (eds) (1953) *Papers in English Monetary History.* Oxford.
Bacon, R. and W. Eltis (1978) *Britain's Economic Problem: Too Few Producers*, 2nd edn. London.
Bain, A. (1882) *John Stuart Mill: a Criticism*. London.
Balassa, B. (1959) 'Karl Marx and John Stuart Mill', *Weltwirtschaftliches Archiv*, 83, 147–65.
Baumol, W. J. (1974) 'The Transformation of Values: What Marx "Really" Meant', *Journal of Economic Literature*, 12, 51–62; also 'Comment' (on Samuelson), ibid., 74–5.

Baumol, W. J. and B. S. Becker (1952) 'The Classical Monetary Theory'. In Spengler and Allen (eds) (1960), ch. 31, 753–72.

Beach, E. F. (1971) 'Hicks on Ricardo on Machinery', *Economic Journal*, 81, December, 916–22.

Bharadwaj, K. (1978) 'The Subversion of Classical Analysis: Alfred Marshall's Early Writings on Value', *Cambridge Journal of Economics*, 2, 253–71.

Black, R. D. C., A. W. Coats, and C. D. W. Goodwin (eds) (1973) *The Marginal Revolution in Economics: Interpretation and Evaluation.* Durham, NC.

Bladen, V. W. (1965) 'Introduction' to J. S. Mill, *Principles of Political Economy*, ed. J. M. Robson. In *Collected Works*, II, xiii–lxiii.

Blaug, M. (1958) *Ricardian Economics*, New Haven, Conn.

— — (1980) *The Methodology of Economics*. Cambridge.

— — (1985) *Economic Theory in Retrospect*, 4th edn. Cambridge.

Bonar, J. (1924) *Malthus and his Work*. London.

Bortkiewicz, L. von(1907) 'Value and Price in the Marxian System', *International Economic Papers*, 1952, no. 2, 5–60.

Boss, H. (1988) *Theories of Surplus and Transfer: Parasites and Producers in Economic Thought.* London.

Boulding, K. E. (1971) 'After Samuelson, Who Needs Adam Smith?', *History of Political Economy*, 3, 225–37.

Bowley, M. (1937) *Nassau Senior and Classical Economics*. London.

— — (1972) 'The Predecessors of Jevons – The Revolution that Wasn't', *The Manchester School*, 40, 9–29.

— — (1973) *Studies in the History of Economic Theory before 1870*. London.

Brewer, A. (1984) *A Guide to Marx's 'Capital'*. New York.

Buchanan, D. H. (1929) 'The Historical Approach to Rent and Price Theory', *Economica*, 9, June. In W. Fellner and B. F. Haley (eds), *Readings in the Theory of Income Distribution*, Philadelphia, 1951.

Caldwell, B. (1982) *Beyond Postivism: Economic Methodology in the Twentieth Century.* London.

— — (ed.) (1984) *Appraisal and Criticism in Economics: a Book of Readings.* London.

Campbell, R. H. and A. S. Skinner (1982) *Adam Smith.* London.

Caravale, G. A. (ed.) (1985) *The Legacy of Ricardo.* Oxford.

Casarosa, C. (1985) 'The "New View" of the Ricardian Theory of Distribution and Economic Growth'. In Caravale (ed.) (1985), ch. 3, 45–58.

Checkland, S. G. (1949) 'The Propagation of Ricardian Economics in England', *Economica*, 16, 40–52.

Chipman, J. S. (1965) 'A Survey of the Theory of International Trade: Part I, The Classical Theory', *Econometrica*, 33, 477–519.

Clark, J. M. (1928) *Adam Smith 1766–1926.* Chicago.

Coase, R. H. (1976) 'Adam Smith's Views of Man', *Journal of Law and Economics*, 19, 529–46.

Coats, A. W. (ed.) (1971) *The Classical Economists and Economic Policy.* London.

Coleman, D. C. (1969) (ed.), *Revisions in Mercantilism.* London.

Collard, D. (1973) 'Léon Walras and the Cambridge Caricature', *Economic Journal*, 83, 465–76.

Collini, S. (1983) 'The Tendencies of Things: John Stuart Mill and the Philosophic Method'. In S. Collini, D. Winch and J. Burrow, *That Noble Science of Politics: a Study in Nineteenth-Century Intellectural History*, Cambridge, 127–59.

Corry, B. A. (1962) *Money, Saving and Investment in English Economics: 1800–1850.* London.

Courtney, W. L. (1889) *Life of John Stuart Mill.* London.

Deane, Phyllis (1978) *The Evolution of Economic Ideas.* Cambridge.

Dempsey, Bernard (1943) *Interest and Usury.* Washington.

Dobb, M. (1973) *Theories of Value and Distribution since Adam Smith.* Cambridge.

Eagly, R. V. (1974) *The Structure of Classical Economic Theory.* New York.

Edgeworth, F. Y. (1910) 'John Stuart Mill'. In R. H. I. Palgrave (ed.), *Dictionary of Political Economy*, London, II, 756–63.

Eltis, W. (1984) *The Classical Theory of Economic Growth.* London.

Endres, A. M. (1985) 'The Functions of Numerical Data in the Writings of Graunt, Petty, and Davenant', *History of Political Economy*, 17, 245–64.

Fetter, F. W. (1965) *Development of British Monetary Orthodoxy, 1795–1845.* Cambridge, Mass.

— — (1969) 'The Rise and Decline of Ricardian Economics', *History of Political Economy*, 1, 67–84.

Flew, A. (1970) Introduction to *(First) Essay on the Principle of Population.* Harmondsworth, 7–56.

Fox-Genovese, E. (1976) *The Origins of Physiocracy: Economic Revolution and Social Order in Eighteenth Century France.* London.

Friedman, M. (1953) 'The Methodology of Positive Economics', *Essays on Positive Economics.* Chicago, 3–43.

— — (1968) 'The Role of Monetary Policy', *American Economic Review*, 58, March, 1–17.

Frisch, R. (1981) 'From Utopian Theory to Practical Applications: the Case of Econometrics', *American Economic Review*, 71, 1–16.

Garegnani, P. (1983) 'The Classical Theory of Wages and the Role of Demand Schedules in the Determination of Relative Prices', *American Economic Review* (Papers and Proceedings), 73, 309–13.

— — (1984) 'Value and Distribution in the Classical Economists and Marx', *Oxford Economic Papers*, 36, 291–325.

— — (1985) 'On Hollander's Interpretation of Ricardo's Early Theory of Profits'. In Caravale (ed.) (1985), ch. 5, 87–104.

Gordon, B. (1975) *Economic Analysis Before Adam Smith: Hesiod to Lessius.* London.

Gordon, D. F. (1959) 'What was the Labour Theory of Value?', *American Economic Review*, 69, May 1959, 462–72.

— — (1965) 'The Role of the History of Economic Thought in the Understanding of Modern Economic Theory', *American Economic Review*, 60, 119–27.

Gottheil, F. M. (1966) *Marx's Economic Predictions*. Evanston, Ill.

Grampp, W. D. (1965) *Economic Liberalism*. New York.

— — (1974) 'Malthus and his Contemporaries', *History of Political Economy*, 6, 278–304.

Groenewegen, P. D. (1983) 'Turgot's Place in the History of Economic Thought', *History of Political Economy*, 15, 585–616.

Harcourt, G. C. (1972). *Some Cambridge Controversies in the Theory of Capital*. Cambridge.

— — (1975) 'Decline and Rise: the Revival of (Classical) Political Economy', *Economic Record*, 51, 339–56.

Harrod, Roy (1961) 'Review of Sraffa', *Economic Journal*, 71, 783–7.

Hayek, F. A. (1931) *Prices and Production*. London.

— — (1951) *John Stuart Mill and Harriet Taylor*. London.

— — (1955) *The Counter Revolution of Science: Studies in the Abuse of Reason*. Glencoe, Ill.

— — (1978) 'Dr Bernard Mandeville', in *New Studies in Philosophy, Politics, Economics and the History of Ideas*. Chicago, ch. 15, 249–66.

Heckscher, Eli F. (1955) *Mercantilism*, 2nd edn. London.

Heertje, A.(1975) 'On David Ricardo', *Transactions of the Jewish Historical Society of England*, 24, 73–81.

Hicks, J. R. (1939) *Value and Capital*. Oxford.

— — (1967) *Critical Essays in Monetary Theory*. Oxford.

— — (1971) 'A Reply to Professor Beach', *Economic Journal*, 81, 922–5.

— — (1974) 'Capital Controversies: Ancient and Modern', *American Economic Review*, 64, 307–16.

— — (1976) '"Revolutions" in Economics'. In Latsis (ed.) (1976), 207–18.

— — (1983) 'From Classical to Post-Classical, the Work of J. S. Mill', *Collected Essays on Economic Theory*, III. Oxford, 60–70.

— — (1985) 'Sraffa and Ricardo: a Critical View'. In Caravale (ed.) (1985), ch. 13, 305–19.

Higgs, Henry (1897) *The Physiocrats*. London.

Hollander, J. H. (1910) *David Ricardo: a Centenary Estimate*. Baltimore, Md.

Hollander, S. (1962) 'Malthus and Keynes: a Note', *Economic Journal*, 72, June, 355–9.

— — (1965) 'On the Interpretation of the Just Price', *Kyklos*, 18, 615–34.

— — (1969) 'Malthus and the Post-Napoleonic Depression', *History of Political Economy*, 1, 306–35.

— — (1973) *The Economics of Adam Smith*. Toronto.

— — (1976) 'The Historical Dimension of the *Wealth of Nations*', *Transactions of the Royal Society of Canada*, 14, 277–92.

— — (1977a) 'Adam Smith and the Self-Interest Axiom', *Journal of Law and Economics*, 20, 133–52.

— — (1977b) 'The Reception of Ricardian Economics', *Oxford Economic Papers*, 20, July, 221–57.

— — (1979) *The Economics of David Ricardo*. Toronto.

— — (1980) 'On Professor Samuelson's Canonical Classical Model of Political Economy', *Journal of Economic Literature*, 18, 559–74.

— — (1981) 'Marxian Economics as "General Equilibrium" Theory', *History of Political Economy*, 13, 121–54.

— — (1982) 'On the Substantive Identity of the Ricardian and Neo-Classical Conceptions of Economic Organization', *Canadian Journal of Economics*, 15, 586–612; also in Caravale (ed.) (1985), ch. 2, 13–44.

— — (1984a) 'The Wage Path in Classical Growth Models: Ricardo, Malthus and Mill', *Oxford Economic Papers*, 36, 200–12.

— — (1984b) 'J. S. Mill on "Derived Demand" and the Wage-Fund Theory Recantation', *Eastern Economic Journal*, 10, 87–98.

— — (1984c) 'Marx and Malthusianism: Marx's Secular Path of Wages', *American Economic Review*, 74, 139–51.

— — (1985) *The Economics of John Stuart Mill*. Oxford.

Horsefield, J. K. (1953) 'The Duties of a Banker, II, The Effects of Inconvertibility'. In Ashton and Sayers (eds) (1983), ch. 3, 16–36.

Hutchison, T. W. (1978a) *On Revolutions and Progress in Economic Knowledge*. Cambridge.

— — (1978b) 'Friedrich Engels and Marxist Economic Theory', *Journal of Political Economy*, 86, 303–19.

Jaffé, W. (1965). 'Biography and Economic Analysis', *Western Economic Journal*, 3, 223–32.

— — (1983). *Essays on Walras*, ed. D. A. Walker. Cambridge.

James, P. (1979) *Population Malthus: His Life and Times*. London.

Kaldor, N. (1960) 'Alternative Theories of Distribution', *Essays on Value and Distribution*. London, 209–36.

Kaushil, S. (1973) 'The Case of Adam Smith's Value Analysis', *Oxford Economic Paper*, 25, 60–71.

Keynes, J. M. (1933) 'Robert Malthus: First of the Cambridge Economists', *Essays in Biography*. London, 81–124.

King, J. E. (1983) 'Utopian or Scientific? A Reconsideration of the Ricardian Socialists', *History of Political Economy*, 15, 345–74.

Knight, F. H. (1956) *On the History and Method of Economics*. Chicago.

Kuhn, T. S. (1970) *The Structure of Scientific Revolutions*, 2nd edn. Chicago.

Laidler, D. (1972) 'Thomas Tooke on Monetary Reform'. In M. Peston and B. Corry (eds), *Essays in Honour of Lord Robbins*, London, 168–86.

— — (1981) 'Adam Smith as a Monetary Economist', *Canadian Journal of Economics*, 14, 185–200.

Lakatos, I. (1970) 'Falsification and the Methodology of Scientific Research Programmes'. In I. Lakatos and A. Musgrave (eds), *Criticism and the Growth of Knowledge*. Cambridge, 91–195.

Landreth, H. (1975) 'The Economic Thought of Bernard Mandeville', *History of Political Economy*, 7, 193–208.

Langholm, O. (1979) *Price and Value in the Aristotelian Tradition: a Study in Scholastic Economic Sources*. New York.

Latsis, S. (ed.) (1976) *Method and Appraisal in Economics*. Cambridge.

Leijonhufvud, A. (1976) 'Schools, "Revolutions", and Research Programmes in Economics'. In Latsis (ed.) (1976), 65–108.

Letwin, W. (1963) *The Origins of Scientific Economics*. London.

Levy, David (1976) 'Ricardo and the Iron Law: a Correction of the Record',

History of Political Economy, 8, 235–52.

Lewis, W. A. (1954) 'Economic Development with Unlimited Supplies of Labour', *The Manchester School of Economic and Social Studies*, 22, May, 139–91.

Link, R. G. (1959) *English Theories of Economic Fluctuations*. New York.

Low, J. M. (1952) 'An Eighteenth Century Controversy in the Theory of Economic Progress', *The Manchester School of Economic and Social Studies*, 20, 311–30.

— — (1954) 'The Rate of Interest: British Opinion in the Eighteenth Century', *The Manchester School of Economic and Social Studies*, 22, 115–38.

McLellan, D. (1974) *Karl Marx: His Life and Thought*. London.

de Marchi, N. B. (1970) 'The Empirical Content and Longevity of Ricardian Economics', *Economica*, 37, August, 257–76.

— — (1974) 'The Success of Mill's Principles', *History of Political Economy*, 6, Summer, 119–57.

— — and R. P. Sturges (1973) 'Malthus and Ricardo's Inductivist Critics: Four Letters to William Whewell', *Economica*, 40, November, 379–93.

Meek, R. L. (1956) *Studies in the Labour Theory of Value*, 1st edn. London.

— — (1962) *The Economics of Physiocracy*. London.

— — (1967) *Economics and Ideology and Other Essays*. London.

— — (ed.) (1971) *Marx and Engels on the Population Bomb*. Berkeley, Ca.

— — (ed.) (1973a) *Precursors of Adam Smith*. London.

— — (ed.) (1973b) *Turgot on Progress, Sociology and Economics*. Cambridge.

— — (1974) 'Value in the History of Economic Thought', *History of Political Economy*, 6, 246–60.

— — (1977) *Smith, Marx and After: Ten Essays in the Development of Economic Thought*. London.

Mehring, Franz (1957) *Karl Marx: The Story of his Life*. New York.

Milgate, M. (1979) 'On the Origin of the Notion of "Intertemporal Equilibrium"', *Economica*, 46, 1–10.

Mitchell, W. C. (1967) *Types of Economic Theory*. New York.

Morishima, M. (1977) *Walras' Economics*. Cambridge.

— — and G. Catephores (1975) 'Is There an "Historical Transformation Problem"?', *Economic Journal*, 85, 309–28.

— — (1980) 'W. Jaffé on Léon Walras: a Comment', *Journal of Economic Literature*, 18, 550–8.

Morrow, G. R. (1928) 'Adam Smith: Moralist and Philosopher'. In J. M. Clark et al., *Adam Smith 1776–1926*, Chicago, ch. 6, 156–79.

Moss, L. S. (1976) *Mountifort Longfield: Ireland's First Professor of Political Economy*. Ottawa, Ill.

Mossner, E. C. (1969) *Adam Smith: the Biographical Approach*. Glasgow.

Myers, M. L. (1983) *The Soul of Modern Economic Man: Ideas of Self-Interest, Thomas Hobbes to Adam Smith*. Chicago.

Myint, H. (1948) *Theories of Welfare Economics*. London.

— — (1977) 'Adam Smith's Theory of International Trade in the Perspective of Economic Development', *Economica*, 44, 231–48.

O'Brien, D. P. (1970) *J. R. McCulloch: a Study in Classical Economics*. London.

— — (1975) *The Classical Economists*. Oxford.

Packe, M. St John (1954) *The Life of John Stuart Mill*. London.

Padover, S.K. (1979) *The Letters of Karl Marx*. Englewood Cliffs, NJ.

Pasinetti, L. (1974) 'A Mathematical Formulation of the Ricardian System', *Growth and Income Distribution: Essays in Economic Theory*. Cambridge, ch. 1, 1-28.

— — (1977) *Lectures on the Theory of Production*. London.

Patinkin, D. (1956) *Money, Interest and Prices*. Evanston, Ill.

Phelps-Brown, E. H. (1972) 'The Underdevelopment of Economics', *Economic Journal*, 82, 1-10.

Phillips, A. (1955) 'The Tableau Economique as a Simple Leontief Model', *Quarterly Journal of Economics*, 69, 137-44.

Planck, Max (1949) *Scientific Autobiography, and other papers*, trans. F. Gaynor. New York.

Popper, Karl R. (1934) *The Logic of Scientific Discovery*. London, 1959.

Porta, P. L. (1984) 'Piero Sraffa 1898-1983', *Rivista internazionale di scienze economiche e commerciale*, 31, 14-20.

Pullen, J. M. (1986) 'Correspondence Between Malthus and his Parents', *History of Political Economy*, 18, 133-54.

Rae, John (1895) *Life of Adam Smith*, with an Introductory 'Guide' by Jacob Viner. New York, 1965.

Rankin, S. (1980) 'Supply and Demand in Ricardian Price Theory: A Reinterpretation', *Oxford Economic Papers*, 32, 241-62.

Raphael, D. D. (1985) *Adam Smith*. Oxford.

Rauner, S. (1961) *Samuel Bailey and the Classical Theory of Value*. Cambridge, Mass.

Reder, M. W. (1961) Review of Sraffa (1960), *American Economic Review*, 51, 688-95.

Reisman, D. A. (1971) 'Henry Thornton and Classical Monetary Economics', *Oxford Economic Papers*, 33, 70-89.

Richardson, G. B. (1975) 'Adam Smith on Competition and Increasing Returns'. In Skinner and Wilson (eds) (1975), 350-60.

Robbins, L. C. (1930) 'On a Certain Ambiguity in the Conception of Stationary Equilibrium', *Economic Journal*, 40, June, 194-214.

— — (1932) *An Essay on the Nature and Significance of Economic Science*. London.

— — (1958) *Robert Torrens and the Evolution of Classical Economics*. London.

— — (1961) *The Theory of Economic Policy in English Classical Political Economy*. London.

— — (1968) *The Theory of Economic Development in the History of Economic Thought*. London.

— — (1970) *The Evolution of Modern Economic Theory*. London.

— — (1981) 'Economics and Political Economy', *American Economic Review* (Papers and Proceedings), 71, 1-10.

Robertson, H. M. and W. L. Taylor (1957) 'Adam Smith's Approach to Value Theory', *Economic Journal*, 67, 181-98.

Robinson, J. (1961) 'Prelude to a Critique of Economic Theory', *Oxford Economic Papers*, 13, February, 53-8.

Robson, J. M. (1968) *The Improvement of Mankind: the Social and Political*

Thought of John Stuart Mill. Toronto.

Roncaglia, A. (1985) 'Hollander's Ricardo'. In Caravale (ed.) (1985), ch. 6, 105–23.

de Roover, R. (1957) 'J. A. Schumpeter and Scholastic Economics', *Kyklos*, 10, 115–46.

Rosenberg, N. (1960) 'Some Institutional Aspects of the *Wealth of Nations*', *Journal of Political Economy*, 68, December, 557–70.

— — (1963) 'Mandeville and Laissez-Faire', *Journal of the History of Ideas*, 24, 183–96.

— — (1965) 'Adam Smith on the Division of Labour: Two Views or One?' *Economica*, 32, 127–39.

— — (1968) 'Adam Smith, Consumer Tastes and Economic Growth', *Journal of Political Economy*, 76, 361–74.

Rosenbluth, G. (1969) 'A Note on Labour, Wages and Rent in Smith's Theory of Value', *Canadian Journal of Economics*, 2, 308–14.

Rubel, M. (1980) *Marx: Life and Works.* London.

Samuels, W. J. (1966) *The Classical Theory of Economic Policy.* Cleveland, Ohio.

Samuelson, P. A. (1965) 'Economic Forecasting and Science'. In *Collected Scientific Papers*, III, Cambridge, Mass., 1972, 774–80.

— — (1971) 'Understanding the Marxian Theory of Exploitation: a Summary of the So-Called Transformation Problem', *Journal of Economic Literature*, 9, 399–431.

— — (1974) 'Insight and Detour in the Theory of Exploitation: a Reply to Baumol', *Journal of Economic Literature*, 12, 62–70; also 'Rejoinder', ibid., 75–7.

— — (1978) 'The Canonical Classical Model of Political Economy', *Journal of Economic Literature*, 16, 1415–34.

— — (1980) 'Noise and Signal in Debates Among Classical Economists: a Reply', *Journal of Economic Literature*, 18, 575–8.

Sayers, R. S. (1953) 'Ricardo's Views on Monetary Questions'. In Ashton and Sayers (eds) (1953), ch. 6, 76–95.

Schumpeter, J. A. (1934) *The Theory of Economic Development.* Cambridge.

— — (1954) *History of Economic Analysis.* New York and London.

Schwartz, Pedro (1972) *The New Political Economy of J. S. Mill.* London.

Scott, W. R. (1937) *Adam Smith as Student and Professor.* New York, 1965.

Shove, G. (1942) 'The Place of Marshall's *Principles* in the Development of Economic Theory'. In Spengler and Allen (eds) (1960), 711–40.

Skinner, A. S. (1965) 'Economics and the Problem of Method: an Eighteenth Century View', *Scottish Journal of Political Economy*, 12, 267–80.

— — (1979) *A System of Social Science: Papers Relating to Adam Smith.* Oxford.

— — (1981) 'Sir James Steuart: Author of a System', *Scottish Journal of Political Economy*, 28, 40–42.

— — and T. Wilson (eds) (1975) *Essays on Adam Smith.* Oxford.

Smith, V. E. (1951) 'The Classicists' Use of Demand', *Journal of Political Economy*, 59, June, 242–57.

Sowell, T. (1972) *Say's Law: an Historical Analysis.* Princeton, NJ.

— — (1974) *Classical Economics Reconsidered*. Princeton, NJ.

Spengler, J. J. (1945) 'The Physiocrats and Say's Law of Markets', *Journal of Political Economy*, 53, 193–211, 317–47.

— — (1954) 'Richard Cantillon, First of the Moderns', *Journal of Political Economy*, LXII, 281–94, 406–24. In Spengler and Allen (eds) (1960), ch. 6, 105–40.

— — (1959–60) 'Adam Smith's Theory of Economic Growth', *Southern Economic Journal*, 25, 397–415; 26, 1–12.

— — (1960) 'Mercantilist and Physiocratic Growth Theory'. In B. Hoselitz (ed.), *Theories of Economic Growth*, New York, ch. 1, 3–64.

— — (1976) 'Adam Smith on Population Growth and Economic Development', *Population and Development Review*, 2, 167–80.

— — and W. R. Allen (eds) (1960), *Essays in Economic Thought*. Chicago.

Spiegel, H. W. (1983) *The Growth of Economic Thought*, revised edn. Durham, NC.

Sraffa, Piero (1960) *Production of Commodities by Means of Commodities*. Cambridge.

Stigler, G. J. (1965). *Essays in the History of Economics*. Chicago.

— — (1965a) 'The Nature and Role of Originality in Scientific Progress', ibid., ch. 1, 1–15.

— — (1965b) 'The Influence of Events and Policies on Economic Theory', ibid., ch. 2, 16–30.

— — (1965c) 'The Ricardian Theory of Value and Distribution', ibid., ch. 6, 156–97.

— — (1982a) 'The Scientific Uses of Scientific Biography, with Special Reference to J. S. Mill', in *The Economist as Preacher and Other Essays*. Chicago, ch. 8, 86–97.

— — (1982b) 'The Successes and Failures of Professor Smith', ibid., ch. 13, 146–59.

Sweezy, Paul (1942) *The Theory of Capitalist Development*. New York.

Taussig, F. W. (1896) *Wages and Capital: an Examination of the Wages Fund Controversy*. New York, 1968.

Taylor, W. L. (1965) *Francis Hutcheson and David Hume as Predecessors of Adam Smith*. Durham, NC.

Tsuru, Shigeto (1956) 'On Reproduction Schemes'. In Sweezy (1942), appendix A.

Tucker, G. S. L. (1960) *Progress and Profit in British Economic Thought 1650–1850*. Cambridge.

— — (1961) 'Ricardo and Marx', *Economica*, 28, 252–69.

Vickers, D. (1970) 'Sir James Steuart's *Works*: a Review Article', *Journal of Economic Literature*, 8, 1190–5.

— — (1975) 'Adam Smith and the Status of the Theory of Money'. In Skinner and Wilson (eds) (1975), 482–503.

Viner, Jacob (1928) 'Adam Smith and Laissez Faire'. In J. M. Clark et al., *Adam Smith 1776–1926*, Chicago, ch. 5, 116–55.

— — (1937) *Studies in the Theory of International Trade*. New York.

— — (1958) *The Long View and the Short*, Glencoe, Ill.

— — (1960) 'The Intellectual History of Laissez Faire', *Journal of Law and Economics*, 3, 45–69.

— — (1963) 'The Economist in History', *American Economic Review* (Papers and Proceedings), 53, 1–22.

— — (1972) *The Role of Providence in the Social Order*. Philadelphia.

— — (1978) *Religious Thought and Economic Society*, eds J. Melitz and D. Winch. Durham, NC.

Wallas, G. (1925) *The Life of Francis Place*. London.

Weatherall, D. (1976) *David Ricardo: a Biography*. The Hague.

Whitaker, J. K. (1975) 'John Stuart Mill's Methodology', *Journal of Political Economy*, 83, 1033–49.

Williams, P. L. (1978) *The Emergence of the Theory of the Firm: From Adam Smith to Alfred Marshall*. London.

Winch, D. N. (1962) 'What Price the History of Economic Thought?' *Scottish Journal of Political Economy*, 9, 193–204.

— — (1970) Introduction to J. S. Mill, *Principles of Political Economy*. Harmondsworth, 11–48.

Wolfson, M. (1982) *Marx: Economist, Philosopher, Jew*. New York.

Wood, J. C. (ed.) (1984) *Adam Smith: Critical Assessments*. Beckenham.

— — (ed.) (1985) *David Ricardo: Critical Assessments*. Beckenham.

— — (ed.) (1986) *Thomas Robert Malthus: Critical Assessments*. Beckenham.

Worland, S. T. (1977) 'Justum Pretium: One More Round in an Endless Series', *History of Political Economy*, 9, 504–21.

Index

484

Index